Hatha Yoga Pradipika
Light on Hatha Yoga

With kind regards, ॐ *and prem*

Swami Niranjan

Hatha Yoga Pradipika

Light on Hatha Yoga

*Including the original Sanskrit text
of the Hatha Yoga Pradipika
with translation in English*

Commentary by

Swami Muktibodhananda

Under the Guidance of

Swami Satyananda Saraswati

Yoga Publications Trust, Munger, Bihar, India

Published by Bihar School of Yoga
    First edition 1985
    Second edition 1993
    Third edition 1998

Published by Yoga Publications Trust
    Reprinted 2000, 2001, 2002, 2003, 2004, 2005, 2006, 2008 (twice), 2009, 2011
    Fourth edition 2012
    Reprinted 2014

ISBN: 978-81-85787-38-1

Publisher and distributor: Yoga Publications Trust, Ganga Darshan, Munger, Bihar, India.

Website: www.biharyoga.net

Printed at Thomson Press (India) Limited, New Delhi, 110001

Dedication

In humility we offer this dedication to
Swami Sivananda Saraswati, who initiated
Swami Satyananda Saraswati into the secrets of yoga.

Contents

xix

Swami Satyananda Saraswati on Hatha Yoga

In yogic literature we have a number of reliable texts on hatha yoga. The *Hatha Yoga Pradipika* by Yogi Swatmarama is a very wellknown one. Another by Yogi Gorakhnath is known as the *Goraksha Samhita*. A third text is *Gheranda Samhita* by the great sage Gheranda. Besides these there is a fourth major text known as *Hatharatnavali* which was written later by Srinivasabhatta Mahayogindra. All these texts are considered to have been written between the 6th and 15th centuries AD.

There are also minor references to hatha yoga in the ancient Upanishads and Puranas. The Upanishads date back to earlier than the Buddhist period, which was around the 6th century BC. The references made in the Upanishads indicate that the science of hatha yoga was known well before this period. There is another very important text known as *Srimad Bhagavatam*, the story of Krishna. In that voluminous book, there are references to hatha yoga in several chapters.

Evidence of hatha yoga has also been found in the pre-Columbian culture of the Americas. Even now, at St. Agustin, a southern province of Colombia in South America, there are large stone figures and carvings depicting hatha yoga practices. However, the systematic form of hatha yoga began to emerge in India some time in the 6th century AD.

This gives us a glimpse of the historical aspect of hatha yoga. For centuries these books have guided spiritual

1

aspirants. Many sects were also formed in India, Nepal and Tibet on the basis of hatha yoga. What is the subject matter of these books? Is it just to maintain a youthful body, or to obtain psychic powers, *siddhis*, or is it to develop the capacity to awaken the potential energy, *kundalini*, and attain supraconsciousness, *samadhi*? As we analyze these texts carefully the purpose becomes very clear.

In ancient times hatha yoga was practised for many years as a preparation for higher states of consciousness. Today, however, the real purpose of this great science has been forgotten altogether. The hatha yoga practices, which were designed by the rishis and sages of old for the evolution of mankind, are now being understood and utilized in a very limited sense. Often we hear people say, "Oh, I don't practise meditation, I only practise physical yoga, hatha yoga." Now the time has come to correct this point. Hatha yoga is a very important science for humanity today.

The culling of hatha yoga

By the 6th century AD a great deal of spiritual evolution had already taken place in India over many centuries. Two great men were born in India in the 6th century BC. One is known internationally as Buddha and the other was Mahavir, the founder of the Jain sect, a tradition in Indian culture. Both of them performed severe austerities and both also preached non-violence, *ahimsa*.

Finally, Buddha formulated his teachings, which are known as the Four Noble Truths. Two of Buddha's systems became widely known all over the world. One is known as *vipassana* and the other is *anapanasati*, contemplation. For this Buddha laid a basic foundation called the Eightfold Path, which was a system of ethics more or less like the *yama* and *niyama* of raja yoga.

As a result of Buddha's popularity, meditation became the main form of spiritual practice on the entire subcontinent. However, the preparatory practices were ignored. Ethics and morality were very much overemphasized. It was at this time that the thinkers of India began to reassess Buddha's system. Indians believe that meditation is the highest path, but they disagree on one point – that one can start meditation immediately. Instead they believe one has to prepare oneself.

Five hundred years after Buddha, and one hundred years before Christ, in India, at Nalanda in Bihar, a great university was established in the Buddhist tradition, devoted to the Hinayana system. *Hinayana* means the 'narrow path', i.e. the orthodox Buddhist system. Many thousands of students from all over the known world came to study religion there.

However, there was another group amongst the Buddhists who did not agree with the orthodox interpretation of the teachings. They thought that it was not what Buddha himself had preached. So they established another university called Vikram Shila, eighty miles east of Munger, in Bihar, which became the teaching centre of the Mahayana tradition. *Mahayana* means 'great path'. They were not orthodox Buddhists, but open-minded, liberal Buddhists. In that Mahayana tradition they also began to include tantra; however, this was not something Buddha had directly preached about, so orthodox Buddhists did not believe in it. From Vikram Shila a sect arose known as *Sahajayana*, the 'spontaneous way', and *Vajrayana*, which includes the sexual matters between a man and woman. So, the practices of the tantric sects were very much misinterpreted by orthodox people.

After about five hundred years or so, the popularity and influence of Buddhism declined and so did these tantric sects and their practices. Then in the 4th, 5th and 6th centuries AD, after the period of Buddhist decadence in India, some great yogis took the science and set out to purify the tantric system. Matsyendranath, Gorakhnath and a few other yogis in the tradition found that this important science was being ignored by serious-minded people and being wrongly taught by others. So they separated the hatha yoga and the raja yoga practices of tantra from the rest and left out the rituals of tantra altogether, not even mentioning them.

3

When they culled the practices, they picked up the useful, practical and noble practices of yoga from the tantric system. At that time it became necessary for them to classify some of the unclassified instructions in tantra.

Although Buddha was a great personality, his teachings later remained merely what we can call psychological experiences. Therefore, it became necessary to reintroduce a proper system of meditation. That is how the system of hatha yoga was established. It was at this time that Matsyendranath founded the Nath cult which believed that, before taking to the practices of meditation, you must purify the body and its elements. This is the theme of hatha yoga.

Science of purification

Of the many authorities on hatha yoga, one outstanding personality is Swatmarama who compiled the *Hatha Yoga Pradipika*. It can also be translated as 'Light on Hatha Yoga'. However, the term *pradipika* actually means 'self-illuminating' or 'that which illumines'. It is a text which illumines a multitude of physical, mental and spiritual problems for aspirants. Gorakhnath, the chief disciple of Matsyendranath, had earlier written books, poems and prose on the hatha yoga system in the local dialect, but Swatmarama compiled the entire wisdom of hatha yoga in Sanskrit. In common with the other texts, he has expounded techniques such as asana, pranayama and shatkarma.

The beauty of the *Hatha Yoga Pradipika* is that it solves a very great problem faced by every aspirant. Swatmarama has completely eliminated the *yama,* moral codes, and *niyama,* self-restraints, which are the starting points in the Buddhist and Jain systems, as well as in Sage Patanjali's raja yoga.

Sage Patanjali was a contemporary of Buddha and his system of yoga was influenced by the Buddhist philosophy of yama and niyama. In the *Yoga Sutras* he divided raja yoga into eight steps. Yama and niyama are the first two, followed by asana and pranayama. Then come pratyahara, dharana, dhyana and samadhi, which are the final four. Sage

4

Patanjali's contention is that you have to first perfect yama and niyama, otherwise asana and pranayama may fail to give desirable results.

What are yama and niyama? Self-control, rules of conduct and observances: truth, non-violence, celibacy, non-stealing, non-aggrandizement, external and internal purity, and contentment, are some of the regulations. However, the authors of texts on hatha yoga, such as Swatmarama, were very much aware of the practical difficulties every person faced in relation to yama and niyama. Moreover, yama and niyama have more to do with religion than with a person's spiritual life.

Experience has taught us that in order to practise yama and niyama, discipline and self-control, a certain quality of mind is needed. Often we observe that when we try to practise self-control and discipline, we create more mental problems in our mind and personality. If we were to take the statistics of patients in mental hospitals, we would find that most of them are religious, because self-discipline and self-control split the personality. Therefore, before you try to practise self-discipline and self-control, you must also prepare yourself.

If harmony is not created in the personality, then self-control and self-discipline will create more conflict rather than peace of mind. Therefore, the principle of antithesis should not be taught to everybody. It has always been expounded as a philosophical or religious principle, but from the spiritual standpoint it has mercilessly failed to assist man when confronted with the dilemma of his own evolution.

Emphasis on shatkarma

In the *Hatha Yoga Pradipika* the first thing we see is that Swatmarama does not worry at all about self-control and self-discipline in the form of yama and niyama. The order here is very different. He begins by saying that you should first purify the whole body – the stomach, intestines, nervous system and other systems. Therefore, shatkarma comes first, i.e. neti, dhauti, basti, kapalbhati, trataka and nauli. Hatha yoga begins with these practices.

5

However, shatkarma alone does not constitute the whole of hatha yoga. After shatkarma you should practise asana and pranayama. Self-control and self-discipline should start with the body. That is much easier. Asana is discipline; pranayama is discipline; *kumbhaka*, retention of breath, is self-control. Sit in *padmasana*, lotus posture, for fifteen minutes. That is self-discipline. Why do you fight with the mind first? You have no power to wrestle with the mind, yet you wrestle with it, thereby creating a pattern of animosity towards yourself.

There are not two minds, there is one mind trying to split itself into two. One mind wants to break the discipline and the other mind wants to maintain the discipline. You can find this split in everybody. When this split becomes greater, then we call it schizophrenia.

This danger was clearly realized by the authorities and masters of hatha yoga. Therefore, they said, first discipline the body. They explained what they meant by the body. The subtle elements, *tattwas*, the energy channels, *nadis*, within the body should be purified. The behaviour of the vital force, *prana*, the entire nervous system and the various secretions in the body should be properly maintained and harmonized.

After this one should go on to practise mudras like vajroli, sahajoli, khechari, shambhavi, vipareeta karani and others. In this way it will be possible to develop deep meditation. These practices will induce pratyahara and lead into dharana, dhyana and samadhi.

Aim of hatha yoga

In order to purify the mind, it is necessary for the body as a whole to undergo a process of absolute purification. Hatha yoga is also known as the science of purification, not just one type of purification but six types. The body has to be cleaned in six different ways for six different impurities. When you clear the body of these impurities, the nadis function and the energy blocks are released. Then the energies move like wave frequencies throughout the channels within the physical structure, moving right up to the brain.

6

Therefore, we consider hatha yoga as the preliminary practice of tantra, raja yoga, kundalini yoga and kriya yoga. When the rishis discovered the science of hatha yoga, they did not have yoga therapy in mind. Although yoga has proved to be very effective in the treatment of many impossible and incurable diseases, the therapeutic effect of yoga is only a byproduct and incidental.

The main objective of hatha yoga is to create an absolute balance of the interacting activities and processes of the physical body, mind and energy. When this balance is created, the impulses generated give a call of awakening to the central force, *sushumna nadi*, which is responsible for the evolution of human consciousness. If hatha yoga is not used for this purpose, its true objective is lost.

The interplay of the inner energy

In order to make the subject clear, it was termed hatha, i.e. *ha* and *tha* yoga, a combination of two bija mantras. It has been explained in hatha yoga that *ha* represents prana, the vital force, and *tha* represents mind, the mental energy. So hatha yoga means the union of the pranic and mental forces. When union between the pranic and mental forces takes place, then a great event occurs in man. This is the awakening of higher consciousness.

Prana shakti, the life force, and *manas shakti*, the mental force, are the two fundamental creators. Every object in the universe, right from the smallest atom to the largest star, is composed of these two *shaktis*, or energies. When they interact with each other, when the interplay of these two shaktis takes place, then creation begins to unfold. When the two shaktis are separated from each other, or they are dissolved back to their source, then creation is dissolved. That is the great *pralaya*, i.e. the total annihilation of matter. In the field of physics also they speak along the same lines.

All matter in this creation is alive. This is the first point. It is also conscious. This is the second point. Therefore, everything has potential consciousness and everything is alive. In yoga, life and consciousness are known as prakriti and purusha; in tantra they are known as Shakti and Shiva. In hatha yoga they are called ida and pingala; in taoism, yin and yang, and in physics, matter and energy. They have their own names in different times, in different philosophies. This physical body as it is seen is the gross perception. If you look at this body with psychic eyes, or with the eyes of specialized and sophisticated electronic equipment, perhaps you would understand that it has its own subtle counterpart also.

What happens internally whenever you start to think? If you have never thought about it, please start thinking now. What is thought? What happens within us when a thought is emerging, and a thought is diminishing, and when one is superseded by another, or when thoughts intercept each other? This is called the interplay of shakti.

Harmony between the positive and negative forces

In hatha yoga there is the concept of harmonizing the twofold shaktis or energies in man, because they normally remain in an unbalanced and unharmonized form. Either the prana shakti is predominant and the mental shakti is subservient, or the mental shakti is predominant and the prana shakti is subservient. Due to this imbalance, either physical diseases occur or mental diseases manifest. When prana is subservient to mental shakti, then people are driven to bouts of insanity. They are admitted to mental hospitals and lunatic asylums. This is because they have too much mental shakti, and too little prana shakti to balance it. When prana shakti is predominant and the mental shakti is subservient, then you will find people becoming angry, quarrelling, creating wars, causing murders, committing crimes and all sorts of violent behaviour. This is the effect of unbalanced prana shakti.

The concept in hatha yoga is, therefore, to bring about a harmony between these two great forces known as ida and pingala. In hatha yoga, first of all the purification of the whole bodily mechanism, the physical complex, takes place.

8

You should always keep in mind that the body, the mind and the spirit are not three, they are one. At one level of existence you see the body. At another level you perceive it as the mind. You should never consider spirit as different from body and body as different from spirit. They are one.

Transcendence through training

The basis of this body is divine, and therefore, through the practices of yoga, a process of transmutation of the physical elements of the body into non-physical elements takes place. Matter is convertible into energy, and vice versa. This is the underlying concept. Similarly, this body is convertible into spirit and spirit is convertible into matter. This is the eternal play of *maya*, power of illusion, and creation. It has been happening eternally. Therefore, there is no reason why anyone should think that this body is impure, and say that he will not meditate. This is a very unscientific way of thinking.

We have examples in history, which you may or may not believe, of great saints, who, at the time when they wanted to leave this earthly existence, transmuted their body into light particles, and then completely disappeared. There was nothing left of their gross physical body. This body is not just flesh and bone, nor just marrow and myriads of secretions, but it is a gross manifestation of the very subtle shakti, polarized into prana and manas shakti.

Therefore, in hatha yoga, first of all we take care of the body and purify it by six methods. The most important point is that the nadis have to be purified for the purpose of meditation. Our body functions along very simple lines. Just as a machine produces wastes, likewise our body continuously produces wastes. These wastes are of three types: mucus, gas and acidity. If we cleanse the body internally from time to time, the excesses of these three metabolic products are removed, and their formation is regulated and balanced. Then perfect health can be maintained.

It is in this sense that the shatkarmas are of very great importance. Cleansing the body of the three types of

9

imbalance in the system is an important aspect of hatha yoga and therapy. In the process of hatha yoga, total training has to be imparted to every part of the body – to the nose, heart, respiratory system, circulatory system and so on. For example, the body has to be made free from any erratic behaviour of the heart; the cardiac behaviour has to be changed. As a preliminary to meditation there has to be change in the unconscious response of the heart. Otherwise, if you are a good meditator, and if you concentrate on one point, then the moment meditation takes place the coronary behaviour will change, and certainly the body will have to suffer.

Not only that, but the nervous system must also be trained, because it is the carrier of impulses through the sensory and motor channels. For an uninterrupted flow of energy to pass throughout the body it is vital that all blockages are removed, because if they are not, then in meditation you will have all sorts of abnormal manifestations.

Many people who have these experiences say, "What is all this? Meditation should be full of beauty and serenity; meditation is supposed to be graceful and very attractive; it is not supposed to be frightening or annoying or disturbing. If it is as beautiful as flowers and as serene as a full moon, then why don't I experience it like that?" This is what they say. Meditation is blissful. It is total bliss, inside and outside also, providing that the correct approach to purification has been made.

There are other people who say, "Oh, I am spiritual. I don't care about the physical body; hatha yoga only makes you body-minded." What is this nonsense? When you are spiritually-minded and you sit for meditation then, when meditation is taking place, you will become aware of your body very forcibly. You may even have to go to a doctor because you may not be able to control it. To transcend the body does not mean to just forget about it. You have to purify it. Therefore, these six kriyas of hatha yoga (neti, dhauti, basti, nauli, kapalbhati and trataka) are necessary for spiritual aspirants.

10

Concentration depends on purification

These then are the basic hatha yoga kriyas which tend to purify the energy patterns and bring a balance between them. When these patterns are well under control, then you can force your mind onto one point. Otherwise, what happens when you try to concentrate on a circle? You start to get a faint image of a circle, but then it starts to change its shape. It becomes elongated; it becomes oval; it starts to break asunder, and starts to go completely out of order. You are not able to form a perfectly steady image of the circle, because the nature of the pranas is fluctuation and the characteristic of the mind is motion.

Prana can never be motionless. The pranas are always moving, and the mind is ever-changing as well. These two highly mobile energies have to be brought into a steady state. You can barely imagine how difficult it is. Concentration is extremely difficult. You may say anything. You may say that you can forget yourself completely, but that is not concentration. You may be able to steer yourself with ease amongst the visions, but that is not concentration. Concentration is unbroken awareness of one point at all times, like one line stretching into the far distance. It does not break, it does not turn, it does not reverse, it is not intercepted. It is unbroken and steady. One idea, the same idea, no other idea, no other thought. That is concentration, and it should happen by itself.

Metamorphosis from gross to subtle

The two forces of mind and prana maintain the rhythm of life and consciousness. This is one stage of evolution, but mankind has yet to evolve further. If civilization is not constructed along evolutionary lines, then man has to face disaster, death and absolute extinction. You cannot deny evolution.

Everything in the universe is evolving, even the rocks. If there is metamorphosis in every part of creation, why shouldn't man's consciousness also undergo this state of metamorphosis? Transformation is a scientific fact. It is

11

not a philosophy, faith or creed. It is the path of evolution, and it gives meaning to life. This physical body constantly undergoes various processes of transformation, which affect each and every molecule of its material substance.

Now people have begun to realize that matter in its ultimate form is energy. Therefore, we will have to re-analyze and redefine what the body is and how far this transformation can be effected. Can the body be turned into light particles? Think about it in terms of science, not in terms of faith or beliefs that you have had, or not had, up until now.

If this body can undergo a state of metamorphosis, then what is the way? The answer is yoga. Through the processes of yoga the body is rendered so subtle and pure that it is transformed into a yogic body which is unaffected by old age and disease.

Hatha yoga is practised in order to initiate a process in this physical body whereby the pranic currents and mental forces which interact with each other in the scheme of life and existence may be transformed. Unless the physical molecules are transformed it is no use discussing compassion or unity.

A great challenge is open to us. If matter in its ultimate form is energy, then this physical body can be transformed into solid energy through the systematic practice of the six cleansing techniques of hatha yoga. After this, asana and pranayama should be practised.

Union of mind and body is yoga
An important point which has been omitted by the commentators is that hatha yoga is not only the union of prana and mind. In fact, it means the union of prana and mind with the Self. Now let us clarify this. In the spine there are three major nadis known as ida, pingala and sushumna. Nadi here does not mean nerve. It is not a physical channel. *Nadi* means flow, like the flow of electricity within a cable. One wire carries the negative force and another carries the positive force of electricity. So, in hatha yoga, ida nadi represents the negative force, the flow of consciousness,

pingala represents the positive force, the flow of vital energy, and sushumna nadi represents the neutral force, the flow of spiritual energy.

The union, the connection between these three flows, occurs in ajna chakra at the eyebrow centre. Therefore, let us revise the literal meaning of hatha yoga. Commentators have stated that union between ida, pingala and sushumna is hatha yoga. When this union takes place there is an instant awakening in mooladhara chakra at the base of the spine. This is the seat of primal energy or *kundalini shakti*. The awakening of kundalini is the subject matter of hatha yoga. Through the practices of hatha yoga, union is brought about. As a result of that union, the awakening of kundalini takes place. When awakening occurs, then kundalini ascends to higher realms of consciousness, and finally it is established in sahasrara chakra at the crown of the head.

When kundalini is established in sahasrara chakra, that is called yoga, not hatha yoga. This is the difference between yoga and hatha yoga. *Yoga* means union of Shiva (consciousness) and Shakti (energy). *Shakti* is kundalini energy; *Shiva* is the Supreme Consciousness seated in sahasrara chakra. When awakening takes place in mooladhara at the base of the spine, then kundalini starts ascending.

She ascends through sushumna, not through ida and pingala. Sushumna is the highway for kundalini. It passes through various chakras, sometimes all of a sudden and sometimes very slowly. When it unites with ida and pingala in ajna chakra, that is called hatha yoga. Then, after this first union, it forges ahead to sahasrara chakra. There it unites with the Supreme Consciousness, Shiva. That is called yoga, which means ultimate union. Therefore, the ultimate object of hatha yoga is to experience yoga.

Arousing potential energy

Awakening of kundalini is a fact, but more important than that is awakening of sushumna. Much more real and important is awakening of the chakras. People do not understand

13

this difficulty at all. Awakening of the chakras must take place first, because the chakras are the junctions through which energy or shakti is distributed to 72,000 circuits.

If the chakras are not functioning properly, if there is a blockage somewhere, then the energy cannot penetrate. If the junction somewhere in your building is faulty, you will not get electricity there. For the whole complex there may be many, many circuits, not merely one or two. Maybe all are intact, but the basic connection may be wrong somewhere near the main switch. Then what will happen? Even the junctions that are intact will not be able to supply electricity. So, purification and awakening of the chakras is essential. This can be accomplished through the practice of pranayama.

Supposing you have purified the nadis by asana and pranayama, and you have also awakened the chakras by pranayama and a few asanas, there then remains the awakening of sushumna, the central channel. Sushumna flows from mooladhara chakra, at the lowest circuit, to ajna, the highest circuit, and it is a very important nadi. The awakened kundalini shakti has to pass through sushumna, but if this highway remains closed, kundalini cannot penetrate beyond mooladhara. Therefore, before awakening kundalini, sushumna should be awakened.

Controlling the mind by controlling the prana

There is another difference between Sage Patanjali's system of raja yoga and the traditional system of hatha yoga. The authors of the hatha yoga texts were very much aware of the difficulty in controlling the fluctuations of the mind. You may manage it for some time, but still you will not be able to succeed all the time.

So they adopted another method. The hatha yoga texts state very clearly that by controlling the pranas, the mind is automatically controlled. It seems that prana and mind exert an influence on each other. When the pranas are restless, it affects the mind and vice versa. Some people find it easier

14

to control the mind than to control the prana. Perhaps a few people may succeed, but most people cannot control the mind by the mind. The more they try, the more the split grows.

There is another important point to be noted. Sometimes you are inspired. You feel very well, very one-pointed, but it does not happen everyday. Therefore, the authors of hatha yoga struck another theme: "Don't worry about the mind. Ignore it. Practise pranayama."

By practising pranayama correctly, the mind is automatically conquered. However, the effects of pranayama are not so simple to manage. It creates extra heat in the body, it awakens some of the dormant centres in the brain, it can alter the production of sperm and testosterone. It lowers the respiratory rate and changes the brain wave patterns. When these changes take place, you may not be able to handle it. Therefore, hatha yoga says that the shatkarmas must be practised first.

The purpose of emphasizing shatkarma is to prepare a base for the higher practices of pranayama. Shatkarma purifies the whole system and removes blockages on the paths of ida and pingala. When there are no mental or vital blockages, the breath in both the nostrils flows systematically. When the left nostril flows it means ida is active and the mind is dominant. When the right nostril flows it means the breath in pingala is active and the pranas are predominating. The flow of the breath in alternate nostrils indicates the state of balance of the sympathetic and parasympathetic nervous systems.

If ida is flowing and you are practising meditation, you will go to sleep and your brain will produce delta waves. If the right nostril is flowing and you are trying to meditate, your brain will produce beta waves and you will be thinking many thoughts at the same time. When both the nostrils are flowing equally, that means sushumna is flowing. When sushumna flows you can meditate without any difficulty. Awakening of sushumna, making sushumna nadi flow, is the most important process in yoga which precedes kundalini awakening.

Dimensions of prana

Shatkarma is the preparation for pranayama. Most people think of pranayama as breathing exercises but it is far more. *Ayama* literally means 'dimension', not 'control'. So pranayama is practised in order to expand the dimensions of prana within you.

Within us are planes of existence, areas of consciousness, which are in absolute darkness. These planes are much more beautiful and creative than the ones we live on now. However, how are we going to penetrate and illuminate them? It is useless to talk about the different stages of consciousness. You must be able to experience them, even as you experience the state of dreams or sleep. When the pranic energy is aroused and awakened through the practice of pranayama, it is circulated to these dark areas of consciousness. Then the inner city is illuminated and man is reborn into a new dimension of existence, a new area of experience.

The practical aspect

If you want to achieve this transcendental experience, the practices of hatha yoga and pranayama should be perfected. The rules and recommendations should also be observed. This does not mean giving up all the pleasures in life, but as you well know, "you can never have your cake and eat it too." So, once you have decided to step into another dimension of consciousness, you must be ready to sacrifice some of those things which are definitely detrimental to the practice of pranayama and hatha yoga. Therefore, remember that the practices of hatha yoga, asana and pranayama are ultimately intended for developing the quality of human consciousness, not just the mind or body.

Philosophy is intellectual and you can never reach the point of evolution through intellect. Intellect becomes a barrier to spiritual awakening, and we have to find a powerful means of transcending it. Hatha yoga is most effective because you are working on the prana and bypassing the mind.

Hatha yoga is a great science which everyone can practise according to his or her own capacity. Maybe not all, but at least a few techniques can be practised each day. Hatha yoga techniques, along with asana and a few pranayama, are sufficient for most people. It is necessary to practise these preparatory limbs first. Then you may go further. If the preparation is perfect, there will be no need to learn meditation from anyone. One fine morning while practising pranayama your mind will be lifted into a new realm of consciousness.

The therapeutic aspect
Hatha yoga is a method of preparing the system for spiritual awakening but it is also a very important science of health. Since ancient times it has been used by yogis and rishis for the relief and elimination of all kinds of diseases and defects. It is true that the practices require more time and effort on the part of the patient than conventional therapies, but in terms of permanent, positive results, as well as saving the enormous expenditure on medicines, they are certainly more worthwhile.

What makes this method of treatment so powerful and effective is the fact that it works according to the principles of harmony and unification, rather than diversity. The three important principles on which physical and mental therapy is based are as follows:
1. Conferring absolute health to one part or system of the body thereby influencing the rest of the body.
2. Balancing the positive and negative energy poles (ida and pingala, prana and apana).
3. Purifying the body of the three types of wastes (doshas).

If you have fifteen grandfather clocks together on the same wall, all with pendulums of identical length and weight, you will notice that after some time all the pendulums become synchronized in their movements. This occurs

17

quite naturally according to the law of mutual rhythms and vibrations.

In this physical body, the various organs and systems all have their own functions to carry out, but there should be complete coordination between them. If any of the organs or systems of the body are not able to coordinate with each other, it means that not one but all the systems and organs are unbalanced. Thus, in any sickness, whether physical or mental, every system is out of coordination.

According to the law of mutual rhythms, all you have to do in order to regain the health of the whole system is to bring one organ or system to a state of health. Then all the others will naturally follow suit.

Ill health of one system creates ill health in the rest of the body. You cannot say that your stomach is bad and every-thing else is alright. Therefore, a sick person with a number of ailments should generally be given treatment for only one of them. If you are able to create health in one system of this body, gradually the whole body begins to improve. This is how hatha yoga therapy should be prescribed.

Most yoga teachers today, however, do not follow this system. Depending on their knowledge of medical diagnosis, they make a very long list of practices – one for constipation, one for nosebleeds, one for something else. They think that by teaching a sick person various hatha yoga techniques for his different ailments, he will get better. Their system is based on the popular concept that various diseases belong to different groups, which does not take into account the interrelationship of all the organs and systems.

Conserving energy in this physical body is another important aspect of health which has been ignored by most of the healing sciences. We have given so much importance to nutrition, but we have missed the real source of energy, which is inherent. This energy is something like positive and negative electrical charges pulsating throughout. The correct balance of these opposite forms of energy creates good health. Whenever these positive and negative flows are suppressed, blocked, dissipated or poorly distributed, disease inevitably results.

The different organs and systems of the body do not subsist merely on food and vitamins. The main source of energy in life is these plus/minus or positive/negative charges. Therefore, the science of physical and mental harmony is known as hatha yoga.

Physical and mental therapy is one of the most important achievements of hatha yoga. So far, hatha yoga has succeeded in diseases like asthma, diabetes and blood pressure where modern science has not. Besides this, hatha yoga has proved very effective in cases of epilepsy, hysteria, rheumatism and many other ailments of a chronic and constitutional nature. In fact, we have found that most diseases of a chronic and constitutional nature can definitely be reversed through hatha yoga.

The psychic and mental diseases which human beings are suffering from are nothing but a state of disharmony in the energetic system. In order to alleviate them we will have to take a new look at our body and enlarge the dimension of modern medical science. We will have to redefine the body, the classification of disease and the system of diagnosis.

What is being discovered more recently is that asana and pranayama are more powerful and effective ways of controlling the whole body. They are the first steps in allowing us to not only alter the mechanisms of one element, but to gain control over the total structure of the brain and mind, the controlling system which allows us to direct every aspect of our lives, and the energy within that.

The real purpose of hatha yoga

In the last forty years hatha yoga has been accepted as a therapeutic science all over the world and many scientific studies have been conducted in this field. Today we teach yoga to people because it is very necessary. Man has become sick and medical science is not able to meet the challenge. Hatha yoga, however, has been helping everybody.

Therefore, we do not want to discourage this aspect, but at the same time we should not forget what hatha yoga really stands for.

Behind every sick man there is a spiritual man. Behind a diabetic there is a yogi. Behind a man suffering from depression there is an aspirant. When a patient comes for help, teach him yoga and make him better. Treat his sickness, but do not stop there. Take him further into the spiritual domain of life.

This is the mistake that most yoga teachers make in the West. They just take a patient with arthritis, rheumatism or insomnia, teach him a few exercises and that is it. Hatha yoga has not been used to treat the total personality. This is why teachers are not able to raise the level of their pupils. Just to improve the physical health is not enough. The mental health must also improve, the nature must change, the personality must change, the psychological and the psychic framework also has to change. You should not merely feel freedom from disease, but freedom from bondage and from the vagaries of the mind. Now, the time has come when teachers in every part of the world must understand and transmit the true spirit of hatha yoga.

अथ प्रथमोपदेशः

Chapter One

Asana

अथ हठयोग प्रदीपिका

श्रीआदिनाथाय नमोऽस्तु तस्मै येनोपदिष्टा हठयोगविद्या।
विभ्राजते प्रोन्नतराजयोगमारोढुमिच्छोरधिरोहिणीव ॥ 1 ॥

*Salutations to the glorious primal (original) guru, Sri Adinath,
who instructed the knowledge of hatha yoga which shines forth as a
stairway for those who wish to ascend to the highest stage of yoga,
raja yoga.*

Sri Adinath is one of the names given to Lord Shiva, who is
supreme cosmic consciousness. In tantra there is the concept
of Shiva and Shakti. Shiva is the eternal consciousness of
the cosmos and Shakti is his creative power. The cosmic
consciousness or universal spirit is known by many names. In
Samkhya philosophy it is Purusha, in Vedanta it is Brahman.
The Shaivites call it Shiva, the Vaishnavites call it Vishnu.

23

It is one and the same, and the original source from which creation and sentient beings evolved. It is that power which resides in all. That force is known as the guru because when the realization of its existence dawns, it takes one out of the darkness of ignorance into the light of reality. The Nath sect of yogis called it Adinath, primal master or protector.

Swatmarama, the author of this text, belonged to the Nath sect, therefore he respects Shiva in the form of Adinath. All knowledge, without exception, emanates from the cosmic consciousness. Tantra and every branch of yoga came from that source, and traditionally the expounder is known to be Shiva. Sanskrit scriptures always start with: "Salutations to the Supreme state of Being". However, the *Avadhoota Gita*, which is vedantic in philosophy, gives another point of view. Dattatreya says: "How shall I salute the formless Being, indivisible, auspicious and immutable, who fills all this with His Self and also fills the self with His Self? Shiva, the Absolute, is ever without white and other colours. This effect and cause are also the supreme Shiva. I am thus the pure Shiva devoid of all doubt. O beloved friend, how shall I bow to my own Self in my Self?"

Few people have reached this stage of evolution, therefore, the first thing you must always remember before starting any spiritual practice is that the cosmic force is guiding all action and that you are the instrument of that force. In both the Orient and the Occident, the tradition is the same. First you pay your respects and then you ask for guidance. When little children pray at night they first remember their parents and guardians, the ones who are protecting them. In the same way, the spiritual aspirant remembers his humble position in relation to the mighty cosmic force.

In India there is an ancient tradition of prostrating oneself before the guru, whether one is worshipping his physical or cosmic form. This is done before undertaking any work so that the divine power can be evoked. It acts like a *sankalpa*, or resolve, constantly reminding one of his ultimate goal and his purpose in life – to attain the same perfected state of being. Such salutations and prostrations are not just an acknowledgement of the superiority of a higher being, but an act done in sincerity, with pure motives, which involves offering one's whole being with love, faith and devotion. This is called *shraddha*. When Yogi Swatmarama salutes Adinath, he is acknowledging that the knowledge revealed in the forthcoming slokas is due to the glory of the guru and not to his own personal attainments. There is humility, absence of ego or the sense of 'I', and this is extremely important for attaining a higher state of consciousness.

Yogi Swatmarama goes on to explain that hatha yoga is to be utilized as a means of preparing oneself for raja yoga, the supreme state of yoga. The word hatha is made up of two Sanskrit roots, ha and tha. *Ha* means 'sun' and *tha* means 'moon'. This is symbolic of the twin energy forces which exist in everything. Hatha represents the forces of mind, and prana or vitality, which constitute the body and mind. The moon is the mental energy of chitta. It is the subtle force which is concerned with the mental layers. The pranic force is like the sun, dynamic and active. The two create the extremities of introversion and extroversion. It is the practice of hatha yoga which enables the fluctuations between these two energies to become harmonious and unified into one force.

In the body there are specific pathways for channelling these two forces. Just as in an electrical circuit you have suitable wires for the conduction of positive-negative electrical energy currents, similarly, there are energy channels within the structure of the body. These are known as *nadis*. *Nad* means 'flow'. The mental energy travels along ida nadi which governs the left side of the body. Pranic energy travels through pingala nadi and this governs the right side of the body. The positive and negative effects of these energies have been equated to the parasympathetic nervous system and sympathetic nervous system. However, although there is a definite relationship between nadis and the nervous system, they are not the same.

If these two separate flowing energies, prana and chitta, can be unified, this creates a suitable condition for kundalini, or spiritual energy, to awaken and ascend through the middle passage, sushumna nadi. Hatha yoga is the process of establishing perfect physical, mental, emotional and psychic equilibrium by manipulating the energies of the body. It is through hatha yoga that one prepares for the higher spiritual experience.

One's whole being, starting from the physical body, has to be refined and strengthened so it can act as a medium for the higher cosmic force. The system of hatha yoga was, therefore, designed to transform the gross elements of the body so they can receive and transmit a much subtler and more powerful energy. If the body is not prepared for this higher form of energy, it would be like running 200 volts of electricity into a machine which only has the capacity to utilize 6 volts. The machine would definitely 'burn out'. So, hatha yoga systematically prepares the body, mind and emotions, so there will be no difficulties when the aspirant is undergoing higher states of consciousness.

Traditionally, hatha yoga consisted only of six kriyas known as shatkarmas. These were the practices of dhauti, basti, neti, trataka, kapalbhati and nauli. Later, hatha yoga also came to include asana, pranayama, mudra and bandha, and the shatkarmas were practised afterwards by advanced practitioners. Through these practices the consciousness can be raised without having to come into a direct confrontation with the mind. Through hatha yoga you regulate the body secretions, hormones, breath, brain waves and prana; then the mind automatically becomes harmonious. Hatha yoga is the means and raja yoga is the goal. Hatha yoga is the stairway leading to raja yoga. Once the sadhaka reaches the stage of raja yoga, hatha yoga ceases to be necessary for him.

प्रणम्य श्रीगुरुं नाथं स्वात्मारामेण योगिना ।
केवलं राजयोगाय हठविद्योपदिश्यते ॥ 2 ॥

Prostrating first to the guru, Yogi Swatmarama instructs the knowledge of hatha yoga only for (raja yoga) the highest state of yoga.

By first prostrating to the guru, Yogi Swatmarama indicates that he is only a tool of transmission for the knowledge which is to be imparted. It is also emphasized that hatha yoga is to be practised for the sole purpose of preparing oneself for the highest state of raja yoga, i.e. samadhi.

Originally, a sadhaka practised hatha yoga for many years to prepare himself for the awakening of kundalini, or in terms of raja yoga, for the experience of samadhi. However, in the last fifty years, with the revival of yoga in the West, it seems that the real aim of hatha yoga has been overlooked or even completely forgotten. Today, yoga is generally practised to improve or restore health, to reduce stress, to prevent the body from ageing, to build up the body or to beautify it. Hatha yoga does fulfil these objectives, but it should be kept in mind that they are certainly not the goal.

As one practises hatha yoga techniques, one's physical and mental potential begins to increase and unfold. We know that man utilizes only one-tenth of his total brain capacity. This means that nine-tenths are lying dormant, waiting to be brought into action. Science calls the dormant brain the 'silent area'. Little is known about its capacity, but neurologists say it has something to do with man's psychic capacity. After long and arduous practice of yoga, the psychic potential manifests, maybe in the form of clairvoyance, clairaudience, telepathy, telekinesis, psychic healing, etc. These are called *siddhis* or perfections. Some people regard them as a grand achievement, but they are only temporary manifestations which can even hinder further spiritual progress. The goal of all yogic sadhana is to discover and experience the universal spirit within, and if siddhis are indulged in, they take one away from the ultimate experience. Therefore, they are better ignored as they are not the desired fruit of hatha yoga.

Although regular practice of hatha yoga can bring about many wonderful changes and desired results, it is essential to remember that they are only side-effects. Hatha yoga is not being taught for its own sake, for therapeutic purposes, or for gaining worldly or psychic powers, and this is something the hatha yoga practitioner should always keep in mind.

भ्रान्त्या बहुमतध्वान्ते राजयोगमजानताम् ।
हठ प्रदीपिकां धत्ते स्वात्मारामः कृपाकरः ॥ 3 ॥

The highest state of raja yoga is unknown due to misconceptions (darkness) created by varying ideas and concepts. In good will and as a blessing, Swatmarama offers light on hatha yoga.

There is a proverb: "Many sages, many opinions". The highest goal in yoga is attainment of kaivalya, the point at which raja yoga culminates. Ultimately, all spiritual practices and branches of yoga lead to that state, but there are as many ways of reaching the goal as there are individuals in the world. If we try to follow and believe that every path is applicable to ourselves, we will never attain the final experience.

A person's individual method has to be systematic. Whether one practises karma yoga, bhakti yoga, kriya yoga, jnana yoga, Zen Buddhism, or a combination of a few varying techniques, one has to have an ordered system and that system has to be followed from beginning to end, without diverging and trying other systems and gurus along the way. Believing in one system, following it for a while and then leaving it for another, leads nowhere.

Yogi Swatmarama offers hatha yoga so that people may be guided along an assured path. The word 'offers' or *kripakara* should be noted. *Kripa* means 'blessing', and a blessing can only be given by someone with spiritual attainment. It can be said that hatha yoga comes in the form of a 'saving grace' to those who are stumbling in darkness. Swatmarama is not preaching or propagating, but humbly showing a way which may be easier for the average person to follow in order to come closer to raja yoga.

हठविद्यां हि मत्स्येन्द्रगोरक्षाद्या विजानते ।
स्वात्मारामोऽथवा योगी जानीते तत्प्रसादतः ॥ 4 ॥

*Yogi Matsyendranath knew the knowledge of hatha yoga. He
gave it to Gorakhnath and others, and by their grace the author
(Swatmarama) learned it.*

In this and the next four verses, Yogi Swatmarama shows the
lineage of the siddhas of hatha yoga. Gorakhnath, who was
probably the guru of Swatmarama, belonged to a very popular
yoga sect called the Nath panth. *Nath* is a general term
meaning 'master'. Members of the Nath sect are commonly
called kanphata yogis. *Kanphata* means 'split-eared' and refers
to the yogis' unique practice of having the cartilage of the ears
pierced for the insertion of huge earrings.

It is believed that the Nath sect came into existence in
the middle of the seventh century, when the influence of the
tantra shastras was prevalent all over India, and yoga was
associated with black magic and sorcery. The Nath sect was
established to save society from the heinous practices that
were being carried out in the name of spirituality. There are
many interesting stories about how the sect was originally
formed. One common belief is that to prevent the decline
of spirituality, Vishnu and Mahesh took the incarnations of
Gorakhnath and Matsyendranath to propagate the message
of yoga.

Although Adinath, who heads the lineage of Naths,
may have been a yogi who preceded Matsyendranath, he
is generally identified with Shiva, and with his name at the
head of the list, this would indicate that the origins of the
sect can be traced back to the greatest of yogis, Lord Shiva.

According to a story in the Puranas, Lord Shiva was
instructing Parvati into the secret sadhanas of yoga while
standing on the seashore. A large fish overheard all that was
said and from this fish, the all-knowing Matsyendranath was
born. Hence his name is *Matsya-indra* or 'lord of the fish'.

There are also many stories concerning the birth of Gorakhnath. It is said that when Matsyendranath was begging for food as a parivrajaka, he met a woman who lamented to him her woe of not having a son. Matsyendranath gave her some siddha vibhooti and told her that if she ate it, she would obtain a son. The woman did not eat the substance but cast it upon a pile of cow dung. Twelve years later, when Matsyendranath was passing through the same village, he called her to see the child. The woman told the yogi what she had done and he asked to be taken to the spot where she had thrown the vibhooti. He called the name 'Gorakhnath' and immediately a radiant twelve-year-old lad emerged from the pile of cow dung.

Gorakhnath became the dutiful disciple of Matsyendranath and later became an expounder of hatha yoga and the founder of the Nath sect. He was an accomplished guru credited with the performance of many miracles. Members of the Nath sect were held in high esteem because of their severe penances, austere yogic lifestyle and the accomplishment of many siddhis.

The effect of the Nath yogis was felt right across the old world. Great Nath yogis journeyed through Persia, Afghanistan and the entire Middle and Far East. Their influence was felt all over India and Nepal and particularly around Gorakhpur and the Nepalese border. Even to this day, Nath yogis can still be found in India although few have the same reputation as the original masters.

श्रीआदिनाथमत्स्येंद्रशाबरानंदभैरवा: ।
चौरंगीमीनगोरक्षविरूपाक्षबिलेशया: ॥ 5 ॥

मंथानो भैरवो योगी सिद्धिर्बुद्धश्च कंथडि: ।
कोरंटक: सुरानन्द: सिद्धपादश्च चर्पटि: ॥ 6 ॥

कानेरी पूज्यपादश्च नित्यनाथो निरंजन: ।
कपाली बिन्दुनाथश्च काकचंडीश्वराह्वय: ॥ 7 ॥

अल्लाम: प्रभुदेवश्च घोडा चोली च टिंटिणि: ।
भानुकी नारदेवश्च खंड: कापालिकस्तथा ॥ 8 ॥

इत्यादयो महासिद्धा हठयोगप्रभावत: ।
खंडयित्वा कालदंडं ब्रह्माण्डे विचरंति ते ॥ 9 ॥

*Sri Adinath (Shiva), Matsyendra, Shabara, Anandabhairava,
Chaurangi, Mina, Goraksha, Virupaksha, Bileshaya, Manthana,
Bhairava, Siddhi, Buddha, Kanthadi, Korantaka, Surananda,
Siddhipada, Charapati, Kaneri, Pujyapada, Nityanath, Niranjan,
Kapali, Bindunath, Kakachandishwara, Allama, Prabhudeva,
Ghodacholi, Tintini, Bhanuki, Naradeva, Khanda, Kapalika. (5–8)
These mahasiddhas (great masters), having conquered time (death) by
the practice of hatha yoga, roam about the universe.* (9)

These mahasiddhas, having accomplished the goal of yoga,
have released their own personalities from the cycle of birth
and death in the physical world. Being *jivanmuktas*, liberated
while still in the confines of prakriti, their will is sufficiently
strong to enable them to do anything, anywhere and at any
time. This is one of the advantages of being beyond the
confines of time and eventually space.

Mahasiddhas are great beings who attained powers
through the perfection of sadhana. In Sanskrit the word
sadhana means 'to practise', and hence the practitioner is
known as a *sadhaka*. What he practises is known as sadhana.
The object of practice is known as *sadhya*, and when the
sadhana has matured, the results which are accomplished

are known as siddhis. Often the word siddhi is interpreted to mean psychic accomplishment but, according to raja yoga, it means perfection of mind, and sadhana means to train and perfect the crude mind.

As far as siddhis go, there are eight major ones which a sadhaka has to master before he is called a siddha:
1. *Anima* – the ability to become as small as an atom
2. *Laghima* – the ability to become weightless
3. *Mahima* – the ability to become as large as the universe
4. *Garima* – the ability to become heavy
5. *Prapti* – the ability to reach any place
6. *Prakamya* – the ability to stay under water and to maintain the body and youth
7. *Vashitva* – control over all objects, organic and inorganic
8. *Ishatva* – the capacity to create and destroy at will.

A mahasiddha becomes omnipresent and omnipotent because he has purified and perfected the functioning of his physical and pranic bodies through mastery of hatha yoga, and has transcended the normal limitations of mind by traversing the path of raja yoga. To one immersed in the ordinary mind as we know it, such a concept as transcendence of the barriers of time and space would appear to be impossible. The human mind has its limitations and is by no means perfect and infallible. However, as the *Yoga Sutras* of Sage Patanjali contend, the imperfect mind can be made more perfect and efficient through the practice of sadhana.

Our present day scientists acknowledge the fact that man is only utilizing one-tenth of his total brain power. If you consider all that man has accomplished in the fields of science and technology, etc., utilizing only one small compartment of the brain, you may gain some idea of how much might be possible with development of the nine silent centres of the brain. As the mind expands, it increases in power and all physical barriers are transcended.

अशेषतापतप्तानां समाश्रयमठो हठ: ।
अशेषयोगयुक्तानामाधारकमठो हठ: ॥ 10 ॥

For those continually tempered by the heat of tapa (the three types of pain – spiritual, environmental and physical) hatha is like the hermitage giving protection from the heat. For those always united in yoga, hatha is the basis acting like a tortoise.

Through the practice of hatha yoga, one's entire being is made fit and strong, as a shelter from the effects of the pains which come in life. The Sanskrit word *tapa* has two meanings: one is 'to heat', the other is 'pain'. Pain itself is a type of heat. It tempers and heats the mind, emotions and physical body. Pain is of three types: *adhyatmik*, 'spiritual', *adhidevik*, 'natural or environmental', and *adhibhautik*, 'physical'.

As long as we feel the separation from our true identity, we will always suffer spiritually. Adhyatmik tapa is that which comes from living without realization of the inner being, and it is essential so that we strive for a purer experience. Pain brought by natural circumstances is also unavoidable. The course of nature always brings some climatic or geological imbalance such as flood, drought, earth tremors, winds, storms, etc., which affect the balance of the body's functions, and generally disturb the normal functioning of life. Business is affected, crop growth is affected and so are many things. Thirdly, there is physical suffering. Nature continually tests the body, sometimes by an imbalance of bacteria, sometimes by accidents, or sometimes by mental and emotional shocks. Therefore, it is essential that the hatha yogi prepares himself, not only physically, but also mentally, emotionally and psychically, in such a way that he can remain unaffected by these three types of external tempering.

The body and mind should be structured in such a way that they remain unaffected by the mundane circumstances of worldly events. In this way the body-mind becomes like a tortoise which can extend its limbs when necessary or retreat into the protection of its hard covering shell when threatened. The limbs are symbolic of the external senses, which should be externalized when necessary, but which, at our command, can be internalized and unaffected by the external happenings of the world. To perfect this condition, Swatmarama advises us to practise hatha yoga because this will enable such strength and control of the body and mind.

The symbology of the tortoise is very significant. The creation of the world we know is said to rest on the tortoise. It is an emblem of patient endurance. According to Hindu mythology, when dissolution of the universe started to take place, the earth lost its support and was threatened with destruction. Lord Vishnu came to the rescue and manifested in the form of a tortoise, supporting the earth on his back. Thereby the earth was saved.

Of course, this legend is not meant to be taken literally. It is the explanation of what happens during the process of creation and evolution, both externally and internally, and of movement back to the centre of being. As the individual consciousness moves closer to the real self, the supports on which the mind is dependent, i.e. the senses and sensorial world, become less influential. Consciousness can fall into a void if the mind completely dissolves without having a base to fall back on. Preservation of the mind and body must take place when the consciousness moves into higher states. The senses must be conditioned to retract and extend at will. The concept of Vishnu is an aspect of existence which links prana and consciousness to the physical body and creation.

According to the *Tantraraja Tantra*, there are four types of *koorma*, 'tortoise', known as para, deshagata, gramaga and grihaga. *Para koorma* is that which supports the earth; *deshagata*, countries; *gramaga*, villages, and *grihaga*, individual households. Verse 88 says: "He who does japa without knowing *koormasthiti* (the position of koorma) not only fails to get the fruit thereof but he meets with destruction."

In order to experience a higher or purer state of existence and still maintain the body-mind in the gross realm so that the consciousness can return, we have to be prepared. The body and senses should be trained in such a way that consciousness is able to withdraw and come back again to continue the sensorial experiences. Hatha yoga is the process through which the body becomes like a tortoise so that the external form is not the breeding place of disease and disharmony, but rather a protective covering.

हठविद्या परं गोप्या योगिना सिद्धिमिच्छताम् ।
भवेद्वीर्यवती गुप्ता निर्वीर्या तु प्रकाशिता ॥ 11 ॥

Hatha yoga is the greatest secret of the yogis who wish to attain perfection (siddhi). Indeed, to be fruitful, it must be kept secret; revealed it becomes powerless.

This sloka is typical of any yogic shastra expounding higher knowledge, i.e. the science should be kept to oneself. Whatever a sadhaka gains or achieves during the period of sadhana should be a private affair. This may seem a little out of context as the book itself appears to be disclosing the secrets of the practices, but in fact, when you learn under the guidance of a guru, you will find that Swatmarama has only stated the bare essentials as guidelines for the practice of asana, etc., so that the science of hatha yoga will be preserved for humanity.

Originally, Gorakhnath had written much about hatha yoga in the form of prose and poetry. Traditionally, a shastra must be in Sanskrit; local dialects are not accepted as authentic works. Therefore, Swatmarama is continuing Gorakhnath's original work. What has been given here is the system of hatha yoga without too much elucidation. It is left up to the practitioner to find out from his guru what is actually involved. Swatmarama is not advocating the performance of a particular sadhana; he merely noted down the system and outlined the correct methods of practice. Your specific sadhana is between you and your guru. When your sadhana is mastered, the result is siddhi or perfection, and whatever you have managed to perfect is your own attainment and what the guru has enabled you to become.

Gorakhnath used to tell his disciples that hatha yoga is the science of the subtle body. It is the means by which the body's energy can be controlled. He said that hatha is the means of controlling the two main energy channels of the positive and negative currents.

The positive-negative nature of energy exists in every part of our being. Hatha yoga not only brings a balance in the energy, but also in the duality of the mind, and between the lower nature and the higher mind, between the individual soul and the universal spirit. It involves your self and the atma, so why bring anyone else into the picture?

In the *Shiva Samhita* it says that the practitioner should keep his practice secret, "just as a virtuous wife keeps her intimate relations between herself and her husband quiet". This develops the love between husband and wife. Similarly, if you have any respect for your own beloved, the pure atma, whatever experience and power you are bestowed with is your own affair and has to be cultivated privately.

This is a purely logical and scientific process. When you have a small light burning in a room at night, the whole room is illumined. If you take your little light outside into the vast, open space, the light is engulfed by the night and absorbed in the darkness. The same principle applies to the power gained through your sadhana. The power may enlighten your own consciousness, but displayed and dissipated in the magnitude of the outside world, it loses strength.

Sadhana is like a seed and siddhis are like flowers. If you want a seed to germinate you have to leave it in the soil. If you dig it up to show your friends and neighbours how it is progressing, it will not grow any further, it will die. Likewise, the siddhi is just the germinating point of your sadhana. If you are trying to cultivate fully bloomed awareness of atma, you will have to act properly. Sadhana is not a biology lesson where you dig up the plant to investigate its roots. Sadhana involves the growth of your own spirit and it is like the process of giving birth. When a foetus is growing in the womb, we cannot peep into the intermediate stage of its development, we have to wait for the final product.

Keeping sadhana and siddhis under cover has a powerful psychological effect. If you talk about and display your attainments, the sense of 'I' or ego becomes very acute. 'I' have achieved, 'I' had this experience, or 'I' can do this.

If you want to experience cosmic consciousness, ego or *ahamkara* is the greatest barrier. Siddhis never last long, they are impermanent. After a certain stage of evolution they disappear. If you associate yourself with the feeling that 'I' have perfected this and that, you will expect yourself to be able to perform a great feat and so will others. You will be living to meet the expectations of others, otherwise they will not think that you are great. One day when the siddhi leaves you, how are you going to cope with the situation? In spiritual life it is very important to keep the ego under control.

Most of the great saints and siddhas who had powers rarely displayed them. Only the people who lived very close to them knew their greatness. Many siddhas who did display their powers were persecuted, e.g., Christ. Therefore, for your own good and for the good of others it is said, as a warning rather than mere advice, that sadhana and siddhis are to be kept secret.

सुराज्ये धार्मिके देशे सुभिक्षे निरुपद्रवे ।
धनुः प्रमाणपर्यन्तं शिलाग्निजलवर्जिते ।
एकान्ते मठिकामध्ये स्थातव्यं हठयोगिना ॥ 12 ॥

The hatha yogi should live alone in a hermitage and practise in a place the length of a bow (one and a half metres), where there is no hazard from rocks, fire or water, and which is in a well-administered and virtuous kingdom (nation or town) where good alms can be easily attained.

Here Yogi Swatmarama has outlined the ideal situation for hatha yoga sadhana and the location of the hermitage the sadhaka should establish. However, we must remember that in the days of Yogi Swatmarama, the whole structure of society and the way of living were very different from what we see nowadays. It is doubtful whether a truly righteous country still exists today; so few countries allow for the growth of the spirit. With the influence of modern politics, everybody is more interested in making money and gaining power and prestige. It seems India is one of the only countries which has catered for spiritual growth and continued the tradition of giving alms. India is still the home of spiritually hungry and spiritually enlightened souls and she continues to feed her children.

In the tradition of ancient India, a man's life was divided into four distinct stages which were called *ashrama*. The first ashrama was for the period up to the age of twenty-five and it was known as *brahmacharya* ashrama. In this ashrama the child went to live with a guru in a spiritual community, where he received an education in both worldly and spiritual subjects. Then, from the age of twenty-five to fifty, he entered *grihastha* ashrama in which he married and lived a family life. From the age of fifty to seventy-five he passed through *vanaprastha* ashrama, where he and his wife left all family ties and lived alone in the forest or jungle, secluded from society. After seventy-five, the two separated and took the life of sannyasa.

In *sannyasa* ashrama one was free from society and independent of its rules and regulations. However, society took care of the sannyasins and gave them food, clothing and shelter if it was required. Those people who had a natural inclination to sannyasa at an early age were permitted to leave society if the family agreed, but they were never allowed to re-enter the framework of society again.

The ashrama tradition was designed to systematically evolve man's consciousness, and in those times society respected those who were spiritually inclined and took care of them. Ashrams were established so those men and women who were dedicated to the life of the spirit and sannyasa could live in a conducive environment aloof from society. Those who were unable to take to such a life showed their respect by offering what they could to maintain the sannyasins. Thus, it was the householder's duty to give *bhiksha*, or alms, when the swamis came for food.

Now, relating Swatmarama's specifications to modern times, the most important factor is environment. He recommends that a sadhaka should live alone and away from others. Let us be practical for present times and suggest that a person who plans to undergo intensive sadhana should dwell in a place which is a comfortable travelling distance from the noise and pollution of industry and the hustle and bustle of a crowded city. The atmosphere should be calm, peaceful and clean, free from the hazards of rocks, fire and water, landslides, volcanoes, earthquakes, bushfires, floods, swamps, etc. The geological and climatic conditions should be conducive to health and sadhana, and the soil should be suitable for growing crops.

Environment plays a major role in influencing the results of sadhana. If sadhana is performed in a disturbing atmosphere and amidst negative vibrations, too much energy is dissipated in simply trying to overcome the negative influences. The body and mind are very susceptible to

41

negativity and it is much easier to fall under the influence of negative vibrations than to rise above them. A positive environment in itself charges one with energy, inspiration and the will to strive forward in the quest for spiritual enlightenment. Amidst people who are mainly motivated by ambition, and who, thirsty for wealth and power, will push you down at any opportunity, it is difficult to keep your head above water, let alone make any significant progress in sadhana. Therefore, it is essential for a sadhaka to choose quiet and pure surroundings away from the materialistic and polluted cities.

It is recommended in the sloka to practise in an area of one and a half metres, where there are no surrounding objects which may cause physical affliction should they be knocked, etc. One should also practise in this same place every day in order to build up the spiritual vibrations. These are the various recommendations stated by the yogis; they are just a matter of common sense and logical thinking, rather than rules that must be adhered to.

अल्पाद्वारमरध्रगर्तविवरं नात्युच्चनीचायतं
सम्यग्गोमयसांद्रलिप्तममलं निःशेषजंतूज्झितम् ।
बाह्ये मंडपवेदिकूपरुचिरं प्राकारसंवेष्टितं
प्रोक्तं योगमठस्य लक्षणमिदं सिद्धैर्हठाभ्यासिभिः ॥ 13 ॥

*This is the description of the yoga hermitage as prescribed by the
siddhas for the hatha yoga practitioners. The room of sadhana
should have a small door, without aperture (window), holes or
cracks, being neither too high nor too low. It should be spotlessly
clean, wiped with cow manure and free from animals or insects.
Outside, there should be an open platform with a thatched roof,
a well and a surrounding wall (fence). The appearance of the
hermitage should be pleasant.*

When we consider the specifications for the yoga hermitage,
we will have to remember that they were probably ideal for
that particular time and those climatic conditions. Needless
to say, if we plan to establish a sadhana place now, we will
have to make certain adaptations to suit present circumstances and facilities. However, we can use Swatmarama's
description as a basic guideline.

Essentially, Swatmarama is saying that the hermitage
should be simple, clean, practical and very natural. 'Having
a small door' is suitable in a country where people grow no
taller than five and a half feet, but some Europeans are six
feet or more, so allowances must be made.

'Without windows, holes or cracks' was probably recommended to keep insects, rats and other pests from entering
the sadhana room. Nowadays, however, windows can have
flyscreens attached, so there would be no harm in having
a window or two as long as there are curtains. 'No window'
may have been recommended so that the atmosphere
would be dark and more conducive to internalizing the
awareness and introverting the mind. A window could be a
great distraction as the sadhaka's attention could often be

drawn to view the outside world and external happenings. The sadhana room should be 'neither too high nor too low'; if it is too high it would be difficult to clean and if it is too low it would be impractical for sadhana and for proper air circulation.

The recommendation that the sadhana room be kept 'spotlessly clean' is as applicable for today as it was then. If the mind is to be kept pure and unpolluted, it is essential that the environment be the same. Even the daily act of cleaning purifies the mind. The very thought of using cow manure may come as a shock to the western mind, but it is a well-known tradition in India. In the villages, even to this day, most homes have floors made of hard-packed earth. Every morning the women clean their homes and wipe the floors with fresh cow manure mixed with a little water. Cow manure is an excellent disinfectant and insecticide which has medicinal properties. What is cow manure anyway? Digested grass and the cow's bodily secretions. Most importantly, it is a natural disinfectant, it does not contain harmful chemicals to give off gases which pollute the air, and it is cheap. Nature provides us with everything, but we have forgotten the simplicities of life.

The sadhana room must be 'free from insects and animals'. At the time of sadhana there is nothing more distracting than mosquitoes, flies or other buzzing, crawling insects. Besides this, some mosquitoes carry malaria and many insects can give a painful sting or cause skin rashes. Animals should not be kept in the hermitage as they can be a great disturbance, requiring care, food and extra thought that can distract one's energy from sadhana. Particularly when you first commence sadhana, the mind always looks for an excuse to stop the practices as it resents being centred on one particular point for too long. It will always try to prevent you from coming closer to the object of meditation. The mind will surely find good reason to be disturbed and externalized by annoying insects and animals, so a sadhaka should definitely avoid this problem.

44

The 'open platform with a thatched roof' has probably been recommended as a sadhana place for the summer months when it is too hot to practise (especially pranayama) indoors. It could also be used for sleeping outside. In India most people prefer to sleep outdoors as it is cooler and closer to nature.

Swatmarama has not omitted the necessity of a well. Not only is a fresh water supply essential for good health, but a practitioner of hatha yoga needs pure water for his daily purificatory practices as well as for drinking, bathing, toilet, cooking, etc. Neti, dhauti and kunjal require fresh water, and if you can avoid chlorinated and fluoridated water, these techniques are much more effective.

Another reason why there should be a well in the hermitage is that a lot of time and energy can be lost if the yogi has to make several long and maybe arduous trips to a river to fetch water. Swatmarama is outlining instructions for intensive hatha yoga sadhana and, therefore, he gives prime importance to minimizing external distractions and conserving vital energy for the inward journey.

If one's hermitage is in a jungle or some other undeveloped area, a surrounding wall would serve the purpose of keeping out unwanted predators, particularly wild animals. Apart from this, if the hermitage is enclosed within a wall, its spiritual vibrations and magnetic power can be maintained and negative external influences will not be able to penetrate so easily. Thus a peaceful atmosphere can be maintained.

All these recommendations have been given by yogis who have traversed the spiritual path and experienced the pitfalls and problems a sadhaka is likely to face. It should also be understood that these recommendations have an esoteric meaning as well. They indicate the way a sadhaka should structure himself and his mind. The mind has to be protected from outside influences and the body should have a good defence mechanism. The mind and body must be kept pure, simple and modest. Then they will cultivate spiritual vibrations, and conditions will be conducive for the atma to manifest itself. The structure of the hermitage is an external symbol of one's own self and of what will be achieved through sadhana. Therefore, a sadhaka should try to live as simply and as self-sufficiently as possible. His possessions should be kept to a minimum and his surroundings should always remain uncluttered and clean. Thereby he will have fewer mental distractions and worries and all his energy can be directed towards spiritual unfoldment.

एवंविधे मठे स्थित्वा सर्वचिंताविवर्जितः ।
गुरूपदिष्टमार्गेण योगमेव समभ्यसेत् ॥ 14 ॥

In this manner, dwelling in the hermitage, being devoid of all thought (excess mentation), yoga should be practised in the way instructed by the guru.

'Dwelling in the hermitage, being devoid of all thought', means that by living in a place of spiritual vibrations the mind is free from unnecessary thoughts cultivated by society and the modern lifestyle. Under normal conditions the mind can never be thoughtless. Swatmarama is actually saying that the mind should be devoid of all thoughts that are irrelevant to spiritual life. Anxieties and worries caused by family and business should be absent during sadhana, as such disturbances affect one's ability to concentrate.

It is a natural tendency of the mind to dwell on past events and to contemplate the future, but this tendency has to be controlled. The mind has to be concentrated on the practice at hand and it must be kept in the present. There is a constant and habitual mental chatter which has to be nullified, and for this the practice of antar mouna is very useful.

An undisciplined mind is like a boisterous child, telling stories, continually distracting you from your sadhana. If you are working in your study, you do not allow the children to come in and disturb you; the same applies when you are practising sadhana. When the mind is assailed by unwanted and irrelevant thoughts, you should cultivate the habit of putting these thoughts aside until later, when you have finished your sadhana. It does not mean that those who have no control of mind are excluded from practising. In fact, most people today suffer from infirmity of mind. Few people have real control of their mind. At man's present stage of evolution the mind is weak. However, we have to start somewhere so it is better not to concern yourself with the mental activities; just do your practices and let the mind do what it likes. If you do not try to constantly block and suppress the mind, it will automatically become obedient and concentrated.

In the days of Yogi Swatmarama, people may have been more sattwic by nature. Nowadays we find that people are either tamasic or rajasic. A sattwic person will have a quiet mind and his sadhana will progress unhindered by the *chitta vrittis* or 'mental modifications'. However, a rajasic person will have a very restless and oscillating mind, while a tamasic person will have a dull and lazy mind. Therefore, we have to make concessions.

We should also remember that in Swatmarama's day, more people were able to devote their whole lives or a considerable portion of their lives to sadhana. It is not possible for people today to leave all their social commitments and simply practise sadhana all day. Few people could even manage to take a month off work to retreat into seclusion for intensive sadhana. This is highly recommended, but if impractical, further modifications have to be made. Let us say that for the average person it is enough to have a room set aside and to devote thirty minutes to sadhana every day.

'Yoga should be practised in the way instructed by the guru.' This is probably the most important sentence in the whole text. Whichever yogic text you pick up, you will read the same thing. The *Shiva Samhita* says: "Having attained the guru, practise yoga. Without the guru, nothing can be auspicious." According to *Skanda Purana*: "The systematic stages of yoga can only be learned from a competent guru." The *Yoga Bija* says that: "He who wants to practise yoga should have a competent guru with him." In the *Sruti* it is written that: "Mahatmas reveal those things only to him who has deep devotion towards his guru as well as God." Thus guru is the most vital element in sadhana.

Guru is not merely a yoga teacher. He is the only one who can enlighten your soul by the luminosity of his own revealed spirit. He reflects the brilliance of your spirit and what you see in him is actually your own self. *Gu* means 'darkness' and *ru* means 'light'. Guru is the one who removes the darkness and ignorance from the mind to reveal the pure light of the inner consciousness. He may be an adept in yoga or any science, or he may be completely illiterate. His social qualifications are unimportant as far as your spiritual experience is concerned. The important factor is your faith in his words and your obedience; then it does not matter whether his instructions seem right or wrong, they will prove fruitful to you.

In the science of hatha yoga there is a specific system which has to be followed, and if you find a hatha guru he will instruct you in the correct manner in which you should practise. It does not mean that the same system should be followed by your neighbour. Your guru knows how to tackle all the individual problems you are having. If no obstacles arise, good, he can guide you quickly. If you are facing certain problems or difficulties, he will know how to guide you step by step in accordance with your own personal evolution.

We have very little understanding of our bodily functions and we are virtually unaware of our mental potential. Consciousness is like an iceberg; we can only see the superficial portion which is above the surface, and because of our limited perception we cannot understand how yoga can evolve the spirit from the gross body and the lower consciousness. Therefore, when we take to sadhana it is essential for us to have the guidance of one who thoroughly understands the process of spiritual unfoldment. There is only one person for this purpose, that is the guru.

अत्याहार: प्रयासश्च प्रजल्पो नियमग्रह: ।
जनसंगश्च लौल्यं च षड्भिर्योगो विनश्यति ॥ 15 ॥

Overeating, exertion, talkativeness, adhering to rules, being in the
company of common people and unsteadiness (wavering mind) are
the six (causes) which destroy yoga.

According to hatha yoga there are six major factors which
prevent *yoga*, or union, from occurring. In hatha yoga, union
means uniting the two energy forces in the body, i.e. the
pranic and mental energy flowing in ida and pingala nadis.
Usually, these two forces do not operate simultaneously;
either the mental force predominates or the vital energy is
dominant. Hatha yoga is the process of balancing the flow
of these two alternating forces to bring perfect physical
and mental equilibrium, and awakening of sushumna and
kundalini. All branches of yoga unite these two energies
and channel them through the third nadi, sushumna. The
three nadis, ida, pingala and sushumna, terminate in ajna
chakra, the psychic centre which is situated in the region of
the medulla oblongata and the pineal gland. Through the
practice of yoga, ida and pingala are equalized, sushumna is
activated and ajna chakra is awakened.

Ida is connected to the left nostril and the right brain
hemisphere. Pingala is connected to the right nostril and
the left brain hemisphere. In the same way that the right
hemisphere governs the left side of the body, on a pranic
level ida also controls the functions of the left side of the
body. Likewise, pingala and the left hemisphere govern the
right side of the body. Just as the brain hemispheres and the
nostrils alternate their functions in ninety minute cycles, so
do ida and pingala.

Ida and the right hemisphere activate an introverted
state of awareness: orientation in space, artistic, creative and
musical ability. Conversely, pingala and the left hemisphere
externalize the awareness. Your approach becomes logical,

sequential, mathematical and analytical. Ida nadi controls the subconscious activities, whereas pingala is responsible for the conscious and dynamic functions. When these forces are balanced and operating simultaneously, then both nostrils are active. This indicates that sushumna nadi is functioning. Usually this occurs for one to four minutes between each ninety minute cycle.

The object of hatha yoga practice is to increase the duration and flow of sushumna and the period when both nostrils flow simultaneously so that a balance is created in the physical and mental functions. When the mind and body are not functioning in harmony, there is a division between the physical and mental rhythms, which inevitably leads to sickness.

When a sadhaka is in the process of uniting the two opposite forces of ida and pingala, he must avoid all activities which waste energy and distract the mind. One major obstacle to yoga, or union, is overeating. When the body is overloaded with food, it becomes sluggish and the mind becomes dull. Over a period of time toxins build up in the body, constipation sets in and the whole physical-mental system becomes blocked. If the body is toxic and lethargic, how can you expect to make progress in sadhana? Whatever sadhana you do will act as a purification, so you will just be spending your time removing toxins and disease. However, if you avoid overeating and its consequences, then the sadhana you are doing will help you to progress more quickly. Swami Sivananda of Rishikesh and many other yogis have said that the stomach should be half filled with food, one quarter with water and one quarter with air.

The next advice is that the hatha yogi should avoid overexerting or overstraining the body and mind. Hard physical labour or intense mental work taxes one of the energy systems and can create further imbalance between the two energies. The hatha yogi has to conserve and build up his store of energy for spiritual purposes and should not waste it in performing any unnecessary physical or mental feats.

51

Too much talking dissipates vital energy and wastes time which could be better spent in awakening the inner awareness. Gossiping with people who have low morals, base consciousness and sensuous desires cannot enlighten your soul, rather, their negative vibrations may influence you. Social situations and irrelevant discussions definitely distract the mind from sadhana.

Although Swatmarama advises that a sadhaka should not adhere to strict rules and regulations, the guru's instructions must be followed. As far as social rituals and religious doctrines are concerned, it is unnecessary that they be maintained for spiritual progress. Sadhana is not dependent on social morals nor are its effects promoted by religious practices. Adhering to rules makes one narrow minded. Yoga is meant to expand the consciousness, not to limit it. A yogi should have a free and open mind.

If you are accustomed to taking a cold bath every morning before practice, and one day you have no water, you should not be disturbed. Take a bath when you can get water. Your mind should be flexible and you should be able to adjust to circumstances.

Unsteadiness means an imbalanced body metabolism, inability to hold one posture for a period of time, and a wavering mind. Obviously yoga cannot be achieved under these conditions. When there is physical, mental, emotional and psychic imbalance, the energy is dispersed, but if the energy is channelled properly, all the bodily systems become stable, and physical and mental steadiness develop automatically. Unsteadiness also means wavering willpower. One day you get up at 3 am and the next morning you sleep in till 7 am because you feel lazy. When there is inconsistency and irregularity in lifestyle further imbalance in the body will ensue. An unswerving mind and steady body cultivate yoga.

If you can live in a hermitage as described in the previous sloka, all these obstacles will be avoided naturally. However, if you are unable to live in such a place, try to develop the habit of avoiding all activities which are useless, time-consuming and energy-depleting, and channel all your desires and actions into spiritual ventures.

Apart from these obstacles, the *Tantraraja Tantra* mentions that: "The six obstacles to yoga are *kama* (lust), *krodha* (anger), *lobha* (greed), *moha* (infatuation), *abhimana* (pride), *mada* (arrogance)." The six obstacles described in hatha yoga and in tantra are interwoven and interlinked. Those of tantra have a broader scope and pinpoint the obstacle to actually be the mental attitude.

उत्साहात्साहसाद्धैर्यात्तत्त्वज्ञानाश्च निश्चयात् ।
जनसंगपरित्यागात्षड्भिर्योग: प्रसिद्ध्यति ॥

*Enthusiasm, perseverance, discrimination, unshakeable faith,
courage, avoiding the company of common people, are the (six
causes) which bring success in yoga.*　　　　　　　　　16 (i)

To succeed in yoga, enthusiasm or, we could say, a positive
attitude is absolutely essential. Constant inspiration and the
ideal of attaining perfection generate energy and help to
maintain regularity in practice. Every day should seem like
the first day of practice. The same zeal should exist between
a sadhaka and his sadhana as between a newlywed couple.
Then the sadhana will be invigorating and exciting. This
spontaneously generates perseverance.

No matter what happens externally, rain, hail or shine,
your sadhana must be done regularly. Whether you are
afflicted with material losses or you acquire valuable
possessions, whether there are visible signs of progress in
your sadhana or not, you must continue with your efforts.
Even if you have practised for fifteen years, you must
continue until you reach the final goal. It may take only one
more month of practice, or it may take a whole lifetime.
Everybody evolves at a different rate, so it is useless to
compare yourself with others. No matter what, your attitude
should always be optimistic.

Discrimination is the third prerequisite for success in
yoga. Everything you do and every aspect of your life,
including your diet, clothing, company, material necessities,
conversations, etc., should be conducive to your sadhana. If
something is going to be detrimental, leave it.

Unshakeable faith in guru and the ultimate truth or
reality is the most important tool for a sadhaka. If you doubt
your guru, how will you succeed in what he has taught you?
If you lose faith in your guru, there is no hope for success in
yoga. Absolute faith in whatever he says and does is the only

key to unlock the door to higher experience. You can doubt your own ability to achieve, but if you have faith in guru and he says you can move a mountain, you will do it.

Once a hermit lived alone on a little island. He was totally absorbed in God consciousness and practised Ishwara pooja daily according to his guru's instructions. One day a very pious and devout religious man rowed to the island. When the religious man saw the hermit practise his pooja, he was horrified. Although the hermit's devotion had reached the utmost heights his ritual was all back to front. The religious man instructed him in the right way and the hermit was truly grateful.

So the religious man rowed away from the island feeling he had done a good deed, but when he was a few hundred metres out to sea, he saw a figure running over the water towards him. It was the hermit and he was very upset. He said in a worried tone, "Now I'm confused. I don't remember if you said it should be like this or like that." The religious man stood aghast and then, gathering himself, he reassured the hermit that however he practised it was correct. The hermit was relieved and proceeded to walk back to his island over the water. Even if faith in guru and your ultimate goal is the only thing you have in your favour, you will surely succeed.

Courage is also recommended for fulfilling yoga, courage to face the inner visions and realizations as they dawn. Courage, perseverance and faith go hand in hand. Not only in the face of internal hardships but the external ones also.

During the period of sadhana you may find it useless to mix with people who have lower aspirations. At that stage, the less you involve yourself with others the more your inner knowledge can grow. Of course, a sadhaka should not consider the others to be inferior, but until his physical, mental, emotional and psychic resistance are developed, it is better to stay away from social interactions and negative influences.

These six factors can be cultivated anywhere, whether living in a city with your family or alone in a hermitage. A householder should modify them to suit his lifestyle.

अथ यमनियमाः ।

अहिंसा सत्यमस्तेयं ब्रह्मचर्यं क्षमा धृतिः ।
दयार्जवं मिताहारः शौचं चैव यमा दश ॥

Non-violence, truth, non-stealing, continence (being absorbed in a pure state of consciousness), forgiveness, endurance, compassion, humility, moderate diet and cleanliness are the ten rules of conduct (yama).   16 (ii)

तपः संतोष आस्तिक्यं दानमीश्वरपूजनम् ।
सिद्धान्तवाक्यश्रवणं ह्वीमती च तपो हुतम् ।
नियमा दश संप्रोक्ता योगशास्त्रविशारदैः ॥ 16 ॥

Penance (austerity), contentment, belief (faith) in the Supreme (God), charity, worship of God, listening to the recitations of sacred scriptures, modesty, a discerning intellect, japa (mantra repetition) and sacrifice are the ten observances (niyama).   16 (iii)

Ten rules of conduct and ten observances, called *yama* and *niyama*, are listed in raja yoga, but hatha yoga does not place much emphasis on them. Raja yoga claims that yama and niyama must be practised before commencing hatha yoga. It says, control the mind and then purify the body, but in this day and age too many problems can arise if an aspirant comes into direct confrontation with his mind at the beginning of his spiritual quest. It is like running from a den of lions into a cage of tigers. Therefore, in hatha yoga the whole system has been designed for the people of Kali Yuga. Hatha yoga commences with purification of the body, the *shatkarmas*, then come asana and pranayama. Yama and niyama can be practised later when the mind has become stable and its outward-going tendencies can be controlled.

Here, Swatmarama is merely listing what is required from a sadhaka at a later stage of practice. He has mentioned the ways in which yoga can be enhanced and the factors that can lead to failure. The yama and niyama are given to verify why he states these causes, so there may be a little repetition on certain points. Swatmarama also advises, "not to adhere to rules". Yama and niyama are rules, and to an extent they are also moral codes. Initially, it is not essential to practise these and it should not be thought that you cannot succeed without them. The yama and niyama have been given as guidelines to keep a sadhaka on the path.

The first yama is *ahimsa*, or 'non-violence': to remain passive in any situation, without the desire to harm anyone or anything, either physically, emotionally, psychologically or psychically. In India, the Jain sect is very firm in this code of conduct. They even sweep the pathway before them so they will not step on any insect and kill it. They strain all their drinking water and cut their vegetables scrupulously so that no form of life can be injured. Ahimsa means not acting with the will to violate anything, even the atmosphere. Harmony and serenity have to be maintained.

There is no need to place any religious connotation on the word 'ahimsa'. It is a process of self-control, self-awareness and awareness of everything that is around you. If you harm another person intentionally, and you lose control of your mind and actions, you are creating an imbalance in yourself. Violence means moving away from your true nature; ahimsa means coming closer to the pure spirit. Mahatma Gandhi was a living example of this doctrine.

'Honesty' is something we rarely find in this modern world of corruption, and it is definitely something which needs to be cultivated and instilled again. If you make a habit of fooling or cheating others, you start to believe the lies yourself. You are only being dishonest with yourself. Basically, honesty means being truthful with yourself and not aiming to cheat others for your own personal gain or to discredit them.

'Non-stealing' is easy to understand: not taking what does not belong to you, not only for social or moral reasons, but to avoid psychological and karmic repercussions. Stealing breeds guilt. In yoga we are trying to release the complexes and samskaras from our mind and personality, so we really do not want to create any more. If you need something and it is truly essential, somehow it will come to you.

'Continence', or *brahmacharya*, is the next yama. Generally, brahmacharya is considered to be abstention from sexual involvement or relationships. Some people even go as far as having absolutely no contact with the opposite sex, neither talking nor looking at a woman or man. However, this is not the true meaning of brahmacharya. Brahmacharya is the combination of two words: *Brahman*, 'pure consciousness' and *charya*, 'one who moves'. Therefore, it means 'one who lives in constant awareness of Brahman'; one whose awareness is absorbed in pure consciousness, whose mind is above the duality of male and female, who sees the atman in all. One who is in constant communion with the atma is a brahmachari.

A true brahmachari can be involved in sexual relationships and maintain awareness of only the supreme experience. Passions do not arise in the mind when he or she comes in contact with the opposite sex. In yoga and tantra they explain this as maintaining the bindu, i.e. not losing the bindu or semen. The bindu has to be kept in the brain centre where it is produced. It should not flow out through the sexual organs, and if it does, it should be drawn back. For this purpose there are many yogic techniques which curb the production of sex hormones and restructure the reproductive organs. Yoga influences the whole endocrine system by regulating the pineal and pituitary glands.

Brahmacharya was generally taken to mean abstention from sexual activity because, by refraining from sexual stimulation, sexual impulses and the production of sex hormones are reduced. Sexual abstinence may be necessary in the beginning while you are trying to gain mastery over body and mind, but once you have managed this, and you can maintain awareness of the higher reality, sexual interaction is no barrier. In fact, in tantra it is never said that sexual interactions are detrimental to spiritual awakening. On the contrary, tantra says that the sexual act can be used to induce spiritual awakening.

By avoiding sexual contact one does not automatically become a brahmachari. You may abstain from sexual interaction for thirty or forty years and still not be a brahmachari. If your mind is haunted by sexual fantasies or you have an uncontrollable loss of semen even while avoiding any sort of contact, then you are definitely not a brahmachari. You are suppressing and causing frustration, and this will do more harm than good.

Therefore, in hatha yoga there are special techniques which aid in brahmacharya by regulating hormonal secretions and the functioning of the glands. Sexual thoughts and desires are then curbed. After all, what causes sexual motivation? A chemical reaction in the brain and body or, let us say, hormones. Control of the hormones induces true brahmacharya. When the bindu is retained in the brain centre, sexual urges are controlled and the mind can remain absorbed in awareness of the supreme. This is real brahmacharya.

The next yama is 'forgiveness', or *kshama*. Forgiveness actually means the ability to let experiences go from the mind and not to hold on to memories of past events. It means living in the present. This yama is not only for the sake of other people, it is more for your own benefit. If you can forgive, life becomes more pleasant and harmonious. Whereas revenge brings anger and remorse and creates karma, forgiveness bring happiness and lightness to your heart.

Swatmarama has already discussed endurance; he called it 'perseverance'. The trials and tribulations of life are often arduous and painful, but they have a positive purpose. If you cannot endure ordinary mundane experiences, how will you cope when the atma reveals itself? A spiritual experience can occur at any moment and you have to be prepared to sustain it on every level. It is not just something which happens to the spirit and leaves the body and mind unaffected.

One has to be ever alert and constant in both practice and aspiration. Even if the whole world collapses around you, it does not matter. If you give up hope and effort, you can never be successful. The divine power is gracious to devotees and disguises itself in many forms just to test their devotion and faith. When we give up hope and belief because the odds seem to have turned against us, we have misunderstood the situation. Due to our concepts of good and bad we assume that a particular experience is negative, and react to it. However, whether circumstances seem to be pleasant or unpleasant, we must maintain faith and continue our practice; only then can sadhana bear fruit.

'Compassion' is kindness to the young and old, rich and poor, worthy and seemingly unworthy. We are all of the one atma. Cruelty to others ultimately rebounds on us. Kindness to others brings divine mercy. If you open your heart to the divine energy and you can feel compassion for every creature, you will make quick progress in your search for the atma.

Swatmarama has previously described humility as 'modesty'. Spontaneous humility comes with divine awareness and surrender of the ego or 'I' awareness. It is ego which creates the feeling of separation from the atma and prevents us from feeling the inner being. Those, like Swami Sivananda of Rishikesh and many other great saints, who found unity in the atma, were as meek as small children. Humbleness or meekness means simplicity of character and lifestyle. The soul needs no lavish accessories, food or praises, and when you seek them they pull you away from your true identity.

'Moderation in diet' means neither overeating nor undereating. It means eating sparingly but comfortably filling the stomach and meeting the requirements of the body. Thus, body and mind remain healthy and balanced. A weak body cannot support a strong mind. A strong and healthy body reflects the nature of the mind. Overeating and greediness for food shows an uncontrolled mind.

Your diet should be simple, pure and not overspiced. Eat what is necessary to maintain your bodily requirements and choose a diet which will be most conducive for your sadhana. However, do not become too food conscious.

The last of the yamas is cleanliness in your whole lifestyle; keeping the body and mind in a pure state. When the body is clean and there are no blockages, it can become a perfect vessel for divine energy and pure consciousness. Not only should the internal body be clean, so should the surroundings in which you live. To clean the body internally, hatha yoga prescribes the six cleansing techniques: neti, dhauti, nauli, basti, kapalbhati and trataka.

These ten yamas are followed by the ten niyamas. The first is *tapah* which means 'to heat' and also refers to austerities. There are three types of tapas: *sharirik*, physical; *vachik*, vocal; and *manasik*, mental; which may again be sattwic, rajasic or tamasic.

In the past, tapas meant standing in cold water on one foot for hours at a time, or wearing a loin cloth in the freezing cold, and suchlike. However, these methods are unnecessary for spiritual evolution and actually they do not help people of this age to come any closer to self-realization. They will only cause physical discomfort and possibly diseases like rheumatism, arthritis, etc., and disbelief in the path of self-evolution. These austerities may help strengthen the mind but there are other less severe methods of doing this.

Austerities for people of this age involve doing those things which test the willpower and strength of mind and body. If you are used to getting up at 7 am and if you change this habit and make yourself get up at 4 am, this is tapas. Once you are accustomed to it, it no longer remains an austerity. Austerity is doing away with comforts and luxuries such as a ten-inch thick foam mattress, expensive clothing, tasty food, television, air-conditioner and heater, and involves taking cold baths in winter, doing tasks which you do not like, etc. Once you adjust yourself to such conditions, they no longer remain austerities for you. These processes mould the body and mind into a purer and more sattwic state and they help in spiritual growth.

'Contentment', or *santosha*, means developing the sense of satisfaction in any situation, whatever may come to you. Whether you have a lot or nothing, if you gain or lose, you should try to feel that you have more than enough. The opposite of this is insecurity, which creates restlessness and unsteadiness. Definitely we are all searching for something. Most people find contentment in material fulfilment, but after a while discontent arises. When you realize that desires can never be satisfied, it is time to search for fulfilment in spirit. This is the only way to truly feel santosha or satisfaction.

'Belief in the Supreme', or *astikyam*, is the same as faith. Some people call the Supreme 'God'. Of course, God is not a man sitting in heaven on a throne. Life and creation are very systematic and scientific. You may call the cosmic power God, Nature or Supreme consciousness, but definitely a higher force exists and controls all lower existences.

Some people have been able to experience the existence and operation of the Supreme and it is the right of everyone to expand their consciousness to such a state. We can only maintain faith that one day, we too shall have this experience. Even an agnostic believes in something. Maybe he disagrees with religion, but he cannot say that he does not believe in a force greater than his own mind and body. He cannot deny the facts of science and nature and, although he will always try to deny the existence of God, he will still seek facts to prove His non-existence or to confirm his own existence. So, he is also searching for the higher experience.

We are all like little children in the supreme vision, and just as a baby trusts its mother, we should also have the same unquestioning faith in the higher force. A mother does not need to explain to her child why she is bathing or feeding it, because it will not understand her explanations. Similarly, the cosmic force has no need to explain anything to us. If you have faith in the will and the work of the Supreme, this faith alone is enough to guide and protect you.

'Charity', or *daanam*, not only means providing material things and financial aid for the poor and underprivileged, it also means helping or serving others in any way required, for example, by offering mental or emotional support. To be truly charitable, one must have a giving, unselfish and sharing attitude but, of course, not to the extent that you exhaust your own resources.

Swami Sivananda calls this *udara vritti*, which means 'having a large heart'. In his word:, "Charity must be spontaneous and unrestrained. Giving must become habitual. You must experience joy in giving. If you give, the whole wealth of the world is yours. Money will come to you. This is the immutable, inexorable, unrelenting law of nature. Some people do charity and are anxious to see their name published in newspapers. This is the tamasic form of charity. You must give with the right mental attitude and realize God (the ultimate reality) through charitable deeds."

'Worship of the Supreme Being', or *Ishwara poojanam*, should not be misunderstood as pertaining to religion. Sage Patanjali calls it *Ishwara pranidhana*, or resignation to the Supreme Being. In India the majority of people do ritualistic pooja to their own deity, but that is not the meaning implied here. The external life we lead is but the manifestation of the Supreme; it is the interplay of energy and consciousness. That should be remembered constantly. Everything is sacred, not just a pooja room, etc.

There is a well-known story of Guru Nanak which illustrates this point. He was doing a pilgrimage to Mecca and just before he reached there, he lay down to rest. A Muslim devotee came by and said, "You can't lie like that, your feet are directed towards the mosque." Guru Nanak told the devotee that he was a very old man and he was tired. He asked the devotee to kindly move his feet away from the direction of the mosque. However, in whichever direction the Muslim devotee moved Nanak's feet, he still saw the mosque in front of them.

This shows the elevated state of Nanak's consciousness. To him there was not one place that was not holy or that did not represent the Supreme. Similarly, worship or pooja should be internal. What is the point of spending hours doing ritualistic pooja, offering flowers, kumkum, rice and incense, and chanting mantras, if you cannot have the awareness of the highest reality in your external life. External pooja is done to awaken the inner consciousness; but if you still argue with the family and friends, cheat others and cause them pain and suffering, then your pooja is meaningless. Pooja means carrying with you awareness and respect for the subtle force, the Supreme, in everything.

The sixth niyama is 'listening to discourses of spiritual scriptures', *siddhanta* or *siddhantavakya shravanam*. Traditionally, siddhanta is a specific section of the Vedas and vedantic philosophy. Siddhanta is the culmination of spiritual knowledge collected in a concise form. Listening to spiritual knowledge and to what ancient sages found in their quest and experience helps develop our higher faculty of knowledge, or jnana. It helps us understand the spiritual path and the way in which the spirit unfolds.

In India there is a tradition where people sit together with a person who has spiritual knowledge and discuss matters of the soul. It is called *satsang*. It is not necessary that only siddhanta be discussed; you can listen to any spiritual topic. Most people waste time and energy in going to the cinema, etc., which only develops the worldly nature. Satsang preserves mental and emotional energy and it keeps one's awareness in the realm of spiritual vibrations and aspirations.

'Modesty', or *hree*, is a part of humility which has already been discussed.

'A discerning intellect', or *mati*, is essential for discriminating between truth and untruth. It means being able to perceive the essential nature or underlying truth of a situation, whether the situation involves other people, or only yourself. It is something like being able to interpret the significance of a dream, i.e. whether it was due to physical imbalance, mental and emotional purging, suppression, or if it was of spiritual significance. Life is also symbolic of the internal world. Understanding its meaning and being able to analyze and judge correctly is to have a discerning intellect.

In some yogic texts the eighth observance is tapo, while in others it is japo. As tapaha has been mentioned in the first place, it seems more likely that the original word is japo. The *Hatharatnavali* and *Srimad Devi Bhagavatam* have also listed japo. *Japa* means 'repetition of mantra'. Mantra can be repeated mentally, whispered, sung or written. Not just any sound can be a mantra, nor are mantras the names of gods or holy words. They are specifically formulated sound vibrations which affect the deeper layers of the mind and consciousness. There are different grades of mantras: some affect the subtle body, some affect the pranic vibrations and others are purely transcendental.

Initially, japa is done consciously and mechanically, but after some time the mantra comes spontaneously from within your own consciousness. You do not have to think about it, it just continues by itself. Awareness will be drawn to the sound and thought of the mantra like a moth to a light.

The universal mantra which can be used by everybody is the mantra *Om*, comprised of the sounds 'A', 'U' and 'M'. It is the cosmic vibration of both the manifest and unmanifest realities. 'A' represents the conscious world and creation, 'U' represents the intermediate realms and subconscious, and 'M' represents the unmanifest and unconscious. The three sounds together represent the existence of the supreme consciousness and manifestation. Everything in creation has its own particular vibrational frequency and mantra, but the combination of the whole universal and vibrational frequencies pulsates to the rhythm of *Om*. There is no greater mantra to repeat.

'Sacrifice', or *hutam*, is the last niyama. It does not mean the ritualistic form of offering oblations in a fire ceremony. It means internal sacrifice, giving up worldly desires and surrendering the ego; sacrificing sensual experiences for spiritual experiences. Sacrifice is giving up the idea that life is for worldly pleasure alone.

65

All the yamas and niyamas stated here constitute twenty mental disciplines and self-restraints which were originally designed to help a sadhaka conserve and build up his store of pranic and psychic energy. Although they were formulated by exponents of yoga, they can also be found in many religions. Those who had higher revelations found these disciplines helpful for preparing aspirants for spiritual experiences. However, they should not be considered as mere religious practices; they are a part of the yogic science.

In the *Yoga Sutras* of Sage Patanjali, only five yama and five niyama are specified: non-violence, truthfulness, honesty, abstinence and non-possessiveness; cleanliness, contentment, austerity, self-analysis and resignation to the Supreme Being. However, the *Hatharatnavali* says there are fifteen yama and eleven niyama: mental pleasure, contentment, keeping silence, control of the senses, compassion, politeness, belief in the Supreme, straightforwardness, forgiveness, purity of thought and emotion, non-violence, abstinence, patience and forbearance; bathing, cleanliness, truth, repetition of mantra, oblations of water, austerity, self-restraint, endurance, reverential salutations, observance of vows, and fasting.

In this day and age it may be difficult to try and force yourself to keep to these rules, therefore, Swatmarama does not stress their importance. However, they can be cultivated with sadhana and spiritual endeavour. The mind should never be forced to accept something which feels unnatural. When it comes spontaneously there will be no suppression. If you force yourself to do something which is going against your nature, you will develop all sorts of psychological complications. Keep the yamas and niyamas in mind and let them develop naturally.

Asana

अथ आसनम्

हठस्य प्रथमांगत्वादासनं पूर्वमुच्यते ।
कुर्यात्तदासनं स्थैर्यमारोग्यं चांगलाघवम् ॥ 17 ॥

Prior to everything, asana is spoken of as the first part of hatha yoga. Having done asana one gets steadiness (firmness) of body and mind; diseaselessness and lightness (flexibility) of the limbs.

Asana is the first part of hatha yoga. In raja yoga, *asana* refers to the sitting position, but in hatha yoga it means something else. Asana is a specific position which opens the energy channels and psychic centres. Hatha yoga is a process through which purification and control of the body take place by restructuring the pranic flows. The hatha yogis also found that by developing control of the body through asana, the mind is controlled. Therefore, asana practice is foremost in hatha yoga. When you practise asana, steadiness develops. Prana moves freely, and there is less chance of disease occurring. Just as stagnant water is the breeding ground for all sorts of creatures, when prana stagnates anywhere in the body, conditions are perfect for bacteria to flourish; prana should move like swift flowing water.

When prana flows freely, the body also becomes supple. Stiffness of the body is due to blockages and an accumulation of toxins. When prana begins to flow the toxins are removed from the system and you will be able to bend and stretch in a relaxed manner without having to do vigorous warming up exercises. When the store of prana is increased to a greater degree, the body will move by itself. You may find yourself spontaneously performing asanas and various bodily postures, mudras or even pranayama. You may find yourself performing postures you could never have done before. This is due to a relaxed state and to a greater vibrational rate of the prana.

वशिष्ठाद्यैश्च मुनिभिर्मत्स्येन्द्राद्यैश्च योगिभि: ।
अंगीकृतान्यासनानि कथ्यन्ते कानिचिन्मया ॥ 18 ॥

I will proceed to describe some of the asana accepted by munis such as Vasishta and yogis such as Matsyendranath.

The yogic tradition says that in all, there are eighty-four lakh of asanas, i.e. there are as many asanas as forms of life. No wonder Swatmarama says he is only going to describe 'some' of the asanas! Asanas were done to evolve the consciousness from the lowest to the highest state. Therefore, some asanas imitate the shapes of the bow or boat; plants like trees and the lotus; reptiles, fish, the foetus, birds, saints like Vasishtha and gods such as Nataraja.

In the yogic texts the maximum number of asanas described is thirty-three. Thus Swatmarama describes those which are essential and which were performed by the founders of hatha yoga.

It is interesting that Swatmarama should narrate asanas practised by munis such as Vasishtha. It is natural that he would discuss those performed by Matsyendranath as he is the founder of this hatha yoga system, but Vasishtha was a jnana yogi, so we would assume that he would have mainly utilized sitting and meditative postures rather than the more dynamic postures. It shows that even those concerned with contemplation and higher wisdom realized the necessity of yogasana. It also implies that the influence of asanas is more than physical. If saints such as Vasishtha were able to become honoured as jnanis, asanas must also be beneficial in the development of higher wisdom. The sloka seems to infer that whether you are specifically practising hatha or any other form of yoga, asana is important and should be incorporated.

SWASTIKASANA (auspicious pose)

जानूर्वोरन्तरे सम्यक्कृत्वा पादतले उभे ।
ऋजुकाय: समासीन: स्वस्तिकं तत्प्रचक्षते ॥ 19 ॥

Placing both soles (of the feet) on the inner side of the thighs, sitting equipoised with a straight body. This is called swastika (asana).

Technique

Sit crosslegged and bring the feet up between the thighs and calf muscles.

Place the hands in jnana or chin mudra.

Though this is a steady sitting position, it affects the whole body. Prana shakti is directed in a particular manner suitable for meditation. The nadis at the back of the legs are stimulated. The exact points of stimulation can be found by pressing along the acupuncture meridians. When you find a particularly tender and sensitive point, that is a centre. These nadis carry energy to centres in the spinal column and the energy is distributed from there. When you sit in any meditative pose you are stimulating the main nadis.

The sciatic nerve is gently massaged in this posture, thereby influencing the lumbar region. The abdominal muscles are also influenced and the inner body temperature is affected.

Swatmarama does not forget to state that the body should be straight, i.e. in alignment. This is of prime importance in any asana practice. For meditation it is essential that the spinal column is straight so that nervous impulses can pass freely to the brain. Furthermore, the main nadi, sushumna, is situated within the spinal cord and the impulses must also be able to run straight up this nadi when the energy wants to rise. If you bend or lean to one side, either ida or pingala will be suppressed and the other will become predominant. The aim is to activate sushumna, therefore, the body must be in alignment and in a balanced position so there is no blockage to the flow of prana.

The symbol of the swastika represents fertility, creativity and auspiciousness. Thus this asana, being so named, induces the same capacity in the body.

Descriptions of swastikasana in the *Gheranda Samhita*, *Hatharatnavali* and *Shiva Samhita* all agree with the sloka.

GOMUKHASANA (cow's face pose)

सव्ये दक्षिणगुल्कं तु पृष्ठपार्श्वे नियोजयेत् ।
दक्षिणेऽपि तथा सव्यं गोमुखं गोमुखाकृति: ॥ 20 ॥

*Place the right ankle next to the left buttock and the left (ankle) next
to the right (buttock). This is gomukhasana and it resembles the face
of the cow.*

Technique

Bend the right knee and place the right foot so that the
left heel touches the side of the left buttock.

Then bend the left leg over the right thigh so that the
heel is placed close to the right buttock. This gives the
impression of a cow's face.

Then join the hands behind the back.

Stretch the left arm up in the air and bring it down
behind the head and back. Stretch the right arm
downward and bring it up the back.

Clasp the two hands together.

In this position the back is automatically straightened. After practising for some time, change the position so that the left leg is underneath, the right leg is on top, the right elbow is pointing up and the left elbow is pointing down.

Alternatively, the hands may rest on the upper knee, one on top of the other.

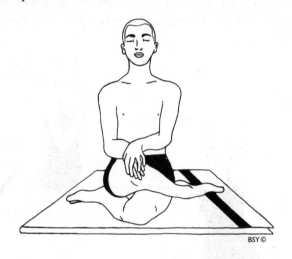

In this position the eyes may be open or closed, or shambhavi mudra may be performed, which will give the mind a point of concentration. Although gomukhasana is not a meditative posture, the longer the position is held the better.

Gomukhasana tones the muscles and nerves around the shoulders and the cardiac plexus. The nadis in the legs are squeezed and the nadis connected with the reproductive organs and glands are also influenced, thus regulating the hormonal secretions. On a pranic level, gomukhasana affects the vajra nadi and prevents prana from flowing outward. Instead, prana is directed to and accumulated in mooladhara chakra. Because the fingers are interlinked prana also cannot escape through the hands. Gomukhasana creates a complete energy circuit flowing in the spinal region. In fact, the arm position is very significant as the arms form the shape of the figure eight or infinity. This represents the complete balance of prana, between the higher and lower forces and the positive and negative aspects.

The various yogic texts agree in their descriptions of gomukhasana, except one step has been omitted from the final position, and that is the arm position.

VEERASANA (hero's pose)

एकं पादं तथैकस्मिन्विन्यसेदुरुणि स्थिरतम् ।
इतरस्मिंस्तथा चोरं वीरासनमितीरितम् ॥ 21 ॥

*Placing one foot by the (opposite) thigh and the other (foot) under
the (same) thigh is known as veerasana.*

Technique 1

Sit on the left heel, bend the right knee and place the
foot beside the left knee.

Place the right elbow on the right knee and the palm
against the right cheek.

The left hand should be placed on the left knee.

Close the eyes and concentrate on the breath.

Hold the position for a minute or two.

Repeat on the other side, changing the leg and arm
positions.

Technique 2

Sit with the left foot behind the left buttock, big toe
under the buttock as in vajrasana.

Place the right foot on the left thigh and keep the knees widely separated.
Keep the hands on the knees, in chin or jnana mudra, spine erect, head straight.
Repeat on the other side, changing the leg position.

There are variations of this asana according to different acharyas of hatha yoga. This is the traditional posture as described by commentators of the hatha yoga texts. The full name of this asana is mahaveerasana, veerasana is an abbreviation. *Maha* means 'great', *veer* means 'valiant' or to display heroic power and the ability to subdue. *Mahaveer* is the name of Hanuman (the monkey god) who was the 'great hero' of the Hindu pantheon. This gives us a clear indication of the benefits and purpose of the asana.

Veerasana stabilizes the energy flow to the reproductive organs and enables control of the sexual energy. It increases willpower and strengthens the body. As in the other sitting positions, specific nadis in the legs which are connected to the sex glands, sex organs and associated brain centres are stimulated.

KOORMASANA (tortoise pose)

गुदं निरुध्य गुतफाभ्यां व्युत्क्रमेण समाहितः ।
कूर्मासनं भवेदेतदिति योगविदो विदुः ॥ 22 ॥

Press the anus firmly with the ankles positioned in opposite directions and sit well-poised. According to the yogis this is koormasana.

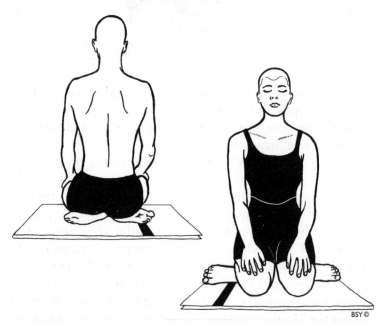

Technique I

First sit in vajrasana with the knees together and the feet under the buttocks.

Then place the feet in such a way that the heels press the anus and the toes point outwards. The weight is on the heels and the sides of the feet. In this way, the body must be well-balanced, straight and relaxed.

If this is too strenuous on the feet, the heels may be kept further apart.

This asana is very good for straightening a curved spine. The heels press the anus close to the vajra nadi and prevent energy from escaping. Thus it is useful for both celibates and householders. It channelizes the sexual energy to higher centres in the body and regulates the sex glands, reproductive and excretory organs. Important nadis in the sides of the feet, which connect to the kidneys and other visceral organs, are pressed and thereby receive gentle stimulation. Those people suffering from lack of energy, sexual and urinary disorders, etc., can practise koormasana to help rectify these problems. However, unless the feet are supple it will be difficult to sit on them comfortably. Anyone who practises moola bandha will find this asana helpful.

Koormasana varies according to different texts. This particular asana is called koorma because the shape of the body resembles that of a tortoise. The description sounds simple but one has to practise it carefully and the feet have to be sufficiently supple.

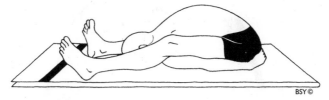

BSY©

Technique 2

Sit on the ground and spread the legs out to the sides as much as possible.

Exhaling, lean forward, bend the knees and slip the arms under the knees, taking the hands back behind the buttocks.

Bring the forehead down to the ground.

Breathe normally in the final position.

This asana is extremely helpful for those who have a slipped disc. It also stimulates the kidneys and the digestive tract. Blood flow is directed to the spine and back muscles, neck and head.

KUKKUTASANA (cockerel pose)

पद्मासनं तु संस्थाप्य जानूर्वोरन्तरे करौ ।
निवेश्य भूमौ संस्थाप्य व्योमस्थं कुक्कुटासनम् ॥ 23 ॥

Assuming padmasana insert the hands between the thighs and calves, planting them (the hands) firmly on the ground, raise the body in the air. This is kukkutasana.

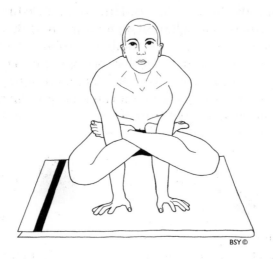

BSY©

Technique

Sit in padmasana.

Insert the right arm between the right thigh and calf muscle, and the left arm between the left thigh and calf muscle.

Place the palms of the hands firmly on the ground with the fingers pointing forward.

Balance the weight of the body on the hands and raise the body off the ground.

The arms and wrists will have to be strong to support the body.

Inhale slowly as you raise the body.

Hold the breath in the final position or breathe normally. Remain in the final pose for as long as is comfortable, keeping the head straight and the eyes fixed on a point in front.

Exhale while lowering the body to the ground.

People with a lot of hair on the legs may find it difficult and painful to insert the arms between the thighs and calves. Shaving the legs or applying oil to them will ease the problem. Those with a lot of fat or muscle on the legs will also have difficulty.

Kukkutasana is known as the cockerel pose as the shape of the body resembles a cockerel. This asana is said to be useful in the process of awakening kundalini. It strengthens the arm and shoulder muscles and gives the sensation of levitation. Normally the body weight is on the legs and feet, but in this asana it is altered and, therefore, the energies of the body flow in a different direction.

UTTANKOORMASANA (stretching tortoise pose)

कुक्कुटासनबंधस्थो दोभ्यां संबध्य कंधराम् ।
भवेत्कूर्मवदुत्तान एतदुत्तानकूर्मकम् ॥ 24 ॥

Sitting in kukkutasana, join both the hands at the shoulders and lie flat on the back like a tortoise. This is uttankoormasana.

Technique 1

First make the body ready as for kukkutasana, but instead of raising the body, slowly roll back onto the floor.
Bring the arms right through between the legs and clasp the shoulders with the hands or join the hands behind the neck.

Technique 2

Lie in shavasana.
Bring the knees up to the chest and do padmasana.

Push the right arm between the right calf muscle and thigh, up past the elbow, and the left arm between the left calf muscle and thigh, up past the elbow.

This is also called garbhasana, the embryo pose.

In the final position the breath will be shallow because the stomach and lungs are pressed tightly.

To come out of the position, first unclasp the hands, then unfold the legs and lie flat in shavasana for a few minutes.

It is essential to perform this asana on a blanket, otherwise you could damage the protruding spinal vertebrae.

Uttankoormasana tones the nervous system and induces relaxation, if the final position is held comfortably. It is particularly recommended for people who suffer from nervous disorders and for those who become angry easily, as it regulates the adrenal glands. Uttankoormasana also stimulates digestion and appetite.

DHANURASANA (bow pose)

पादांगुष्ठौ तु पाणिभ्यां गृहीत्वा श्रवणावधि ।
धनुराकर्षणं कुर्याद्धनुरासनमुच्यते ॥ 25 ॥

Holding the toes with the hands, pull them up to the ears as if drawing a bow. This is called dhanurasana.

Just as there are different stages of drawing a bow, there is a progression for the various techniques of dhanurasana.

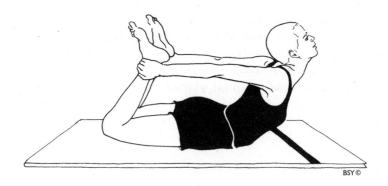

Technique 1: Saral Dhanurasana (easy bow pose)

Lie flat on the stomach with the forehead resting on the floor.

Bend the knees and hold both ankles.

Separate the knees.

Inhale while slightly raising the knees, head and chest, at the same time pull the feet away from the hands and upwards.

The whole body should move simultaneously into the posture.

Exhale while lowering the body and relaxing on the floor.

Technique 2: Dhanurasana (bow pose)

Repeat the same process as for Technique 1, but raise the legs, head and chest as high as possible.
Hold the final position and hold the breath.
Exhaling, slowly come down.

Technique 3: Poorna Dhanurasana (full bow pose)

Hold the toes of one foot only and twist the elbow outwards and upwards.
Do the same with the other foot.
Hold the final position for as long as possible, breathing normally.
Slowly release the posture while exhaling.

83

The final position of each stage can be held either with normal breathing or internal breath retention. The body can also be gently rocked forward and backward. Concentration should be on vishuddhi chakra in the back of the neck, or on manipura in the abdominal region, or on the midpoint where the back is bending.

Dhanurasana is very important for stimulating the solar plexus. It regulates the digestive, eliminatory and reproductive organs. It massages the liver and pancreas and is thus very useful for yogic management of diabetes. The kidneys are stimulated and the whole alimentary canal is toned. By lying on the diaphragm with the arms stretched back, the heart is given a gentle massage and, because the chest is fully expanded in this posture, dhanurasana is useful in the treatment of various chest ailments. It stimulates and regulates the endocrine glands, particularly the thyroid and adrenal glands, and it induces production of cortisone.

The backward bend of the spine adjusts the vertebral column, straightening a hunched back and drooping shoulders. It is also recommended for treating certain types of rheumatism. Dhanurasana helps to regulate the menstrual cycle and also to correct female infertility, if the cause is not due to deformity of the reproductive organs themselves.

MATSYENDRASANA (spinal twist pose)

वामोरुमूलार्पितदक्षपादं जानोर्बहिर्वेष्टितवामपादम् ।
प्रगृह्य तिष्ठेत्परिवर्तितांग: श्रीमत्स्यनाथोदितमासनं स्यात् ॥ 26 ॥

Place the right foot at the base of the left thigh, the left foot at the side of the right knee. Take hold of the left foot with the right hand, pass the left arm behind the waist and remain with the body turned. This asana is described by Sri Matsyendranath.

Matsyendranath supposedly practised this asana and thus it is named after him. In English it is called the spinal twist. There are variations in the placement of the arms and hands and the degree of twisting in the spine.

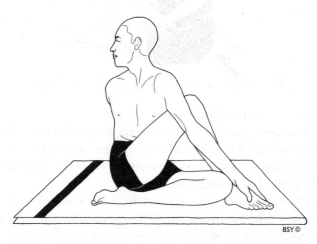

BSY©

Technique 1: Ardha Matsyendrasana (half spinal twist)

Keep the right foot by the side of the left buttock, the left leg on top, with the foot in front of the right knee and the left knee raised upward (or the left foot can be placed by the outside of the right knee or right thigh). Inhale while raising the arms shoulder high, keeping the elbows straight.

85

Exhaling, twist to the left, place the right arm by the outer side of the left knee and hold the left ankle with the right hand.
Take the left arm behind the back and rest the back of the left hand against the right side of the waist.
Hold the position.
Practise on both sides, changing the leg and arm position.

BSY©

Alternate arm positions are:
1. Take the right arm around the front of the left knee, then underneath the bent left knee, and take the left arm around the back of the waist to meet the right hand. Clasp the hands together.
2. Place the right arm around the left knee and the palm of the right hand on the left thigh, take the left arm around the back of the waist as described above.

Technique 2: Poorna Matsyendrasana (full spinal twist pose)
Sitting in padmasana, the lotus posture, raise the knee of the uppermost leg and place its foot slightly by the side of the thigh it is resting on.
Utilize the same arm positions as described above.

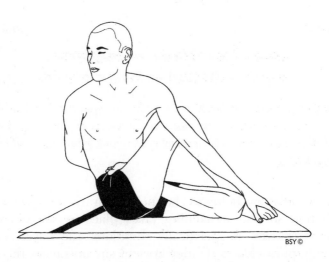

The final position of each stage should be held while breathing naturally. Hold the position for as long as comfortable, concentrating on either ajna chakra, the mid-eyebrow centre or the natural breath. Remember to practise on both sides of the body. That is, if you first twist to the right, make sure you twist to the left next, and hold the posture for the same length of time.

मत्स्येन्द्रपीठं जठरप्रदीप्तिं प्रचंडरुग्मंडलखंडनास्त्रम् ।
अभ्यासत: कुंडलिनीप्रबोधं चन्द्रस्थिरत्वं च ददाति पुंसाम् ॥ 27 ॥

Practice of this asana (matsyendrasana) increases the digestive fire to such an incredible capacity that it is the means of removing diseases and thus awakening the serpent power and bringing equilibrium in the bindu.

Matsyendrasana helps to channel the prana in a particular direction so that awakening takes place in the dormant energy centres. It specifically stimulates the navel centre or manipura chakra. Under normal circumstances the rate of pranic vibration is slow. Performing those asanas which direct the prana to the navel centre is very important for the awakening of kundalini. The navel centre is responsible for maintaining the body. When it is underactive or overactive, body functions are not harmonious and if it is sluggish, diseases develop in other areas. If the capacity of manipura is increased systematically, it not only eliminates imbalances and disease, but the dormant potential of sushumna nadi can be awakened.

Manipura is directly connected to the digestive system. Proper digestion and assimilation is the key to good health. Many texts talk about the 'fire' of manipura, i.e. the digestive fire. It is said that a certain fluid produced in the higher brain centres is consumed by this fire, and the result is old age, disease and death. This fluid refers to the neuro-hormones of the pituitary and pineal glands which activate the other endocrine glands. In yoga it is said that this fluid is stored in bindu visarga and it is often associated with semen or ova. If one can prevent that fluid from falling into the fire of manipura, vitality can be increased and longevity can be cultivated.

The navel region is powered by samana vayu. Samana is responsible for the assimilation of nutrients and prana from the air and food. Above the region of the body where samana operates, prana vayu pervades, and one of its functions is to absorb prana. In the region of the body below the navel, apana vayu is located and its chief function is elimination. Prana and apana are the two major forces and normally move in opposite directions. One of the aims of yoga is to make prana and apana move towards each other so they meet in the navel and connect with samana.

Prana vayu is positive energy, apana is negative and samana is neutral. When the two opposite energies are brought together in manipura chakra, there is an explosion of energy and the energy forces its way through sushumna nadi. That is why manipura is such an important centre in the process of awakening kundalini. It is even said that kundalini awakening starts from manipura and not in either of the lower centres. The chakras below manipura are concerned with the animal instincts and those above are connected with the higher qualities of the mind. Manipura is midway between the two and is said to be the midpoint between heaven and earth. Matsyendrasana increases the vital capacity of manipura so it can sustain the effects of kundalini awakening.

The other important physiological aspects of this asana are that it stimulates the pancreas, liver, spleen, kidneys, stomach and ascending and descending colons. It is useful in the treatment of diabetes, constipation, dyspepsia and urinary problems. It tones the nerve roots, and adjusts and realigns the vertebral column. The back muscles are pulled and stretched in a different direction than usual and this relieves them of tension. Matsyendrasana is, therefore, recommended in cases of lumbago, rheumatism and slipped disc. In fact, it is a powerful asana and its vitalizing effects can be felt quickly.

PASCHIMOTTANASANA (back stretching pose)

प्रसार्य पादौ भुवि दंडरूपौ दोभ्यां पदाग्रद्वितयं गृहीत्वा ।
जानूपरिन्यस्तललाटदेशो वसेदिदं पश्चिमतानमाहुः ॥ 28 ॥

Stretching the legs (in front) on the ground, like a stick; bending forward, holding the toes with both hands and placing the forehead on the knees, is called paschimottanasana.

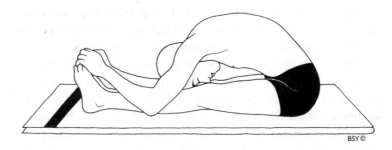

Technique I

Sit with the legs stretched out in front of the body, hands on the knees.

Inhale while raising the arms above the head and keeping the back straight.

Exhale while bending forward from the hips and keep the head between the shoulders so that the spinal column is stretched.

Clasp the big toes or ankles with the hands and bring the head down to rest on the knees.

If this is not possible, hold the calf muscles.

The back should not curve or hunch.

In the final position you can hold the breath or breathe normally, concentrating on the navel.

When releasing the position inhale and raise the arms above the head while sitting up.

Exhale while bringing the hands down to the knees.

This is the passive form of paschimottanasana. In the *Shiva Samhita* it is called ugrasana. *Ugra* means 'stern'.

Technique 2: Gatyatmak Paschimottanasana (dynamic back stretch pose)

The dynamic form of paschimottanasana involves rocking and rolling backwards and forwards.

Sit in the starting position.

Inhale while raising the hands above the head.

Exhaling, slowly lie down on the ground, keeping the hands stretched above the head.

Inhale while sitting up. Keep the arms above the head.

Exhale as you bend forward and grasp the toes.

Inhaling sit up, exhaling lie down.

Continue in this way, concentrating on the inhalation and exhalation.

Technique 3

Spread the legs wide apart.

Keep both hands on the right knee and practise in the same way as Technique 1 except that you are facing the right leg.

Then place both hands on the left knee and practise on the left leg.

Then practise by keeping the left hand on the left knee, right hand on the right knee.

Inhaling, raise the hands above the head, exhaling, lean forward, hold the toes and bring the head down towards the ground between the knees.

Return in the same way as described in Technique 1.

Technique 4

Spread the legs and clasp the hands behind the back.

Inhale; now exhaling, bend forward and lift the arms up and straighten the elbows, keeping the hands clasped together.

It is more difficult to practise paschimottanasana in the morning than in the afternoon because the back muscles and nerves have not had time to loosen. Therefore, it is usually performed after having practised some other asana or physical movement so that the spine and hamstrings are sufficiently supple. The knees must be kept straight throughout the practice. If it is not possible to bring the head down without bending the knees, then bring it down as far as is comfortable and hold the knees or calf muscles. Remember to keep the back straight and not hunched. The whole body should be relaxed in the final position.

Chapter 1

इति पश्चिमतानमासनग्र्यं पवनं पश्चिमवाहिनं करोति ।
उदयं जठरानलस्य कुर्यादुदरे कार्श्यमरोगतां च पुंसाम् ॥ 29 ॥

Paschimottanasana is the best among asanas. By this asana the pranic currents rise through sushumna, the digestive fire increases, the abdomen becomes flat, and the practitioner becomes free from diseases.

Paschimottanasana activates manipura chakra and releases the prana through sushumna, which in turn strengthens the digestive organs and tract. Of course, this does not happen after practising only once or twice; practice has to be on a regular daily basis. Paschimottanasana stretches the whole spinal column and central nervous system through which sushumna runs, thus enabling nervous and pranic impulses to pass directly up to the higher centres.

The back, shoulder, arm and leg muscles are toned by stretching them in a relaxed manner without straining. The visceral organs are massaged, in particular the pancreas, spleen, kidney, liver, reproductive organs, the adrenal glands and abdominal muscles. Therefore, it is very useful in the yogic management of digestive disorders, especially diabetes, constipation, flatulence, and loss of appetite. The reproductive organs are toned and sexual disorders can be relieved. Women can utilize this asana to regulate the menstrual cycle.

Paschimottanasana, particularly the dynamic form, helps remove excess fat deposits from the abdomen and thighs. When there is a lot of tension in the body and mind, paschimottanasana helps remove it by regulating the adrenal glands and the whole system. In fact, the numerous effects promote health and harmony.

MAYURASANA (peacock pose)

धरामवष्टभ्य करद्वयेन तत्कूर्परस्थापितनाभिपार्श्वः ।
उच्चासनो दंडवदुत्थितः खे मायूरमेतत्प्रवदन्ति पीठम् ॥ 30 ॥

*Lie on the stomach, placing both hands on the ground (under
the body) and the elbows at the sides of the navel. Raise the body
high, keeping it like a stick. This is called the peacock pose by the
exponents of yoga.*

Technique I

The wrists and forearms must be strong to support the
body in this asana and, therefore, men will find it easier
than women.
Start by assuming marjariasana with the palms of the
hands on the ground and the fingers pointing backwards.
Place the elbows at each side of the navel and waist.
Stretch the legs backward.
Exhale and inhale while raising the legs up off the
ground.
Try not to jerk the body into the position.
Lift the legs as high as possible.
Hold the position for as long as is comfortable and
breathe normally.

Concentrate either on manipura chakra or on maintaining balance of the body.
Exhale while coming down.
Lie in shavasana and relax the whole body.

Technique 2: Padma Mayurasana (lotus or bound peacock pose)

First sit in padmasana, then place the weight of the body on the hands as described above and slowly lift the knees off the ground, into the air.

Mayurasana should not be done at the beginning of asana practice. Do it after performing other asanas or any inverted postures.

हरति सकलरोगानाशु गुल्मोदरादी-
नभिभवति च दोषानासनं श्रीमयूरम् ।
बहु कदशनभूक्तं भस्म कुर्यादशेषं
जनयति जठराग्निं जारयेत्कालकूटम् ॥ ३१ ॥

Mayurasana quickly alleviates all diseases like enlargement of the glands, dropsy and other stomach disorders. It rectifies imbalance of the humours (vata, pitta, kapha). It reduces to ashes all food taken indiscriminately, kindles the gastric fire and enables destruction of kalakuta (a deadly poison).

This asana has not only been given its name because the practitioner resembles a peacock, but also because the effects of its practise enable one to develop the characteristics of the peacock's digestive system. The peacock has the remarkable ability to eat poisonous substances and digest them completely without adverse effects. In fact, the peacock prefers to eat poisonous snakes, poisonous insects, reptiles and scorpions. The peacock's digestive system must be very strong, secreting ample digestive juices and having very efficient elimination. Practice of mayurasana promotes digestion and elimination of toxins so that poisonous substances are not circulated or stored.

Mayurasana purifies the blood, alleviates constipation, flatulence, indigestion, dyspepsia and chronic gastritis. It stimulates the liver, kidneys and gallbladder. Diabetic patients who are able to perform it can quickly improve their condition.

When mayurasana is practised the heart is massaged, the circulation is improved and metabolism is stimulated. The endocrine glands are regulated and their secretions are harmonized. The back muscles and spinal column are strengthened and in fact, muscles all over the body are strengthened. Mayurasana invigorates the entire system.

It is advisable to make the diet very pure before commencing mayurasana. As this asana eliminates the buildup of toxic materials, the cleansing process will be much more effective if the diet is pure to start with or laghoo shankhaprakshalana is practised. Foods which produce a lot of toxins, such as meat, alcohol, pungent spices, etc., are considered as poisons. Pure food is one which cleans the system, such as grains, cereals, pulses, vegetables, fruit, and spices such as turmeric. Actually, a simple vegetarian diet will maintain a toxin-free system, but if one is forced by social conditions to take toxic foods, mayurasana will maintain the system.

People suffering from peptic ulcers, hernia, heart disease, high blood pressure, brain tumours or ear, eye or nose infections must first cure their condition before attempting mayurasana.

It is also said that mayurasana can awaken kundalini. However, if you cannot do this practice it does not mean that your kundalini will not awaken.

SHAVASANA (corpse pose)

उत्तानं शववद्भूमौ शयनं तच्छवासनम् ।
शवासनं श्रान्तिहरं चित्तविश्रान्तिकारकम् ॥ 32 ॥

Lying flat on the ground with the face upwards, in the manner of a dead body, is shavasana. It removes tiredness and enables the mind (and whole body) to relax.

Shavasana is the corpse pose. *Shav* means 'corpse'. This asana has been adapted from the tantric practice of shavasana in which the sadhaka sits on the corpse and practises his mantra. Shavasana is also known as the pose of relaxation and it is essential to practise this in between other asanas or after a busy day.

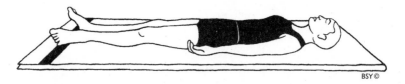

Technique

    Lie flat on the back.

    Separate the feet slightly, place the hands by the sides of the body, about one foot away, with the palms facing upwards.

    The legs, back and head should be aligned, not crooked.

    Relax the whole body, keep the eyes and mouth closed.

    Breathe naturally through the nose.

    Concentrate on the natural breath and feel the body becoming looser and lighter with each exhalation.

    Keep the awareness on the breath and the physical body.

Shavasana is a very simple practice but most people find it almost impossible to completely relax the body. There is a tendency to hold tension in some part. The whole body must relax, then the breathing will simultaneously slow down. Try to ignore the mental chatter and concentrate only on the breath and body.

This practice is useful for developing body awareness and pratyahara. When the body is completely relaxed, awareness of the mind develops. Its effects influence the physical as well as the psychological structure. It is very useful in yogic management of high blood pressure, peptic ulcer, anxiety, hysteria, cancer and all psychosomatic diseases and neuroses. In fact, shavasana is beneficial no matter what the condition is, even in perfect health, because it brings up the latent impressions buried within the subconscious mind, and the mind which operates during waking consciousness relaxes and subsides. It is, therefore, necessary to practise shavasana for developing dharana and dhyana. Even though it is a static pose it revitalizes the entire system.

चतुरशीत्यासनानि शिवेन कथितानि च ।
तेभ्यश्चतुष्कमादाय सारभूतं ब्रवीम्यहम् ॥ 33 ॥

Eighty-four asanas were taught by Shiva. Out of those I shall now describe the four important ones.

According to *Hatharatnavali*: "The Almighty Shambhu has described eighty-four asanas, taking examples from each of the 8,400,000 kinds of creatures." (3:6) The *Goraksha Satarka* says: "Every one of the 8,400,000 asanas has been told by Shiva. Of these, eighty-four postures have been selected. Amongst all these, two have been selected." (v. 9,10).

Of all the hatha yoga texts, *Gheranda Samhita* describes the most asanas (thirty-two), although *Hatharatnavali* lists the names of the eighty-four asanas. These are siddha, bhadra, vajra, simha, shilpasimha, bandhakara, samputita, shuddha, (four varieties of padma), danda parsva, sahaja, bandha, pinda, mayura, ekapadamayura, (six varieties of mayurasana), bhairava, kamadahana, panipatra, karmuka, swastika, gomukha, veera, manduka, markata, matsyendra, parshva matsyendra, bandha matsyendra, niralambana, chandra, kanthva, ekapadaka, phanindra paschimatana, shayita paschimatana, vichitrakarani, yoga mudra, vidhunana, padapindana, hamsa, nabhitala, akasha, utpadatala, nabhilasitapadaka, vrischika, chakra, utphalaka, uttana-koorma, koorma, baddha koorma, kabandha, goraksha, angustha, mustika, brahmaprasadita, panchachuli, kukkuta, ekapadaka kukkuta, akarita, bandha chuli, parshva kukkuta, ardhanarisvara, baka, chandrakanta, sudhasara, vyaghra, raja, indrani, sharabha, ratna, chitrapitha, baddhapaksisvara, vichitra, nalina, kanta, sudhapakshi, sumandaka, chaurangi, krauncha, dridha, khaga, brahma, nagapitha and shavasana.

It should be noted that although *Hatharatnavali* is a Sanskrit text, it was written by a yogi from South India and some of the names of the asanas vary from those which are given in texts that were written in the north.

सिद्धं पद्मं तथा सिंहं भद्रं वेति चतुष्टयम् ।
श्रेष्ठं तत्रापि च सुखे तिष्ठेत्सिद्धासने सदा ॥ 34 ॥

Siddhasana, padmasana, simhasana and bhadrasana, these are the four main asanas. Always sit comfortably in siddhasana because it is the best.

A correct meditative posture is most important to a yogi, therefore, Swatmarama advises that any follower of Matsyendranath must practise these four asanas. *Hatharatnavali* also lists these four as the most important. The *Shiva Samhita* says siddhasana, padmasana, ugrasana (paschimottan-asana) and swastikasana are most important. The *Goraksha Satarka* mentions only two asanas as most important – siddhasana and padmasana.

Siddhasana is practised by men. The equivalent for women is siddha yoni asana. The other three asanas can be practised by both. Siddhasana is known as the pose of the perfectionist or the pose of perfection; padmasana is the lotus posture, also called kamalasana; simhasana is the lion posture and bhadrasana is the gracious pose.

SIDDHASANA (adept's pose)

तत्र सिद्धासनम्

योनिस्थानकमङ्घ्रिमूलघटितं कृत्वा दृढं विन्यसे-
त्मेण्ढ्रे पादमथैकमेव हृदये कृत्वा हनुं सुस्थिरम् ।
स्थाणुः संयमितेन्द्रियोऽचलदृशा पश्येद् भ्रुवोरन्तरं
ह्येतन्मोक्षकपाटभेदजनकं सिद्धासनं प्रोच्यते ॥ 35 ॥

Press the perineum with the heel of one foot, place the other foot on top of the genitals. Having done this, rest the chin on to the chest. Remaining still and steady, with the senses controlled, gaze steadily into the eyebrow centre; it breaks open the door to liberation. This is called siddhasana.

Technique

The traditional method of siddhasana is done in the following manner.

Sit with the heel of the left foot pressing the perineum, the area between the anus and the genital organ.

Place the right foot so that the heel presses the pubis, directly above the generative organ.

Push the toes and edge of the right foot in between the left thigh and calf muscles.
Make sure the body is comfortable and steady, spine erect.
Lower the chin towards the collarbone, relax the head.
Gaze into the eyebrow centre – shambhavi mudra.

Today siddhasana is commonly known as described above but without lowering the head, i.e. the head remains erect, eyes closed.

Siddhasana can only be practised by men. Its equivalent for women is called siddha yoni asana. It is practised in

103

the same way as siddhasana except that the lower heel is pressed into the opening of the vagina and the upper heel rests against the clitoris. The toes of both feet are inserted between the thigh and calf muscle.

According to Swami Sivananda, in the practice of siddhasana, one heel should be pressed into the anus and the other placed at the root of the generative organ. Both ankles are then resting one on top of the other.

Siddhasana is very important for stimulating ajna chakra and controlling nervous and pranic impulses from mooladhara and swadhisthana chakras. When ajna is awakened, the realm of pure consciousness is experienced. It is beyond the effects of *prakriti*, or nature, and is, therefore, the door to liberation.

Siddhasana is a purely meditative posture. It is designed to channel the *prana*, or vital energy, directly to ajna chakra. Shambhavi mudra stimulates ajna chakra so that the pranic impulses coming up from the lower centres can be received. When the chin is placed on the chest, a simplified form of jalandhara and ujjayi pranayama is automatically performed. This adjusts the heart rate, blood pressure and brain wave pattern.

When you first start to practise meditation other postures can be utilized, but in the final stages, when the external consciousness drops and inner consciousness begins to pervade, siddhasana is the best posture as it enables you to handle the changes that take place in the body during deep meditation.

When the mental fluctuations cease, inner consciousness blooms forth and exterior consciousness withdraws, the body metabolism alters. The brain waves, inner body temperature and skin resistance undergo tremendous changes and the effects on the consciousness can be detrimental if one is not careful.

Siddhasana prevents nervous depression from occurring during meditation, as it stops the blood pressure from falling too low, regulates the production of the male hormone testosterone, and helps maintain the inner body temperature. It stabilizes the two lower psychic centres – mooladhara chakra and swadhisthana chakra, redirecting prana upwards towards the higher centres. Blockage of energy within these two centres is responsible for many health problems; it also poses a barrier which has to be crossed in spiritual life. Mooladhara is the root centre in which an infinite source of pranic energy lies dormant while swadhisthana is the centre responsible for the sexual and emotional metabolism in which our psychic energy most spontaneously manifests itself. When our emotional life does not extend beyond this plane, blood pressure and cardiac function remain unstable and our role and purpose in life remain ill-defined and unclear. On a pranic level, siddhasana balances the alternating flows of ida and pingala nadis, thus activating sushumna.

Many people consider padmasana as the ultimate posture for meditation, however, siddhasana is easier to practise and maintain. In siddhasana the feet are less likely to fall asleep and the body is locked firmly in its position. Siddhasana also stabilizes cardiac function, and if practised throughout life, it bestows protection from emotional ravages and stabilizes the passions, preventing later cardiac demise.

Swami Sivananda has said that siddhasana is actually the best practice for most people, even those with large thighs, and it is essential for those who wish to observe celibacy. If one can master this asana, one will acquire siddhis.

मेण्ढ्रादुपरि विन्यस्य सव्यं गुल्फं तथोपरि ।
गुल्फान्तरं च निक्षिप्य सिद्धासनमिदं भवेत् ॥ 36 ॥

According to others, placing the heel above the penis and the other (heel) on top of that is siddhasana.

This is a modified version of siddhasana, best for those who are unable to sit in the way previously described. *Hatharatnavali* agrees that some people consider this variation to be siddhasana, but other hatha yoga texts, such as *Goraksha Satarka* and *Shiva Samhita*, describe siddhasana with one heel pressing the perineum and the other on top. It is the most widely practised form of siddhasana, even today, and the Nath yogis use only that.

एतत्सिद्धासनं प्राहुरन्ये वज्रासनं विदुः ।
मुक्तासनं वदंत्येके प्राहुर्गुप्तासनं परे ॥ 37 ॥

This is called siddhasana, others know it as vajrasana, some call it
muktasana and lastly it is called guptasana.

Vajrasana, muktasana and guptasana are three different
postures. Siddhasana is the pose of perfection; vajrasana,
the thunderbolt pose, regulates the vajra nadi; muktasana is
the pose of liberation and guptasana is the secret pose. The
leg and feet positions vary in all four postures. Perhaps what
this sloka is trying to express is that some say siddhasana is
essential, others think vajrasana, others muktasana and still
others say guptasana.

Muktasana is not described in this text, but the *Gheranda
Samhita* states it is done by placing the left heel under the
anus and the right heel above it.

Vajrasana is done by kneeling and placing the buttocks between the heels, the right big toe overlapping the left.

In guptasana the feet are placed between the thigh and calf muscles so that the heel underneath presses the anus. However, when the left heel presses the perineum, it is siddhasana. Siddhasana is most useful because it exerts a constant pressure on the perineum.

यमेष्विव मिताहारमहिंसां नियमेष्विव ।
मुख्यं सर्वासनेष्वेकं सिद्धा: सिद्धासनं विदु: ॥ 38 ॥

Just as moderate diet is the most important of the yamas, and non-violence, of the niyamas, so the siddhas know that siddhasana is the most important of the asanas.

Moderate diet is the basis of self-control as it brings balance to the body and mind and controls lust. Non-violence is the basis of controlled conduct because it checks the expression of the mind and emotions. When the basic tendencies of mind and prana are channelled, psychic and spiritual experiences awaken. When these experiences occur you should be adequately prepared with siddhasana.

चतुरशीतिपीठेषु सिद्धमेव सदाभ्यसेत् ।
द्वासप्ततिसहस्राणां नाडीनां मलशोधनम् ॥ 39 ॥

Of all the eighty-four asanas, siddhasana should always be practised. It purifies the 72,000 nadis.

Even if you practise no other asana, siddhasana must be performed. Although there are other asanas which purify the body-mind complex, siddhasana balances the energy level by equalizing the mental and pranic forces. An unhealthy lifestyle leads to a buildup of toxins in the body and negative thinking, which subtly manifest as blockages in the nadis. If sushumna is to awaken, the nadis must be purified so that the energy flows freely and ida and pingala are balanced. Siddhasana is essential for achieving this.

How can a sitting position purify the nadis? Pressure on the perineum stimulates mooladhara chakra, the point at which the three major nadis originate, and while the posture is being maintained, electrical and pranic impulses are constantly flowing up to the brain, purifying the nadis and removing all blockages. Also, meridians in the feet are stimulated and they are connected with the visceral organs, e.g. the stomach, gallbladder, liver, spleen, kidneys, etc., and all these organs have important roles to play in purifying the blood.

आत्मध्यायी मिताहारी यावद्द्वादशवत्सरम् ।
सदा सिद्धासनाभ्यासाद्योगी निष्पत्तिमाप्नुयात् ॥ 40 ॥

The yogi who meditates on the self or atma, takes moderate and pure food and practises siddhasana for twelve years, attains perfection or siddhi.

Twelve years sounds like a long time to have to practise one thing before perfecting it, but it should be taken into consideration that it also takes many years of study and practice to become a qualified practitioner of medicine or law. In comparison to the rest of one's life, twelve years is not a long time if it is going to culminate in perfection and the awakening of a higher state of consciousness. If people can devote a whole lifetime to the pursuit of material goals, why not dedicate twelve years for the development of higher awareness and the unfoldment of the spirit?

It takes many years for the body and mind to change. After a cycle of seven years all body cells have been completely replaced. We can say one has a new body. However, it takes longer to restructure the mind and remould the awareness. Many shastras say that sadhana takes twelve years to fructify. Twelve years enables gradual and complete restructuring of the body, mind, emotions and psyche.

In spiritual life, twelve years is an important cycle. Perhaps it takes that amount of time to purify and prepare the pranic and psychic bodies for spiritual awakening. In the guru-disciple tradition also, the disciple is meant to spend twelve years training with his guru.

Two other specifications are also given here: moderate diet and contemplation on atma. A pure and moderate diet helps establish equilibrium and creates conditions conducive for higher experiences. In fact, the basic cause of disease can be attributed to faulty diet. If people took more care about their diet, many physical and psychological problems could be averted.

Yogi Swatmarama recommends meditation on the self or atma. As all spiritual aspirants are heading towards the experience of atma, it is a good idea to prepare oneself for that realization right from the beginning. The practice channels one's internal energy in a positive direction, makes the mind one-pointed and keeps one moving towards the ultimate goal.

Mind is not static; it is a vibrating mass of conscious energy and is moulded into whatever shape you give it. When a person lives for material pleasure, the mind becomes absorbed in the material reality. If it is absorbed in negative and debauched things, then it becomes that way. If it is absorbed in the subtler experiences then it can come closer to the atma. This is a process which involves the total restructuring of the entire organism right down to the minutest cell.

Of course, the idea of meditating on the atma has a vedantic tinge, and is similar to the idea in Samkhya philosophy that the ultimate is purusha. A shakta would probably advise meditation on Shakti. Similarly, according to the individual sadhaka's nature, a guru might recommend an entirely different object of meditation and not suggest contemplation on atma.

Actually, the aspect of guru has been omitted here. If you have no guru and sit for one hundred and twelve years you may not make much headway, unless you are already enlightened. Only a man with spiritual insight can guide you on the inward path. If you want to experience another state of mind beyond this sensorial experience, the finite perception has to be altered. How can the finite mind concentrate on the infinite? Swatmarama says concentrate on atma, but atma is formless and infinite. This is where the guru is essential, because the light of his atma illumines your own; without that there can be no self-realization.

किमन्यैर्बहुभि: पीठै: सिद्धे सिद्धासने सति ।
प्राणानिले सावधाने बद्धे केवलकुंभके ।
उत्पद्यते निरायासात्स्वयमेवोन्मनी कला ॥ 41 ॥

*When perfection is attainable through siddhasana, what is the use of
practising many other asanas? When the flow of prana is stabilized,
the breath stops spontaneously (kevala kumbhaka) and a mindless
state (unmani) arises by itself.*

By practising only siddhasana and pranayama a higher
state of awareness can be aroused. However, everybody has
individual requirements depending on whether his nature
is basically tamasic, rajasic or sattwic. Ultimately, when the
mind is quiet and the body is fit for prolonged meditation,
then all you need is siddhasana.

Swatmarama is not asking the purpose of practising any
other asana, but just pointing out the fact that for one who
is established in siddhasana, it is unnecessary to spend time
in asana practice. Previously siddhasana was recommended
in combination with atma dharana. Whatever the form of
concentration may be, complete concentration and absorption in the object of meditation results in cessation of the
breath. Conscious breath restraint and self-contemplation
result in kevala kumbhaka; self-awareness diminishes,
individual experience subsides. Therefore, Yogi Swatmarama
is saying that if one experiences this in siddhasana, then time
should be spent practising siddhasana rather than other
postures.

However, people belonging to the tamasic or rajasic
categories need to practise a series of asanas and other
forms of yoga to raise their pranic and conscious capacity.
Siddhasana and raja yoga are perfect for the sadhaka who
has a psychic temperament, but those who are emotional,
devotional, extrovert, dynamic or analytical will need
other forms of yoga as well. Karma yoga and bhakti yoga

harmonize the body, mind and emotions and help to subdue sensorial experiences. If the mind is basically tamasic or rajasic it needs a proper outlet of expression, otherwise during meditational practice it will cause havoc, wander here and there or just become dull and sleepy.

To attain higher experience the mind has to become totally absorbed in the point of concentration. If you are performing siddhasana and practising pranayama, there comes a stage when the two pranic forces, apana and prana, meet and the alternating tendencies of ida and pingala unite in ajna chakra. At that moment the mind becomes unified and the breath stops. However, the mind must have a definite point of focus such as a psychic symbol, the guru, a mantra or yantra, etc., otherwise it will enter a state of void, or *shoonya*. So, we find that it is a combination of various elements which creates higher experience, not just an asana and stopping the breath.

तथैकस्मिन्नेव दृढे सिद्धे सिद्धासने सति ।
बंधत्रयमनायासात्स्वयमेवोपजायते ॥ ४२ ॥

Thus, through securing siddhasana, the three bandhas occur by themselves.

The three bandhas indicated are moola, uddiyana and jalandhara bandhas. *Moola bandha* is contraction of the perineum, *uddiyana* is contraction of the lower abdomen and *jalandhara* is the chin lock. These three bandhas are specific methods of accumulating a greater pranic supply and, whether you know about them or not, they occur spontaneously when you are established in siddhasana.

In fact, when prana is awakened, the body is naturally guided into various mudras, bandhas and pranayama techniques which may not even be previously known to the practitioner. There are now a few well-known yoga systems which work largely on arousing this spontaneous movement through yoga practices by activating the pranic level to a higher intensity.

नासनं सिद्धसदृशं न कुंभ: केवलोपम: ।
न खेचरीसमा मुद्रा न नादसदृशो लय: ॥ 43 ॥

There is no asana like siddhasana, no kumbhaka like kevala, no mudra like khechari and no laya or dissolution of mind like nada, the inner sound.

Here the full sadhana of samadhi has been described. This final description of siddhasana emphasizes its importance and greatness, and stresses that it is foremost amongst asanas, just as kevala is the superior form of kumbhaka, khechari is the foremost mudra and nada is the best dissolvant of mind.

We will not clarify kevala kumbhaka, khechari mudra or nada here, as kumbhaka and pranayama are discussed in detail in Chapter 2, khechari in Chapter 3 and nada in Chapter 4.

PADMASANA (lotus pose)

अथ पद्मासनम् ।

वामोरुपरि दक्षिणं च चरणं संस्थाप्य वामं तथा
दक्षोरुपरि पश्चिमेन विधिना धृत्वा कराभ्यां दृढम् ।
अंगुष्ठौ हृदये निधाय चिबुकं नासाग्रमालोकयेत्
एतद्व्याधिविनाशकारि यमिनां पद्मासनं प्रोच्यते ॥ 44 ॥

*Place the right foot on the left thigh and the left foot on the right
thigh, cross the hands behind the back and firmly hold the toes. Press
the chin against the chest and look at the tip of the nose. This is
called padmasana, the destroyer of a yogi's diseases.*

उत्तानौ चरणौ कृत्वा ऊरुसंस्थौ प्रयत्नतः ।
ऊरुमध्ये तथोत्तानौ पाणी कृत्वा ततो दृशौ ॥ 45 ॥

*Place the feet on the thighs, soles upward, palms in the middle of the
groin, facing upward.*

नासाग्रे विन्यसेद्राजदंतमूले तु जिह्वया ।
उत्तंभ्य चिबुकं वक्षस्युत्थाप्य पवनं शनैः ॥ 46 ॥

*Gaze at the nosetip, keeping the tongue pressed against the root of
the upper teeth and the chin against the chest, and slowly raise the
prana upward.*

इदं पद्मासनं प्रोक्तं सर्वव्याधिविनाशनम् ।
दुर्लभं येन केनापि धीमता लभ्यते भुवि ॥ 47 ॥

*This is called padmasana, destroyer of all diseases. Ordinary
people cannot achieve this posture, only the few wise ones on this
earth can.*

Padmasana is a very well-known asana which is also called kamalasana. *Padma* and *kamala* mean 'lotus'. When one thinks of a yogi one usually imagines somebody sitting in padmasana as it is the traditional meditative posture. The body is locked firmly in its position and physical movements are reduced to a minimum. The lower back is naturally held straight and one can almost feel the balancing effect on the body.

The asana described in verse 44 is commonly known as baddha padmasana. In this asana the legs are positioned as in padmasana but the arms are placed differently. In padmasana the hands are kept either in jnana, chin, bhairavi, bhairava or yoni mudra.

Before attempting padmasana, the legs, ankles and knees have to be very flexible. If the knees are slightly stiff, precautions should be taken. You must always be gentle with the knees when assuming padmasana because once the kneecaps or ligaments are damaged you may have a permanent problem. The legs should be warmed and loosened by some of the pawanmuktasana exercises, i.e. knee rotation, crow walking, butterfly, etc.

Technique I

Bend the right knee and bring the foot up to the right buttock.

The foot should be either on or a little above the floor.

Then place the right foot so that the ankle rests high up on the left thigh close to the hip.

Bend the left leg in the same way and place the foot high up on the right thigh close to the hip.

Now the legs are locked securely into position.

Place the hands on the knees in either chin or jnana mudra.

To practise chin mudra, curl the index fingers so that the tips touch the inside root of the thumbs. Straighten the other three fingers of each hand so that they are relaxed and slightly apart. Place the hands on the knees with the palms facing upward.

118

Jnana mudra is performed in the same way as chin mudra except that the palms of the hands face down.

To practise bhairavi mudra, place the left hand on top of the right hand, the palms of both hands should face upward, hands in the lap.

Bhairava mudra is done with the opposite hand on the top.

For yoni mudra, the last three fingers are interlaced, the first fingers join at the tips and the tips of the thumbs join.

The thumbs point upward and the first fingers point forward, so a triangular space is formed between the thumbs and fingers.

Bend the head forward in a relaxed position, keeping the spine erect.

Practise *nasikagra drishti*, also known as nosetip gazing.

This is the traditional practice of padmasana.

Today padmasana is commonly practised by sitting as described above except that the head remains erect and the eyes closed.

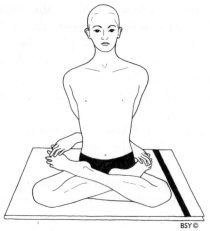

Technique 2: Baddha Padmasana (locked lotus pose)

Place the legs correctly in padmasana.

Take the arms behind the back and cross them over each other.

With the right hand, hold the right toes (or just the big toe) and with the left hand, hold the left toes (or just the big toe).

This is the upright position of baddha padmasana.

In the final position of baddha padmasana bend forward, resting the forehead on the ground.

Technique 3

Place the legs correctly in padmasana and put the palms of the hands on the knees.

Practise jalandhara, uddiyana and moola bandha with vajroli mudra.

Gaze at the mid-eyebrow centre or the tip of the nose.

Khechari mudra can also be performed throughout.

In order to raise the prana, one should practise uddiyana (with bahir kumbhaka), jalandhara and moola bandhas, i.e. maha bandha. 'Raising the prana' means to draw up the energy which normally flows downward and outward. The purpose of hatha yoga is to reverse the free flowing downward movement of apana and the upward movement of prana, i.e. to hold the apana before it flows out and the prana before it moves up, within the area of samana, the navel region. This causes a pranic reaction and a more potent energy is created which rises through sushumna. Padmasana alone is not enough to induce this 'rise of prana', therefore, pranayama, bandha and mudra have to be incorporated.

Though padmasana and siddhasana may be considered equally good, siddhasana is more useful in the process of reversing the pranic flow because the vajra nadi is pressed, thus preventing an outward energy flow. Both asanas, however, are designed for effective dharana, dhyana and samadhi.

Padmasana specifically balances prana, and siddhasana maintains blood pressure and balances both the pranic and mental forces.

Padmasana is the 'destroyer of disease'. It brings about changes in the metabolic structure and brain patterns and this helps create balance in the whole system. Like siddhasana, it also presses and stimulates the acupuncture meridians of the stomach, gall bladder, spleen, kidneys and liver. Perfect functioning of these organs is essential for good health. Padmasana tones the sacral and coccygeal nerves by supplying them with an increased flow of blood. Blood flow to the legs is decreased and directed to the abdominal region. This is helpful for people with emotional and nervous disorders. However, people with sciatica or sacral infections should not do padmasana until the problem is alleviated.

Yogi Swatmarama says: "Ordinary people cannot achieve padmasana, only the few wise ones can." What does he mean by that? He means the average person. Of course, if you look around you will find that very few people can perform padmasana, and only those who are regular practitioners of yoga can maintain the posture for long periods of time. If you keep the legs supple you will be able to do it.

कृत्वासंपुटितौ करौ दृढतरं बद्ध्वातु पद्ममासनं
गाढं वक्षसि सन्निधाय चिबुकं ध्यायंश्च तच्चेतसि ।
वारंवारमपानमूर्ध्वमनिलं प्रोत्सारयन्पूरितं
न्यंचन्प्राणमुपैति बोधमतुलं शक्तिप्रभावान्नरः ॥ 48 ॥

(Sitting in padmasana) keeping the palms one above the other, chin on the chest and concentrate the mind (chitta) on Him (the Self). Repeatedly draw the vital air up from the anal region and bring the inhaled prana downwards. (Thus joining the two) one gets the highest knowledge by awakening the Shakti.

By practising padmasana in the described manner and reversing the natural flow of prana and apana, the potential force in the pranic system and the higher faculties of the mind are awakened. Everyone has this potential, but most people only operate on a very low current of energy and thus only utilize a very small portion of the brain's capacity. To awaken the dormant centres of the brain the energy level has to be increased, and to increase the prana, the positive and negative energies have to be brought together. When they unite an explosion occurs, releasing a greater quantum of energy. This union must take place in one of the vital centres so that the released energy travels through sushumna to the higher brain centres. This energy is called kundalini. What Swatmarama has described is the process which takes place through practising uddiyana bandha and moola bandha.

Swatmarama is giving the basic technique for the practice of further kriyas. Correct sitting position is the first prerequisite for the practices of pranayama, mudra, bandha, dharana and dhyana.

पद्मासने स्थितो योगी नाडीद्वारेण पूरितम् ।
मारुतं धारयेद्यस्तु स मुक्तोनात्र संशय: ॥ 49 ॥

*The yogi who, seated in padmasana, inhales through the entrances
of the nadis and fills them with maruta or vital air gains liberation;
there is no doubt about it.*

Maruta is another word for prana but it also has other
meanings. The Upanishads say that there are forty-nine
maruta. They are described as being brothers of Lord Indra.
Indra represents the individual mind and the controller of
the senses or indriyas, thus the maruta represent the forty-
nine essential faculties or powers of the mind. They are also
represented by the forty-nine letters of the Sanskrit alphabet,
and each part of the body is associated with a particular
letter. Every part of the body has a corresponding centre in
the brain and its own bija mantra located in the psychic body
and mind.

To absorb maruta is to withdraw the extroverted energy
of the body and senses into the nadis. This prevents an
outward flow of prana, the associated brain centres are
not activated and the energy is channelized into the brain
centres responsible for higher consciousness. When a
practitioner establishes himself in padmasana and reverses
the pranic process, the consciousness is liberated from
individual experience and existence. Mind and prana are
intricately linked.

Just as there are two poles of energy, the negative
and positive forces, so there are two poles of individual
consciousness – time and space. The left hemisphere of the
brain functions according to the sequence of time and the
right hemisphere of the brain operates according to the
principle of space. When these two opposite poles come
together there is a higher awakening. This means, for the
whole brain to be active, both hemispheres must function at
the same time.

Hatha yoga accomplishes this by uniting the two poles of shakti: the passive and the dynamic force, ida and pingala. This creates a third force, known as kundalini. It is man's potential spiritual energy which is responsible for all the higher qualities of mind. The shakti is created in the lower body centres and rises to the higher brain centres, thus manifesting the pure consciousness. When this takes place, the finite awareness operating through the senses and the sensory experiences ceases to function. The poles of duality no longer exist because they have been united; only the higher awareness exists. This is what is called emancipation.

The raja and dhyana yogi aims to achieve this through concentration of mind, but the hatha yogi achieves it by uniting the pranas, whereby the mind automatically becomes still. He does not have to come into confrontation with the gross tendencies of the lower mind; mind is transcended by concentrating on the physical aspect of prana.

Liberation is not a religious word. It indicates a scientific process of uniting two opposite forces. When these opposite forces combine, an explosion occurs which releases potential energy. In tantra the forces are called Shiva and Shakti; in yoga, prana and chitta; in Samkhya, purusha and prakriti; in Vedanta, Brahman and jiva; and in physics, time and space.

These two forces cannot meet at any point, they must unite in the nucleus of matter. When the opposite forces of shakti unite in mooladhara or manipura chakra, then the explosion which occurs releases the potential energy from that centre. Science has seen, when time and space meet in the nucleus of matter, that matter explodes into thousands and thousands of particles. This is the basis of creation. It is how each and every one of us was born, and by the same process the potential consciousness can be liberated from the gross mind.

All living matter is the combination of two forces, prana and consciousness. With evolution of the body, the consciousness becomes more apparent, and in this world

125

man is the closest to developing pure consciousness. Through the 'fire of yoga' the consciousness can be liberated from the gross matter of mind and body. This is the experience of atma anubhuti, atma darshan, self-realization, moksha or samadhi. Call it what you like, it is one and the same process which commences with the practice of asana and the perfection of a comfortable meditative posture such as padmasana.

SIMHASANA (lion pose)

अथ सिंहासनम् ।

गुल्फौ च वृषणस्याध: सीवन्या: पार्श्वयो: क्षिपेत् ।
दक्षिणे सव्यगुल्फं तु दक्षगुल्फं तु सव्यके ॥ 50 ॥

*Place the ankles below the scrotum, right ankle on the left side, left
ankle on the right side of the perineum.*

हस्तौ तु जान्वो: संस्थाप्य स्वांगुली: संप्रसार्य च ।
व्यात्तवक्रो निरीक्षेत नासाग्रं सुसमाहित: ॥ 51 ॥

*Place the palms on the knees, fingers spread apart, keep the mouth
open and gaze at the nosetip with a concentrated mind.*

सिंहासनं भवेदेतत्पूजितं योगिपुंगवै: ।
बन्धत्रितयसंधानं कुरुते चासनोत्तमम् ॥ 52 ॥

*This is simhasana, held in great esteem by the highest yogis. This
most excellent asana facilitates the three bandhas.*

There are two traditional methods of performing simhasana.

Technique 1

Keep the left foot under the right buttock so that the heel presses the right side of the perineum, or in women it will press the right side of the vagina.

Place the right foot in the same manner, pressing the opposite side of the perineum or vagina, so that the feet cross each other.

For this position the feet and ankles need to be very flexible.

Place the palms of the hands on the knees and spread the fingers apart.

Bend the head forward into semi-jalandhara bandha and focus the eyes on the nosetip in nasikagra drishti.

Open the mouth wide and extend the tongue as far as possible.

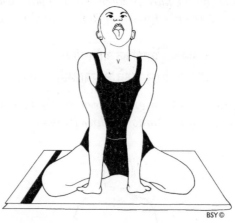

BSY©

Technique 2: Simhagarjanasana (roaring lion pose)

Place the right foot under the right buttock and the left foot under the left buttock and separate the knees widely.

This is the sitting position of bhadrasana.

The hands can be positioned as in Technique 1 or the palms can be placed on the ground with the fingers pointing towards the body. In this position there is pressure on the balls of the palms.

128

Raise the chin two or three inches, practise shambhavi mudra, extend the tongue as far as is comfortable.

Inhale deeply through the nose and exhale making a roaring sound like a lion – 'aaahhhh'.

The sound should not be forceful, nor should it irritate the throat.

To stimulate the throat more, move the tongue from side to side.

Swatmarama considers Technique 1 as one of the four major asanas. Both techniques induce the practice of bandhas. The position of the feet, especially in Technique 1, induces a natural moola bandha by creating pressure on the perineum. As the head is bent forward, jalandhara is performed, and by keeping the hands on the knees and arms stretched, the back straight and the body leaning slightly forward, uddiyana bandha is induced.

Simhasana is useful for alleviating numerous throat, mouth, nose and even ear diseases. Technique 2 is particularly good for toning the throat and eradicating stammering. It also helps to externalize introverted people. This asana is more effective when performed outside in front of the rising sun.

BHADRASANA (gracious pose)

अथ भद्रासनम् ।

गुल्फौ च वृषणस्याध: सीवन्या: पार्श्वयो: क्षिपेत् ।
सव्यगुल्फं तथा सव्ये दक्षगुल्फं तु दक्षिणे ॥ 53 ॥

*Place the ankles below the genitals on the sides by the perineum, left
ankle on the left (side) right ankle on the right (side).*

पार्श्वपादौ च पाणिभ्यां दृढं बद्ध्वा सुनिश्चलम् ।
भद्रासनं भवेदेतत्सर्वव्याधिविनाशनम् ।
गोरक्षासनमित्याहुरिदं वै सिद्धयोगिन: ॥ 54 ॥

*Then hold the feet, which are on their sides, firmly with the hands and
remain motionless. This is bhadrasana which destroys all diseases. The
yogis who are perfected (siddhas) call it gorakshasana.*

Bhadra means 'gracious and blessed'. According to
Swatmarama it is also referred to as gorakshasana, and
some call it moola bandhasana, but in these postures the foot
position varies slightly.

130

Technique

Sit in vajrasana and separate the knees as wide as possible. Then place the heels underneath the scrotum or the sides of the vagina. Heels of the feet are kept together, and the balls of the feet are under the buttocks.

When the sitting position is accomplished, hold the toes from behind the back and make the body steady.

Close the eyes and concentrate on the breath, a given symbol or mantra.

BSY©

Gorakshasana, however, is slightly different because you sit with the feet in front of the groin, the balls of the feet on the ground, heels together pointing upwards. The right hand is placed on the left heel and the left hand on the right heel. Moola bandha asana is also a variation of bhadrasana. You sit on the feet, the soles of the feet together, heels pressing the anus, sides of the feet pressing the perineum or vagina and toes pointing out in front.

These asana positions are for advanced practitioners and those with very supple ankles. Bhadrasana spontaneously induces moola bandha and tones the reproductive organs, alleviating ailments pertaining to those organs. The benefits of bhadrasana are similar to those of padmasana, siddhasana and vajrasana.

131

एवमासनबंधेषु योगीन्द्रो विगतश्रमः ।
अभ्यसेन्नाडिकाशुद्धिं मुद्रादिपवनक्रियाम् ॥ 55 ॥

*Thus the best of yogis, being free from fatigue in practising asana
and bandhas, should practise purification of the nadis, mudras and
pranayama.*

आसनं कुंभकं चित्रं मुद्राख्यं करणं तथा ।
अथ नादानुसंधानमभ्यासानुक्रमो हठे ॥ 56 ॥

*Asana, the varieties of kumbhaka, practices called mudras and
concentration on the inner sound (nada) comprise the sequence of
hatha yoga.*

When asanas and bandhas are practised one should feel
an energy boost afterwards rather than an energy loss. If
one experiences tiredness, it means some practices are
being done incorrectly. After asanas, pranayama should be
practised to purify the nadis. For this purpose nadi shodhana
(nadi purification) pranayama is best. Then mudras should
be performed to channelize the energy and create specific
attitudes of mind, and bandhas to force the energy upward.
In hatha yoga the sequence is asanas first, then pranayama,
mudras and bandhas. Lastly, one should sit quietly in a
meditative pose and concentrate on a symbol. If the inner
sound can be heard, concentrate on that.

Listening to the inner sound is called nada anusandhana,
and it can be practised by sitting on a slightly raised
platform, blanket or cushion, with the knees bent, the elbows
resting on the knees and the ears closed with the fingers.
Make a slight humming sound, then concentrate on the
sound vibrations. This helps awaken awareness of the inner
sound.

So, in the systematic science of hatha yoga, you must
firstly prepare the physical body because it is the grossest
manifestation of prana. Activate the prana through asana,

then practise pranayama to purify the energy channels and to process and balance the prana. Then perform mudras to channel the prana and arouse different faculties of the mind, and bandhas to draw prana upward from the lower centres. When the full capacity of prana or shakti is released, the high vibrational rate creates an audible sound in the inner ear. If you can hear it, it is a sure sign that kundalini has awakened.

ब्रह्मचारी मिताहारी त्यागी योगपरायण: ।
अब्दादूर्ध्वं भवेत्सिद्धो नात्र कार्या विचारणा ॥ 57 ॥

One who is brahmachari, takes moderate and pure food, is regular and intent on yoga and renounces (attachment to sensual experience) becomes perfected (siddha) after a year.

Brahmachari means 'one whose consciousness is absorbed in Brahma', the purest state of consciousness, not necessarily one who abstains from sexual interaction. So, one who keeps his mind above the existence of duality and sex, takes agreeable and sweet (mitahara) food, practises his sadhana regularly and maintains detachment from the affairs of mundane life, will definitely achieve perfection within a short period of time. It is certainly no easy task as we have previously discussed; there are many trials and obstacles to face on the path to perfection.

सुस्निग्धमधुराहारश्चतुर्थांशविवर्जितः ।
भुज्यते शिवसंप्रीत्यै मिताहारः स उच्यते ॥ 58 ॥

Mitahara is defined as agreeable and sweet food, leaving one fourth of the stomach free, and eaten (as an offering to please Shiva).

'Sweet food' means fresh, pleasant tasting food, not particularly that which has extra sugar. Food which is disagreeable means that it is either bad tasting, poisonous to the system or not agreeable to one's metabolism. The stomach should never be overloaded, it should be half filled with food, one quarter with water and one quarter with air. Eating 'to please Shiva' means that when taking food the yogi should not feel that he is eating for himself. He should cultivate the attitude that he is nourishing the body for its maintenance so his consciousness can continue its process of unfoldment and spiritual evolution.

Shiva is the inner consciousness, the atma. Everything the yogi eats should be considered as prasad or an offering from the supreme being. This is very important for eradicating the sense of ego: 'I' want and 'I' eat. Food is not taken for sense gratification but to sustain the vehicle of the indweller, the atma. Therefore, eating should be considered as part of one's sadhana. Life itself is a sadhana.

Many people indulge in food as a means of escape for the mind. When they are tense, frustrated or insecure they eat to relieve the problem. A yogi should always regard food as a medicine which will purify and fuel the body and mind for the maintenance of life and progress in sadhana. Thus at all times he will eat cautiously, with awareness and with a higher purpose than sensual pleasure.

Mitahara means 'sattwic food', light food which is easy to digest. As Swami Sivananda of Rishikesh points out: "Heavy food leads to a tamasic state and induces sleep only. There is a general misapprehension that a large quantity of food is necessary for health and strength. Much depends upon the power of assimilation and absorption. Generally, in the vast majority of cases, most of the food passes away undigested along with faeces . . . Almost all diseases are due to irregularity of meals, overeating and unwholesome food." His maxim is that through overeating you become a rogi, through sattwic diet a yogi.

कट्वम्लतीक्ष्णलवणोष्णहरीतशाकसौवीरतैलतिलसर्षप मद्यमत्स्यान् ।
अजादिमांसदधितक्रकुलत्थकोलपिण्याकहिंगुलशुनाद्यमपथ्यमाहुः ॥ 59 ॥

*The foods which are prohibited (for the yogi) are: those which are
bitter, sour, pungent, salty, heating, green vegetables (other than
those ordained), sour gruel, oil, sesame and mustard, alcohol, fish,
flesh foods, curds, buttermilk, horse gram, fruit of jujube, oil cakes,
asafoetida and garlic.*

A yogi's diet should be simple and bland. Anything that
is highly concentrated, causes acidity in the stomach and
overheats the whole system should be avoided, i.e. greasy,
spicy and stale foods. Foods which create toxins and putrefy
in the intestines, such as meat, should definitely be avoided.
Asafoetida and garlic are considered aphrodisiacs as they
supposedly stimulate the production of sex hormones. Of
course, they are not harmful and in small quantities they
are medicinal, but they are strong and leave an odour in the
body. In particular, it is said that garlic should not be taken
at night because it arouses sexual fantasies. One who is trying
to maintain awareness of the higher aspects of reality should
definitely refrain from taking such substances until he is
established in that state of awareness.

Alcohol should be avoided, not specifically because it
intoxicates the mind, but more for the reason that it destroys
liver and brain cells, which do not reproduce themselves.
Once brain cells are destroyed they are not replaced and in
hatha yoga one aims at maintaining and sustaining the body,
thus alcoholic substances are better left untouched.

भोजनमहितं विद्यात्पुनरस्योष्णीकृतं रूक्षम् ।
अतिलवणमम्लयुक्तं कदशनशाकोत्कटं वर्ज्यम् ॥ 60 ॥

Unhealthy diet should not be taken, that which is reheated after becoming cold, which is dry (devoid of natural oil), which is excessively salty or acidic, stale or has too many (mixed) vegetables.

When food is cooked and again reheated after it has gone cold, bacterias have set in, and if this food is eaten it creates fermentation in the stomach, resulting in indigestion, wind and acidity. Dry food means that which has absolutely no natural oil or water left in it. Oil is necessary in minimum quantities. Excess salt and acidity imbalance the system, in fact, salt directly affects the heart rate. If salt is taken in excess it makes the heart beat faster and heats the body.

Many different types of vegetables should not be cooked together as the resulting chemical reactions can upset the digestive system and disturb body functions. Digestion should always be a quick and smooth process which does not overstrain or overheat the system, and prana should not be wasted on digestion.

वह्निस्त्रीपथिसेवानामादौ वर्जनमाचरेत् ।
तथाहि गोरक्षवचनम् ।
'वर्जयेद् दुर्जनप्रान्तं वह्निस्त्रीपथिसेवनम्।
प्रातःस्नानोपवासादि कायक्लेशविधिं तथा' ॥ 61 ॥

Fire, women and long pilgrimages should be avoided. Therefore Gorakhnath said: bad company, mixing with women, bathing in the early morning, fasting and tasks which produce pain in the body should be avoided.

Anything which demands excess energy and depletes the system should be avoided. Standing or working near a fire exhausts the prana. 'Bad company' means those who live an antispiritual life or who think negatively. People without any purpose in life, who are unaware of the importance of spiritual evolution, do not enlighten one's soul and should be avoided by a sadhaka.

Involvement with the opposite sex and sexual intercourse for pleasure alone, deplete energy and tax the nervous system. Sexual desire can never be fulfilled and when you feed that desire it is like throwing kerosene on a fire. It is not the physical act which is 'bad' but the mental repercussions which can be harmful for the sadhaka. Thus it is better not to indulge for some time if one wants to awaken prana through hatha yoga.

One is also advised not to undergo long journeys or pilgrimages. Of course, it should be remembered that when *Hatha Yoga Pradipika* was written, jets and fast cars were not in existence. People travelled by foot, physically exhausting the bodily and pranic reserves. A pilgrimage implies a religious search to find God somewhere else. The hatha yogi can realize that highest state without travelling anywhere.

'Bathing early in the morning should be avoided', but the sentence is incomplete without adding 'with cold water when the weather is wintery'. In India most people bathe in water from the well or water reserve, few take a hot bath. Particularly when it is very hot, nobody wants to bathe in warm water. However, in winter it is cold in the early morning and if one bathes in cold water it strains the nervous system and lowers the body temperature. Hot water baths weaken the body's resistance to the outside temperature and can make one feel very lethargic and sluggish.

The hatha yogi should eat regular meals and not make a habit of fasting too often. However, fasting can be useful to stimulate the digestive system, to eliminate toxins and to help bring the senses and mind under control. In sickness it stimulates the body to produce the necessary antibodies to fight disease and rebalance the body structure.

In India many people follow the age-old tradition of fasting in conjunction with the phases of the moon. There are particular days which are conducive for either a full or half day fast, e.g. the fourth, ninth, eleventh, fourteenth and fifteenth day of either the bright or dark fortnight. Swami Sivananda says: "Occasional fasting once a month or when passion troubles you much, will suffice."

Though fasting has a lot to offer and many people advocate it, one who devotes many hours to hatha yoga sadhana should not strain the body in such a way. Any actions which are strenuous and create pain or extreme conditions in the body should not be undertaken by the yogi. Without being fanatical, one should take proper care of the body and avoid any unnecessary strain or injury, as the body is the vehicle to higher consciousness. Of course, one has to be sensible about all these instructions and take into account the situation and conditions.

गोधूमशालियवषाष्टिकशोभनान्नंक्षीरराज्यखंडनवनीतसितामधूनि ।
शुंठीपटोलकफलादिकपंचशाकंमुद्गादिदिव्यमुदकंच यमींद्रपथ्यम् ॥ 62 ॥

(The most conducive foods for the yogi are:) good grains, wheat, rice, barley, milk, ghee, brown sugar, sugar candy (crystallized sugar), honey, dry ginger, patola fruit (species of cucumber), five vegetables, mung and such pulses, and pure water.

Whole grains and rice supply essential carbohydrates and vitamin B complex. Fresh milk and ghee maintain the mucous lining of the digestive tract and alimentary canal which is washed away by shatkarma practices, and neutralize any acidity or heat in the stomach which the practices may create. Sugar is necessary for the efficient functioning of the brain as well as other bodily processes. Honey is recommended as it is an easily digestible, whole food. Dried ginger is also agreeable.

In the *Gheranda Samhita* (5:20) the 'five vegetables' are said to be balasaka, kalasaka, patolapatraka, vastaka and himalochika. These are leafy vegetables which are similar to spinach. Light, easily digestible pulses such as mung, red lentils, etc., are recommended as they supply protein, but pulses and gram such as horse gram, which are hard to digest and create flatulence, are to be avoided. Pure water which is free of chemicals, excess minerals and harmful bacteria is essential, particularly for the purification practices.

141

पुष्टं सुमधुरं स्निग्धं गव्यं धातुप्रपोषणम् ।
मनोभिलषितं योग्यं योगी भोजनमाचरेत् ॥ 63 ॥

*The yogi should take nourishing and sweet food mixed with ghee
and milk; it should nourish the dhatus (basic body constituents) and
be pleasing and suitable.*

The most important attribute of the diet is that it should
nourish the dhatus. There are seven dhatus or basic body
structures: skin, flesh, blood, bone, marrow, fat and semen
or ova. Anything which destroys their natural balance should
not be taken.

Although milk and ghee are recommended, large
quantities should not be taken. Too much milk creates a
mucous problem and excess ghee is stored in the body as fat.
On the other hand, if you have an allergic reaction to milk
do not take it. If rice creates swelling in the abdomen or fluid
retention, leave it.

'Pleasing and suitable food' means that which suits the
individual body metabolism and which makes one feel
healthy, mentally content and stable. Diet differs according
to each individual, so you may have to experiment with
different foods and quantities before you find the correct diet
for yourself.

Of course, it has to be taken into consideration that the
diet given here is suitable for the climate and environmental
conditions of India. It is also the diet of the hatha yogi who is
devoted to many hours of constant sadhana, and not of those
who do a one hour yoga class once a week and have other
household commitments. Nevertheless, most of the foods
mentioned are available all over the world, and even if you
are a householder, such a diet will help purify the body and
stabilize the mind and passions.

युवा वृद्धोऽतिवृद्धो वा व्याधितो दुर्बलोऽपि वा ।
अभ्यासात्सिद्धिमाप्नोति सर्वयोगेष्वतंद्रित: ॥ 64 ॥

Whether young or old, very old, sick or feeble, one can attain perfection in all the yogas by practising.

क्रियायुक्तस्य सिद्धि: स्यादक्रियस्य कथं भवेत् ।
न शास्त्रपाठमात्रेण योगसिद्धि: प्रजायते ॥ 65 ॥

Perfection results from practical application. Without practising how can it happen? Just by reading the shastras perfection in yoga will never be attained.

न वेषधारणं सिद्धे: कारणं न च तत्कथा ।
क्रियैव कारणं सिद्धे: सत्यमेतन्न संशय: ॥ 66 ॥

Neither by wearing the garb of a siddha, nor by talking about it (is perfection attained). Only through practical application does one become a siddha. This is the truth without a doubt.

There is a saying that practice makes perfect and that is exactly what is being expressed here. You may read as many principles as you can absorb intellectually, but until they are put into practice there is no experience of their reality nor manifestation of their inherent potential. A doctor does not become a doctor until he can practise all that he has learned theoretically. An engineer cannot make a machine just by reading instructions on how to do it. The final product will not be perfect until one has tried many times.

Regular practice of any yoga technique creates a pattern in the body and mind, and after many years of practice, perfection is attained, regardless of the initial circumstances. One should not be deterred from practising yoga because of feeling physically inadequate. It does not matter if the body is old or young, sick or feeble, everybody is eligible to practise hatha yoga and to attain self-realization. If one has an inner desire to experience the truth of existence one will succeed regardless of physical conditions.

Where truth exists there is no place for illusion or delusion. One cannot become a yogi just by assuming the external appearance, nor can one fool others into believing it; the lack of inner strength and understanding will expose anyone who is a fraud. One may delude oneself by looking like a yogi or ascetic but the atma cannot be deluded, nor can the cloth give power and knowledge. It can only come by training the body and refining the gross consciousness.

पीठानि कुंभकाश्चित्रा दिव्यानि करणानि च ।
सर्वाण्यपि हठाभ्यासे राजयोगफलावधि: ॥ 67 ॥

Asanas, various types of kumbhaka, and the other various means of illumination should all be practised in the hatha yoga system until success in raja yoga is attained.

This chapter on asanas concludes perfectly with a reminder of the purpose for practising hatha yoga. As it is said in the beginning, it is solely for the attainment of raja yoga. Hatha yoga is the basis of raja yoga. The fact that it should be practised until attainment in raja yoga is achieved means they are intricately connected. In fact, it would seem that they are one yoga; hatha being the dynamic and preparatory aspect while raja yoga is the passive and culminating stage.

However, hatha and raja yoga have become two different systems. Raja yoga says yama and niyama first, then asana, pranayama, pratyahara, dharana, dhyana and samadhi. Hatha yoga starts with asana, pranayama and shatkarma and does not emphasize any moral disciplines. It only states how to live most conducively for the practice and perfection of sadhana. There is no moral code causing tension in the mind.

Hatha yoga leads on to raja yoga, then one starts the practice of yama and niyama and continues the sadhana of asanas, etc. Therefore, hatha yoga precedes raja yoga. Until one reaches realization in raja yoga one has not achieved perfection in hatha yoga. Perfection and realization through hatha yoga means samadhi, i.e. perfection of raja, dhyana, laya and samadhi yoga.

अथ द्वितीयोपदेशः

Chapter Two

Shatkarma and Pranayama

अथासने दृढे योगी वशी हितमिताशन: ।
गुरूपदिष्टमार्गे प्राणायामान्समभ्यसेत् ॥ 1 ॥

*Thus being established in asana and having control (of the body),
taking a balanced diet; pranayama should be practised according to
the instructions of the guru.*

Only when the body is regulated by asana and moderate diet
should a sadhaka begin the next stage of hatha yoga, i.e.
pranayama. It should not be started until the guru indicates
the appropriate pranayama to be practised. Pranayama
is more than simple breathing exercises and it must be
practised systematically and under proper guidance.

The word prana is a combination of two syllables, *pra* and
na. Prana denotes constancy, it is a force in constant motion.
Prana is the vital life force and pranayama is the process
by which the internal pranic store is increased. *Pranayama*
is comprised of the words *prana* and *ayama*, which means
'pranic capacity or length'. It is not merely breath control,
but a technique through which the quantity of prana in the
body is activated to a higher frequency.

In yogic terminology it is said that whatever is manifest is
the *sthula roopa* or 'gross form' of the subtle, cosmic energy,
known as prana. In yoga and tantra there is an eternal truth:
the basis of existence depends on two forces, *Shiva* and
Shakti, or 'consciousness' and 'energy'. Ultimately they are
not two forces but one; Shakti or prana is the creative force
of consciousness or Shiva. The purpose of hatha yoga is to
realize Shiva or consciousness by means of Shakti or prana.

Pranayama is practised in order to understand and control
the pranic process in the body. Breathing is a direct means of
absorbing prana and the manner in which we breathe sets off
pranic vibrations which influence our entire being.

Diet control is specified along with the practice of
pranayama. Eating is a direct means of pranic absorption,
which affects the body, mind and pranic vibrations.

चले वाते चलं चित्तं निश्चले निश्चलं भवेत् ।
योगी स्थाणुत्वमाप्नोति ततो वायुं निरोधयेत् ॥ 2 ॥

*When prana moves, chitta (the mental force) moves. When prana is
without movement, chitta is without movement. By this (steadiness
of prana) the yogi attains steadiness and should thus restrain the
vayu (air).*

Prana and mind are intricately linked. Fluctuation of one
means fluctuation of the other. When either the mind
or prana becomes balanced the other is steadied. Hatha
yoga says, control the prana and the mind is automatically
controlled, whereas raja yoga says, control the mind and
prana becomes controlled. These are two paths of yoga.

The mind is equated with a wild monkey, jumping here
and there. Because of this inborn tendency it is very difficult
to hold it still. Hatha yoga says let the mind be, concentrate
on the autonomic body functions and vital energy, and the
mind will become quiet by itself. When the nervous impulses
are steady and rhythmic, the brain functions are regulated
and the brain waves become rhythmic.

The breathing process is directly connected to the brain
and central nervous system and it is one of the most vital
processes in the body system. It also has some connection
with the hypothalamus, the brain centre which controls
emotional responses. The hypothalamus is responsible for
transforming perception into cognitive experience. Erratic
breathing sends erratic impulses to this centre and thus
creates disturbed responses.

There are also certain areas of the nasal mucous membrane
which are connected to the visceral organs. When impulses
coming from the nose are arrhythmic, the visceral organs,
particularly those connected to the coccygeal plexus, respond
in the same manner, arrhythmically. Being disturbed, these
organs again send irregular impulses to the brain and cause
more disharmony and imbalance. This cycle is continuous.

By becoming aware of the nature of the breath and by restraining it, the whole system becomes controlled. When you retain the breath you are stopping nervous impulses in different parts of the body and harmonizing the brain wave patterns. In pranayama, it is the duration of breath retention which has to be increased. The longer the breath is held, the greater the gap between nervous impulses and their responses in the brain. When retention is held for a prolonged period, mental agitation is curtailed.

Actually, Sage Patanjali defines pranayama as the gap between inhalation and exhalation. Pranayama is usually considered to be the practice of controlled inhalation and exhalation combined with retention. However, technically speaking, it is only retention. Inhalation and exhalation are methods of inducing retention. Retention is most important because it allows a longer period for assimilation of prana, just as it allows more time for the exchange of gases in the cells, i.e. oxygen and carbon dioxide.

Sage Patanjali further says that retention of breath after expiration removes the obstacles to yoga. Yoga is the union of the two poles of energy within us. In mundane awareness these poles are separate from each other. In transcendental awareness these poles come closer together, and during retention the poles come closest together. Breath retention must be developed in order to stop the fluctuations of the brain and mind so that a more expansive type of experience can develop.

When you go further into yoga, there comes a time when you must have some control of the mind so you can dive deeper within yourself. When you try to practise mantra or meditation, the fluctuating mental waves create a barrier between you and the object you are trying to focus your awareness on. So how to control the mind?

For many, many centuries, people have known that through pranic restraint you can control the influxes of the mind and through mental restraint you can control the influxes of prana, but various spiritual systems have

151

been debating which is the best method to harness the two energies and induce unity. Christ and Lord Buddha said the same thing – 'Lead a good life and your mind will be controlled.' Of course what they said is true, but people today are exposed to so many disturbing external factors that this approach does not work for them. There are many good, charitable, pure-minded and compassionate people, but if you ask them to sit quietly, still the mind and meditate, they can't do it. Yama and niyama do help, but they are difficult for modern day man to uphold, and for this age, these disciplines have not proved to be a very powerful method for developing mind control.

However, it has been found that through pranayama, mudras, bandhas and certain postures which regulate the prana, the mind can be brought under control. In many spiritual traditions, including Sufism, Buddhism and yoga, it was discovered that by concentrating on the breath, one can still the mind, develop one-pointedness and gain entry into the deeper realms of the mind and consciousness.

यावद्वायु: स्थितो देहे तावज्जीवनमुच्यते ।
मरणं तस्य निष्क्रांतिस्ततो वायुं निरोधयेत् ॥ 3 ॥

As long as the vayu (air and prana) remains in the body, that is
called life. Death is when it leaves the body. Therefore, retain vayu.

Death is not total. The physical body dies or the mind dies,
but not the soul. Death is not extinction, it is a process
of disintegration. The components of the body, the five
tattwas: *akasha*, ether, *vayu*, air, *agni*, fire, *apas*, water, and
prithvi, earth; which are associated with the five prana vayus,
disintegrate and go back to their original source. Akasha
tattwa goes back to akasha, vayu to vayu, agni to agni, apas
to apas, prithvi to prithvi, and then the jivatma moves out.

This jivatma, spirit, ego, astral body, or whatever you
might like to call it, is something which survives death.
The pranas also do not die, they move out of the body and
return to their source. If death is to be averted the process
unlinking all the three components i.e. prana, mind and
soul, has to be stopped.

In this sloka we are told to retain the vayu. *Vayu* means
'air', but it does not refer only to the gross air and its
chemical properties; it indicates pranic air. In the pranic
body, pingala channelizes prana shakti, but prana vayu
moves throughout the whole body like waves of energy. It can
be likened to an electromagnetic field where the energy is in
constant motion.

There are five main vayu functions, known as apana,
prana, samana, udana and vyana. They are the different
processes and manifestations of the one vayu, just as the
various limbs of a man comprise the one body.

Pranic absorption takes place on a major scale in
the thoracic region and is the function of prana vayu.
Elimination takes place largely through the urinary, excretory
and reproductive organs and is powered by apana. In
between apana and prana, in the stomach region, is the area

of assimilation, which is the function of samana. Movement in the throat and facial expressions are due to udana. Circulation is powered by vyana which pervades the whole body.

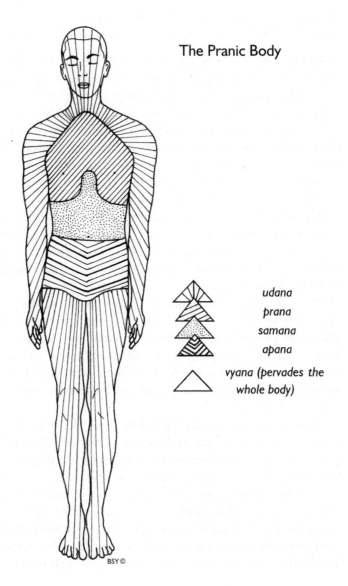

The Pranic Body

udana
prana
samana
apana
vyana (pervades the whole body)

BSY©

All the processes which affect absorption or inward movement of the subtle cosmic force are due to prana. Those which affect elimination or outward movement are due to apana. Assimilation, preservation and continuation are the work of samana. Ascension and refining are the work of udana, and pervasiveness is the property of vyana. These actions occur within the various realms of existence. The vayu, however, is specifically concerned with the pranic body or pranamaya kosha.

In the Upanishads, prana vayu is also called the 'in breath', apana the 'out breath', samana the 'middle breath', and udana the 'up breath'. Prana vayu is inhalation, apana exhalation, samana the time between inhalation and exhalation, and udana, the extension of samana. According to the *Maitri Upanishad* (11:6): "Samana is the higher form of vyana and between them is the production of udana. That which brings up or carries down what has been drunk or eaten is udana."

From a yogic point of view the most important vayu is samana. It is related to sushumna nadi. Prana vayu is related to ida, apana to pingala, and ascension of kundalini to udana. Samana vayu has to be developed. This takes place by suspending apana and prana within the region of samana. Each vayu is interdependent and interconnected. In the *Chandogya Upanishad* it is asked: "On what are you (body and senses) and yourself (soul) supported? On prana. On what is prana supported? On apana. On what is apana supported? On vyana. On what is vyana supported? On samana."

On account of these five main movements, five subsidiary or *upapranas* are produced. These are known as *koorma* which stimulates blinking, *krikara* which generates hunger, thirst, sneezing and coughing, *devadatta* which induces sleep and yawning, *naga* which causes hiccups and belching, and *dhananjaya* which lingers immediately after death.

From the time of conception up until four months, the foetus survives purely on the mother's prana. It is like a tumour in the mother's body. After four months it is said that prana enters the foetus and individual life begins. As the individual pranas begin to move, so the individual body functions become active. However, the child is only independent once it is born and starts breathing.

The moment prana completely leaves the body, consciousness departs, because prana and consciousness are the two poles of the one source, the Self. The *Prashnopanishad* says: "This prana is born of the Self. Just as there can be a shadow when a man is there, so this prana is fixed on the Self . . . " (3.3) At death, when the breath stops and the prana leaves, the magnetic force which held the body together deteriorates and along with it, so does the body. Therefore, the breath and prana are likened to a thread in the *Brihadaranyaka Upanishad*: "Verily by air, as by a thread, this world, the other world and all beings are held together. Therefore it is said, when an individual dies his limbs have been loosened because they are held together by air like a thread."

When prana leaves the body there is no force to animate it. As long as prana is retained the body will not die. Life is generated with inhalation, with exhalation there is loss of prana. When the breath is held, the prana does not move out or in, it becomes stabilized.

Prana is the basis of life and can be directly controlled through the breath. The yogis who go underground for days together in a place where no air can penetrate, completely stop the breath. These yogis concentrate on the prana as a point of light in the mid-eyebrow centre. When their consciousness is completely absorbed in that light, the breath stops automatically. Prana still remains in the body, but there is no breathing process. There is no absorption of prana, no elimination, no function of prana and apana; only of vyana. The body functions are suspended as long as consciousness remains absorbed in the point of light. It is a state of suspended animation. The moment the awareness starts to come back to the physical body, the breath starts and the yogi has to come out. Through the breath, prana and

156

consciousness are essentially linked; they can be separated by a scientific means which starts with the yogic technique of learning to retain the breath.

Prana is the tangible manifestation of the higher Self. Hatha yoga uses prana as the key to expand the awareness of consciousness and realize the Self. Some systems of yoga aim at self-realization by purifying and concentrating the mind, others by purifying and channelizing the emotions, and some by purifying the intellect and developing wisdom. There are so many ways of redirecting the vital life force from the lower to the higher centres. Hatha yoga achieves it by a means which is most practical for everybody – through the physical body and by working directly on the pranic movements.

मलाकुलासु नाडीषु मारुतो नैव मध्यगः ।
कथं स्यादुन्मनीभावः कार्यसिद्धिः कथं भवेत् ॥ 4 ॥

The vital air does not pass in the middle channel because the nadis are full of impurities. So how can the state of unmani arise and how can perfection or siddhi come about?

If our perception was finely attuned to the pranic body, we would see a light body in which there were thousands of fine, wirelike structures conducting shakti. These wirelike structures are the nadis. *Nadi* is a flow of energy. The *Shiva Samhita* says that altogether there are 350,000 nadis in the body, the *Prapanchasara Tantra* says 300,000 and the *Goraksha Satarka* says 72,000. There are thousands upon thousands of nadis within the superstructure of the gross body and they distribute consciousness and prana to every atom. However, as stated here and in the *Gheranda Samhita*: "When the nadis are full of impurities, vayu does not enter them."

What are these impurities? They are waste and residue of sensuous living and desires. Just as excess fats accumulate around blood vessels and can eventually obstruct the flow of blood, similarly on a pranic level also there is an accumulation of wastes. With the build up of waste matter, the body's capacity to circulate energy lessens. The body becomes lethargic, the energy level decreases and activation of the chakras and higher brain functions is prevented.

Supposing you have a one litre plastic bottle and inside it some areas are coated with cement, and you try to fill it with a litre of nitric acid, two things will happen. One , the full litre of nitric acid will not fit, and two, the plastic will melt. Similarly, if kundalini shakti is released when the nadis are blocked and weak, you will not be able to handle the experience. Therefore, the whole body and network of nadis have to be purified and the energy channels have to be made strong.

The pranic body is the intermediate link between the physical body and the mind. Therefore, it can be approached from either side. It is, however, easier to control and purify the pranic body through the physical body. By strengthening the sympathetic and parasympathetic nervous systems, ida and pingala nadis are directly affected, and by developing the central nervous system, sushumna is activated. Therefore, the most important practices of hatha yoga are those which arouse the central nervous system and sushumna.

शुद्धिमेति यदा सर्वं नाडीचक्रं मलाकुलम् ।
तदैव जायते योगी प्राणसंग्रहणे क्षमः ॥ 5 ॥

When all the nadis and chakras which are full of impurities are purified, then the yogi is able to retain prana.

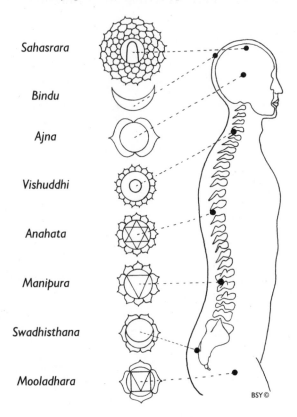

Sahasrara

Bindu

Ajna

Vishuddhi

Anahata

Manipura

Swadhisthana

Mooladhara

BSY©

Location of the Chakras

In the process of awakening kundalini, the sadhaka has not only to clear the nadis, energy channels, but also increase the quantity and quality of prana and store it. Prana is accumulated in six main centres along the spinal column.

These centres are located in the subtle body and correspond to the nerve plexuses in the physical body. In the subtle body they are known as chakras. *Chakra* means 'a circling motion or wheel'. Prana shakti and manas shakti collect in the chakras and form swirling masses of energy. Each chakra is a conjunction point for many nadis. There are numerous chakras in the body but the seven major ones situated along sushumna nadi are specifically concerned with human evolution.

In deep meditation, the yogis have seen these chakras and they described them as lotus flowers. Though the chakras are situated in the subtle body, their influence extends to the gross and causal bodies. Each chakra vibrates at a particular rate and velocity. The chakras at the lowest point of the energy circuit operate on a lower frequency and are said to be grosser and to create grosser states of awareness. Chakras at the top of the circuit operate on a high frequency and are responsible for subtle states of awareness and higher intelligence.

Some yogic texts describe only five or six chakras, others describe seven. The lowest chakra is within the perineal floor in the male body and the cervix in the female body. It is a four-petalled red lotus called *mooladhara*, and it influences the excretory and reproductive organs, reproductive glands and hormonal secretions. Mooladhara is directly connected to the nose and sense of smell and with our animal instincts. At mooladhara human evolution begins and kundalini emerges.

Two fingers width above mooladhara and closely associated with it, is *swadhisthana* chakra, a six-petalled vermilion lotus. It is connected to the sacral plexus, urinary and reproductive organs and glands. Swadhisthana is associated with the tongue and the sense of taste. Its influence on the deeper personality arouses a selfish sense of ego.

The next chakra is behind the navel, within the spinal column. It is a ten-petalled yellow lotus called *manipura* and it is associated with the solar plexus. Manipura influences the digestive process and the assimilation of food and prana. It is also connected to the eyes and sight. At the level of manipura the consciousness is still bound by the grosser levels of existence and sensualities, ambition and greed.

Above manipura, in the proximity of the heart, is *anahata* chakra, with twelve blue petals. It is connected to the cardiac plexus, heart, respiration and thymus gland and is responsible for emotions of love and hate, compassion and cruelty, etc. Anahata is also connected to the sense of touch and the hands.

Within the middle of the throat is the fifth chakra *vishuddhi*, with sixteen purple petals. It is associated with the cervical plexus and thyroid gland and it maintains purity in the body and mind. Vishuddhi is connected to the ears and sense of audition, throat and speech. It arouses acceptance of the adversities of life, mental balance and sensitivity to the needs of others.

At the top of the spinal column, at the medulla oblongata, is one of the most important chakras, *ajna* chakra, which has two silvery grey or clear petals. Above vishuddhi the chakras are mainly concerned with higher intelligence. Some authorities do not even consider them as chakras because, as the veiling power of prana shakti decreases, manas shakti becomes more predominant. Ajna chakra is the command centre. It operates in conjunction with the reticular activating system, medulla oblongata and the pineal gland. Ajna chakra is the third eye through which the whole subtle world can be perceived. It is known as the gateway to liberation.

When kundalini shakti passes beyond ajna, duality and ego cease to exist. It reaches the highest centre, *sahasrara*, the thousand-petalled lotus. Sahasrara is situated at the crown of the head and is associated with the pituitary gland. When this chakra is fully activated by kundalini it is the highest experience of human evolution.

Between ajna and sahasrara there are three other chakras which are briefly mentioned in the Tantras. Opposite the uvula is *lalana* chakra, which is a twelve-petalled lotus. Above ajna is *manas* chakra, a six-petalled lotus, and above that, at the mid-cerebrum is *soma* chakra of sixteen petals. These chakras are concerned with the flow of nectar from bindu visarga (which is discussed later), and they are responsible for higher states of consciousness and intelligence.

Through hatha yoga all these chakras are influenced and stimulated, and blockages are removed. The influence of each chakra can be felt in the body and seen in a person's behaviour. Correct balance of energy in each of the chakras is extremely important.

Dr. Hiroshi Motoyama of Japan has devised instruments which can detect the activity of these chakras and he has found that depletion of energy and the paranormal functioning of any of the chakras causes imbalance or disease in the associated physical organs and body functions. This is exactly what is stated in the hatha yoga texts.

Purification of the chakras and nadis is the first step to physical and mental health and the awakening of kundalini. Therefore, the chakras and nadis have to be strengthened so they are capable of conducting the kundalini shakti.

प्राणायामं ततः कुर्यान्नित्यं सात्त्विकया धिया ।
यथा सुषुम्नानाडीस्था मलाः शुद्धिं प्रयांति च ॥ 6 ॥

Therefore pranayama should be done daily with a sattwic state of
mind so that the impurities are driven out of sushumna nadi and
purification occurs.

There are three modes of nature and mind known as *guna*:
tamas, rajas and sattwa. *Tamas* is inertia, *rajas* is dynamism
and *sattwa* is steadiness. For example, a rock represents
tamas, man represents rajas and divinity represents sattwa.
The dull mind or the mind in which there is no awareness
is tamasic or inert, the mind which oscillates between
awareness and no awareness is rajasic or dynamic, and the
steady, one-pointed mind is sattwic. Tamas is the first stage
of evolution and it evolves into rajas and then sattwa. In the
state of tamas, rajas and sattwa are potential forces. In the
rajasic state there are traces of tamas and sattwa, and in the
sattwic state, tamas and rajas do not exert any influence.

During pranayama practice the mind should be steady
and aware and not moving from thought to thought. Then
the whole system is receptive. When the mind is inert
or tamasic, some of the nadis remain inert and closed,
impurities collect and the energy cannot pass. However, this
does not mean that if you are tamasic you cannot practise
pranayama. Whether you are tamasic or rajasic, pranayama
should be practised to remove the blockages and to lift
you out of the tamasic and rajasic states. When the mind
is sattwic, the inner awareness grows quickly and prana
accumulates.

When sushumna awakens, this represents sattwa, when
pingala functions it represents rajas and when ida functions,
tamas. Thus it is best to practise pranayama when sushumna
is flowing. When the breath is flowing naturally through
both nostrils, it means sushumna is active. We do not always
breathe through both nostrils, usually one nostril is open and

the other is partially or fully closed. Science calls it 'alternate rhinitis'. In yoga it is known as swara.

The science of swara yoga says that the breath alternates from ida to pingala every hour. Modern science has also observed the same alternating process and its association with the activation of the right and left brain hemispheres. The cerebrum alternates its activities every sixty to ninety minutes as indicated by the nostril functions. When the breath is flowing through the left nostril it indicates that ida and the right brain hemisphere are active. When the right nostril is flowing it means pingala and the left brain hemisphere are active.

Pingala is the dynamic, male principle and ida the passive female principle. The left brain hemisphere operates on the same principle as pingala. It processes information logically, sequentially and functions according to time sequence. The right hemisphere is concerned with intuition, mental creativity and orientation in space. When both nostrils operate simultaneously the energy is being transferred from one hemisphere to the other. It passes through a thin sheet of membrane between the two hemispheres called the corpus callosum. At this time the whole brain can function and perception will not be limited to one mode of processing.

According to swara yoga, during the flow of ida one should do quiet tasks and those requiring mental creativity. During the flow of pingala, physical work should be done and during the flow of sushumna the most suitable and productive activity is yoga abhyasa and dhyana.

Factors which influence pranic flow in the nadis are: lifestyle, diet, desires, thoughts and emotions. Hatha yoga influences the nadis directly, but one's entire external life should be taken into consideration. When the personality is balanced and there are no extreme conditions in the mind and body, the breath will also be harmonized.

NADI SHODHANA PRANAYAMA
(alternate nostril breathing)

बद्धपद्मासना योगी प्राणं चंद्रेण पूरयेत् ।
धारयित्वा यथाशक्ति भूय: सूर्येण रेचयेत् ॥ 7 ॥

Sitting in baddha padmasana, the yogi should inhale through the left nostril and hold the breath to capacity, and then exhale through the right nostril.

प्राणं सूर्येण चाकृष्य पूरयेदुदरं शनै: ।
विधिवत्कुंभकं कृत्वा पुनश्चंद्रेण रेचयेत् ॥ 8 ॥

Then inhaling through the right nostril, gradually fill the abdomen, perform kumbhaka as before, then exhale completely through the left nostril.

येन त्यजेत्तेन पीत्वा धारयेदतिरोधत: ।
रेचयेच्च ततोऽन्येन शनैरेव न वेगत: ॥ 9 ॥

Inhale with the same nostril through which exhalation was done, hold the breath to utmost capacity and exhale through the other nostril slowly and not forcibly.

The first pranayama practice is nadi shodhana pranayama, alternate nostril breathing, which activates and harmonizes ida and pingala nadis. *Shodhana* means 'to purify'. In English this practice is called 'nadi purification' pranayama.

If you have never done pranayama before, in order to learn and practise it correctly, it is essential that you become fully acquainted with the natural breathing process first. This can be done by practising the following technique.

Simple breath awareness technique

    Lie down in shavasana and relax the whole body.
· Bring the awareness to the breath moving in through the nostrils, down the trachea and into the lungs.

Feel the lungs expand with inhalation, the stomach rise and a slight tension in the chest region.

While exhaling, feel the stomach drop, the lungs contract and the whole body relax as the air passes up to the nose and out through the nostrils.

Let the breath be natural.

Practise for five to ten minutes.

Many people have the tendency to take shallow breaths without filling their lungs to capacity. When you breathe in, the lungs should expand fully and the stomach should extend outwards. During exhalation the stomach should relax completely and the lungs should expel as much air as possible. This process will be developed through the above practice. When you have perfect awareness and regulation of the breath, practise in a sitting position.

Technique I

Sit in siddhasana/siddha yoni asana.

With the right hand thumb, close the right nostril and breathe in slowly and fully through the left nostril and out through the left nostril.

Practise this ten times and then repeat the same process with the opposite nostril by closing the left nostril with the third finger of the right hand, leaving the two middle fingers bent and free.

Develop breath control so that inhalation and exhalation continue for exactly the same length of time.

Count up to 3,4,5 or 6 while inhaling and then exhale for the same count. This is a ratio of 1:1.

Practise up to ten rounds.

Later on the ratio of inhalation to exhalation will be adjusted and then kumbhaka (retention) will also be added. However, first you must be able to equalize inhalation and exhalation. The progressive ratios are – 1:1, 1:2, 1:2:2, 1:4:2, 1:4:2:3.

167

There are two ways of closing the nostrils. One is by using the thumb and third finger of the right hand with the middle fingers folded. The second is by performing *nasagra* or *nasikagra mudra*, in which the first and second fingers are placed between the two eyebrows at the root of the nose. The thumb is used to close the right nostril and the third finger is used to close the left. In either technique the right hand is always used, even if you are left-handed in other tasks.

Technique 2
Stage 1: Inhale as in Technique 1, through the left nostril. Then exhale through the right nostril.
Practise in this way ten times.
Stage 2: Inhale through the right nostril and exhale through the left ten times.
Practise five to ten rounds .
Then continue the practice for a few more rounds making the inhalations and exhalations completely equal.

Technique 3
Combine the two stages of Technique 2. That is, inhale through the left nostril, exhale through the right, inhale through the right and exhale through the left. This is one round.
Practise five to ten rounds.

After these preliminary stages have been perfected, nadi shodhana with breath retention can be commenced. When the breath is being retained, both nostrils should be held closed so that the nostrils are slightly pinched. Press them a little above the lower edge and make sure they are sealed properly. The *Gheranda Samhita* says: "After inhalation hold the two nostrils with the thumb, little and ring fingers, not using the middle and index fingers, so long as the breath is retained." (5:53)

While practising, be sure that the head and body do not tilt in any direction. If the right arm becomes tired, support the elbow in the left palm. When you have prolonged the duration of inhalation and exhalation and have full breath control, you are ready to add kumbhaka to the practice. However, you must never strain; kumbhaka must be developed gradually.

Technique 4

Sit in siddhasana/siddha yoni asana.

Practise as in Technique 3, but add breath retention after inhalation.

Start with the ratio 1:2:2. After a month or so begin 1:4:2.

Though the recommended sitting position in this sloka is padmasana, the most practical is siddhasana/siddha yoni asana for the majority of people. Padmasana should be used by those people who can sit in the position for at least fifteen minutes without the slightest discomfort.

169

प्राणं पिबेदिडया पिबेत्रियमितं भूयोऽन्यया रेचयेत्
पीत्वा पिंगलया समीरणमथो बद्ध्वा त्यजेद्वामया ।
सूर्याचन्द्रमसोरनेन विधिनाभ्यासं सदा तन्वतां
शुद्धा नाडिगणा भवंति यमिनां मासत्रयादूर्ध्वत: ॥ 10 ॥

When the prana is inhaled through the left nostril, then it must be exhaled through the other. When it is inhaled through the right, hold it inside and then exhale through the other nostril. The yamini who practises in this way, through the right and left nostrils, alternately purifies all his nadis within three months.

If you are just learning pranayama, you may easily be confused about which nostril you should be breathing through. You have to maintain awareness of what you are doing. After inhalation, the breath is retained and then exhaled through the opposite nostril. Then you inhale through the same nostril through which you exhaled. After a few weeks of practise it becomes a rhythmic pattern and there will be no confusion.

An important factor has been omitted in this verse, and that is the correct ratio for inhalation to retention to exhalation. It is not sufficient to practise pranayama just by breathing in and out. The length of each breath must be counted. Start cautiously with the ratio 1:1:1, even if you are capable of retaining the breath for longer. After a week or more you can increase the ratio to 1:2:2 and progress from there.

The duration of each breath should be increased gradually. For example, supposing you start by breathing in for a count of 3, holding for 6, exhaling for 6, every three days you can increase the length of each phase by one count until you reach your capacity. Pranayama must be developed slowly and systematically so the lungs and nervous system are never harmed in any way. That is why it is always recommended that pranayama only be practised under the guidance of a teacher or guru.

According to the *Gheranda Samhita*: "There are three stages of pranayama. In the first stage, inhalation is for 12 *matras* or counts, retention 48 and exhalation 24. In the second stage, inhalation is 16 matras, retention 64 and exhalation 32. The highest stage is inhalation 20 matras, retention 80 and exhalation 40." (5:55) In the complete and final stage of pranayama, retention is also done after exhalation.

The time of one matra or count is very important. Today a metronome can be used, but traditionally there were four ways to judge the time: 1) the time taken to circle the knee and snap the fingers, 2) the time taken to clap the hands three times, 3) the time taken for the breath to go in and out while in deep sleep, 4) the time taken to chant Om. Of course, during pranayama practice it is not practical to snap your fingers, etc. Counting has to be done mentally in a calm manner – one, Om, two, Om, three, Om . . .

When pranayama is performed without repetition of mantra it is known as *nigarbha*. When mantra is repeated with inhalation, exhalation and retention, that is known as *sagarbha*. The method of sagarbha nadi shodhana given in the *Gheranda Samhita* is done by: "Inhaling (through the left nostril) while repeating the vayu bija mantra (*yam*) for 16 matras, holding the breath while repeating *yam* for 64 matras, and exhaling through the right nostril while repeating the bija mantra for 32 matras. Then raising the 'fire' from the root of the navel, contemplate on its light associated with the earth element. Repeating the agni bija (*ram*) for 16 matras inhale through the right nostril and retain the breath while repeating *ram* for 64 matras." This is the traditional method and there are variations.

Swami Sivananda of Rishikesh, for example, describes a method of nadi shodhana which includes visualization of the process of purification. Contemplate the luminous orb of the moon at the tip of the nose. Inhale through the left nostril repeating *tham* for 16 matras. Perform retention while repeating *vam* for 64 matras and imagine nectar flowing through the nadis and purifying them. Then exhale

171

through the right nostril while steadily contemplating on the *lam* mantra for 32 matras, i.e. ratio 1:4:2. However, such high proportions of inhalation, exhalation and retention are unnecessary. The ratio has to be adjusted to individual capacity.

During pranayama practice try to reduce the movement of the breath to a minimum and increase the duration of breathing to the maximum. If you find yourself gasping or becoming restless and exhausted you are forcing the breath and should reduce your ratio and counting. If boils, pimples, diarrhoea, constipation or fever occur, it is most likely due to the nadis rebalancing and purifying themselves. However, you should check that your lifestyle and diet are suitably balanced and regular, and that your asana practice is systematic.

Yogi Swatmarama states that nadi shodhana will purify the nadis within three months. Of course, other conditions have to be met for this to take place. You need to practise regularly for extended periods, devoting many hours to the practice of pranayama only. Perhaps if the final stage of nadi shodhana with the ratio 20:80:40:60 were practised, the nadis would be purified within three months. For most people it will take longer. If you revert back to an indulgent lifestyle, again the nadis will become impure. Certain disciplines have to be maintained until the kundalini is awakened, otherwise old conditions will recur.

प्रातर्मध्यदिने सायमर्धरात्रे च कुंभकान् ।
शनैरशीतिपर्यन्तं चतुर्वारं समभ्यसेत् ॥ 11 ॥

Retention should be practised perfectly four times a day: early morning, midday, evening and midnight, so that retention is gradually held up to eighty (counts in one sitting).

Those who are completely dedicated to a life of hatha sadhana should practise pranayama at the four specified times but, of course, with our present social commitments and way of life, few of us would find this possible. For the average person it is sufficient to practise once a day. It is best to get up early in the morning, take a bath, do neti/kunjal if necessary, then asanas and pranayama. If you also have the opportunity to do sadhana in the evening, then do it before eating.

The specified times for practice are important in correlation to body rhythms and solar-lunar activities. At these times there is a changeover of body and external energy rhythms, and sushumna nadi is more likely to become active.

Early morning means an hour and a half before sunrise and it is called *brahmamuhurta*, 'the period of Brahma'. At this time the subconscious mind is active and if you are sleeping then, you will most likely be dreaming. It is a time when unconscious experiences are more likely to manifest.

Evening, around the time of sunset, is called *sandhya*. Sandhya is the meeting of day and night. It represents the time when ida and pingala merge with sushumna in ajna chakra. The external influences of the sun setting or the evening commencing affect body rhythms and functions, making it conducive to the merging of the pranas in sushumna.

Similarly, at midnight and midday there is a changeover in the external and internal energies. All becomes tranquil. Midnight in particular is the time for sadhakas to awaken shakti. It is called the 'witching hour' because the 'ghosts' in the mind become active. Brain functions operate differently at night and different chemical hormones are released.

At these specified times there is a change in the levels of energy in ida and pingala. During each cycle of ida and pingala there are high and low phases when energy reaches either a peak or an ebb. In between each cycle there is a period when the energy is stable and, therefore, it is the most appropriate time for sadhana and breath retention. So the times recommended for the practice of retention have been chosen on account of the biological and pranic activities that are taking place then.

For most people, it is not advisable to practise pranayama at midnight unless specified by the guru. If you practise then, it will disturb the normal pattern of living and the people living around you will consider you absurd. Also, because the unconscious mind becomes active at this time, if negative impressions come to the surface you might have frightening experiences which you may not be able to cope with.

If you practise pranayama in the morning or evening and live a simple life, your pure thoughts will exorcize these 'ghosts' so that positive experiences unfold. Until the mind and body are purified, go slowly with your practices according to the guru's instructions. Do not be over-enthusiastic.

Pranayama should be done in correct proportion to other practices and your routine daily activities. Other forms of yoga should also be integrated into your sadhana so there will be balanced development of your personality. A person who goes 'headlong' into sadhana cannot maintain the schedule for many years. Gradually increase your sadhana according to time available and your mental, physical and psychic capacity.

Not only are particular times of the day specified for pranayama practice, there are also seasonal recommendations. The *Gheranda Samhita* enumerates the times of the year when hatha yoga should be practised: "One should not begin the practice of yoga in these seasons, viz. *hemant* 'early winter', *shishira* 'late winter', *grisma* 'summer' and *varsha* 'monsoon'. If practised, yoga causes sickness. It is said that one should begin the practice of yoga in *vasant* 'spring' and *sharad* 'autumn'. Thereby the yogi attains success and verily he becomes free from diseases." (5:8,9)

174

कनीयसि भवेत्स्वेद: कंपो भवति मध्यमे ।
उत्तमे स्थानमाप्नोति ततो वायुं निबंधयेत् ॥ 12 ॥

At first there is perspiration, in the middle stage trembling, in the highest stage complete steadiness, and therefore the breath should be withheld.

When the body and mind are purified, and the quantum of prana is increased, then various physical symptoms manifest during pranayama. The body becomes hot due to increased activities of the sympathetic nervous system. If it perspires irrespective of cool weather, pranic awakening has definitely taken place. It is possible for hot flushes to occur or you may not even notice any excess heat.

In the second stage, there may be quivering or sensations in the spine, or perhaps twitching of the hands, face and various other muscles. When the mind, body and breath become completely steady the practice is nearly perfect. The final stage is when the breath stops moving by itself.

Initially, when the pranic flow becomes intense, the peripheral parts of the body may vibrate. Impulses rush through the central nervous system and create itching or tingling sensations. The prana accumulates in different regions and may create strange sensations in the chest, abdomen, intestines or excretory organs, and sometimes whining sounds come from the lower intestines or excretory passage.

Gheranda Samhita states that: "The first stage of pranayama gives heat, the middle stage gives rise to tremor, particularly in the spinal column, whilst the final stage of pranayama leads to levitation." (5:56) The *Shiva Samhita* further states that: "Through the strength of constant practice the yogi obtains bhoochari siddhi (control of the earth element). He moves as a frog jumps over the ground when frightened by clapping hands." (3:46) Various siddhis or perfections may be attained with the awakening of the different chakras.

The first centre or chakra which should be activated is mooladhara. Mooladhara is the source of the earth element. What does the earth element represent? Earth signifies the quality of cohesion, weight and gravity. It is associated with the sense of smell and controls the basic physical structure of the body. When kundalini rises from mooladhara, levitation is said to occur because the magnetic force within you, which normally holds you down, undergoes a change. You become light like a feather.

The flow of prana can be understood in terms of light rays. Science has so far defined light in two ways: one as waves, the other as particles. The waves and particles are said to vibrate at different velocities and frequencies, thus creating the various colours of the light spectrum, but when the waves or particles move simultaneously in a straight line then there is a laser beam. Similarly, in the body ida and pingala represent the fluctuating light waves. If the intensity of their vibration is increased and they function together rather than alternately, they will move together through the central passage, sushumna, like a laser beam. That is kundalini and at that time there can be no extreme condition in the body.

When the kundalini shakti reaches the highest centre, sahasrara, it stays there for a period of time. Everything becomes still, there is no creation, no breath. Prana is held in the highest brain centre, united with consciousness.

जलेन श्रमजातेन गात्रमर्दनमाचरेत् ।
दृढता लघुता चैव तेन गात्रस्य जायते ॥ 13 ॥

Rub the body with the perspiration from the labour (of pranayama).
The body derives firmness and steadiness from this.

When the body is unclean, impurities are excreted through the pores of the skin in the form of perspiration. When the body has been purified, only water, salt and hormones are excreted through the skin. When the body becomes hot due to pranayama, excess water may be lost. The *Shiva Samhita* states: "When the body perspires, rub it well, otherwise the yogi loses his dhatu."

There are seven dhatu known as *sapta dhatu*: blood, fat, flesh, bone, marrow, skin and semen or ova. To maintain these, certain chemical hormones are produced and when they cannot be stored they are expelled from the system. If there is perspiration due to pranayama, chemical hormones are released unnecessarily. Therefore, the perspiration should be rubbed back into the skin so they are reabsorbed through the pores. This also helps to rebalance the system and tone the nerves and muscles.

अभ्यासकाले प्रथमे शस्तं क्षीराज्यभोजनम् ।
ततोऽभ्यासे दृढीभूते न तादृङ्नियमग्रहः ॥ 14 ॥

*In the beginning stages of practice, food consisting of milk and
ghee is recommended. Upon being established in the practice such
restrictions are not necessary.*

When a sadhaka starts to practise pranayama the body
metabolism undergoes a change. The heart rate and blood
pressure are activated and all body processes are energized.
Digestive secretions and excretory processes are stimulated.
To help maintain balance until the body adjusts, it is advised
to take milk because it has a neutralizing effect on the body
and helps lubricate the system. Milk products help increase
the fats which are important for insulating the body when
the prana is increased. Otherwise, if fats are quickly utilized
you may 'blow a fuse' in the energy system. If the fats are
burnt up before they are distributed, lymphatic mechanisms
are increased. The lymphatic system releases fats into the
body from the digestive tract. Pranayama directly affects this
mechanism.

There is another important factor; milk contains animal
hormones which have a direct effect on the body and mind.
Pranayama can awaken an altered state of consciousness,
but the animal hormones help maintain normal conscious
functioning. If psychic experiences occur too rapidly, before
your mind is ready, you will have difficulties coping. Once
the whole system is adjusted, it is not necessary to take milk.

The *Gheranda Samhita* further states that: "Food should
be taken twice a day, once at noon and once in the evening."
(5:32) When practising pranayama the stomach must be
completely empty, and after the practice food should not be
taken for at least half an hour. Light, easily digestible and
nourishing food facilitates pranayama practice.

यथा सिंहो गजो व्याघ्रो भवेद्दश्य: शनै:शनै: ।
तथैव सेवितो वायुरन्यथा हन्ति साधकम् ॥ 15 ॥

Just as lions, elephants and tigers are gradually controlled, so the prana is controlled through practice. Otherwise the practitioner is destroyed.

It is very difficult to train a wild animal, especially a lion, tiger or elephant, but if from a young age they are given calm and continual training, they will respond to their master's commands. Control of prana is also a tedious and delicate process which requires alertness, awareness, patience and constancy.

When prana moves through the body freely and sporadically, like a roaming lion or tiger, it does not respond to your will. For example, you may want to sleep at night but your prana makes you active. Or you may have to work but your prana is inactive and you feel sleepy or ill. Therefore, prana has to be controlled so that it acts in accordance with your desire and will. The method you employ has to be safe, sure and systematic, just as if you were taming a wild and unpredictable beast.

If prana is left unrestrained, the eventual result is that the prana is exhausted and sickness and death occur. The life force and physical elements are 'burnt up' as you expend your energy in mundane and worldly affairs. Prana has to be channelized and redirected so it is not wasted.

प्राणायामेन युक्तेन सर्वरोगक्षयो भवेत् ।
अयुक्ताभ्यासयोगेन सर्वरोगसमुद्भवः ॥ 16 ॥

By proper practice of pranayama etc., all diseases are eradicated. Through improper practice all diseases can arise.

If performed properly and systematically any yogic technique will activate a greater pranic capacity and thus eliminate disorders and malfunctioning in the physical body, but if the practices are done incorrectly and unsystematically, more physical disturbances will develop. If practice is irregular or incorrect it can be very harmful and it is better not to practise at all.

Even if you fail to observe one simple rule, sickness can result. For example, you should always practise on an empty stomach, whether you are performing asana, pranayama, mudra or bandha. If you stand on your head after meals, you are definitely going to damage your digestive system. You must be very careful about the rules and precautions for pranayama and the sequence in which any of the hatha yoga techniques are to be done.

Remember, hatha yoga is the science of the body, mind and spirit and it should be approached as such, and never in a haphazard or careless manner. It is dangerous to try and learn it by following instructions from books. For harmonious development you must have the guidance of a teacher with a comprehensive knowledge of yoga and enough sensitivity to recognize what your individual needs are.

हिक्का श्वासश्च कासश्च शिर:कर्णाक्षिवेदना: ।
भवन्ति विविधा रोगा: पवनस्य प्रकोपत: ॥ 17 ॥

Hiccups, asthma, coughs, headache, ear and eye pain, and various other diseases are due to disturbances of the vital air.

The processes of respiration, digestion and assimilation are the outcome of the harmonious interaction of the pancha pranas or vital airs. If the prana vayu between the throat and diaphragm is disturbed, various symptoms will manifest. These include hiccups, wheezing, coughs, headache and pain in the ears and eyes. If disturbance or imbalance between prana and apana is not rectified, then various symptoms, complexes and ailments of the respiratory and upper digestive systems will manifest. These include migraine headache, indigestion and hyperacidity, asthma and infections of the ears, nose and throat. These diseases may become chronic and medicines fail to give lasting relief, unless the underlying disturbance in the prana vayu is corrected.

युक्तं युक्तं त्यजेद्वायुं युक्तं युक्तं च पूरयेत् ।
युक्तं युक्तं च बन्धीयादेवं सिद्धिमवाप्नुयात् ॥ 18 ॥

The vayu should skilfully be inhaled, exhaled and retained so that perfection or siddhi is attained.

When pranayama is performed correctly and systematically, in the proper proportion, and in a steady sitting position, prana is channelized into the higher brain centres which are responsible for greater psychic capacity. Nothing can ever be attained by just inhaling and exhaling in any fashion as we do all the time. The word *yuktam* is used repeatedly in this verse to emphasize the necessity of precision. Just as an engineer who works with precision becomes perfect in his profession, in the same way, the sadhaka who practises pranayama precisely and systematically develops physical, mental and psychic perfection or siddhi.

यदा तु नाडीशुद्धिः स्यात्तथा चिह्नानि बाह्यतः ।
कायस्य कृशता कान्तिस्तदा जायेत निश्चितम् ॥ 19 ॥

*When the nadis are purified there are external symptoms. Success is
definite when the body becomes thin and glows.*

यथेष्टंधारणं वायोरनलस्य प्रदीपनम् ।
नादाभिव्यक्तिरारोग्यं जायते नाडिशोधनात् ॥ 20 ॥

*When one is able to hold the vayu according to one's will, the
digestive power increases. With the nadis purified, thus the inner
sound or nada awakens and one is free from disease.*

Purification of the nadis means the shakti can flow throughout the body unhindered. Just as a light bulb glows with
the flow of electric current (positive and negative ions), the
body emits radiance from the flow of positive and negative
shakti. The stronger the flow the brighter the glow. When
you practise hatha yoga there will be visible changes in your
physical appearance, in the nature of hunger and thirst, in
the frequency of urination and evacuation, in the quality or
smell of perspiration, in the structure of the body related to
the accumulations of fats, etc., in the quality of voice, in the
quality of thoughts and meditation, and also in the quantity
of sleep. When other forms of yoga are practised, such as
bhakti, karma and jnana yoga, the indications are different.

When there is 'thinness' of the body due to practice of
hatha yoga it does not mean you are reduced to skin and
bone. It means the body becomes firm and without excess
fat. Increase of digestive power does not mean you become
ravenously hungry and eat excessively. It means you have
greater capacity to assimilate food and utilize the nutrients.
In fact, when there is pranic awakening the urge to eat
decreases as prana is absorbed directly from the cosmos.

As you proceed further in the practice of hatha yoga,
you develop control over the prana, and the symptoms that

manifest represent the awakening of kundalini and psychic experiences. By increasing the shakti in every chakra, you develop greater mental and psychic capacity and your consciousness can move freely in the subtle realms of existence. Experiences which normally take place through the senses take place directly through the mind itself. You can smell without the nose, see without the eyes, speak without the mouth and tongue, taste without the tongue, feel without the hands and skin, and hear without the ears.

Shakti has two characteristics – frequency and form. When the shakti in the body is activated and increased, the consciousness becomes attuned to the frequency, then an audible sound is heard. That sound is known as nada and it becomes apparent in the later stages of yoga when the mind is totally concentrated. This nada is discussed in detail in Chapter 4.

According to the *Shiva Sutras*, in the practices of prana yoga, which include pranayama, prana vidya, concentration on prana and pranic centres, purification of nadis and chakras, there are five distinct indications which characterize the awakening of prana. These are: *ananda* 'the experience of bliss and delight', *udbhava* 'levitation', *kampan* 'tremoring', *yoga nidra* 'sleep with awareness' and *ghurni*, 'reeling with bliss'.

मेदश्लेष्माधिक: पूर्वं षट्कर्माणि समाचरेत् ।
अन्यस्तु नाचरेत्तानि दोषाणां समभावत: ॥ 21 ॥

When fat or mucus is excessive, shatkarma: the six cleansing techniques, should be practised before (pranayama). Others, in whom the doshas, i.e. phlegm, wind and bile, are balanced should not do them.

There are three humours in the body: *kapha*, mucus, *pitta*, bile and *vata*, wind. In yoga and ayurveda they are called *tridosha*. A balanced proportion of these three facilitates body functions, but if there is an excess of one and a shortage of another, ailments develop due to overheating or not enough heat in the body.

Before commencing pranayama, any imbalance in the doshas should be removed – excess body fat should be reduced, mucus blocking the respiratory tract should be removed, gas in the stomach and intestines eliminated, etc. In hatha yoga there are six particular practices which were specifically designed for this purpose. They are called shatkarma. *Shat* is six, *karma* is action. These techniques regulate the production of the doshas.

If the doshas are already balanced there is no need to practise the shatkarma. However, they should be learned, simply so the sadhaka will know how to practise them if they are needed. If they are practised unnecessarily, as a part of one's daily sadhana, they will not be so effective when genuinely required. Just as you would not have your tonsils or appendix removed if they were functioning perfectly, similarly, the shatkarma are really only for those people who have disturbances or imbalances in the doshas.

धौतिर्बस्तिस्तथा नेतिस्त्राटकं नौलिकं तथा ।
कपालभातिश्चैतानि षट् कर्माणि प्रचक्षते ॥ 22 ॥

Dhauti, basti, neti, trataka, nauli and kapalbhati; these are known as shatkarma or the six cleansing processes.

Hatha yoga is famous for these six cleansing techniques. Although only six in number, each has a variety of practices.

Dhauti is divided into four parts. According to the *Gheranda Samhita* they are called *antar* (internal) *dhauti, danta* (teeth) *dhauti, hrid* (cardiac) *dhauti* and *moola shodhana* (rectal cleaning).

Antar dhauti is divided into four practices: *vatsara dhauti,* expelling air through the anus, *varisara dhauti,* evacuating a large quantity of water through the bowels, *vahnisara dhauti,* rapid expansion and contraction of the abdomen, *bahiskrita dhauti,* washing the rectum in the hands.

Hrid dhauti is divided into three practices: *danda dhauti,* inserting a soft banana stem into the stomach, *vastra dhauti,* swallowing a long thin strip of cloth, *vaman dhauti,* regurgitating the contents of the stomach.

The last practice of dhauti, moola shodhana can be performed in two ways. It is done either by inserting a turmeric root or the middle finger into the anus.

The second karma, *basti* is divided into two parts: *jala* (water) *basti* and *sthala* (dry) *basti*. In jala basti you suck water into the large intestine through the anus and then expel it. In sthala basti you suck air into the large intestine.

The third karma, *neti*, has four practices: *jala* (water) *neti,* passing warm saline water through the nose, *sutra* (thread) *neti,* passing a soft thread through the nose, *ghrita* (ghee) *neti,* passing clarified butter through the nose, *dugdha* (milk) *neti,* passing milk through the nose.

The fourth karma is *trataka*, which is steady and continuous gazing at a point of concentration. It has two practices: *antar* (internal) and *bahir* (external) *trataka*.

The fifth karma is *nauli*, in which you isolate and churn the abdominal muscles. It has three practices. When the muscles are isolated to the right it is *dakshina nauli*, to the left, *vama nauli* and in the middle it is *madhyama nauli*.

The last karma is *kapalbhati*, which has three practices: *vatkrama kapalbhati*, which is similar to bhastrika pranayama, *vyutkrama kapalbhati*, sucking water in through the nose and expelling it through the mouth, *sheetkrama kapalbhati*, sucking water in through the nose.

These six fundamental cleansing techniques are the most important aspects of hatha yoga and are the original hatha yoga. However, today asana and pranayama are more widely known and few people are now proficient in the shatkarma.

कर्मषट्कमिदं गोप्यं घटशोधनकारकम् ।
विचित्रगुणसंधायि पूज्यते योगिपुंगवैः ॥ 23 ॥

These shatkarma which effect purification of the body are secret. They have manifold, wondrous results and are held in high esteem by eminent yogis.

The shatkarma are very powerful practices that can never be learned from books or taught by inexperienced people. In India there is the tradition that only those who are instructed by the guru can teach others. One may think he has the capacity to teach, but actually, he may not have adequate experience or knowledge to guide others proficiently, and this applies to the shatkarma in particular. If unqualified people teach them, they are likely to make serious mistakes. Also one can make mistakes if one practises them independently without the instructions of the guru.

The shatkarma are said to be secret practices as one must be personally instructed to do them and taught how to perform them and how often, according to individual need. For this a qualified and experienced teacher is essential. Those who sincerely want to learn the shatkarma will have to find a guru of hatha yoga and they will have to search well because few teachers are expert in shatkarma. Of course, as it has been said in a previous sloka, one should not divulge one's personal sadhana, one should keep it secret.

The shatkarma specifically increase the vital capacity of the practitioner. They were never designed for therapy alone, but to create harmony in the body and mind and to prepare one for further practices. As they bring about smooth and perfect functioning of the bodily systems, it is inevitable that through their practice the mind will become free from turbulence and disturbances and thus be better able to concentrate and to move towards dhyana.

The effects of shatkarma can be summed up in one word – purification. When the different systems of the body have been purified, the overall result is that energy can flow through the body freely. One's capacity to work, think, digest, taste, feel, experience, etc., increases, and greater awareness develops. It is no wonder that the yogis who have achieved perfection and know the real extent of human capacity, regard the shatkarma with great esteem.

DHAUTI (internal cleansing)

अथ धौतिः ।

चतुरंगुलविस्तारं हस्तपंचदशायतम् ।
गुरूपदिष्टमार्गेण सिक्तं वस्त्रं शनैर्ग्रसेत् ।
पुनः प्रत्याहरेच्चैतदुदितं धौति कर्म तत् ॥ 24 ॥

A strip of wet cloth, four angulas wide (i.e. seven to eight centimetres) and fifteen handspans (i.e. one and a half metres) in length is slowly swallowed and then taken out, as instructed by the guru. This is known as dhauti.

The practice described here is actually *vastra dhauti*. *Vastra* means cloth. This practice must only be performed under expert guidance and in full accordance with the instructions given. The cloth should be finely woven cotton which is unused and clean. Synthetic material should definitely not be used. The cloth must also be trimmed neatly so that no loose threads fray on the sides. It should be no wider than the tongue or it will fold as it passes down the throat, and should be at least one metre in length and no more than a metre and a half.

Technique: Vastra Dhauti (cloth cleansing)

Wash and rinse the cloth well, then boil it in water.
Keep the cloth in a container of warm water while you are practising.
Assume a squatting position with the heels flat on the ground and the buttocks off the ground or resting on a brick or something about the same height.
Relax the body.
Keep the cloth spread and not folded as you utilize it.
Spread one end over the tongue and start swallowing the cloth.

Shatkarmas

DHAUTI	**Antar dhauti** (internal)	vatsara (plavini) varisara (shankha-prakshalana) vahnisara (agnisara kriya) bahiskrita (rectal cleaning)
	Danta dhauti (teeth)	jihva (tongue) karna (ear) kapalrandhra (frontal sinuses) chakshu (eyes)
	Hrid dhauti (cardiac)	vastra (cloth) danda (stick) vaman (kunjal & vyaghra kriya)
	Moola shodhana (anal)	
BASTI	**Jala** (water) **Sthala** (dry)	
NETI	**Sutra** (thread) **Jala** (water) **Dugdha** (milk) **Ghrita** (ghee)	
TRATAKA	**Antaranga** (internal) **Bahiranga** (external)	
NAULI	**Dakshina** (right) **Vama** (left) **Madhyama** (middle)	
KAPALBHATI	**Vatakrama** (breathing) **Vyutkrama** (reversed) **Sheetkrama** (cooling)	

If the cloth catches in the throat and will not pass down, take a sip of warm water but do not drink a large quantity. The stomach is to be filled with the cloth and not with water.

The cloth may tend to stick in the lowest point of the throat, so keep swallowing the cloth and resist the urge to vomit. Once the cloth passes a little further down the oesophagus the problem will end.

When two thirds of the cloth have been swallowed, leave the remaining few inches hanging out of the mouth and stand up ready to practise nauli.

The cloth can be left in the stomach for five to twenty minutes but no longer.

Practise dakshina (right) and vama (left) nauli; then rotation and madhyama nauli.

Five to ten minutes is sufficient time to clean the stomach.

Sit in a squatting position and slowly take the cloth out.

This is the practice of dhauti which is given in *Hatha Yoga Pradipika*, however, the *Gheranda Samhita* describes all the practices of dhauti:

Vatsara dhauti is performed by breathing in slowly through the mouth in kaki mudra, and then swallowing the air into the stomach while expanding the abdomen. It can be done up to ten times or until the stomach is fully expanded. Then the air should be passed through the large intestine. To do this it is helpful to assume an inverted posture. Pashinee mudra is the best. The air should then pass out of the anus easily.

Varisara dhauti is more commonly known today as *shankhaprakshalana*. In this practice you drink a total of sixteen glasses of warm salty water and evacuate it through the bowels. First drink two glasses and perform a series of five specific asanas: tadasana, tiryaka tadasana, kati chakrasana, tiryaka bhujangasana, and udarakarshan asana. After every two glasses of water the asanas should be performed until the water starts flowing out of the anus. Once clear water starts coming through, you will know that the stomach and intestines are perfectly clean and you can stop the practice.

Forty-five minutes after completing the practice of shankhaprakshalana, a saltless liquid mixture of cooked rice, mung dal and ghee has to be eaten until the stomach is completely full. There are dietary restrictions to observe for a week after this practice, and as it is a 'major operation', it must be done under expert guidance.

There is a shorter technique called *laghoo shankhaprakshalana*. *Laghoo* means 'short'. In this practice only six glasses of warm saline water are taken. After every two glasses the same series of asanas are to be performed as in *poorna* or 'full' shankhaprakshalana.

The *Hatharatnavali* mentions the use of jaggery water or milk water (1.50) instead of salt water. There are also various other herbs and juices which could be used, such as a few drops of lemon, onion or garlic juice. Laghoo shankhaprakshalana could be done with carrot or celery juice.

Vahnisara dhauti, also known as *agnisara kriya*, involves moving the 'fire' in the body. *Vahni* and *agni* mean 'fire'. *Sar* is 'essence'. 'The essence of fire' is located in the navel region. On a physical level, the practice involves conscious movement of the abdominal muscles and organs and this creates internal heat. The practice is very useful as a preparation for kapalbhati and bhastrika pranayama.

The *Gheranda Samhita* says to: "Push the navel against the spine a hundred times . . ." (1:19) The practice can be done standing or sitting in bhadrasana. Jalandhara bandha is performed first, then the abdomen is pushed out and in rapidly while the breath is held. It can be done while breathing through the mouth with the tongue extended, panting like a dog and moving the abdomen in rhythm with the breath. For most people it is unnecessary to practise one hundred times; fifty is sufficient.

Bahiskrita dhauti is very difficult unless you are an extremely advanced hatha yoga practitioner. It involves standing navel-deep in clean water, pushing the rectum out and washing it in the hands. The *Gheranda Samhita* says: "It is not easily available, even to the gods." (1:23)

Danta dhauti is the cleaning of the teeth with a special stick, usually of neem or babool. A toothbrush and tooth-paste or powder can be used. Danta dhauti includes *jihva dhauti* – cleaning the tongue by rubbing it with the joined first finger and thumb in a downward motion and then squeezing it, *karna dhauti* – cleaning the ears with the middle finger and nothing smaller, *kapalrandhra dhauti* – cleaning the upper back portion of the palate, *chakshu dhauti* – bathing the eyes with tepid, saline water or with urine.

Hrid dhauti, according to the *Gheranda Samhita*, is threefold. One should perform it with a stick, by vomiting, and with a piece of cloth. The first practice is *danda dhauti* which has been mentioned in the commentary on verse 22. Although a soft banana stem is traditionally used, the *Gheranda Samhita* advises that a sugarcane stick or a turmeric root can be used. Today, some people use a thin catheter as a substitute.

Vaman dhauti or *vyaghra kriya* is the second practice of hrid dhauti. *Vaman* 'to vomit', *vyaghra* is 'tiger'. Just as a tiger regurgitates its food a couple of hours after eating, in this practice you vomit the food from the stomach three hours after a meal. If it is difficult you can drink a glass or two of warm saline water and then tickle the back of the throat with the first two fingers to induce vomiting. Traditionally, after performing this practice a sweet milk rice pudding should be eaten. *Kunjal kriya* is almost identical to vyaghra kriya except it is performed on an empty stomach. You drink two to four glasses of warm saline water and vomit it out. There are no dietary restrictions afterwards.

The third practice of hrid dhauti is vastra dhauti which has already been described in full detail.

Moola shodhana is done by inserting the middle finger into the rectum and rotating it clockwise then anticlockwise. Make sure the fingernail is cut short, and if necessary you can put some non-irritating oil on the finger to lubricate the anus. The *Gheranda Samhita* also recommends the use of a turmeric root instead of the finger and to start by sitting in utkatasana.

This is the full series of dhauti practices.

कासश्वासप्लीहकुष्टं कफरोगाश्च विंशतिः ।
धौतिकर्मप्रभावेण प्रयांत्येव न संशयः ॥ 25 ॥

There is no doubt that coughs, asthma, diseases of the spleen, leprosy and twenty kinds of diseases caused by excess mucus are destroyed through the effects of dhauti karma.

The combination of all the practices of dhauti cleans the entire digestive tract and respiratory tract. It removes excess and old bile, mucus and toxins and restores the natural balance of the body's chemical composition, thus alleviating ailments caused by such imbalances. The various practices help remove infectious bacteria from the mouth, nose, eyes, ears, throat, stomach, intestines and anus. The results are a reduction of excess fatty tissue and relief from flatulence, constipation, poor digestion and loss of appetite.

Dhauti is even said to cure leprosy. Although this disease is not prevalent in many countries today, the point is that even such insidious diseases can be alleviated through this powerful practice. The equivalent of leprosy today could be considered as cancer.

The *Gheranda Samhita* states that dhauti can cure abdominal ailments and fever. Of course it is not advisable to practise dhauti during a fever or acute visceral infection. However, if it is practised after recuperation it will prevent recurrence of the problem.

There are certain conditions in which antar dhauti must not be practised. These are: stomach or intestinal ulcers, hernia, heart disease and high blood pressure.

BASTI (yogic enema)

अथ बस्तिः

नाभिदघ्नजले पायौ न्यस्तनालोत्कटासनः ।
आधाराकुंचनं कुर्यात्क्षालनं बस्तिकर्म तत् ॥ 26 ॥

Sitting in utkatasana, navel deep in water, insert a tube into the anus and contract the anus. This cleansing with water is called basti karma.

Although there are two forms of basti, *jala* and *sthala*, only one is mentioned in this sloka. We will describe both here. To perform basti, first you have to be adept in uddiyana bandha and nauli.

Technique 1: Jala Basti (yogic enema with water)

As it is not practical to sit in a river these days, jala basti can be done sitting over a bucket of water. Beginners will have to start by inserting a 0.8 cm catheter into the rectum. Traditionally, a bamboo tube was used. Plastic tubing or a catheter are suitable but organic material is always preferable. The tube should be at least 13–15 cm long, perfectly smooth and hollow. Wipe it with beeswax or a non-irritating oil such as vaseline or ghee for lubrication.

Insert 4 cm of the tube into the anal passage, or as much as comfortable. Then squat over the bucket in utkatasana. Exhale and perform uddiyana bandha. If the water is not sucked up through the tube into the bowel, then do madhyama nauli and hold. If the water is still not sucked up, do vama or dakshina nauli. When you can no longer hold kumbhaka, remove the catheter or tube, without exhaling. Then stand up and exhale slowly through the nose. When you expel the water it is best to squat over the toilet because stool in the lower intestine will also come out. If the catheter is not removed before exhaling, the water will pass out and the tube may get blocked by pieces of stool.

After much practice the catheter will not be necessary, you will be able to suck water into the bowel directly, but that is at a very advanced stage which may take years to perfect.

When practising without the catheter, you have to push the rectum out as far as possible, then draw it in with uddiyana. First open the sphincter muscles with the fingers, perform uddiyana and remove the hand. Maintain kumbhaka for as long as possible and then slowly exhale.

After the practice make sure all the water is expelled. Then lie in shavasana on a blanket. Slowly assume pashinee mudra, placing the knees beside the ears and balancing on the backs of the shoulders, hands clasped together behind the back of the knees. This releases air from the bowel and induces a bowel action if there is any water remaining.

Come out of the position slowly and lie in shavasana again. Then fold the knees to the chest, hold them and slowly rock from side to side, or rock with the arms stretched out to the sides at shoulder height.

Lie in shavasana again and when you are ready, perform bhujangasana slowly three to five times. This exerts pressure on the lower intestine and releases any remaining water or air. It is not essential, but mayur-asana is also recommended after basti. Pashinee mudra is the most suitable counterpose.

It is extremely important that the water used in basti is perfectly clean and neither hot nor too cold. In cold weather, lukewarm water should be used. It is not necessary to add salt to the water, but the catheter must be sterilized before and after use.

Basti can be done in warm or hot weather, especially if you are also doing intense pranayama and bandhas. Basti generates energy but also removes heat from the system. It must not be done during cloudy, rainy, windy or stormy weather.

Technique 2: Sthala Basti (dry yogic enema)

Sthala basti is performed while lying on the back. Assume vipareeta karani mudra but position the back at a 60 degree angle to the floor. Then bring the knees down to the chest. Push the sphincter muscles out and in so that air is sucked into the bowel. This is not an easy practice and jala basti has to be perfected first.

Sthala basti can also be practised in pashinee mudra or paschimottanasana, performing ashwini mudra. In the beginning uddiyana may also be required. It is not easy to suck in air while in paschimottanasana as there is pressure on the anus, so it is best to start in an inverted asana.

The *Hatharatnavali* says that after practising basti, food should not be taken for three *ghatis*, i.e. seventy-two minutes.

गुल्मप्लीहोदरं चापि वातपित्तकफोद्भवा: ।
बस्तिकर्मप्रभावेण क्षीयन्ते सकलामया: ॥ 27 ॥

Enlargement of the glands and spleen, and all diseases arising from excess wind, bile and mucus are eliminated from the body through the practice of basti.

धात्विंद्रियान्त:करणप्रसादं दधाच्च कांतिं दहनप्रदीप्तिम् ।
अशेषदोषोपचयं निहन्यादभ्यस्यमानं जलबस्तिकर्म ॥ 28 ॥

By practising jala basti the appetite increases, the body glows, excess doshas are destroyed and the dhatu, senses and mind are purified.

Basti completely washes the bowel and removes excess bacteria, old stool, threadworms and heat from the lower intestines. Most importantly, it pushes apana vayu upward. When the apana rises it can be felt in the navel region and as a great pressure on the stomach. Basti cures digestive disorders and is particularly useful for removing constipation, stimulating sluggish digestion, controlling nervous diarrhoea and strengthening the solar plexus.

When the body is purified the chemical constituents are in balanced proportion and the brain functions are simultaneously influenced and altered. When the body is pure the mind becomes stable, emotional reactions to external stimuli are altered and you will respond in a more relaxed and controlled manner. Thus, shatkarma enable control over unruly senses. They make the *karmendriya*, organs of action, keen and the *jnanendriya*, organs of knowledge, more perceptive and sensitive. The shatkarma not only purify the body elements or dhatu, they also influence the subtle body.

According to yoga, human existence extends through five layers or sheaths which are called *koshas*. The physical body and its elements comprise the first layer, *annamaya* kosha. *Anna* is 'food', *maya* means 'comprised of'. The shatkarma directly influence this kosha and penetrate the next layer, *pranamaya* kosha, as they allow free flow of prana. The third layer, *manomaya* kosha, the mental sheath, is indirectly affected through pranayama. Purification of these sheaths opens the fourth kosha, *vijnanamaya* or the sheath of intuition. However, the fifth kosha, *anandamaya* or the sheath of bliss, is unaffected by any physical influence because it is a transcendental realm.

These five sheaths are interlinked; whatever happens in one affects the others. When annamaya and pranamaya are cleansed there are no blockages between them and mano-maya. Mind, body and energy can work in unison and that removes the barrier to vijnanamaya kosha.

The first four koshas are the extension of anandamaya. When there are blockages between any of the koshas, communication and integration are hindered. Annamaya and pranamaya are gross manifestations while manomaya and vijnanamaya are subtle. Pranamaya is the link between the gross and subtle and manomaya is the bridge to the higher mind. When you practise the shatkarma you are establishing integration of your whole being, physically, emotionally, mentally, psychically and cosmically.

NETI (nasal cleansing)

अथ नेति: ।

सूत्रं वितस्तिसुस्निग्धं नासानाले प्रवेशयेत् ।
मुखान्निर्गमयेच्चैषा नेति: सिद्धैर्निगद्यते ॥ 29 ॥

*Insert a soft thread through the nose to the length of one handspan
so that it comes out of the mouth. This is called neti by the siddhas.*

This practice of passing a length of thread through the nose
is called *sutra neti. Sutra* means 'thread'. There is another
form of neti known as *jala neti* and it is done with water.

To practise sutra neti a specially prepared thread has to
be used. It should be made of cotton, not synthetic fibre,
tightly wound together and wiped with melted beeswax. The
width should be about 4 mm and length 36 cm. However, it
is more convenient to use a thin rubber catheter lubricated
with ghee so that it slides easily through the nasal passage.
It is also a good idea to practise jala neti before sutra neti to
make sure the nostrils are clear.

Technique 1: Sutra Neti (nasal cleansing with thread)

Squat on the heels, tilt the head slightly back and insert
the thread or catheter straight into the left nostril.

The thread should not be forced through the nose but
gently pushed so that it slowly passes down into the
throat.

When it reaches the back of the throat, put the first two
fingers into the mouth and pull the thread out through
the mouth leaving a few inches of thread hanging out of
the nose.

Slowly and gently pull the thread backwards and
forwards thirty to fifty times.

Take it out slowly and perform in the same way through
the opposite nostril.

Pranayama should be practised after completing this practice.

According to the *Hatharatnavali* (1:38), once the thread has been pulled out of the mouth the two ends should be joined and the thread rotated through the nasal passage and mouth. However, it is very difficult to join the two ends securely while still being able to pass it through the nose comfortably. Therefore, it is probably quite sufficient to pull the thread forwards and backwards.

For jala neti you require a special neti *lota* or pot which has a nozzle designed specifically so that it will fit into the nostril. The lota should be filled with warm saline water. The salt should be just enough to taste.

Technique 2: Jala Neti (nasal cleansing with water)

Stand squarely, legs apart, body weight evenly distributed between the two feet and lean forward.

Tilt the head to the right side and place the lota's nozzle in the left nostril.

Open the mouth slightly and breathe through the mouth. Keep the whole body relaxed and let the water pass out through the right nostril.

When you have used half of the water, remove the lota, remain bending forward, centre the head and let the water run out of the nose.

Close the right nostril with the fingers and blow gently through the left nostril so that all the remaining water comes out.

Practise in the same way passing the water through the right nostril.

Throughout the whole practice keep breathing through the mouth and do not attempt to breathe through the nose. When blowing the nose, do not blow very hard, otherwise any remaining water may be pushed into the ears. It is important to remove all the water after the practice so irritation of the sinuses and mucous membrane does not occur. Although you can practise neti in a squatting posture, it is best to stand.

If you experience pain in the nose during the practice, the quantity of salt is incorrect. Too little salt will create pain and too much salt will cause a burning sensation.

Instead of water you can use warm milk to practise *dugdha neti*, or warm ghee to practise *ghrita neti*. If oil is used instead of ghee, it must be unconcentrated and with no added chemicals. These two practices are classified as variations of jala neti. However, the most powerful form of jala neti is with urine. Though it is not mentioned in the hatha yoga texts, it is particularly useful for curing inflammation of the nasal passage and sinuses, and bleeding.

Neti can be practised every day if you are suffering from sinusitis, colds, insensitivity to smell, nosebleed, headache, eyestrain or eye infections, otherwise it is best to practise only once or twice a week. People suffering from chronic haemorrhage should not attempt neti unless under expert guidance.

It is advisable to practise bhastrika or kapalbhati pranayama after jala neti. This will dry the nose and generate heat in the nostrils.

कपालशोधिनी चैव दिव्यदृष्टिप्रदायिनी ।
जत्रूर्ध्वजातरोगौघं नेतिराशु निहंति च ॥ 30 ॥

Neti cleanses the cranium and bestows clairvoyance. It also destroys all diseases which manifest above the throat.

Sutra and jala neti exert a profound physiological effect on the body, mind and personality. On the physical level, irrigation of the nasal mucosa removes accumulated mucus from the nostrils, associated passages and sinuses, allowing air to flow without obstruction.

The membrane lining the nostrils secretes a protective film of sticky mucus. Tiny hair-like cilia promote the movement of this mucus, along with the pollutants, dust etc., which adhere to its surface. The nasal membrane is highly innervated by nerve fibres and is perhaps the most sensitive area of the whole body.

These nerve fibres include not only the fibres of the olfactory nerve (the first cranial nerve) responsible for the sense of smell, but also numerous other autonomic fibres which relay information to the brain about the inflowing breath. Not only smells, but also environmental temperature, humidity and allergens in the air are all sensed by the nose as the inflowing breath is drawn across this mucous membrane.

Neti exerts a relaxing and irrigating effect upon the eyes by stimulating the tear ducts and glands. It also clears the entrance to the eustachian tubes in the nasopharynx. The sinuses, important bony cavities within the facial and frontal bones, are also lined with mucous membranes and help to make the skull light and the voice resonant. Neti promotes drainage of the sinuses, preventing stasis of mucus and keeping them clean and functional.

Regular practice of neti maintains healthy secretory and drainage mechanisms of the entire ear, nose and throat area. This helps to ward off colds and coughs, allergic rhinitis, hayfever, catarrh and tonsillitis. It also gives resistance to various diseases of the ears, eyes and throat, such as myopia, tension headache due to eyestrain, certain cases of deafness such as glue ear and middle ear infections, inflammation of the adenoids, as well as inhibiting the formation of nasal polyps. Where there is weakness or deficiency in these areas, even in children, or stemming from childhood, neti stimulates and restores natural functioning. Mouth breathing in children, leading to poor memory, concentration and development is overcome by neti.

Neti relieves muscular tension of the face and nervous tics, and helps maintain facial youth and freshness. It releases emotional tension and is beneficial in anxiety, depression, epilepsy and hysteria.

Of course, the practice of neti promotes a balance between the left and right nostrils and consequently the right and left hemispheres of the brain. This induces a state of harmony and balance throughout the entire central nervous system and the systems governing respiratory, circulatory, digestive and excretory functions.

The frontal lobes of the cerebrum, responsible for the higher mental faculties, begin to function optimally. Integration of the higher mental faculties leads to genius, intuition, creativity and so on.

According to Yogi Swatmarama, perfection of neti leads to *divya drishti*. *Divya* means 'divine' and *drishti* is 'sight' or 'vision'. Divya drishti is the faculty of clairvoyance which manifests with the awakening of ajna chakra. It is a faculty of the higher intuitive mind or the 'third eye'. The practice of neti is said to stimulate ajna chakra, remove its blockages and bring it into fuller functioning.

TRATAKA (concentrated gazing)

अथ त्राटकम् ।

निरीक्षेत्रिश्चलदृशा सूक्ष्मलक्ष्यं समाहित: ।
अश्रुसंपातपर्यन्तमाचार्यैस्त्राटकं स्मृतम् ॥ 31 ॥

Looking intently with an unwavering gaze at a small point until tears are shed is known as trataka by the acharyas (teachers).

Trataka means to gaze steadily. There are two forms of the practice, one is *bahiranga* or external trataka and the other is *antaranga* or internal trataka. Bahiranga is simpler to practise because you just have to gaze at an object or symbol. However, antaranga trataka involves clear and stable inner visualization of an object. Swatmarama has not indicated whether he is referring to the external or internal practice, therefore we will discuss both.

Swatmarama says to gaze at a small point or *sukshma lakshyam*. *Sukshma* can mean 'small' or 'subtle'. In the practice of trataka an object is gazed at until its subtle form manifests in front of the closed eyes.

The point of concentration is usually a symbol or object which activates the inner potential and can absorb the mind. The object most commonly used is a candle flame, because even after closing the eyes, the impression of the flame remains for some time and antaranga trataka can easily be practised. The purpose of focusing the eyes on an external object is to arouse the internal vision and to make that vision steady by stopping the eye movements.

There are other equally effective symbols or objects such as a crystal ball, a shivalingam, yantra, mandala, full moon, a star, the rising or setting sun (when it is an orange-red ball and not yellow), a chakra, the symbol of Om, or your own shadow. These are the most effective; but trataka can also be done on a rose, a tree, a mountain, the sea, or lightning.

In fact, when people worship a particular deity and gaze steadily at the form, it is also bahiranga trataka.

Of all the symbols and objects, the most suitable for general use is a candle flame because a symbol, yantra or mandala leaves an impression in the mind and stimulates particular centres. If you concentrate on Kali you will arouse that aspect of your inner being if you are not beyond it. You may even manifest Kali and be terrified by her fearsome form. Therefore, a steady flame of light is most practical unless the guru says otherwise.

At a certain stage of concentration you will see a point of light in front of the closed eyes. This has to be developed and made steady because initially it tends to waver or even disappear.

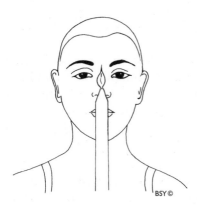

Technique 1: Bahiranga Trataka (external concentrated gazing)

Practise in a dark room which is free from draughts and insects.

Place a candle two to three feet in front of you with the flame at eye level.

It is vital that the flame is still and does not flicker at all.

Sit in a comfortable meditative pose, preferably siddhasana/siddha yoni asana, and place the hands on the knees in either jnana or chin mudra.

Relax your whole body, close your eyes and prepare yourself as for any meditative practice.

Make yourself calm and quiet and be prepared to keep your body perfectly still throughout the whole practice. Practise kaya sthairyam (steadiness of the body) for a few minutes.

Then open your eyes and gaze at the middle portion of the candle flame, just above the wick.

Try to keep the eyes perfectly steady. Do not blink.

Lower the eyelids if the eyes become sore or tired.

Stare as long as possible, five or ten minutes, or if you can gaze longer without closing the eyes, do so.

Only when you really need to, should you close the eyes.

Try to keep the mind empty. If any thoughts come, put them out of the mind immediately.

Remain the silent witness, *sakshi*, throughout the whole practice.

When you finally close the eyes keep them fixed on the impression of the flame in front, in chidakasha.

If it moves bring it back to the centre and continue gazing until the impression disappears.

Once you can stabilize the image, study it and look intently at the colour.

Sometimes you may not see light, but an impression which is blacker than chidakasha itself.

Keep the mind completely devoid of thought. Only be aware of the object of concentration. When thoughts come, let them pass and remain uninvolved.

Practise for fifteen to twenty minutes unless the guru has advised you to do it for a longer period.

Trataka can be done at any time, but it is more effective when performed on an empty stomach. The most suitable time is between four and six a.m. after asana and pranayama practice. If you want to delve deeper into the mind, trataka should be done late at night before going to bed and before japa or meditation.

If there is an uncontrollable flow of thoughts during trataka, mantra japa should also be done at the same time. If the eyes feel strained, imagine that you are breathing through the mid-eyebrow centre to and from ajna chakra. When you close your eyes and gaze at the counter-image, continue the same awareness of the breath – breathing to and from the image through the eyebrow centre.

Technique 2: Antaranga Trataka (internal concentrated gazing)

Prepare yourself in the same way as for bahiranga trataka.

Keep your eyes closed throughout the practice and concentrate on your symbol.

If you have no symbol, then try to visualize a point of light, like a twinkling star or a crescent or full moon.

Try to see the object clearly and steadily in the dark space in front of the closed eyes.

Practise for five to twenty minutes.

This practice has to be cultivated and it can take a long time. If the symbol has been given by the guru the process will be quicker.

मोचनं नेत्ररोगाणां तन्द्रादीनां कपाटकम् ।
यत्नतस्त्राटकं गोप्यं यथा हाटकपेटकम् ॥ 32 ॥

Trataka eradicates all eye diseases, fatigue and sloth and closes the doorway creating these problems. It should be carefully kept secret like a golden casket.

Trataka benefits not only the eyes, but a whole range of physiological and mental functions. It is therapeutic in depression, insomnia, allergy, anxiety, postural problems, poor concentration and memory. Its most important effect is on ajna chakra and the brain. The *Gheranda Samhita* mentions that it promotes clairvoyance or perception of subtle manifestations.

Trataka is a process of concentrating the mind and curbing its oscillating tendencies. The purpose is to make the mind completely one-pointed and to arouse inner vision. One-pointed concentration of mind is called *ekagrata*. There are numerous distractions which obstruct ekagrata. In fact, distraction only occurs when the senses are tuned to the external world, which means an energy leakage is occurring. Association and identification through the eyes and sight are major contributing factors to this leakage. Furthermore, the eyes constantly move either in large movements – saccades, or tremors – nystagmus. Even when the eyes are focused on an external object the view perceived is always fluctuating because of these spontaneous movements. When the same object is constantly seen, the brain becomes accustomed or habituated and soon stops registering that object. Habituation coincides with an increase of alpha waves indicating diminished visual attention to the external world; when they are produced, particular areas of the brain have ceased functioning.

Vision depends not only on the eyes, but upon the entire optic tracts. The lens of the eye is only the medium of external visual perception. Via the lens, an image is projected onto the retina. This is a stimulus which excites the retina to fire impulses back to the visual cortex of the brain where an inner image is mapped out. If you close your eyes and gently push and release them, you will also see flashes of light, not because light is entering the eyes, but because the optic nerve has been stimulated. When the image of an external object is stabilized on the retina, after a period of time, perception of the image will completely disappear and a suspension of the mental processes occurs.

In fact, if there is absolutely no visual stimulus, e.g. if you sit in a pitch black room or cover the eyes with opaque cups, after some time the mind will turn off just as in sleep. Therefore, during the practice of trataka it is essential to maintain the inner awareness so that when the mind is suspended all that remains is the awareness.

This is not only in relation to trataka but in any practice of concentration; when the awareness is restricted to one unchanging sense stimulus, like touch or sound, the mind is 'turned off'. Complete absorption in a single perception induces withdrawal of contact with the external world.

In trataka, the result is a blanking out of visual perception, and in the wake of this suspension, the central nervous system begins to function in isolation. This experience is known by yogis as sushumna awakening. When the brain is isolated from the sense modalities and from the associated mental processes, ideas, memories, etc., triggered by these thought impressions, then the spiritual conscious-ness emerges. The higher brain, liberated from time and space, is experienced. Sushumna is awakened.

The body must be firmly locked in a steady sitting asana and the practice done in a quiet place, so that distraction from other sense modalities will not interfere in the process of trataka.

Trataka unlocks the inherent energy of the mind and channelizes it to the dormant areas of consciousness. Yogi Swatmarama mentions the arousal of clairvoyance but other capacities such as telepathy, telekinesis, psychic healing, etc., can develop. Not only that, further results of one-pointedness of mind are strong willpower, improved memory and concentrative ability. Physiologically, trataka relieves eye ailments such as eyestrain and headache, myopia, astigmatism and even early stages of cataract. The eyes become clear and bright, able to see the reality beyond appearances.

NAULI (abdominal massaging)

अथ नौलिः ।

अमन्दावर्तवेगेन तुन्दं सव्यापसव्यतः ।
नतांसो भ्रामयेदेषा नौलिः सिद्धैः प्रचक्ष्यटे ॥ 33 ॥

Lean forward, protrude the abdomen and rotate (the muscles) from right to left with speed. This is called nauli by the siddhas.

Nauli is the practice of contracting and isolating the rectus abdomini muscles. In the *Gheranda Samhita* it is known as *lauliki*. The root word *nala* means the 'navel string' i.e. rectus abdomini muscles. It also means a tubular vessel. Lauliki comes from the word *lola* which means 'to roll' or 'agitate'.

When the rectus abdomini muscles are rotated from left to right (anticlockwise), it is called *dakshina nauli*. When they are rotated from right to left (clockwise), that is *vama nauli*. When the muscles are pulled together and the middle group of muscles protrude, it is *madhyama nauli*. Before attempting nauli you must be able to perform uddiyana bandha properly.

The rectus abdomini are the two long vertical muscles situated in front of the abdomen, which run from under the centre of the ribcage near the diaphragm to the pubic bone. Though these are the muscles you are manipulating in nauli, the external oblique and traverse abdomini are also utilized.

At first nauli is practised with the hands just above the knees and the body bent forward. Once this is perfected you can practise in a more erect position, hands placed on the upper thighs.

Stage I: Vama and Dakshina Nauli (left and right isolation)

Stand with the feet 45 to 60 centimetres apart.
Bend the knees and rest the palms of the hands just above the knees, thumbs on the insides of the thighs, fingers touching the outsides, or as shown in diagram.

215

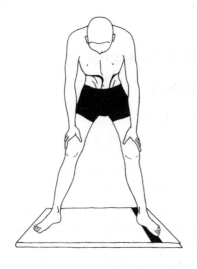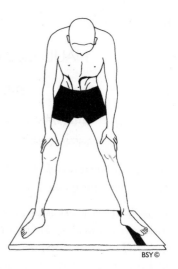

Keep the head up and the eyes open.

Breathe in deeply through the nose and exhale quickly through the mouth, slightly pursing the lips.

Perform jalandhara bandha while maintaining bahiranga (external) kumbhaka.

Suck the abdomen and stomach in by performing uddiyana bandha.

Lift the right hand slightly off the knee, keeping all the pressure on the left hand and knee, but do not lean to the left side. This will automatically isolate the rectus abdomini muscles on the left.

Then release uddiyana bandha, raise the head slowly, stand up and inhale slowly.

This is vama nauli.

Practise in the same way on the right side.

Keep the right hand resting above the knee and slightly lift the left hand to isolate the rectus abdomini muscles on the right. This is dakshina nauli.

In between each round of nauli, release uddiyana first, then jalandhara, raise the head, stand erect and then breathe in very slowly through the nose. Take a few normal breaths before practising the next round.

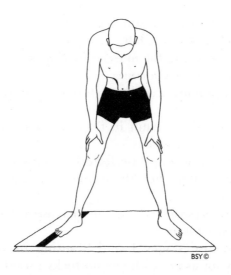

Stage 2: Madhyama Nauli (central abdominal contraction)

Practise vama or dakshina nauli as in stage 1, and then start to roll the muscles to the other side, but before they reach the opposite side hold them in the middle. In order to roll the muscles, slowly bring the weight back onto the hand which was lifted from the knee.

While holding the muscles in the centre, both hands should rest above the knees.

This is madhyama nauli.

Stage 3: Practise in the same way as stages 1 and 2 but learn to control the contraction of the muscles and to isolate the muscle groups without lifting the hands from the legs.

First try by just releasing the pressure off the hand without moving it from the leg.

Gradually begin to control the practice so that the hands remain fixed on the legs. Then practise with the hands on the upper thighs.

Stage 4: Abdominal rotation or churning

Stand in the same position as in Stage 1, keeping the hands on the legs above the knees throughout the whole practice.

217

Practise vama nauli and then roll the muscles to the right and back to the left.

Continue rotating the muscles in a clockwise direction. This is known as 'churning'.

Start by practising it three times consecutively, then release.

Practise dakshina nauli in the same way, rotating the muscles anticlockwise.

When this churning is perfected, practise it three times with vama nauli, then three times with dakshina nauli and release.

When this is perfected you can increase to ten rotations, then twenty rotations.

Stage 5: Practise stages 1 and 2 sitting in siddhasana/ siddha yoni asana with the buttocks raised slightly by a cushion.

Initially it will be difficult to control the muscles in the sitting position, so it is better to first perfect the practice of nauli in the standing position.

मन्दाग्निसंदीपनपाचनादिसंधापिकानन्दकरी सदैव ।
अशेषदोषामयशोषणी च हठक्रिया मौलिरियं च नौलि: ॥ 34 ॥

Nauli is foremost of the hatha yoga practices. It kindles the digestive
fire, removing indigestion, sluggish digestion, and all disorders of
the doshas, and brings about happiness.

Shatkarma and asanas stimulate digestion, but nauli is
said to be the best for this. It quickly tones the abdominal
muscles, nerves, intestines, reproductive, excretory and
urinary organs. In fact, there is not one part of the internal
system which is not stimulated by this practice. When the
abdominal muscles are manipulated, not only are they toned,
but all the internal organs are massaged.

Asana and pranayama practice definitely generates
energy, but nauli activates the system in a much shorter time
and with greater force. Its effects are particularly noticeable
on the digestive and excretory systems. It generates heat in
the body, stimulates digestion, assimilation and absorption,
thereby reducing excretion. It balances the endocrine system
and helps control the production of sex hormones.

Nauli is especially useful for alleviating constipation,
indigestion, nervous diarrhoea, acidity, flatulence, depression, hormonal imbalances, sexual and urinary disorders,
laziness, dullness, lack of energy and emotional disturbances.
Through its practice one can control one's appetite and
sensual desires and strengthen one's willpower. If this can
be attained, the practitioner will definitely find deeper
satisfaction within.

However, nauli cannot be practised by everyone. Those
who are suffering from heart disease, hypertension, hernia,
gastric or duodenal ulcers, or who are recovering from some
internal injury or abdominal surgery, cannot do it.

KAPALBHATI (frontal brain cleansing)

अथ कपालभाति: ।

भस्त्रावल्लोहकारस्य रेचपूरौ ससंभ्रमौ ।
कपालभातिर्विख्या कफदोषविशोषणी ॥ ३५ ॥

Perform exhalation and inhalation rapidly like the bellows (of a blacksmith). This is called kapalbhati and it destroys all mucous disorders.

The last of the six shatkarma is kapalbhati. In the *Gheranda Samhita* it is known as *bhalabhati*. *Bhala* and *kapal* mean the 'cranium' or 'forehead'. *Bhati* is 'light' or 'splendour', but it also means 'perception and knowledge'. Kapalbhati is a pranayama technique which invigorates the entire brain and awakens the dormant centres which are responsible for subtle perception. In English it is called the 'frontal brain cleansing' technique. It is a similar practice to bhastrika pranayama except that exhalation is emphasized and inhalation is the result of forcing the air out. In normal breathing, inhalation is active and exhalation is passive. This practice reverses that process so that exhalation becomes active and inhalation passive.

As described in the sloka, the breathing should be done like the pumping action of a pair of blacksmith's bellows. When the bellows are closed the air is pushed out and when they are opened the air is sucked in due to the vacuum effect that is created. Similarly, when you inhale in kapalbhati, it should be the reaction to the forced exhalation. In bhastrika, inhalation and exhalation are equal, but in kapalbhati it is not so.

According to the *Gheranda Samhita* there are three forms of kapalbhati: *vatakrama*, *vyutkrama* and *sheetkrama*. *Hatha Yoga Pradipika* describes only vatakrama. *Vata* means 'wind' or 'air'.

Technique 1: Vatakrama Kapalbhati (air cleansing)

Sit in a comfortable meditative pose, preferably siddhasana/siddha yoni asana and prepare yourself as for meditation.

Close the eyes and relax, keeping the spine erect.

Place the hands in either jnana or chin mudra.

Practise kaya sthairyam, i.e. steadiness of the body.

Inhale deeply and perform fifty fast respirations through both nostrils placing more emphasis on exhalation.

Inhalation should be short.

After the last exhalation, inhale deeply through the nose and exhale quickly through the mouth, slightly pursing the lips.

With kumbhaka, perform jalandhara bandha, moola bandha, and uddiyana bandha in this order, but almost simultaneously.

Maintain kumbhaka and the bandhas for as long as possible and count the duration.

Before inhaling, release moola bandha, uddiyana and jalandhara in this order.

When the head is raised, inhale slowly through the nose.

Practise three rounds of fifty breaths.

When this is perfected you can increase it to five rounds.

You can increase the practice by ten breaths each week, so that after five weeks you are practising one hundred breaths per round.

After completing the practice concentrate on the space in front of the closed eyes.

In kapalbhati a greater number of respirations can be taken than in bhastrika pranayama because hyperventilation does not occur. It can be increased to two hundred breaths with months of practice, unless advised otherwise by your guru. Kapalbhati should be done after asana or neti, but before concentration or meditation.

If you experience dizziness while practising, it means you are breathing too forcefully. If this is the case, stop the

221

practice and sit quietly for a few moments. When you begin to practise again, do it with more awareness, and with less force. Inhalation should be spontaneous and not controlled, and exhalation should not make you feel breathless before completing the round. This is important. You should feel as if you could continue breathing in this manner beyond one hundred breaths.

The effects of kapalbhati and bhastrika are similar, but due to the forced and longer exhalation, kapalbhati affects the brain differently. Andre van Lysebeth has quoted a physiological phenomenon that during normal inhalation the fluid around the brain is compressed and so the brain contracts very slightly. With exhalation this cerebrospinal fluid is decompressed and the brain very slightly expands. This is the mechanical influence of the respiratory cycle on the structure of the brain. Forced exhalation in kapalbhati increases the massaging effect on the brain by enhancing the decompression effect on every exhalation.

The average number of breaths being fifteen per minute means the brain is compressed and decompressed that many times, but here you are breathing fifty to one hundred times, stimulating the brain three to seven times more than normal per round. Kapalbhati also expels more carbon dioxide and other waste gases from the cells and lungs than normal breathing.

In the *Gheranda Samhita* the method of practising vatakrama kapalbhati is slightly different. Instead of breathing in rapidly through both nostrils, you inhale through the left and exhale through the right, inhale through the right and exhale through the left, as in nadi shodhana pranayama, except that inhalation and exhalation is done rapidly.

The *Hatharatnavali* clarifies these two different processes. It says: "Fast rotation of the breath from left to right (right to left), or exhalation and inhalation through both nostrils together, is known as kapalbhati." (1:55) Thus the two systems are correct. However, to accelerate the breath while doing alternate nostril breathing is very difficult.

Technique 2: Vyutkrama Kapalbhati (sinus cleansing)

The second practice of kapalbhati, *vyutkrama*, is similar to jala neti and is sometimes given as part of neti. *Vyutkrama* means 'expelling system'.

For this practice you need a bowl of warm saline water rather than a neti lota.

Lean forward, scoop the water up in the palm of the hand and sniff the water in through the nostrils.

Let the water flow down into the mouth and then spit the water out from the mouth.

Practise in this way several times.

It is important to relax while sucking the water in.

There should be absolutely no fear.

If there is pain in the nose during the practice it usually means that the water contains either too little or too much salt.

Technique 3: Sheetkrama Kapalbhati (mucus cleansing)

The third practice, *sheetkrama* is the reverse of vyutkrama. *Sheet* means 'cool' or 'passive'.

In this practice you take a mouthful of warm, salty water and instead of swallowing it, you push it up through the nose and let it flow out.

Remember to remain relaxed the whole time.

Vyutkrama and sheetkrama should both be done standing rather than squatting. Afterwards, make sure all the water is removed from the nose in the same way prescribed for jala neti, or practise vatakrama kapalbhati.

The *Gheranda Samhita* says that not only do these practices rid the sinuses of old mucus, but they make one attractive and prevent the ageing process from occurring. Kapalbhati helps relax facial muscles and nerves. It rejuvenates tired cells and nerves, keeping the face young, shining and wrinkle-free. The effects of vyutkrama and sheetkrama are the same as jala neti. Spiritually they help awaken ajna chakra.

षट्कर्मनिर्गतस्थौल्यकफदोषमलादिक: ।
प्राणायामं तत: कुर्यादनायासेन सिद्ध्यति ॥ 36 ॥

By the six karmas (shatkarma) one is freed from excesses of the doshas. Then pranayama is practised and success is achieved without strain.

If the body is clogged with old mucus, bile and wind, the energy gained through pranayama practice will be utilized for rectifying your disorders. In fact, if you have any mucous blockages it may create such an acute problem that you cannot practise pranayama. First you have to rid yourself of excess mucus and bile and eliminate the toxins from your system. Proper assimilation and excretion have to be established. Pranayama is more effective in a healthy body.

The body has three faults – *kapha*, mucus, *pitta*, acid and *vata*, wind. An imbalance in these causes disease. In the same way, the mind has three faults. The first one is *mala*, impurity, the second is *vikshepa*, distraction, and the third is *avarana*, ignorance.

Impurity is the psychological stuff which manifests when you sit for meditation. There are five types: *kama*, sensual desire, *krodha*, anger, *moha*, infatuation, *mada*, arrogance or pride, *matsarya*, envy.

When visions float across your mind and the mind cannot be made steady because it keeps oscillating, that is vikshepa. When the mind is unable to understand itself, that is called ignorance, avarana.

Through the practice of shatkarma the centres in the physical body which are responsible for arousing these doshas in the mind are stabilized. Shatkarma works on the physical body to influence the mind, brain waves and blockages of energy.

प्राणायामैरेव सर्वे प्रशुष्यन्ति मला इति ।
आचार्याणां तु केषांचिदन्यत्कर्म न संमतम् ॥ 37 ॥

*According to some teachers, pranayama alone removes impurities
and therefore they hold pranayama in esteem and not the other
techniques.*

Here Yogi Swatmarama points out that there are two differing
opinions about the necessity of practising the shatkarma prior
to pranayama. Some hatha yoga teachers say that you should
first clean the nadis through shatkarma so pranayama will
be effective. Others believe pranayama alone will remove the
blockages in the nadis and balance all elements of the body.
Both opinions are correct, but which to follow?

Shatkarma provides a quick method of rebalancing mucus,
bile and wind. If you cleanse the body through shatkarma first,
pranayama will maintain its state of cleanliness. If you have
excess mucus, bile or wind and practise pranayama only, the
energy you generate through pranayama will all be spent in
rectifying your state of imbalance. However, if your body is
healthy, nadis clean and the whole system is functioning in
harmony, then pranayama can be practised without any need
for shatkarma. If there is a slight imbalance, pranayama alone
will be sufficient to rectify any problem.

Excess mucus is the major obstacle which prevents
pranayama practice. When the nose or respiratory tract
is completely blocked, pranayama is impossible, so you
will definitely have to resort to neti, kunjal or even laghoo
shankhaprakshalana. For nasal congestion, neti and kunjal are
sufficient, but for respiratory congestion, asthma, bronchitis or
eosinophilia, the three karmas will be necessary.

Although the shatkarma are very powerful and effective
purifiers and harmonizers, pranayama will have to be
practised afterwards to maintain the balance they have
created. Otherwise impurities will reaccumulate and the body
will fall back into its old patterns.

GAJA KARANI (elephant stomach cleansing)

अथ गजकरणी ।

उदरगतपदार्थमुद्वमन्ति पवनमपानमुदीर्य कंठनाले ।
क्रमपरिचयवश्यनाडिचक्रा गजकरणीति निगद्यते हठज्ञै: ॥ 38 ॥

Vomiting the things in the stomach by moving the apana into the throat is called gaja karani by those who have attained knowledge of hatha yoga. Thus, being accustomed to this technique, control of the nadis and chakras is brought about.

Gaja karani is a technique of vaman dhauti. The description given in the verse is a variation of the practice. Gaja karani is an advanced form of kunjal kriya. In gaja karani the water is regurgitated due to contraction of the abdomen, whereas in kunjal the back of the tongue is rubbed with the fingers. Both are done on a completely empty stomach. This variation, however, specifies "vomiting the things in the stomach", indicating that it is practised after eating.

There are generally three ways vaman dhauti can be done: in kunjal kriya one drinks water on an empty stomach and regurgitates it by rubbing the back of the tongue; in vyaghra kriya one drinks water and regurgitates the contents of the stomach three to four hours after eating; and in gaja karani one drinks water on an empty stomach and regurgitates it by contracting the upper abdomen while simultaneously inhaling. This variation, which is practised three to four hours after eating, is a fourth method.

Yogi Swatmarama says to move the apana up to the throat so as to vomit, but he has failed to reveal the method. Often, in the shastras, we find that vital information has been omitted or left out. Such omissions were deliberate to prevent unauthorized people from practising. The methods used to move apana up to the throat are: to gently rub the back of the tongue with the first two fingers, or, to inhale and simultaneously contract the upper abdomen. Both methods induce vomiting. In the process of vomiting, apana vayu automatically moves upward. Using the fingers is the easier method; few people master the technique of contracting the abdomen.

Another important factor which has been omitted is that half an hour after vomiting you should eat a liquid (not thick) preparation of boiled rice and milk with sugar added. This is like a medicine which restores the natural balance of enzymes in the stomach, as your whole digestive system can be disturbed by the practice.

Gaja karani strengthens the solar plexus, the nerve centre which is connected with manipura chakra. Many texts state that all the nadis emanate from the navel region or the 'navel wheel'. The regurgitating reflex pulls the prana up from mooladhara chakra to the throat and stimulates vishuddhi chakra. This upward movement activates all the chakras within the vertebral column and the surrounding nadis. Nerve impulses rush up from the base of the spine to the medulla oblongata and ajna chakra.

It is important that this variation of gaja karani is done three to four hours after eating; assimilation of food takes place and what is difficult to digest is removed before further energy is spent on digestion. This decreases the amount of excrement produced and reduces the work load of the intestines and excretory organs, thereby preventing an overflow of energy in the lower centres. Of course, this practice should not be done after every meal but only as directed by the guru, otherwise it may weaken the digestive system.

ब्रह्मादयोऽपि त्रिदशा: पवनाभ्यासतत्परा: ।
अभूवन्नंतकभयात्तस्मात्पवनमभ्यसेत् ॥ 39 ॥

Even Brahma and other gods in heaven devote themselves to practising pranayama because it ends the fear of death. Thus it (pranayama) must be practised.

In order to emphasize the importance and value of pranayama, Swatmarama says that Brahma and the other gods practise it. Brahma is one of the holy trinity, the creator. Brahma, Vishnu and Mahesh or Shiva, who comprise the trinity, are the three aspects of the macro and microcosmos.

Swatmarama says that through the practice of pranayama fear of death can be overcome, and for a spiritual aspirant this is a very important achievement. In the *Yoga Sutras* of Sage Patanjali, fear of death or *abhinivesha* is listed as one of the five basic causes of pain. It is known as a *klesha* and kleshas have to be dissolved before enlightenment takes place. "Abhinivesha is the desire for life, sustained by its own force which dominates even the learned." (2:9)

According to Sage Patanjali: "The modification of the kleshas are reducible through meditation." (2:11) However, Swatmarama claims that fear of death can be eradicated through pranayama. Pranayama has a definite strengthening effect on the brain centres responsible for emotion and fear.

228

यावद्बद्धोमरुहे यावच्चित्तं निराकुलम् ।
यावद्दृष्टिर्भ्रुवोर्मध्ये तावत्कालभयं कुत: ॥ 40 ॥

As long as the breath is restrained in the body, the mind is devoid of thought and the gaze is centred between the eyebrows, why should there be fear of death?

If the mind and prana are absorbed in the centre which is responsible for the experience of universal consciousness or atma, what can cause fear of death? When the individual soul or *jivatma* has merged into its source, experience is total, there is no individuality. Any thought of death cannot occur because 'you' do not exist. Fear only comes with the experience of duality. When you think you have something to lose, when there is a feeling of separation and no knowledge of unity, then there is fear of death.

Bodily processes are drastically altered when the mind and prana are totally absorbed during the experience of oneness. The breath is retained spontaneously, the eyeballs roll back as if gazing at the eyebrow centre, blood pressure, heart rate, pulse, metabolism and visceral functions are all altered. The body goes into a state of suspended animation and time and space do not exist in the mind. The body appears as if dead, but it is not because it has the capacity to regenerate prana. It is only suspended for a short while.

By practising breath retention and shambhavi mudra and focusing the mind on a single point, you are inducing the state of complete absorption. If a superconscious state occurs and you return to mundane awareness, the thought of death has less significance. Whether the body is dead or alive is irrelevant to one who has realized the atma.

विधिवत्प्राणसंयामैर्नाडीचक्रे विशोधिते ।
सुषुम्नावदनं भित्त्वा सुखाद्विशति मारुतः ॥ 41 ॥

By systematically restraining the prana (breath) the nadis and chakras are purified. Thus the prana bursts open the doorway to sushumna and easily enters it.

Constant, continual and correct practice of pranayama activates sushumna. Normally the energy in the nadis fluctuates from ida to pingala, but when the energy is equally balanced in both they cease to function and the energy rises through sushumna.

If pranayama is practised incorrectly, it could create an imbalance but nothing disastrous will happen; if done specifically as instructed by the guru, it will definitely arouse kundalini in this lifetime. When pranayama is done correctly, it is like sowing potential seeds in fertile soil. When practised incorrectly, it is like planting small stones in the soil, believing them to be seeds and expecting plants to grow. No matter how much you water the stones they will never develop into plants. Similarly, when practised correctly, pranayama will yield fruits within the course of time, but improper practice will bear nothing.

MANONMANI (mind devoid of thought)

अथ मनोन्मनी ।

मारुते मध्यसंचारे मन:स्थैर्यं प्रजायते ।
यो मन:सुस्थिरीभाव: सैवावस्था मनोन्मनी ॥ 42 ॥

The breath (prana) moving in the middle passage makes the mind still. This steadiness of mind is itself called the state of manonmani – devoid of thought.

When the shakti moves through pingala the left brain hemisphere is activated and only certain faculties of the mind operate. When ida flows, the right brain hemisphere is active and other faculties operate. However, when the energy is passing through the corpus callosum, from one hemisphere to the other, then there is equilibrium. When a steady flow of energy or prana moves through sushumna, the mind becomes still.

When the particular frequency of the energy is such that it arouses perfect stillness of thought activities and no awareness of the external or internal world, that is *manonmani avastha*. *Manonmani* means 'absence of individual mind'; absence of fluctuations in the individual consciousness, and absence of conscious, subconscious and unconscious states.

By cutting off the external stimuli to the brain over a long period of time, the conscious functions of the brain 'turn off' and *shoonya* or void is experienced. This state of shoonya or nothingness often leads to the more positive experience of manonmani.

तत्सिद्धये विधानज्ञाश्चित्रान्कुर्वन्ति कुंभकान् ।
विचित्र कुंभकाभ्यासाद्विचित्रां सिद्धिमाप्नुयात् ॥ ४३ ॥

By practising the various kumbhakas wondrous perfections are obtained. Those who are the knowers practise the various kumbhakas to accomplish them.

अथ कुंभकभेदाः ।

सूर्यभेदनमुज्जायी सीत्कारी शीतली तथा ।
भस्त्रिका भ्रामरी मूर्च्छा प्लाविनीत्यष्टकुंभकाः ॥ ४४ ॥

The eight kumbhakas are suryabheda, ujjayi, sheetkari, sheetali, bhastrika, bhramari, moorchha and plavini.

There are various ways in which pranayama can be practised and utilized with retention or *kumbhaka*. The yogis devised eight specific techniques and these have become the traditional hatha yoga practices of pranayama.

The most important aspect of pranayama is kumbhaka. The manner in which you breathe in and out is also significant, but it is the retention which has to be developed. Kumbhaka arouses the inherent potential in the higher regions of thebrain, and in fact it affects the whole brain. Each type of pranayama can arouse a different faculty and body function.

There are more than eight ways in which pranayama can be practised but there are only two ways to perform kumbhaka. The breath can either be held internally or externally. External retention is known as *bahiranga kumbhaka* and internal retention is *antaranga kumbhaka*. These forms of kumbhaka are both performed consciously by control of the breath, but there is another form of kumbhaka which occurs spontaneously through the practice of pranayama. It is called *kevala kumbhaka*.

When pranayama is done with effort and not spontaneously, it is called *sahita pranayama*. The eight practices of sahita pranayama are: suryabheda, ujjayi, sheetkari, sheetali, bhastrika, bhramari, moorchha and plavini. There are other forms of pranayama such as nadi shodhana (which has previously been described in this chapter), viloma, anuloma viloma, pratiloma and kapalbhati but they are not traditional techniques of pranayama. Although kapalbhati is a pranayama technique, traditionally it is considered as a shatkarma.

In the practice of suryabheda pranayama, inhalation is done through the right nostril, activating pingala nadi, and exhalation is through the left. Ujjayi is deep breathing with contraction of the epiglottis. Sheetkari is performed by breathing in slowly through the mouth and teeth. Sheetali is done by breathing in through the rolled tongue. Bhastrika is rapid breathing. Bhramari is performed by making a humming sound with exhalation. Moorchha emphasizes retention to create a fainting feeling, and plavini is done by swallowing air into the stomach.

More recently, pranayama has been categorized into balancing practices, vitalizing practices and tranquillizing practices. Of course the overall effects of any pranayama are tranquillizing, however, some particularly activate pranic movement and the sympathetic nervous system, while others pacify or cool the system. The vitalizing practices rapidly create heat in the physical and subtle bodies, and such practices are more suitable for middle to advanced sadhakas. Beginners should always start with nadi shodhana to balance the breath and ida/pingala, or the sympathetic/parasympathetic nervous systems.

Tranquillizing pranayama practices are those which pacify the body and mind. They simultaneously increase the pranic flow and arouse awareness of the subtle vibration of energy. Such forms of pranayama stimulate activity in the parasympathetic and central nervous systems. These techniques should be performed once the pranic flow is balanced and therefore they generally involve breathing through both the nostrils.

233

पूरकांते तु कर्तव्यो बन्धो जालंधराभिधः ।
कुंभकांते रेचकादौ कर्तव्यस्तूड्डियानकः ॥ ४५ ॥

At the end of inhalation, jalandhara bandha is done. At the end of kumbhaka and beginning of exhalation, uddiyana bandha is done.

अधस्तात्कुंचनेनाशु कंठसंकोचने कृते ।
मध्ये पश्चिमतानेन स्यात्प्राणो ब्रह्मनाडिगः ॥ ४६ ॥

By contracting the perineum, contracting the throat and drawing the abdomen up, the prana flows into the brahma nadi.

Pranayama actually involves the practice of breath control in combination with bandhas and mudras. Without bandhas, pranayama is incomplete. Either the three bandhas – jalandhara, uddiyana and moola bandha should be done together or in different combinations.

After completing inhalation, when you are about to hold the breath, the head should be dropped forward so that the chin is close to the collarbone and the throat is blocked. If both hands are on the knees the elbows should be straightened and the shoulders raised. This is jalandhara bandha.

According to Yogi Swatmarama, uddiyana or sucking in of the abdomen should be done after retention and beginning of *rechaka* or exhalation. Once exhalation is complete, jalandhara bandha should be done and uddiyana fully employed. Uddiyana bandha is only practised with external retention or bahiranga kumbhaka, then the stomach and lungs are completely empty and the abdomen can easily be drawn in and up.

Moola bandha or contraction of the muscles of the perineal body or cervix can be done with either antaranga or bahiranga kumbhaka. After inhalation, jalandhara and moola bandha are practised together, and after exhalation the three bandhas – jalandhara, uddiyana and moola

234

are performed. When the three bandhas are practised in combination, this is called *maha bandha*. However, in certain pranayama practices the three bandhas cannot be done together. For example, it is inappropriate to perform uddiyana bandha in moorchha pranayama.

Though the bandhas are utilized in pranayama they are considered as separate practices. Bandhas are powerful practices that generate and accumulate prana in specific parts of the physical and subtle bodies; they are essential in the practices to awaken the chakras and sushumna nadi.

Brahma nadi is the innermost core of sushumna nadi and is extremely significant in the process of spiritual awakening. The outer surface of the middle nadi is sushumna, inside that is vajra nadi, within that chitrini, and in the very centre, brahma nadi. Sushumna represents tamo guna or inertia; vajra nadi, rajo guna or dynamism; chitrini, sattwa guna, and brahma nadi represents the pure unconditioned state of consciousness.

If the prana can be made to penetrate brahma nadi there will be total absorption of the individual consciousness with the cosmic source. Prana is the life force of the individual and when it merges back into its original source there is complete unity of every aspect of your being.

आपानमूर्ध्वमुत्थाप्य प्राणं कंठादधो नयेत् ।
योगी जराविमुक्त: सन्षोडशाब्दवया भवेत् ॥ 47 ॥

*Raising the apana upward and bringing the prana down from the
throat, the yogi becomes free from old age and appears as if sixteen
years of age.*

If you can reverse the downward flowing tendency of apana
vayu and the upward movement of prana vayu, you can
reverse the ageing process. When the prana flows down and
up there is loss of vital energy, but if it flows inward, then it
is retained and this vitalizes the whole body.

If the body could remain in the same condition as
a child's, ageing would not occur. It is the secretion of
certain hormones or chemicals from the pituitary gland
and endocrinal system which causes ageing. In this
sloka Swatmarama is indicating that by the use of the
three bandhas the body is influenced in such a way that
degeneration no longer occurs.

SURYABHEDA PRANAYAMA
(vitality-stimulating breath)

अथ सूर्यभेदनम् ।

आसने सुखदे योगी बद्ध्वा चैवासनं ततः ।
दक्षनाड्या समाकृष्य बहिःस्थं पवनं शनैः ॥ 48 ॥

Sitting comfortably, the yogi should become fixed in his posture and slowly breathe the air in through the right nostril.

आकेशादानखाग्राच्च निरोधावधि कुंभयेत् ।
ततः शनैः सव्यनाड्या रेचयेत्पवनं शनैः ॥ 49 ॥

Retention should then be held until the breath diffuses to the roots of the hair and tips of the nails. Then slowly exhale through the left nostril.

कपालशोधनं वातदोषघ्नं कृमिदोषहृत् ।
पुनःपुनरिदं कार्यं सूर्यभेदनमुत्तमम् ॥ 50 ॥

Suryabheda is excellent for purifying the cranium, destroying imbalances of the wind dosha and eliminating worms. It should be done again and again.

Surya is 'the sun' and it also refers to pingala nadi. *Bheda* has three meanings: secret, discrimination and to pierce. In this pranayama pingala nadi is activated by breathing in through the right nostril. Suryabheda pierces pingala and activates prana shakti in this nadi.

Technique

Sit in a comfortable meditative pose, preferably siddh-asana/siddha yoni asana.

Relax the body and practise kaya sthairyam.

Perform nasikagra mudra, closing the left nostril and leaving the right open.

Inhale slowly and deeply through the right nostril.
At the end of inhalation hold both the nostrils closed and lower the head to perform jalandhara bandha.
Retaining the breath inside, perform moola bandha.
Hold for as long as possible.
Release moola bandha then jalandhara and raise the head.
Keep the right nostril closed, open the left and slowly exhale through the left.
If necessary a few normal breaths can be taken between rounds while the hands remain relaxed on the knees, the eyes remain closed and you concentrate on the space in front of the closed eyes.
Then commence another round. Breathe in through the right nostril, hold and breathe out through the left nostril.
Practise up to ten rounds.

Suryabheda can also be practised by inhaling and exhaling through the right nostril only. However, when you breathe only through the right nostril, this might shut off ida nadi and functions of the left nostril. By exhaling through the left nostril you release energy and any impurities that remain in ida. By inhaling through the right nostril you draw the prana into pingala, and by retaining the breath after inhalation, you keep the prana in pingala.

Of course, this pranayama should only be done on an empty stomach, and it should only be done on the instructions of the guru. If your pingala nadi naturally predominates during the day, it is not advisable to practise this pranayama. When pingala flows, the mind and senses are extroverted, the left brain hemisphere functions, the sympathetic nervous system is active and the body is heated. Pingala should not be made to function excessively, it should be in harmony with the functioning of ida.

Unlike nadi shodhana pranayama which balances the breath and brain hemispheres, suryabheda predominantly works on half the system. It stimulates the sympathetic nervous system and decreases the parasympathetic functions.

Swatmarama says that suryabheda eliminates imbalance of the wind dosha, but it also balances the other two doshas, mucus and bile. Stimulation of the sympathetic nervous system and pingala nadi removes dullness from the body and mind, and the heat produced through the practice burns up impurities in the body. The *Gheranda Samhita* says suryabheda, "Prevents old age and death, increases the body heat and awakens kundalini." (5:62,63)

If this pranayama is practised in the reverse manner, inhaling though the left nostril and exhaling through the right, it activates ida nadi and is known as *chandrabheda pranayama*. In this text, nothing has been written about this pranayama because if ida is awakened the mind can introvert completely and the body will become lethargic. It is quite safe to activate pingala nadi through suryabheda pranayama, but it can be dangerous to activate ida through chandrabheda unless the guru has specifically advised it.

UJJAYI PRANAYAMA (psychic breath)

अथोज्जायी ।

मुखं संयम्य नाडीभ्यामाकृष्य पवनं शनै: ।
यथा लगति कंठात्तु हृदयावधि सस्वनम् ॥ 51 ॥

*Closing the mouth, inhale with control and concentration through
ida and pingala, so that the breath is felt from the throat to the heart
and produces a sonorous sound.*

पूर्ववत्कुंभयेत्प्राणं रेचयेदिडया तथा ।
श्लेष्मदोषहरं कंठे देहानलविवर्धनम् ॥ 52 ॥

*Do kumbhaka as before and exhale through ida. This removes
phlegm from the throat and stimulates the (digestive) fire.*

नाडीजलोदराधातुगतदोषविनाशनम् ।
गच्छता तिष्ठता कार्यमुज्जाय्याख्यं तु कुंभकम् ॥ 53 ॥

*This pranayama, called ujjayi, can be done while moving, standing,
sitting or walking. It removes dropsy and disorders of the nadis and
dhatu.*

Ujjayi means 'victorious'; *ujji* is the root which means 'to
conquer' or 'acquire by conquest'. In English ujjayi is
known as the 'psychic breath' because of its effect on the
mind. Though it is described here as a specific practice,
this pranayama occurs spontaneously when concentration
becomes deep and intense. The practice of ujjayi is so simple
that it can be done in any position and anywhere.

Ujjayi is often used in combination with mantra
repetition, i.e. japa on your guru mantra or *soham, hamso*. It
is used in meditation practices, kriya yoga and yoga nidra
because it helps relax the physical body and the mind, and

240

develops awareness of the subtle body and psychic sensitivity. Ujjayi promotes internalization of the senses and pratyahara. When used in meditation, kumbhaka is omitted and ujjayi is performed through both the nostrils with natural inhalation and exhalation.

Technique 1

Sit in a comfortable meditative pose or lie in shavasana. Become aware of the natural breathing process and feel the air passing down through the windpipe.

Slightly contract the region at the back of the throat as you do when you swallow.

Inhalation and exhalation are done through the nose, but there is a partial contraction of the glottis which produces a light snoring sound. The sound must come from the throat and not forced to come through the nose.

Make the inhalation and exhalation long, deep and controlled.

Practise full yogic breathing and concentrate on the sound.

Continue for as long as you can, maintaining full awareness.

Technique 2

Practise as in Technique 1 but incorporate khechari mudra by folding the tongue back so that the tip of the tongue presses the back of the soft palate.

Technique 3

Sitting in a meditative pose, prepare yourself as for meditation.

Practise in the same way as in Technique 1, but after inhalation retain the breath, closing both nostrils with the right hand, and lower the head to perform jalandhara bandha.

Release jalandhara, raise the head and with ujjayi, exhale slowly through the left nostril only.

Technique 4

Practise Technique 3 with khechari mudra.

Techniques 1 and 2 can be practised for any length of time. They are very simple, and unlike any other pranayama can be done in any position, under any circumstances. If breath retention is incorporated the number of rounds must be restricted.

Simple ujjayi is done with japa or repetition of *soham*. As you breathe in and feel the breath move up the spine, mentally repeat *so*, and as you exhale and feel the breath move down the spine, mentally repeat *ham*. This form of breathing can also be incorporated with asana practice for specific therapeutic purposes, e.g. when practising makarasana for sciatica or spinal spondylitis, or shashankasana for menstrual tension, insomnia or emotional disturbance. It can also be incorporated into asana practice purely to increase the awareness and to stimulate sushumna. When it is practised for relaxation and concentration of mind, it should be done after other pranayama techniques and before concentrating on a psychic symbol.

Ujjayi is especially recommended for people who have insomnia and mental tension. The simple form, without retention, is a must in the yogic management of heart disease. However, anyone with low blood pressure must first correct their condition before taking up the practice.

SHEETKARI PRANAYAMA (hissing breath)

अथ सीत्कारी ।

सीत्कां कुर्यात्तथा वक्त्रेप्राणेनैव विजृंभिकाम् ।
एवमभ्यासयोगेन कामदेवो द्वितीयकः ॥ 54 ॥

By drawing the breath in through the mouth, make a hissing sound, without gaping the mouth, and exhale through the nose. By practising this, one becomes a second Kaamadeva (god of love).

In sheetkari pranayama the sound 'see' or 'seet' is made during inhalation. The Sanskrit word *kari* means 'that which produces'. The practice produces the sound 'see' and it also produces coolness. In English this practice is usually called 'the hissing breath'.

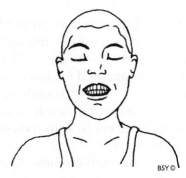

Technique I

Sit in a comfortable meditative pose, preferably siddhasana/siddha yoni asana and close your eyes.

Keep the hands on the knees throughout the practice in either jnana or chin mudra.

Practise kaya sthairyam for a minute or so.

Press the lower and upper teeth together and separate the lips as much as is comfortable.

Breathe in slowly through the gaps in the teeth.

Listen to the sound of the breath as the air is being drawn in.

Close the mouth at the end of inhalation and slowly exhale through the nose.

Repeat the same process up to twenty times.

Technique 2

Practise in the same way as Technique 1, but after inhalation retain the breath.

Perform jalandhara bandha, lowering the head, raising the shoulders and straightening the arms.

Perform moola bandha.

Hold for as long as possible.

First release moola bandha, then jalandhara, and exhale slowly through the nose when the head is perfectly straight.

Practise up to twenty rounds.

Sheetkari cools the body and should therefore be practised during warm seasons, not in winter unless particularly specified by your guru. If the weather is extremely hot it can be practised for more than ten minutes. In moderate heat, ten to fifteen rounds is sufficient. It is often done after bhastrika pranayama (especially if bhastrika is practised during summer) to counterbalance the excess heat produced in the body.

When you breathe through the mouth, as in this pranayama, it has a cooling effect, just as an animal pants in the heat to cool the body. Of course, those who have many teeth missing or no teeth at all will find this practice impossible.

When air enters through the mouth it cools the tongue and lowers the temperature of the blood leaving the lungs and thus of the whole body. Heat produced in the lower energy centres, particularly those connected to the reproductive and excretory organs, is reduced and, therefore, people who suffer from chronic constipation are advised not to practise. Sheetkari establishes harmony in the endocrine system and regulates the hormonal secretions of the reproductive organs.

This pranayama also has another important effect. When the breath is taken in through the mouth, the nerves in the nose which register the moisture, temperature, ions, etc., in the air are not stimulated, though of course the ions and air are nevertheless absorbed into the body.

Yogi Swatmarama mentions that the practitioner of sheetkari becomes Kaamadeva the second. In Hindu mythology Kaamadeva is the god of love and passion. He is something like Cupid and is the personification of sensual desire and affection. Of course this does not mean that sheetkari pranayama will make you lustful, rather it will make you virile and attractive. Passion is a form of heat in the body and mind, which in sensual life is expressed and discharged in the natural way. This results in an energy loss. However, through sheetkari the mental and emotional inflammation of passion is reduced. One is able to maintain vital energy and control and have a magnetic and attractive aura.

योगिनी चक्रसमान्य:सृष्टिसंहारकारक: ।
न क्षुधा न तृषा निद्रा नैवालस्यं प्रजायते ॥ 55 ॥

He is adored by the circle of yoginis and becomes the controller of creation and dissolution, being without hunger, thirst, sleep and laziness.

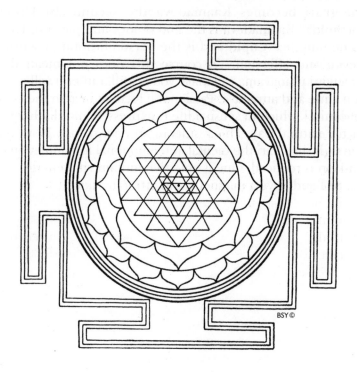

According to this sloka, the perfectionist of sheetkari is adored or worshipped by the chakra or circle of yoginis, but what exactly is the chakra of yogini? *Chakra* usually refers to a particular circle which is a source of energy. *Yogini* is a female yogi, the embodiment of Shakti, the cosmic, creative force. In tantra there is an order of sixty-four yoginis who represent the sixty-four tantras and sixty-four perfections of yoga.

246

The aspects and evolution of cosmic Shakti from its source are represented by the Sri yantra or chakra. Sri yantra is the formula of creation, manifestation and dissolution of the macro and microcosmos. It is constituted by a number of interlacing triangles which are known as yoginis. They represent the cosmic Shakti and manifestation of human existence. Sri yantra also represents each individual.

The chakra of yoginis symbolizes every function of the gross and subtler bodies, the functions of mind and integration with the soul. Our entire existence is controlled or operated by various forms of Shakti or a specific yogini or devi. Each individual person is a manifestation of the chakra of yoginis.

Thus it is said that through the practice of sheetkari the whole body comes under the control of the practitioner. In fact, perfection of any of the pranayamas leads to control of the body mechanisms, stabilization of the mental tendencies and deeper awareness of the mind-body complex.

Sheetkari particularly works on the heat and cold aspect of the body. Control of any two opposite forces in the body or mind leads to control of the other aspects of the physical, mental, emotional and psychic makeup. Swatmarama specifically mentions that sheetkari eliminates indolence and the need and desire to eat, drink and sleep.

भवेत्सत्त्वं च देहस्य सर्वोपद्रववर्जित: ।
अनेन विधिना सत्यं योगींद्रो भूमिमंडले ॥ 56 ॥

And the sattwa in the body becomes free from all disturbances. Truly, by the forementioned method one becomes lord of yogis on this earth.

There are three qualities or *gunas* of the body-mind and nature which bind the consciousness – tamas, rajas and sattwa. Each of us has these three qualities but they do not exist in equal proportions; one always predominates. In order to achieve higher states of consciousness, sattwa has to become predominant, although ultimately one also has to go beyond that.

Most people in this kali yuga are tamasic (dull and lethargic) or rajasic (dynamic and ambitious) by nature, but through yoga and other evolutionary sciences, sattwa (balance, harmony and one-pointedness) can be developed. Sattwa represents the highest point in the evolution of the human mind.

Here, Yogi Swatmarama is saying that through the practice of sheetkari pranayama, the body and mind can both be brought into a state of harmony and thereafter sattwa will become the dominating quality. One who has completely transcended tamas and rajas and is ruled by sattwa, is indeed a great yogi.

SHEETALI PRANAYAMA (cooling breath)

अथ शीतली ।

जिह्वया वायुमाकृष्य पूर्ववत्कुंभसाधनम् ।
शनकैर्घ्राणरंध्राभ्यां रेचयेत् पवनं सुधी: ॥ 57 ॥

The wise inhale air through the tongue and practise kumbhaka as (described) before, then exhale the air through the nostrils.

गुल्मप्लीहादिकान् रोगान् ज्वरं पित्तं क्षुधां तृषाम् ।
विषाणि शीतली नाम कुंभिकेयं निहंति हि ॥ 58 ॥

This kumbhaka called sheetali cures an enlarged stomach or spleen and other related diseases, fever, excess bile, hunger and thirst, and counteracts poisons.

Sheetali means 'the cooling breath' and it also means calm, passionless, unemotional. Like sheetkari, this pranayama was specifically designed to reduce the body temperature. However, these practices not only cool and calm the physical body, they also affect the mind in the same way.

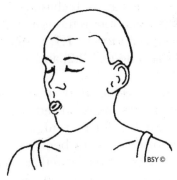

Technique I

Sit in a comfortable meditative posture, preferably siddhasana/siddha yoni asana and close your eyes.

Keep the hands on the knees in either jnana or chin mudra.

Protrude the tongue from the mouth and extend it to a comfortable distance.

Roll the sides up so that it forms a tube.

Then breathe in slowly and deeply through the tube-like tongue.

At the end of inhalation close the mouth and breathe out through the nose.

Practise nine rounds initially. Later on you can practise for up to ten minutes.

Technique 2

Practise in the same way as Technique 1, but retain the breath after inhalation.

Practise jalandhara and moola bandhas and hold the breath for as long as comfortable.

Release moola bandha then jalandhara bandha, and when the head is erect, breathe out through the nose in a controlled manner.

Practise for the same duration as Technique 1.

Technique 3

Practise in the same way as Technique 2, but count the duration of the inhalation, retention and exhalation.

Initially practise to a ratio of 1:1:1. When this becomes easy, increase the ratio to 1:2:2, and later 1:4:2.

Sheetali should be done after asana or any heating pranayama, but it can also be practised at any time during the day. It can even be done at night during summer months, especially for therapeutic benefits.

The benefits of sheetali and sheetkari are basically the same. These two practices are unique because inhalation is done through the mouth. In every other yogic practice and in breathing in general, we are told to always breathe through the nose. When the breath is taken through the

250

nose, the nose heats up and cleans the incoming air. This infringement is acceptable providing you do not practise in a dirty, polluted atmosphere or in excessively cold weather.

When you breathe through the teeth or tongue the air is cooled by the saliva and this cools the blood vessels in the mouth, throat and lungs. In turn, the stomach, liver and whole body are cooled. Because sheetali and sheetkari soothe away mental tension, they are useful techniques for alleviating psychosomatic disease such as high blood pressure. They also purify the blood and, of course, improve digestion.

There is only a slight difference between sheetkari and sheetali. In sheetkari awareness is focused on the hissing sound and in sheetali it is kept on the cooling sensation of the breath. There are also minor differences which affect different parts of the nervous system, but ultimately the impulses are sent to the central nervous system and brain.

BHASTRIKA PRANAYAMA (bellows breath)

अथ भस्त्रिका ।

ऊर्वोरुपरि संस्थाप्य शुभे पादतले उभे ।
पद्मासनं भवेदेतत्सर्वपापप्रणाशनम् ॥ 59 ॥

Placing both soles of the feet on top of the thighs is padmasana which destroys all sins (bad karma).

सम्यक्पद्मासनं बद्ध्वा समग्रीवोदर: सुधी: ।
मुखं संयम्य यत्नेन प्राणं घ्राणेन रेचयेत् ॥ 60 ॥

Sitting properly in padmasana, keeping neck and abdomen in alignment, exhale prana through the nose.

यथा लगति हृत्कंठे कपालावधि सस्वनम् ।
वेगेन पूरयेच्चापिहृत्पद्मावधि मारुतम् ॥ 61 ॥

And again the air should be quickly inhaled up to the heart lotus. Accordingly, the resounding is felt from the heart and throat up to the cranium.

पुनर्विरेचयेत्तद्वत्पूरयेच्च पुन: पुन: ।
यथैव लोहकारेण भस्त्रा वेगेन चाल्यते ॥ 62 ॥

In that way it (the breath) is inhaled and exhaled repeatedly, with the same motion as a pair of bellows being pumped.

तथैव स्वशरीरस्थं चालयेत्पवनं धिया ।
यदा श्रमो भवेद्देहे तदा सूर्येण पूरयेत् ॥ 63 ॥

Thus, in this way, one keeps the breath moving with mindfulness (awareness) and body steadiness. When the body is tired then inhale through the right nostril.

यथोदरं भवेत्पूर्णमनिलेन तथा लघु ।
धारयेन्नासिकां मध्यातर्जनीभ्यां विना दृढम् ॥ 64 ॥

Accordingly, when the abdomen becomes full of air, then quickly hold the nostrils (and breath) firmly, without using the index and middle fingers (i.e. using the thumb and ring finger as in nasikagra mudra).

विधिवत्कुंभकं कृत्वा रेचयेदिडयानिलम् ।
वातपित्तश्लेष्महरं शरीराग्निविवर्धनम् ॥ 65 ॥

Having performed (pranayama and) retention systematically, exhale through the left nostril. Thereby imbalances of wind, bile and mucus are annihilated and the digestive fire increased.

Bhastrika is the name of the pranayama which imitates the action of the *bhastra* or 'bellows' and fans the internal fire, heating the physical and subtle bodies. Bhastrika pranayama is similar to vatakrama kapalbhati, but in bhastrika, inhalation and exhalation are equal and are the result of systematic and equal lung movements. The breath has to be sucked in and pushed out with a little force. In kapalbhati, inhalation is the result of forced exhalation.

Bhastrika should not be done so forcefully that the nostrils are sucked in with inhalation. The air creates a sound as it passes in and out of the nose, but it should not be a heavy sound. It should come from the nose and not the throat.

Throughout the practice the body should remain steady. The shoulders and chest should not move at all, only the lungs, diaphragm and abdomen should move.

The correct sitting position for bhastrika is padmasana, but if it cannot be practised, ardha padmasana or siddhasana/siddha yoni asana are good alternatives. In padmasana and siddhasana the body is firmly locked so that physical movement is restricted and the spine remains straight. Nervous impulses are then able to travel directly up through the central nervous system. Siddhasana also maintains the blood pressure.

Preparation

Sit comfortably in your meditative posture with the hands on the knees and the eyes closed.

Take a slow deep breath in.

Breathe out quickly and forcefully through the nose, but do not strain, and immediately afterwards breathe in with the same force.

When you breathe out the abdomen comes in and the diaphragm contracts. When you breathe in the diaphragm relaxes and the abdomen moves out. These movements should be slightly exaggerated.

Continue to breathe in this manner counting ten breaths. At the end of ten breaths, take a deep breath in and out slowly. This is one round.

Practise three to five rounds.

As you become accustomed to this style of breathing, gradually increase the speed but keep the breath rhythmic. Inhalation and exhalation must be equal.

Technique 1

Stage 1: Sit comfortably in your meditative pose, relax and prepare yourself for pranayama. Keep the head and spine straight.

Place the right hand in nasikagra mudra and close the right nostril.

Inhale slowly and deeply through the left nostril and then breathe in and out as described in the preparation, counting twenty breaths.

After completing the last exhalation, breathe in slowly and deeply, close both nostrils and bend the head forward into jalandhara bandha, but do not raise the shoulders.

Hold for as long as comfortable.

Raise the head and exhale slowly through the right nostril. Take a deep inhalation through the right nostril and practise in the same way as you did through the left nostril, counting twenty breaths.

After the last exhalation, inhale slowly and deeply through the right nostril.

When inhalation is complete, close both the nostrils and practise jalandhara, hold, and release as before. Complete one round by practising on both sides. Perform three rounds.

Stage 2: Practise as in stage 1, but after practising through the right nostril, practise through both nostrils together counting up to forty breaths. Practise three rounds.

Stage 3: Practise as in stage 2, but during retention add moola bandha after jalandhara.

On completion of retention, release moola bandha then jalandhara.

Practise three to five rounds.

Stage 4: Practise five rounds of stage 3 and increase by ten respirations every week until you are breathing in the ratio of 50:50:100 in each round.

Technique 2

Practise Technique 1 stage 4, but omit breathing through alternate nostrils, only breathe through both, one hundred times.

Instead of performing antar kumbhaka (internal retention), practise bahir kumbhaka (external retention). That means, after the last exhalation of bhastrika, inhale slowly and deeply, and exhale rapidly through the mouth. Perform jalandhara and moola bandha.

Release in the same way as described previously.

Practise five rounds.

After a week or so of practice add uddiyana bandha after jalandhara, so that you now perform maha bandha with external kumbhaka.

Release moola bandha, then uddiyana, then jalandhara.

Between each round concentrate on the natural breath or mid-eyebrow centre.

Practise five rounds of up to a hundred breaths unless your guru asks you to practise more.

255

Bhastrika should be performed after asana and nadi shodhana pranayama, but before sheetkari, sheetali or ujjayi. During warm seasons it should be followed by a few rounds of sheetali or sheetkari so that the body does not overheat. The number of rounds of bhastrika may also need to be reduced.

Those people with high blood pressure, heart disease, brain tumor, vertigo, stomach or intestinal ulcers, glaucoma, dysentery or diarrhoea must not attempt this practice. If dizziness is experienced during the practice it means it is being performed incorrectly. Bhastrika must always be done in a relaxed manner with full awareness and the mind should not be allowed to wander.

In *Hatharatnavali* it is said that after the practice of bhastrika you should listen "with the right ear to welcome internally aroused sounds of crickets, flute, thunder cymbals, a black bee, bell, gong, trumpet, drum."

कुंडली बोधकं क्षिप्रं पवनं सुखदं हितम् ।
ब्रह्मनाडीमुखे संस्थकफाद्यर्गलनाशनम् ॥ 66 ॥

This (bhastrika) quickly arouses kundalini. It is pleasant and beneficial, and removes obstruction due to excess mucus accumulated at the entrance to brahma nadi.

सम्यग्गात्रसमुद्भूतग्रंथित्रयविभेदकम् ।
विशेषेणैव कर्तव्यं भस्त्राख्यं कुंभकत्विदम् ॥ 67 ॥

This kumbhaka called bhastrika enables the three granthis (psychic, pranic knots) to be broken. Thus it is the duty of the yogi to practise bhastrika.

The most important physiological effect of bhastrika is on the brain and heart. Bhastrika stimulates the circulation of cerebral fluid and increases the compression and decompression upon the brain, creating a rhythmic massage. The rhythmic pumping of the diaphragm and lungs stimulates the heart and blood circulation. Accelerated blood circulation and rate of gas exchange in each cell produces heat and 'washes out' waste gases. Hyperventilation begins to occur and excites the sympathetic nerves in the respiratory centre, but because there is an increased release of carbon dioxide, the centre is subsequently relaxed and hyperventilation does not take place. If exhalation were to become less than inhalation, then there would be hyperventilation. Therefore, in bhastrika inhalation and exhalation must remain equal.

The rapid and rhythmic movement of the diaphragm also stimulates the visceral organs and this creates a massaging effect throughout the whole system. Bhastrika and kapalbhati are the most dynamic and vitalizing pranayama techniques.

Bhastrika heats the nasal passages and sinuses, clearing away excess mucus and building up resistance to colds and

257

all respiratory disorders. Therefore, it is useful in the yogic management of chronic sinusitis, pleurisy, asthma and bronchitis. Bhastrika improves digestion and stimulates a sluggish system. It increases the appetite, accelerates the metabolic rate and strengthens the nervous system. Bhastrika also helps in cases of tuberculosis, constipation, sciatica, spondylitis, arthritis, rheumatic problems, cancer and physical and mental tension.

Pranic movement, particularly in the coccygeal, navel, thoracic and brain centres, is accelerated by the practice of bhastrika and this increases physical vitality and bestows clarity of mind. The tremendous heat generated by the practice clears sushumna nadi and prepares it for the ascent of kundalini.

Within sushumna there are three granthis or psychic, pranic knots which prevent the passage of kundalini shakti. One is found in mooladhara chakra. It is called *brahma granthi* and it ties the awareness to sensual perception and the physical world. Another is in anahata chakra and it causes the desire for emotional security, expression and fulfilment. It is called *vishnu granthi*. The third granthi is located in ajna chakra and is associated with attachment to siddhis, psychic phenomena and experiences. It is called *rudra granthi*. The shakti produced by bhastrika is said to break these granthis so that kundalini can move on unobstructed.

Through the practice of bhastrika, the indriya: *jnan-endriya*, sensory organs, and *karmendriya*, motor organs, become less influential in motivating one's behaviour, and the need for sensual enjoyment decreases. The nervous system becomes stronger, the emotions are harmonized and deeper inner satisfaction results. This occurs when brahma and vishnu granthis begin to unknot. When psychic experiences begin, bhastrika helps one to remain as a silent uninvolved witness who is not attached to any of these experiences. As rudra granthi starts to unfold, this attitude of *sakshi*, the witness, develops.

258

It is not easy to loosen the granthis because there are many physical, emotional and mental barriers. For the average person it is almost impossible to control sensual desires and to live without emotional security and fulfilment. As for psychic experiences, those who have them often end up in a mental hospital because they have no guru to guide them through their spiritual awakening.

So, although bhastrika helps loosen the granthis which obstruct kundalini's ascent, it is not enough just to practise bhastrika for hours together; a guru's guidance is necessary.

BHRAMARI PRANAYAMA (humming bee breath)

अथ भ्रामरी ।

वेगाद्घोषं पूरकं भृंगनादं भृंगीनादं रेचकं मंदमंदम् ।
योगींद्राणामेवमभ्यासयोगाच्चित्ते जाता काचिदानंदलीला ॥ 68 ॥

Breathe in quickly, making a reverberating sound like the male black bee, and exhale slowly while softly making the sound of the female black bee. By this yogic practice one becomes lord of the yogis and the mind is absorbed in bliss.

This is *bhramari*, the humming bee pranayama, so called because the sound you make during respiration imitates that of a black bee.

Technique I

Sit in any comfortable meditative pose, relax the body and practise kaya sthairyam.

Keep the eyes closed throughout the practice.

Inhale slowly and deeply through the nose, listening to the sound of the breath.

Close the ears with the index and middle fingers by pressing the middle outer part of the ear ligament into the earhole.

Keep the ears closed and exhale, making a deep soft humming sound.

Concentrate on the sound, keeping it low pitched.

When exhalation is complete, lower the hands to the knees and breathe in slowly.

Continue to practise in the same way, performing ten to twenty rounds.

When finished, keep the eyes closed and listen for any subtle sounds.

Technique 2

Stage 1: Practise in the same way as Technique 1, but after exhalation perform bahir kumbhaka and jalandhara bandha.

Practise ten to twenty rounds, taking a few normal breaths between rounds if necessary.

Stage 2: Practise as in stage 1, but add moola bandha after jalandhara.

Technique 3

Stage 1: Practise Technique 1 with *shanmukhi mudra*. That is, after inhalation do kumbhaka and close the ears with the thumbs, the eyes with the first fingers, the nostrils with the middle fingers and the mouth with the ring and little fingers.

Hold for as long as comfortable, then exhale maintaining the same hand position.

Keep your awareness on the subtle sound vibrations or any images that may appear in front of the closed eyes.

Stage 2: Practise stage 1 with shanmukhi mudra, but add moola bandha.

Bhramari should be practised after asana, nadi shodhana and dynamic forms of pranayama, and before meditation or sleep. It is best to practise on an empty stomach. Bhramari helps to awaken psychic sensitivity and awareness of subtle vibrations, therefore, it is better to practise in the early hours of the morning or late at night. The sound produced in bhramari is very soothing and thus the practice relieves mental tension and anxiety and helps reduce anger.

MOORCHHA PRANAYAMA (swooning breath)

अथ मूर्च्छा ।

पूरकांते गाढतरं बद्ध्वा जालंधरं शनै: ।
रेचयेन्मूर्च्छनाख्येयं मनोमूर्च्छा सुखप्रदा ॥ 69 ॥

At the end of inhalation gradually become fixed on jalandhara bandha, then exhale slowly. This is called the fainting or swooning pranayama as it makes the mind inactive and (thus) confers pleasure.

Moorchha is 'to faint' or 'swoon'. Through this pranayama the experience of conscious unconsciousness is meant to arise, but it must be learned under expert guidance. The other root word, *moorchha*, means 'to expand', 'pervade and congeal'. Thus the purpose of this pranayama is to expand the consciousness and store prana.

There are two methods of practice. Here jalandhara bandha has been included, but it is not included in the *Gherand Samhita*.

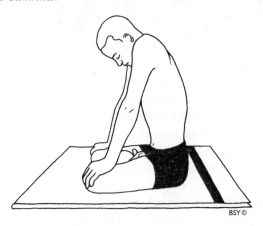

Technique I

Sit in padmasana or siddhasana/siddha yoni asana and prepare yourself for pranayama.

263

Place the palms of the hands on the knees and close the eyes.

Inhale slowly and deeply through the nose.

Practise antar kumbhaka with jalandhara bandha and shambhavi mudra.

Keep holding the breath for even longer than is comfortable.

Close the eyes, release jalandhara, raise the chin slightly and exhale in a very controlled manner.

Breathe normally for a minute or two before commencing the next round. Concentrate on the void sensation.

BSY©

Technique 2

Prepare yourself as in Technique 1, making sure the body is firmly locked in position.

Breathe in slowly through both nostrils while raising the chin up, and head slightly back, but not so far that the position is strenuous.

Practise kumbhaka while straightening the elbows, raising the shoulders and performing shambhavi mudra.

Retain the breath slightly longer than is comfortable.

Then close the eyes, slowly lower the head and shoulders, and exhale in a controlled manner.

Breathe normally before commencing the next round and concentrate on the sensation of voidness.

Moorchha pranayama is only to be done by advanced practitioners who have purified their bodies and who have a good capacity to retain the breath. With practice, the number of rounds can be increased and gradually extended from five minutes up to ten minutes. However, whenever you feel lightheaded you must stop the practice.

The sensation of fainting occurs for two reasons. One is that continued retention lowers the oxygen concentration in the blood reaching the brain, i.e. hypoxia. Second, by compressing the great vessels in the neck, jalandhara bandha influences the pressure receptors in their walls and the heart rate and blood pressure are adjusted by the reflex response.

The word *moorchha* implies insensibility of mind, i.e. the conscious mind. This pranayama clears the mind of unnecessary thoughts and reduces awareness of the senses and external world. Therefore, it is an excellent preparation for meditation and enhances *dharana*, concentration, practices. It helps reduce anxiety and mental tension and induces relaxation and inner awareness. Anyone suffering from heart disease, high blood pressure or vertigo must not attempt this practice.

PLAVINI PRANAYAMA (gulping breath)

अथ प्लाविनी ।

अन्तः प्रवर्तितोदारमारुतापूरितोदरः ।
पयस्यगाधेऽपि सुखात्प्लवते पद्मपत्रवत् ॥ 70 ॥

The inner part of the abdomen being completely filled with air, one can float like a lotus leaf on water.

Plavana means 'to float'. According to the hatha yoga texts, plavini pranayama enables one to float on water. It is an unusual form of pranayama which is similar to vatsara dhauti, except the air is retained in the stomach and intestines and not expelled immediately.

In *Hatharatnavali*, it is called *bhujangi mudra*. This pranayama is rarely taught and little has ever been written about it. It is a practice that is generally handed down from guru to disciple.

Technique

Sit in any meditative pose and prepare yourself for pranayama.

Inhalation can be done in one of two ways. Either inhale slowly through both nostrils and gulp the air into the stomach, or inhale through the mouth in kaki mudra, i.e. pursing the lips in the shape of a crow's beak. After inhalation the air has to be swallowed as you swallow food, retained inside and not belched out.

Practise as many times as possible without expelling the air.

While retaining the air inside the stomach there should be absolutely no physical movement or the air will escape.

Try to retain the air in the stomach for at least thirty to ninety minutes.

Plavini should be practised after asana and all other pranayama techniques, or it can be practised during the day if you are fasting. This will keep the stomach full and prevent hunger pangs and the desire to eat.

Plavini is useful in cases of gastritis and stomach acidity. Some yogis practise plavini before going into samadhi for days together so that the stomach remains full during their natural fast.

Floating on water is traditionally done in shavasana. If you can reach this stage of perfection it means there has been a pranic awakening and that swadhisthana chakra is awakened, because swadhisthana controls the water element.

प्राणायामस्त्रिधा प्रोक्तो रेचपूरककुंभकै: ।
सहित: केवलश्चेति कुंभको द्विविधो मत: ॥ 71 ॥

*Pranayama is said to be of three types: exhalation (rechaka),
inhalation (pooraka) and retention (kumbhaka). Kumbhaka is again
of two types: connected (sahita) and unconnected (kevala).*

यावत्केवलसिद्धि: स्यात्सहितं तावदभ्यसेत् ।
रेचकं पूरकं मुक्त्वा सुखं यद्वायुधारणम् ॥ 72 ॥

*Until kevala kumbhaka is perfected, sahita kumbhaka has to be
practised. When (you are) freed of inhalation and exhalation then
the breath or prana is retained easily.*

प्राणायामोऽयमित्युक्त: स वै केवलकुंभक: ।
कुंभके केवले सिद्धे रेचपूरकवर्जिते ॥ 73 ॥

*Perfection of isolated retention is freedom from inhalation and
exhalation. This pranayama spoken of is verily kevala kumbhaka.*

न तस्य दुर्लभं किंचित्त्रिषु लोकेषु विद्यते ।
शक्त: केवलकुंभेन यथेष्टं वायुधारणात् ॥ 74 ॥

*Nothing in the three planes of existence is unobtainable by him
who has mastery of kevala kumbhaka and can retain the breath as
desired.*

When kumbhaka is practised with conscious effort it is
called *sahita* or connected retention. When it happens
by itself, without any apparent reason or association with
either pooraka or rechaka, then it is *kevala* or unconnected,
unsupported retention.

The purpose of all pranayama practices is to create
a perfectly still state in the body so that inhalation and
exhalation stop with the cessation of pranic movement.
Control of the breath, prana and body means control of
the wavering tendencies or oscillations of the mind. All

hatha yoga techniques eventually lead to this state of kevala kumbhaka, when prana and mind stop moving.

Vijnana Bhairava Tantra explains that: "When the middle state (sushumna) develops by means of dissolution of all dichotomizing thought constructs (vrittis), the prana shakti of exhalation does not leave the centre (sushumna), nor does the shakti of inhalation enter (the body). In this way, by means of Bhairavi (kundalini shakti) in the form of cessation of prana and apana (inhalation and exhalation), there supervenes the state of Bhairava (Shiva, conscious unconsciousness). By the fusion of the two breaths there arises finally a condition in which there is complete cessation of both (kevala kumbhaka)." (2:73)

Sahita pranayama is divided into two divisions: *sagarbha*, with mantra repetition, and *nirgarbha*, without mantra repetition. Throughout the eight pranayama practices in *Hatha Yoga Pradipika*, Yogi Swatmarama has not referred to mantra repetition, therefore all the practices are forms of nirgarbha pranayama. However, in the *Gherand Samhita* and *Hatharatnavali* sagarbha is referred to.

"When there is perfection of pranayama (kevala kumbhaka), nothing in the three planes of existence is unobtainable." The three planes are the conscious, subconscious and unconscious – jagrat, swapna and sushupti. Sahita pranayama influences the conscious and subconscious levels, i.e. the body, prana, mind and psyche. Kevala kumbhaka results in the awakening of the unconscious mind and body and leads to a state beyond that. If there is awakening in all three planes, then what cannot be achieved or known in this world?

राजयोगपदं चापि लभते नात्र संशय: ।
कुंभकात्कुंडलीबोध: कुंडलीबोधतो भवेत् ।
अनर्गला सुषुम्ना च हठसिद्धिश्च जायते ॥ 75 ॥

*There is no doubt, the state of raja yoga is also attained (through
kevala kumbhaka). By retention kundalini is aroused, sushumna
becomes unobstructed and perfection of hatha yoga takes place.*

हठं विना राजयोगो राजयोगं विना हठ: ।
न सिध्यति ततो युग्ममानिष्पत्ते: समभ्यसेत् ॥ 76 ॥

*There can be no perfection if hatha yoga is without raja yoga or
raja yoga without hatha yoga. Therefore, through practice of both,
perfection is attained.*

The cessation of breath coincides with the cessation of
mental activity. For most people this only happens at the
time of death. Through practice of hatha and raja yoga the
body and mind are trained to withstand this experience, so
that potential life does not leave the body and awareness is
maintained. Raja yoga is the result of total one-pointedness
of mind, and this total one-pointedness can only be
maintained when the body has been fully prepared.

Hatha yoga is the process of uniting *ha*, the sun or
pingala nadi, and *tha*, the moon or ida nadi, with sushumna
in ajna chakra. Before the union takes place, there has to
be purification of all the body elements, and for this to
occur they must first be separated. The process also involves
separation of the mind from matter, liberating the energy.

In the *Yoga Sutras* of Sage Patanjali it says when
consciousness, *purusha*, and matter or energy, *prakriti*, live
together, there is perception, cognition, knowledge, action
and creation. Separate them and that is samadhi (raja yoga).
It may seem strange to call this science yoga, i.e. union, when
it involves a process of separation.

Consciousness and matter are eternally interacting with each other and as a result there is creation in the body, the mind and the universe. By yoga you separate these two forces within you on every level and then samadhi takes place. However, the secret of this separation is union. Only by uniting the mind on one point in meditation can the separation take place. You have to separate yourself from the idea that you and the object are different. That means you have to unify the mind and idea with the object.

Hatha yoga is a system which separates the elements of shakti or prakriti which constitute the body-mind through purification; it separates consciousness from cognition of the form of energy and unites the two in ajna chakra. Then there is raja yoga or samadhi. Raja yoga is a system which teaches you to unite the mind on the point of concentration. Then separation will take place. After this separation one reaches the highest state which is called kaivalya. It represents the journey from ajna to sahasrara through sushumna.

कुंभकप्राणरोधांते कुर्याच्चित्तं निराश्रयम् ।
एवमभ्यासयोगेन राजयोगपदं व्रजेत् ॥ 77 ॥

By stopping the prana through retention, the mind becomes free from all modifications. By thus practising (this yoga), one achieves the stage of raja yoga (supreme union).

Thoughts, emotions and desires are not the mind, they are modifications of the mind and are like waves on the ocean. The ocean is not one little wave, or even hundred of waves. It is the total volume of water. Thoughts are the result of *vrittis* or modifications – mental movements in the sub-conscious and unconscious mind. All mental activities are due to the external or internal experiences which arouse the samskara or vasana; they are not due to the mind. The mind is like a lump of clay which can be moulded into any shape. Whichever way you shape it, it is still clay.

Sage Patanjali clarifies the five basic vrittis or modifications from which all thoughts and emotions originate. They are: right knowledge or *pramana*, wrong knowledge or *viparyaya*, fancy or *vikalpa*, sleep or *nidra,* and memory or *smriti*. As long as there is identification with these modifications you can only experience mundane existence and individuality, but if all these modifications are blocked then there is no individual experience. Therefore, Sage Patanjali says: "*Yogaschittavrittinirodha*", i.e. "Blocking of the mental modifications is union or yoga." (1:2) Only then can awareness be infinite or homogeneous.

When the prana in the body is moving, it creates ripples or movements in the mind. It is like rain falling on a pool of water; it constantly creates ripples on the surface. Individual awareness is the absorption of awareness in the chitta vrittis. If you remove the vrittis or waves, the awareness is reabsorbed in the totality of consciousness.

When you go deep in meditation, the mind stops; it ceases to have any association with objects, time and space, and with ego also. Then the breath stops, maybe for one minute, two, three or four. That is kevala kumbhaka. It is a real and very significant event in the life of a yoga aspirant, for when the breath stops light immediately dawns. A light manifests in the eyebrow centre and the whole frontal passage is illumined, as though it were daybreak.

If through raja yoga you can control the mind, prana is automatically suspended, but this is very difficult, particularly in the beginning. It is not easy for anyone to control, unify or isolate the mind from the sense experiences and ego. Therefore, through hatha yoga we try another approach – first control the prana, so that suspension of the mind takes place. That signifies success in yoga.

वपु: कृशत्वं वदने प्रसन्नता नादस्फुटत्वं नयने सुनिर्मले ।
अरोगता बिंदुजयोऽग्निदीपनं नाडीविशुद्धिर्हठसिद्धिलक्षणम् ॥ 78 ॥

Perfection of hatha yoga is achieved when there is leanness of the body, tranquil countenance, manifestation of the inner sound, clear eyes, diseaselessness, control of bindu (semen or ova), active digestive fire and purification of nadis.

When kundalini shakti passes through sushumna, all the nadis and chakras and the entire body emanate that shakti. It is like replacing a twenty-five watt bulb with a fluorescent tube and bringing greater illumination into a small room. When kundalini ascends through sushumna, the whole body becomes luminous, not only the consciousness. Changes manifest in every aspect of your being.

When kundalini moves through mooladhara the sense of smell becomes very acute. One may even be able to manifest different smells just by concentrating on them. As one gains mastery over the earth element, i.e. cohesion and gravity, levitation may take place. Intuitive knowledge of the past, present and future arises in the mind; writing ability develops and states of natural ecstasy occur.

When kundalini passes through swadhisthana chakra the sense of taste becomes very sharp and different tastes can be created at will. Because swadhisthana awakening gives power over the water element, there is no fear of deep waters and some people have even been known to be able to walk on water. Psychic ability and control of the senses develop. Perception of the astral realm and intuition become keen and even death can be controlled.

When kundalini is in manipura chakra the body becomes completely diseaseless and is imperishable by fire. Excretion, hunger and thirst decrease and the body can survive for days on prana alone. Excess fat is lost and the skin becomes radiant.

In anahata, kundalini arouses the inner sound or *nada*. Pranic healing becomes apparent and one becomes very sensitive towards others and the external vibrations. Immense compassion and love for all beings arises and even the ability to enter another's body can develop.

When vishuddhi is penetrated by kundalini the voice becomes melodious and resonant, and one's words become totally captivating. The body can destroy poisonous substances and is unaffected by any extreme conditions of heat and cold, pain and pleasure, night and day.

When kundalini reaches ajna chakra, pure knowledge and wisdom unfold and all past karmas are destroyed. It is said the eight major siddhis and thirty minor siddhis are acquired. Then when kundalini dwells in sahasrara, perfection is attained, and when it is redirected down to mooladhara, every virtue descends upon the yogi. That is *dharma megha samadhi.*

अथ तृतीयोपदेशः

Chapter Three

Mudra and Bandha

सशैलवनधात्रीणां यथाधारोऽहिनायक: ।
सर्वेषां योगतंत्राणां तथाधारो हि कुंडली ॥ 1 ॥

As the serpent (Sheshnaga) upholds the earth and its mountains and woods, so kundalini is the support of all the yoga practices.

The phenomenon of kundalini is the basis of tantra and yoga. Kundalini yoga is the process of bringing together the two opposite poles of energy in the body so that they meet in the nucleus of matter, mooladhara chakra, and release the inner potential energy. That energy is called *kundalini shakti*. Tantra is made up of two syllables: *tan* 'to expand', *tra* 'to liberate'. Tantra is the process of expanding consciousness and liberating energy, and is the oldest science known to man. It has been, and still is, practised even among illiterate and so-called uncivilized tribes. Kundalini, the inherent power in every individual, is only just coming to be investigated and accepted by modern science. However, the ancient rishis understood kundalini and explained it through the scientific and systematic process of tantra.

Yogi Swatmarama has compared the existence of kundalini to the serpent which upholds the earth. According to Hindu belief, there is a thousand-headed snake wound around the earth resting on a tortoise and apparently maintaining the earth in its respective orbit. Of course, this is a symbolic explanation of the function of the earth's axis, north and south poles, and equator. It represents the distribution of cosmic energy in and around the earth. Without this force there could be no earth, no vegetation, nor inhabitants, etc. Similarly, every being has a central axis and centre of balance created by the internal energy force. Without kundalini shakti, without prana, there could be no consciousness and no life.

सुप्ता गुरुप्रसादेन यदा जागर्ति कुंडली ।
तदा सर्वाणि पद्मानि भिद्यंते ग्रंथयोऽपि च ॥ 2 ॥

Indeed, by guru's grace this sleeping kundalini is awakened, then all the lotuses (chakras) and knots (granthis) are opened.

Even today, yogic minded people talk about activating chakras and raising kundalini to penetrate the deeper layers of the mind, body and spirit. They may go from one yoga teacher to another and from one form of yoga to another in search of a way, yet they never manage any tangible experience. The key word given in this sloka is 'guru'. He is the one who can show you the pure essence of life and give you experience of the universal self or atman. He is the link to the guru within and the detonator of kundalini.

Only if it is the guru's will can kundalini awaken and ascend through sushumna nadi to illumine the silent areas of the brain. Of course, people have awakened kundalini without a guru, but it has been a disturbing and hazardous affair. Unless all the chakras are opened and sushumna is clear, kundalini should not be awakened, and if it is, it will not reach its final destination in sahasrara. The guru's guidance must be there, otherwise there is no force to raise the consciousness, and psychological blockages will manifest. For a sadhaka, the greatest problem to tackle is *ahamkara* or 'ego', and if there is no guru to keep the ego trimmed, it will prove to be an insurmountable barrier. When you live according to guru's will, things that could prove to be obstacles can no longer hinder your spiritual progress.

The guru will ensure that an aspirant is properly prepared before he graces him with an awakening of the divine spiritual force, kundalini. He will guide the sadhaka through all stages of physical, mental, emotional and psychic preparation. The sadhaka has to purify the physical and pranic bodies, strengthen the nervous system, harmonize the mind and emotions and develop intuition or a strong link with the inner guru. All the chakras can then be activated within the spinal cord and sushumna will awaken. However, it is up to the guru to decide when the aspirant is ready to cope with the force of kundalini.

People who awaken kundalini without a guru have no direction or aim in life. They do not know how to utilize and harness the immense quantity of energy that has developed within and they do not understand what is happening to them. They become lost in a maze of meaningless and intense experiences and may end up in a mental hospital classified as lunatics.

If kundalini ascends through ida instead of sushumna, they may have fantastic psychic experiences and become so introverted and withdrawn that they cannot function in the external world. Or if kundalini rises through pingala they may become lost in pranic phenomena and the experiences of the external world. Kundalini can never reach sahasrara without direction from the guru.

Guru may be external or internal, but for most people it is easier to follow the verbal instruction of one who is physically present than to trust any guidance that comes from within. Both the inner guru and the outer guru guide the disciple through ajna chakra. If kundalini is to travel up to the higher brain centres, ajna must already be functioning.

Mooladhara is the negative energy pole and ajna is the positive. If the negative pole is awakened, then the positive pole must also be awakened to create the force of attraction. It is the law of nature that energy of the negative pole is attracted to the positive. Therefore, when ajna awakens, the energy which resides in mooladhara will be drawn towards it.

This same principle of attraction exists between the guru and disciple; the disciple represents the negative pole of energy and guru is the positive. An aspirant may have a keen desire for transcendental knowledge, but it is only on finding a guru that one can move towards the higher experience. One will be drawn closer and closer to the guru internally, and thereby the guru can help remove internal blockages.

281

However, guru's instructions must be followed implicitly. The disciple must be like a patient under anaesthesia in an operating theatre and let the guru be the surgeon. The patient who screams and runs away in terror can never be helped. Likewise, a disciple has to be subservient to the guru's commands and his actions must be in accordance with the guru's will.

प्राणस्य शून्यपदवी तदा राजपथायते ।
तदा चित्तं निरालंबं तदा कालस्य वंचनम् ॥ 3 ॥

*Then indeed sushumna becomes the pathway of prana, mind is free
of all connections and death is averted.*

When the chakras are activated, sushumna is clear and
kundalini shakti awakens in mooladhara, there is only one
way for it to move, straight up the centre. At that time the
mind becomes unsupported or free of all connections. The
mind is the composite structure of twenty-four elements: five
karmendriyas, five jnanendriyas, five tanmatras, five tattwas,
ahamkara, chitta, manas and buddhi. If you separate these
elements and eliminate their function the mind has no base
to operate from; it is unsupported. With the awakening
of kundalini, the elements of the mind are separated,
one's perception alters and the consciousness undergoes a
different experience.

With the awakening of kundalini, both hemispheres and
the dormant areas of the brain become active, perception
becomes independent of the sense organs, deeper states
of consciousness are entered, and then there is cosmic
experience. When individual consciousness has been
transcended and only cosmic experience exists, there is no
comprehension of individuality. Death is an experience of
the individual mind and body. If consciousness is universal,
then the individual body and mind are like one of the
millions of tiny body cells.

When a body cell dies or is reproduced, you do not feel
that you have died or you have just been born. However, if
your consciousness was limited to the cells, then you would
experience death and birth every minute. Because your
consciousness exists in the body as a whole, you do not feel
this momentary death and birth process. Therefore, when
you experience the cosmos as a whole, there can be no death
and no birth, only experience of the process in its entirety.

सुषुम्ना शून्यपदवी ब्रह्मरंध्रं महापथ: ।
श्मशानं शांभवी मध्यमार्गश्चेत्येकवाचका: ॥ ४ ॥

Sushumna, shoonya padavi, brahmarandhra, maha patha, shmashan, shambhavi, madhya marga, are all said to be one and the same.

There are various names given to sushumna. The potential of sushumna is present in every aspect of our being from the physical to the subtle levels. On the physical level it functions in accordance with the central nervous system. On the pranic level it is the period when the breath flows through both nostrils and is also known to be the gap between inhalation and exhalation. It is when apana and prana are brought together. According to biorhythms, it is the period between the high and low cycles which is called the 'caution day'.

Sushumna functions at the time when there is a changeover from one brain hemisphere to the other. Then the whole brain is active and the mind is neither fully extroverted not introverted; it operates in both states and there is equilibrium between mental and physical energy. It is the period between the dream and waking states, when you are awake but beyond empirical consciousness and control, when you are drifting.

This condition is known as the path of void, or *shoonya padavi*; the great pathway, *maha patha*; cremation ground, *shmashan*; the attitude of Shiva, *shambhavi*; the middle pathway, *madhya marga*. Sushumna is associated with the subtlest aspect of existence, the soul or atma, and it is related to the faculty of wisdom.

Sushumna is the central point, state, or condition between all extreme conditions, internal and external. It is the period when day meets night at sunrise or sunset, known as *sandhya*. In tantra it is related to the subterranean river called Saraswati. Geographically sushumna is represented by the equator.

In the following chart the different manifestations representing sushumna, ida and pingala are given.

Sushumna	Ida	Pingala
androgynous	feminine	masculine
sunrise/sunset	night	day
tao	yin	yang
kundalini shakti	chitta shakti	prana shakti
supramental	mental	vital
neutral	negative	positive
cosmic light	moon	sun
temperate	cold	hot
wisdom	intuition	logic
knowledge	desire	action
unconscious mind	subconscious mind	conscious mind
centred	internal	external
balanced	passive	active
awareness	subjective	objective
central nervous system	parasympathetic nervous system	sympathetic nervous system
Saraswati	Ganga	Yamuna
yellow	blue	red
Rudra (in dormancy)	Brahma	Vishnu
tamas	sattwa	rajas
sattwa (after awakening)	tamas	rajas
'M'	'U'	'A'
nada	bindu	bija
pratyaya	shabda	artha

तस्मात्सर्वप्रयत्नेन प्रबोधयितुमीश्वरीम् ।
ब्रह्मद्वारमुखे सुप्तां मुद्राभ्यासं समाचरेत् ॥ 5 ॥

Therefore, the goddess sleeping at the entrance of Brahma's door should be constantly aroused with all effort by performing mudra thoroughly.

Mudra is a specific body position which channels the energy produced by asana and pranayama into the various centres, and arouses particular states of mind. Some mudras are done separately after asana and pranayama and others are performed with asana and pranayama to help awaken the chakras and arouse kundalini shakti. They can also arouse specific emotions. When the pranic level is increased and the conscious mind withdraws, mudras occur spontaneously. The hands, feet, eyes, arms and legs move slowly into definite positions like those of Indian dancers. Through mudras you invoke specific qualities of Shakti or Devi and can become overwhelmed by that power.

Kundalini is often depicted as a goddess. At the level of mooladhara it manifests as Kali and Dakini. In the tantra shastras it says that the Shakti in mooladhara is in the form of a sixteen-year old girl in the first full bloom of youth, with large, beautifully shaped breasts and adorned with various types of jewels. She is red in colour with ever restless eyes. In *Kankalamalini Tantra* it says that the Shakti in front of Brahma's door is resplendent like millions of moons rising simultaneously, has four arms and three eyes and is seated on a lion.

As kundalini ascends through each chakra her form changes until she unites with her lord, Shiva, in sahasrara. Then there is no individuality; energy and consciousness are one and they manifest in the form of pure light. The various aspects of Shakti indicate different stages in the evolution of energy and consciousness, and as an aspirant awakens each chakra he will manifest some of the attributes of the related devi.

286

महामुद्रा महाबंधो महावेधश्च खेचरी ।
उड्डीयानं मूलबंधश्च बंधो जालंधराभिध: ॥ 6 ॥

Maha mudra, maha bandha, maha vedha, khechari, uddiyana, moola bandha and jalandhara bandha.

करणी विपरीताख्या वज्रोली शक्तिचालनम् ।
इदं हि मुद्रादशकं जरामरणनाशनम् ॥ 7 ॥

Vipareeta karani mudra, vajroli and shakti chalana, verily, these are the ten mudras which destroy old age and death.

If one makes a study of the different hatha yoga texts, there is likely to be some confusion when it comes to mudras and bandhas. Some practices are referred to as mudras in one text and as bandhas in another. In different texts the same practices may be described, but they might also have different names.

In particular, one could easily be confused about jalandhara, uddiyana and moola bandhas. In the ancient tantric scriptures these practices were defined as mudras (attitudes), not bandhas. Then, during the periods when tantric practices were prevalent, it seems they were not considered as separate practices, but their combination was called *maha mudra* 'the great attitude'.

When the system of hatha yoga was culled from the tantric practices, some of the practices were redefined and mudras and bandhas were separated. Now jalandhara, uddiyana and moola are defined as bandhas, but their combination becomes a mudra.

In this sloka, the most important mudras and bandhas have been listed: *maha mudra*, the great attitude, *maha bandha*, the great lock, *maha vedha mudra*, the great piercing attitude, *khechari mudra*, the attitude of dwelling in supreme consciousness, *uddiyana bandha*, the abdominal retraction lock, *moola bandha*, perineum or cervix retraction lock, *jalandhara bandha*, throat lock, *vipareeta karani mudra*, the attitude of reversing, *shakti chalana mudra*, the attitude of moving or circulating the energy. One more important mudra of hatha yoga which is not listed here is *shambhavi mudra*, eyebrow centre gazing. This is discussed in Chapter 4 in connection with samadhi.

आदिनाथोदितं दिव्यमष्टैश्वर्यप्रदायकम् ।
वल्लभं सर्वसिद्धानां दुर्लभं मरुतामपि ॥ 8 ॥

*Adinath said they are the bestowers of the eight divine powers. They
are held in high esteem by all the siddhas and are difficult for even
the gods to attain.*

Perfection of asana and pranayama results in minor
siddhis, or perfections, i.e. vitality, good health, mental
and emotional equilibrium, clairaudience, etc. However,
perfection of mudras and bandhas results in attainment
of major siddhis such as anima, mahima, garima, prapti,
prakamya, vasitva, ishatva, which are described in Chapter 1.

In the *Yoga Sutras* also these eight siddhis are listed and
are called *ashta siddhi*. However, Patanjali emphasizes that
siddhis should not be sought and, if they develop, they
should virtually be ignored and definitely not exhibited.
According to him, they are obstacles on the path to samadhi
and they can completely hinder one's spiritual evolution.
Therefore, although mudras and bandhas can bestow divine
powers, they should not be practised for this purpose.

गोपनीयं प्रयत्नेन यथा रत्नकरंडकम् ।
कस्यचिन्नैव वक्तव्यं कुलस्त्रीसुरतं यथा ॥ 9 ॥

These must remain secret just like precious stones, and not be talked about to anyone, just as one does not tell others about his intimate relations with his wife.

We are repeatedly reminded that neither the practices, the siddhis, nor the sadhana can be divulged to anyone. It is the guru's decision who should be given the knowledge, and it can only be gained through experience. There is no merit in trying to share one's spiritual experiences with another.

MAHA MUDRA (the great attitude)

अथ महामुद्रा ।

पादमूलेन वामेन योनिं संपीड्य दक्षिणम् ।
प्रसारितं पदं कृत्वा कराभ्यां धारयेद्दृढम् ॥ 10 ॥

Press the left heel into the perineum (or vagina), straighten the right leg, and with the hands, firmly take hold of the outstretched foot.

कंठे बंधं समारोप्य धारयेद्वायुमूर्ध्वतः ।
यथा दंडहतः सर्पो दंडाकारः प्रजायते ॥ 11 ॥

By locking the throat and retaining the breath, the prana rises straight, just like a snake beaten with a stick becomes straight.

ऋज्वीभूता तथा शक्तिः कुंडली सहसा भवेत् ।
तदा सा मरणावस्था जायते द्विपुटाश्रया ॥ 12 ॥

So the kundalini shakti becomes straight at once. Then the two (ida and pingala) become lifeless as the shakti enters sushumna.

ततः शनैः शनैरेव रेचयेन्नैव वेगतः ।
महामुद्रां च तेनैव वदंति विबुधोत्तमाः ॥ 13 ॥

Then exhale slowly and gradually, not quickly. Indeed this is described as maha mudra by the great siddhas.

Although maha mudra is a technique of hatha yoga it is also one of the kriya yoga practices. It involves asana, kumbhaka, mudra and bandha, and makes a powerful pranic lock which spontaneously arouses meditation.

BSY©

Technique I

Sit with the right leg stretched in front, bend the left knee and press the heel into the perineum or vagina. This posture is called utthanpadasana.

Exhaling, lean forward and grasp the big toe of the right foot.

Keep the head erect, eyes closed and the back straight. Relax in the position.

Perform khechari mudra, then slowly inhale, tilting the head slightly backwards and perform shambhavi mudra (gaze at the eyebrow centre).

Hold the breath inside (antar kumbhaka) and perform moola bandha (contraction of the perineum or cervix).

Rotate your awareness from the eyebrow centre to the throat and base of the spine, mentally repeating 'ajna, vishuddhi, mooladhara' or 'shambhavi, khechari, moola', while retaining the breath.

Continue for as long as you can hold the breath without straining.

Then close the eyes, release moola bandha, lower the head into its normal position and exhale slowly.

This is one round.

Practise three times with the left leg folded, change the position and do it on the right side three times. Then keep both legs stretched in front, as in paschimottan-asana and again perform the practice three times.

Maha mudra should be done after asana and pranayama and before meditation. You should only increase the number of rounds when instructed by your teacher or guru.

Technique 2

If you cannot sit comfortably in utthanpadasana you can practise in siddhasana/siddha yoni asana.

Sit with the hands on the knees in jnana or chin mudra and practise in the same way, but without bending forward.

Practise five to ten times.

The kriya yoga practice of maha mudra incorporates ujjayi pranayama, khechari mudra, awareness of arohan and awarohan passages and the chakras, and unmani mudra. The hatha yoga variation is a good preparation for the kriya yoga technique which should not be attempted without the guru's instruction.

इयं खलु महामुद्रा महासिद्धै: प्रदर्शिता ।
महाक्लेशादयो दोषा: क्षीयंते मरणादय: ।
महामुद्रां च तेनैव वदंति विबुधोत्तमा: ॥ 14 ॥

*Maha mudra removes the worst afflictions (the five kleshas) and the
cause of death. Therefore it is called 'the great attitude' by the ones
of highest knowledge.*

From the practice of maha mudra the combined benefits
of shambhavi mudra, moola bandha, kumbhaka, paschimottanasana and utthanpadasana are gained. In the *Yoga
Chudamani Upanishad* it says: "Maha mudra is a practice
which purifies the entire network of nadis, balances ida and
pingala and absorbs rasa or health-giving fluid so that it
pervades one's entire being." (v. 65)

Maha mudra clears the nadis and particularly stimulates
the flow of sushumna. It increases one's vitality, stimulates
digestion and harmonizes all bodily functions. It also
increases one's awareness, brings about clarity of thought and
helps one to overcome depression.

चंद्रांगे तु समभ्यस्य सूर्यांगे पुनरभ्यसेत् ।
यावत्तुल्या भवेत्संख्या ततो मुद्रां विसर्जयेत् ॥ 15 ॥

After practising on the left side, practise on the right side. When the number of rounds is even, discontinue and release the mudra.

As in all asana and pranayama practices, it is important to practise an equal number of times on both sides. Some people have misinterpreted this sloka by saying the practice should be done first by breathing through the left nostril and later the right. The words indicating left side are *chandra anga*. *Chandra* is 'moon', *anga* 'part', 'limb' or 'side'. Chandra can also mean ida nadi or the left nostril. Similarly, *surya anga* indicates the right side. Surya or sun is pingala nadi and can mean the right nostril. Thus there is some discrepancy whether a particular side of the body or flow of breath is being intimated.

However, it should be understood that the correct method of practising maha mudra is with the left leg folded first and then the right leg. Let us examine this from a practical point of view. How can you possibly practise comfortably while holding the nose and the toes? It may be possible to breathe in through the left nostril while sitting straight, but it is not usual to practise in such a way. You should breathe through both nostrils and hold the toes of the outstretched leg with both hands. After practising three to twelve rounds on one side, the same number of rounds should be performed on the other side. Then the same number of rounds should be repeated with both legs stretched in front of the body.

न हि पथ्यमपथ्यं वा रसा: सर्वेऽपि नीरसा: ।
अपि भुक्तं विषं घोरं पीयूषमपि जीर्यति ॥ 16 ॥

For one who practises maha mudra, there is nothing wholesome or unwholesome. Anything can be consumed, even the deadliest of poisons is digested like nectar.

Through the practice of maha mudra, digestion and assimilation of both food and prana are stimulated. Although it is said that the practitioner can even consume deadly poisons and be unaffected, it would surely take many years of practice to achieve this state. The benefits of maha mudra are equal and above those of mayurasana, and it is essentially more dynamic on a pranic and psychic level.

क्षयकुष्ठगुदावर्तगुल्माजीर्णपुरोगमा: ।
तस्य दोषा: क्षयं यान्ति महामुद्रां तु योऽभ्यसेत् ॥ 17 ॥

Abdominal disorders, constipation, indigestion and leprosy, etc., are alleviated by the practice of maha mudra.

कथितेयं महामुद्रा महासिद्धिकरा नृणाम् ।
गोपनीया प्रयत्नेन न देया यस्य कस्यचित् ॥ 18 ॥

Thus maha mudra has been described as the giver of great siddhis. It must be kept secret and not disclosed to anyone.

Maha mudra stimulates the shakti in the energy circuit from mooladhara to ajna chakra and its effects can be strongly felt on a psychic level. Physiologically it stimulates the digestive capacity; pranically it generates circulation of energy in the chakras; psychologically it develops the mind and inner awareness, and psychically it arouses receptivity.

Maha mudra rapidly eliminates mental depression as it removes all energy blockages which are the fundamental cause of the problem. The practice stills the mind and body and increases one's sensitivity to subtle experiences. It is therefore a highly recommended and powerful preparatory practice for meditation.

MAHA BANDHA (great lock)

अथ महाबन्ध: ।

पार्ष्णिं वामस्य पादस्य योनिस्थाने नियोजयेत् ।
वामोरूपरि संस्थाप्य दक्षिणं चरणं तथा ॥ 19 ॥

Press the heel of the left foot in the perineum/vagina and place the right foot on the left thigh.

पूरयित्वा ततो वायुं हृदये चुबुकं दृढम् ।
निष्पीड्यं वायुमाकुंच्य मनोमध्ये नियोजयेत् ॥ 20 ॥

Thus breathing in, bring the chin to the chest (jalandhara bandha), contract the perineal/cervical region (moola bandha) and concentrate on the eyebrow centre (shambhavi mudra).

धारयित्वा यथाशक्ति रेचयेदनिलं शनै: ।
सव्यांगे तु समभ्यस्य दक्षांगे पुनरभ्यसेत् ॥ 21 ॥

Having retained the breath as long as comfortable, exhale slowly. Once completing the practice on the left side, practise again on the right side.

मतमत्र तु केषांचित्कंठबंधं विवर्जयेत् ।
राजदंतस्थजिह्वाया बंध: शस्तो भवेदिति ॥ 22 ॥

Some are of the opinion that the throat lock (jalandhara bandha) is unnecessary and it is sufficient to keep the tongue against the front teeth.

Maha bandha is the 'great lock'. According to these slokas, the *Gherand Samhita* and *Hatharatnavali*, it consists of internal breath retention or antar kumbhaka, jalandhara, moola bandha and shambhavi mudra. However, maha bandha is also done with external breath retention, jalandhara, uddiyana and moola bandhas, which is later referred to in slokas 74 to 76. Today maha bandha is generally practised with external breath retention and the three bandhas; shambhavi mudra is optional. According to the *Gherand Samhita*, when uddiyana bandha is employed, then the practice becomes maha vedha mudra but the *Hatha Yoga Pradipika* says maha vedha is an entirely different practice.

Again we have to remember that any discrepancy in the practices of mudra and bandha is due to the fact that the techniques were extracted from tantra in which there was no distinction between mudra and bandha.

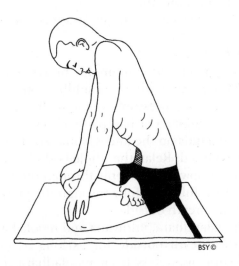

Technique 1: Hatha yoga technique

Sit in half padmasana with the left heel pressing the perineum/vagina and the right foot on top of the left thigh.

Prepare yourself as for any meditation practice.

Breathe in slowly through the left nostril and perform antar kumbhaka (internal breath retention), then jalandhara and moola bandhas and shambhavi mudra.

The eyes may be kept closed throughout the practice with concentration on bhrumadhya during retention.

Hold kumbhaka, the bandhas and shambhavi for as long as comfortable.

Before exhaling, release shambhavi mudra, then moola bandha and lastly jalandhara.

When the head is upright and the shoulders are relaxed, exhale slowly through the right nostril.

Then breathe in slowly through the right nostril and practise as described above. When exhaling, breathe through the left nostril.

This is one round. Before starting the next round, breathe normally for a minute or two and concentrate on the natural breath.

Practise three rounds initially and increase up to five.

Technique 2

Maha bandha is most commonly practised as follows:
Preferably sit in siddhasana/siddha yoni asana as this posture applies pressure to mooladhara, or you can assume padmasana or half padmasana.

Keep the hands on the knees, spine erect, head straight and eyes closed. Relax the whole body.

Breathe in slowly and deeply through the nose.

Exhale forcefully and fully through the pursed lips.

Retain the breath outside.

Perform jalandhara, uddiyana and moola bandhas.

Keep the breath outside for as long as possible and rotate your awareness from mooladhara to manipura to vishuddhi, mentally repeating the names of these chakras as you concentrate on each.

When you can no longer retain the breath, release moola, uddiyana and lastly jalandhara, and inhale slowly in a controlled manner.

Keep the eyes closed, make sure the body is completely relaxed and breathe naturally, concentrating on the spontaneous breath.

Then practise again following exactly the same process.
Perform three rounds in the beginning.

After many months, when you are proficient, increase by one round every second, third or fourth day, until you are practising nine rounds. Continual practice over the years will result in spontaneous cessation of the breath, even after kumbhaka is released. You may take one or two normal breaths and then the breathing will stop automatically. Let this happen and just watch how long it lasts.

Maha bandha can be practised between each round of bhastrika pranayama. In fact, it is better to practise it in conjunction with bhastrika because kumbhaka can then be easily held for a longer time.

Before attempting maha bandha you will need to be proficient in the practice of the three individual bandhas. People suffering from high or low blood pressure, hernia, stomach or intestinal ulcer, or those recovering from any visceral ailment, will have to correct their condition before attempting maha bandha. In fact, good health is necessary for this practice.

अयं तु सर्वनाडीनामूर्ध्वं गतिनिरोधक: ।
अयं खलु महाबंधो महासिद्धिप्रदायक: ॥ 23 ॥

This stops the upward movement of energy in the nadis. Verily this maha bandha is the bestower of great siddhis.

कालपाशमहाबंधविमोचनविचक्षण: ।
त्रिवेणीसंगमं धत्ते केदारं प्रापयेन्मन: ॥ 24 ॥

Maha bandha frees one from the bonds of death, makes the three nadis unite in ajna chakra and enables the mind to reach the sacred seat of Shiva, Kedara.

In maha bandha, shakti is locked within the torso; it cannot leak out through any channel and it recirculates upwards. When the hands are also in chin or jnana mudra, prana cannot leave the body through the hands, it flows back up the arms to the heart. Moola bandha forces the prana upwards and prevents it from escaping through the lower outlets, and jalandhara prevents an upward leakage. When uddiyana bandha is added, prana and apana are forced towards each other, to eventually meet in the navel centre. When the two opposite poles of energy unite in the navel centre, they are forced upward to ajna. This affects the hormonal secretions of the pineal gland and regulates the entire endocrinal system. The decaying, degenerating and ageing processes are then checked and every cell of the body is rejuvenated.

From a psychological point of view, when ida and pingala merge with sushumna in ajna, the limited external and internal awareness is transcended and the attitude of the witness, *sakshi*, automatically develops. More than this though, Yogi Swatmarama says that 'the mind attains the seat of Shiva'. Shiva is pure consciousness and represents the highest conscious capacity of man. It is also another way of saying that the individual soul, or *jivatma*, returns to the paramatma or that one attains cosmic consciousness.

रूपलावण्यसंपन्ना यथा स्त्री पुरुषं विना ।
महामुद्रामहाबंधौ निष्फलौ वेधवर्जितौ ॥ 25 ॥

Just as an extremely beautiful woman is nothing without a husband, so maha mudra and maha bandha are unfruitful without maha vedha mudra.

Maha bandha is a complete practice which can awaken the entire pranic capacity in the main chakras, but it should be followed by another systematic practice, maha vedha mudra. The purpose of maha vedha mudra is to channel the prana accumulated through maha mudra and maha bandha. When you perform these practices without maha vedha mudra, it is like having a car full of petrol, turning the ignition on but keeping the foot on the brake. To get the car moving you must slowly release the brake and steer it in a calculated manner. Similarly, when kundalini shakti has been awakened through maha mudra and maha bandha, it must be released and directed by the practice of maha vedha mudra.

Yogi Swatmarama compares the necessity and inter-relationship of these practices to a woman without a husband. A woman who is husbandless is unproductive and her beauty is not fully appreciated either by herself or a husband. Or, if she uses her beauty for the pleasure of many men, her charm and prana will quickly diminish. The same applies to maha bandha and maha mudra. Maha vedha channels the shakti created by these two. If many other practices are performed, the energy may go back into ida or pingala or may even go down to mooladhara again. Therefore, you must know the correct sequence for gaining the most from these practices.

MAHA VEDHA MUDRA (great piercing attitude)

अथ महावेध: ।

महाबंधस्थितो योगी कृत्वा पूरकमेकधी: ।
वायूनां गतिमावृत्य निभृतं कंठमुद्रया ॥ 26 ॥

*The yogi, in the position of maha bandha, should inhale, make the
mind steady and stop the movement of prana by performing the
throat lock.*

समहस्तयुगो भूमौ स्फिचौ संताडयेच्छनै: ।
पुटद्वयमतिक्रम्य वायु: स्फुरति मध्यग: ॥ 27 ॥

*Placing the palms of the hands on the ground, he should slowly
beat the buttocks gently on the ground. The prana (then) leaves the
two nadis (ida and pingala) and enters into the middle channel
(sushumna).*

सोमसूर्याग्निसंबंधो जायते चामृताय वै ।
मृतावस्था समुत्पन्ना ततो वायुं विरेचयेत् ॥ 28 ॥

*Ida, pingala and sushumna become united and verily, immortality is
attained. A death-like state occurs; then the breath should be exhaled.*

Maha vedha means 'the great piercer'. Through this practice
the kundalini shakti is forced into sushumna and up to
ajna chakra by gently beating the buttocks on the floor.
The hatha yoga technique described here should not be
confused with the kriya yoga practice of maha bheda mudra
which is similar to maha mudra. The technique described in
this sloka is similar to tadan kriya of kriya yoga. Today the
practice is usually adapted and taught without jalandhara
bandha. However, Swatmarma's technique is as follows.

Technique

Sit in padmasana. If you have not perfected padmasana, you will not be able to practise properly.

Relax the body and keep the eyes closed.

Place the palms of the hands on the floor beside the thighs.

Inhale slowly and deeply through the nose.

Retain the breath inside and perform jalandhara bandha.

Raise the body by placing all the weight on the hands, straighten the arms, and gently beat the buttocks on the ground from three to seven times, keeping your awareness in mooladhara. Then rest the buttocks on the floor, release jalandhara bandha, sit quietly and exhale slowly and deeply.

This is one round.

Let the breathing return to normal, then again inhale and repeat the process.

Practise three rounds in the beginning. After a few months you can gradually increase up to five rounds but no more.

When beating the buttocks you must be gentle. The buttocks and the backs of the thighs should touch the ground simultaneously. The spine must be kept straight and jalandhara bandha maintained. When you complete the practice, sit quietly and concentrate on mooladhara chakra for a few minutes.

महावेधोऽयमभ्यासान्महासिद्धिप्रदायक: ।
वलीपलितवेपघ्न: सेव्यते साधकोत्तमै: ॥ 29 ॥

This is maha vedha, and its practice bestows great perfections.
Wrinkles, grey hair and the trembling of old age are evaded, thus
the best of practitioners devote themselves to it.

Actually, all the practices of hatha yoga which help relax
the body and mind and which stimulate pranic capacity,
slow down the ageing process. Maha mudra and maha
vedha mudra are powerful techniques which introvert the
mind and awaken psychic faculties. They affect the pineal
and pituitary glands and thus the whole endocrinal system.
By activating the pineal gland, the pituitary is kept under
control, hormonal secretions are regulated and catabolism
is curtailed. Then the symptoms of old age are either
annihilated or reduced.

एतत्त्रयं महागुह्यं जरामृत्युविनाशनम् ।
वह्निवृद्धिकरं चैव ह्यणिमादिगुणप्रदम् ॥ 30 ॥

These are the three great secrets which destroy old age and death,
increase the digestive fire and bestow the siddhis of anima, etc.

अष्टधा क्रियते चैव यामे यामे दिने दिने ।
पुण्यसंभारसंधायि पापौघभिदुरं सदा ।
सम्यक्शिक्षावतामेवं स्वल्पं प्रथमसाधनम् ॥ 31 ॥

They should be done daily at every yama (three hour period). They
bring out the virtues and destroy vices. Those who have perfect
instructions should practise them gradually.

According to the yoga shastras, the twenty-four hour period
of a day is divided into sixteen parts, each of ninety minutes,
called *ghariya*; or eight periods of three hours, called *yama*.
In each period the flow of energy throughout the body varies
and different organs function more actively. Of course, as the
brain hemispheres alternate their functioning every sixty to
ninety minutes, one's mode of thinking also changes.

Yogi Swatmarama specifies that maha mudra, maha
bandha and maha vedha mudra should be practised during
each three hour period. Because they are then being
performed during different phases of the brain's cycle,
they must surely induce radical changes in the brain and
psychological structure of the practitioner.

It is obviously impossible for the average person to practise
so frequently, and it is not really recommended. It is quite
sufficient to practise in the morning and in the evening also if
time allows. We must keep in mind that the specifications laid
down in this text are for a recluse who lives away from society,
free from family and social obligations, and who is practising
directly under the guidance of a guru. If a householder were
to perform these practices so frequently, there would by very
little time and energy for anything else.

The man of today does not need to practise hatha yoga for hours and hours together. He is dynamic and needs to express himself through action and various interrelationships with people. Yoga must meet the demands of the various elements of his personality, and for this reason he needs a balanced combination of hatha yoga, karma yoga, bhakti yoga and jnana yoga.

Therefore, when we read the yoga texts, we have to view them in a very practical manner. We can practise the techniques according to the instructions given, but which techniques we should do and how much we practise has to be decided upon according to our own physical and mental capacity and the amount of time we can devote to sadhana. Of course, it is preferable if one has a guru to make the decisions.

KHECHARI MUDRA
(attitude of dwelling in supreme consciousness)

अथ खेचरी ।

कपालकुहरे जिह्वा प्रविष्टा विपरीतगा ।
भ्रुवोरंतर्गता दृष्टिर्मुद्रा भवति खेचरी ॥ 32 ॥

Khechari mudra is turning the tongue backwards into the cavity of the cranium and turning the eyes inwards towards the eyebrow centre.

छेदनचालनदोहै: कलां क्रमेण वर्धयेत्तावत् ।
सा यावद्भ्रूमध्यं स्पृशति तदा खेचरीसिद्धि: ॥ 33 ॥

The tongue should be exercised and milked and the underneath part cut away in small degrees. Indeed khechari is perfected when the tongue touches the eyebrow centre.

स्नुहीपत्रनिभं शस्त्रं सुतीक्ष्णं स्निग्धनिर्मलम् ।
समादाय ततस्तेन रोममात्रं समुच्छिनेत् ॥ 34 ॥

With a clean thin blade, gently cut away the membrane under the tongue. Cut it by a fine hair's breadth each time.

तत: सैन्धवपथ्याभ्यां चूर्णिताभ्यां प्रघर्षयेत् ।
पुन: सप्तदिने प्राप्ते रोममात्रं समुच्छिनेत् ॥ 35 ॥

Then rub in a mixture of powdered rock salt and turmeric. After seven days, again cut a hair's breadth.

एवं क्रमेण षण्मासं नित्यं युक्त: समाचरेत् ।
षण्मासाद्रसनामूलशिराबंध: प्रणश्यति ॥ 36 ॥

One should continue doing this regularly for six months, then the membrane at the root of the tongue will be completely severed.

Khechari mudra is also known as *nabho mudra*, and Swami Sivananda has called its practice *lambhika yoga*. There are two forms of khechari mudra. The one described here which involves the gradual cutting of the frenum and elongation of the tongue is the hatha yoga form, and only those who have detoxified their body and are advised by the guru should attempt it.

It is taught from an early age, twelve to sixteen years, during the period when the body is still developing. First the tongue has to be massaged and this is done by holding it with a piece of cloth and gently stretching it, and pulling it from side to side. Then the frenum lingue is very gradually cut with a sharp and sterilized blade. The process draws a little blood but there is no pain. After this the wound is wiped with turmeric powder and/or powdered rock salt, so that there can be no infection and healing will be quick.

The process of 'milking', i.e. rubbing and stretching, is done every day; cutting is done on alternate days, or every few days. When the tongue becomes elongated it is not possible to move it by itself into the nasal cavity, for this the fingers or a thin hooked instrument has to be used. In order for the tongue to reach the 'eyebrow centre', it takes many years of practice.

The raja yoga form of khechari mudra is much simpler and can be performed by anyone. It is done by turning the tongue back so that the under surface touches the upper back portion of the soft palate and the tip of the tongue is inserted into the nasal orifice at the back of the throat if possible. The position should be maintained for as long as comfortable. At first it will be necessary to release the tongue every now and then, relax it and resume the mudra. This form of khechari is usually practised in conjunction with other practices such as japa, meditation and ujjayi pranayama and it is used in most of the kriya yoga techniques.

कलां पराङ्मुखीं कृत्वा त्रिपथे परियोजयेत् ।
सा भवेत्खेचरी मुद्रा व्योमचक्रं तदुच्यते ॥ 37 ॥

Having turned the tongue back, the three channels of ida, pingala and sushumna are controlled. This is khechari mudra and it is called the centre of ether.

Once the tongue has been sufficiently elongated, it has to be inserted into the nasal cavity at the back of the throat. This is not an easy process and at first it will be necessary to push the tongue into position with the fingers. When the tongue is strengthened, it can be pushed right into the back of the nasal cavity by itself, and when prana is awakened in the body, the tongue will move into that position spontaneously.

When the tongue is inserted right up into the nasal cavity, the breath can be directed into either nostril by the tip of the tongue. The tip of the tongue will be able to block the right or left passage or be placed a little lower so that both nostrils are open. To actually elongate the tongue to the extent that it can move up to the eyebrow centre will take many years of consistent practice.

रसनामूर्ध्वगां कृत्वा क्षणार्धमपि तिष्ठति ।
विषैर्विमुच्यते योगी व्याधिमृत्युजरादिभिः ॥ 38 ॥

The yogi who remains with the tongue going upwards for even half a second is freed from toxins, disease, death, old age, etc.

न रोगो मरणं तंद्रा न निद्रा न क्षुधा तृषा ।
न च मूर्च्छा भवेत्तस्य यो मुद्रां वेत्ति खेचरीम् ॥ 39 ॥

One who accomplishes this khechari mudra is neither troubled by diseases, nor death, lassitude, sleep, hunger, thirst or unconsciousness.

If the tongue can reach the eyebrow centre internally, the pineal gland, and also ajna chakra, will be stimulated. There is a close relationship between the pineal gland, the throat centre and another psychic centre situated in the upper palate, known as *lalana chakra. Bindu visarga*, the psychic centre at the top back of the head, is also influenced by khechari mudra. *Bindu* is said to be the place where the moon resides and when it is full it sheds its nectar or ambrosial fluid down to permeate the entire body, just as the external moon pours its light over the surface of the earth at the time of the full moon.

Khechari mudra exerts a controlling influence upon the network of endocrine glands throughout the body. This is achieved by regulating the production of the powerful secretions of the brain itself, which are produced in tiny amounts to control the pituitary gland and thereby the whole orchestra of glands associated with the centres below ajna. These dependent glands include the thyroid, mammary, thymus, adrenal and reproductive glands, as well as many other dependent processes which continually go on in the body.

The practice of khechari mudra also influences the centres in the hypothalamus and brain stem which control autonomic breathing, heart rate, emotional expression, appetite and thirst. The hypothalamus is strongly connected with the thalamus and the RAS (Reticular Activating System), which assumes a vital role in sleep and wake mechanisms and all degrees of central nervous system activities, including the ability to concentrate.

The practice also influences the salivary gland and the faculty of taste, which in turn are also connected to the lower nerve plexuses involved in the digestive and assimilative processes. Knowing these neuro-endocrinal functions of the brain, we can better understand this sloka concerning the powerful effects of khechari mudra on human psycho-physiology and destiny.

पीड्यते न स रोगेण लिप्यते न च कर्मणा ।
बाध्यते न स कालेन यो मुद्रां वेत्ति खेचरीम् ॥ 40 ॥

*One who knows khechari mudra is unafflicted by disease, unaffected
by the laws of cause and effect (karma) and free from the bonds of
time (death).*

चित्तं चरति खे यस्माज्जिह्वा चरति खे गता ।
तेनैषा खेचरी नाम मुद्रा सिद्धैर्निरूपिता ॥ 41 ॥

*Mind moves in Brahman (khe) because the tongue moves in
space (khe). Therefore, the perfected ones have named this mudra
khechari, moving in space or Brahman.*

One who knows khechari mudra is one who has experienced
and perfected it. The Sanskrit word *vetti*, meaning
'knowledge', refers to knowledge through experience, not
knowledge through an intellectual concept.

The benefits attributed to khechari mudra are those
which result from experience of supraconsciousness or
samadhi. Here we are told that khechari is so powerful that
the practitioner can reach a state beyond karma (i.e. cause
and effect), time, death and disease. These are all aspects
of the influence of Shakti or maya. The state of supraconsciousness is that of universal awareness, beyond duality
and the finite mind. It is called kaivalya, nirvana, moksha,
samadhi or Brahma. These are all synonymous terms
indicating the final stage or accomplishment of raja yoga.

Khechari mudra directly influences brain functions and
awakens the higher centres of awareness. Our mind functions
within the confines of time and space, ida and pingala, but
it is possible to transcend these two poles of duality. Normal
brain functions have to undergo a transformation and
restructuring so that supernormal functioning takes place.

Time and space are concepts of the finite mind and
perception. In yoga and tantra they are said to be the tools

of maya, prakriti or Shakti. They are laws of nature, and the finite mind is a product of nature. If you can expand the consciousness beyond the awareness of the finite mind and natural phenomena, the consciousness will enter the realm of the infinite.

खेचर्या मुद्रितं येन विवरं लंबिकोर्ध्वतः ।
न तस्य क्षरते बिन्दुः कामिन्याः श्लेषितस्य च ॥ ४२ ॥

When the upper cavity of the palate is sealed by khechari mudra,
the bindu or semen cannot be lost even if one embraces a beautiful
woman.

चलितोऽपि यदा बिंदुः संप्राप्तो योनिमंडलम् ।
व्रजत्यूर्ध्वं हृतः शक्तया निबद्धो योनिमुद्रया ॥ ४३ ॥

Even when there is movement of the bindu and it enters the genitals,
it is seized by closing the perineum and is taken upward.

The effect of khechari mudra on the endocrine system and
the pineal gland has already been discussed. If one has
control of the reproductive fluid, one has control of nature,
the body and the mind. Of course, it is not easy to develop
this control, but hatha yoga provides the methods. Khechari
mudra regulates hormonal production and activity in the
brain centres and there are other practices to directly control
the secretory behaviour of the reproductive organs.

ऊर्ध्वजिह्व: स्थिरो भूत्वा सोमपानं करोति य: ।
मासार्धेन न संदेहो मृत्युं जयति योगवित् ॥ 44 ॥

With the tongue directed upwards, the knower of yoga drinks the
fluid of the moon. Within fifteen days physical death is conquered.

नित्यं सोमकलापूर्णं शरीरं यस्य योगिन: ।
तक्षकेणापि दष्टस्य विषं तस्य न सर्पति ॥ 45 ॥

The yogi's body is forever full of the moon's nectar. Even if he is
bitten by the king of snakes (Takshaka), he is not poisoned.

'Drinking the fluid or nectar of the moon' is drinking or
assimilating the fluid released from bindu visarga. Bindu
is always depicted as a full moon. The nectar produced in
bindu is said to intoxicate the conscious mind and make the
body resistant to toxins in the system.

At a certain stage of spiritual evolution this is an
inevitable process which takes place irrespective of the type
of yoga you practise. There is a well-known story about
Meera Bai, one of the greatest saints and bhaktas of India.
Her devotion to Lord Krishna was so intense that she lived
in constant ecstasy through remembering him. Even when
her mother-in-law fed her deadly poison she remained
unaffected. People say that Lord Krishna turned the poison
into rose water or milk. Actually, her system was immune to
it because of the 'flow of nectar from the bindu'.

According to hatha yoga, if the practice of khechari
mudra can be perfected, after two weeks the process of
degeneration in the body is reversed. However, it takes a
long time to perfect khechari, but one should consider the
fact that during the process of perfecting it, the body is
slowly readjusting itself and, once it is perfected, it will only
take a short time to release the fluid from bindu.

इंधनानि यथा वह्निस्तैलवर्त्तिं च दीपक: ।
तथा सोमकलापूर्णं देही देहं न मुंचति ॥ 46 ॥

Just as fuel kindles fire and oil a lamp, so the indweller of the body does not vacate while the body is full of the moon's nectar.

गोमांसं भक्षयेन्नित्यं पिबेदमरवारुणीम् ।
कुलीनं तमहं मन्ये चेतरे कुलघातका: ॥ 47 ॥

By constant swallowing of the tongue he can drink amaravaruni. I consider him of high lineage (heritage). Others destroy the heritage.

In the previous slokas it has been said that death occurs when prana leaves the body. It is the twofold force of prana which maintains life; the vital life-giving aspect and the force of will or desire. As long as desires remain unfulfilled, as long as the will to live is strong, and so long as the vitality exists, the consciousness remains in the body. Through the practice of khechari, the prana is maintained in the body even while the consciousness moves into the higher realms during samadhi. This is achieved by channelling the total pranic force through sushumna.

The process involves the release of the body fluid the yogis call amaravaruni. *Amara* refers to immortality or the moon and *varuni* is wine. *Amaravaruni* is the wine of immortality or of the moon. This wine is the chemical fluid secreted by bindu visarga. It is the nectar of pure consciousness.

Just as the result of the union between a man and a woman is the release of reproductive secretions, so the union of ida and pingala with sushumna in ajna chakra releases the fluid from bindu. At that time one experiences the climax of spiritual experience which is more fulfilling than any empirical experience. With the release of amaravaruni the body is impregnated with spiritual or cosmic force and gives birth to higher consciousness or atman.

The physical body is the feminine principle of Shakti. Mind is the masculine principle of Shiva, consciousness. The union of the two is realization of the indweller, the Self.

Yogi Swatmarama says that the person who can drink amaravaruni is from a worthy or high lineage. Those who live, procreate and die without attaining any spiritual knowledge have not been fulfilling the purpose of life or evolution. They are only continuing the generations of families. However, once a person endeavours to know the spirit or pure consciousness, the whole physical structure undergoes a rearrangement and even the genes of that person change, consequently, the generations that follow are influenced by the achievements made in sadhana. The children of such a person, and their children, have a greater chance of achieving the same perfections. Therefore, the person who can drink amaravaruni is truly venerable to their family.

गोशब्देनोदिता जिह्वा तत्प्रवेशो हि तालुनि ।
गोमांसभक्षणं तत्तु महापातकनाशनम् ॥ 48 ॥

*The word 'go' means tongue (and also means cow). When it enters
into the upper palate, it is 'eating the flesh of the cow'. It (khechari)
destroys the great sins.*

Here Yogi Swatmarama clarifies the meaning of 'eating cow's
flesh'. *Gomansa* is the tongue and should not be literally
interpreted to mean 'cow's meat'. When the tongue is
swallowed back up into the nasal cavity that is called 'eating
cow's meat' in hatha yoga.

Of course, if you ask a non-vegetarian to eat meat it
would not sound unusual, but to the majority of Hindus it
would be considered sacrilegious. In fact, for any Hindu, to
eat cow's meat is one of the worst crimes and it incurs the
worst karma. A Hindu considers a cow most sacred; it is
worshipped as a form of Devi. Therefore, Swatmarama has
had to elucidate on the practice of eating cow's meat.

The practice of khechari is said to destroy 'the great
sins'. What are these sins? There are many variants of
five great sins described in both yogic and Buddhist texts
alike. Some define these as killing a Brahmin (one who
upholds spiritual values), drinking alcohol and losing your
senses, theft, adultery with the guru's wife and being in the
company of people who do such things. However, this is a
social and moralistic interpretation. In other texts we find
more personal reference to the five great sins as defects in
character, overt crimes are not stated but their cause within
the individual is defined – lust, greed, anger, fear, ignorance
and/or jealousy. These are also known as the 'six enemies' in
some texts.

How does khechari destroy the great sins? No matter how
much you practise khechari, once your desire or emotion
has pushed you into action and one of these defects has
manifested in your behaviour, or even one such sin has

been committed, it is not going to alter what you have done. However, becoming established in khechari can bring about a change in your consciousness so that you learn from the mistake and do not make it again, so that you learn how to manage these inner forces properly without an unnecessary residue of guilt or anxiety.

Khechari helps to overcome gross emotions and passions that compel you to react with anger, greed, etc. You can overhaul the very pattern of your thoughts and desires. In this way, we can say the sins are destroyed. However, let us not misunderstand sin in this context due to religious connotations; rather, let us see sins as obstacles to spiritual progress. These 'negative modes' of mind which grip the body and force you to act can become a powerful bondage to lower levels of awareness and can hinder further development. They are not to be suppressed, yet they have to be overcome and khechari mudra gives a direct method of doing so, by recognizing their subtle forms.

जिह्वाप्रवेशसंभूतवह्निनोत्पादितः खलु ।
चंद्रात्स्रवति यः सारः सा स्यादमरवारुणी ॥ 49 ॥

When the tongue enters the cavity, indeed heat is produced and the nectar flows from the moon.

By practising khechari mudra, heat is produced in the physical and subtle bodies. This is the same type of heat as that discussed previously in relation to pranayama. This heat is extremely important for the release of the 'nectar from the moon'. Just as metal becomes liquid when it is heated, ice becomes water and paraffin wax becomes liquid paraffin; so the nectar in the body which has 'solidified' begins to run like a fluid when it is heated. The release of this fluid within the body is extremely important for arousing a higher state of consciousness.

चुम्बंती यदि लंबिकाग्रमनिशं जिह्वारसस्यंदिनी
सक्षारा कटुकाम्लदुग्धसदृशी मध्वाज्यतुल्या तथा ।
व्याधीनां हरणं जरांतकरणं शस्त्रागमोदीरणं
तस्य स्यादमरत्वमष्टगुणितं सिद्धांगनाकर्षणम् ॥ 50 ॥

*When the tongue constantly presses the cavity, the moon's nectar
(flows and) has a saline, pungent and acidic flavour. It is like
(the consistency of) milk, ghee, honey. Fatal diseases, old age and
weapons are warded off. From that, immortality and the eight siddhis
or perfections manifest.*

The particular tastes attributed to the nectar are related
to the pancha tattwas. Each of the five tattwas – earth,
water, fire, air and ether, creates a definite flavour when
it predominates. Tattwas represent specific pranic flows
associated with the five vayus and each can be tasted when it
is active. According to the flavour, you can know which tattwa
is active. Earth tattwa is characterized by a sweet flavour,
water is astringent, fire is bitter, air is acidic and ether is
pungent or hot.

Apart from this factor, khechari mudra stimulates the
flow of mucus in the nasal cavity. When the mucus first
begins to flow, it is thick, but as the area becomes stimulated
and cleaned by the tongue, the mucus becomes more
refined.

मूर्ध्नः षोडशपत्रपद्मगलितं प्राणादवाप्तं हठा-
दूर्ध्वास्यो रसनां नियम्य विवरे शक्तिं परां चिंतयन् ।
उत्कल्लोलकलाजलं च विमलं धारामयं यः पिबे-
न्निर्व्याधिः स मृणालकोमलवपुर्योगी चिरं जीवति ॥ 51 ॥

*Fluid drips into the sixteen petalled lotus (vishuddhi chakra) when
the tongue is inserted into the upper throat cavity; the paramshakti
(kundalini) is released and one becomes concentrated in that
(experience which ensues). The yogi who drinks the pure stream of
nectar is freed from disease, has longevity, and has a body as soft and
as beautiful as a lotus stem.*

The sixteen petalled lotus spoken of in the sloka is vishuddhi
chakra. It describes the mechanism of consuming the
nectarine flow by khechari mudra. This is the technique of
preservation and rejuvenation adopted by the yogis to gain
radiant health, longevity and physical attractiveness.

When the tongue becomes flexible and can be inserted
into the upper epiglottis, a nectarine secretion begins
to flow. It drips from bindu visarga to soma, lalana and
vishuddhi chakras. Yogic texts are pervaded by the theme
of an immortal nectar and the techniques and practices by
which it can be trapped and consumed within the human
body. The divinization of man is considered to be a process
of physiology rather than a philosophical or religious idea.

The symbology of vishuddhi chakra and the nectar
is well-known in India. When the devas and asuras were
churning the ocean they extracted fourteen elements, two
of which were nectar and deadly poison. Neither of the two
parties wanted the poison, but both wanted the nectar. When
it came to the distribution of the nectar the devas and asuras
sat in two lines. Lord Vishnu disguised himself as a beautiful
young maiden and danced between the two lines, discreetly
pouring the nectar only into the glasses of the devas. One
asura sat in the deva's line and also received the nectar.

However, as he swallowed and it reached his throat, the Sun and Moon, who had been watching the whole situation, told Vishnu, who then destroyed the asura before the nectar had time to circulate through the body and endow him with immortality.

Now when the poison was extracted everyone was afraid. Whoever drank the poison would be finished, and yet there was no safe place to discard it either. If it was thrown away the three worlds would be burnt. So they took the poison to Lord Shiva to ask his help because he was the only one able to drink it without being destroyed. Shiva drank the poison and retained it in his throat. Therefore, he is often depicted with a blue throat and called 'Nilakantha'. This myth signifies the capacity of the yogi who has awakened vishuddhi chakra to assimilate both positive and negative aspects of life; to retain balance, health and equanimity in the midst of the dualities of pain and pleasure, light and dark, life and death, body and mind, etc.

Physiologically the myth has relevance to the thyroid gland in the front of the neck and its relationship with the pituitary gland. The thyroid gland is responsible for regulation of the body's metabolic rate. It differs from other endocrine glands in that it has the capacity to secrete and store the hormones synthesized by its secretory cells within the follicles of the gland itself, and these pooled secretions can be visualized as the nectar of vishuddhi.

The gland absorbs and concentrates iodine from the blood and uses it in the synthesis of two vital hormones: tri-iodothyronine (T3) and thyroxine (T4), which are the metabolically active products. Under the microscope, several week's supply of the concentrated hormonal stores, in colloidal form, are readily seen within the substance of the gland. Excess or inhibited secretion or consumption of thyroxine results in the two extremes of thyroid disease.

Thyroxine is essential in maintaining the normal activities of the central nervous system, body growth and movement, memory, thought process and speech, emotional and behavioural stability. It also exerts important effects upon the biochemistry of the liver, heart and skeletal muscles. It is essential in maintenance of the cells of the anterior pituitary, and has other important functions as well. Thus thyroid imbalance has far-reaching effects throughout the body.

Symptoms of hyperthyroidism (thyrotoxicosis) include tremulous personality, unstable emotions, poor memory, anxiety, palpitations and accelerated heart rate, accelerated gastric motility with diarrhoea, loss of weight, etc. In hypothyroidism, on the other hand, there is a general slowing of the mental and physical processes, including slowing of the speech and thought processes, obesity and heaviness, reduced and slowed physical movements, constipation, etc.

It is interesting to note that Swatmarama mentions the body becoming as soft as a lotus stem with the trapping of nectar because thyroxine maintains skin pliability and texture. In hypothyroidism the skin becomes dry and puffy, and with hyperthyroidism the skin becomes warm, moist and clammy. Correct proportion of thyroxine is clearly essential for balanced functioning of the body and mind. This is a part of the physiological aspect of the 'dripping of nectar'. Other effects of khechari have been discussed previously and will be discussed further in relation to bindu and amrit.

यत्राालेयं प्रहितसुषिरं मेरुमूर्धान्तरस्थं
तस्मिंस्तत्त्वं प्रवदति सुधीस्तन्मुखं निम्नगानाम् ।
चंद्रात् सार: स्रवति वपुषस्तेन मृप्युर्नराणां
तद्बध्नीयात्सुकरणमधो नान्यथा कार्यसिद्धि: ॥ 52 ॥

*The nectar is secreted from the topmost part of the Meru
(Sushumna), the fountainhead of the nadis. He who has pure
intellect can know the Truth therein. The nectar, which is the
essence of the body, flows out from the moon and hence death ensues.
Therefore khechari mudra should be practised, otherwise perfection
of the body cannot be attained.*

Meru is the name of a mythological mountain described in
the Puranas. It is also called *Sumeru*. Its fame is comparable
to Olympus in the north of Greece. The summit of Meru
is the abode of Brahma, devas and rishis. According to the
Tantraraja Tantra: "In the middle of Bhuloka (this physical
world and body) is the Meru made of gold, around which the
earth extends . . . and the seven oceans." All the planets are
said to revolve around the Meru. The river Ganga falls from
heaven onto its summit and flows down in four streams in
the four directions – north, south, east, west.

Although this story of Meru is mythological, it has
significance in relation to the physical and subtle bodies.
Meru is sushumna, the central axis. The summit is in the
middle of the head, in the region of ajna, lalana, soma and
manas chakras. Ganga is the descent of consciousness. Nectar
drips from bindu to lalana and then down to vishuddhi, etc.
It is actually not the flow of 'the moon's ambrosia' which
causes death, but its transformation into 'poison' which then
flows through the body.

सुषिरं ज्ञानजनकं पंचस्रोत:समन्वितम् ।
तिष्ठते खेचरी मुद्रा तस्मिन्शून्ये निरंजने ॥ 53 ॥

Five nadis convene in this cavity and it is the source of knowledge. Khechari should be established in that void, untainted (by ignorance).

When the tongue extends into the nasal cavity through the practice of khechari mudra, then four chakras in that area are affected: ajna – medulla oblongata; lalana – just below ajna and opposite the uvula (the fleshy appendage which projects from the soft palate); manas – directly above ajna; and soma – above manas, in the mid-cerebrum above the sensorium.

The five nadis which convene in this cavity are ida, pingala, sushumna, gandhari and hastijihva, which all merge into ajna.

एकं सृष्टिमयं बीजमेका मुद्रा च खेचरी ।
एको देवो निरालम्ब एकावस्था मनोन्मनी ॥ 54 ॥

There is only one seed of creation and one mudra – khechari; one deva independent of everything and one state – manonmani.

Bindu is the seed of creation and khechari mudra maintains bindu in the brain centre. This leads to the expansion of finite consciousness and realization of Shiva, Brahman, Atman. This is a state that transcends the mind; it is samadhi.

This sloka indicates the experience of oneness, union with the Supreme, which is realized by the yogi. There is an experience of oneness which is to be realized. There is only unity amidst seeming diversity; the many fragmentary experiences, seeming realities, individuals and distinctions we confront, are only elements of a greater Self, which includes all diversities and relative contradictions within itself. A yogi gains this experience by grasping within himself the bindu of consciousness. The unity of consciousness, creation and mind is comprehended by one who realizes the bindu; the seed from which all thoughts, minds, bodies, deities, devas and mudras spring forth.

The one who has steadied the bindu comprehends in a single, eternal, crystalline experience all the scattered and fragmentary pieces of individual and collective perception, knowledge and aspiration. He alone sees the world through the eye of Lord Shiva, the one who wishes well to all beings and sees only unity amidst apparent diversity.

Different men appear separate and distinct from one another, with distinguishing features and characteristics. However, from a greater standpoint these distinctions fall away and we can see that all men are essentially the same – all are born by the same process, with the same hopes and aspirations, fears and desires. Similarly, individual minds and personalities can be endlessly defined by their differences, but it is to their similarity that a yogi directs his attention. All minds are only minute parts and expressions of a single collective mind. To realize this collective mind in operation is called manonmani.

How is the yogi to realize within himself the entire creation in all its diversity, which has been studied in a thousand disciplines? Physics, chemistry, history, biology, geology, etc., are just a few of them. Even a lifespan of academic study could not hope to keep abreast of all these fields of research. Yogically, these types of knowledge are not absolute in themselves, but are the various aspects of a single creative seed and source, like rays emerging from the sun. The realization of creation, time and space, including his own body and mind, as the outpouring of the one cosmic maha bindu, is the attainment of a yogi.

Similarly, all the mudras and other practices of hatha yoga lead towards khechari, the attitude of unsupportedness in space; consciousness existing alone and independently; without a second. In the same way, all the devas, deities, gurus and evolved personalities are to be realized as the workpieces of a single absolute consciousness and experience.

How is the yogic aspirant to gain this experience of yoga? How to realize the one containing the many, and the unity within diversity? How to realize that he is none other than all names, forms, ages, times and personalities which have ever existed or will exist, to have the experience that all these are already within himself? How to span the seemingly infinite chasm between the individual and cosmic awareness? By realizing the bindu, the seed, the nada within his own body, mind and consciousness. By the outpouring of the bindu, one has become many. By its retention, many again become one.

UDDIYANA BANDHA (abdominal retraction lock)

अथोड्डीयानबन्धः ।

बद्धो येन सुषुम्नायां प्राणस्तूड्ड्डीयते यतः ।
तस्मादुड्ड्डीयनाख्योऽयं योगिभिः समुदाहृतः ॥ 55 ॥

Uddiyana bandha is so-called by the yogis because through its
practice the prana (is concentrated at one point and) rises through
sushumna.

उड्डीनं कुरुते यस्मादविश्रान्तं महाखगः ।
उड्डीयानं तदेव स्यात्तत्र बंधोऽभिधीयते ॥ 56 ॥

The bandha described is called the rising or flying bandha, because
through its practice, the great bird (shakti) flies upward with ease.

Yogi Swatmarama moves on to discuss the principal bandhas.
Bandha is generally considered to mean 'lock' as it literally
means 'to bind', 'to hold captive' or 'to contract'. Bandha is
a technique through which the opposite poles of energy, or
shakti, are bound together. Through contraction of muscles
and organs in the physical body, the shakti is accumulated
in a particular centre.

    Uddiyana means 'to rise up' or 'fly'. In the practice of
uddiyana bandha the abdominal organs are pulled up and
in, creating a natural upward flow of energy, therefore, it is
often translated as 'the stomach lift'.

    Movement of shakti in the body is described as a bird.
In the Upanishads, alternating activities of ida and pingala
nadis are said to ensnare the consciousness like a bird which
is tied to its perch. It tries to fly away time and time again,
but it is constantly pulled down. However, if the shakti of ida
and pingala can be brought together and released through
sushumna, it will ascend and ultimately it will be freed in
sahasrara chakra, the highest heaven.

Uddiyana bandha changes the course of the downward moving apana vayu and unites it with prana vayu and samana vayu in the navel centre. When the two opposite energies of apana and prana meet in the navel region, there is an explosion of potential force which travels upward through sushumna nadi. Powered by udana vayu, it is taken up to the higher centres. Of course, this is a major event in the course of one's sadhana and it does not take place with one or two rounds of practice. It requires patient and ardent performance in combination with other techniques.

उदरे पश्चिमं तानं नाभेरूर्ध्वं च कारयेत् ।
उड्डीयानो ह्यसौ बंधो मृत्युमातंगकेसरी ॥ 57 ॥

Pulling the abdomen back in and making the navel rise is uddiyana bandha. It is the lion which conquers the elephant, death.

Uddiyana bandha involves the sucking in and pulling up of the abdomen and stomach. It can be done while sitting, standing or lying flat on the back. Initially it should be practised standing. It must always be done on a completely empty stomach and the bowels should preferably be evacuated first.

Technique 1: Standing abdominal contraction

Stand with the feet approximately half a metre apart.

Bend the knees slightly and rest the hands above the knees with the thumbs facing inwards and the fingers outwards.

The spine must remain straight, not curved, and the head should be kept up and eyes open.

Inhale deeply through the nose, then exhale quickly through slightly pursed lips, but do not be forceful.

Having fully exhaled, perform jalandhara bandha by moving the chin down to the chest and raising the shoulders.

Then pull the abdomen and stomach inward towards the spine and up.

Hold for a few seconds.

Before inhaling, relax the stomach and abdomen, release jalandhara by raising the head, and stand straight.

Then inhale through the nose slowly and with control.

Before repeating another round, breathe normally for a minute or two.

Practise three rounds at first. Over a period of a few months you can gradually increase to ten rounds.

334

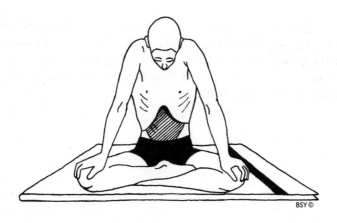

Technique 2: Uddiyana Bandha

Sit in bhadrasana, siddhasana/siddha yoni asana or padmasana.

If seated in siddhasana/siddha yoni asana or padmasana, sit on a cushion so that the buttocks are raised.

Keep the palms of the hands on the knees and the spinal cord upright and straight.

You can practise with the eyes opened or closed.

Perform uddiyana bandha as in Technique 1.

Practise three to ten rounds, concentrating on the natural breath for a minute or two between rounds.

Bandhas should be done after asana and pranayama or in combination with either; however, any bandha should be perfected before it is incorporated with asana or pranayama. It is easier to practise uddiyana bandha perfectly if an inverted asana is performed first. If the bowels have been emptied beforehand, there will be greater suction of uddiyana. It is necessary to perfect uddiyana before practising nauli.

Jalandhara must always be done with uddiyana. During the practice you can concentrate on either the throat or navel. When the practice has been mastered, the bija mantra of manipura, *Ram*, can be repeated mentally a specific number of times while you concentrate on the navel.

Anyone suffering from stomach or intestinal ulcers, hernia, high blood pressure, heart disease, glaucoma or raised intracranial pressure must not practise this bandha. Uddiyana is an advanced practice and it should only be taught to capable sadhakas.

उड्डीयानं तु सहजं गुरुणा कथितं यथा ।
अभ्यसेत्सततं यस्तु वृद्धोऽपि तरुणायते ॥ 58 ॥

Uddiyana is easy when practised as told by the guru. Even an old person can become young when it is done regularly.

नाभेरूर्ध्वमधश्चापि तानं कुर्यात्प्रयत्नतः ।
षण्मासमभ्यसेन्मृत्युं जयत्येव न संशयः ॥ 59 ॥

The region above and below the navel should be drawn backward with effort. There is no doubt that after six months of practice, death is conquered.

If bandhas are to be practised perfectly, they must be learned from a guru or qualified teacher. In the yoga texts, full details are always omitted, and if one tries to practise according to instructions given in books, one will never know if it is actually practised correctly and according to individual needs and capacity. For perfection of all yogic practices there are two basic requirements: the guru and regular practice.

With regular practice of uddiyana the effects become visibly apparent. Vitality increases as uddiyana has a powerful toning effect on the visceral organs, muscles, nerves and glands. The suction created stimulates blood circulation and absorption. The heart is squeezed and gently massaged by the upward pressure of the diaphragm. The suction or negative pressure in the thorax draws venous blood up from the abdomen into the heart and at the same time, arterial blood is drawn into the internal organs. The autonomic nerves comprising the solar plexus are strengthened. The processes of digestion, assimilation and elimination are directly affected.

Improper functioning in the alimentary canal is the most basic cause of disease. Uddiyana effects optimal functioning in this area, thereby overcoming many related diseases. Uddiyana bandha also strengthens the diaphragm and other respiratory muscles and renders them more mobile. Improper respiration and gas exchange is the other major cause of disease and degeneration. The lungs are tightly squeezed during uddiyana and this induces a greater efficiency of gas exchange, i.e. absorption of oxygen and expulsion of carbon dioxide. Because the brain is deprived of oxygen for a short period during retention, its capacity to absorb oxygen is also increased.

On a pranic level, uddiyana pulls the apana vayu up from the abdominal and reproductive organs towards the chest. Through uddiyana and jalandhara the prana is carefully locked into the navel region where union of prana and apana with samana can occur and induce the awakening and ascent of kundalini.

With so many wonderful benefits, it is not surprising that uddiyana can slow down the natural process of degeneration and ageing and make even an old person look young. However, we should face the fact that old age and death are natural processes and today there are few adept yogis who have perfected themselves to the extent of reversing the ageing process and overcoming death. Also, those who have done so nevertheless usually submit themselves to the natural laws of the body.

According to the sloka, after six month of practise, death can be averted. First uddiyana has to be perfected and it is not perfect until you can retain the breath for more than three or four minutes. Then it has to be practised regularly for months and months in combination with other practices and a conducive diet. However, even if the degenerative process is not completely reversed, at least there will be noticeable physiological and psychological benefits and the ageing process is definitely retarded.

सर्वेषामेव बंधानामुत्तमो ह्युड्डियानक: ।
उड्डियाने दृढे बद्धे मुक्ति: स्वाभाविकी भवेत् ॥ 60 ॥

*Of all the bandhas, uddiyana is the best. Once it is mastered, mukti
or liberation occurs spontaneously.*

Uddiyana should not be practised on its own, it should
always be performed with jalandhara bandha. In fact, it
is even more effective when moola bandha and/or vajroli
mudra are also added. Uddiyana is said to be the most
powerful of all the bandhas because it can draw apana
upward within a short time and bring about the awakening
of kundalini. Due to its suction force, the shakti can be
pushed through sushumna to ajna chakra, the great door to
liberation.

MOOLA BANDHA
(perineum/cervix retraction lock)

अथ मूलबंध: ।

पार्ष्णिभागेन संपीड्य योनिमाकुंचयेद्गुदम् ।
अपानमूर्ध्वमाकृष्य मूलबंधोऽभिधीयते ॥ 61 ॥

Pressing the perineum/vagina with the heel and contracting the rectum so that the apana vayu moves upward is moola bandha.

अधोगतिमपानं वा ऊर्ध्वगं कुरुते बलात् ।
आकुंचनेन तं प्राहुर्मूलबंधं हि योगिन: ॥ 62 ॥

By contracting the perineum the downward moving apana vayu is forced to go upward. Yogis call this moola bandha.

गुदं पाष्ण्या तु संपीड्य वायुमाकुंचयेद् बलात् ।
वारंवारं यथा चोर्ध्वं समायाति समीरण: ॥ 63 ॥

Press the heel firmly against the rectum and contract forcefully and repeatedly, so that the vital energy rises.

When the muscles of the perineum are contracted the whole pelvic floor is pulled up. In the text we are told to press the perineal/vaginal region, or *yoni*, and contract the rectum. The word *gudam* indicates 'rectum'; but it also means anus, bowels, or lower intestine. However, it should be clearly understood that in moola bandha there should be absolutely no anal contraction.

Contraction of the anus is known as *ashwini mudra*. Ashwini mudra indicates the movement a horse makes with its rectum during evacuation of the bowels. In the *Gherand Samhita* it is said to "contract and relax the anal aperture again and again. This is called ashwini mudra." (3:64)

When moola bandha is initially practised there is a tendency to contract the two areas, i.e. the perineum and the anus. Moola bandha takes place in the centre of the body, neither in the front nor back. Then mooladhara chakra is directly contacted. Controlled systematic contraction of the perineal body/cervix produces heat in the subtle body and this awakens the potential of kundalini.

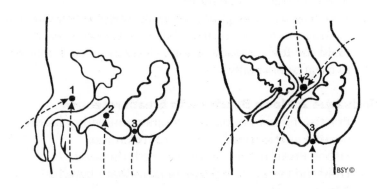

Technique I: Moola Bandha
Stage I: Sit in any comfortable meditative pose, but preferably siddhasana/siddha yoni asana as they contact mooladhara chakra.

Keep the hands on the knees in either jnana or chin mudra and close the eyes.

Make sure the body is completely relaxed and the spine is erect.

For men, the area just inside the perineum has to be contracted, so it is best to concentrate on this area for a few minutes first.

Women should concentrate on the cervix as it is the cervix and vaginal muscles which have to be contracted. After a few minutes of concentration start to gradually contract and release the muscles of the perineum/cervix. Contraction will last for a few seconds.

Keep the breath normal.

Contract and release up to twenty times.

341

Stage 2: Prepare yourself as for the previous practice.
Contract the muscles of the perineum/cervix and hold.
Continue to breathe normally, do not hold the breath.
Hold the contraction for as long as possible, then release.
Practise up to twenty times.

Stage 3: Contraction should start off gently and only partially.
Contract just a little and hold without releasing.
Then contract a little more.
Continue like this, gradually increasing the tension and contraction ten times, until full contraction is reached.
Hold the full contraction for as long as possible and try to breathe normally.

Technique 2: Moola Bandha with breath retention

Practise moola bandha in conjunction with jalandhara bandha and internal or external retention.
Sitting erect, inhale deeply through the nose.
Hold the breath and perform jalandhara bandha.
Now practise stage 3.
Before exhaling, release moola bandha then jalandhara.
When the head is straight exhale slowly.
The same sequence can be done with external retention.

Technique 3: Moola Bandha with uddiyana bandha

With external kumbhaka and jalandhara bandha, practise five rounds of Technique 1 (stage 2).
Then practise five rounds of Technique 1 (stage 3).
Now add uddiyana bandha to the practice.
Do five rounds of stage 2, then five rounds of stage 3.
It takes months of practice to become fully acquainted with moola bandha and years to perfect it. The greatest difficulty is overcoming the tendency to contract all the muscles of the urinary and excretory complex. It takes a lot of practice before one can isolate the different muscles in this area and control them so that movement only takes place in the area associated with mooladhara chakra.

Moola bandha is meant to be used in combination with pranayama practices, kumbhaka, jalandhara and uddiyana bandhas. It can also be used in certain asana practices. Moola bandha should be performed with jalandhara bandha during antar (internal) kumbhaka and with uddiyana and jalandhara during bahir (external) kumbhaka. However, it should be perfected as an individual practice before it is incorporated into other techniques.

प्राणापानौ नादबिन्दू मूलबंधेन चैकताम् ।
गत्वा योगस्य संसिद्धिं यच्छतो नात्र संशय: ॥ 64 ॥

*There is no doubt that by practising moola bandha, prana and apana,
and nada and bindu are united, and total perfection attained.*

The union of prana and apana has been discussed previously,
but what are bindu and nada? Bindu is an important aspect
of tantra and yoga. *Bindu* means 'point' or 'nucleus', and
refers to the nucleus in each individual which contains
the potential consciousness and creative force. What is the
potential within the nucleus? It can be compared to the DNA
molecule which contains the potential of creating an entire
universe in the form of a new being.

Bindu has a different form of manifestation in each of
the three realms; physical, subtle and causal. In hatha yoga,
bindu often refers to sperm or ova in the physical body, but
these are understood to be the grossest manifestation of the
subtle bindu which drips as nectar from bindu visarga, the
point at the top back portion of the head. From this point,
the bindu moves down through the chakras until it materially
manifests as the cellular components within the reproductive
secretions. According to tantra, bindu can be experienced
and controlled from these two points, i.e. bindu visarga and
the reproductive organs.

In its aspect as semen, it is called white or *shukla bindu*. In
its aspect as ova it is known as red or *rakta bindu*. The union
of the two is *mishra bindu* and that union produces nada
or sound vibration. The *Chudamani Upanishad* states that:
"Bindu is of two types; white and red. The white is shukla
and the red is maharaja. The white bindu represents the
male aspect, Shiva, purusha or consciousness and semen.
The red bindu represents the female aspect, Shakti, prakriti
or energy and menses. The red bindu is established in the
sun and the white bindu in the moon. Their union is difficult
indeed." (v. 60,61)

The terms white and red should not only be taken literally, they are also symbolic. White bindu resides in the head, red bindu in mooladhara. "He who realizes the essential oneness of the two bindus, when red bindu merges with white bindu, alone knows yoga (union)." (*Chudamani Upanishad*, v. 64). In terms of the male and female bodies, the red bindu in the mooladhara of a man is shukla bindu and the red bindu in the mooladhara of woman is rakta. In the practice of vajroli mudra during maithuna, the aim is to unite the two bindus so that the nada (subtle sound vibration) created returns to its source in the mahabindu seated within the brain.

It is not the physical bindu, i.e. sperm or ova, which is to be taken up into the brain. This is often misinterpreted. It is the subtle essence from the union of these two poles of energy. It is the energy of the reproductive impulse which has to be channelled through the central nervous system through sushumna.

Two important bandhas are to be perfected, moola and jalandhara. When moola bandha is performed in conjunction with jalandhara, the sushumna passage between mooladhara and vishuddhi is isolated. Jalandhara bandha prevents prana vayu from passing upwards beyond vishuddhi. Moola bandha prevents the apana from escaping downwards below mooladhara. These two vayus are forced together and their union in manipura is gradually accomplished.

This awakening of manipura chakra is a definite milestone in the spiritual life of a yogic aspirant. With this, kundalini is considered to have risen from mooladhara and become established in manipura, and this affects the source in the brain where the nectar flows from bindu visarga. In physiological terms, this flow of nectar is associated with the release of hormones from the pituitary gland into the bloodstream.

The principle of 'feedback inhibition' of hormones upon their source is well-known to scientists; it means that a hormonal end product, such as testosterone in the male,

345

or oestrogen/progesterone in the female, is produced by the testes or ovaries due to the stimulus of gonadotrophins from the pituitary. As well as their primary effects upon the reproductive system, these reproductive hormones are also found to 'feedback' upon the pituitary to inhibit further release of the same pituitary hormones which have stimulated their production.

In this way, hormonal effects are exerted in the body in a 'fits and starts' manner, with a continuing state of imbalance between production and consumption of hormones. This fluctuating system of self-regulation is considered as 'normal' by medical science today, but because of its inherent imbalance, ageing and degeneration result in the body.

However, as union of prana and apana in manipura is induced, the behaviour of the lower chakras and the instinctive functions they govern, undergo modification. Production of the reproductive hormones diminishes to a steady baseline level, so that inhibition upon the pituitary secretion is released. The pituitary then begins to secrete its stimulating hormones without 'fits and starts'. This is the physiological explanation of the flow of nectar from bindu visarga becoming continuous and undisrupted.

As a result, the stream of consciousness becomes one-pointed and continuous. This is the emergence of continuous nada in the brain. The gross bindu in the reproductive secretions has been withdrawn and transmuted into nada, the blissful, eternal 'seed sound' emanating within the brain. Bindu has become nada, control of the sexual impulses has been attained, consciousness has been liberated into new realms of experience and simultaneously the dependent glands and organs of the body are preserved.

The *Sarada Tilaka* states: "Mahabindu (the great bindu, i.e. Brahman) divides itself into three: one division is predominated by Shiva (consciousness), the other by Shakti (energy), the merging of the two is nada (transcendental sound vibration)." The original mahabindu in the cosmic realm is the primal source of pure consciousness, with energy

346

in a passive state. On the differentiation of this supreme bindu, nada or unmanifest sound bursts forth. The bindu visarga is the highest manifestation of consciousness in the individual. It is the source of creation.

By performing moola bandha and thereby controlling the release of the sex hormones and the sexual impulses, a constant flow of nectar is induced from bindu visarga. This is experienced as transcendental sound. By controlling bindu visarga, you are controlling creation within the microcosmos.

अपानप्राणयोरैक्यं क्षयो मूत्रपुरीषयो: ।
युवा भवति वृद्धोऽपि सततं मूलबंधनात् ॥ 65 ॥

*With constant practice of moola bandha, prana and apana unite,
urine and stool are decreased and even an old person becomes
young.*

All the practices which unite the two opposite forces, prana
and apana, generate and release immense heat in the body.
This increases the metabolic rate for a short period, and
as a result, elimination and degeneration are decreased;
absorption and assimilation improve, and the nervous
system, blood circulation and brain functions are greatly
stimulated. The mind becomes alert, sensual desires and
the need for sleep decrease, and even during the dream
state, there is greater awareness. When moola bandha is
practised regularly the physiological need for food decreases
and the same symptoms which appear due to perfection of
pranayama and uddiyana bandha, manifest.

अपान ऊर्ध्वगे जाते प्रयाते वह्निमंडलम् ।
तदाऽनलशिखा दीर्घा जायते वायुनाऽऽहता ॥ 66 ॥

Apana moves up into the region of fire (manipura chakra, the navel centre), then the flames of the fire grow, being fanned by apana vayu.

ततो यातो वह्न्यपानौ प्राणमुष्णस्वरूपकम् ।
तेनात्यंतप्रदीपतस्तु ज्वलनो देहजस्तथा ॥ 67 ॥

Then, when apana and the fire meet with prana, which is itself hot, the heat in the body is intensified.

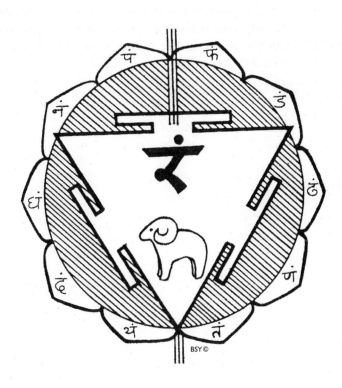

The ultimate effect of moola bandha and jalandhara is the same as uddiyana and jalandhara. Actually, the three bandhas should be performed together in maha bandha for the best results, even though they can be practised separately, and should be, until each is individually perfected.

When the perineal body is constantly contracted, the prana shakti which normally escapes through this passage is redirected to the navel centre, which is the seat of the fire element or *agni tattwa*. When any chakra is activated, heat will be produced, but manipura becomes excessively hot because of the fire element. This centre is responsible for maintaining the body temperature and regulating the digestive fire. The nervous impulses sent from the coccygeal plexus are said to 'fan the fire'.

Moola bandha and uddiyana bandha are techniques which redistribute and rechannel pranic heat and nervous impulses from the lower to the higher centres or from the grosser to the subtler centres.

तेन कुंडलिनी सुप्ता संतप्ता संप्रबुध्यते ।
दंडाहता भुजंगीव निःश्वस्य ऋजुतां व्रजेत् ॥ 68 ॥

Through this, the sleeping kundalini is aroused by the extreme heat and it straightens itself just as a serpent beaten with a stick straightens and hisses.

बिलं प्रविष्टेव ततो ब्रह्मनाड्यंतरं व्रजेत् ।
तस्मान्नित्यं मूलबंधः कर्तव्यो योगिभिः सदा ॥ 69 ॥

Just as a snake enters its hole, so kundalini goes into brahma nadi. Therefore the yogi must always perform moola bandha.

When kundalini is awakened the whole central nervous system becomes active and charged with energy. Energy passes from the firing of one neuron to the next and the chains of nerve fibres straighten with the force of the energy. Thus it is said: "Kundalini straightens like a snake which is suddenly beaten with a stick."

The normal amount of energy which passes through the central nervous system is of a low frequency compared to that of kundalini. Most of our energy flows outwards through the sense organs. Through the practice of moola bandha, that same energy can be redirected upwards to the higher brain centres which normally do not receive much of a charge.

In the average person, the energy which flows through the central nervous system is of such a low voltage that it is only sufficient to power the instinctive consciousness and body functions. To manifest the so-called superhuman qualities, the entire pranic capacity has to be increased and the central nervous system and brain have to be charged with the high voltage energy of kundalini shakti.

In order to purify and strengthen the chakras, moola bandha, jalandhara bandha, uddiyana bandha and kumbhaka are practised. Then, when kundalini rises it will pass through brahma nadi, the innermost layer of sushumna.

JALANDHARA BANDHA (throat lock)

अथ जालंधरबन्ध: ।

कंठमाकुंच्य हृदये स्थापयेच्चिबुकं दृढम् ।
बंधो जालंधराख्योऽयं जरामृत्युविनाशक: ॥ 70 ॥

*Contracting the throat by bringing the chin to the chest is the bandha
called jalandhara. It destroys old age and death.*

बध्नाति हि शिराजालमधोगामि नभोजलम् ।
ततो जालंधरो बंध: कंठदु:खौघनाशन: ॥ 71 ॥

*That is jalandhara bandha which catches the flow of nectar in the
throat. It destroys all throat ailments.*

Jal is 'throat', *jalam* is 'water', *dhara* means 'supporting' or 'a
tubular vessel in the body.' Jalandhara bandha is the throat
lock which helps prevent the fluid of bindu from flowing
further down than vishuddhi. Although it is easy to perform,
jalandhara is a very important practice.

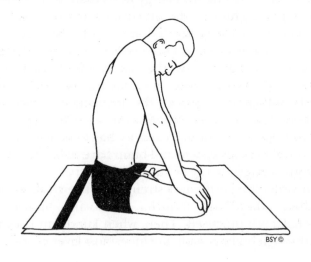

Technique

Sit comfortably in siddhasana/siddha yoni asana, padmasana, sukhasana or vajrasana.

Place the palms of the hands on the knees and allow the whole body to relax.

Inhale slowly and deeply and retain the breath.

Lower the chin so that it touches the chest, or more specifically the collarbone.

Simultaneously, straighten the elbows and raise the shoulders.

Hold for as long as is comfortable.

Then release jalandhara by slowly raising the head and relaxing the shoulders.

Exhale in a very slow and controlled manner.

Practise five rounds, breathing normally for a minute or two between each round.

Then practise five rounds with external retention.

Jalandhara can be done in the same standing position as used for uddiyana bandha or nauli karma. However, it is usually practised in conjunction with pranayama and other major kriyas involving breath retention. Initially it can be done separately until you become accustomed to it. As it is such an easy practice, this will not take long.

Jalandhara bandha is extremely useful for alleviating throat disorders such as inflammation, stuttering, excess mucus in the throat, tonsilitis, etc. It also improves the quality of the voice and increases the quantum of prana in the thoracic region. Because jalandhara has a powerful effect on the blood pressure, people with high blood pressure or heart disease should not practise without the guidance of a teacher.

Many major nerve fibres pass through the neck. When jalandhara is performed it exerts pressure on them and the flow of nervous impulses to the brain is restricted. These impulses collect in the cervical plexus and when the bandha is released they flood into the brain. The force of these impulses helps to activate higher centres in the brain.

353

जालंधरे कृते बंधे कंठसंकोचलक्षणे ।
न पीयूषं पतत्यग्नौ न च वायुः प्रकुप्यति ॥ 72 ॥

Having done jalandhara bandha by contracting the throat, the nectar does not fall into the gastric fire and the prana is not agitated.

When the hormonal secretions of the pituitary flow through the blood stream to the various endocrine glands, the life process associated with these centres is set into motion. These processes of metabolism, the response to stress, instinctual life, etc., endured and experienced throughout a lifetime, cause the body to become degenerate, exhausted and decrepit. This is easy to understand. Just as a car or piece of machinery is worn out at a rate proportional to its mileage or intensity of usage, so too the human body obeys such natural laws of performance and decay.

The experiences of life demand that heat be produced in the body. So the gastric fire is kindled by the consumption and combustion of fuel, and the pranas governing the different parts and processes, for example, assimilation, digestion, excretion and circulation, become agitated. This is the mechanism of experience of external reality mediated through the sensory and motor organs. It is also the medium leading inevitably to decay and death of the body.

The throat region is intermediate between the brain and the digestive and assimilative processes. It is here that a brake or governor can be exerted upon the rate at which the bodily processes are activated. The thyroid gland secretes the hormone thyroxine (T4), which is responsible for the rate of tissue metabolism (i.e. the rate of nutrient consumption and of cell turnover and tissue ageing). This gland is situated precisely here, in the front of the neck, where the yogis visualize the pool of nectar.

By applying jalandhara bandha this fleshy gland is squeezed. The nerve stimuli and blood flow to and from the gland are modified, and the secretory responses of the gland are modulated.

The parathyroid glands, which regulate calcium metabolism and control the density of the body by regulating the amount of calcium in the blood and bones, are situated on either side of the thyroid gland. They are also influenced.

Many of the chronic and complex diseases seen in later life occur due to the inherent imbalance between production and consumption of hormones in the body over many decades. Jalandhara bandha is a means to consciously influence the rate of metabolism. The influence of thyroxine pervades the body's tissues right down to the microscopic level where it activates the enzymatic and oxidative processes of the cells.

This is the meaning of the yogic concept of capturing the nectarine flow at the throat level, thereby moderating the rate of decay of the body's organ systems. Of course, the flow of nectar from bindu cannot be entirely equated with the hormonal secretions from the pituitary gland, just as prana cannot be equated with nervous impulses. These terms refer also to subtle processes taking place in the pranic, mental and psychic bodies. Therefore, it should not be understood only on a physiological basis. However, by understanding the physiological concomitants of these psychic and pranic processes a clearer insight is gained.

कंठसंकोचनेनैव द्वे नाड्यौ स्तंभयेद् दृढम् ।
मध्यचक्रमिदं ज्ञेयं षोडशाधारबंधनम् ॥ 73 ॥

By firmly contracting the throat, the two nadis, ida and pingala are paralyzed and the sixteen adharas of the middle chakra are locked.

When jalandhara bandha is performed, the flow of shakti in ida and pingala is arrested and prevented from flowing between the head and the body. There is a subtle restructuring in the energy circuit, and the energy which had been flowing in ida and pingala is induced to flow through sushumna. Thus ida and pingala are described as becoming inert or paralyzed. Jalandhara bandha causes prana to collect in vishuddhi chakra, the middle chakra between the physical body and the brain centres.

Vishuddhi is described as a deep purple lotus which has sixteen petals called *adharas* which means 'support' or 'receptacle which contains a particular fluid'. Each petal or adhara has a specific potential power or force. The eighth petal is said to contain poison, the sixteenth, *amrit* (nectar). The potential force of each petal is represented by the bija mantras: Am अं, Aam आं, Im इं, Eem ईं, Um उं, Oum ऊं, Rim ऋं, Reem ॠं, Lrim ऌं, Lreem ॡं, Em एं, Aim ऐं, Om ओं, Aum औं, Ah अः, Amh अं:. These bija mantras relate to various bodily functions, mental and psychic and even subtler capacities. It is said that the realization through the first fifteen letters is the dissolution of conscious, subconscious and unconscious into Atma, i.e. Om.

Sixteen petals or adharas are also found on the Sri Yantra and the shakti, or potential forces, of each are: desire, intellect, ego, sound, touch, form, taste, smell, chitta, steadfastness, memory, attraction by speech, growth, the subtle body, revivification and the gross body. These are also called the adhi devatas of the pancha tattwas, jnanendriya and karmendriya.

In the *Subhagodaya* the sixteen petals are called nityas, i.e. they are the fifteen days of the waxing moon (kalas of the fifteen tithis of shukla paksha) culminating in poornima. The sixteenth petal, known as Adya Satchidananda roopini, is in the form of the Supreme Self. These petals, as the phases of the waxing moon, denote ambrosia, life giving, growth, contentment, nourishment, attachment, constancy, containing the man in the moon, light spreading, effulgent, moonlight, prosperity, delight, limb developing, fullness, and full of nectar.

Vishuddhi is referred to as the middle chakra in this sloka, because below vishuddhi the chakras are concerned with the four grosser tattwas or mahabhutas but above vishuddhi, shakti comes directly into contact with conscious-

357

ness. Vishuddhi chakra contains the subtlest of the tattwas or elements, i.e. ether or akasha, the sound principle. Manipura is also called the middle chakra because it is midway between the earth (mooladhara) and sky (vishuddhi). Rather manipura is concerned with the intermediate realm between gross and subtle. Vishuddhi is the middle chakra between manifest Shakti (in the form of tattwas) and the unmanifest Shakti in the form of mahat (consciousness). It is also via the voice box in the throat that thought is converted into audible sound. So, this chakra draws the unmanifest Shakti into a manifest form.

मूलस्थानं समाकुंच्य उड्डियानं तु कारयेत् ।
इडां च पिंगलां बद्ध्वा वाहयेत्पश्चिमे पथि ॥ 74 ॥

By contracting the perineum, performing uddiyana and locking ida and pingala with jalandhara, sushumna becomes active.

अनेनैव विधानेन प्रयाति पवनो लयम् ।
ततो न जायते मृत्युर्जरारोगादिकं तथा ॥ 75 ॥

By this means the prana and breath become still. Thus death, old age and sickness are conquered.

Prana is in a constant state of flux in the body, sometimes being directed through the external senses, sometimes towards the internal organs. Sometimes prana shakti in pingala predominates and sometimes chitta shakti in ida, and this creates various biorhythms and states of mind. The yogic practices moderate these fluctuations between the extremes of ida and pingala. It is most important to remain aware of these extremes. It means developing the state of balanced awareness where mind is neither extrovert nor introvert, no matter whether you are working, thinking, eating or practising asana or meditation. If you cannot maintain a state of conscious awareness while awake, then in deeper states also, the awareness will be lost. When sushumna awakens or when the breath stops, it should be a conscious experience, only then can the experience of death be altered.

बंधत्रयमिदं श्रेष्ठं महासिद्धैश्च सेवितम् ।
सर्वेषां हठतंत्राणां साधनं योगिनो विदुः ॥ 76 ॥

The great siddhas practise these three best bandhas. Of all the sadhanas in hatha yoga and tantra, the yogis know this practice (maha bandha).

Though there are many techniques for establishing a state of equilibrium and union between mind and body, the most effective is said to be the combination of these three bandhas. Maha bandha is the culmination of asana, pranayama, mudra and bandha. Perfection in it induces a state of perfect equanimity which unfolds into pratyahara or even spontaneous dhyana.

There are innumerable techniques which can be practised in the path of self-realization but many involve either forced mental concentration or sensual restrictions. Therefore, it is difficult for the average person to apply himself to accomplish the task. However, it can be achieved by learning to control the body in such a way as given here, without mental conflicts.

Tantra approaches the problem of higher experience by being a friend of the mind and not an enemy. Therefore, no matter what a yogi's personal philosophy may be, the three bandhas are considered as important as eating and sleeping, and are as well known as ABC.

यत्किंचित्स्त्रवते चंद्रादमृतं दिव्यरूपिण: ।
तत्सर्वं ग्रसते सूर्यस्तेन पिंडो जरायुत: ॥ ७७ ॥

That nectar which flows from the moon has the quality of endowing enlightenment, but it is completely consumed by the sun, incurring old age.

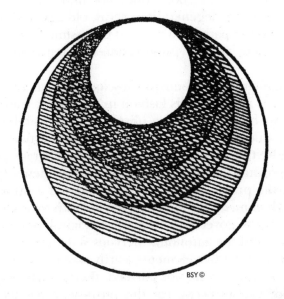

BSY©

In various ancient texts of yoga and tantra, we come across the word ambrosia or nectar. This nectar is a fluid which is secreted from the top of the brain. Its source is the centre named bindu visarga. In short it is called bindu and it is symbolized by the crescent moon. Awareness of this tiny centre has been maintained in India for many thousands of years, but with a religious accent. Hindus even today keep a tuft of hair at this point, which indicates their faith and religion. However, it has a much deeper significance.

Bindu visarga literally means the 'oozing point of the nectar drop'. It is said that at this particular point, a tiny amount of fluid forms. It is like a tiny drop. This nectar begins to flow downwards and in the course of the life span it is consumed by the lower centres and old age is incurred.

However, this process is not inevitable. This nectar has the capacity to enlighten the individual consciousness, but for that to occur the consumption of the falling nectar must be averted so that it can be assimilated into the body. If this is accomplished, consciousness in that body becomes enlightened and the body does not undergo the fate of mortal flesh, viz. degeneration, decay, old age and death. It follows another path. As a result of the assimilation of nectar into the body, cellular preservation and rejuvenation take place.

Enlightenment of human consciousness has never been interpreted in a religious fashion in the tantric tradition. It has always been known as a physiological possibility which can be induced within the body by certain practices. This is why in the tantric system, as opposed to religious philosophies, purification of the body, its five elements (pancha tattwa), the pranas and nadis, is considered a prerequisite for enlightenment. If the body is loaded with toxic elements; if the pranas governing vital physiological functions are disrupted and the autonomic nervous system is in a state of imbalance; if the five elements (earth, water, fire, air, ether) or the five chakras are not purified, then enlightenment of that body cannot occur. For this purpose, a few particular practices or kriyas are indicated in hatha yoga, kriya yoga and tantra.

VIPAREETA KARANI MUDRA
(reversing attitude)

अथ विपरीतकरणी ।

तत्रास्ति करणं दिव्यं सूर्यस्य मुखवंचनम् ।
गुरूपदेशतो ज्ञेयं न तु शास्त्रार्थकोटिभिः ॥ 78 ॥

There is a wonderful means by which the nectar is averted from falling into the opening of the sun. This is obtained by the guru's instructions and not from the hundreds of shastras (treatises).

उर्ध्वंनाभेरधस्तालोरूर्ध्वं भानुरधः शशी ।
करणी विपरीताख्या गुरुवाक्येन लभ्यते ॥ 79 ॥

With the navel region above and the palate below, the sun is above and the moon below. It is called vipareeta karani, the reversing process. When given by the guru's instructions it is fruitful.

The moon emits its nectar and due to the natural body processes it falls into the sun. The moon not only represents bindu but also consciousness. The sun not only represents manipura but also prana, the body. From this it can also be understood that the consciousness streams into the body and is wasted through the sense organs.

Through the practice of vipareeta karani mudra we are directly concerned with reversing the flow of a fluid from the brain centre. The process is reversed by reversing the natural upright body position. The force of gravity naturally pulls all body fluids down to the lower parts. By inverting the body so that the head is down and the feet are up, all the fluids flow back towards the head without undue force or pressure.

There are various asanas which can also effect this, but the two most effective are vipareeta karani and sirshasana. However, the effects of vipareeta karani differ from sirshasana as it creates pressure in the throat which stimulates the thyroid and awakens vishuddhi chakra. Sirshasana directly affects the cerebrum and sahasrara chakra. Vipareeta is also a simpler posture than sirshasana but it should be learnt from the guru directly.

The practice of vipareeta karani is similar to the shoulder stand, sarvangasana. The major difference is the angle of the back to the floor. In sarvangasana the back and legs should be perpendicular; in vipareeta karani the back is maintained at a forty-five degree angle to the floor and legs. This means the throat is not completely blocked and allows the flow of blood to the brain. Vipareeta karani mudra is the first kriya practised in kriya yoga. In kriya yoga a particular concentration and visualization is utilized in the practice which is omitted in the hatha yoga technique.

Technique

Stage 1: Lie in a relaxed supine position on a blanket, i.e. shavasana.

Then bring the legs together, palms of the hands on the floor beside the body.

Raise the legs, bringing them a little behind the head so that the back rises, and support the back with the hands.

Raise the legs in the air, feet towards the ceiling, not pointed, making the back at a forty-five degree angle to the floor.

Support the lower back with the hands, keeping the elbows behind on the floor.

The hands can be adjusted so that you are steady.

Either they should hold the buttocks or the sides of the waist.

Remain in the position as long as possible, breathing normally.

Concentrate on the throat centre.

When you come out of the position, slowly lower the back onto the floor, keeping the legs raised.

Keep the palms of the hands on the ground and slowly lower the legs, keeping them straight.

If this is too strenuous, bend the knees to the chest and place the soles of the feet on the floor, then slide the legs onto the ground.

Completely relax the body in shavasana.

Stage 2: Practise stage 1 and include ujjayi pranayama in the final position.

Stage 3: Practise stage 2 and include khechari mudra with ujjayi pranayama.

The practice is more powerful when ujjayi and khechari are utilized. In kriya yoga the practice becomes more effective by utilizing concentration. While inhaling, visualize that a hot fluid is being drawn up from the navel into the throat. Retain the breath for a second or two while experiencing this hot fluid becoming cool. When it becomes icy cold, exhale the fluid up to bindu and on to sahasrara. Again bring the awareness back down to the navel and inhale in the same way. This is repeated twenty-one times.

People suffering from high blood pressure, heart disease, enlarged thyroid or excessive toxins in the system should never attempt an inverted posture. If you have constipation it is advisable to empty the bowels first by drinking warm saline water or practising laghoo shankhaprakshalana. Then vipareeta karani helps relieve the tendency to further constipation. It is a powerful practice and is better done when the body is completely healthy. However, it can be used in the case of hypoactive thyroid to rebalance the functions. It should always be done on an empty stomach, at least three hours after taking a meal.

The most appropriate time to practise any inverted asana is in the morning after evacuating the bowels and bathing are completed. At that time the body is relaxed and rested. Later in the day when food has been consumed and the body is at peak activity, different hormonal secretions are flowing throughout the system and if these flow down to the throat and head, imbalance may be created. It may be performed in the afternoon after first relaxing in shavasana for ten minutes, provided the stomach has been empty for more than three hours and you have not been doing strenuous physical work.

नित्यमभ्यासयुक्तस्य जठराग्निविवर्धिनी ।
आहारो बहुलस्तस्य संपाद्य: साधकस्य च ।
अल्पाहारो यदि भवेदग्निर्दहति तत्क्षणात् ॥ 80 ॥

Digestion is strengthened by continual, regular practice and therefore, the practitioner should always have sufficient food. If one takes only a little food, the heat produced by the digestion will destroy the system.

अध:शिराश्चोर्ध्वपाद: क्षणं स्यात्प्रथमे दिन ।
क्षणाच्च किंचिदधिकमभ्यसेच्च दिने दिने ॥ 81 ॥

Therefore, on the first day, one should only stay a moment with the feet up and head down. The practice should be done daily, gradually increasing the duration.

There are a number of basic rules which have to be followed if you practise any of the hatha yoga techniques, and these are often omitted in the texts. It is therefore important to learn under expert guidance. The practices have a specific effect on the body and mind which has to be watched by the person who is guiding you.

All the practices of hatha yoga will release an internal heat in the course of time. Swami Muktananda of Ganeshpuri describes how, as a result of asana, pranayama, mudra, bandha and meditation, a type of fire was liberated in his body. No matter what he did to cool himself, still his body burnt internally. Consequently his body became emaciated. He had to adjust his diet, taking boiled rice water rather than solid food. This reiterates that yoga practices are very powerful and the sadhaka must be guided by a guru.

One of the initial positive effects of vipareeta karani is an increased capacity to digest and assimilate food. Digestive secretions and appetite are definitely increased and, therefore, a moderate diet should be taken at regular intervals. Food should be taken after practising hatha yoga.

If food is not taken, if you fast, the gastric acids and digestive enzymes will burn the lining of the stomach and duodenum. However, it is unlikely to happen when vipareeta karani is practised for a few minutes. Regularity of meal timings and quantities is necessary for the advancing hatha yogi, and fasting is contraindicated.

Vipareeta karani has a powerful draining influence on the visceral organs. Due to the force of gravity, the lower dependent parts of these organs tend to pool blood, and the body fluids also aggregate in the dependent parts of the body such as the pelvis and legs. Vipareeta karani flushes these dependent parts, returning pooled cellular fluid to the circulation. This cannot be induced in the upright or lying positions, and this is why inversion is so powerful physiologically. Inversion of the body also contracts visceroptosis (protrusion of the abdominal organs), haemorrhoids, varicose veins and hernia, all of which are mediated by the downward force of gravity. The inverted position, while draining the lower body, simultaneously enhances blood flow to the brain, especially the cerebral cortex and the intracranial glands, i.e. the pituitary and pineal. Cerebral insufficiency and senile dementia are counteracted. However, elderly people are not advised to commence inversion in later life because of the possibility of stroke.

Inversion also profoundly influences the entire vascular network. The constant dragging force upon the arteries and veins continues throughout life, but is released completely during inversion. Regular practice prevents atheriosclerosis (arterial degeneration) by restoring vascular tone and elasticity.

Inversion also reverses the polarity of the electromagnetic field created within the upright body. The energy field generated by the electrical activity of the brain is integrated with the geomagnetic field of the earth's surface. This has a revitalizing influence upon the human aura.

वलितं पलितं चैव षण्मासोर्ध्वं न दृश्यते ।
याममात्रं तु यो नित्यमभ्यसेत् स तु कालजित् ॥ ८२ ॥

After six months of practise, grey hairs and wrinkles become inconspicuous. One who practises it for yama (three hours) conquers death.

Vipareeta karani mudra should be done daily at the same time, preferably in the morning. Hold the final position for a few minutes in the beginning or until discomfort arises. Over the period of a few months slowly increase the duration of practice. When pressure builds up in the head, slowly come down. Count the number of respirations taken during the practice and increase by an extra breath each day.

According to the sloka, if it is performed for three hours, death can be overcome, but do not practise for such a long duration on this basis because the body will be unable to cope with its influence. It takes years of sadhana to reach this stage. Most important is that during the practice the position is perfect and concentration is one-pointed.

On completion of the practice, it is advisable to practise a backward bending posture such as matsyasana, bhujangasana or ushtrasana. However, this is not as necessary as it is after sarvangasana, and, if vipareeta is practised only for one or two minutes, backward bending is not essential.

To gain full benefit from the practice it is necessary to go slowly. Gradually build up the duration and adhere to the rules of the practice.

VAJROLI MUDRA (thunderbolt attitude)

अथ वज्रोली ।

स्वेच्छया वर्तमानोऽपि योगोक्तैर्नियमैर्विना ।
वज्रोलीं यो विजानाति स योगी सिद्धिभाजनम् ॥ 83 ॥

*Even one living a free lifestyle without the formal rules of yoga,
if he practises vajroli well, that yogi becomes a recipient of siddhis
(perfections).*

Vajra is 'thunderbolt' or 'lightning'. It is also the weapon of
Lord Indra and means 'mighty one'. Vajra in this context
refers to vajra nadi which governs the urogenital system. It
is the second innermost layer of sushumna nadi. Vajra nadi
is the energy flow within the spine which governs the sexual
systems of the body. In mundane life it is responsible for the
sexual behaviour and this aspect has been termed 'libido'
by Dr Freud and 'orgone' by Dr Reich. In tantric sadhana
this energy is not suppressed, it is awakened and redirected.
Vajroli, sahajoli and amaroli are mudras which specifically
sublimate sexual energy into ojas, vitality, and kundalini
shakti.

According to the *Shatkarma Sangraha* there are seven
practices of vajroli. The practice involves years of preparation which commences with the simple contraction
of the urogenital muscles and later the sucking up of
liquids. Only after the sixth practice is perfected can the
seventh be successfully attempted by the yogi; that is the
practice included in maithuna, yogic intercourse. Through
this practice of vajroli, the sexual energy, hormones and
secretions are reassimilated into the body. Its outcome is the
union of the negative and positive poles of energy within
one's own body.

By and large, people have inherited a concept that these
practices are unnatural or bad. Many commentators on the

Hatha Yoga Pradipika avoid discussing these slokas, dismissing them as obscene practices indulged in by lowcaste tantrics. Obviously they have an incorrect understanding of the practice. People have concocted the notion that spiritual life is separate from mundane life and the physical body because of past religious conditioning which has become perverted. These people must realize that spiritual life is not anti-sexual and sexual life is not anti-spiritual.

Of course, celibacy has its own rewards but according to tantra it should arise spontaneously, not out of suppression. Spiritual life means developing awareness by applying the higher mind to the experiences of the body. Whatever we do should be a means of creating yoga in our being. Why should sexual life be excluded? According to this sloka, sexual life can be elevated from the sensual to the spiritual plane if it practised in a particular way, and for this vajroli has been described.

A person who has perfect control of body and mind is a yogi in every situation. A person who gorges himself on food, for example, is just as 'obscene' as a person who indulges in uncontrollable sexual acts. Sexual life has three purposes which should be understood: for the tamasic person it is for progeny; for the rajasic person it is for pleasure; for a sattwic person it is for enlightenment.

The desire to release semen is an instinctual urge experienced throughout nature, not only by humans. Therefore, there should be no guilt or shame associated with it. Animal consciousness is not the end stage in the evolutionary destiny for a human being. Man's potential for bliss can be extended beyond the momentary experience which accompanies the release of semen. Semen and ova contain the evolutionary potential and if these can be controlled, not only the body but also the mind can be controlled.

Nature has provided the mechanism of seminal release, but although it is generally not known, nature has also provided a means to control this mechanism through various

371

practices of hatha yoga. If the release of semen and ova can be controlled, a new range of experience dawns. Those experiences are also endowed by nature, even if only a few people have gained them. Therefore, the techniques should not be considered to be against the natural order.

Although medical science has generally failed to acknowledge the fact, uncontrolled release of semen throughout life does contribute to premature deterioration of the vital capacities of the brain, overburdens the heart and depletes the nervous system. Actually it is a matter of degree and there is no limit to perfection. Many men die prematurely of physical and mental exhaustion with their dreams unfulfilled and their goals unattained. However, if the process of seminal release can be arrested, so that energy and spermatozoa do not escape through the generative organ but are redirected upwards into the higher brain centres, then a greater awakening can take place; a greater vision can be realized, and a greater vital power can be directed towards accomplishments in life.

According to the sloka, if vajroli is well practised, even in an otherwise free lifestyle, that yogi's attainments in life will be greater, and a greater source of vital and mental power will become available to him. A few great yogis and masters had these experiences and have, therefore, instructed their disciples in the oli mudras and other hatha yoga techniques.

In mundane life, the climax of sexual experience is the one time when the mind becomes completely void of its own accord and consciousness beyond the body can be glimpsed. However, that experience is so shortlived because the energy is expressed through the lower energy centres. This energy which is normally lost can be used to awaken the dormant power of kundalini in mooladhara. If the sperm can be withheld, the energy can be channelled through sushumna nadi and the central nervous system, to the dormant areas of the brain and to the sleeping consciousness.

The sexual act is the one means to totally concentrate and captivate the mind, but in tantra it should not be the ordinary experience. The experience has to be more than the gross or sensual one. Awareness and control have to be developed. The senses have to be utilized but only as the means of awakening the higher consciousness, not the animal consciousness, and for this, vajroli mudra and various tantric rituals are to be perfected.

Vajroli mudra is an important practice today in the kali yuga when man's ability and need to express himself in the material and sensual world is predominating. We have to act in the external world and simultaneously develop inner awareness. The purpose of life should be to attain a deeper and more fulfilling experience beyond the empirical sensory experience alone.

Man has four basic desires known as *purushartha* or *chaturvarga*, the first of which is *kaama* or 'sensual gratification'. This needs to be fulfilled to a certain extent, but it should not pull the consciousness down. It should be a means to accomplish a greater result. Every action, including the sexual act, should be directed towards realizing the truth of existence. Then you are living a spiritual life. Spiritual life does not depend on living up to puritanical morality.

If you can follow such puritanical ideals and attain enlightenment, then practise them, but do not condemn others who cannot. The moment you create rigid ideals that the spiritual path has to be like this, and cannot be like that, you are limiting your own ability to have a total experience.

Spiritual unfoldment is the process of evolution. It can happen slowly through millions of years as the process of nature, or it can be accelerated through the practices of yoga. Vajroli mudra accelerates this rate of evolution. The practice of vajroli regulates the entire sexual system. Testosterone level and sperm production are influenced. Even if the yogi is a householder, he does not lose the semen. Therefore, whether one has sexual interactions or not, vajroli should be practised.

तत्र वस्तुद्वयं वक्ष्ये दुर्लभं यस्य कस्यचित् ।
क्षीरं चैकं द्वितीयं तु नाडी च वशवर्तिनी ॥ 84 ॥

There are two things hard to obtain, one is milk and the second is a woman who can act according to your will.

This sloka need not be understood on face value. There are two essential requisites in the tantric practice of vajroli. One is milk and the second is an 'obedient' woman. Milk is *kshira*; in this context it refers to the flow of fluid or nectar from bindu, and it also means semen. The difficulty lies in it being maintained in one's own body, even after its release. Secondly, it is difficult to find a woman who is equally adept in the practice, if not more so, than the man. According to the ritual of vama marga tantra the practice is led by the woman, as she is the manifestation of Shakti and the spark of creation or kundalini comes from her. The third unmentioned requisite is the guru.

Actually, vajroli, amaroli and sahajoli have purposely been preserved secretly because of social beliefs which consider them to be immoral behaviour. Initiation into the practice is only given to ardent and dedicated yogis, not to the common person or the casual enquirer.

The system of hatha yoga consists of a substratum of tantric practices. Only ritual has been omitted. It is not a coincidence that the system has been handed down from a tantric guru. In hatha yoga the basic techniques for uniting the positive and negative energies within the individual have been maintained.

मेहनेन शनै: सम्यगूर्ध्वाकुंचनमभ्यसेत् ।
पुरुषोप्यथवा नारी वज्रोलीसिद्धिमाप्नुयात् ॥ 85 ॥

*By practising gradual upward contractions during the emission in
intercourse, any man or woman achieves perfection of vajroli.*

In the tantric system it is said that the husband and wife
should practise tantra together, and for that purpose they
must master certain techniques. The man has to master
vajroli and the woman has to master sahajoli, in combination
with moola bandha and uddiyana bandha (not as bandha but
as mudra).

Perfection of vajroli means being able to withdraw the
seminal fluid during the height of climax. This involves the
practice of contracting and controlling the muscles of the
urogenital complex. It should be practised daily in siddhasana or siddha yoni asana in the same progressive stages as
given for moola bandha. Initially the muscles of the genital,
excretory and urinary organs tend to contract simultaneously.
The muscular contractions have to be isolated in three
distinct areas. Eventually contractions become so forceful
that upward suction is created. In the female body the labia
minora should move upwards with complete contraction.
Practice of uddiyana bandha before vajroli creates greater
suction and tighter contraction.

According to the *Gheranda Samhita*, vajroli is an entirely
different practice. Perhaps the full details have been omitted.
You have to balance the body on the buttocks and place
the feet behind the head. The arms remain in front of the
body and palms on the ground. In this position the urinary
complex is compressed and automatic contraction of the
urogenital muscles occurs. However, it is not specifically
stated that these muscles are, or should be, contracted.
Neither is the retention of reproductive fluid hinted at.

Vajroli for women is called sahajoli. The yogini practises
sahajoli to regulate the hormones secreted from the ovaries.

This is the principle of preservation, and hatha yoga believes this to be the important point. Man must preserve his *veerya*, semen, and the female must preserve her secretions, *rajas*. Abstention from sexual life is not advocated. This is one of the most important points which everyone will have to understand very clearly, because it is a scientific point. It is not that celibacy is out of the question. Celibacy has its own merits, but it is not good for all. It is opposing the very realities and processes of nature. Then, what to do? Hatha yoga came up with a suggestion. It is called the principle of preservation. If you are able to master the technology of preservation, you are a brahmachari.

You can be a brahmachari even if you are married and a householder, if you are able to handle the technology of preservation. Preservation is important, the act is not important. If a negative experience occurs, that is due to loss, not due to the act. So for that, sahajoli has been prescribed for women and vajroli for men.

यत्नत: शस्तनालेन फूत्कारं वज्रकंदरे ।
शनै: शनै: प्रकुर्वीत वायुसंचारकारणात् ॥ 86 ॥

*By slowly drawing in air through a prescribed tube inserted into
the urethra of the penis, gradually air and prana traverse into the
vajra kanda.*

Preparation for vajroli must specifically be done under the
guidance of a guru and not just any teacher. In fact this form
of vajroli is rarely taught. The *Hatharatnavali* states that it
should only be taught to one "whom the guru feels like his
own prana. It should not be given to one's son without the
guru-disciple tradition." (2:75) Therefore even though the
instructions and techniques are given here it should not be
attempted out of curiosity.

The *Hatharatnavali* states that vajroli/sahajoli should
be done by men/women. However, the following practice
is specifically for men. The complete method of practice is
not given in this sloka, but in the *Hatharatnavali* there are
detailed descriptions: "According to the author of *Hatha Yoga
Pradipika*, one should blow with effort through the urethra
with a prescribed tube. This should be done repeatedly. If
the tube is made of green grass then insufficient air will pass,
but if the passing of air is not important then a tube of green
grass can be used. A tube of gold, silver or pure copper is
recommended by Srinivasa Yogi. This tube should be three
palas weight and twelve cubits long. The tube should be
smooth, bright and soft and made like an umbrella. It should
be introduced into the urethra for a moment, cautiously,
but without fear. This will give stability and strength to the
generative organ as well as increasing semen." (2:80–84)

A tube of one of the stable metals is specifically
recommended because these are chemically inert and will
not irritate or contaminate the urethra. Suitable substances
for this purpose must have been difficult to procure in
ancient times, as the risks of irritation and of introducing an

ascending infection into the bladder by using an unsterile catheter of an unsuitable material are considerable. In this age of medical technology, we can suggest that stainless steel, such as is used for surgical instruments, will be a satisfactory substitute, and in practice, a sterile rubber urinary catheter (size number 4 in width) about twenty centimetres long, is acceptable. Later, the catheter width can be increased up to size number 8. Whatever material is decided upon, it should be well sterilized before use.

Traditionally, the catheter was then smeared with almond oil or ghee to lubricate it so that it passed easily along the urethra without damaging the delicate lining. In our own day and age, catheterization of the bladder is routinely performed by doctors under sterile conditions. The entire surrounding genital area is first scrubbed and isolated by sterile drapes and sterile gloves are worn. The procedure is not without inherent difficulties, and we can suggest the yogi's body and hands be cleansed with soap and dried on a clean towel, with a clean sheet beneath the body. The sterilized catheter may then be lubricated with a diluted solution of a non-irritant germicidal such as Savlon.

It is said that the catheter should be gently passed to a distance of twelve angulas (17 centimetres) while two angulas (3 centimetres) remain outside the tip of the penis. This will depend on individual body size and structure. The important point is that the catheter should be passed until it enters the bladder, and there must be some remaining outside the body so that liquid can be drawn up into the bladder.

Initially only a fraction of the catheter should be inserted, one or two centimetres per day. If there is no unpleasant sensation or obstruction, then insert a little further. While negotiating the rim of the bladder, resistance may be encountered. This is due to the prostate gland which encircles the urethra at that point. This should not be overcome by force, as the urethra can definitely be torn in this way. Gentle manipulation is required and the male organ should be held at the same angle as during the erect state.

The process must be gradually accomplished, day by day. Do not hurry or force the procedure, as serious injury is possible. Only by consistent gentle application is success attained.

Once that resistance is passed, the catheter is felt to pass freely into the bladder, and a volume of urine may be immediately passed through the catheter, provided the bladder was not emptied prior to commencing the practice. This urine should be collected in a clean bowl.

Uddiyana and nauli should now be practised in a standing position. This sucks air into the bladder. Later, suction power can be increased by practising uddiyana in the squatting position (ukatasana). Only when you are able to suck up air should the same practice be done by placing the end of the catheter in a bowl of clean tepid water and sucking the water up through the catheter. After this, various liquids of increasing density and viscosity are to be drawn up.

In the hatha yoga tradition, first air is drawn into the bladder, then water, later oil, honey and finally liquid mercury. According to some authorities, it is neither essential nor advisable to use any liquid other than water. Instead of drawing further viscous liquids into the bladder, pure water may be used while varying the suction exerted by increasing the height to which the liquid is raised. Pulling water up thirteen centimetres is equivalent to raising mercury through one centimetre, because the specific gravity of mercury is thirteen times that of water.

The use of mercury as a medical agent is commonly mentioned in ancient ayurveda and also in alchemy, where it was one of the three base elements which was transformed into gold. In the ancient ayurvedic science of India, the ashes of various elements (*bhasma*) were incorporated into the body, and it was claimed that by assimilation of mercury into the body, immortality could be obtained. Siddhanagarjuna and Nityananda, two of the Nath siddhas, are said to have attained immortality in this way.

In modern times, mercury has been recognized as a powerful poison by medical scientists and, therefore, some researchers now consider that these ancient prescriptions were allegorical references to secret techniques which produce immortal consciousness (gold). It is more than possible that the ancients were referring in veiled terms, not to the internal consumption of mercury, but to its use in the perfection of vajroli mudra as a bestower of immortality.

नारीभगे पतद्विंदुमभ्यासेनोर्ध्वमाहरेत् ।
चलितं च निजं बिंदुमूर्ध्वमाकृष्य रक्षयेत् ॥ 87 ॥

*The bindu (semen) that is about to fall into the woman's vagina
should be made to move upwards with practice. And if it falls, the
semen and the woman's fluid should be conserved by drawing it up.*

The bindu or semen is not supposed to be released but if
this occurs then it must be drawn up through the generative
organ by vajroli. The flow of bindu can be reversed at various
stages, for example, through practices of vipareeta karani
mudra, khechari mudra, etc., as has already been discussed.
Vajroli is the last technique to be described.

In the previous slokas it has been stated that so long
as bindu falls into the 'sun', decay and death are the end
result, as it is consumed by the fire during the lifespan.
The sun represents rajas in manipura, but rajas also refers
to vaginal secretions. Therefore, if the bindu falls into the
rajas, the practice of vajroli has not been successful. When
bindu falls to manipura, what is actually consumed by the
fire are its sattwic nectarine qualities which enlighten the
body and bestow immortality. Below manipura the chakras
are concerned with instinctive animal functions and tamasic
qualities, and if the bindu is spilled here it becomes a
poison, causing suffering and death. Therefore, during
the practice of maithuna a sattwic state of mind has to be
maintained at all costs, even though the lower chakras are
activated; the rajasic and tamasic tendencies of those centres
are to be recognized and controlled.

The *Shiva Samhita* states: "The practice of vajroli bestows
deliverance even upon those who are bound by worldly
attraction. It is therefore the duty of all yogis to ensure that
it is practised with due care. The wise should first absorb into
their body the ovarial fluid in the vagina by contracting the
duct of their own organ and thereafter perform coitus without
ejecting the seminal fluid. Should the latter tend to issue,

it must be restrained by the means of yoni mudra (vajroli). Next, the same seminal fluid should be diverted to the channel on the left (ida) and the coitus stopped for a while. Thereafter, in accordance with the instructions of the guru, they should, with a long intake of apana, extract with one triumphal effort the remaining ovarial fluid in the vagina." (4:79–84) In this text there is no mention of the preparatory stages of vajroli using a tube and water.

Comparison of all the texts gives a clearer picture of vajroli. First uddiyana, nauli and moola bandha have to be perfected. Then vajroli should be practised by sitting on the buttocks, raising the legs, etc., as described in the *Gheranda Samhita*. After this, it should be practised by muscular contraction of the urethra and then with a tube or catheter. When all these have been perfected it is the guru who will indicate further practices.

एवं संरक्षयेद् बिन्दुं मृत्युं जयति योगवित् ।
मरणं बिंदुपातेन जीवनं बिंदुधारणात् ॥ 88 ॥

Therefore, the knower of yoga conquers death by preserving the bindu (semen). Release of the bindu means death; conservation of semen is life.

This sloka demands detailed discussion. The word *bindu* means point or nucleus. The nucleus of every cell is this same bindu. It contains the chromosomes which encode the entire memory and evolutionary potential of the species. Of course, it is not only loss of semen which causes death. Cell degeneration, death and replacement is continually occurring at a certain rate in all the tissues of the body (except in the central nervous system where the neurones are not replaced). Semen and menses are specifically referred to because their rate of formation and turnover far overshadows the turnover rate of the other cells, and therefore has the most metabolic significance.

What is the connection between the semen and im-mortality? It is twofold. In common life, union of these germ cells creates another bindu, another individual and another universe. This is the glimpse of immortality through one's progeny. Secondly, according to Swatmarama, if seminal release from the body can be quelled, a man has tapped within his own body that same primal source of life.

Both medical science and modern psychology have dismissed the ancient belief in the value of retaining the semen as an old wives' tale. However, from the yogic experience, this myth contains more essential truth than all the medical and psychological tomes ever published.

There have been 'experts' who have nevertheless remained ignorant about the purpose of existence. The modern age is no exception. There may be intellectual giants, there may be compassionate and even heroic men, there may be dedicated humanists, but this is not enough if they have failed to grasp transcendental experience. Their endeavours and achievements remain within the realm of empirical consciousness and the lower mind.

Why has Swatmarama made a claim that loss of semen is the cause of death? The semen contains an enormous force in molecular or potential form. It can be compared to the potential contained within an atomic bomb. The seminal fluid discharged in a single emission contains an average of 400 million spermatozoa. Each of these minute sperm possesses enough energy to swim 3,000 times its own length. In relative terms that is the same amount of energy used up by a six-foot man swimming one and a half miles. That is the amount, proportionally, of the body's vital energy packed into a single sperm cell expelled from the body in a single seminal emission.

When the shedding and ejaculation of semen is habitual, frequent and uncontrolled, that individual is being constantly drained of a quantum of highly potent living essence which the body has no option but to continually replace using a constant supply of metabolic energy.

Where has this energy which is lost in the semen come from? From the nutritional viewpoint, it is derived from the dietary nutrients, broken down in digestion, assimilated into the blood and constituted into the nucleic acids and the fatty protein structure of the spermatozoa. Metabolic energy is consumed every step of the way. Constant replacement of discharged semen demands that a diet rich in fats and proteins be consumed. This imposes a heavy working burden upon the digestive organs and glands, such as the liver and pancreas, as well as on the heart, circulatory and eliminative systems.

As a result, the cells and tissues of the bodily systems demand replacement more rapidly, and the higher overall cell turnover leads to greater expenditure of metabolic energy, accelerates the metabolic rate and elevates the basal body temperature. According to gerontologists, who investigate the ageing and degenerative process, elevation and acceleration of these factors are the major cause of rapid physical degeneration and early death of the human body.

According to Swatmarama, preservation of the semen in the body conserves energy and bestows upon the yogi a power and experience not known to a man accustomed to losing semen throughout his life. He declares that semen which is withheld is the very nectar of immortality.

How many men die prematurely with desires unfulfilled and dreams unaccomplished because vitality has deserted their body, clarity has escaped their minds, acuity has vanished from their senses and exhaustion has overcome their will? Could it be that seminal retention sustains a greater conscious power in the body, mind and will of a yogi? Does seminal retention create an indwelling fountain of joy, power and bliss which enlightens the human brain? These are the questions which modern scientists will have to ask themselves. It is not sufficient to dismiss the claims and experiences of yogis as unscientific myths. The materialistic scientific vision of man as nought beyond blood, bone, bile and fat is sustained by the uncontrolled loss of semen.

Why control the semen? Certainly not for any moralistic reason. Note well that Swatmarama is not recommending celibacy, only the retention of semen; if a man can escape from the slavish compulsion to expel the semen, he can realize within himself the source of freedom, immortality and bliss.

The entire *Hatha Yoga Pradipika* sets out the method to preserve the body and mind. Let those who would realize the truth seek a guru and practise according to initiation and instructions.

सुगंधो योगिनो देहे जायते बिंदुधारणात् ।
यावद् बिन्दुः स्थिरो देहे तावत् कालभयं कुतः ॥ 89 ॥

As long as the bindu or semen is steady in the body, then where is the fear of death? The yogi's body smells pleasant by conserving the bindu or semen.

Fear of death is one of the most fundamental motivating forces governing human personality and behaviour. These have been termed as *kleshas* by Sage Patanjali. Fear of death stems from identification of the self with the physical body. Release of semen strongly reinforces this identification. When a yogi can control the bindu, preventing its release from the body even in maithuna, identification with the body ceases, and consciousness is freed from physical identification. Then the fear of death dissolves.

Even though a person may say that he does not fear death, nevertheless his body's reactions and responses betray that he is still governed by this fear. It remains a subconscious determinant of his behaviour. To convince the conscious mind that 'I am fearless' in the face of death is not difficult. It is only a psychological matter. How can we convince the deeper mind and overcome the physiological responses of fear which are subconsciously determined? For that, tantric and yogic sadhana are necessary and a competent guru should be sought.

The second segment of the sloka states that conservation of the bindu alters the smell of the yogi's body. How can this occur? The cyclic phases of the reproductive process liberate chemicals from the body which have particular odours. These have been isolated by scientists and are known as pheromones. Normally we are unaware of these odours unless they are potent, but they exert a subliminal influence upon the unconscious brain. Scientific investigations have revealed that the odour emitted from one woman's armpits at the onset of her menstruation triggers off a chain reaction in other women living in close proximity. It has also been found that the pheromones released from a man's armpit cause a psychoemotional response in a woman depending on the stage of her menstrual cycle.

With the release of reproductive secretions, new cells are produced and the odour cycle begins. However, if the semen is maintained in the body the quality of the pheromones changes. It is something like cultivating perfume. Premature cultivation does not give a pleasant smell, but once perfectly cultivated it will give off a fragrant odour. Similarly the body of a yogi emits a highly fragrant odour.

Of course, as well as conservation of semen, other factors influencing body odour have to be taken into consideration. Pure and moderate diet, regular bathing and keeping the clothes clean also influences body odour, but Swatmarama is talking of something beyond this.

चित्तायत्तं नृणां शुक्रं शुक्रायत्तं च जीवितम् ।
तस्माच्छुक्रं मनःश्चैव रक्षणीयं प्रयत्नतः ॥ 90 ॥

A man's semen can be controlled by the mind and control of semen is life-giving. Therefore, his semen and mind should be controlled and conserved.

Yogis have always claimed that autonomic body functions can be consciously controlled, but it takes time and effort. It is only recently that science is proving this true. The easiest method is to work with pranayama, as the rate and depth of the breath influences the physiological systems of the body, brainwave patterns and modes of thinking. Function of the reproductive organs can also be influenced and eventually controlled by yoga practices over a sustained period of time. The easiest functions to control are those concerned with the voluntary nervous system. For this the system of asana has been developed. Release of reproductive secretion is not only a physiological process. The mind is also involved. Without mental involvement the release cannot occur.

The role of sensory pathways, *jnanendriya*, and mental imagery in initiating sexual responses must be witnessed. Control of mind begins by becoming aware of the process. By isolating awareness, the mind remains unexcited in the midst of sensory perception. When the mind can be witnessed in this way, excitation of the motor responses, *karmendriya*, can be controlled, and semen can be withheld. Control of mind means control of the whole process.

By the practice of vajroli one can learn to control the physical mechanism, but side by side with this, mental control must be developed. When the mind wanders in useless fantasy, energy is dissipated. When the mind is totally concentrated on a specific object, symbol or point, pranic movements are channelled and the bindu is maintained. In hatha yoga the mind has to be kept on the aim of the practices in order to induce total one-pointedness.

ऋतुमत्या रजोऽप्येवं निजं बिंदुं च रक्षयेत् ।
मेंढ्रेणाकर्षयेदूर्ध्वं सम्यगभ्यासयोगवित् ॥ 91 ॥

The knower of yoga, perfect in the practice, conserves his bindu and the woman's rajas by drawing it up through the generative organ.

It is not just a matter of control during maithuna which can awaken the higher centres. It is the appropriate combination of the opposite elements and energies. When hydrogen gas and oxygen combine there is an instant explosion. Similarly in the physical body when the positive and negative elements combine there is an explosion. When the union takes place in the nucleus of mooladhara chakra, kundalini shakti is released. At that time, if vajroli is practised, the energy rises up sushumna and the central nervous system to ajna chakra in the brain. The purpose of the practice is neither indulgence nor birth control but specifically to expand the consciousness. The experience has an impact that can last for hours, days or weeks. When vajroli has been perfected, the expanded state of consciousness becomes a permanent experience.

The *Shiva Samhita* states: "Know that the seminal fluid is the moon and the ovarian fluid is the sun. It is necessary to coalesce the two within one's own body. In fact I (Shiva) am the seminal fluid and the ovarian fluid is Shakti. When the two are united in the body of the yogi, he attains a divine body." (4:86, 87) There are two processes: one is the process of uniting the sun and the moon through vajroli and maithuna. Secondly, that process has to take place within one's own body. Only the guru can further illumine this to the disciple.

SAHAJOLI MUDRA
(attitude of spontaneous arousing)

अथ सहजोलि: ।

सहजोलिश्चामरोलिर्वज्रोल्या भेद एकत: ।
जले सुभस्म निक्षिप्य दग्धगोमयसंभवम् ॥ 92 ॥

Sahajoli and amaroli are separate techniques of vajroli. The ashes of burnt cow manure should be mixed with water.

वज्रोलीमैथुनादूर्ध्वं स्त्रीपुंसो: स्वांगलेपनम् ।
आसीनयो: सुखेनैव मुक्तव्यापारयो: क्षणात् ॥ 93 ॥

After performing vajroli during intercourse, (being in a comfortable position), the man and woman should wipe the ashes on specific parts of their bodies during the leisure time.

सहजोलिरियं प्रोक्ता श्रद्धेया योगिभि: सदा ।
अयं शुभकरो योगो भोगयुक्तोऽपि मुक्तिद: ॥ 94 ॥

It is called sahajoli and the yogis have complete faith in it. This is very beneficial and enables enlightenment through the combination of yoga and bhoga (sensual involvement).

Sahaj means 'spontaneous'. Sahajoli is an essential part of vajroli, just as jalandhara is part and parcel of uddiyana. The description of sahajoli here differs from other texts. Here it is the practice done by both the man and woman which entails the application of ash. In tantra, vajroli is done by men and the same practice when done by a woman is sahajoli. In the *Shiva Samhita* also it is said that: "When the yogi is able to control and stop the discharge of seminal fluid by means of yoni mudra (vajroli), it is called sahajoli. It is a secret preserved in all the tantras. These (sahajoli and amaroli) are only different in name, in effect they are the same.

Therefore, either can be used by the yogi – but all with due care." (4:97,98) Amaroli and sahajoli are two different means of preserving bindu. Amaroli is discussed in the next sloka.

In the ancient tradition of Shaivism, ash is wiped onto the body and in particular onto the forehead. This is not only a mark to indicate that they are followers of Shiva, but also to raise the consciousness within the body, and awaken the higher faculty of mind. Just as the application of sindhur, which contains mercury, stimulates ajna chakra, so the particular ash applied onto the body in sahajoli influences the subtle elements, *tattwas*, of the body.

In preparation for tantric sadhana, purification of the body is achieved by a process called *bhuta shuddhi*, which means purification of the pancha tattwas (five elements). This involves pranayama, meditation, application of ash, mantra and fasting. In the *Srimad Devi Bhagavatam* application of ash is known as 'the bath of fire' and is considered as one of the highest forms of sadhana. It is not any ash which is used. It has to be ash of cow manure, and in this Purana the breed of cow it should be taken from and when, according to the moon phase, is delineated.

The application of ash is not mentioned in conjunction with maithuna, however, the use of ash is greatly praised. "The yogi who takes the bath of ashes all over his body at the time of the three sandhyas, quickly develops the state of union (yoga). This bath of ashes is many times superior to a water bath . . . This is first mentioned by Shiva, who took the bath himself . . . He who applies the ash on his head attains the state of Rudra (Shiva, pure consciousness) while living in the body of five elements (pancha tattwa) . . . The ash bath cleanses not only external but also internal uncleanliness."

There are two main paths to realize the truth: one is pravritti, the other is nivritti. *Pravritti* is the path of spiritual evolution by involvement in desires, ambitions, emotions and all the modifications of the mind, *vrittis*, without renouncing any aspect of worldly life. Nivritti is resignation, the path of total retirement from the vrittis, worldly life and society.

391

According to the concept given in the Vedas, the first two stages of a man's life, *brahmacharya* and *grihastha ashramas*, taking one up to the age of fifty, belong to the pravritti *marga*, or path. In these two stages the desires, cravings and ambitions are necessary and you evolve through expressing them. Then a period of transition has to come from pravritti to nivritti. This is *vanaprastha ashrama*, the third stage of life from fifty to seventy-five years of age, in which you reflect on your life. You begin to doubt and rethink, leading to resignation, the fourth stage, or *sannyasa ashrama*.

The *Bhagavad Gita* makes it quite clear that you can reach the ultimate reality either by pravritti or nivritti. Pravritti or involvement is described in terms of *karma*, or action and expression. Nivritti is the path of Samkhya, or awareness and experience. However, there is a contention made by some authorities that the Supreme or ultimate reality cannot be attained by pravritti, active involvement, but can only be experienced by nivritti, passive awareness. However, the *Bhagavad Gita* clearly states that those who work and those who renounce will both reach that end provided they resign their ego, surrender their lower self, purify their mind and discipline their senses. If they detach or renounce themselves from the idea of doership i.e. 'I am doing', then ordinary householders can reach the higher path.

The path of pravritti or involvement is not for sensual pleasure and enjoyments. Sensual life is a byproduct. The real purpose is illumination, but it is a path which takes a long time. It is circuitous and not dangerous. Nivritti marga is very difficult and even precipitous, but it is short.

Here in this sloka of the *Hatha Yoga Pradipika*, we are shown that the combination of yoga, awareness, and bhoga, sensual involvement, are compatible. In fact, as long as you are involved in the external world the inner awareness must be developed and yoga or union must be the objective. This is where hatha yoga becomes extremely useful, whether one is following the path of involvement or resignation.

392

अयं योग: पुण्यवतां धीराणां तत्त्वदर्शिनाम् ।
निर्मत्सराणां वै सिध्येत्र तु मत्सरशालिनाम् ॥ 95 ॥

Verily this yoga is perfected by virtuous and well-conducted men who have seen the truth and not those who are selfish.

Vajroli and maithuna were never meant for the general public because most people are victims of their emotions and passions. The first requirements for the practice is a passionless state of mind. Maybe one or two people today can fit into this category. Only those who have entered the highest states of samadhi know what a passionless state is.

These practices result in greater personal power and if used by selfish people they will incur catastrophes upon themselves and others. The story of Milarepa is a very good example. Though he attained his power through other tantric means, nevertheless the intent in his mind was to punish those who had caused his mother and family hardship. He put his power to an evil end with disastrous results which far exceeded those earlier inflicted upon his own family.

The purpose of liberating the energy through vajroli is to go beyond personal identity and the limitations of the ego. If yoga is practised only to gain psychic power, or if vajroli is an excuse for any lesser fulfilment, the practices are being misused.

However, there is another important point. There is a saying 'knowledge purifies'. Even a person with the most selfish, criminal tendencies, if he practises yoga, no matter what his intentions may be, his consciousness will evolve towards perfection much more quickly than if no practice is adopted. The higher faculties of consciousness and awareness will begin to operate and the personality will slowly change as defective conditioning and unpleasant habits are restructured in the brain. The *Shiva Samhita* states that: "People under delusion, and being in constant prey of decay and death in this world, can make their pleasure and pain equal by control of the seminal fluid." (4:91)

A novice will not be able to find a guru to teach him the traditional method of this practice. Nor will a guru teach any person who is untrustworthy or cannot understand the purpose of the practices. Likewise we have to be careful when we read about these practices as interpreted by non-yogis because incorrect descriptions have surely been given, "The priest then, in the presence of all, behaves towards the female in a manner which decency forbids to be mentioned; after which the persons present repeat many times the name of some god, performing actions utterly abominable and here this most diabolical business closes." Precisely for this reason many people have a misconception concerning vajroli. Only those who can comprehend the subtle laws of tantra, kundalini, energy and consciousness can appreciate its significance and necessity.

AMAROLI MUDRA (attitude arousing immortality)

अथामरोली ।

पित्तोल्बणत्वात्प्रथमांबुधारां विहाय निःसारतयांत्यधाराम् ।
निषेव्यते शीतलमध्यधारा कापालिके खण्डमतेऽमरोली ॥ ९६ ॥

*According to the Kapalika sect, amaroli is practised by drinking
the cool midstream of urine. The first part of the urine is left as
it contains bile, and the last part is left as it does not contain
goodness.*

अमरीं यः पिबेन्नित्यं नस्यं कुर्वन्दिनेदिने ।
वज्रोलीमभ्यसेत् सम्यक्सामरोलीति कथ्यते ॥ ९७ ॥

*One who drinks amari, takes it through the nose and practises
vajroli, is said to be practising amaroli.*

The various hatha yoga texts have different views as to what
constitutes the practice of amaroli. *Amara* means 'immortal',
'undying' or 'imperishable'. Thus amaroli is the practice
leading to immortality. The *Hatha Yoga Pradipika* designates
that 'according to the Kapalika sect' amaroli is the practice
of drinking the midstream of urine. The *Shiva Samhita* states
that amaroli is the practice of withdrawing the seminal fluid
from the woman after it has been released. However, this
has previously been described as vajroli. Amaroli is most
commonly accepted as the practice described here.

Urine has been used as a healing agent in many cultures
for centuries but little has ever been spoken about it, as urine
is generally considered to be unclean. Definitely the urine
of people who take an unwholesome diet, and those whose
bodies are impure, will be offensive because it contains toxins
and metabolic wastes that are harmful to drink, or even
apply on the body. However, the midstream urine of a yogi
is pure and inoffensive.

In tantra and yoga, amaroli is also known as *shivambhu*, i.e. the basic element of one's self. The drinking of the midstream of urine is highly regarded in yoga. There is also a science of urine therapy, but medical science has yet to look more deeply into it.

The *Jnanarnava Tantra* states that: "After realizing the exact knowledge of dharma and adharma, healthy and unhealthy lifestyle, every aspect of the (material) world becomes holy – stool, urine, nails, bone, all are holy aspects in the sight of that person who has explored mantra. O Parvati, deities (divine powers) are living in that water from which urine is made, then why is urine said to be contaminated?" (Ch.22)

People believe urine to be unclean because they think of it as a waste product, of the same quality as faeces. We should review this concept thoroughly. Both anatomically and physiologically, it is not correct to class urine and stool together, because the two are produced in completely different ways and leave the body by distinct and separate portals.

Urine is an ultra-filtrate of the blood. It contains water, hormones, enzymes, electrolytes, minerals and byproducts of protein and fat breakdown, which exceed the body's capacity to recycle them at that time. Therefore, these may be termed as wastes only in the same sense that grains harvested by a farmer are surplus because they exceed the capacity of the granary to store them for later use. It is not that they are wastes in the sense of being unclean, but only that their potential value has had to be sacrificed. Vital biomolecules such as hormones, amino acids and enzymes are synthesized at great metabolic cost to the body and their loss from the body must be considered as a waste indeed.

Furthermore, the human bloodstream is an absolutely clean living substance, from which the urine is filtered and collected in absolutely sterile conditions by the kidneys. Nor is there any question of bacterial contamination in the ureters, bladder or urethra provided, of course, no infection is present. Therefore, which part of this process can be termed dirty? Medical scientists will have to consider this carefully if they wish to understand the rejuvenating power of amaroli.

Solid waste is formed in an entirely different way. The digestive tract is unsterile from the mouth to the anus, and at no time has this solid matter actually entered inside the body, or into the general circulation. It has remained only within the hollow digestive pipe, yielding up its nutrients without being itself assimilated into the body.

Then what is offensive about the urine? Urine which contains a high concentration of urea, uric acid and bile salts has a definite pungent taste and objectionable quality. However, these constituents are the byproducts of protein and fat metabolism and are contained in only very small amounts in the urine of a yogi who consumes a diet low in protein and devoid of animal products. That is the first requirement for amaroli. The diet should be completely fresh and natural, without excess salt, spices and condiments. Highly refined and processed foods should also be avoided. Under these circumstances, the quality of the urine is transformed. It is not that the practice becomes ineffective or prohibited by a heavy, rich diet. However, objectionable qualities of the urine are avoided if a lighter diet is adopted.

It is not possible to overcome mental conditioning about urine just by thinking intellectually. However, practice of amaroli rapidly dissolves subconscious blockages. If you feel that your own urine is impure, it betrays your deep subconscious belief about your own body and its origin. Subconsciously, you have inherited the conviction that your body is impure. This deep rooted defect must be eradicated, and if amaroli is practised for a fixed period of time according to the guru's instruction, this surely occurs.

Scientists who study the body's biorhythms have discovered that during the day and night, various hormones are secreted sequentially. For example, pituitary hormones such as the growth hormone are released during sleep, while ACTH which activates the adrenal glands and TSH which

397

activates the thyroid, become prominent during daytime activity. Pineal hormones follow a similar diurnal pattern.

The various hormones are filtered into the urine over the nocturnal sleep period and are reassimilated into the blood when amaroli is practised on rising in the morning. This urine will accurately mirror the hormonal activities which have occurred during sleep. In this regard, it is the hormones secreted in the night and, specifically, in the very early morning hours, which are of most value, because in this physiological lull period, consciousness is withdrawn from the lower centres and the secretions of the cerebral glands become prominent.

The influence of vajroli and amaroli upon the human reproductive system is profound. The levels of reproductive hormones from the pituitary (gonadotrophins) follow a monthly rhythm in the female body to secrete oestrogen and progesterone sequentially, which initiate and maintain the menstrual cycle. In the male body the pituitary gonadotrophins cause the formation of the spermatozoa and the secretion of testosterone by the testes. Their levels in the bloodstream vary according to the rate of sperm formation and release.

Amaroli and vajroli have always been known to yoginis as an effective oral contraceptive. This occurs because the reassimilation of the urine containing oestrogen and progesterone effectively inhibits ovulation, in the same way that the oral contraceptive pill, which contains synthetic oestrogen and progesterone, prevents ovulation from occurring. The difference is that in amaroli these hormones are the body's own natural products, and many of the side effects of the synthetic preparations do not occur.

Similarly, in the male, reassimilation of testosterone in the urine creates negative feedback upon the pituitary, inhibiting the further release of gonadotrophins. As a result, further production of testosterone and spermatozoa is temporarily inhibited, reducing the sperm count, although seminal fluid continues to be formed.

We have to remember that amaroli has always been a closely guarded secret revealed to yogis by initiation, but not to others. It is part of a system which evolves the human body into an illumined state over a number of years.

What is the overall effect of long term practice of amaroli upon the human psychophysiology? Medical science has yet to establish it, but we can postulate that it rectifies the inherent imbalance between the process of production and consumption of hormones in the body which is the fundamental cause of the ageing process. Scientists have always dreamed of a 'perpetual motion machine' which would run indefinitely on its own products, thus conserving energy for other purposes, but they have been unable to create it. Amaroli is based upon this principle.

There are a few rules for those who wish to practise amaroli. First of all, amaroli sadhana is not suitable for all and, therefore, it should be adopted according to a guru's instructions. Secondly, the amount and duration of the practice will be indicated by the guru. Thirdly, regular habits and lifestyle are necessary. Finally, amaroli is a secret sadhana. Once you are practising, it should not be discussed in public. Certain experiences will come to you in yoga sadhana which are known to the guru and can be discussed with him, but not with others.

अभ्यासात्रि:सृतां चांद्रीं विभूत्या सह मिश्रयेत् ।
धारयेदुत्तमांगेषु दिव्यदृष्टि: प्रजायते ॥ 98 ॥

The practitioner should mix the semen with the ashes of burnt cow manure and wipe it on the upper parts of the body, it bestows divya drishti (clairvoyance or divine sight).

After performing vajroli, a little of the semen should be released, mixed with prepared ash of cow manure and wiped onto the body. Here the sloka says to wipe it on the 'uttam' parts, which can either mean the best parts or the upper parts. If taken to mean the best parts, these are the forehead, throat, chest, upper arms, navel, upper thighs, anus, back and feet. The upper parts indicate either the forehead only, or include the throat, chest and upper arms. In tantra this is always accompanied by the repetition of mantras. The effects of mantra are mainly on the subtle body, but it also cools the physical body and has a strong psychological effect as it reminds the practitioners that what is being practised is in the cause of awakening the higher spirit.

Tantra has been grossly maligned by moralists and puritans in the past. Tantric practices have been called decadent, sinful, depraved and perverted. However, at best, these judgements are social and religious concepts which have scant bearing upon self-realization. Those with an eye to see deeper can grasp that tantra is none of these.

By and large, religions have failed mankind because they have failed to show their adherents the path by which an earnest seeker can evolve a divine body and realize himself. 'I may be a good, kind and peaceful man by religious dictum, but what good are all these social and moral conventions for me if I fail to attain self-realization?' This is the standpoint of tantra.

A paper rose can be sprinkled with fragrant water so that it bears a passing semblance to a real rose bloom, but no one who looks closely can be deceived for very long. In the same way, one may practise virtue, righteousness and morality for a whole life span. However, unless one has confronted the subconscious mind and awakened the dormant energy there, one can only ever remain an imitation.

A fragrant rose can be cultivated only after its roots have been established in rich earth. To cherish the rose while disdaining the roots is called schizophrenia, and this is the sickness which puritans and moralists have inherited. Who are those blessed ones who can glimpse the realities of human evolution, who can see the sublime and compassionate purpose of the tantric system? One who has attained self-realization, let him live by any system or by none. It does not matter, for he will be a system unto himself. He will exude the fragrance of enlightenment everywhere and unconditionally, for that is his nature. Truth and virtue will be his being, but not his practice or commitment.

If I am a debauchee or a criminal, perhaps not openly but in the secret recesses of my mind and heart, then why should I suppress it? Is it because of inherent goodness that I do not express my subconscious desires and personality, or is my suppression due to fear? This is the question which sincere religious people will have to ask themselves now.

Religions demand you to suppress yourself, but if you do so that is where your evolution is arrested, the internal energy becomes blocked, and it can remain so for an entire lifetime. Such suppression brings anxiety, depression and disease upon an individual, and fear, hatred, cruelty, and violence upon society. This is why tantra proclaims: accept yourself in totality. Then the cultivation of a real and immortal rose can begin.

पुंसो बिंदुं समाकुंच्य सम्यगभ्यासपाटवात् ।
यदि नारी रजो रक्षेद्द्वज्रोल्या साषि योगिनी ॥ 99 ॥

If a woman practises vajroli and saves her rajas and the man's
bindu by thorough contraction, she is a yogini.

Just as a man should be adept in the practice, the woman
also has to be well-practised and adept. There are few
references in the hatha yoga texts that the practices are
meant for women but here it is clearly stated. Just as a
man should practise gradual contractions of the urogenital
muscles so should the woman. According to tantra that is
sahajoli.

   The *Hatharatnavali* states that: "Rajas is permanent,
like red lead, in the reproductive organ of a woman. The
rajas should be saved during menstruation like bindu is
to be saved. The woman should practise vajroli, after that
she should draw up the rajas if possible. The nada in her
body moves like bindu. Bindu and rajas produced in the
body should be mixed through the vajroli practice of yoga.
Then success is at hand. The woman who does not know
the science of yoga should not practise vajroli. This yoga is
successful to the courageous and pious yogis who have an
insight into reality." (2:93, 101–103)

   Just as a man prepares for vajroli by practising contractions and then drawing up air and water through a catheter
via the urethra, so a woman can practise in a similar way.
Instead of inserting a catheter into the urethra, however, a
tube (0.8 centimetres wide and ten centimetres long) should
be inserted into the vagina so that a portion of it extends
outside. Then sit on a bucket of water and practise uddiyana
bandha. If water is not sucked into the vagina through this
process, then practise vama, dakshina and madhyama nauli.
When this has been perfected, try to retain the water inside
for as long as possible. Try to hold it while standing upright.
Then practise nauli by churning the abdominal muscles. This

cleanses the vagina of old secretions. After these practices are perfected, practise without the use of a tube. Only sit on the bucket and practise uddiyana or nauli. Again try to retain the water inside and stand erect. When the water can be retained inside only by the practice of moola bandha and without uddiyana, the perineal muscles associated with moola bandha and vajroli/sahajoli have become strong.

तस्या: किंचिद्रजो नाशं न गच्छति न संशय: ।
तस्या: शरीरे नादश्च बिंदुतामेव गच्छति ॥ 100 ॥

*Without doubt, not even a little rajas is wasted through vajroli, the
nada and bindu in the body become one.*

The sloka refers to the perfection of vajroli in maithuna.
The important point here concerns the manifestation of the
gross and subtle bindu. Rajas refers to the ovum, which is the
physical manifestation of the bindu in the female body. The
ovarian follicle which nurtures and surrounds the ovum is
responsible for the menstrual cycle. The menses and vaginal
secretions are dependent manifestations of the ovum, because
the ovarian follicle secretes the hormones, oestrogen and
progesterone, which induce the proliferation of the uterine
lining and its expulsion during the menstrual period.

Therefore, the ovum is the rajas; the menstrual and
vaginal fluids are the dependent secretions of that rajas, and
in vajroli it is the ovum which is withdrawn as the bindu. In
the male body the physical bindu is the spermatozoa, which
are supported in the medium of the seminal fluid. By vajroli
the spermatozoa are withdrawn from the semen to become
the bindu.

The important point in this sloka is that if the bindu is
totally withdrawn, neither energy nor fluid are lost from the
body. Actually it is not the retention or release of the fluids
which is vitally important, but the conservation of energy. If
the production of spermatozoa has been halted by vajroli or
amaroli sadhana, then the bindu, i.e. the energy nucleus, has
been withdrawn. The seminal fluid is devoid of spermatozoa,
so that even if released from the body, energy loss does not
occur.

Similarly in the female body, if ovulation has been
suppressed by sahajoli or amaroli, then the bindu of energy
has been withdrawn. Then any residual menstrual loss is an
insignificant drain upon the body.

For fertility and the production of progeny, a high sperm count and a rich menstrual loss may be most desirable, and as yet this has been the viewpoint of medical science, which considers a sperm count of less than 400 millions per millilitre to be deficient and a menstrual period of less than four or five days to be scanty. However, for the performance of vajroli in maithuna, where the goal is spiritual illumination, semen with very low or absent spermatozoa, and ovulation which has been naturally suppressed, are desirable prerequisites.

Even from the human standpoint, where sexual intercourse occurs for the giving and receiving of pleasure, a sperm-rich semen and heavy menstrual loss are not desirable, as too much vital energy is being needlessly sacrificed. When there is loss of energy from the body, a dissolution of awareness occurs. This is experienced as a 'fall' because the power of consciousness has fragmented and the physical vitality has dissipated.

In sloka 87 it has been stated that even if the bindu should be lost into the vaginal secretions, consciousness can be resurrected, energy regained and the fragments of the shattered bindu reaggregated, if the mixed secretions lying inside the vagina can be drawn up into the male body through vajroli. However, the present sloka emphasizes the indwelling perfection of the retained bindu, resplendent like the full moon, and for this to be restored perfected vajroli demands that not even a little of the mixed secretions be left behind in the vagina.

The second part of the sloka is also very important as it refers to the experiences of the bindu in vajroli. How and where is the bindu which has been withdrawn from the rajas (ova/spermatozoa) to be experienced? It has to be traced to its origin through vajroli. It is a point in consciousness. It is not in the body, nor in the mind, but it is experienced through the body and the mind.

When mooladhara chakra awakens in maithuna, the bindu of consciousness must be raised by vajroli, away from the sensual experiences. How to control the manifestation of this bindu? How to sustain and prolong this experience and realize its source? The bindu or semen is the interface between matter, energy and consciousness. If you try to focus your awareness onto that experience in mooladhara, is the semen the material you are trying to isolate, or your consciousness, or is it an experience of energy which you are undergoing? Or is it the point of your own consciousness that is being located? It is the bindu, that is all. That bindu must be withheld, withdrawn and redirected upwards by vajroli.

Where does the point of consciousness go when vajroli is performed? Try to remember or re-experience it. Where is it experienced? Does it retreat upwards towards its source? Or was its source in mooladhara and by vajroli it is being enticed to rise? By vajroli, this bindu rises to ajna chakra. It manifests at the eyebrow centre and can be experienced there in ajna.

Ajna is not the source of bindu, but through vajroli its form will manifest there. By sustaining vajroli that bindu goes beyond ajna, where it becomes subtler than audible sound or nada in the consciousness, i.e. *ashabda*. The sound, or *nada*, released from the chakras below ajna, is traced back to its source where the bindu and nada are one. It is somewhere in the totality of consciousness, above, beyond and within, where the mind has dissolved, time and body do not exist, but only consciousness in the form of soundless sound.

To conclude, the practice of vajroli brings equilibrium in the mind and body. It revitalizes the body, activates all the energy centres and awakens sushumna nadi. The higher faculties of the brain are activated. In fact, it could be the most powerful practice in the awakening of kundalini and higher consciousness, However, unless the practitioner maintains a sattwic state of awareness, it is useless.

स बिंदुस्तद्रजश्चैव एकीभूय स्वदेहगौ ।
वज्रोल्यभ्यासयोगेन सर्वसिद्धि प्रयच्छत: ॥ 101 ॥

The bindu and that rajas in one's own body unite through the union
by practice of vajroli, thus bestowing all perfections or siddhis.

Perfection of vajroli is the union within one body of the two
opposite forces, prana and mind, which results in the ascent
of kundalini. As kundalini travels up to sahasrara through
the various energy and psychic centres, specific perfections
of mind and body become apparent. The signs and siddhis
have already been described.

Now the union of the opposite poles to awaken mooladhara is to be accomplished within the body of the yogi
alone by a more subtle process. In this context, the terms
rajas and bindu are redefined. In this stage of vajroli, the
union is to be established between consciousness (Shiva) and
energy (Shakti) within the yogi's body.

The *Goraksha Satarka* states that: "Bindu is Shiva
(consciousness), rajas is Shakti (energy). Bindu is the moon
(ida) and rajas is the sun (pingala). From the mingling
of these two, one obtains the highest state. Shukra bindu
(semen) is joined with bindu (the brain centre), and rajas
(prana shakti) is joined with the sun (manipura). One who
knows how to unite the two is an adept." (v. 74, 76)

Therefore, when vajroli in maithuna is accomplished,
the further perfection of vajroli within the adept is then to
be accomplished in three stages. Whereas in maithuna the
rajas of the female practitioner is the manifest Shakti, now
Shakti becomes the mind. Shiva remains the male body, as
in maithuna, and mooladhara is now awakened by concentrating the mind upon the trigger point of mooladhara in
the perineum. For this purpose, various specific yantras,
forms and mantras are concentrated upon there, as in kriya
yoga. Secondly, when mooladhara awakens, ida nadi (the
mind) and pingala nadi (the vitality or prana) are drawn

together at each successive chakra by vajroli mudra so that the bindu rises through the sushumna nadi (spinal passage) to bindu visarga, manifesting there as eternal nada.

Shiva (pure consciousness) now resides in the brain as nada while the total Shakti (energy or rajas) is now awakened in the sun (manipura). The awakening within the adept's body is stabilized at this level. Consciousness remains elevated within the spine of the adept. Mind at ajna is raised to Shiva (pure consciousness) issuing from bindu as nada (transcended semen). Rajas (Shakti) is raised from mooladhara and established in manipura and the bindu has been withdrawn from the two lower chakras.

In the final stage, union of the pure consciousness at bindu and the total energy (Shakti) at manipura is to be accomplished. Accomplishment of the first two stages involves the withdrawal of the bindu from the mooladhara and swadhisthana chakras. Shakti which formerly manifested in these centres as sense gratification, instinctual desire and passion, now manifests through manipura chakra as will (ichchha shakti) and anahata chakra as compassion. Will is transcended sensuality, compassion is transcended passion, and enlightenment is transcended mind. Will, universal love and higher awareness become the basic instinct, desire and mind of the adept.

Perfection of vajroli is not accomplished until final union between the Shakti at manipura and the Shiva at bindu is accomplished. Yogi Gorakhnath states clearly that this union is the highest state. This is the final union of yoga, because it means that the yogi's will, intuition, intellect and emotions become conscious manifestations of the cosmic or divine intelligence. He is a medium of divine power. Personal desires have been sacrificed in the ascent of kundalini to become the willpower of Shakti. Having surrendered his mind at ajna in that ascent, it has been superseded by the cosmic intelligence (Shiva).

Paradoxically, this surrender allows an enormous cosmic power to manifest. The body and mind of the adept have become the possession and expression of Shakti, while individual consciousness has merged with pure consciousness (Shiva). According to Yogi Gorakhnath, it is possible for a sadhaka to accomplish successive stages by ardent practice of vajroli, with guru's blessings and guidance. No yogic text can be more explicit than this in describing the higher stages of tantric sadhana, because the role of the guru in these attainments can never be adequately revealed.

In hatha yoga and tantra, the satguru is worshipped both internally and externally as Lord Shiva because he has attained that status. Such a guru leads, guides and cajoles his disciple at every step of the way. In attaining the higher states, it is not that the disciple is only following the guru's instructions and receiving his best wishes. A transmission of the guru's consciousness and energy into the disciple is occurring. The guru is revealing, sharing and bequeathing something which he has attained.

A light can only be kindled from one which is already burning. This is why, in the yogic tradition, no adequate repayment can ever be made to that illumined one who kindles the divine light in his disciples.

रक्षेदाकुंचनादूर्ध्वं या रज: सा हि योगिनी ।
अतीतानागतं वेति खेचरी च भवेद् ध्रुवम् ॥ 102 ॥

*She is verily a yogini who conserves her rajas by contracting and
raising it. She knows past, present and future and becomes fixed in
khechari (i.e. consciousness moves into the higher realm).*

All the attainments which a man attains by perfection of
vajroli, a woman can also achieve. A woman is normally
compelled to experience the mental and physical fluctuations of the menstrual cycle. The loss of energy which
accompanies the shedding of menses is obligatory. However, if the ovum is withdrawn by the practice of vajroli,
this continuing loss of energy is averted and the menstrual
loss diminishes. Whereas a man is bound to the grosser
dimensions of awareness by his instincts and passions, which
cause his body to produce and shed spermatozoa within the
semen, the woman is bound to physical consciousness by the
menstrual cycle.

A yogini who withdraws the bindu (ovum) overcomes this
bondage. She experiences the awakening of a higher energy
force within her body and her consciousness effortlessly
expands into transpersonal awareness. This occurs very
readily because a woman can intuit the nature of higher
consciousness and understands the hidden power underlying
acceptance and surrender, whereas for a man the barrier of
personal ego many times proves insurmountable.

Traditionally, woman has been regarded as the weaker
sex but it is clear that she has a greater capacity to suffer,
sacrifice and endure. Up to the menarche, the female body is
as strong as the male, but with the descent of bindu and the
commencement of ovulation, vitality begins to be drained in
the menses.

A yogini who has perfected vajroli and withdrawn the
bindu becomes very powerful. Siddhis manifest more easily
to a woman because her intuitive faculties are by nature more

highly evolved. She has actually always been aware of them in a rudimentary, dormant form. A woman is more aware of her own subconscious mind and that of others and if she can withdraw the bindu by vajroli, the individual consciousness very easily moves into the universal mind space (chidakash), and the attitude of khechari mudra spontaneously occurs. As the tongue moves back into the upper palate, becoming fixed there without support, so the mind moves from the centres below vishuddhi and enters the total space of consciousness where the barrier of time dissolves and the past, present and future become known.

देहसिद्धिं च लभते वज्रोल्यभ्यासयोगतः ।
अयं पुण्यकरो योगो भोगे भुक्तेऽपि मुक्तिदः ॥ 103 ॥

By the yoga of vajroli practice, perfection of the body fructifies. This auspicious yoga even brings liberation alongside with sensual involvement (bhoga).

This important sloka states a basic concept of tantra that contradicts and shatters puritanical ideas. The very idea that the ultimate experience can unfold through sensual experience is not one that many people in the last few centuries, or even earlier, have been able to accept. Some commentaries on the hatha yoga texts refuse to accept this as a part of the science of yoga and completely omit the slokas pertaining to vajroli and maithuna, yogic intercourse, from the original text stating that they are obscure and repugnant practices followed by only those yogis who lack the willpower to reach their goal otherwise.

However, according to tantra, *bhoga*, or sensual involvement, can be the means to yoga. Sense interaction can lead to higher awareness. We have a physical body and cannot deny its existence. Until one knows the experiences of the senses how can deeper and subtle awareness evolve? Experience is of the mind and not the physical body.

First we have to know what the physical experience is. Then by increasing the subtle perception, the experience can be reawakened in the mind without involving the physical senses. During the day we see with our eyes but what happens at night when we dream? We are not seeing through the eyes but nevertheless, the mind is experiencing. We are re-experiencing what has been perceived. Therefore, in tantra the physical body is the means to delve deeper into the mind and the reality of existence.

It is repeatedly advocated that the reproductive secretions must be drawn up into the body through the practice of vajroli, so that bindu and rajas, i.e. consciousness and energy remain within the body. This enables the sexual impulses to travel up through the central nervous system to the higher centres of the brain.

The *Hatharatnavali* states that: "Semen as well as chitta (consciousness) should be preserved with effort. The person should love mentally that lady only with whom he practises vajroli . . . this semen is the only reason for creation, sustenance and destruction. Through this only a person can become a raja yogi." This form of vajroli has nothing to do with obscene conduct or ritual. Vajroli, amaroli, sahajoli and maithuna are scientific practices to unite the negative and positive poles of energy within the nucleus of consciousness. If the potential of the bindu can be exploded, a greater awakening unfolds. In the practice of vajroli in maithuna, man is the positive pole of energy. He represents the factor of time, and woman is the negative pole and represents space; but these two polarities also exist within each individual.

Mooladhara chakra is the seat of Shakti and sahasrara is the abode of consciousness, Shiva. During maithuna, mooladhara is directly stimulated so that the kundalini shakti can rise to sahasrara. Even if it fails to reach sahasrara it will still awaken dormant centres of perception because each of the ascending chakras is directly connected to specific centres of experience in the brain. This is one path leading to the expansion of consciousness.

The other is on the basis of connecting the two poles within your own being. When kundalini awakens, whether you are a puritan or a debauchee, a believer or a non-believer, a scientist, a priest or a beggar, is irrelevant. They are only intellectual convictions and mundane experiences. They are qualifications of the lower mind. They have no bearing upon what you are. Awakening of kundalini is a process of the higher mind which is triggered in the human nervous system. It is the experience of the greater mind and intelligence which is lying beyond the fence surrounding your own mind and personality.

In the course of evolution it has to become known to you; it is inevitable because it already exists suppressed within you. It is physiological unfoldment and a scientific destiny. Ultimately the fusion of the two poles within the seat of your own consciousness has to take place in order to realize reality.

What is reality? If we are to discuss ultimate reality, then that will not be ultimate, because you have to state a point and say 'this is the end' – but that cannot be the end because there could be something else beyond that. It is the same as an astronaut who can probe the universe to a certain distance. A light telescope can perceive those stars existing up to a certain range. A radio telescope can peer a little further, but can he draw any absolute conclusion about the dimensions of the universe? No, he can only speak about what falls within the range of his telescope. Neither should we make any conclusive statement about the ultimate reality.

There is no ultimate reality. Nor can there be only one way to realize it. Nor can there be only one form of God. There are as many forms as there are individuals to reflect on them. There is a totality as far as your mind can go. That is the extent of your acceptance. Beyond that there is nothing else for you. If you can stretch your mind a little further, and can see a little beyond, then that becomes the extent of the ultimate reality for you. When the mind becomes homogeneous and when mind merges into infinity, who is going to experience ultimate reality?

Ultimate reality is a concept which has something to do with the mind, not with mindlessness. When the body dies, when the mind is completely dissolved, when the individual ego evaporates, and when there is no more 'I', 'you', 'he', 'she', then who is going to see whom? Who is going to know whom? Who is going to smell whom? By whom will you be smelled? How can you know the knower by which you know everything? How can you know the known by which you know everything? How can you know him? It is a very difficult thing.

414

In the *Brihadaranyaka Upanishad* there is a dialogue. Yajnavalkya was a great sage who had two wives. The eldest one was Katyayani and the younger was Maitreyi. One day he wanted to renounce. He called both of them and said, "I am going now. I want to distribute the property between you two." Katyayani accepted but Maitreyi asked, "Will I become immortal by this property which you are now ordaining?" Yajnavalkya was quiet for a moment. She asked again, "Will I experience immortality by what you are giving away to me?" He said, "No". Then she asked, "Why don't you teach me the Brahmavidya; knowledge of the Supreme?" He said, "Maitreyi, you are not only my wife, you are my disciple as well. Come and sit down, I will teach you."

During the discussion between Yajnavalkya and Maitreyi comes this question – the nature of ultimate reality, the nature of its experience. Yajnavalkya said, "As long as you have a nose you can smell but if your mind is in disorder, you cannot understand the smell. If you have eyes you can see the form, but if your mind is not in order, you cannot understand the form. If the senses and the mind are both withdrawn, and the ego is withdrawn, and duality in the form of 'I', 'you', 'he' and 'she' is withdrawn, then time, space and object do not exist. When time, space and object do not exist, where is an experience? The basis of our experience is the mind, but mind cannot have an experience unless it can have the notion of time, space and object. If you withdraw the concept of time, space and object, mind becomes dull. For an experience there has to be the interaction between mind and the object. For an experience, there has to be an interaction between mind and space, mind and time.

"There is another important thing. Time, space and object are not independent. They are categories of the mind. If there is no mind there is no time, space and object. Then where is the knower? The knower cannot be known." This is the answer which Yajnavalkya gave to Maitreyi.

When salt is put into water, it completely dissolves. It completely and totally loses its identity. An experience means duality. When there is non-duality there cannot be an experience. It is a very simple thing to understand. For an experience there have to be two objects – the experiencer and the object of experience. Where there is only one, who is going to experience whom? That knower is not suffering from narcissism. He is pure.

It is much better to discuss the ultimate reality, without concluding anything. Otherwise a conclusion will be a philosophical error.

अथ शक्तिचालनम् ।

कुटिलांगी कुण्डलिनी भुजंगी शक्तिरीश्वरी ।
कुंडल्युरंधती चैते शब्दा: पर्यायवाचका: ॥ 104 ॥

*Kutilangi, kundalini, bhujangi, shakti, ishwari, kundali, arundhati
are all synonymous terms.*

There are many names of the kundalini shakti. In the
Hatharatnavali other names are also given: phani, nagi,
chakri, saraswati, lalana, rasana kshetra, lalati, shakti, raji,
bhujangi, sheshu, kundali, mani, adhara shakti, kutila karali,
pranavahani, ashtavakra, sadadhara, vyapini, kalanodhara,
kunti, shankini, sarpini.

Kutilanga is made up of two roots, *kut* which is 'to tear
asunder', and *anga* which is 'part'. It refers to the great
force and its route through the body which eliminates the
functions of ida and pingala. Kundalini is made up of the
roots *kund* which is a particular type of pit for preserving fire,
and *kundalin* is a snake. Mooladhara is the kund and the fire
released rises like a snake. Kundalini, bhujangi, nagi, phani,
sarpini are all names of a female serpent. Shesha is also a
snake but it is particular to Vishnu for he reclines on Shesha.
Shakti is the cosmic energy. Ishwari is the creative force of
Ishwara, the cosmic causal body. Arundhati is made up of
the words *arun* which means 'dawn' and *dhati* which means
'to generate' or 'create'. *Arundhata* means 'unobstructed'.

उद्धाटयेत्कपाटं तु यथा कुंचिकया हठात् ।
कुंडलिन्या यथा योगी मोक्षद्वारं विभेदयेत् ॥ 105 ॥

Just as a door is opened with a key, similarly the yogi opens the door to liberation with kundalini.

Without generating kundalini shakti there is no possibility of transcending empirical existence. The average mind and body function on a very low 'voltage' of energy. For higher experience to take place a super boost of energy is required to activate the brain centres. It can only be accomplished when the fluctuating energies of ida and pingala are absorbed into mooladhara and exploded through sushumna nadi in the centre of the spinal axis.

Activation of sushumna indicates that the whole brain will awaken. If kundalini goes through either ida or pingala then only half the brain and nervous system has been activated. Kundalini must ascend through sushumna so that the central nervous system is activated, not only the parasympathetic or sympathetic nervous system. Kundalini is not just a mystical name. It is the name of the potential force inherent in every human being. Man has not yet utilized his full capacity to live and experience. Opening the door to liberation is not an easy task. There must first be preparation. The spinal pathway of sushumna has to be cleaned. The chakras have to be opened and activated. If the door is opened before this has taken place, consciousness may enter into a dark, dingy dungeon instead of a sparkling, illumined palace. One should practise hatha yoga under the guidance of an adept guru. This is the only way and it is the short way.

येन मार्गेण गंतव्यं ब्रह्मस्थानं निरामयम् ।
मुखेनाच्छाद्य तद्द्वारं प्रसुप्ता परमेश्वरी ॥ 106 ॥

The sleeping Parameshwari rests with her mouth closing that door, through which is the path to the knot of brahmasthana, the place beyond suffering.

कंदोर्ध्वे कुंडली शक्ति: सुप्ता मोक्षाय योगिनाम् ।
वंधनाय च मूढानां यस्तां वेत्ति स योगवित् ॥ 107 ॥

The kundalini shakti sleeps above the kanda. This shakti is the means of liberation to the yogi and bondage for the ignorant. One who knows this is the knower of yoga.

In these two slokas, a clearer glimpse of mooladhara chakra is given. 'With her mouth closing the door' indicates that it is impossible for the consciousness of the aspirant to pass further without rousing the sleeping kundalini from her slumber. Mooladhara must be awakened. There is no other way to explode the spiritual awareness except through this most powerful experience of the senses. Just as a man and woman completely possess each other at the point of sexual climax, so the consciousness of the aspirant must directly encounter the great Shakti in mooladhara and be engulfed by her.

Out of fear, an aspirant may be looking for some way to avoid this encounter, but in order to enter into the path which unfolds the mysteries of consciousness, he must go to her, enter into her and go through her, because her mouth is closing the doorway to liberation.

In the psychophysiology of yoga, three knots, *granthis*, are encountered in the awakening of kundalini and the ascent to higher consciousness. These are three locations where consciousness and energy are tightly knotted or intertwined, and must be unravelled if the reality of higher consciousness is to be experienced. The first is *Brahma granthi*, the knot of creation, located in mooladhara. In this sloka it is termed as the knot of Brahmasthana. It is the psychophysical barrier imposed by attachment and identification of the consciousness with the physical body and sense experiences. This misidentification leads the consciousness back into the painful cycle of rebirth in another body. The three granthis are discussed in Chapter 4, slokas 70–76.

The Brahmasthana is described as the place beyond suffering because if this granthi can be pierced, the realization of deathless consciousness existing distinct from time, space and individuality, occurs. Out of this grows dispassion for the objects of sense craving, and the desire for liberation.

According to Swatmarama, a yogi is one who has become aware that the same kundalini shakti is responsible for bondage and liberation. The ignorant are bound to the intoxication of mundane sexual life, leading to rebirth of individual consciousness, but those who arouse the same shakti in mooladhara and practise vajroli, gain the secret means to liberation. This is the meaning of the statement in *Hevajra Tantra*: "One should rise by that which one falls."

The physical body is the storehouse of prana shakti, the mind is the storehouse of manas shakti, and atma is the storehouse of atma shakti. Our entire being consists of these three energies, and the three energies interact with and depend upon each other. Whatever the mind dwells upon, the entire shakti becomes absorbed in that. As the *Chandogya Upanishad* states: "As one thinks so he becomes."

Manas shakti is *ichchha shakti*, the force of desire or will. We have to be very clear about what we desire or will, because our entire shakti becomes absorbed in that. That is why those people who continually strive for higher knowledge and experience eventually develop that state of consciousness. Even if they are not able to attain liberation, they do become evolved souls. However, if your goal is material and aimed at sensual fulfilment, your prana and mind will be absorbed in that. You have to decide what you are going to plug your positive and negative wires into, the soul or the senses.

420

When the full force of atma shakti is released, its form becomes visible to the inner eye. In tantra it is known as *atma darshan*, vision of the atma. When this happens, the atma appears before you in some form. You are able to see it because the liberated energy and consciousness are freed from the physical body. It may take the form of your guru, ishta devata, or somebody very dear to you, or even someone you do not know. Actually it is the force of your own atma. It is the result of intense aspiration for higher experience.

Contrary to this desire, if your purpose for living is to gain sensual pleasure, money, worldly security, name and fame, etc., your vital energy will be lost in accomplishing that. The fruits of this purpose perish in time and likewise your energy is lost with them. However, atma is the eternal existence and force. Therefore, if one lives in hope of experiencing that, time and energy can never be wasted. 'One who knows this (atma) is the knower of yoga'. Knowing means more than intellectual knowledge. It means knowledge based on experience.

कुण्डली कुटिलाकारा सर्पवत्परिकीर्तिता ।
सा शक्तिश्चालिता येन स मुक्तो नात्र संशय: ॥ 108 ॥

Kundalini is said to be coiled like a snake. Without a doubt, one who makes that shakti flow obtains liberation.

BSY©

While kundalini is asleep in mooladhara, she is depicted as a snake, usually a cobra, coiled three and a half times around a smoky grey shivalingam, known as the *dhumralingam*. The three and a half coils present the form of the *Om* mantra. These three coils are the three states of existence and experience; conscious, subconscious and unconscious; *jagrat*, *swapna* and *sushupti*, i.e. waking, dream and deep sleep; objective experience, subjective experience and nonexperience; past, present and future. The three coils also represent the three qualities of nature, prakriti or Shakti – tamas, rajas and sattwa. The half coil represents that which is beyond the play of nature, *turiya* or the fourth dimension which includes any other dimension beyond the third. The smoky shivalingam around which kundalini is coiled is the subtle body or sukshma sharira, also known as the astral body, but its ill-defined, smoky quality indicates that the inner consciousness is obscured in the changing realities of the three realms of experience.

In an unaware individual the kundalini has her head downward, but in the yogi the head is lifted up as she begins to awaken. When the kundalini serpent wakes up she should rise through sushumna, until she is perfectly straight from the tip of her tail, anchored in mooladhara, to the top of the head which fills the skull. It indicates pervading conscious- ness which is not limited by any influence or subject to any modification.

While kundalini lies dormant in mooladhara the connection to ajna chakra takes place through ida or pingala nadis. Sometimes the connection does not even take place as there is a blockage. Once kundalini has risen up so that the head is completely immersed in the brain, the connection is direct (sushumna), the three states of experience merge into the fourth (transcendental), as the coils of the kundalini are straightened. Then there is no separate existence of any of the gunas, there is no longer separation of anything. It all becomes one eternal cosmic experience.

गंगायमुनयोर्मध्ये बालरण्डां तपस्विनीम् ।
बलात्कारेण गृह्णीयात्तद्विष्णो: परमं पदम् ॥ 109 ॥

*Between Ganga and Yamuna is the young widowed Balarandam
practising austerity. She should be seized forcibly, then one can reach
the supreme state of Vishnu.*

इडा भगवती गंगा पिंगला यमुना नदी ।
इडापिंगलयोर्मध्ये बालरण्डा च कुंडली ॥ 110 ॥

*Ida is the holy Ganga, pingala the river Yamuna. Between ida and
pingala in the middle is this young widow, kundalini.*

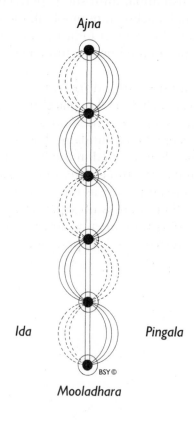

Ajna

Ida   Pingala

Mooladhara

424

In yogic and tantric lore, the river Ganga is known as ida, and Yamuna as pingala. Ida and pingala are the two major nadis sustaining the individual body-mind. A third, subterranean river, Saraswati, is also described. This is sushumna nadi, the hidden channel conducting spiritual energy. In this way, the geography of the subtle body has been incorporated into the mythology of the people who lived beside these two great rivers since the dawn of civilization. Ganga and Yamuna have always been the source of life-sustaining water, while Saraswati is the subtle undercurrent of spiritual awareness which so tangibly permeates life on the Indian subcontinent.

Ida is dark in colour, just as the river Ganga is deep blue at its origin. Ganga is fathomless, mysterious and raging like the mental force. The mythology of Ganga's first descent on the earth describes her as wild and uncontrollable, capable of demolishing anything standing in her way. When she was released from her homeground in the Himalayan heavens, Lord Shiva had to catch her in his matted locks. After some time, he released her and Bhagirathi guided her gently down to the earth (through the body). Likewise the force of ida, if not controlled, can make a person turn into a lunatic. The tendency of Ganga to spill her banks and flood in every direction is an indication that she represents space, the unique quality of ida and the right brain hemisphere.

There is no such story about the origin of the Yamuna river in relation to pingala nadi. Like the male or positive aspect of pingala, Yamuna is sober in nature. It is the river by which Lord Krishna lived for many years. He overpowered the great serpent Kaliya in Yamuna and danced on her fan. Kaliya represents time, the quality of pingala nadi and the left brain hemisphere. Yamuna, too, is deep but there are times in summer when it becomes dry, just as the prana shakti (vitality) also is sometimes lost and must be regenerated.

These two rivers are terrestrial, just as ida and pingala nadis are manifest forces. Sushumna nadi lies deep within

425

the central axis of the spine just as the subterranean Saraswati river lies within the earth. These three rivers convene at Prayag, near Allahabad in northern India. It is a powerful energy point in the geological structure of the earth and is associated with the union of ida, pingala and sushumna in ajna chakra in the subtle body.

The kundalini is described in this sloka as a young widow practising austerity midway between Ganga and Yamuna or ida and pingala. She is said to be youthful because the potential of kundalini is likened to the irresistible power of a young and attractive woman. She is widowed because her husband, Shiva, remains in the lofty heavens, at Mount Kailash, the sahasrara chakra. She practises austerity in the sense that separation from her husband is the greatest penance, or *tapasya*, a young and beautiful widow has to endure. She longs to be united again with her husband in Kailash. This is symbolic of the bliss to be attained with the ascent of kundalini from mooladhara to sahasrara chakra. Mooladhara is the source of energy or Shakti and sahasrara is the abode of consciousness, Shiva.

पुच्छे प्रगृह्य भुजगीं सुप्तामुद्बोधयेच्च ताम् ।
निद्रां विहाय सा शक्तिरूर्ध्वमुत्तिष्ठते हठात् ॥ 111 ॥

*By seizing the tail of kundalini serpent, she becomes very excited.
Abandoning sleep that shakti is released and rises up.*

If you hold any snake by its tail it will definitely become
alarmed and immediately rise up and attempt to break
loose from the grip. The tail end represents mooladhara
chakra. By activating mooladhara, the energy is agitated
and will seek to rise up out of its bondage there. Ida and
pingala must be closed. Sushumna must be opened or
cleared. Whether or not sushumna is open can be judged
by the natural flow of breath through the nostrils. When
both nostrils are open simultaneously, sushumna's door is
open. Therefore at the conclusion of your sadhana, when
you are sitting for concentration, make sure both nostrils are
functioning. If they are imbalanced, try to manipulate the
breath so that it flows evenly.

SHAKTI CHALANA MUDRA
(attitude of moving the energy)

अवस्थिता चैव फणावती सा प्रातश्च सायं प्रहरार्धमात्रम् ।
प्रपूर्य सूर्यात् परिधानयुक्त्या प्रगृह्य नित्यं परिचालनीया ॥ 112 ॥

Breathing in through the right nostril (pingala) the serpent (shakti) should be seized through kumbhaka and rotated constantly for an hour and a half, morning and evening.

This practice of shakti chalana is carefully undisclosed here. There are two methods of practice: one according to hatha yoga, the other, kriya yoga. Kriya yoga utilizes mental visualization whereas hatha yoga does not. Of course this does not mean it may not be incorporated. In the practice of kriya yoga, shakti chalana is known as shakti chalini. Sit in siddhasana/siddha yoni asana, practise khechari mudra and ujjayi pranayama; inhale up to bindu and maintain antar kumbhaka. Then performing yoni mudra, visualize a thin green serpent in arohan and awarohan passages, with the mouth biting its own tail. Then visualize this serpent rotating through arohan and awarohan passages until the breath can no longer be held. Then, releasing yoni mudra, exhale back down to mooladhara.

The practice in hatha yoga is different. The techniques used in hatha yoga are moola bandha, antar and bahir kumbhaka, siddhasana/siddha yoni asana and nauli. The *Gheranda Samhita* describes the practice in the following manner: "Smearing the body with ashes and assuming siddhasana (siddha yoni asana) one should inhale through both the nostrils and forcibly join prana with apana. Then by ashwini mudra one should slowly contract the anus till the vayu is forced into the sushumna and gives a particular experience. Then by restricting the vayu, kundalini feels choked and rises upwards. Without shakti chalana, yoni mudra is ineffectual. So one should practise shakti chalana and then practise yoni mudra." (3:66–70) The use of ashwini mudra is mentioned here. Ashwini mudra has not been previously described in the *Hatha Yoga Pradipika*. Moola bandha is used instead.

Technique

Sit in siddhasana/siddha yoni asana.

Keep the eyes closed throughout the practice.

Inhale slowly and deeply through the right nostril and perform internal breath retention, antar kumbhaka.

Perform moola bandha as tightly as possible, concentrating on the area of contraction.

Hold the breath and moola bandha as long as possible.

Exhale slowly.

Perform jalandhara and uddiyana bandha.

Then practise 'churning' nauli, moving the rectus abdomini muscles clockwise in a circular motion from left to right, then directly back to the left and again circling to the right side, counting the number of rotations up to ten.

Before inhaling, come back to uddiyana, slowly release uddiyana and jalandhara bandhas. Only after the head is raised should inhalation proceed very slowly.

This is one round.

Though it is stated in the text that shakti chalana should be practised for ninety minutes, this will not be possible, nor is it advisable. Initially five rounds can be practised. After seven months of continual practice gradually increase the number of rotations per round. Up to twenty rotations can be performed. Increase one rotation every two or three days. The number of rounds can also be increased very gradually up to ten rounds over a period of one year.

429

उर्ध्वं वितस्तिमात्रं तु विस्तारं चतुरंगुलम् ।
मृदुलं धवलं प्रोक्तं वेष्टितांबरलक्षणम् ॥ 113 ॥

The kanda, situated above the anus, one hand span high and four fingers breath wide, is soft and white as if enveloped in cloth.

Kanda means 'root' like the root of a plant. The kanda in the body is the root source from where all the nadis spring. It is said to be nine inches high and three inches wide, soft and white, but it does not consist of physical elements. Its manifestation is entirely in the subtle body. The base of the kanda is just above the perineal floor, in which the perineal body is situated anterior to the anus. The middle of the body is sometimes considered to be four centimetres above and in front of the anus, and four centimetres below and behind the root of the male genital organ. Try to locate the consciousness at this point. The kanda extends upwards from this point supporting all the nadis and is sometimes described as being egg-shaped. Those who have witnessed the shivalingam in one of the temples of Lord Shiva can visualize this.

Some of the texts describe manipura chakra, or the navel wheel, as the source from where the nadis emanate. However, the kanda being nine inches high, terminates at the level of manipura.

According to Swami Sivananda of Rishikesh, the kanda is just above mooladhara in the junction of sushumna and mooladhara, which is called *granthi sthana*. *Sthana* means 'base' or 'platform' and *granthi* means 'knot'. The petals of mooladhara lotus spring from the side of the base of the kanda. Within the spine at the level of the upper back the spinal cord tapers off into a group of long silken nerve filaments, known as *cauda equina* (horse's tail). Long hairlike filaments cascade from the central mass of the tail as it continues down towards the base of the vertebral column. This structure in the physical body is said to correspond to the kanda in the subtle body.

430

सति वज्रासने पादौ कराभ्यां धारयेद् दृढम् ।
गुल्फदेशसमीपे च कन्दं तत्र प्रपीडयेत् ॥ 114 ॥

Firmly seated in vajrasana, holding the ankles, one should squeeze
the kanda close to the anus.

The position of practice is vajrasana. The left big toe lies
over the right big toe, heels are by the sides of the buttocks,
hands are on the knees. Perform moola bandha or ashwini
mudra or both. When moola bandha is performed correctly
the muscles around the perineal body tighten. The perineal
body is located exactly in the base of the kanda, so that
when the contraction is performed, the base of the kanda is
grasped and squeezed.

वज्रासने स्थितो योगी चालयित्वा च कुंडलीम् ।
कुर्यादनन्तरं भस्त्रां कुंडलीमाशु बोधयेत् ॥ 115 ॥

In the position of vajrasana, the yogi should move the kundalini.
Having done bhastrika pranayama the kundalini is soon aroused.

First, moola bandha or ashwini mudra should be performed
in vajrasana or siddhasana (males), or siddha yoni asana
(females), with kumbhaka, to locate the base of the kanda
within mooladhara chakra. This grasps the tail of the
sleeping kundalini and incites her to move. Then bhastrika
pranayama is to be practised to activate her.

भानोराकुंचनं कुर्यात्कुण्डलीं चालयेत् ततः ।
मृत्युवक्त्रगतस्यापि तस्य मृत्युभयं कुतः ॥ 116 ॥

Contracting the sun in manipura, kundalini should be moved. Even if such a person should be on the verge of death, where is the need to fear death?

This important sloka indicates the means to raise kundalini beyond the level of manipura chakra. The sloka indicates the precise order in which the two important bandhas are to be applied. Firstly, manipura should be contracted. This indicates that after bhastrika pranayama has been practised and external breath retention (bahir kumbhaka) is maintained, uddiyana bandha should be performed. Then kundalini should be moved in mooladhara chakra by moola bandha as already described in the previous sloka.

Practise of uddiyana bandha awakens the sushumna passage at manipura chakra by converging the vital and mental energies at the solar plexus. Then kundalini can arise beyond this centre.

Various practices which purify manipura chakra such as uddiyana and nauli are prescribed in hatha yoga. These strengthen the solar plexus and increase vitality and longevity. They give strength and resilience to the body and radiance to the personality. There is no doubt that the dominating and shining qualities of the sun manifest in the individual who performs these practices daily.

How is the universal fear of death overcome when this chakra is awakened by a yogi? To understand it, the *tattwas*, elements, composing the universe and the individual personality must be considered. The earth element governs mooladhara chakra, water governs swadhisthana and fire, manipura. The chakras beyond manipura are governed by air, ether and mind. The human personality is a combination of these tattwas, from gross to subtle. Individual consciousness identifies a component of itself with each element.

433

When consciousness has been withdrawn to manipura, awareness and identification with the gross physical body has ceased, and so the need to fear death is also lost. Death is the eventual destiny of every physical body. A yogi accepts the dissolution of matter as the universal process of nature. However, consciousness is eternal and thus the yogi, while in a body, seeks to realize and identify with that underlying consciousness, by the process of *tattwa shuddhi*, purification of the elements.

Once manipura is awakened, consciousness beyond the physical body is established, and the previously all-embracing fear of death evaporates like mist on the earth at sunrise.

मुहूर्तद्वयपर्यन्तं निर्भयं चालनादसौ ।
ऊर्ध्वमाकृष्यते किंचित्सुषुम्नायां समुद्गता ॥ 117 ॥

By moving the kundalini fearlessly for an hour and a half, it is drawn into sushumna and rises up a little.

This sloka indicates that a sadhana specifically designed for the successful awakening of kundalini requires one and a half hours of practice each day. The precise sadhana to be practised has purposely not been designated, but from prior slokas many indications have been given and practices have been indicated. The systematic technique remains to be given directly by the guru.

Though hatha yoga is guaranteed to awaken kundalini when practised under the given conditions, there is an even more powerful practice for those who are predominantly rajasic, and who should not force their minds directly into concentration. It is known as kriya yoga and is the combination of the asanas, pranayama, mudras and bandhas, which specifically induce pratyahara, i.e. siddhasana, padmasana, ujjayi pranayama, khechari, shambhavi, vajroli and yoni mudras, nasikagra drishti, uddiyana, jalandhara, moola and maha bandhas. Kriya yoga is an ancient intitiation and practice for which adequate preparation is required.

A series of twenty or more kriyas are learned and practised sequentially in a daily rite or ritual until the conscious mind is completely absorbed and the great awakening manifests. There are three distinct phases in the practice of kriya yoga. The preliminary kriyas induce mental relaxation, *pratyahara*, sense withdrawal, and awaken sushumna. The intermediate group of kriyas directly arouse kundalini in sushumna, and the final six kriyas absorb the mind in *dharana*, concentration, and *dhyana*, meditation.

The total time for the practice is three hours; of this the first hour induces sense withdrawal and mental relaxation.

Subsequently, the actual raising and movement of kundalini in sushumna consumes ninety minutes as described in the sloka. Then the meditative experiences of expanded consciousness in the final kriyas are arbitrarily limited to thirty minutes.

The key point of the sloka is that kundalini must be moved fearlessly. To awaken kundalini requires tremendous faith and conviction, as well as a powerful and enlightened guru. Both must be present or nothing substantial will happen. In order to move kundalini fearlessly, one must have total commitment to what one is practising. It means that the aspirant is to go on with determination, one-pointedness and conviction for the required period each day, without wavering or succumbing to the negative states of mind, which invariably arise to oppose the ongoing discipline of daily yoga sadhana. This determination only comes when the practice has been received from a guru in whom you have developed a trust.

If one were to commence the practices of kundalini yoga alone, without a guru's guidance, one's confidence in the technique one has desired to follow would definitely be found lacking after a short time. Even if one should succeed in arousing kundalini, it is very difficult to integrate the experiences and sustain the awakening. At a certain point, fear for one's sanity is overwhelming, and only the guru's form can dispel it. Therefore, to move kundalini fearlessly, the aspirants must first be aware of who their guru is.

Unflinching regularity in the practice is the absolute prerequisite. If the practice lapses, everything is lost. To sustain this discipline for the required period in the midst of the distractions of modern life is extremely difficult. For this reason, it is usually easier to undertake the discipline of kundalini sadhana in the environment of an ashram where external distractions are minimized, diet is simple and regulated and guidance is at hand.

It is interesting that Swatmarama indicated that ninety minutes is the prerequisite for kundalini sadhana. Modern

436

researchers have found that the alternating cycle of predominance of the breath between left and right nostrils and associated hemispherical dominance in the brain, follows a cycle of one and a half to three hours. This means that sushumna nadi is activated spontaneously once in this time period for a few minutes, while the breath crosses from one nostril to the other. In that time, the flow of breath through both nostrils is balanced and both hemispheres are active and synchronized. Then the interconnecting bridge of nerve fibres between the two hemispheres (corpus callosum) becomes active.

In mental or physical sickness this cycle may be grossly disturbed, and preponderance of one nostril and its contralateral hemisphere may even extend for eight to twelve hours before sushumna is activated. By yoga practices, however, it is usually possible to induce balance in the nostrils and the awakening of sushumna willfully. From the outset of kriya yoga, both prana and mind are directed towards the awakening of sushumna. This enables the energy awakened by arousing kundalini to pass through the spinal cord into both hemispheres via the corpus callosum. The result is that the mind becomes spontaneously one-pointed and various experiences and faculties of the awakened mind manifest.

तेन कुंडलिनी तस्या: सुषुम्नाया मुखं ध्रुवम् ।
जहाति तस्मात्प्राणोऽयं सुषुम्नां व्रजति स्वत: ॥ 118 ॥

*In this way, it is easy for kundalini to issue from the opening of
sushumna. Thus the prana proceeds through sushumna of its own
accord.*

Awakening of kundalini by yoga practices is a systematic
and stepwise process. The important point here is that when
kundalini is awakened, she issues easily from the kanda and
proceeds through sushumna by the help of the previously
described practices. Only through practice does perfection
or siddhi in asana, pranayama, mudra, bandha and
concentration develop; only when the body posture becomes
stable in sushumna does the energy of kundalini issue from
the kanda into the chakras.

It has always been possible to invoke kundalini by
unsystematic, drastic and even tragic means. However, full
and sustained awakening never occurs in this way. Herbs,
drugs and chemicals, sleep and food deprivation and even
intense and prolonged pain may give some glimpses, but
these experiences are never sustained and cannot be directed
or controlled. A treasure chamber may be forcibly plundered
but in exploding the door to the chamber prematurely and
without adequate preparation, the treasure beyond may be
damaged or lost forever.

In order to issue forth easily and willingly from the kanda
into the chakras, as permanent sources of power and bliss
within the aspirant, the sleeping kundalini must be patiently
aroused by devotion to daily yogic sadhana.

तस्मात्संचालयेन्नित्यं सुखसुप्तामरुंधतीम् ।
तस्या: संचालनेनैव योगी रोगै: प्रमुच्यते ॥ 119 ॥

In that way the sleeping kundalini should be regularly moved. By her regular movement, the yogi is freed from disease.

Regular practice at the appropriate time creates harmony in the body-mind and likewise, irregular practice at the wrong time creates imbalance. By regular practice, pranic intensity is activated and, even if kundalini does not rise up in sushumna, the vital capacity of the nadis and chakras is nevertheless increased. The whole body system is activated; the immune system operates as a powerful army. The heart, lungs, stomach and all the other internal organs are strengthened. Muscles remain flexible. Each living cell becomes a vital source of energy. Even if you do not awaken kundalini these practices will at least bring optimal health and tranquility of mind.

This sloka indicates that the benevolence of kundalini is twofold. Firstly, if she is aroused and moved regularly, the supreme experience of awakening and spiritual illumination of the body is within reach.

Swatmarama also indicates the secondary or subsidiary benefit from the practice, and has foreseen that the therapeutic application will emerge. Radiant health and freedom from disease is a great boon which the practitioner of kundalini yoga possesses almost coincidentally. Freedom from disease is the very least of the benefits derived from kundalini arousal.

Millions of people in the world suffer from terrible and insidious diseases. They are pronounced incurable by medical science, despite powerful drugs and bolstered nutrition. The cause of these diseases remains elusive because although they are experienced in the physical body the cause often does not lie there. They are due to imbalance and blockage of energy in the subtle body. Diminution of vitality and onset of disease in the different systems of the physical body is only the gross and inevitable manifestation.

Good health is a particularly positive state of physical and mental vitality. It does not merely mean absence of disease symptoms. That is a purely negative definition.

Regular practice under correct conditions increases the voltage of prana in the nadis and chakra circuits. The entire energy function of the body is amplified. All organs and systems of the body function optimally. Muscles remain flexible and skin tone is enhanced. The responses of the immune system are sharpened. Each living cell is permeated by greater energy. The radiance of health is an important by-product of moving the kundalini upward, but it is not the spiritual objective of the practice.

येन संचालिता शक्ति: स योगी सिद्धिभाजनम् ।
किमत्र बहुनोक्तेन कालं जयति लीलया ॥ 120 ॥

The yogi who moves the shakti regularly, enjoys perfection or siddhi.
He easily conquers time and death. What more is there to say?

By regularly generating the shakti in ida and pingala, the
different chakras become active and manifest specific psychic
abilities according to the corresponding regions of the brain.
The states of dharana and dhyana become deeper, until
samadhi is achieved. With the unfoldment of samadhi one
goes out of the barriers of body and limited mind, beyond
duality and perception of time and space. This is the point
of view of raja yoga.

According to one who is already self-realized, there is no
beginning or end, but only the one continual state and any
other experience is false. The *Avadhoota Gita* states that: "I
was not born nor do I have death. I have no acts good or
evil. I am Brahman, stainless, without qualities. How can
there be bondage or liberation? The whole universe shines
undivided and unbroken. O, the maya, the delusion – the
imagination and the non-duality. Always 'not this, not this'
to both the formless and the formed. Only the absolute
exists, transcending difference and non-duality. There is no
state of liberation, no state of bondage, no state of virtue, no
state of vice. There is no state of perfection and no state of
destitution. Why do you, who are the identity in all, grieve in
your heart?" (1:59, 61, 62, 5:19)

This is true for a self-realized avadhoota but we are far
from that state of realization. We need to do something to
awaken the higher brain centres and it can only be achieved
by generating a greater flow of energy. When the ultimate
realization of man can be achieved through the practice of
hatha yoga, then what more is to be added?

Our mundane perception of night and day is a biological
process. They are not conditions of the soul. Death belongs

to the physical body but not to the inhabitant, the consciousness and energy. It is well known that different hormones are released during the day and night which affect our perception and bodily functions. The pituitary and pineal bodies are largely responsible for this, and the pineal reacts to the light and dark cycles. Just as a plant responds automatically to the light and dark cycles, so also our body reacts. Experiments have shown that light enters the pineal gland and stimulates it. Modern science is considering how the presence of light within the brain is a mechanism to alter ordinary awareness.

For a state of consciousness to arise where the duality of day and night, pleasure and pain, life and death, cease to exist, it means that the pineal body must undergo some type of change. How this change is to take place, yogis have explained through hatha yoga, which illumines the inner light.

ब्रह्मचर्यरतस्यैव नित्यं हितमिताशिनः ।

मंडलाद् दृश्यते सिद्धिः कुंडल्यभ्यासयोगिनः ॥ 121 ॥

One who enjoys being brahmacharya and always takes moderate diet and practises arousal of kundalini, achieves perfection in forty days.

One who enjoys brahmacharya is one who has contentment from living in continual awareness of the supreme state or Brahman, one who sees everything as part of the divine consciousness and the interplay of Shakti or nature. One whose energy is sublimated, who has control over the animal nature, can perfect the process of awakening kundalini within forty days.

The sloka prescribes the three requirements for this vastly accelerated awakening. Firstly is brahmacharya which is enjoyable. This is not sexual continence achieved by suppression but that which is spontaneously occurring because the experience of bliss of the Self is all consuming, and therefore not even sexual interaction will cause the consciousness and bindu to move.

The second requirement is to always take a moderate diet. The important word is 'always'. The third requirement is the systematic arousal of kundalini as has already been discussed in detail.

To live in such a state is not possible for people today and there are many preparatory stages and practices which have to be accomplished first. Nevertheless the sloka boldly asserts that by fulfilling these requirements only forty days are required to attain the supreme accomplishment. The legends of the great avatars such as Rama and Krishna reveal the transcendental bliss and pleasure of the illumined ones and provide hope, joy and inspiration for the yogis. Even great yogis, such as Paramahamsa Ramakrishna, are known to have awakened kundalini only by intense struggle and perseverance in sadhana, requiring years rather than a few days.

Even if you are able to awaken kundalini within forty days, are you ready to cope with that experience, before which all the mundane experiences of joy, sorrow, pleasure and tragedy in human life pale into insignificance? Awakening of kundalini is not a small happening, and you have to be adequately prepared for it.

In order to hasten the awakening, yogis seek out austere and humble circumstances, such as an ashram or an isolated cave or hermitage where external distractions are minimal. Even in such circumstances, according to the sannyasa tradition, twelve years is to be set aside in order to surrender the ego, discipline the senses and exhaust the karmas. It is not that the awakening cannot be precipitated quickly. A powerful guru can even bestow it in a day, but the unpurified body, undisciplined mind and senses and unbridled ego will never survive it.

In comparison, the amount of time we are going to be able to devote each day to the practices is minimal, and our lifestyle has many distractions. Therefore, the effects on the mechanisms releasing kundalini shakti are likely to be gradual rather than drastic. This is the sensible and desirable approach for most people.

The awakening of kundalini will take longer than forty days for most people. It may take months, years or even a lifetime, but is there any other goal worth striving for? Never be in a hurry, never expect or demand results from your sadhana. Follow the guru's instructions closely, and let the awakening occur in its own time.

कुंडलीं चालयित्वा तु भस्त्रां कुर्याद्विशेषतः ।
एवमभ्यसतो नित्यं यमिनो यमभीः कुतः ॥122॥

Bhastrika pranayama with kumbhaka should specifically be practised to activate kundalini. From where will the fear of death arise for a self-restrained practitioner who practises daily with regularity?

The number one practice in the awakening of kundalini is bhastrika. If you have never practised pranayama before, then you will have to first take up other preliminary practices. Nadi shodhana should be practised as the preliminary pranayama, gradually increasing the ratios and duration of retention. Nadi shodhana can be continued during any season and, excluding retention, it may be done by anyone. There are specific requirements for bhastrika pranayama, and one should not perform it without the guru's instructions.

This breathing technique powerfully influences the nervous system and brain, as has been discussed in Chapter 2. By regular practice it can completely alter habitual neuronal firing patterns in the brain, particularly in the regions of the recticular activating system and hypothalamus. It thereby modifies the basic and deep-rooted emotional responses of the personality, of which fear of death is primal.

However, the process of emergence of a yogic personality is an evolutionary transformation which is gradual and painstaking. It is said that a yogi transcends the fear of death altogether, and it becomes a challenge for death to overtake him.

द्वासप्ततिसहस्त्राणां नाडीनां मलशोधने ।
कुत: प्रक्षालनोपाय: कुंडल्यभ्यसनादृते ॥ 123 ॥

*What other methods are there to cleanse the 72,000 nadis of dirt
besides the practice of arousing kundalini?*

This sloka indicates the uniqueness of hatha yoga and
tantra as a system of spiritual evolution. Many patriarchal
religious scriptures and philosophies have talked about
spiritual emancipation and higher life beyond body, but
they invariably create a split between consciousness and
matter, between soul and body. They suggest that divinity
is to be somehow attained beyond the body, but they
never affirm that the body itself is the divine experience
and manifestation. Tantra insists that the way to higher
consciousness is by purifying the body and expanding
the awareness of its experiences, rather than denying
them. Religions hold that man's body is tainted in its very
conception; that along with his body, man has inherited a
'fall' from which his consciousness must be redeemed. From
the tantric viewpoint, these beliefs lead to suppression, guilt,
mental and physical sickness.

Tantra asserts that body and spirit are not two, but
one. Consciousness permeates the 72,000 nadis of the
body. Enlightenment is to be attained by first removing
the blockages and impurities within the nadis through
the practices of hatha yoga. Then the nervous system is
capable of sustaining the greater voltage of consciousness
which accompanied the arousal and awakening of kundalini
shakti.

There may be methods to gain emancipation or
deliverance from the body, but why is the body to be
rejected? Is human birth innately defiled? Should spiritual
awareness begin by struggling with the mind or by purifying
the body? This is what spiritual aspirants will have to decide.
Hatha yoga exists for those who wish to purify consciousness

in order to experience health and enlightenment. What other method is there?

This sloka must be carefully understood. Some people will maintain that by adhering to a suitable lifestyle in conjunction with some philosophical ideas or religious beliefs, their body is kept clean and healthy; therefore, kundalini need not be aroused. However, they have substituted an ethical lifestyle for a greater spiritual awakening.

The crucial point is that for illumination to occur, consciousness must evolve and the body must be transformed into a more subtle substance altogether. The process commences with shatkarma, and proceeds through the work of kundalini shakti within the nervous system. What is the spiritual benefit of dietary and lifestyle regulation? That is not yoga; it may be stagnation rather than evolution. Of course, it is good as far as it goes, but where is the impetus for higher consciousness to be found? Without arousing kundalini, the power to transcend within the mundane life is lacking. This type of life is only a facsimile, based on suppression of natural desires.

This is the fundamental difference between a religious, ethical or natural lifestyle, and a lifestyle devoted to the direct experience of illumination. The experience of a greater reality is all important for a yogi, not adherence to beliefs. That is why he espouses kundalini.

इयं तु मध्यमा नाडी दृढाभ्यासेन योगिनाम् ।
आसनप्राणसंयाममुद्राभि: सरला भवेत् ॥ 124 ॥

This middle nadi, sushumna, easily becomes established, (straight)
by the yogi's persistent practice of asana, pranayama, mudra and
concentration.

Sushumna is to be purified and awakened by the sequential
and systematic application of the practices as described
throughout the text. The consecutive order should be
followed, starting with shatkarma and progressively continuing through to dharana or concentration.

With the straightening of sushumna, the awareness of the
yogi is established in relation to the flow of energy within the
spinal axis, on a more or less continual basis. Straightening
the nadi means it becomes functional, in the same sense that
a length of hose which is entangled and kinked will not carry
water, but when it is disentangled and stretched from end to
end, the water will flow.

What are these kinks and entanglements which obstruct
the sushumna passage? In psychological terms, they are the
barriers and blockages within the individual mental and vital
makeup which are opposing the uninhibited expression of
the greater personality.

Straightening of sushumna is not accomplished without
difficulties, and it takes time. Nor is it an easy process, but
it is the inevitable outcome of continuing the practices.
Establishing sushumna awareness may take months or years,
depending upon dedication to the practices, and the nature
of the deeper karma and samskaras of the aspirant. However,
once sushumna awareness is functioning throughout the
twenty-four hours, it becomes the medium through which
the maha shakti awakens and ascends.

In the awakening of sushumna, the lifestyle and habits
must be regulated, because these definitely affect the flow of
consciousness and prana in the nadis. Extremes of lifestyle,

which disrupt the flow of awareness, are to be sacrificed, and the aspirant discovers for himself precisely how this is to be done in relation to his own lifestyle and goals.

Practices such as shankhaprakshalana exert a profound cleansing and purifying effect upon the subtle body, and demand dietary regulation if the states of awareness generated are to be preserved and consolidated. What is the point in doing shankhaprakshalana if after a week one again begins to eat greasy and tamasic foods, and starts smoking? Unhealthy habits only maintain blockages in the nadis. The practices of hatha yoga are very powerful, and they demand responsibility and self-discipline. Otherwise, it is not only a waste of time, but also foolhardy and dangerous. Therefore, along with the initial practices of hatha yoga, a lifestyle which is conducive must gradually emerge.

Hatha yoga starts with the physical body and gradually works its way to the mind. The order should always be shatkarma, asana, pranayama, mudra, bandha, pratyahara, dharana, dhyana, samadhi. After bandha, concentration commences. First is pratyahara, in which the external mind is consciously withdrawn from the sensory channels.

In one of the tantric scriptures there is a dialogue between Shiva and Parvati. Parvati asks Shiva, "How does one transcend the awareness of the objects; how does one annihilate the ego; how does one realize the homogeneous totality and absoluteness of one's own Self?" In reply Shiva tells her, "There are 125,000 practices and all these practices ultimately withdraw the mind from the sense objects."

These practices which are taught in yoga are all practices of pratyahara, not meditation. They are preparations for meditation, i.e. dhyana. After pratyahara, when the mind has been totally withdrawn from the sense objects and is isolated, and is roaming within and experiencing itself without any external aid, then there are other practices for meditation which the guru will indicate.

What is the difference between pratyahara and dhyana? In pratyahara, the mind is trying to withdraw itself from the

449

experience of sense objects. In meditation you are trying to fuse the trinity of experiences into one unity. When you are in meditation there are only three things that are surviving for you: the meditator, the act of meditation and the object of meditation. This is the trinity in meditation and other than these three, nothing is surviving for you. There is no fourth experience, no experience of distraction or experience of dissipation, no knowledge or experience of time and space. The experience is just of the meditator and the object, and the process of meditation.

Pratyahara is a Sanskrit term. It is 'a retreat'. Retreat means 'to return to'. Senses usually run towards objects; eyes after the form, ears after the sound, nose after the smell. This is how the senses run after their respective sense objects. The knowledge of the sense object is then transferred to the mind and thus stimulation is constantly sent to the different centres of the brain, thereby disturbing the mind. As a result the mind is agitated, active and dynamic all the time. If you have to silence the mind you will have to delink the mind from the senses. This delinking process between the mind and the senses is known as pratyahara.

Dharana is 'concentration', fixing the mind on an object and holding the awareness on that object for a particular period of time, so that the mind which has an idea, transforms itself into the form. The idea is converted into a form; it is given a form. When mind is able to hold a concept for a particular period of time, then ego withdraws itself. The objective awareness has already withdrawn by this time, because without withdrawing the objective awareness you cannot hold a concept. To be able to hold an idea for a period of time, it is necessary that you have withdrawn completely and annihilated any objective awareness. After that the ego is withdrawn; then dhyana, total awareness occurs.

Dhyana literally means 'total, non-dual, absolute aware-ness'. When you see the object in meditation, the awareness

450

is total. Now the awareness is not total because there is awareness of yourself, of the room, of time; that is partial awareness. In dhyana the awareness is not partial, finite or limited. It is total awareness. Awareness of one thing only, not of three things. When this happens, the principles of existence are affected. Karma which is responsible for incarnation, pleasure, pain, destiny, happiness and unhappiness, is affected. The seed of karma, the samskara, the totality of man's life and existence is within himself in the seed form. As long as you have that seed you will continue to exist.

After meditation or dhyana has been accomplished, you enter the domain of samadhi. When consciousness tries to annihilate itself; when the trinity of experience, of meditation, meditating, and the object of meditation also disintegrates, the boundaries are broken. At that time the seed of individual existence dissolves. That is the highest point, called *samadhi*, nirvana, emancipation. It has no name and it has every name.

अभ्यासे तु विनिद्राणां मनो धृत्वा समाधिना ।
रुद्राणी वा परा मुद्रा भद्रां सिद्धिं प्रयच्छति ॥ 125 ॥

For those who are alert and the mind one-pointed (disciplined) in samadhi, rudrani or shambhavi mudra is the greatest mudra for bestowing perfection.

All the mudras expand consciousness, but for the aspirant whose mind remains disciplined and whose awareness remains alert when all internal and external barriers have been dissolved in samadhi, shambhavi is the greatest perfection. *Shambhu* refers to Lord Shiva, 'the one born of peace', and *bhava* is 'divine emotion', or the elevation of human emotion into intense spiritual longing. Shambhavi is the energy principle of Shambhu. The mudra is adopted by gazing at the eyebrow centre, known as *bhrumadhya*, and instils peace. It may be performed externally with the eyes open or internally with closed eyes. The practice is described in Chapter 4, slokas 36 and 37.

Meditation becomes samadhi when awareness merges with the object of meditation and duality dissolves. In that state, sense perception is completely non-existent, and the eyeballs turn upwards, spontaneously fixed in shambhavi mudra. This is an external sign of the inner mental tranquility.

Scientists have discovered that mental fluctuations in the form of changing thoughts, ideas and images cause rapid flickering movements of the eyeballs. During dreaming sleep, when the awareness is completely withdrawn into the mental realm and dreams are occurring, rapid eyeball movement (REM) are also produced. Similarly, during the waking state, when the external world is being perceived visually, the eyes are constantly blinking and following the external objects. These eye movements have been correlated with fluctuations in the electrical discharge of the brain, especially with prominent bursts of high frequency beta waves on the electroencephalogram (EEG).

During practices of concentration and meditation, when lower frequency alpha and theta waves emerge in steady, fixed patterns, the eyeballs are found to become spontaneously steady and fixed. Likewise, by stilling the eyeball movements, either externally or internally, it is possible to bring the brainwaves into the meditative pattern and induce the experience of meditation. It is on this basis that shambhavi mudra is practised.

After pratyahara has been established, it is very easy for the isolated awareness to be consumed by the internal mental modifications. Visionary and psychic experiences will manifest according to the samskaras and desires of the meditator, and their appearance is endless. Their appearance does not indicate a meditative state. It is a trance. It is only that laziness and lack of discipline have been transferred from the external world of sensory perception into the internal psychic and mental realms.

Meditation is to remain one-pointed and disciplined in the midst of these inner experiences as well, and this discipline must continue through the succeeding stages of samadhi. For this purpose the inner gaze is to be fixed upon a particular psychic symbol, the *ishta devata*, in shambhavi mudra. This symbol is chosen by the aspirant according to his own inclination, or it may be assigned by the guru. That symbol becomes the focus of pure consciousness for the aspirant. It becomes a real illumined object in his consciousness by one-pointedness and discipline.

Otherwise, meditation does not occur and the samadhi attained is of tamasic quality. It is to be remembered that the awareness is being constantly assailed by psychic experiences, visions and even divine beings, and that these experiences increase as meditation deepens. To hold onto the chosen symbol is very difficult, and the meditator fails many times in this regard. Nevertheless, he should press on to perfection in shambhavi mudra.

The symbols of Lord Shiva are many indeed. The crystal shivalingam or the lingam whose substance has been transmuted into light, are just two of them. Sri Ramana Maharshi of South India was one of the greatest yogis in modern times. He lived at the base of the mountain Arunachala in Thiruvannamalai, which is a geological symbol of Lord Shiva. This mountain became his ishta devata, and every day he used to circumambulate its base. He lived in constant awareness of its presence, both internally and externally. It became the channel of his bhavana and the basis of his samadhi. It was his symbol of the supreme consciousness, and his poems reveal this wonderfully. Similarly, many mountains and natural places in India are considered as sacred to Lord Shiva. Any form or symbol may be used as the ishta devata according to the inclination or belief of the aspirant. The important point is not so much the symbol, but the devotion and aspiration to realize it.

राजयोगं विना पृथ्वी राजयोगं विना निशा ।
राजयोगं विना मुद्रा विचित्रापि न शोभते ॥ 126 ॥

The earth without raja yoga, night without raja yoga, even the various mudras without raja yoga are useless, i.e. not beautiful.

Without raja yoga the value of this life cannot be had. The final stage of samadhi is raja yoga, and it is the only purpose of existence on this earth. Without that experience, the real nature of this empirical world cannot be grasped. Samadhi can be had by following any path of yoga, such as karma, jnana, bhakti yoga, etc. They all terminate in the experience of a totally one-pointed mind, i.e. samadhi. Raja yoga means not only the particular system of Sage Patanjali's ashtanga yoga, but it means the complete absorption in dhyana by any means. Without withdrawing the sensory awareness and experiencing the inner world in meditation it is impossible to appreciate the external. Without striving for the inner experiences it is meaningless to live for the external experience because that is limited by the senses. The internal world is vast and limitless. Through dhyana the external experience expands and becomes part of the internal. The deeper you can go into dharana and dhyana the more you can appreciate the purpose and beauty of life.

मारुतस्य विधिं सर्वं मनोयुक्तं समभ्यसेत् ।
इतरत्र न कर्तव्या मनोवृत्तिर्मनीषिणा ॥ 127 ॥

All the pranayama methods are to be done with a concentrated mind. The wise man should not let his mind be involved in the modifications (vrittis).

During the practice of pranayama the mind has a natural tendency to run away in the multitude of thoughts and emotions which arise. This happens particularly during the practice of bhastrika pranayama. Thoughts come very rapidly and the awareness is easily swept away by their force. It is not sufficient to merely perform pranayama mechanically, while the awareness is dissipating and rambling in the quagmire of illusory thoughts and visions. There must be concentration upon the present moment. Mind, body and prana must cooperate together so that the three start to work in unison. Therefore, there has to be a method for concentration throughout the practice.

During nadi shodhana pranayama the awareness is to be fixed either on a mantra or on counting the ratio of the inflowing and outflowing breath. Try for the ratio 1:2. Breathe in repeating *Om* mentally four times, then breathe out repeating *Om* eight times. Like this, the awareness has to move with the breath.

During bhramari pranayama, concentrate on the source of the sound in the brain and the effect of the gentle humming vibrations. With ujjayi pranayama, listen to the subtle sound of the breath, repeating *So* with the inflowing breath and *Ham* with the outflowing breath while moving the awareness and prana up and down in the spinal passage. Mantra repetition and sound vibration help in holding the concentration.

How to concentrate during bhastrika pranayama? It is not possible to do japa with the speed of each inhalation and exhalation. Concentration must be upon counting the

456

breaths, up to 100, 200, 300, 400, etc. Hold kumbhaka with uddiyana, jalandhara and moola bandhas and concentrate upon mooladhara, then manipura and then vishuddhi, and then release the bandhas correctly. Start a second round and keep the awareness on the counting as before. If you can hold the awareness it improves the quality and depth of dharana. In fact dhyana will result from deep concentration in bhastrika.

Single-minded concentration is essential in all the practices whether pranayama, asana or mudra. It is the essence of perfection in every form of yoga. There is a short parable which illustrates this. Once a disciple asked his guru to write down the greatest wisdom. The guru wrote 'attention'. The disciple asked if that was all and if the guru could add something more, as it was very brief. The guru then wrote, 'attention, attention'. Still the disciple failed to understand and asked if there was a deeper explanation. So the guru wrote three times, 'attention, attention, attention.' The disciple was completely puzzled and again questioned what it meant. The guru said, 'attention means attention'. In every situation, not only while practising pranayama, we must pay attention and become aware of the experiences, actions and thoughts in that moment. Development of awareness while awake leads to constant awareness in the deeper states of dhyana and samadhi.

इति मुद्रा दश प्रोक्ता आदिनाथेन शंभुना ।
एकैका तासु यमिनां महासिद्धिप्रदायिनी ॥ 128 ॥

*Thus the ten mudras have been told by Adinath Shambhu. Each one
is the bestower of perfection to the self-restrained.*

This completes the section on mudra. All have been
described as powerful practices which awaken kundalini
shakti and bestow perfection by regular practice combined
with self-control in life.

Although all the mudras have been described, it is not
necessary that all be practised. They are to be initiated first
by the guru according to the nature and level of the aspirant.

The necessity of self-restraint and purification have been
repeatedly emphasized by Swatmarama. This is because the
premature attainment of this power in an unpurified body
produces unimaginable diseases and, in an unrestrained
and unevolved mind, leads to demonic manifestations and
insanity. Some of the cruellest figures of history have been
empowered by a prematurely awakened kundalini. Self-
restraint is the abiding quality of perfection.

उपदेशं हि मुद्राणां यो दत्ते सांप्रदायिकम् ।
स एव श्रीगुरु: स्वामी साक्षादीश्वर एव स: ॥ 129 ॥

One who instructs mudra in the tradition of guru-disciple is the true
guru and form of Ishwara.

Perfection in mudra and awakening of the shakti through
mudra depends upon the initiation of the guru and then the
practice of the sadhaka. When mudra or any other practice
is passed on from the guru to disciple it is sure to bear fruit
when practised, because the guru's words themselves are the
very shakti which, manifests in concrete form. The external
guru is the only means to understanding your internal guru.
He is considered as the manifestation of Ishwara. Of course,
the inner guru, the atman, has no form or shape. In order
to perceive it we have to give some form and identity to it.
Atman with form is known as Ishwara.

Ishwara is the supreme being, the causal or sattwic body of
the cosmic consciousness and Shakti. Ishwara is said to be the
God presiding over the universe we know. *Ishwara* is commonly
translated as God. To the yogi, however, God has no religious
connotation, it is purely the highest state or experience. Sage
Patanjali's *Yoga Sutras* state: "God is a special soul untouched
by afflictions, acts, their traces and their fruits." (1:24) Through
guru you can reach that state of experience, therefore it is said
that he is that. Externally, guru has a physical body, ego and
mind, just like anyone else but his individual consciousness
is illumined by the light of atma. He has realized his own
inner guru, and therefore by contemplation on his form, by
following his words and instructions, that experience can also
come to you. For the disciple, the guru represents the supreme
experience and existence, Ishwara.

It is Lord Shiva who witnesses through the eyes of the
guru established in sahaja samadhi. Those who can recognize
this have perceived the true nature of their guru and joyfully
pay homage and worship at his lotus feet.

459

तस्य वाक्यपरो भूत्वा मुद्राभ्यासे समाहितः ।
अणिमादिगुणैः सार्धं लभते कालवंचनम् ॥ 130 ॥

*By following explicitly his (guru's) words, and practising mudra,
one obtains the qualities of anima, etc., and overcomes death/time.*

This sloka clearly indicates the necessity of the guru-disciple
relationship in attaining the fruits of mudra practice, viz.
siddhi and immortality. Once the disciple has chosen the
guru and the guru has recognized the disciple, only the
meaning and application of the guru's advice and instructions, and the regularity of the practices have utmost
importance in the disciple's life. The interaction with the
inner and outer personality of the guru is all important
in removing egocentricity. The deep-rooted and inherited
impressions, or samskaras, which stand as blockages to the
greater flow of awareness and limit the expression of greater
energy in the practices are to be systematically exposed and
rooted out.

How is the guru to be approached? The disciple has to
use any and every means to bring himself into the light of
the guru's awareness. His aspiration and efforts will be noted
by the guru, who will give specific cues which the disciple
must be attuned to receive. The greatest capacities for the
aspirant are to be able to discriminate and so recognize a
fine guru and guide, and then to surrender his ego and
conditioning at the guru's feet.

Just as a sick person whose bowels are strangulated
must soon find an accomplished surgeon, so the aspirant
who wants to experience the greater consciousness has to
submit his own psychophysiological personality before the
guru. Only a fool will consent to an anaesthetic without
trusting in his surgeon. So the guru-disciple relationship
must be established by a process of trust and surrender if the
practices are to bear the greater fruit.

460

अथ चतुर्थोपदेशः

Chapter Four

Samadhi

अथ समाधिपाद:

Chapter Four

Samadhi

नम: शिवाय गुरवे नादबिन्दुकलात्मने ।
निरंजनपदं याति नित्यं तत्र परायण: ॥ 1 ॥

Salutations to the Guru Shiva, who is regarded as nada, bindu, kalaa (sound, nucleus and emanating ray). One wholly devoted to them, goes into the eternally stainless state.

Shiva is the mantram of the ultimate state of existence and non-existence, manifest and unmanifest. "Shiva is beyond prakritic attributes, i.e. beyond nada, bindu, kalaa, but also beyond the source from where they emerge; eternal and ever-omnipresent, without change, immutable; unattainable but by yoga (union)." (*Srimad Devi Bhagavatam*) It is something impossible to define or conceive by the finite mind. Shaivites praise Shiva; Vaishnavites, Vishnu; Vedantins, Brahman; Shaktas and tantrics, Shakti; followers of Samkhya philosophy, Purusha. They are the names of the same reality.

Veneration of Shiva originates from the Vedas in which he is known as Rudra. The mantra *Shiva* came after the *Rig* and *Atharva Vedas*. In the Vedas, Rudra is depicted as a wild nature god, controlling the environmental elements. His origin seems Dravidian and was inherited by the Kapalikas. Only after 200 BC in the *Yajur Veda*, does he take the form of Shankara, Shiva, Mahadeva, and is considered to be Ishwara.

In the *Atharva Veda* and Brahmanas, Rudra is known as *Pashupati*, the controller of the animal instincts. By the time of the Upanishads he had become the Creator. Shiva represents the principle of consciousness. Thus, throughout the gradual historical emergence of Shiva, we see the evolution of individual consciousness from primal under-standing to enlightenment.

Shiva and guru are synonymous terms indicating the existence of supreme consciousness and reality. It is within everybody and yet beyond every body and object. When that reality is realized the inner guru or Shiva becomes known. Such a person is entitled to be called guru.

Traditionally, there are three lines of guru: divine guru or *divyaugha*, siddha guru or *siddhaugha* and human guru or *mahavaugha*. Sadhakas devoted to a particular *devata* (form of God), or spiritual path will have a guru of a different lineage. Shiva is the *Adiguru*, the first source of everything, and though he is the guru of gurus and beyond lineage, a lineage has descended from him.

According to tantra, Shiva, or consciousness, cannot exist alone. Side by side with Shiva is the aspect of Shakti. Shiva, or consciousness, is inactive and inert. Shakti is the active and changing aspect, and is actually none other than the reflection or energy of Shiva. In the scheme of creation whether manifest or potential, Shakti is the opposite polarity to Shiva. Consciousness is the silent witness, Shakti is the doer.

The mid-point between these two polar tensions is the bindu. When the two polarities meet in the bindu or nucleus, the nucleus is exploded and manifests *nada*, sound and *kalaa*, emanating ray. Nada is the first manifestation of prana, the beginning of creation.

Bindu is both macrocosmic and microcosmic. Ultimately there is *maha bindu*, the entire conscious creation, then *para bindu*, the form of Ishwara, *sukshma bindu*, the individual mind, and *sthula bindu*, the gross bindu in the form of ovum or sperm. The emergence of bindu is the evolution of the primordial Shakti into manifestation of mind and matter.

In the initial maha bindu, called Shiva, Brahman, Parameshwara, consciousness and Shakti are not different but one. The consciousness is known as *chit* and the Shakti is *chidroopini*, through which consciousness experiences itself. Here Shakti is coordinate, not subordinate and is called *parasamvit* or *samyavastha*, which indicates total equilibrium.

When movement, or *spandana*, takes place in Shakti, the shiva tattwa or element and shakti tattwa or element, emerge as separate identities. When they unite, the 'thrill of the union' is nada. This is the first movement of Shiva-Shakti, and the product is called *sadashiva tattwa* or *turiya brahman*. It contains the potential of nada. Though Shakti is still unmanifest, a very subtle and pure notion of existence or being arises. After this point the shakti tattwa becomes predominant. *Sadakhya,* the combined Shiva-Shakti, evolves into bindu shakti which is the Ishwara tattwa, para bindu, in which knowledge, or *jnana shakti*, predominates. This para bindu is known as *ghanavastha shakti*, i.e. the totality of Shakti. It is what is called Shabda Brahman, *vak*, the word, the cosmic causal body and the causal body of nada, the realm of satyaloka, shoonya.

From Ishwara emerge the three bindus known as nada, bindu and bija or kalaa. It is the movement of nada and bindu together which forms kalaa or the emanating ray. They are the three qualities or *gunas* of sattwa, rajas and tamas and are also known as the three devatas, Brahma, Vishnu and Maheshwara or Shiva. These three bindus are predominated by the shakti tattwa. The nada, or shabda as it is often called, is described by Sir John Woodroffe as the 'stress' or the attracting force between bindu and bija or kalaa. The union of bindu with bija is manifest sound or *dhwani*.

The evolution of individual consciousness means bringing the 'stress' or the tension between the two polarities of Shiva and Shakti, time and space, or consciousness and prana, closer together. When they meet in the nucleus or bindu, the total potential of consciousness and Shakti explodes. Only then can the true experience of Shiva be attained.

From bindu, consciousness is expressed by means of Shakti. When consciousness and prana meet in the nucleus of matter (mooladhara), bindu, kalaa and nada emerge. Kalaa is primal Shakti, the power through which thirty-six principles of creation come into manifestation and the movement of prana in the physical body. Nada is the stream of consciousness flowing from the bindu to the object. By uniting these two within the framework of our body and consciousness, one returns to the original bindu, shoonya. When that is attained, it is *moksha*, liberation. In the Guru Gita of the *Skanda Purana* it states, "Prostrations to the Guru who is pure knowledge, eternal, peaceful, beyond space, full of light, unattached, beyond bindu, nada, kalaa." That is what is to be realized.

Evolution of the Bindu

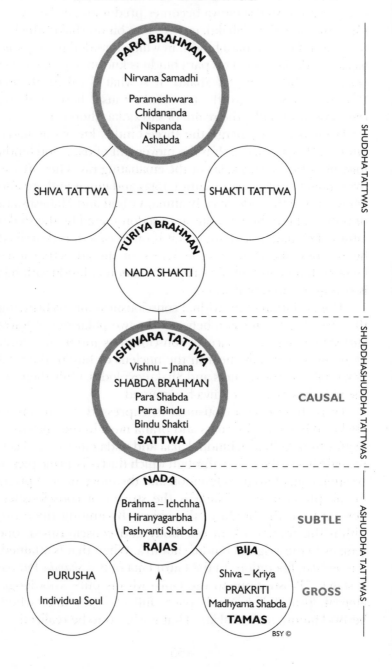

PARA BRAHMAN

Nirvana Samadhi

Parameshwara
Chidananda
Nispanda
Ashabda

SHIVA TATTWA — — — — — — SHAKTI TATTWA

TURIYA BRAHMAN

NADA SHAKTI

ISHWARA TATTWA

Vishnu – Jnana
SHABDA BRAHMAN
Para Shabda
Para Bindu
Bindu Shakti
SATTWA

NADA

Brahma – Ichchha
Hiranyagarbha
Pashyanti Shabda
RAJAS

BIJA

Shiva – Kriya
PRAKRITI
Madhyama Shabda
TAMAS

PURUSHA

Individual Soul

SHUDDHA TATTWAS

SHUDDHASHUDDHA TATTWAS

ASHUDDHA TATTWAS

CAUSAL

SUBTLE

GROSS

BSY ©

अथेदानीं प्रवक्ष्यामि समाधिक्रममुत्तमम् ।
मृत्युघ्नं च सुखोपायं ब्रह्मानन्दकरं परम् ॥ 2 ॥

Thus, I shall now expound the best process of samadhi which eliminates death and takes one to the greatest bliss of Brahma.

Now we come to the culmination of hatha yoga and raja yoga: samadhi. The word *samadhi* is made up of two roots, *sama* which means 'equal' and *dhi* which is 'reflection' or 'to perceive'. The *Hatharatnavali* states that, "When the mind becomes motionless as a result of (deep) concentration, that is called samadhi." (4:3) *Gheranda Samhita* states that, "Detaching the mind from the body, one should make it one with the Paramatma. That is known as samadhi, which is not a state of any kind of consciousness as we understand this word." (7:3)

The word samadhi does not indicate liberation but it is a field of awareness comprising supraconsciousness. It is the result of total one-pointedness of mind and expansion of consciousness from the mundane perception to that of cosmic awareness. It is the final experience of every human being and that which we are all evolving towards. Through yogic and tantric practices this process is accelerated. Just as scientists have developed the means to release nuclear energy from the uranium atom, similarly the yogis found the scientific system to release the energy and consciousness from the bindu within the body.

Samadhi is the experience of that which exists beyond temporal experience, which is beyond the influence of nature. It is a timeless state beyond birth, death, beginning, end. Samadhi starts with total concentration on the object of meditation, with no other thought and no awareness of the witness remaining.

According to Sage Patanjali's *Yoga Sutras* there are six stages of samadhi: savitarka, nirvitarka, savichara, nirvichara, ananda and asmita. They are names of very subtle fluctuations taking place before the superior samadhi – nirvikalpa.

467

Samadhi is neither trance nor ecstasy. Samadhi is that state of consciousness in which there is no fluctuation. A thought is a fluctuation, objective awareness is fluctuation, subjective awareness is fluctuation. A dream is fluctuation, a spiritual vision is fluctuation, psychic forms are fluctuation. The knowledge of 'I' in the depth of meditation is fluctuation. In deep meditation when you become unconscious of everything, that is also fluctuation. It is called sankalpa-vikalpa, i.e. thought and counterthought, awareness and counterawareness.

In the deepest mental states the sankalpa-vikalpa keep on taking place, but when sankalpa-vikalpa dies then a state emerges that is called samadhi. Samadhi is either savikalpa or nirvikalpa. *Savikalpa* is samadhi or supraconsciousness with vikalpa, counterawareness. *Nirvikalpa* is samadhi without any vikalpa, or counterawareness. In savikalpa samadhi there is higher awareness but the four main types of vikalpa continue. These vikalpas are not like passion or fear but they are very slight modifications termed vitarka, vichara, ananda and asmita by Sage Patanjali.

When samadhi begins, the consciousness moves beyond the awareness of the physical and pranic sheaths, i.e. annamaya and pranamaya koshas, and abides in the mental sheath of manomaya. Later, the awareness develops into *prajna* or intuition, the higher mind in vijnanamaya kosha, then transcendental awareness in anandamaya and then beyond that. Samadhi is progressive, transcending the spheres of object, motion, thought and instinct.

The entire range of samadhi is classified into two divisions: savikalpa, which is also known as *sabija*, i.e. 'with seed'. The seed is *samskara*, the trace of ego, which manifests as the vikalpa. The unfoldment from vitarka to asmita is called sabija or savikalpa or salambana samadhi because the consciousness still has a base support or *pratyaya*. Consciousness operates within the koshas and is therefore still entangled with Shakti, prakriti or maya. Nirbija is beyond that, devoid of awareness and consciousness. Rather, it is conscious unconsciousness. It is without vibration or movement, there is complete stillness of everything.

Each stage of sabija has a positive and negative aspect. Positive samadhi is *samprajnata*. Samprajnata indicates that there is consciousness of the object of meditation, or pratyaya. *Asamprajnata* is negative samadhi which means there is unconscious awareness of the object. It is called *virama pratyaya*. It is not complete absence of the symbol. The symbol of concentration is in the mind but there is no awareness. It is a dynamic state which intercepts vitarka and vichara, vichara and ananda and asmita and nirvikalpa. It is a state of shoonya or laya, characterized by the presence of samskara but the dropping of object or pratyaya. It is an impermanent state preceding the ascension into a higher or deeper state. However, descent into a grosser state may also result and this should be remembered. The concluding point of samprajnata samadhi always unfolds through asamprajnata.

In the first stage of sabija samadhi, i.e. savitarka, also known as *vitarka samprajnata*, mind is absorbed in the object, subject and sense of perception, or 'known, knower and knowing'. There is no distinction between the three. Chitta or memory exists and confuses the subject, object and idea, so they appear to be one. In this state the concept still exists in language and gross form.

When knower, known and knowing become unconfused and memory is free of any past impressions concerning the object, it is nirvitarka or *vitarka asamprajnata*. The gross form of the object and knowledge of it shines in the mind but there is no awareness or language. The faculty of memory is checked.

Savichara or *vichara samprajnata* begins when the subtle layer of the object appears. However, mind is not totally fixed on the subtle object, i.e. *sukshma artha*, because of association with time, space and idea. There is infusion and awareness of each aspect (knower, known and knowing) separately. Vichara is direct reflection without the basis of language. It is *pratyabhijna*, 'illumined knowledge', which guides all the processes in the deeper states of supraconsciousness.

When time, space and idea (knower, known and knowing) are removed, and the essential nature of thought remains, it is nirvichara or *vichara asamprajnata*. At the culmination of this samadhi, the chitta is illumined and intellect ceases.

Nirvichara develops into ananda or *sanandan* samadhi when chitta has penetrated beyond the subtle existence of the object and there is only awareness of the existence of the vritti 'I am' (aham asmi). It is sattwic ahamkara or ego, a state of pure existence and awareness without word or idea.

Ananda becomes asmita when there is no differentiation between the object of consciousness and the consciousness. Awareness and consciousness are absolute but there is still the seed of ego. It is the highest sattwic state of consciousness.

At the end of this samadhi there is a state which is called dynamic samadhi. Before making a jump from savikalpa to nirvikalpa, there is a gap and that gap is complete shoonya or void; there is no experience. The self is dynamic potential, and it is after this gap that nirvikalpa samadhi dawns.

However, before nirvikalpa there are a few other samadhis. One of them is known as *dharmamegha* samadhi. *Megha* is 'cloud', *dharma* is 'virtue'. Dharmamegha samadhi is emergence of a consciousness where the virtues pour down upon you. The virtues are not religious or other virtues, but all the good qualities automatically come to you, because it is very necessary before nirvikalpa. If the dawn of virtue does not take place before nirvikalpa samadhi, then you are going to enter nirvikalpa samadhi with all the rubbish that you carry in your life. In order to remove that dirt, it is necessary to achieve dharma megha samadhi.

Nirvikalpa or nirbija samadhi is the disappearance of the last trace of samskara and vikalpa. Individual consciousness is eliminated just as a fire which has consumed its fuel dies out. From dharma megha samadhi onwards, there is complete freedom from karma and kleshas (ignorance, egoism, attachment, aversion, clinging to life). There is no desire to become liberated, but nevertheless, nirvana, kaivalya or moksha ensues. That is timeless, changeless – the supreme samadhi.

470

Progressive Stages of Samadhi

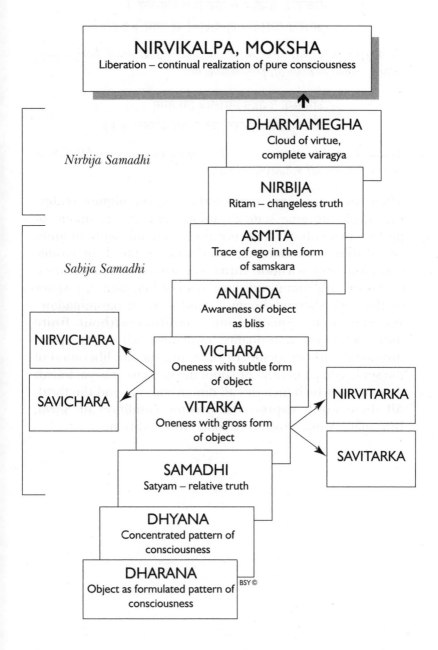

राजयोग: समाधिश्च उन्मनी य मनोन्मनी ।
अमरत्वं लयस्तत्त्वं शून्याशून्यं परं पदम् ॥ 3 ॥

*Raja yoga, samadhi, unmani, manonmani, amaratwa, laya, sahaja
tattwa, shoonyashoonya, parampadam.*

अमनस्कं तथाद्वैतं निरालम्बं निरंजनम् ।
जीवन्मुक्तिश्च सहजा तुर्या चेत्येकवाचका: ॥ 4 ॥

*Amanaskam, advaitam, niralamba, niranjana, jivanmukti, sahaja
and turiya are all synonymous terms.*

There are many yogic terms indicating the highest reality:
raja yoga, supreme state of union; samadhi, complete or
perfect perception, concentration; unmani, without individual mind; manonmani, mind without mind, or cosmic
consciousness without finite consciousness; amaratwa,
beyond death, immortal; laya, dissolution; tattwa, essence
or thatness; shoonyashoonya, voidless void; parampadam,
supreme state; amanaskam, condition without finite
mind; advaitam, non-duality; niralamba, without support;
niranjana, without quality or stain; jivanmukti, liberation of
the soul; sahaja, natural or spontaneous state; turiya, fourth
dimension, which includes all dimensions beyond the third.
All these words express the pristine condition of Shiva,
Brahman, Atma, which is beyond any condition.

सलिले सैन्धवं यद्वत्साम्यं भजति योगत: ।
तथात्ममनसोरैक्यं समाधिरभिधीयते ॥ 5 ॥

As salt merges in the sea, likewise the mind and atma are considered united in samadhi.

यदा संक्षीयते प्राणो मानसं च प्रलीयते ।
तदा समरसत्वं च समाधिरभिधीयते ॥ 6 ॥

When the movement of prana is completely annihilated, then mind is reabsorbed and then samadhi is considered attained.

तत्समं च द्वयोरैक्यं जीवात्मपरमात्मनो: ।
प्रनष्टसर्वसंकल्प: समाधि: सोऽभिधीयते ॥ 7 ॥

When the twofold nature of the individual soul and cosmic soul becomes one, all desires and ideations are destroyed and that is considered samadhi.

Shiva or purusha is the true state. Individual mind is but a transmutation of pure consciousness. In order for the individual consciousness to return to its original state the process of transmutation has to be retraced, or it can be said that a process of involution has to take place.

Pure consciousness, Shiva, is known as *avyakta* or 'unmanifest reality'. From that evolves *mula prakriti* or *avyakritam*, unmanifest Shakti, which has been described as sadakhya tattwa in sloka 1 of this chapter. Then comes sattwic ahamkara and prana which is the macrocosmic causal body, or *karana sharira*, i.e. Ishwara; then the karana sharira of the *jiva*, or individual soul, and later tamasic ahamkara which divides into *avarana shakti*, the 'veiling power' and *vikshepa shakti*, the 'projecting power'. From vikshepa shakti come the pancha tattwas and tanmatras and the manifest universe.

Individual mind is the combination of different elements. Therefore, in order to dissolve individual awareness,

473

these elements have to be separated. Mind is said to be composed of the twenty-four elements: five jnanendriya, five karmendriya, five tanmatras, five tattwas and antah karana, i.e. chitta, buddhi, ahamkara and manas. It means that perception through the senses has to be isolated from the mind, cognition of the tanmatras eliminated, manas separated from chitta, chitta separated from buddhi, buddhi separated from ahamkara. Dissociation of each function has to occur. Only then can individual consciousness dissolve again into its pure source.

Just as the matrix of sodium ions and chloride ions combined together in a crystal lattice makes an individual substance, i.e. salt, but when added to water the ions separate into solution by binding with the hydrogen and hydroxide ions of water, so the elements of individual mind merge with the universal mind in nirvikalpa samadhi. The *Avadhoota Gita* states: "Just as when water has been poured into water, no distinction remains, so purusha and prakriti appear non-different to me." (1:51)

According to Vedanta, buddhi is the closest aspect of mind to atman. It receives information from manas, which in turn receives information from the karmendriyas and jnanendriyas. If the information from the senses is cut off by pratyahara and intellect is made to become still by dharana, only the shining atma will remain. In yoga, the first step to samadhi is control of the sense impulses feeding the mind. The easiest method to achieve this is by control of the pranic flow.

Chitta shakti is responsible for ichchha or desire; prana shakti is responsible for kriya or action. When both these functions are arrested but awareness is maintained, what remains is pure knowledge. Therefore, in raja yoga it is essential for the body to become perfectly steady in the asana and the practice of kumbhaka to be prolonged. During samadhi the body appears as if dead because the functions of prana, apana, samana and udana withdraw into vyana. In order to induce the state of samadhi the bandhas and mudras, etc., were devised.

In the *Hatharatnavali* it is stated that, "In this stage (samadhi), jivatma and paramatma are held in the state of equilibrium, in which there is complete cessation of mental activity." (4:2) In order to fuse the individual mind with paramatma, the cause creating individuality has to be eradicated. Individuality occurs when fluctuation, *vritti*, and desire, *vasana*, exist in the mind. The more powerful the vasana, the less clarity of consciousness remains and the more the mind is drawn into the grosser modifications. Unless the mind is crystal clear, free from these influences, concentration, meditation and samadhi cannot take place.

The wavering tendencies of the vrittis have to be diminished. It is the condition of the mind to attach itself to an object. Thus, the fewer the objects it is attached to, the more one-pointed it becomes. Sage Patanjali's *Yoga Sutras* state that, "Samapatti is a state of complete absorption of mind which is free from vrittis into (the three types of objects such as) cognizer, cognized and senses; just as a polished crystal takes the colour of that on which it rests." (1:41) Mind has to become subtle and clear as crystal so that it reflects the paramatma and not the vrittis or vasanas.

Cosmic consciousness is always with us. We constantly receive cosmic impulses but they are filtered through the RAS (reticular activating system) at the junction of the spinal cord and brain. What is received by the higher brain is but a trickle of the total torrent of messages, enough so that mundane awareness and biological survival is possible. As the contemporary psychologist, Robert E. Ornstein says in his book, *The Psychology of Consciousness*: "We cannot possibly experience the world as it fully exists; we would be overwhelmed. We are restricted by our physical evolution to only a few sensory dimensions. If we do not possess a 'sense' for a given energy-form, we do not experience its existence. It is almost impossible for us to imagine an energy-form or an object outside our normal receptive range."

In order to expand our limited state of perception, the normal range of brain functions has to be expanded by a safe and sure science. We should not consider this as a paranormal event. Just as it was considered a supernormal feat to voluntarily control the blood pressure but it is now an accepted phenomenon, so this expansion of awareness enabling 'extraordinary' communication is becoming reknown.

राजयोगस्य माहात्म्यं को वा जानाति तत्त्वत: ।
ज्ञानं मुक्ति: स्थिति: सिद्धिर्गुरुवाक्येन लभ्यते ॥ 8 ॥

Who really knows the magnitude of raja yoga? Through the guru's words, inner knowledge, liberation, perfection fructify.

दुर्लभो विषयत्यागो दुर्लभं तत्त्वदर्शनम् ।
दुर्लभा सहजावस्था सद्गुरो: करुणां विना ॥ 9 ॥

Without the compassion of the true guru, renunciation is impossible, perception of the truth inaccessible and sahaja samadhi unobtainable.

Only when a person has experienced the fruits of raja yoga can he know its real value. Those who have never experienced it will be unable to appreciate its worth. Swatmarama has divulged the secret of inner awakening – guru. No matter how much you practise yoga, if there is no guru, there can be no enlightenment. The quickest method to evolve the inner consciousness is through devotion and service to one's guru. He may not be a literate or educated person, his external personality may not be in accordance with yours, but the light of his soul will enlighten all devoted to him. His words are the atma shakti which is transmitted to you. They are the seeds which you water when you apply and practise what he has said. When the seeds bloom forth his words become the living reality.

A living guru is the manifestation of your own atma, and atma only appears when you have reached a certain stage of inner awareness. What the external guru says and wants for you is the voice of your own atma. Therefore, without his will there is nothing you can do. Guru can give you instant awakening if he wants to. Therefore, the one way to samadhi is grace or *anugraha* from the guru.

The *Gheranda Samhita* states that: "Samadhi, the supreme yoga, is attained by great merit earned previously. It is achieved by the grace of the guru and by devotion to him. That yogi soon acquires this exquisite experience, who is convinced by what he has learnt and heard from his guru, who has developed self-confidence and whose mind is becoming more and more enlightened." (7:1,2)

Grace or anugraha is also known as *shaktipat*. The intensity of shaktipat depends on the intensity of a disciple's desire to attain realization, and his previous samskaras. Spiritually evolved souls can attain enlightenment through intense or *tivra shaktipat* without performing much sadhana. Those who are less evolved receive *madhyama shaktipat* to help them realize their guru and to be initiated into yoga. Through regular practice of sadhana and patience they can attain liberation. The third type of shaktipat is moderate or *manda* which instils a yearning for spiritual knowledge and if the desire and perseverance in the quest is pursued there can be enlightenment.

Grace has to be earned by spiritual discipline and desire. It cannot be bought, nor can the guru be cheated. There are four main ways or *upayas* described in the *Shiva Sutras* to purify the body and mind and earn this grace. They are known as anavopaya, shaktopaya, shambhavopaya and anupaya.

Anavopaya includes physical discipline, such as hatha yoga, which purifies the body and awakens sushumna. It is therefore also known as *kriyopaya*. *Shaktopaya* is for a person whose mind and body are already considerably pure. It consists of only concentration, mantra repetition and instilling the idea: "I am the supreme consciousness. The universe is none other than the expansion of the Self." This is also known as *jnanopaya* because it utilizes the aspect of jnana. Kundalini rises by means of the higher intellect and, therefore, it includes jnana yoga and other higher stages of raja yoga. *Shambhavopaya* is for those who are highly evolved, who can become realized by simply concentrating on the idea of pure consciousness or the Shiva tattwa. Through constant self-analysis, awareness and reflection, they are led to self-realization. This is the path of Advaita philosophy.

Anupaya is direct realization through one simple action of the guru. *An* denotes something minute, 'the nucleus of the nucleus'. Thus anupaya infers the grace which is attained by nominal effort. A well-known example of this, is when Balakrishna opened his mouth and his adopted mother, Yashodha, saw the entire universe. Anupaya is, therefore, also known as *anandopaya* because it instils instant bliss.

विविधैरासनै: कुंभैर्विचित्रै करणैरपि ।
प्रबुद्धायां महाशक्तौ प्राण: शून्ये प्रलीयते ॥ 10 ॥

When the maha shakti is aroused by the various asanas, pranayamas and mudras, the prana dissolves into shoonya.

Shoonya is void, but it is not a state of nothingness. It is a very deep and dynamic state of consciousness. It is the cause and origin of that which constitutes the manifest universe. It is bindu or the nucleus. According to Sage Patanjali's *Yoga Sutras*, shoonya is the step before the final samadhi. The word shoonya is used generally to describe the unfolding process between asmita samadhi and nirvana. Shoonya also describes the state of asamprajnata samadhi or the negative phase of samadhi. Just as the word samadhi describes the range of supraconsciousness, so shoonya describes all the negative phases of samadhi in which there is unconscious supraconsciousness. Awareness of the object, onlooker and looking are absorbed into one, the symbol shines in the consciousness, but there is no consciousness of it. That awareness is held by the subtle existence of vasana in the causal body or unconscious mind.

The *Vijnana Bhairava Tantra* states: "O goddess, if one, after casting one's gaze on some object, withdraws it slowly and eliminates the knowledge of that object along with the thought and impression of it, he abides in shoonya, the void." (Dharana 95, v. 120) At this point of samadhi you become totally helpless.

According to Buddhism there are four types of shoonya which are described as:
1. Phenomena and shoonya
2. Clearness and shoonya
3. Bliss and shoonya
4. Consciousness and shoonya.

However, Mahayana Buddhism has categorized shoonya into eighteen stages:

1. Shoonya of internal sensory response
2. Shoonya of external sensory perception
3. Shoonya of both internal and external sensory stimuli
4. Shoonya of shoonya
5. The great shoonya of space
6. Real shoonya
7. Compounded shoonya, as of the universe
8. Uncompounded shoonya of the unmanifest
9. Infinite shoonya
10. Beginningless shoonya
11. Remainderless shoonya
12. Natural shoonya
13. Shoonya of phenomena
14. Shoonya of predication
15. Shoonya of non-thought
16. Shoonya of immateriality
17. Shoonya of reality
18. Shoonya of non-substantiality of reality.

This is a very involved classification compared to the yogic definition in which there are three distinct stages, which intercept and come after vitarka samadhi, vichara samadhi and asmita samadhi.

उत्पन्नशक्तिबोधस्य त्यक्तनि:शेषकर्मण: ।
योगिन: सहजावस्था स्वयमेव प्रजायत ॥ 11 ॥

The sahaja state is conquered on its own (occurs by itself) in him whose remaining karmas are abandoned and who experiences the rising of shakti.

सुषुम्नावाहिनि प्राणे शून्ये विशति मानसे ।
तदा सर्वाणि कर्माणि निर्मूलयति योगवित् ॥ 12 ॥

When prana is flowing through sushumna, mind is in pure shoonya. Then all the karmas of the one knowing yoga are uprooted.

In the process of samadhi, the evolution of individual consciousness and shakti is very rapid and systematic. It is a process of refining the ego, vasanas and mind which are intricately linked. Once mind and prana are reabsorbed into the source, the vasanas also become non-existent. The *Shiva Samhita* states: "He who always contemplates on the hidden ajna lotus, at once destroys all the karmas of his past life without any opposition." (5:11) The store of karmas and vasanas is not entirely burnt until dharma megha samadhi has taken place.

When kundalini shakti reaches sahasrara chakra then the last traces of karma, vasana and ego are destroyed. As the kundalini moves up sushumna the various samskaras stored in each of the chakras are pulled forth into manifestation. These samskaras are expressed through the ego. The process of samadhi is involution of shakti into pure consciousness. It is a process of eliminating the base supports of individual mind.

Vasana is not something bad. It is responsible for the will to live. If it is completely eradicated before self-realization takes place you will be removing your will to live. In vedic and tantric philosophy there are said to be four main desires deep-rooted within every person. These are: *artha,* acquirement of wealth and commodities; *kaama*, gratification of sensual desire; *dharma*, to perform social, ethical, moral and natural duty; *moksha*, liberation.

Our desires are expressions of one of these four aspects. Some desires are superficial but the deep-rooted desires or vasanas are hidden within the deepest levels of consciousness, in the causal body. Desires lead to action and these actions create samskaras or impressions in the mind. *Samskara* is residue of experience, like a seed buried in the soil. Each experience we have is recorded and stored in the unconscious mind and body in a symbolic form. When samskaras are not re-experienced they are transferred deep within the subtle body, and if they are not re-expressed they are buried deeper. These suppressed samskaras are expressed in our dreams, behaviour patterns and diseases.

In Samkhya, Vedanta and Hindu philosophy, samskara is considered to be the primal form of existence. Every action is an expression of our previous samskaras. The force of desire to experience is channel through ida nadi, and the force which leads to action is channelled through pingala nadi. The two nadis have to be brought together; it is not a matter of eradicating them or suppressing them. The force channelled through both these nadis has to be channelled through sushumna. Only then can their influences be nullified. In hatha yoga we approach the problem of desire, vasana; impression, samskara; karma, action and reaction, by uniting these two channels of chitta and prana shakti.

According to the *Vijnana Bhairava Tantra* samskara has to be handled by directly controlling the mind through meditation, "Having observed a desire that has sprung up, the aspirant should put an end to it immediately. It will be absorbed in that very place from which it arose. When a desire or knowledge of it appears, the aspirant should, with the mind withdrawn from all objects, fix his mind on it (the desire) as the Self. Then he will have the realization of the essential reality. If one succeeds in immobilizing his mind (i.e. makes it one-pointed), when under the sway of

483

desire, anger, greed, infatuation, arrogance and envy, the reality underlying these states alone subsists." (73:96, 75:98, 78:101)

Man has freedom of thought and action, freedom of will, inherent in him, but at the same time he is totally subject to the laws of cause and effect, i.e. karma, the law of destiny. Everything in this world, everything in this universe, is subject to the laws of cause and effect, and man is no exception. That is called destiny.

According to the doctrine of karma, karmas are of three types: accumulated karmas, current karmas and fructifying karmas. It can be compared to having 10,000 dollars and putting it in a fixed deposit account. That fixed deposit is one form of karma. From that you get interest at the point of maturity, and that is another form of karma. On top of this, what you are earning is current karma. It is always being deposited into your current account. These three types of karma are constantly accumulating and being expressed. Our present state of life is, therefore, the effect of a previous cause, but at the same time it is also a cause for some further effect.

Destiny and free will always act together and they have to be combined together. They move together and cannot be separated from each other. Up to a certain level of evolution you cannot do anything to modify your destiny, but when you are exposed to spiritual life and you practise concentration and your mind attains strength and willpower, then you are in a position to implement free will together with destiny.

You suffer and you enjoy your past karmas, but at the same time, through your willpower you are integrating new types of karma with the day to day experiences you are now having. This is how the doctrine of karma and the law of spiritual evolution operates. Man is a slave of destiny and a master of his own willpower, but through the practices of yoga he can influence the underlying forces governing his existence.

अमराय नमस्तुभ्यं सोऽपि कालस्त्वया जित: ।
पतितं वदने यस्य जगदेतच्चराचरम् ॥ 13 ॥

O immortal one, salutations to you who have mastery over time, by whose jaws the animate and inanimate alike are devoured.

The sloka pays homage to the yogi who has realized the Self – that which is the origin of all, which is beyond the effects of duality, time and space, and which encompasses all. There is nothing manifest or unmanifest which is not a part of it. Nothing can be taken from it because wherever you put that which has been removed, it remains a part of that Supreme.

According to the Vedas, the universe we know exists during the Day of Brahma. In comparison to the lifespan of Brahma, which is considered as one hundred years, our own life and death is like that of a minute body cell. Each day of his life is divided into four maha yuga cycles which occur one thousand times; satya or krita yuga (1,728,000 earth years), treta yuga (1,296,000 years), dwapara yuga (864,000 years) and kali yuga (432,000 years). We have just entered the kali yuga; we are just on the threshold. In terms of universal time, the time we understand is almost meaningless, it is only relevant to our present reality. For an astronaut in space the whole concept of time is altered. Similarly when you go deep into your own consciousness, the concept of time is altered. The deeper you go, the less influence it has on awareness. At the very centre of creation and your own being, time cannot exert an influence. When time ceases to exist, so does creation.

The *Avadhoota Gita* states that there is no such thing as animate and inanimate, there is only one true state of pure consciousness: "All this is verily the absolute Self. Distinction and non-distinction do not exist. How can I say it exists, it does not exist? I am filled with wonder." (1:4) "The destroyed and undestroyed are both false. The born and unborn are both false. If there is only one indivisible and all comprehensive absolute, how can there be perishable and imperishable?" (6:5)

485

चित्ते समत्वमापन्ने वायौ व्रजति मध्यमे ।
तदामरोली वज्रोली सहजोली प्रजायते ॥ 14 ॥

When mind is in equanimity and (prana) vayu proceeds through sushumna, then amaroli, vajroli and sahajoli are attained.

The purpose of vajroli, sahajoli and amaroli is to reverse the natural downward flow of apana so that the vayu flows upward through sushumna. When it is achieved the external mind becomes instantly tranquil and the awareness enters the inner dimensions. Mental equanimity means a steady mind, peaceful and unflinching in every circumstance. Reversal of apana vayu through sushumna is the primary accomplishment, yet it is more difficult to cope with that experience and positively sustain it. In this sense, vajroli, sahajoli and amaroli are not physical practices but indwelling attitudes or states of perfection.

A strong yet flexible mind can never be an 'overnight' attainment. The process takes many years. It has been said many times that the mind which wavers under the influence of the mundane joys, sorrows and tragedies of human existence will certainly be found lacking in the face of the greater experience. The mind which habitually flees from pain, clings to pleasure, rests in indolence and fails in self-discipline, is not an evolved mind. It will inevitably fail to sustain the experience of greater awareness and power, should it occur. This is why many years are traditionally allotted for the perfection of the mudras and for attaining contentment.

The greatest and most desirable guru is actually not the one who can precipitate the awakening through shaktipat. It is the one who guides, inspires, understands, coaxes and cajoles the disciple systematically through the obstacles, disciplines and karmic experiences, so that sustained awakening and descent of power occurs without mishap in a disciple whose life already reflects virtue, self-restraint, wisdom, benevolence and contentment.

ज्ञानं कुतो मनसि संभवतीह तावत्
प्राणोऽपि जीवति मनो म्रियते न यावत् ।
प्राणो मनो द्वयमिदं विलयं नयेद् यो
मोक्षं स गच्छति नरो न कथंचिदन्य: ॥ 15 ॥

How can there be inner knowledge in the mind, as long as prana is alive and mind is not dead? As long as the twofold nature of mind and prana can be quiescent, liberation is attained. It is not possible for any other person.

Inner knowledge becomes effulgent of its own accord because it is always there, just as the sun on a cloudy day has not ceased to exist, but has only become obscured. When the mind becomes quiescent the prana becomes steady; it is revealed. The task is not to struggle for illumination, but only to quieten the mind and steady the body and its prana, then the light will inevitably shine forth. The very nature of the mind is split; on account of this, a constant struggle appears to go on. The lower instinctive subconscious mind demands one thing and the discriminative higher mind dictates the opposite.

Similarly, the pranas are subject to constant modification by the sense perceptions and experiences, and these uphold and sustain the mental turmoil. Therefore, conflict and disharmony between mind and body, ida and pingala, are inherent in human existence before enlightenment.

Conflict is the unavoidable characteristic of the twofold nature before union is achieved. This conflict is the driving force not only in individual evolution, but also in social evolution and planetary evolution. Without friction and conflict there is no life.

However, the problem of bondage and suffering arises when we fail to appreciate the significance of conflict in the personal and cosmic pageant. We become identified with the conflict; we take sides; we pay fluctuating allegiance to one side or the other and so pass into bondage because we lose sight of the greater role of conflict within the total scheme of existence.

Liberation remains impossible within the confines of duality. Dual experience, twofold nature, inherently causes struggle, but the moment the two opposing natures cooperate, inner knowledge and union are experienced.

Are not night and day opposing one another, and thus sustaining our planetary environment? Do not two brothers struggle within the greater unfoldment of the family life? Do not two supporting teams oppose one another within the framework of a greater spectacle and competition? Is there not conflict in the marital relationship within the confines of a greater union?

Therefore, for realization it is important to be able to recognize and appreciate the greater union which is being forged out of apparent opposition and conflict. This is the meaning of spiritual perspective.

Thought, desire and action have to coordinate and co-operate if there is to be inner wisdom and illumination. So long as there is conflict there is no room for anything else. One could hardly expect to sit quietly with a man of wisdom in a crowded room, with many stray animals and beggars coming and going. So long as your pranas are running wild, so long as the vrittis of the mind are turbulent, how can unfoldment take place? Inner awakening can only occur when there is complete stillness and steadiness in body, mind and soul.

The *Drig-Drishya-Viveka* states: "Buddhi (higher intellect) appears to possess luminosity on account of the reflection of consciousness within it. Buddhi is twofold; one is designated ahamkriti (egoism), the other as antah karana (mind)." (v. 6) As long as these two modifications of buddhi exist, the consciousness illuminating it cannot be perceived. Inner knowledge means perceiving that from which the mind and prana have sprung. "This consciousness does neither rise nor set. It does not increase, nor does it suffer decay. Being self-illumined, it illumines everything else without any other aid." (v. 5)

ज्ञात्वा सुषुम्नासब्द्धेदं कृत्वा वायुं च मध्यगम् ।
स्थित्वा सदैव सुस्थाने ब्रह्मरंध्रे निरोधयेत् ॥ 16 ॥

Staying in the most suitable place, having found out how to penetrate sushumna and make the prana flow through the middle passage, it should be blocked in the brahmarandhra, the centre of higher consciousness.

The place of sadhana has to be conducive for your practice. It must be quiet and free from disturbance which can distract your practice. This has been discussed in Chapter 1. When the way to arouse kundalini has been discovered, experiences will unfold by themselves as each of the chakras is pierced. The union of Shakti, or energy, and Shiva, or consciousness, in the higher brain centres is depicted in tantra as man and woman, Shiva and Shakti, in an interlocking embrace. The final union and samadhi takes place in sahasrara chakra. This is at the crown of the head. The very upper portion is called *brahmarandhra*. The energy and consciousness must remain there, if they pass beyond, there is no return to the physical body. Therefore, it is stated that kundalini should be held in the brahmarandhra.

Swami Sivananda describes brahmarandhra as the 'hole of Brahman' and 'dwelling house of the human soul'. It is the tenth door, also known as *dasamdwara*. In a newborn child the brahmarandhra is very pronounced. It is the soft space at the crown of the head between the parietal and occipital bones called the anterior fontanelle. At the time of death when a yogi permanently leaves the body, the prana bursts out from the brahmarandhra. That is known as *kapala moksha*, literally meaning 'liberation from the skull'. "A hundred and one are the nadis of the heart, of them one (sushumna) has gone out, piercing the head. Going up through it, one attains immortality." (*Kathopanishad*)

However, kundalini must return back down to mooladhara chakra under the guidance of ajna, otherwise the

489

spirit or atma will leave the body for good. When kundalini returns, the yogi once again assumes his life in the mundane world, but with an altered and elevated state of consciousness and awareness. Nothing changes externally, the transformation has taken place internally. There is a Zen proverb: "Before enlightenment, chopping wood and carrying water; after enlightenment, chopping wood and carrying water."

सूर्याचंद्रमसौ धत्त: कालं रात्रिंदिवात्मकम् ।
भोक्त्री सुषुम्ना कालस्य गुह्यमेतदुदाहृतम् ॥ 17 ॥

The sun and moon divide time into day and night. Sushumna is the consumer of time. This is the conveyed secret.

The external sun and moon divide each twenty-four hours into night and day, and the internal sun and moon, i.e. ida and pingala, are responsible for our perception of night and day, that is duality. Ida nadi predominates at night, the parasympathetic nervous system is active, there is a greater release of melatonin hormone within the brain and the subconscious mind is active. During the daylight hours pingala predominates, the sympathetic nervous system is more active and seratonin hormone is released within the brain which brings conscious functions to the fore and the subconscious mind submerges.

The two nadis, ida and pingala, and the nervous systems, pull the awareness from one extreme to the other, binding us to the duality of mundane circumstances because of the interconnection and interrelationship with the external force of the sun and moon. The entire biological system is programmed to the movements of the sun and moon cycles. However, a yogi can develop control of the autonomic nervous system so that the body and mind are not swayed to the extremes. It means developing the voluntary and central nervous systems, activating sushumna nadi and ajna chakra. Such a person lives in a perfectly balanced state of being.

The period of time when day meets night is known as *sandhya*. It can be seen as an external event but it is an internal event. It represents the period of sushumna. We cannot alter the external happenings but a yogi can make the moment when ida and pingala merge a prolonged experience. In the *Shivaswarodaya* it is said: "Sandhya is not the external sandhya when day meets night, it is that period when the two opposite pranas meet." (v. 238) When the two pranas flow through sushumna, when time and space are not separate identities in the mind, then there is no difference or extremity.

Sushumna is said to be 'the consumer of time'. Time is called *kaala*. It is a particular stage of the evolution of unmanifest Shakti. When the primordial Shakti is manifesting it has to create limitation in order for manifestation to take place. The material universe we perceive is considered as the 'contraction' of the unmanifest Shakti. Contraction or limitation of Shakti is called *kanchuka*. *Kanchuka* means a 'sheath' or 'envelope'. There are five such kanchukas; kaala or time is the first. It is temporal limitation. Empirical time is the force which urges growth, development, maturity. It creates division or delineation. To be more specific, it is called *karya kaala*, 'the active aspect of time'.

Transcendental time is *akhanda kaala*, 'time which is without end'. Through the development of the five tattwas (ether, air, fire, water, earth) comes temporal time. When the kundalini shakti in mooladhara chakra is released through sushumna, Shakti is involuting back to its original infinite state. It is therefore called the consumer of time.

द्वासप्ततिसहस्राणि नाडीद्वाराणि पंजरे ।
सुषुम्ना शांभवी शक्ति: शेषास्त्वेव निरर्थका: ॥ 18 ॥

There are 72,000 nadis throughout the cage of this body. Sushumna is the Shambhavi, the remaining nadis are unimportant.

There is not one nadi in this body which is insignificant, just as every speck of life in this world is significant. A beggar is no less important than a king in terms of human life. However, in terms of important duties and obligations to society, a king is more important. Similarly sushumna's role is greater than any of the other nadis because it is the 'royal road' for the highest force, kundalini. It is the 'main freeway' from the depths of the earth to the heights of heaven.

According to the sloka it is the path of Shambhavi, i.e. the Shakti pertaining to Shambhu. Shambhu is the name of Shiva, meaning, 'one born of peace'. Shambhavi is also the name of Durga, an aspect of the great cosmic shakti. Shambhavi means, 'that power which grants peace' or 'existing for the peace and welfare of all'.

The *Shatchakra Nirupana* describes: "In the space inside the meru, placed on the left and right are the two siras, shashi (ida) and mihira (pingala). The nadi sushumna, whose substance is the threefold gunas, is in the middle. She is the form of the sun, moon and fire (ida, pingala, sushumna). Her body, a string of blooming datura flowers (the chakras), extends from the middle of the kanda (mooladhara) to the head and the vajra inside her extends, shining from the medhra (male sex organ) to the head.

"Inside her is chitrini who is lustrous with the lustre of prana and attainable in yoga by the yogis. She (chitrini) is as subtle as a spider's thread and pierces all the lotuses (chakras) which are placed within the backbone, and is pure intelligence. She (chitrini) is beautiful by reason of these (lotuses) which are strung on her. Inside her is the

Brahma nadi, which exists from the orifice of the mouth of Hara (mooladhara) to the place beyond, where Adideva is (sahasrara).

"She is beautiful like a chain of lightning and fire, like a (lotus) fibre and shines in the minds of the sages. She is extremely subtle, the awakening of pure knowledge, the embodiment of all bliss, whose true nature is pure consciousness. The brahmadwara shines in her mouth. This is the place of entrance to the region sprinkled by ambrosia, and is called the knot as also the mouth of sushumna." (v. 1–3)

After sushumna, the next two major nadis are ida and pingala. Thereafter: gandhari, hastijihva, poosha, yashaswini, alambusha, kuhu and shankhini. The location and purpose of other major nadis are briefly mentioned in the Upanishads and various yogic texts, but are not as clearly defined.

- *Gandhari*: From the 'navel wheel' (collection of nadis behind the navel) to the left eye, behind ida, this nadi is associated with sight, joins 'Ham' petal of ajna chakra.
- *Hastijihva*: From the 'navel wheel' to the right eye, in front of ida, associated with sight, joins 'Ksham' petal of ajna.
- *Poosha*: From the 'navel wheel' to the right ear, behind pingala, associated with audition.
- *Yashaswini*: Between poosha and saraswati, running from the left big toe to the left ear, associated with audition.
- *Alambusha*: Runs from the kandasthana to the mouth.
- *Kuhu*: In front of sushumna, flows down to the reproductive organs.
- *Shankhim*: Between gandhari and saraswati, below sahasrara and connects to swadhisthana.
- *Koorma*: In the region of the sternum bone, stabilizes the mind.
- *Payaswini*: Between poosha and saraswati, runs from the edge of the right ear to the right big toe.
- *Shura*: From the 'navel wheel' to the eyebrow centre.
- *Varuni*: Between yashaswini and kuhu, flows downward from the navel to mooladhara, aids defecation.

- *Vishwadhari*: Between hastijihva and kuhu, runs from the navel to kandasthana, said to carry four kinds of nourishment.
- *Saumya*: Runs to the tips of the toes.
- *Kaushiki*: Terminates at the toes.
- *Jihva*: Courses upwards.
- *Raka*: Absorbs water, collects mucus in the throat and sinuses, and creates hunger and thirst.
- *Chitra*: Flows down from the navel, associated with ejaculation.
- *Vilamba*: Around the 'navel wheel'.
- *Vijnana nadis*: Channels of consciousness.
- *Iltalaa*: Extends from mooladhara off the petal *Sam*.
- *Kaaladhamini*: Extends from mooladhara off the petal *Sham*.
- *Sutra*: Extends from swadhisthana off the petal *Ram*.
- *Vishwaa* and *ivantikaa*: Extend from manipura off the petal *Bham*.
- *Ilikaa, yukta* and *shukra*: Extend from manipura off the petal *Nam*.
- *Kali, vijolika* and *iltaa*: Extend from manipura off the petal *Tam*.
- *Taaraka*: Extends from manipura between the petals *Rnam* and *Tam*.
- *Maadhavi*: Extends from manipura between the petals *Rnam* and *Rdham*.
- *Taaraa*: Extends from anahata between the petals *Dam* and *Pham*.
- *Atitaa*: Extends from anahata between the petals *Pham* and *Pam*.
- *Naaga*: Extends from anahata between the petals *Pam* and *Nam*.

The following nadis all extend off vishuddhi chakra.
- *Shrikhati*: Between the petals *Aim* and *Em*.
- *Amritaa*: Between the petals *Em* and *Lreem*.
- *Saraswati*: Between the petals *Reem* and *Rim*.
- *Baalaa*: Between the petals *Rim* and *Oom*.
- *Tiktaa*: Between the petals *Oom* and *Eem*.

- *Maatrikaa*: Between the petals *Eem* and *Im*.
- *Eshamaarikaa*: Between the petals *Im* and *Aam*.
- *Kumaarikaa*: Between the petals *Ah* and *Am*.
- *Sitaa*: Between the petals *Am* and *Aum*.
- *Shiva*: Between the petals *Aum* and *Oum*.

वायु: परिचितो यस्मादग्निना सह कुंडलीम् ।
बोधयित्वा सुषुम्नायां प्रविशेदनिरोधत: ॥ 19 ॥

When the vayu is increased then the gastric fire (samana) should be taken along with kundalini in the aroused sushumna and blocked.

सुषुम्नावाहिनि प्राणे सिद्ध्यत्येव मनोन्मनी ।
अन्यथा त्वितराभ्यासा: प्रयासायैव योगिनाम् ॥ 20 ॥

When the prana flows in the sushumna this state of manonmani (consciousness devoid of mind) is established. Therefore, other forced practices are just laborious to the yogi.

No matter what you practise and how much you practise, until kundalini shakti has been aroused and moves up through sushumna, whatever you practise will be a conscious effort; it is not spontaneous. When you perform breath retention it is done by conscious effort, but when kevala kumbhaka occurs it is a spontaneous happening. Awakening of the shakti means spontaneity.

The pranas can only merge when the time is ripe and a yogi can only wait for that moment. Just as day and night meet at a designated moment and not just when you think it would be a suitable time, similarly ida, pingala and sushumna will only merge at an appointed time.

Therefore, a yogi has to adopt a peculiar and expectant attitude, like a servant awaiting his master. It is a state of relaxed preparedness. He remains poised and ever ready for an event which will occur inevitably in its own time. He accepts that to precipitate that event is not within his control or power, yet it is his destiny that it will occur and he must be ever vigilant in sadhana. It should not be interpreted as fatalism or laziness, but as a state of surrender and readiness which is to be sustained by constant awareness.

That is why relaxation in yoga is a sattwic experience and not a tamasic one. Relaxation for a yogi is not inertia, indolence, laziness or 'turning off'. Rather it is a state of equipoise, balance and receptivity.

The merging of the pranas results in a state called *manonmani*, which literally means mind without mind. Or rather, to be more explicit, it is consciousness or awareness devoid of the individual functioning of the mind. Manonmani means to experience that, at a certain instant, the barrier or fence which delineates or encircles the individual mind and its functions has been vaulted or dissolved, and a greater mind beyond that fence has been revealed and has assumed control.

पवनो बध्यते येन मनस्तेनैव बध्यते ।
मनश्च बध्यते येन पवनस्तेन बध्यते ॥ 21 ॥

Through restraining the prana, thought and counterthought are restrained and through restraint of thought and counterthought, prana (air) is restrained.

हेतुद्वयं तु चित्तस्य वासना च समीरण: ।
तयोर्विनष्ट एकस्मिंस्तौ द्वावपि विनश्यत: ॥ 22 ॥

Chitta has two causes, vasana and prana. When one of the two is destroyed or inactivated the other also will become immobile.

मनो यत्र विलीयेत पवनस्तत्र लीयते ।
पवनो लीयते यत्र मनस्तत्र विलीयते ॥ 23 ॥

Where mind is stilled, then the prana is suspended there, and where prana is suspended, there the mind is still.

दुग्धांबुवत्संमिलितावुभौ तौ तुल्यक्रियौ मानसमारुतौ हि ।
यतो मरुत्तत्र मन: प्रवृत्तिर्यतो मनस्तत्र मरुत्प्रवृत्ति: ॥ 24 ॥

Mind and prana are mixed like milk and water. Both of them are equal in their activities. Where there is pranic movement or activity there is mind (consciousness). Where there is consciousness there is prana.

तत्रैकनाशादपरस्य   नाश   एकप्रवृत्तेरपरप्रवृत्ति: ।
अध्वस्तयोश्चेन्द्रियवर्गवृत्ति: प्रध्वस्तयोर्मोक्षपदस्य सिद्धि: ॥ 25 ॥

Therefore, if one is annihilated, the other is eradicated; if one is active, the other becomes active, and while they exist, all the senses are active. If they are controlled, the state of moksha or liberation is attained.

The word for mind is *manas*. However, it is used to indicate a particular aspect of mind. The total individual mind is known as *antah karana*. Manas is a part of the antah karana. It is thought and counterthought. The word *chitta* is also used to indicate mind, individual consciousness and an aspect of antah karana which is memory. Some scholars even consider chitta and buddhi as identical. Let us not become confused here with terms and details.

We are considering the whole finite mind, or finite consciousness. In order to dissolve the whole finite mind each of the elements or *tattwas* constituting it has to be separated. Just as if you were to separate hydrogen and oxygen from water, then water as a whole substance would no longer remain, similarly when the principles constituting mind are separated, there is no longer finite perception.

What we call spiritual evolution is a process of mental involution because we are trying to dissolve the individual process of perception. The process has to be a conscious experience, otherwise you will just be entering a deep sleep. By working on the subtle, underlying structure of the mind and body, these principles constituting the mind are gradually disintegrated. Through shatkarma, asana, prana-yama, mudra and bandha, the physiological and subtle elements are controlled.

Ida nadi channels the force of will and desire or *ichchha shakti*; pingala nadi distributes the force to act or *kriya shakti*. If these two 'lines' are operating, the mundane experience of individual body and mind is sustained. If they are disconnected there is no consciousness and no activity, as occurs in deep sleep. If they are 'plugged' into sushumna, consciousness and activity do take place, but it is no longer confined within the limitations of the individual body and mind. That is the experience of moksha.

Sense experience occurs when the consciousness or chitta is carried by shakti to the sense organs. If the shakti does not carry the consciousness, there is no sensory experience, unless it is experienced psychically, directly through the

500

higher brain centres. If there is no impetus to send the chitta shakti, the sense organs will not operate. The motivating force which moves the chitta shakti is desire and will. It is a vicious circle. Impressions or samskaras and deep-rooted desires or vasanas motivate the sense organs, and the sense organs create more impressions and samskaras by their contact with the memory. When these deep-rooted impressions are eliminated, then perhaps you can control the mind directly, through the mind. Until this is achieved it is necessary to control the flow of prana through the sense organs. In fact, it is not until the highest stage of samadhi is achieved that these vasanas have no effect.

रसस्य मनसश्चैव चंचलत्वं स्वभावत: ।
रसो बद्धो मनो बद्धं किं न सिद्ध्यति भूतले ॥ 26 ॥

Mercury and mind are unstable by nature. By stabilizing (seizing or fixing) mercury and mind what cannot be perfected?

मूर्च्छितो हरते व्याधीन्मृतो जीवयति स्वयम् ।
बद्ध: खेचरतां धत्ते रसो वायुश्च पार्वति ॥ 27 ॥

O Parvati, when mercury and prana are made steady, disease is wiped out. When they are made torpid that is life-giving. When they are seized, one moves in space (Brahman).

What is this 'mercury' which is spoken of? Biologically, the element mercury exists in the body in minute proportions. However, the metal, its vapours and salts in greater concentration are highly toxic.

In the science of alchemy, mercury is one of the three important elements involved in the process of transformation and transmutation of base metal into gold, signifying the transformation of the basic nature of man into the gold of illumined spirituality.

Mercury is an interesting and unique substance. It is a brilliant metal which is liquid at room temperature, and remains so even at minus 39 degrees Centigrade. It has a high expansion coefficient and is therefore used extensively in thermometers and barometers. Mercury is a good conductor of heat and electricity, having a low oxidation potential, and is considered to be one of the noble metals. It occurs in nature most frequently in combination with sulphur as mercurous sulphate, a brilliant red powder known as cinnabar or vermilion. Only the strongest of acids, viz. nitric and hot, concentrated sulphuric acid, have the power to induce mercury to react.

The attributes and qualities of mercury have been known in yoga and tantric medicine in India for thousands of years, and even today the metal and its ashes and salts are used therapeutically. Clearly its significance was known to Swatmarama and the Nath yogis, who were also 'alchemists' involved in the same task of transformation of the lower nature and the gross body into the finest substance – pure illumined consciousness, the divine body. This suggests that alchemy (which was practised in secret by small numbers of initiates throughout Europe in the Dark Ages of religious persecution, prior to the Renaissance) was part of a worldwide tantric tradition, extending from Europe throughout West Asia to India.

In chemistry, mercury acts as a catalyst in many organic and inorganic reactions. A catalyst is an agent which facilitates or promotes a reaction, but remains itself unchanged in the reaction. In the alchemical process, the three fundamental elements involved in the conversion of metals are mercury, sulphur and salt. Alchemy considers that mercury itself contains sulphur and salt, sulphur contains mercury and salt, salt contains mercury and sulphur. In the subtle process of conversion, mercury is a symbolic catalyst to which either the fluctuating prana or wavering mind is bound, so that the pure consciousness can be extracted. It should also be noted that a definite differentiation has been made in the slokas, between the effects of stabilizing mind and mercury, and stabilizing prana and mercury.

Here sulphur refers to the mind (mentality), manas shakti, salt refers to the body (vitality), prana shakti. Now what is this catalytic agent, mercury, which is able to combine with either the human body or mind, in order to bring about

503

transformation of awareness from gross into subtle and from base into noble? What is it which, when fixed in the mind, enables any perfection or siddhi to be achieved and when steady in the body cures all diseases and is life giving? Certainly this ethereal, alchemical essence is the bindu.

The gross manifestation of the bindu in semen in the male body can be considered to have many of the characteristics of mercury. It is a glistening irradiant liquid which is very heavy, in the sense that it is difficult to stop it from falling down in the body. The use of mercury in the perfection of vajroli has already been discussed in Chapter 3. Mercury, therefore, refers to the bindu as the catalyst or vehicle upon which transformation of consciousness is accomplished.

According to alchemy, the correct combination or relation between mercury, sulphur and salt, i.e. bindu, body and mind, plus an energy additive called 'azoth' (which has the same characteristics as prana) will transform the base mundane consciousness into gold, which represents the illumined consciousness of Atman.

Therefore, when the alchemists refer to the substance mercury, it is symbolic of a subtler manifestation, just as the semen is the physical manifestation of a mental and physiological process. We can have a better understanding of what mercury and various elements represent by studying the information in the following chart.

Realm	Father (consciousness)	Son (individual consciousness)	Mother (body)
1. God (divine)	Father (atma)	Son (jivatma)	Holy ghost (prana)
2. Man	Spirit (atma)	soul (jivatma)	body (prana)
3. Elements	air	fire	water
	or fire	air	water
	or air	water	earth
4. Chemicals	mercury	sulphur	salt
	or sulphur	mercury	salt

In the same way that the metal gold is either naturally occurring or may be transmuted from other metals by scientific means, so the universal consciousness may be realized through 1. Natural evolution, which is a long and tedious process, or 2. Through incessant yogic abhyasa, which is the catalyst to the process. Basic understanding of this alchemy of metal into gold gives a deeper insight into yoga.

Alchemy is the science of transmutation based on the physical phenomena of expansion, which is the same as the tantric concept of expansion of mind and liberation of energy. Alchemy states that: "Nothing from nothing comes." Alchemy works on the basic chemical elements to produce the purest essence, just as in hatha yoga the basic elements of the body are utilized to reveal the subtlest essence, atma. Alchemy, like yoga, is the science of increasing and improving that which exists.

The basic philosophy of alchemy coincides with tantra: "The Supreme (Shiva) manifests Himself through expansion because of the inner urge to expand outward (spandana), the struggle for expression and manifestation (of Shakti)." Alchemy teaches that the Supreme (Shiva) is in everything, and manifests through an infinity of forms (due to Shakti), "like a spiritual seed planted in the dark earth of the material universe". Through faith, *shraddha*, and contentment in the Supreme or pure consciousness, individual mind can be transmuted from the base instincts, desires, passions and emotions, which are represented by the different planetary metals, into gold, i.e. cosmic consciousness.

Base metals have the same qualities as do ignorance (avidya) and if these can be transformed into pure gold, then why should it not be true that the different states of finite mind and perception can be transformed into the highest consciousness? Alchemy states that: "The inferior agrees with the superior and the superior agrees with the inferior." This is the fundamental maxim of tantra – that which exists in the macrocosmos exists in the microcosmos, and vice versa.

The metal mercury which we have been considering as a substance is a means of procuring a more subtle transformation in the realm of mind, energy and consciousness. Mercury is often equated with buddhi or the higher intellect. According to Vedanta the higher aspect of buddhi is the closest to atman.

Another aspect which has to be considered is the planet Mercury. Mercury, because of its gravitational pull on the earth, also exerts a particular effect on each individual. Astronomically Mercury is the closet planet to the sun, just as buddhi is the closest to Atman. It is the smallest planet, just as buddhi is the most subtle aspect of mind, being one and a half times the size of our own moon, and it has the greatest linear speed, taking only eighty-eight days to orbit the sun. In comparison with the earth, which rotates upon its polar axis once in twenty-four hours creating the alternating periods of day and night, Mercury has always been thought of as perfectly round, without an axis of rotation. One side of the planet is always facing the sun and the other is perpetually in darkness; one part of buddhi always reflects the Atman, the other, individual consciousness.

The dual nature of the planet Mercury accurately portrays man's dual nature, his higher and lower self, ida and pingala nadis, conscious and unconscious mind, jivatma and paramatma. It has given rise to the expression 'mercurial', referring to a personality or disposition which is given to polar extremes.

However, in 1974 data from the Mariner 10 space probe somewhat modified this ancient conception, showing that the planet does rotate very slowly upon a polar axis, so that one entire Earth year consists of only one 'day' and half a 'night' on Mercury. Such is the wonder of our intelligent creation that this scientific discovery has been made at a time when thinking people in all cultures are realizing that the pre-existing patterns of human belief, of sharply defined 'black and white, good and bad, right and wrong' are not universal laws of nature. They are merely man-made cultural

506

superimpositions from the past, which have attempted to encapsulate and control nature, which can never be only black and white, but also manifesting every colour and shade in between.

In Grecian mythology, Mercury is the god Hermes, the son of Jupiter and Maica, i.e. the product of union between Shiva or pure consciousness and Shakti or energy. This agrees with the tantric concept of bindu in relation to Shiva and Shakti.

According to astrology, Mercury is physiologically associated with the central nervous system and the whole brain in general, also with the respiratory system, thyroid gland and all the sense perceptions and sensory organs. In the subtle body it is sushumna nadi. The characteristics of Mercury are the urge to know, to be conscious and to communicate knowledge to others. Mercury is unemotional. It is also the principle of communication through mental and nervous attunement. It signifies transmission.

Thus we can understand that if these mercurial elements within us are controlled and stabilized, we will be able to accomplish whatever desire the mind is set upon. When the prana shakti is stabilized, these aspects of mercury will definitely balance the metabolism, eradicate disease and awaken kundalini.

The symbol for mercury is also interesting. It contains a semicircle, representing individual consciousness or jivatma, above a full circle, representing consciousness; below that is the cross, representing matter, manifest energy, ida, pingala and sushumna. This cross is derived from the caduceus where two serpents are intertwined around the vertical rod, indicating the two forms of shakti around sushumna. The symbol of mercury contains the answer to the riddle of life. It is similar to the Om symbol.

Thus, when the word mercury is used in these two slokas we have to understand all the possible implications.

मन: स्थैर्ये स्थिरो वायुस्ततो बिन्दु: स्थिरो भवेत् ।
बिंदुस्थैर्यात्सदा सत्त्वं पिंडस्थैर्यं प्रजायते ॥ 28 ॥

*When mind is still, prana is still, then bindu is still. By bindu being
held still, there is always a sattwic state which produces steadiness
in the body.*

The source of bindu in the body is sahasrara chakra. The
particular centre from which it issues its nectar is bindu
visarga, at the top back portion of the head. Bindu manifests
in the lower centres of the body also. When it is stable in the
brain centre then bindu in the lower regions is stable.

The commentary of *Anandalahari* (v. 32) explains that:
"The moon travelling through the left nadi, ida, bedews the
whole system with her nectar and the sun travelling through
the right nadi, pingala, dries the nectar." The yogi who
can confine the flow of chitta shakti in ida at its source has
stabilized the bindu so that nectar is not shed, and the nectar
is, therefore, not dried by the prana.

It is said that when prana is held in the entrance of
sushumna and the moon and nectar held in sahasrara,
kundalini is deprived of both nectar and prana, and is woken
up. Kundalini hisses angrily and rushes up to the source
of nectar, whereupon the nectar begins to flow down in an
unbroken stream to ajna chakra, whence the whole system
is saturated. The result is a state of blissful intoxication.
It is a process of transformation of experience due to the
permeation of the body and mind with nectar which is
triggered when the bindu is restrained and withheld. The
body and mind become steady, and this is the foundation for
monumental accomplishment in spiritual life.

There is a well-known story of a great sannyasin in India
at the close of the last century, known as Swami Dayananda.
He was the founder of the Arya Samaj, a popular spiritual
movement which holds that the divine is to be sought
directly in the nameless, formless, vibration of *Om*, and

need not be approached by deity worship and temple ritual. He was a very powerful spiritual revivalist in Hindu society. One day he was speaking about the necessity of brahmacharya as the basis for power and accomplishment in life. Some of his audience remained unconvinced, and at the conclusion of the satsang they were preparing their vehicle to depart. They found that the animals were seemingly unable to move their carriage so that their homeward journey could commence. In spite of whipping and exhortations the animals could not budge the cart a single inch. Then they turned around to find that the swami was holding onto the rear of the cart. Such is the steadiness of the body and purpose of one who has accomplished steadiness of bindu, as is referred to in this sloka.

इंद्रियाणां मनो नाथो मनोनाथस्तु मारुत: ।
मारुतस्य लयो नाथ: स लयो नादमाश्रित: ॥ 29 ॥

Mind is the ruler of the senses, prana is the ruler of the mind.
Dissolution is the lord of the prana and that dissolution (laya) is the
basis of nada.

सोऽयमेवास्तु मोक्षाख्यो मास्तु वापि मतांतरे ।
मन: प्राणलये कश्चिदानन्द: संप्रवर्तते ॥ 30 ॥

This is verily called liberation or moksha, but others might not call
it so. Nevertheless, when prana and mind are in laya, indescribable
ecstasy is created.

Finite mind is the operator of the senses and Shakti is
responsible for the finite mind. If the mind could realize
its initial state as Shakti it would be dissolved in that, and
nada, the vibration of Shakti, would be perceived. Swami
Sivananda of Rishikesh describes *laya* as: "the state of mind
when one forges all the objects of the senses and becomes
absorbed in the object of meditation. Laya enables one to
have perfect control over the five tattwas, mind and indriya
or senses. The fluctuations of mind will stop. The mind,
body and prana will be entirely subdued."

Laya is the absorption of the two polarities: mind
and prana, meditator and the object of meditation, the
unmanifest Shakti and manifest shakti. There is absorption
in the source from which the two have originated. The witness
(meditator), that which is witnessed (meditated upon) and
the act of witnessing (meditating) become a single, continual
awareness rather than three experiences. It is the state of
samadhi.

When individual prana and mind are absorbed in their
origin there is no conscious, subconscious or unconscious
existence. Then what remains? It is not death, because at
death the prana, will and consciousness are absorbed into

the karana sharira or causal body. For this reason death is not moksha. During death the jiva or individual soul is still entrapped within the laws of prakriti. However, the laya state means absorption in that which exists beyond the causal body, *hiranyagarbha*, the cosmic body. It is the absorption of prana and consciousness in the higher chakras.

There are two major paths which arouse self-knowledge. The first is known as *vikas* or 'active effort', and the other is by complete absorption or laya. The path of vikas includes many different yoga practices which can be taught by most yoga teachers. However, laya is a process of tantra which can only be taught by one who is a *jnani guru* or 'guru of knowledge and wisdom'.

Swatmarama states that the experience of ecstasy created by the process of laya is none other than moksha, even though others who follow other paths of active effort or vikas will dispute the quality of the laya samadhi. Depending on the psychological makeup of the disciple, and on the power of the guru, it can be accomplished without other active effort, beyond the absorption of the body and mind into a greater cosmic mind and body.

प्रनष्टश्वासनि:श्वास: प्रध्वस्तविषयग्रह: ।
निश्चेष्टो निर्विकारश्च लयो जयति योगिनाम् ॥ 31 ॥

*When inhalation and exhalation are stopped (finished), enjoyment
of the senses annihilated, when there is no effort, and a changeless
state (of mind) occurs, the yogi attains laya or absorption.*

For the state of laya to arise, kevala kumbhaka has to take
place spontaneously for an extended period, not just for a
few seconds. When this happens, mind will automatically
become absorbed in the point of concentration. Side by side,
sense perception diminishes. All these processes lead into
laya or samadhi.

Perhaps this sloka should be worded: when breathing
is suspended for a prolonged period, mind and prana
become absorbed in a subtle and unconditioned state of
consciousness. Conditioned awareness can be compared
to the breaking of white light into all the colours of the
spectrum. Just as there are various coloured rays, so there
are various aspects of mind. Perceiving the original unified
and undifferentiated condition of light as white light is
absorption of prana and mind in consciousness.

When there is no awareness of mundane reality, the body
and senses, then the animal functions cease to operate.
However, once the awareness returns to the conscious state,
the body, prana and sensory functions begin to operate
again. Laya arises where the entire prana of the body is in
union with the cosmic prana. Just as in a financial takeover
the smaller company and its operations are absorbed by
the superstructure of a larger parent company, even while
that company still trades under its original name, form and
premises, nevertheless the highest management has now
been superseded.

When the individual vibrational rate of prana is totally
harmonized with the unconditioned cosmic prana then there
is a merging, but until the individual tattwas of earth, water,

fire, air and ether are dissolved, the breath, mind and prana will continue to fluctuate. The *Vijnana Bhairava Tantra* states that: "When the ideating mind (manas), the ascertaining intellect (buddhi), the prana shakti (vital life force) and the limited empirical 'I' (ahamkara), this set of four, dissolves, then the previously described state of Bhairava (Consciousness) appears." (v.138)

उच्छिन्नसर्वसंकल्पो निःशेषाशेषचेष्टितः ।
स्वावगम्यो लयः कोऽपि जायते वागगोचरः ॥ 32 ॥

All the prominent desires being entirely finished, and the body motionless, results in the absorption or laya, which is only known by the Self, and beyond the scope of words.

यत्र दृष्टिर्लयस्तत्र भूतेन्द्रियसनातनी ।
सा शक्तिर्जीवभूतानां द्वे अलक्ष्ये लयं गते ॥ 33 ॥

Where the sight is directed, absorption occurs. That in which the elements, senses and shakti exist externally, which is in all living things, both are dissolved in the characteristicless.

The *Vijnanabhairava Tantra* states that: "Successively, in this way, wherever there is mindfulness on either void, on a wall, or on some excellent person, that mindfulness is absorbed by itself in the Supreme and offers the highest benefaction. Wherever the mind finds satisfaction, let it be concentrated on that. In every such case the true nature of highest bliss will manifest itself." (Dh. 10:33, Dh. 51:74)

Satisfaction is *tushti*, which indicates a deep moving joy where there is no mental agitation or fluctuation. In such a state there is total oblivion to the external world and thoughts or *vikalpas*, imaginations and ideas.

It is impossible to eliminate desire from the mind. Desire is rooted deep and the store is inexhaustible. Mind is constituted of desire. Superficial desire for material gain, achievement and fulfilment can be simplified and sublimated. There are three predominant forms of desire in most people. In the shastras they are called: *viteshara*, desire for property and money; *pitreshara*, desire for children, grandchildren, tribe; and *baleshwara*, desire for husband or wife.

These are very common desires. The fourth is *lokeshwara*, desire for name, fame, power. It is not present in most people; it is present in only a few people. When there is lokeshwara you want to be very famous, very powerful, like Napoleon or Hitler.

Vasana is 'latent desire' or 'seed'. From vasanas spring desire, greed, anger, then desire for liberation, and then finally moksha or liberation itself. The desire to know, or *vijnana*, and the desire for liberation are positive and sattwic desires. They are necessary for evolution. They should not be suppressed under any circumstance. Never make that mistake because sometimes while you are trying to suppress your vasanas, you are almost giving a death blow to your personality. How can we do this? It poses a problem because vasanas cannot be satisfied.

Desires are insatiable. There is no end to gratification of vasanas. Even if you are given the lifespan of the whole earth to enjoy vasanas, still there will be no end, but if there were no vasanas or desires, man would not strive; he would not work, he would not become active. It is only in the sattwic person who has attained the sattwic mind that there will be fewer or no vasanas. However, when one is rajasic or tamasic in evolution one must have vasanas. If a man is lazy (tamasic), and if he does not have desires, he will become yet more lazy, but if he has desires, he is goaded to work. Vasanas compel him to become active. So, in the tamasic state, vasanas should be stimulated; in the rajasic or dynamic state they should be balanced; and in the sattwic state or balanced state, they should be eliminated gradually.

How are you going to know if you are sattwic, rajasic or tamasic? It is very difficult to judge oneself. Everyone thinks themselves to be sattwic, but there are certain indications by which you can judge whether you belong to that phase or category. If you have greed, you cannot say that you are sattwic. If you are involved in many sorts of activities, or the mind is restless, never at peace, then these are a few indications by which you can know that you are a rajasic type, i.e. your temperament is rajasic.

How do you know that you are tamasic? You will be prone to procrastination and laziness. Those people who sleep too

515

much are tamasic. When you are aware of dhyana, inner peace, and many other things, that is an indication of sattwa. So when a person is lazy or procrastinating, he should be injected with vasana, because without vasana he is not going to evolve at all.

Evolution is from *tamas*, the static state, into *rajas*, the mutative state, and not directly from tamas to *sattwa*, the sentient state. First a tamasic man must change into a rajasic man, and then into a harmonized man, sattwic. After that you become *trigunateetha*, 'having transcended the three states'. You cannot transcend all the vasanas all of a sudden. Most people in the world are a mixture of these three states – predominantly rajasic, sometimes a little tamasic, and a little sattwic. Very few people are predominantly sattwic. So according to one's predominant quality one should be given the appropriate sadhana and dharma. Either the vasanas should be curtailed or they should be fulfilled or sublimated.

So, vasanas are not out of place in our life; desires and passions are necessary for man's evolution. Just as you take a thorn out with another thorn and then throw them both away, the learnt vasanas in the tamasic state should be extricated by vasana, for too much involvement in vasana eventually develops *vairagya*, or dispassion. If you suppress the vasanas, you maintain the state of tamas. You have a taste for it; you have a liking or *raga* for it. You may not fulfil it in your daily life but you can dream, and you may fantasize. This is so-called fulfilment.

Life should be planned in such a way that there is a time when you should fulfil one type of vasana, and another time for another type of vasana, etc. Playing games, the activities of marital life, family, children, opening hospitals, going to Gangotri or sitting in meditation are also vasanas.

How can we stop the *karmas*, cause and effect, and *samskaras*, impressions, from entering the subconscious and unconscious mind? Why try to do it? Why waste your time? You will only be removing samskaras for something else to come in and take their place. It is like being in a railway station or airport; one plane coming, another going. It is the same with the samskaras. Can you close your eyes to them? As long as you are still centred in the nature of your experience, or in your desires, how can you stop the samskaras?

Rather than blocking the samskaras, you should stop your production of them. However, you cannot stop producing samskaras; consciously and unconsciously you produce them. So, instead of blocking the samskaras, or interfering with them, or trying to eliminate them, it would be far better to develop, create or initiate stronger and spiritually uplifting samskaras. Thus the positive will overcome the negative.

When you are trying to develop the inner experience, you are developing strong samskaras. It is possible to fix the samskaras, but for the majority of people it is dangerous. For sometimes in the effort of fixing and adjusting, pacifying and eliminating the samskaras, you are eliminating your whole personality, and you run the risk of developing a very abnormal personality.

Whether it is through mantra, yantra, tantra, hatha yoga or even religious practices, do not make the mistake of fighting with the samskaras. You will only be disturbing the structure of trillions of archetypes in your brain. What are you going to do with these trillions of archetypes in your brain? Be very positive; don't fight with the basis of life. After some time the vasanas should be sublimated. First the vasanas are related to the body, family and career, but later they should be sublimated. How can we sublimate these vasanas?

There are three ways of sublimating the vasanas, be sure that you do not make an error in life. Go the sure way! The surest way is to develop the higher, more noble and sublime attitude in life and then all these positive samskaras will follow you. All will be transformed in time. You don't have to kill any samskara. You don't have to destroy the basis of your existence, that is a destructive way.

Second is by karma yoga where you do social service, like Mahatma Gandhi and such people. The other way is to attain final samadhi. Practise half an hour of meditation, and shoonya (the void). These are the three methods for sublimating the vasanas. In samadhi the vasanas are burnt completely; in karma yoga the vasanas are dissipated and they become weak.

Then there is a fourth way. That is very difficult. You leave everything to God, the divine cosmic will. Let him do what he likes!

लयो लय इति प्राहूः कीदृशं लयलक्षणम् ।
अपुनर्वासनोत्थानाल्लयो विषयविस्मृतिः ॥ 34 ॥

Some say 'laya, laya' but what is the characteristic of laya or absorption?
Laya is the non-recollection of the objects of the senses when the
previous deep-rooted desires (and impressions) are non-recurrent.

In the state of meditation, when the meditator, that which
is meditated upon, and the process of meditation are not
three separate experiences but one experience, then there
are no thoughts in the mind. Mind is totally absorbed and
that is laya. In the vedic and tantric tradition the absorption
of the tattwas is said to be laya. It means the absorption of
the gross and individual energy or shakti into its original
cosmic state. Others say absorption of mind in consciousness.
Both are referring to the same thing. Individual mind is
the product of shakti and the original state of shakti is in
total equilibrium with consciousness. However it is defined,
it should be understood as a state of total unification and
identification with the object of concentration, where the
experience of 'I' is non-existent.

This requires a state of mental purity. It is a process of
elimination of both the external impressions and the subtle
realm. The problem every sadhaka is faced with is how
to make the mind, which is full of vikalpas or imaginary
thoughts, become still. *Abhinavagupta* states that: "When
there is vikalpa, neither accept nor reject, it will retire of its
own self, and you will find yourself to be what you are."

In the *Shiva Sutras* this practice is known as *shambhavopaya*. You should concentrate on one pure thought or
shuddha vikalpa. *Ashuddha vikalpa* is a thought which binds
you to individual experience, whereas shuddha vikalpa is
that which arouses in you the idea that you are in fact the
universal self. Practice of shuddha vikalpa, according to
the *Shiva Sutras*, is shaktopaya and jnana yoga because one
directly uses the mind and chitta shakti.

519

Swami Sivananda defines laya as deep sleep, but it is not an unconscious state. The description of nirvikalpa samadhi given by Swami Sivananda is the same as that of laya described here, because in nirvikalpa samadhi there is no re-occurence of impressions, samskaras or vasanas. Through experience of that samadhi, desires no longer influence the consciousness: "I am the fire that burns the karma of one who is beyond all karma, I am the fire that burns the sorrow of one beyond all sorrow. I am the fire that burns the body of one who is devoid of the body. I am the nectar of knowledge, homogeneous Existence, like the sky." (*Avadhoota Gita*, 3:9)

वेदशास्त्रपुराणानि सामान्यगणिका इव ।
एकैव शांभवी मुद्रा गुप्ता कुलवधूरिव ॥ 35 ॥

The Vedas, shastras and Puranas are like common women, but shambhavi is secret like a woman of good heritage.

Of course, this sloka is not ridiculing the Vedas, etc. It is merely stating that anyone can read these shastras and understand what he may, but those intent on getting into substantial spiritual experience will have to practise. For this purpose shambhavi mudra is recommended, but it will have to be learned from the guru. If you practise shambhavi with sincerity and perseverance, it is bound to awaken higher experiences. The word Shambhavi is the name of the creative power of consciousness, Shiva. Shambhavi can stir Shambhu or supraconsciousness. Shambhavi mudra is also known as bhrumadhya drishti, i.e. gazing at the eyebrow centre.

In Chapter 3, three mudras have been listed as the most important mudras, but shambhavi was not included there. It has instead been included in the chapter on samadhi for a good reason. In the state of samadhi, shambhavi mudra takes place of its own accord. Swami Muktananda Paramahamsa has described how his eyeballs rolled back into the head when he was in deep states of consciousness, without any effort on his part.

Shambhavi is likened to a woman of good heritage or *kula*. The tantras explain Shakti, the female aspect and principle as kula. Shiva the male principle is akula, without heritage. The union of the two is *kaula*, where the branch of kaulacharya arose. That is known as vama marga tantra. Shambhavi is a technique employed in tantra to arouse deeper states of experience. Only the initiated are taught these practices. Therefore, what is being said in the sloka is that scriptures such as the Vedas are for the general public, but shambhavi is for the initiated.

SHAMBHAVI MUDRA (eyebrow centre gazing)

अथ शांभवी ।

अंतर्लक्ष्यं बहिर्दृष्टिर्निमेषोन्मेषवर्जिता ।
एषा सा शांभवी मुद्रा वेदशास्त्रेषु गोपिता ॥ 36 ॥

*With internalized (one-pointed) awareness and external gaze
unblinking, that verily is shambhavi mudra, preserved in the
Vedas.*

अंतर्लक्ष्यविलीनचित्तपवनो योगी यदा वर्तते
दृष्ट्या निश्चलतारया बहिरध: पश्यन्नपश्यन्नपि ।
मुद्रेयं खलु शांभवी भवति सा लब्धा प्रसादाद्गुरो:
शून्याशून्यविलक्षणं स्फुरति तत्तत्त्वं परं शांभवम् ॥ 37 ॥

*If the yogi remains with the chitta and prana absorbed in the
internal object and gaze motionless, though looking, he is not
seeing, it is indeed shambhavi mudra. When it is given by the guru's
blessing, the state of shoonyashoonya arises. That is the real state of
Shiva (consciousness).*

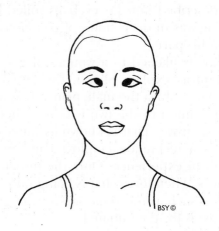

Technique

Sit in any meditative posture and prepare yourself as for meditation.

Then open the eyes and gaze upward at the eyebrow centre. Keep the eyes steady and hold for as long as possible.

When the eyes become tired, close them and keep your gaze fixed on the chidakasha, the space in front of the closed eyes.

After some practice a light will appear when the eyes are open.

After more practice still, the light will appear when the eyes are closed. Concentrate on that point of light. Once the light appears it must be concentrated upon and held in the centre.

Shambhavi mudra can be practised on its own or in combination with other practices of pranayama, bandha and asana. It is also used in kriya yoga. Once you can practise it externally without the eyes tiring, practise it with closed eyes.

श्रीशांभव्याश्च खेचर्या अवस्थाधामभेदत: ।
भवेच्चित्तलयानंद: शून्ये चित्सुखरूपिणि ॥ 38 ॥

Shambhavi and khechari states, though there is a difference in the place of concentration or influence, both bring about ecstasy, absorption in void, in the experience of chit sukha or the pleasure of consciousness.

Khechari directly stimulates lalana and bindu, which releases a nectarine fluid that is responsible for creating the state of ecstasy. Lalana and bindu are in close proximity to ajna chakra. Shambhavi mudra directly awakens ajna. Both shambhavi and khechari cause the external mind to 'turn off' and both awaken the inner awareness. Swami Muktananda states that during the period of his sadhana, secretions sometimes flowed profusely from the cranial region, and his eyeballs would spontaneously roll upwards into shambhavi. In deep meditation his tongue would automatically go upwards through the nasal pharynx, and a voice from within instructed that this would create a greater state of experience by opening the passage to sahasrara.

तारे ज्योतिषि संयोज्य किंचिदुन्नमयेद् भ्रुवौ ।
पूर्वयोगं मनो युंजन्नुन्मनीकारकः क्षणात् ॥ 39 ॥

With perfect concentration, the pupils fixed on the light by raising the eyebrows up a little, as from the previously described (shambhavi), mind is joined and instantly unmani occurs.

What is perfect concentration? When the totality of awareness knows only the object upon which it is concentrated. Perfect concentration is meditation, perfect meditation is samadhi. When you gaze at the eyebrow centre for an extended period a small light appears. That has to be seen with the eyes closed and concentrated upon until nothing else exists except the light. When samadhi is achieved through the practice it is called unmani.

केचिदागमजालेन केचिन्निगमसंकुलै: ।
केचित्तर्केण मुह्यन्ति नैव जानंति तारकम् ॥ 40 ॥

Some people are confused by the agamas, some are confused by the nigamas and logic. They are bewildered, not knowing how to be liberated.

Agamas are the shastras of Shaivism in which Shiva teaches Shakti, Shiva being the guru and the ultimate reality. *Nigamas* are the shastras of the Shaktas in which Shakti instructs Shiva, Shakti being the guru and source of self-realization.

In the agama, Shiva is the supreme, just as in Vedanta it is Brahman. However, nigama says that Shiva is 'lifeless' without Shakti and therefore Shakti should be realized first, for without that realization Shiva cannot be attained. People who are bound to either one of these concepts are limiting their capacity to realize and understand, because Shiva and Shakti, though two opposite aspects, are ultimately one and the same force.

In each yuga there has been a particular part of the Vedas specifically allotted for the people of that age, to guide them in spiritual and worldly life. During the satya yuga, *dharma* or the 'right way of living' was given in the shruti; during the treta yuga, in the smriti; during the dwapara yuga, in the purana; and during the kali yuga, in the agama, nigama and the sixty-four tantras.

The sadhanas and the style of imparting spiritual knowledge in each of these shastras pertains only to the people of that yuga. If the sadhana suited to one particular yuga is adopted in another yuga, it will not bear fruit because the capacity of the individual for faith and concentration changes from age to age. In the *Mahanirvana Tantra* it is said that if a person of the kali yuga should perform the same yajnas (fire ceremonies) that were formerly done in the satya yuga, they would not bear the desired fruit because of the absence of *pashubhava*, or control of the animal instincts.

Even today in the kali yuga, the spiritual knowledge and sadhanas given in the agama, nigama and tantras can be understood by very few people. People as a whole are unable to involve themselves in sadhana and the spiritual quest. They are more able to understand what they read in the newspapers. Nevertheless, they are collectively more attuned to the possibility of spiritual evolution by the practices of tantra and yoga than by austerities, conduct and observances, which were most suitable for other ages and other generations of people.

अर्धोन्मीलितलोचनः स्थिरमना नासाग्रदत्तेक्षण-
चंद्रार्कावपि लीनतामुपनयन्त्रि ष्पंदभावेन यः ।
ज्योतीरूपमशेषबीजमखिलं देदीप्यमानं परं
तत्त्वं तत्पदमेति वस्तु परमं वाच्यं किमत्राधिकम् ॥ 41 ॥

*Mind steady, eyes semi-open, gaze fixed on the nose tip, the moon
(ida) and sun (pingala) suspended, without any movement (physical
or mental), that one attains the form of light (jyoti) which is endless
and is complete, radiant, the Supreme. What more can be said?*

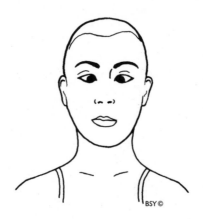

'Gaze fixed on the nose tip': is the description of *nasikagra
mudra*, which has not been previously listed amongst the
ten mudras, but is a practice of hatha yoga which directly
awakens the kundalini shakti in mooladhara. Sitting either in
siddhasana/siddha yoni asana, gaze steadily at the tip of the
nose. The eyes will become slightly convergent and the two
sides of the nose are seen. Concentration should be centred
in the very middle. At first the vision will be unsteady and
the eyes will tire quickly. With a little practice each day the
eyes will become accustomed. As you gaze at the nose tip,
concentrate on the movement of breath through the nostrils
and determine through which nostril the breath is flowing.

528

When both nostrils are open, i.e. sushumna is flowing, the practice is taking effect.

After five to ten minutes close the eyes and look into the dark space in front of the closed eyes, the chidakasha. If you see light in the darkness, concentrate on that, because that is the light which can completely absorb the consciousness.

Meditation is the spontaneous result of concentration of the mind. Dharana or concentration can be practised but meditation cannot. Dhyana or meditation occurs when the mind stops oscillating off the point of concentration, when the witness, witnessed, and process of witnessing alone remain. Dhyana is ekagra or one-pointedness of mind, when the vrittis or mental movements are confined to the process and the object of concentration.

By external gazing at the nose tip, vision of the inner light is aroused because the flow of shakti in the mind and body becomes concentrated. When you turn on the light switch, the light emanates from the bulb. The same applies in the physical body. When the kundalini shakti is released from mooladhara it is drawn up to ajna chakra, and there the inner light appears. That light, when seen, should be concentrated upon, because it is the essence of being, the inner light or jyoti. The purpose of practising nasikagra mudra is to arouse that experience.

दिवा न पूजयेल्लिंगं रात्रौ चैव न पूजयेत् ।
सर्वदा पूजयेल्लिंगं दिवारात्रिनिरोधतः ॥ ४२ ॥

Worship the lingam neither by day nor by night. By blocking the day and night the lingam should always be worshipped.

"Worship the lingam neither by day nor by night" is an ambiguous sentence which should not be taken on face value. 'Worship the lingam' means concentration upon atma, the highest consciousness, and/or practices leading to its realization. 'Day and night' means ida and pingala, though of course it can be taken literally. The best time to practise is during the flow of sushumna at sunrise, sunset, midday or midnight. Practise at other times inevitably proves fruitless because these are the only times when both the subtle bodies and subtle states of mind become readily accessible.

'By blocking the day and night' means stopping the flow of shakti in ida and pingala nadis; stopping awareness or consciousness of day and night, time and space and all other dualities associated with mundane consciousness. Then only will subtle awareness arise.

530

Worship of the shivalingam has been misinterpreted by indologists and researchers since they began to study the spiritual practices of the people of India in the last few centuries. Unfortunately, in the Sanskrit dictionary, one of the meanings given for the word 'shivalingam' is 'phallus, the male organ of Shiva'. When these first researchers, who were not well versed in Sanskrit, its history or grammar, came to explain and record their thesis on shivalingam, they just took the dictionary and came to the conclusion that it refers to phallus worship. In their wake, other research scholars have made the same mistake repeatedly. They even thought that perhaps there was some primitive tribal rite of the Hindus where all females worshipped the male organ. This is how a very unclassical and under-developed brain works.

According to Sanskrit grammar and the philosophy connected with it, the term *lingam* means a state which is invisible, which is unseen, but which is in existence. Many thinkers and most artists and poets can understand this concept very well. You cannot see emotions, frustrations, or joys. If they are in you, you can feel them. If they are not in you, you cannot feel them although they exist in the other person. This means that ordinary human emotion should have a form, although it is invisible.

Similarly, consciousness is formless and abstract. Here consciousness does not mean human consciousness. It means the total cosmic consciousness. Any word can be used to indicate that consciousness – Brahman, God, Allah, etc. The consciousness is invisible, abstract and infinite. It cannot be comprehended by the finite mind. The ultimate reality is incomprehensible to anyone, even to a saint or a yogi, or to a paramahamsa. If you want to comprehend that ultimate reality there is only one way. You have to become that, and not otherwise. Therefore, that consciousness which cannot be comprehended by just any means or anyone should be comprehended by its symbol. That symbol is known as lingam in Sanskrit. It is not a phallic symbol, but it is called shivalinga. Shiva means absolute, ultimate, total, cosmic or universal consciousness. These are all just names, shiva-lingam is the representative or symbol of that cosmic one.

Today in India, the shivalingam is worshipped, venerated and meditated upon by a majority of Hindus but not by any other religion. However, if you go back into history to the civilizations which flourished in the Middle Ages and even in the primitive ages in Europe, you can find substantial evidence that the worship of the shivalingam was once prevalent throughout the world. In the ancient pre-Columbian civilization, in the cultural philosophy of the Aztecs, Incas and Native Indian tribal families and even in Mexico, the worship of Shiva was prevalent. Last century and early this century, when some of the churches in England were excavated after damage, the shivalingam was found underneath. This shows that worship of the lingam was not confined only to the Hindu religion. However, it is the Hindus who have preserved it.

The oval-shaped stone of the shivalingam is not carved. It is found exactly in that shape, ranging from a few inches to about fifteen feet, i.e. five to six metres high. Its source is along the banks of the river Narmada, which originates in central India and flows towards the west, ultimately merging in the Arabian Sea. From there shivalingams are taken and established in Shiva temples. The temples are not constructed just because somebody has the money to do it. Somebody has a revelation in a dream or in meditation, etc., and is told where to find the shivalingam and where to build a temple.

The shivalingam is not a god. It has nothing to do with ritualistic worship. It is an ancient replica of an event which triggered man into conscious awareness and brought him from the state of apeman to man. In the depth of human consciousness and in the centre of the brain there is an unseen force, an invisible power or an invisible substance, without which you are not human. You know that you are. You know that you know that you are. You know that you know that you know that you are. An animal does not know it, but you know it.

In Shaivism, i.e. the Shiva cult, it is said that the real shivalingam is made from crystal. In Sanskrit it is called *sphatik lingam*. Crystal has many scientific effects on matter, on substance and on the brain. It is not just a simple piece of stone or glass. It possesses the power to grasp all the sound vibrations, gross and subtle. Any vibration passing though the sound matrix, through the dimension of sound, will hit crystal objects. It may be a crystal, a small crystal ball, a crystal mala, crystal beads or maybe a crystal lingam.

When you expose yourself to a sphatik lingam something then begins to happen in your brain and within your consciousness. Whenever you concentrate on the sphatik lingam, it explodes the images from the unconscious within you. The source of these experiences and images is within your unconscious. It is beyond the conscious mind, beyond the subconscious mind. It is in the unconscious, the anandamaya kosha, the causal body. In Samkhya and Vedanta philosophy the causal body is called *linga sharira*, i.e. linga body, which is there but which you cannot see. Therefore, concentration and meditation on the shivalingam, either gross or subtle, is considered very important, because it can explode that inner source of awareness where infinite knowledge is hidden and where the possibility of the great evolution of man is stored.

In India, there are thousands and thousands of temples with this oval shaped shivalingam, but of those, twelve are considered as jyotirlingam. *Jyoti*r means 'light'. *Jyotirlingam* means 'illuminated lingam'. They are situated at eleven different places in India and one in Kathmandu, Nepal.

The external shivalingam is responsible for the awakening of your inner shivalingam. According to the science of tantra, kundalini and yoga, there are twelve places in the physical body where shivalingam is located in the same shape. Out of those twelve, three are considered very important. One is in mooladhara chakra (swayambhulingam), the second in ajna chakra (itaralingam) and the third in sahasrara chakra (paralingam). It is said that in sahasrara chakra the finest consciousness resides in the shape of an illuminated shivalingam. Maybe after some time, scientists will discover it, and certainly they are going to discover that man's body and his evolution, man's nature and its transformation, man's consciousness and its awakening, are not influenced by external social factors such as religion, politics, ethics and morality, but they are manifested from somewhere within you. That somewhere is the Shiva in you, the finest matter in you, you in the physical body.

Lingam refers to the causal body. Broadly speaking everyone has three bodies. Finite existence is classified into three main bodies which are then subdivided into ten bodies. It is not just in the Hindu philosophy that this truth is embedded, but in many ancient cultures and civilizations. It is a part of the traditions of the Rosicrucians and Freemasons and even of the Celtic traditions, before Christianity came.

These three bodies are known as: the gross or material body, *sthula sharira*, the subtle or astral body, *sukshma sharira*, and the causal, etheric or Shiva body, *karana sharira*. Each body can be separated, or the consciousness can be led from one body to another. Beyond the tenth or beyond the causal there is the bodiless Self, Atma, God, Brahman, the Absolute. It is not within these bodies, it is beyond them. If you have to arrive at that point and experience who or what is beyond these, then it is important that you jump nine times beyond the fence.

If you want to get out of this level of consciousness in which you are confined, then you have to use some means which will have a direct effect on the inner force. That inner force is called Shiva and this is the philosophy about shivalingam.

अथ खेचरी ।

सव्यदक्षिणनाडिस्थो मध्ये चरति मारुत: ।
तिष्ठति खेचरी मुद्रा तस्मिन्स्थाने न संशय: ॥ 43 ॥

When the prana which is in the right and left nadis moves in the middle nadi (sushumna) that is the condition for khechari mudra.

इडापिंगलयोर्मध्ये शून्यं चैवानिलं ग्रसेत् ।
तिष्ठते खेचरी मुद्रा तत्र सत्यं पुन: पुन: ॥ 44 ॥

The fire (of shakti) being swallowed (suppressed) midway between, ida and pingala, in that shoonya (of sushumna), is in truth the condition for khechari mudra.

सूर्याचन्द्रमसोर्मध्ये निरालम्बान्तरे पुन: ।
संस्थिता व्योमचक्रे या सा मुद्रा नाम खेचरी ॥ 45 ॥

The middle of the sun (pingala) and moon (ida) is the 'unsupported', in which is situated vyoma chakra or centre of ether (void). This mudra is called khechari.

सोमाद् यत्रोदिता धारा साक्षात् सा शिववल्लभा ।
पूर्येदतुलां दिव्यां सुषुम्नां पश्चिमे मुखे ॥ 46 ॥

In the flow from the moon (bindu) is the beloved of Shiva (consciousness). The opening of the unequalled divine sushumna should be filled from behind (by the tongue).

पुरस्ताच्चैव पूर्येत निश्चिता खेचरी भवेत् ।
अभ्यस्ता खेचरी मुद्राप्युन्मनी संप्रजायते ॥ 47 ॥

The sushumna being completely filled at the rear (upper palate) also is khechari. The practice of khechari mudra is followed by the state of unmani (consciousness devoid of mind).

The methods indicated here in the *Hatha Yoga Pradipika*, i.e. shatkarma, asana, pranayama, are intended to awaken sushumna nadi. By that time, everything is set properly. The chakras are clear, the pathways of the nadis are unblocked, and awakening can take place. Mudras and bandhas are intended to awaken kundalini, which arouses meditation spontaneously.

Even if you do not know how to meditate, or you do not have sufficient willpower, if you practise khechari mudra, after some time a 'serum' flows into the body. When it mixes with the blood and other secretions, the state of mind and flow of prana changes. You begin to feel 'high', and the brain-wave patterns alter. Even with your eyes open, you begin to have an altered experience. With the eyes closed you are able to have inner experience. You can hear music internally. You can see the beauty of flowers in any season, anywhere. You can see the moon even when there is none. It is not hallucination, it is a real and conscious experience. The body becomes quiet and the mind steady. Mudra is one of the very important aspects that hatha yoga has inherited from tantra to expand the consciousness.

Khechari mudra, or *nabho mudra* as it is called, is originally a tantric practice. It can be practised in two ways as has been described. Either the root of the tongue is cut, elongating the tongue which can then be inserted into the epiglottis like a cork, or the tip of the tongue simply presses the back of the upper palate.

Meditation may be a spiritual practice but its effects on the body are definite and physiologically verified. Alpha waves become intense, respiration becomes minimal, consumption of oxygen decreases, blood pressure and temperature drop. The rishis realized these effects and therefore instructed the use of particular asanas for meditation and also the use of mudras, especially khechari. When sushumna is active, the heart rate and blood pressure drop, and at that time khechari must be employed. Mudras definitely affect the quality of meditation. You can verify this by experiment. Practise meditation of a passive type for six months. Then change your practice to an active type incorporating mudras like maha vedha, and others, especially khechari mudra. The nature of your experiences will definitely alter.

When meditation becomes deep and the mind is absorbed in the point of concentration, unmani occurs. That is the beginning of samadhi, which has been previously discussed.

भ्रुवोर्मध्ये शिवस्थानं मनस्तत्र विलीयते ।
ज्ञातव्यं तत्पदं तुर्यं तत्र कालो न विद्यते ॥ 48 ॥

*In the middle of the eyebrows is the place of Shiva, there the mind
is quiescent. That state is known as turiya or the fourth dimension.
There, time is unknown.*

The external point of the eyebrow centre is the trigger
point of concentration arousing the ajna chakra or guru
chakra. Ajna chakra is situated in the brain in the region
of the pineal gland and medulla oblongata. If this chakra
is awakened by the kundalini shakti the experience is
altogether beyond the scope of the five lower elements. It is
the centre of consciousness. Its bija mantra is *Om*. It is the
terminating point of ida and pingala. Beyond ajna the two
nadis merge with sushumna, indicating the possibility of
experiencing steady, unwavering awareness of atma.

Paramshiva or Shambhu is said to dwell at this point of awareness. His Shakti is known as Hakini, who is white, has six red faces, with three eyes on each face. She has six arms and holds a rudraksha mala, a human skull, a *damaru* (small drum), a book and the other two hands are in vara and abhyasa mudras. She is seated on a white lotus, above her is the itara lingam (jet black) within an inverted triangle. It is the inner atma. On the three sides of the triangle, sparks of light emanate. Above this is manas, chakras, and above that is the region of the moon in which Paramshiva and his Shakti are seated on a *hamsa* (white swan).

The *Shat-chakra-nirupama* states: "This is the incomparable and delightful abode of Vishnu (i.e. the ishta devata). The excellent yogi at the time of death joyfully places his vital breath (prana) here and enters (after death) that supreme, eternal, birthless, primeval Deva, the Purusha, who was before the three worlds, and who is known by the Vedanta." (v. 38) "The excellent sadhaka, whose atma is nothing but a meditation on this lotus (ajna chakra), is able to quickly enter another's body at will and becomes the most excellent among munis and all-knowing and all-seeing. He becomes the benefactor of all and versed in all the shastras. He realizes his unity with Brahman and acquires excellent powers. Full of fame and long-lived, he ever becomes the Creator, Destroyer and Preserver (Brahma, Maheshwara, Vishnu) of the three worlds." (v. 34)

Ajna chakra has two petals: in the left is the full moon and the bija mantra *Ksham*, in the right, the sun and the bija mantra *Ham*. It is the centre of the Rudra granthi, of bindu, nada and shakti. It corresponds to tapoloka.

Swami Sivananda stated that by concentrating on this centre the karmas of past lives are destroyed, the practitioner becomes a jivanmukta and acquires all the eight siddhis as well as thirty-two other minor siddhis.

Ajna means 'command'. From this centre the bodily systems and states of awareness are controlled. It is responsible for intuitive knowledge and most importantly it is the residence of kundalini shakti after it has reached sahasrara chakra.

In India many people wear a red mark at the point of ajna chakra between the eyebrows. The women wear a single dot, the men a vertical line. It is made of sindhur, containing mercury. This is to help develop higher awareness and awaken ajna chakra.

In yoga there is total emphasis on ajna chakra. Concentration on the mid-eyebrow centre is known as shambhavi mudra. It can be developed through trataka. There are also other ways. If you can handle ajna chakra properly, you can manage the different systems in the body – excretory, respiratory, nervous, coronary system and brain. You can control and manage them all. That is the precise method of yoga. Of course, asana, pranayama, mudra, bandha, meditation, concentration and relaxation are practised but the most important point is that you must become the master of this command centre at the pineal gland.

The pineal gland is the guru, the master, and the pituitary gland is the disciple. This should be the relationship. As long as this relationship exists, everything is going to be alright with you. When the pineal gland becomes the disciple and the pituitary becomes the guru, then all kinds of problems beset you. Emotional problems, mental problems, psychic problems and physical problems, overactive or underactive thyroid, hyperactivity or depression of the adrenals; metabolism and catabolism are all totally out of balance. There is a state of anarchy in the body, mind and life. It is a generalized state of 'dis-ease'. The doctor makes a diagnosis and prescribes drug after drug – antibiotics, sedatives, tranquilizers, etc. Doctors themselves do not know exactly what they are doing, or what is going on, because they consider this body to be bone, marrow, blood and flesh alone.

However, in yoga we consider this body as a manifestation of two energies: awareness and life; mind and prana. To maintain a balance between these two, ajna chakra should be awakened by concentration.

Swatmarama has described the quiescent state of mind as turiya. *Turiya* mentioned here means the all expansive and encompassing 'fourth dimension' in which Shakti neither contracts nor expands, but is in union with Shiva or consciousness. Turiya is Ishwara or bindu. In the third dimension, Shakti has expanded and contracted. The *Avadhoota Gita* states that, the Absolute is even beyond this fourth dimension, "Where there are neither the three states of consciousness nor the fourth, there one attains the Absolute in the Self. How is it possible to be bound or free where there is neither virtue nor vice?" (1:74)

अभ्यसेत् खेचरीं तावद्यावत् स्याद्योगनिद्रितः ।
संप्राप्तयोगनिद्रस्य कालो नास्ति कदाचन ॥ 49 ॥

Khechari should be practised until yogic sleep occurs. For one who has attained yogic sleep, time becomes non-existent.

Yogic sleep or yoga nidra is the state in which conscious mind subsides but awareness remains. Today yoga nidra has become a specific practice of yoga where one lies in shavasana and consciously relaxes the whole body, part by part, and then concentrates on the natural breath. By this method the subconscious mind comes to the surface, and the conscious mind drops away. In the beginning, the practitioner will find that he falls asleep, but with practice he will be able to maintain conscious awareness while in the state of sleep.

Yoga nidra is the state where one is consciously aware during the *swapna avastha* or 'dream state' and, deeper still, conscious awareness is preserved during the *sushupti avastha* or 'deep sleep state'. For most people this is an impossibility. However, with practice it is possible to be aware while in the subconscious or dream state. Most people will have experienced the sensation of 'falling' just before they go to sleep. It is a semiconscious state, or the state of awareness as you drift into sleep. Here you are still awake and aware, but the conscious mind has totally relaxed to the point of dissolution. This is the state of yoga nidra.

Sleep is a biological factor which can be induced psychologically. Sleep is spontaneous pratyahara, i.e. sense withdrawal, which occurs with physical and mental relaxation. At this time there are specific changes in most of the bodily systems with predominance of the parasympathetic nervous system.

As one is 'falling asleep', sense modalities gradually disengage in a systematic order and awareness is led into the deeper layers of mind. During the descent into sleep the wakeful ego state slowly disintegrates. In yoga nidra wakefulness is not lost, but only the external influences upon the ego dissolve. In sleep there is total unawareness of the ego.

Scientific researchers have described sleep in four distinct stages. In the first stage there is an altered state of consciousness and relaxation in the body, in which alpha brain waves become predominant (frequency 7.5–12 c.p.s.). Alpha waves correspond to relaxation and are produced in states of meditation. In the second stage, when dreaming occurs, there is psychic activity and physical movement, and theta waves (4.7 c.p.s.) are produced by the brain. In deep sleep, stages three and four, awareness moves into the unconscious mind which is characterized by delta waves (0–3.5 c.p.s.).

Initially, the state of yoga nidra is dominated by alpha waves, but later on, a yogi can maintain awareness during the experience of delta waves and deep sleep. Therefore, nidra or sleep can be induced biologically, i.e. by a chemical reaction within the body which inhibits the brain's central mechanisms, reticular activating system and cerebral cortex, or psychologically through mental control.

Entry into yoga nidra by khechari is a combination of physiological and psychological induction. However, the use of khechari alone demands considerable practice in order to induce the yoga nidra state. It should be practised with ujjayi pranayama, and concentration upon a particular symbol and form.

निरालम्बं मन: कृत्वा न किंचिदापि चिंतयेत् ।
सबाह्याभ्यंतरे व्योम्नि घटवत्तिष्ठति ध्रुवम् ॥ 50 ॥

Having made the mind unsupported without even a thought, indeed, one is like a pot filled inside and out with space.

Unsupported mind is that state of mind which has no influencing samskaras or vrittis to disturb it. It becomes a perfect receptacle of the cosmic vibrations and consciousness. Just as you have a bottle and fill it with any liquid, and the more you fill it the less air it contains, so it is with the mind. The more you fill your mind with worldly thoughts, desires, etc., the less pure or cosmic vibrations can penetrate it. Therefore, it is essential to empty the mind of the concept of ego, memory, thought and counterthought, and intellect.

Unsupported mind is the state of *niralamba* or *nirbija* samadhi. That is a state devoid of the manifestation of shakti, ego, intellect, memory etc. It is the state of unmanifest Shakti and consciousness. The *Mandukya Upanishad* states that: "Just as space confined within jars merges completely on the disintegration of the jars, so do the individual souls (jivas) merge here in this self (Atman)." (3:4) Because of awareness of the jar (mind-body), the space (atman) within is considered different from the space (atman) without. Once there is realization that the space (atman) within is the same as the space (atman) without and that the jar (mind-body) cannot create a difference, the space (atman) becomes the reality. That is disintegration of the jar (mind-body identification).

Adi Shankaracharya has further clarified this illusion of individuality in his commentary on the *Mandukya Upanishad*: "Just as the spaces within jars emerge into being with creation of the jar, or just as the spaces within the jar disappear with disintegration of the jar, similarly individual souls emerge into being along with the creation of the aggregates of body, and they merge here in the Self on the disintegration of those aggregates."

बाह्यवायुर्यथा लीनस्तथा मध्यो न संशय: ।
स्वस्थाने स्थिरतामेति पवनो मनसा सह ॥ 51 ॥

When the external breath is suspended, likewise the middle one (i.e. shakti in sushumna is suspended). Without a doubt, prana and mind become still in their own place (i.e. Brahmarandhra).

एवमभ्यसमानस्य वायुमार्गे दिवानिशम् ।
अभ्यासाज्जीर्यते वायुर्मनस्तत्रैव लीयते ॥ 52 ॥

Verily, practising with the breath (prana) day and night through the course of prana (sushumna), prana and mind become absorbed there.

These slokas summarize what has been discussed on pranayama in Chapter 2.

अमृतैः प्लावयेद् देहमापादतलमस्तकम् ।
सिद्ध्यत्येव महाकायो महाबलपराक्रमः ॥ 53 ॥

The whole body from the soles of the feet to the head should become filled with nectar. Thus, the one who perfects this has a superior body, superior strength and immense valour.

What exactly this nectar is, science is unable to say. The yogis call it ambrosia or amrit. *Mrit* is 'death', *amrit* is 'that which is beyond death and never dying.' Death is the process of maya or prakriti. That which is beyond the influence of decay and birth is beyond maya. There is only one thing beyond death and maya, that is atma. When the body is filled with this nectar the mind becomes intoxicated with the experience of atma. Swami Muktananda tells how, in the state of deep meditation, ambrosial milk sometimes trickled through his palate and entered the gastric fire and nadis. He saw the nectar fill the body like a 'blended light spreading through the 72,000 nadis with lightning speed.' From this arose the vision of kundalini shakti in many forms, and his body 'became increasingly light, slim, agile, strong and immune to disease.'

In Hindu mythology there are many stories of great saints who, intoxicated with the idea of the highest atma, survived circumstances in which the average person would definitely have died. Even in the Bible and other religious books there are such stories. Though one's personal idea of the image of God will vary, it is the faith in the higher cosmic will which is one and the same, and this faith can move mountains when both wills are in unison.

शक्तिमध्ये मन: कृत्वा शक्तिं मानसमध्यगाम् ।
मनसा मन आलोक्य धारयेत्परमं पदम् ॥ 54 ॥

Having made shakti the centre of mind and mind the centre of shakti, observe the mind making the supreme state the object (of concentration).

खमध्ये कुरु चात्मानमात्ममध्ये च खं कुरु ।
सर्वं च खमयं कृत्वा न किंचिदपि चिन्तयेत् ॥ 55 ॥

Making the atma the centre of Brahman, and making Brahman the centre of atma, and making everything Brahman; remain without even a single thought (in samadhi).

When kundalini is in ajna, bindu or sahasrara, Shakti is in the middle of mind, and mind is in the middle of Shakti. The mind and all its components that we experience is the product of Shakti. It is this shakti in the form of mind which reflects the objects shown to it. The *Tantraraja Tantra* states that: "Upon the mass of the sun, Parashiva being reflected in the pure vimarsha mirror, the maha bindu appears on the chitta wall, illumined by the reflected rays." (v. 4) Here Shakti is compared to a mirror. This mirror is the chitta wall (the mind screen). The mind should contain nothing, then it will function as a mirror directed to the sun, i.e. it will reflect pure consciousness. Otherwise it reflects gross, subtle and causal manifestations. When mind is undifferentiated, shakti reflects the light of atma; it is that light which is experienced as illumination. Therefore, atma should be the object of concentration.

The word *kha* is used here to mean Brahman, but it can also mean akasha or ether. It means the highest cause. "Making atma the centre of Brahman and Brahman the centre of atma." i.e. realizing the individual existence as the whole, remain without any individualized concepts. It has to be realized that atma is always the centre of Brahman and vice versa. However, this is unperceived when the mind is full of vrittis or movement. It is like looking into a pool of water on a rainy day and trying to see your own reflection. When the vrittis cease, when rain stops disturbing the water, then the vision can come, which brings us back to verse 2 of Sage Patanjali's Yoga Sutras: *Yogaschitta vritti nirodha* – Yoga is the cessation of the fluctuating patterns of the mind.

The *Avadhoota Gita* of Dattatreya states that: "Space is pervaded by It (Brahman), but It is not pervaded by anything. It is existing within and without. It is individual and continuous." (2:14) "Mind is indeed the form of space. Mind is indeed the omnifaced. Mind is past. Mind is all. But in reality there is no mind." (1:9) "Union and separation exist neither to you nor to me. There is no you, no me, nor is there universe. All is verily Self alone." (1:15)

What the average person considers to be reality, separate from supraconsciousness, is in fact part and parcel of supraconsciousness, but it is without distinction because nothing can exist on its own. In order to exist individually it has to be defined in relation to something else. It is always a part of something greater and beyond and in essence that something is Brahman. Individuality cannot be denied but neither can collectivity.

A single apple represents the whole tree from which it came. Just because you cannot see the tree when you look at the apple does not prove the tree does not exist. On the other hand, as the tree grows, the apple appears and then falls and dissolves back into the earth from whence it has sprung. We could say there was no individual existence of apple but only the tree's growth and development are real. It is like that with the coming and going of souls. Just as the potential of the tree and the apple expands and contracts, so does the entire universe of individual names, forms and beings within it.

Another way of saying, "Centre the atma in Brahma", is "Realize that atma is the potential of Brahma, realize Brahma", just as the apple and tree are potentially no different from each other.

अन्त: शून्यो बहि: शून्य: शून्य: कुंभ इवांबरे ।
अन्त: पूर्णो बहि: पूर्ण: पूर्ण: कुम्भ इवार्णवे ॥ 56 ॥

Within is void, without is void; like an empty vessel in space, completely full internally, completely full externally, just like a pot in the ocean.

बाह्यचिंता न कर्तव्या तथैवांतरचिंतनम् ।
सर्वचिंतां परित्यज्य न किंचिदपि चिंतयेत् ॥ 57 ॥

Without thought of the external or even internal thought, all thoughts abandoned, without even a single thought.

संकल्पमात्रकलनै जगत समग्रं
संकल्पमात्रकलनैव मनोविलास: ।
संकल्पमात्रमतिमुत्सृज निर्विकल्प-
मश्रित्य निश्चयमवाप्नुहि राम शांतिम् ॥ 58 ॥

The entire world is only the fabrication of thought. Play of mind is only created by thought. By transcending the mind which is composed of constructed thought, definitely peace will be attained, O Rama!

The *Ishavasya Upanishad* explains everything as the 'full' from which nothing can ever be separated because everywhere is still a part of that fullness. The whole of this world, universe, the galaxies and stars, etc., are the total unfoldment of nature (i.e. Shakti), and though it is in constant motion and transformation, with forms appearing and disappearing, nothing is ever lost from the total; the whole remains one. This is the philosophy of tantra, yoga and Vedanta.

The subtle essence of the purest existence is within and without all. The *Ashtavakra Samhita* states: "Just as the same all-pervading space is inside and outside a jar, so the eternal all-pervasive Brahman is in all things." In actuality, that is the only one real state and all other qualifications are only relative definitions which are ultimately illusory. The *Avadhoota Gita* even denies the reality of individual existence altogether. It states: "There is no pot, there is no pot's interior space. Neither is there an individual soul, nor the form of an individual soul. Know the absolute Brahman, devoid of knowable and knower." (1:32) "As the space within a pot dissolves in the universal space when the pot is broken, so a yogi, in the absence of the body, dissolves into the Supreme Self, which is his true being." (2:25) "There is no pot's space or pot, no individual body or individual soul. There is no distinction of cause and effect (karana and karya). Why do you, who are the identity in all, grieve in your heart?" (5:6)

In the ultimate state of experience there is no differentiation between anything; it is all part of the total. That is from an absolute point of view. However, when there is ignorance of the total experience, then the experience of separation of consciousness and the experience of duality cannot be denied.

Dattatreya asks: "How can He, the One and All-pervading, who moves effortlessly all that is moveable, be differentiated?" When you consider that every object is made up of a matrix of particles and it is the combination of every particle which makes the universe what it is, then how can a single object be separate, for it is part of the whole. In the same way, the Absolute is everything manifest and unmanifest; all that was, is and shall be.

The *Avadhoota Gita* further states: "There is no imagined division of bodies. There is no imagined division of worlds. I am indeed the Absolute and supreme truth . . ." (6:24) "You are He who is exterior and interior. You are the auspicious One existing everywhere at all times. Why are you running hither and thither deluded like an unclean spirit?" (1:14) "When the pot is broken, the space within it is absorbed in the infinite space and becomes undifferentiated. When the mind becomes pure, I do not perceive any difference between the mind and Supreme being." (1:31)

550

At the end of sloka 58 in the *Hatha Yoga Pradipika*, Swatmarama has exclaimed: "O Rama", which indicates by the appellation that it has been taken directly from another classical text, the *Yoga Vasishtha*. This text takes the form of a dialogue between Lord Rama and his guru Vasishtha, on the nature of reality, in which Vasishtha uses the simile of a pot to define consciousness and individuality.

The sublime philosophy of an indivisible, eternal and infinite reality, and the illusoriness of individuality, separation, duality and death is the subject matter of the Advaita tradition. This philosophy is also known as Vedanta. Yoga and tantra are the means to proceed from the state of duality to the experience of reality, union, oneness. Separation is not denied, and neither is the Absolute. The fact that Swatmarama has used the teachings of the *Yoga Vasishtha* shows the link between hatha yoga and jnana yoga, and that with the physical awakening of kundalini the mind expands its boundaries.

कर्पूरमनले यद्वत्सैन्धवं सलिले यथा ।
तथा संधीयमानं च मनस्तत्त्वे विलीयते ॥ 59 ॥

As camphor (dissolves) in fire, and salt (dissolves) in the sea, in samadhi mind dissolves into 'Thatness' (tattwa).

Imagine yourself as a teaspoon of salt, having separate self-identity as salt, but when you are mixed into the sea, you become a part of that. Still there is the flavour of the salt, but your separate identity as a quantity of salt is lost. The same applies to the inherent consciousness of the individual mind. When the consciousness has merged into the totality of consciousness, only that consciousness remains. Still there is the 'flavour' of consciousness as salt can be tasted in the sea, but the separation of awareness no longer exists. Swami Yogananda Paramahamsa explains: "In savikalpa samadhi yoga (or union) you will drown your self (ego consciousness) in your Self (universal consciousness). In nirvikalpa samadhi yoga (or union) you will find your-self (ego consciousness) in your Self (universal consciousness)."

ज्ञेयं सर्वं प्रतीतं च ज्ञानं च मन उच्यते ।
ज्ञानं ज्ञेयं समं नष्टं नान्य: पंथा द्वितीयक: ॥ 60 ॥

*All that can be known, all that is known and the knowledge, is
called mind. When the knower and that which is known are lost
together, there is no dual or second way.*

मनोदृश्यमिदं सर्वं यत्किंचित्सचराचरम् ।
मनसो ह्युन्मनीभावाद् द्वैतं नैवोपलभ्यते ॥ 61 ॥

*All that is in this world, animate and inanimate, is the appearance
of mind. When mind attains unmani, duality is lost.*

ज्ञेयवस्तुपरित्यागाद्विलयं याति मानसम् ।
मनसो विलये जाते कैवल्यमवशिष्यत ॥ 62 ॥

*All the known objects being abandoned, mind goes into absorption
or is dissolved. When the mind is dissolved, then there will be
kaivalya.*

एवं नानाविधोपाया: सम्यक् स्वानुभवान्विता: ।
समाधिमार्गा: कथिता: पूर्वाचार्यैर्महात्मभि: ॥ 63 ॥

*Thus, there are many various methods, depending on individual
experience, of the path to samadhi, told by the great ones
(mahatmas).*

When the three states of knower, knowing and known merge
as one experience, that is one-pointedness of mind, which
becomes the state of cosmic or universal consciousness.
When the three perceptions exist there is individual mind.
Sage Patanjali states that: "Samapatti is a state of complete
absorption of the mind (which is free from vrittis) into
cognizer, cognized and the senses, just as polished crystal
takes the colour of that on which it rests." This state of
samapatti precedes samadhi.

The three states all emerge from the one state of consciousness. Knower is the subject, known is the object and the knowing is the link between the two. When the experience of subject and object is one undifferentiated experience there is unification of consciousness. Knower, knowing and known is represented by the symbol Om; the formula of the four states of jagrat, swapna, sushupti and turiya. The *Kama-kala-vilasa* states that: "Knower, knowing and known are the three bindus and forms of bija (mahabindu)." (v. 13)

The three bindus: red, white and mixed (Shiva, Shakti and Shiva-Shakti in union), manifest on all levels of existence. One bindu is considered positive, one negative, the other neutral. The three states of mind are similarly divided. Just as the three bindus are from the one undivided energy, so the states of mind come from the one undivided source of consciousness. That is the state of mahabindu.

As Shakti and consciousness manifest in their different forms through the various realms, so there are as many different means to re-establish unity. Either through the physical body, prana or mind and by any of the various sadhanas, but ultimately it demands the unification of all three. Which sadhana to follow depends on what attracts your entire attention.

However, from the vedantic point of view, in reality there is no knower, knowing or known. The *Avadhoota Gita* says: "Know the absolute Brahman, devoid of knowable and knower." (1:32) "The existence of duality is denied. Some seek non-duality. They do not know the truth which is the same at all times and everywhere, which is devoid of both duality and non-duality." (1:37) "Know the Self to be everywhere, one and unintercepted. I am meditator and the highest object of meditation. Why do you divide the indivisible?" (1:12) "If the self is the negation of difference and non-difference, if it is the negation of known and knowable, if there is only the one indivisible all-comprehensive Absolute, how can there be the third (causal), how can there be the fourth (turiya)?" (6:7)

What Vedanta holds is that in reality there is only Brahman. Anything and everything else is false knowledge: "If it is the nature of the not-Self, how can there be samadhi? If it is the nature of the Self, how can there be samadhi? If all is one and of the nature of freedom, how can there be samadhi?" (1:23)

So, there are two points of view; the first is that of tantra and yoga in which there is individual consciousness, there is higher consciousness, there is mind, there are tattwas and various stages to self-realization. This is dvaita. The second view is that everything is none other than Brahman, the supreme state; then there can be no second, i.e. duality. This is advaita. However, tantra and yoga consider both points of view. Advaita explains the reality after realization has taken place. Tantra and yoga explain the reality before and after self-realization.

सुषुम्नायै कुंडलिन्यै सुधायै चन्द्रजन्मने ।
मनोन्मन्यै नमस्तुभ्यं महाशक्त्यै चिदात्मने ॥ 64 ॥

Salutations to sushumna, kundalini, the nectar flowing from the moon, to the mindless state of mind (manonmani), to the great Shakti, to the atma.

अशक्यतत्त्वबोधानां मूढानामपि संमतम् ।
प्रोक्तं गोरक्षनाथेन नादोपासनमुच्यते ॥ 65 ॥

I will describe the concentration on nada as told by Gorakhnath which is attainable by even the unlearned who are unable to comprehend Thatness (tattwas).

श्रीआदिनाथेन सपादकोटिलयप्रकारा: कथिता जयंति ।
नादानुसंधानकमेकमेव मन्यामहे मुख्यतमं लयानाम् ॥ 66 ॥

There are one and a quarter crore ways told by Sri Adinath to attain laya, but we think the one and only thing is nada anusandhana or the exploration of nada.

Salutations were first given to Shiva, which could lead to the assumption that hatha yoga developed from a background of Shaivism. However, the continual emphasis on absorbing the mind in prana shakti and the praises of kundalini reveal it to be a combination of Shaivite and Shakta philosophies.

Gorakhnath was a tantric guru who had attained unimaginable power and insight into the subtle realms of mind and creation. He had wondrous experiences and faced many obstacles in the path of spiritual evolution. According to him and other evolved souls, the easiest way to laya is through absorption in nada.

In the *Yoga Taravali*, Shankaracharya states that: "Sadashiva has spoken of 20,000 kinds of laya, but most important is nada anusandhana for it leads to samadhi." Now we begin an entirely new aspect of hatha yoga. At this stage hatha yoga is coming into the range of raja yoga because from here on we are dealing with higher states of consciousness and samadhi.

The ways of concentrating the mind vary to suit the different temperaments and personalities. According to Nath yogis there is one way suitable for all, i.e. laya in nada. Shakti is the tool to liberation because she is the vehicle of consciousness. On a subtle level it manifests as sound. Therefore, Gorakhnath says to absorb the mind in that sound.

Sound is known as *nada*, it is called *shabda*. To be more precise, nada is the imperceptible sound and shabda is perceptible. When shabda is language it is called *nama*. Nada is the creative power of the highest consciousness. It exists in each individual and throughout the cosmos. Individual nada is called *pinda*; cosmic nada is called *para*.

Nada refers to the 'flow' from mahabindu. Its quality is sound and its form is light. The form is called *artha* or *prakasha*, and when this form is perceptible in a shape, it is called *roopa*. Shabda is subject and artha is object.

Mahabindu consists of Shiva and Shakti in total union. Then a split occurs within the mahabindu and a threefold Shakti appears: nada, bindu and kalaa. Bindu in man contains the same potential as the mahabindu. When the nada issues from bindu within your own body then the inner sound can be heard. It is the release of the inner potential and when it takes place then your whole perception of this world undergoes a change.

The manifestation of sound has been categorized into four states: para, pashyanti, madhyama and vaikhari. Para nada is soundless sound or *nih shabda*. It is the state when mahabindu or *nirvana bindu*, i.e. param shiva, splits. Mahabindu is before manifestation of sound, para nada is the appearance of Shakti from the mahabindu. When para nada begins to move without particular direction, *samanya spanda*, it is pashyanti nada. When this movement in nada becomes differentiated, *vishesha spanda*, it is madhyama nada. When this sound manifests in a gross or sthula form of *sparshta tara spanda*, it is *vaikhari* or *virat shabda*. The *Subhagodayavasana* describes that: "Para, as pashyanti, is the creeper born in the earth (mooladhara chakra). As madhyama, she is the fragrance from the flower bunch, as vaikhari she is the letter of the alphabet. Thus does she excel all."

There is an important difference between subtle and gross sound. The subtle sound is not caused by two things being struck together, whereas gross sound can only occur by two objects coming together. Produced or struck sound is *dhwani*, it is *ahata nada*. Unproduced sound is *anahata nada*. Subtle sound is heard by the consciousness itself. Gross sound is heard through the ear sending vibrations to the brain.

By developing awareness of the witness within you, i.e. subjective mind, you are developing shabda. When *sthula artha* or 'gross object' is presented to the mind it forms an impression and vritti or modification. Yogic practices aim at stopping the vrittis and impressions of the sthula artha. The external object is artha but its internal impression is also artha, and the part of the mind which cognizes is shabda. Thus, by blocking the artha, shabda is revealed.

The particular method in nada yoga of nada anusandhana reveals this inner sound to the mind. Nada anusandhana, as mentioned here, should not be confused with the technique in kriya yoga called nada sanchalana. They are two different practices but can achieve the same result. *Anusandhana* means 'exploration' or 'search'. The idea is to explore the sound in all dimensions. The sound has to be followed until you reach the subtlest vibration. It has to be followed from vaikhari back to para. Each level of sound is joined and dependent upon the other.

It is said that beyond senses, beyond what the eyes can see and the ears can hear, there are objects that can be seen and there are sounds that can be heard. These sounds are either of a very high frequency or a very low frequency. Your ears are adjusted to a certain frequency and beyond that you cannot hear. So, these sounds which are beyond or below the frequency range of the ear can be heard by adjusting the concentration. Either you bring the concentration to a low level, or you bring it to a high level. Either you intensify the perception of the mind or you withdraw the perception of the mind. So, these nadas are occurring in the mind and the sound is to be heard there.

You cannot create these sounds, they are already there. However, you have to attune your mind. You tune the capacity of the *indriya*, or sense of audition. What can be heard by the physical ear is called vaikhari sound. What can be felt by ears but is heard in the mind is called madhyama sound. What cannot be heard by others but is felt in meditation is called pashyanti sound. For example, you are playing a flute and someone hears it; that is vaikhari sound. When someone is playing a flute somewhere and you can feel that someone is playing a flute, that is called madhyama. When nobody is playing the flute and yet you hear it, that is called pashyanti. What is heard in transcendental states is called para.

So, nada anusandhana means the search for transcendental sound. *Para* refers to 'transcendental'. *Apara* is 'the empirical'. Lower sound is apara. Para means beyond. Beyond what? Beyond mind and senses is para. Apara is within the range of mind and the senses. What is transcendental? Transcendental means that which is beyond the category of the mind, feeling, emotion, senses and the body. You cannot comprehend it by the karmendriya, jnanendriya, the mind, the buddhi, the chitta and ahamkara, not even in dream. Sometimes you can practise nada anusandhana directly by plugging the ears, or the nada can be revealed to you by practising certain hatha yoga kriyas.

When the mind follows the nada it becomes absorbed in that sound. There is union of consciousness and energy; there is yoga. Nada yoga is sometimes called dhwani yoga, and this tradition is stated in some of the tantras. Kabir talks about it and calls it surati shabda. It is also known as surat shabda. The use of sound to create various states of mind, emotions, etc., and to communicate to other people, animals and plants is as old as the existence of man himself.

559

Nada anusandhana has been described by Yogi Gorakh-nath who is a great figure in the history of yoga. His disciples and devotees will never divulge when he actually lived because he is considered to have been beyond a simple human birth. Gorakhnath is said to have lived in the satya yuga at Peshwar, Punjab; in the treta yuga at Gorakhpur, Uttar Pradesh; in the dwapara yuga at Hurmuj, Gurajat; and in the kali yuga at Kathiawar, Uttar Pradesh. However, his spiritual descent is referred to in several places. Throughout the north of India, Gorakhnath's fame is extremely well-known and there are many legends regarding his paranormal and superhuman powers. In fact, there has probably been no other tantric yogi to surpass him. When Swatmarama states that this nada anusandhana is recommended by Gorakhnath, this is sufficient to emphasize its importance to hatha yoga sadhakas.

मुक्तासने स्थितो योगी मुद्रां संधाय शांभवीम् ।
शृणुयाद् दक्षिणे कर्णे नादमंतास्थमेकधी: ॥ 67 ॥

The yogi, sitting in muktasana, concentrated in shambhavi, should listen closely to the nada heard within the right ear.

श्रवणपुटनयनयुगलघ्राणमुखानां निरोधनं कार्यम् ।
शुद्धसुषुम्नासरणौ स्फुटममल: श्रूयते नाद: ॥ 68 ॥

Closing the ears, nose and mouth, a clear, distinct sound is heard in the purified sushumna.

By sitting down and plugging the ears, with practice one can begin to hear various ranges, qualities and forms of sound. In the practice of nada yoga, it is necessary to sit on a hard, round pillow, as you would ride a horse, so that the perineum is pressed. The elbows are placed on the knees and the index fingers inserted into the ears. The pressure should not be forceful; the ears are plugged and the mind withdrawn. Then whatever sound can be heard at the first moment is listened to. In the hatha yoga practice, siddhasana/siddha yoni asana is utilized and shanmukhi mudra, which is the closing of all the facial orifices with the fingers, is practised.

Most people hear some sound, but if no sound can be heard initially, then bhramari pranayama can be practised for some time. Bhramari is practised by producing a humming sound in the same melodious way as the honey bee. It should not be a strong and forced sound. During practice one should also try to discover if there is any other sound to be heard.

Whichever sound you first pick up, keep on following that as far as you can. After some time another sound will be experienced emerging from the background. As soon as you discover this next sound, leave the first and follow the next. In this way go on discovering sound after sound and the sound behind the sound. These sounds eventually become so tangible that you can hear them clearly and vividly.

BSY©

Technique 1

Sit in siddhasana/siddha yoni asana.

Inhale deeply and slowly and perform antar kumbhaka.

Perform shanmukhi mudra by closing the ears with the thumbs, eyes with the index fingers, nose with the middle fingers and the mouth with the ring and little fingers.

Concentrate on any perceivable subtle sound.

If a sound is heard it should be listened to.

Try to differentiate from which ear you are hearing the sound, or concentrate on the sound coming from the right ear.

Before exhaling release shanmukhi mudra, and then breathe out in a controlled manner.

This is one round. Practise five to ten rounds.

Technique 2

Sit on a rolled blanket or folded cushion.

Keep it under the buttocks, knees raised, in a squatting type position, utkatasana, so that there is a steady pressure in the perineum.

Perform shanmukhi mudra as described in Technique 1.

562

Additional Techniques

Practise Technique 1 or 2 and perform vajroli mudra and moola bandha during internal breath retention and shanmukhi mudra, i.e. naumukhi mudra.

Alternatively, either moola bandha or vajroli mudra can be incorporated.

Or include khechari mudra throughout the practice.

Try bhramari pranayama during exhalation while holding shanmukhi mudra but opening the nostrils.

Instead of antar kumbhaka, practise shanmukhi or naumukhi mudra with bahir kumbhaka.

Or plug the ears only and practise shambhavi mudra.

These are the various techniques to reveal and enhance the inner sound. You may even develop your own method.

In the kriya practice of nada sanchalana, the sadhaka sits in siddhasana or siddha yoni asana. During inhalation the awareness ascends with the breath up through the frontal passage of arohan and pierces each of the chakra kshetrams up to vishuddhi and bindu. From bindu the mantra *Aum* is chanted. The *Au* has to explode from the bindu. The awareness then travels back down from bindu to ajna with the sound *Au* and then from ajna to mooladhara with a prolonged *mmm*.

Though it is stated in these slokas that the nada is heard in the right ear, it is actually heard within the mind. You should not be very concerned about which ear perceives it. Baba Muktananda of Ganeshpuri once asked his guru if hearing nada from the left ear was really a premonition of death as people said. Sri Nityananda replied that the distinction between left and right was irrelevant because nada originated in the akasha of sahasrara chakra, the supreme abode of consciousness.

It could be said that for a bhogi the subtle sound heard in the left ear indicates death. However, for the yogi the occurrence of nada indicates the ascension of Shakti and consciousness, i.e. the movement of kundalini shakti.

563

When the kundalini awakens, sometimes inner voices or narrative can also be heard from the deeper levels of consciousness. The actual phenomenon is difficult to explain at an intellectual level as it is more a feeling that is experienced rather than a physical sound. It is something like two trees talking to each other. This is a higher state. Ultimately the inner voice becomes pure vibration, which is neither picture, idea nor sound, but still there is an understanding through it, as if you were speaking a language.

There are certain nada yogis who can answer any question by the vibration they receive. A type of revelation comes to the mind but this does not happen at an intellectual level. The inner voice may also come in the form of symbols which are more difficult to translate.

The Bible was originally a revelation; God spoke. In the same way, the Koran was also revealed; Allah spoke to Mohammed. The Vedas were also revealed by Hiranyagarbha. Rishis heard the verses and jotted them down. Many people can hear a mantra, a sound or music and some can hear narratives. The deeper you go, the more you come into contact with the cosmic mind.

The outer mind is the individual and empirical mind. The inner mind is the universal and transcendental mind. This particular mind through which we talk and understand is the individual mind. This mind has its own particular limitation. The knowledge gained through this mind is conditioned. Unless someone speaks you cannot hear what he is saying. However, as you transcend the empirical mind, then not only can you hear the mantra, you can also hear higher commands. Here a Veda, Koran, or Bible may be revealed to you because the speaker is the cosmic mind. The cosmic mind is the unconscious, symbolized by the four-headed Brahma.

Previously, and even today in occidental countries, if a person heard some inner voices or broken sounds or spoke some irrelevant or incoherent sentences, other people thought that person was going crazy and should be sent immediately to a mental hospital. However, this attitude is beginning to change and some thinkers in the West feel that this may be a spiritual or psychic phenomenon.

In India and in other ancient cultures it is different. If a person began to hear voices or sounds from the inner dimensions, elders at once took notice of it. Such an individual was not treated for mental illness. He was given spiritual initiation because they considered that he had arrived at a particular point of mental evolution. If he is then initiated properly this attainment can be streamlined.

Therefore, if you sometimes hear broken sounds, very unclear conversation, off and on utterances or half-sentences, just continue with your usual practice. The nature of the experience will change. Do not take much notice of it. You may hear music, bits of conversation or someone calling very loudly within you. Don't take any notice of these things. Continue your usual practice until you arrive at a point where your perception of the inner sound becomes systematic, clear and vivid.

The various types of sound that are heard during nada yoga relate to the level of one's spiritual and psychic attainment. Of course, the biological structure also has a part to play because the physical and mental bodies interact with each other up to a certain stage. For the average person, it is not possible to trace these sounds properly. Initially the nada or sound that is heard is the result of the communication between the biological and psychological systems. However, once the awakening of kundalini takes place the sounds have no biological or even psychological basis. They are purely transcendental.

आरंभश्च घटश्चैव तथा परिचयोऽपि च ।
निष्पत्ति: सर्वयोगेषु स्यादवस्थाचतुष्टयम् ॥ 69 ॥

In all the yogic practices there are four stages; arambha, beginning; ghata, vessel; parichaya, increase; nishpatti, consummation.

The four stages of progressive experience of nada yoga are outlined here. The fourth stage verges on samadhi. These four stages are known as *bhava* or 'spontaneous unfoldment'. Each stage is more subtle and refined than the preceding one. These stages are said to apply to all yogic practices, but the *Shiva Samhita* applies them particularly to pranayama.

During each different stage, sound manifests in the inner ear. In the *Shiva Sutras* it is said that through nada anusandhana on the anahata nada (unstruck sound), which is represented by the mantra *Om*, nine stages of yoga or union unfold progressively. These stages of experience of the nine subtler forms of nada are: 1. bindu, 2. ardha chandra, 3. rodhini, 4. nada, 5. nadanta, 6. shakti, 7. vyapini (anji), 8. samana (avatara roopa), 9. unmani. Stages 1 to 5 are said to be in the cosmic causal realm of nada and shakti, and 6 to 9 are in the transcendental realm.

As kundalini shakti rises through the chakras to centres of higher consciousness in the brain, there are four definite stages. These stages relate to the four realms of existence and the four *koshas*, or bodies. Para nada exists in the cosmic causal body or Ishwara tattwa; pashyanti in the cosmic subtle body, hiranyagarbha; madhyama is sukshma, subtle or psychic sound; vaikhari is sthula or gross sound, words and letters.

Para, pashyanti and madhyama are the manifestations of inner nada and speech which precede sensorial perceived sound. Spoken and written language and produced sound is vaikhari nada. Vaikhari, madhyama and pashyanti are also equated to *srishti, sthithi* and laya or *samhara*, i.e. creation, upholding of creation and dissolution, in both the macrocosmos and microcosmos (para and pinda).

ARAMBHA AVASTHA (beginning stage)

अथारंभावस्था ।

ब्रह्मग्रंथेर्भवेद्भेदो ह्यानंद: शून्यसंभव: ।
विचित्र: क्वणको देहेऽनाहत: श्रूयते ध्वनि: ॥ 70 ॥

*The Brahma granthi being pierced, the feeling of bliss arises from
the void; wondrous, tinkling sounds and the unstruck sound
(anahata) are heard within the body.*

दिव्यदेहश्च तेजस्वी दिव्यगंधस्त्वरोगवान् ।
संपूर्णहृदय: शून्य आरम्भे योगवान्भवेत् ॥ 71 ॥

*When the yogi experiences arambha in the void of the heart,
his body becomes lustrous and brilliant with a divine smell and
diseaseless.*

The aroused kundalini unties the Brahma granthi and
activates mooladhara chakra. 'To pierce' means to make a
passageway through. When this occurs, the barriers of the
physical body and ego or *swayambhulingam* are broken. Inner
sounds are heard resembling tinkling bells but other sounds
may also be heard. In *Theories of the Chakras*, Dr Hiroshi
Motoyama writes that he had the experience and sensation
'like the buzzing of bees around the coccyx'. The *Yoga
Shikka Upanishad* states: "A sound arises in Her (kundalini in
mooladhara) as if a sprout were shooting out from the tiny
seed." There will be many different experiences according
to each individual.

This sloka states that 'the unstruck nada is heard'.
'Unstruck' means anahata, but it is not referring to the
anahata chakra. The nada of anahata chakra comes at a later
stage. Anahata nada is the inner, subtle, pure form of nada,
and is depicted by Krishna playing his flute. It represents
transcendental, eternal sound. From mooladhara, sound

manifests as letters or *varna* of the alphabet and language. The *Svachchanda Tantra* explains that: "There is one varna in the form of nada in which lie all the varnas or letters latently in an undivided form. As it is ceaseless it is called anahata, i.e. unstruck, natural, uncaused." (Tan. 61226) By concentrating on the undivided sound, consciousness too becomes undivided.

GHATA AVASTHA (vessel stage)

अथ घटावस्था ।

द्वितीयायां घटीकृत्य वायूर्भवति मध्यग: ।
दृढासनो भवेद् योगी ज्ञानी देवसमस्तदा ॥ 72 ॥

In the second stage, when ghata is achieved, the Shakti goes into the middle nadi. Being fixed in his asana the wise yogi is comparable to a divine being.

विष्णुग्रन्थेस्ततो भेदात् परमानंदसूचक: ।
अतिशून्ये विमर्दश्च भेरीशब्दस्तदा भवेत् ॥ 73 ॥

When the Vishnu granthi is pierced the greatest bliss is revealed. Then from the void the sound of the kettledrum manifests.

Ghata is a vessel for holding water, which recalls the earlier statement, 'like a vessel immersed in water, inside and outside is water.' This symbolizes the state of mind in which the second stage of nada is perceived. The same nada which flows through the entire universe flows throughout our entire being. In the second stage, ghata, mind is like a vessel and consciousness is able to perceive the flow of nada within and without. The nada is always there but we just do not perceive it. Like a high frequency radio which has not been finely adjusted, mind is as yet attuned only to the sensorial impulses. When the Vishnu granthi in anahata chakra is untied the mind becomes attuned to the subtler sound frequencies.

The *Paduka-panchaka* states that: "In my heart (anahata chakra) I meditate on the jewelled altar (manipitha) and on nada and bindu . . . Its substance is chit (pure consciousness)." (v. 3) By following the nada from mooladhara to anahata chakra and unknotting the Vishnu granthi, consciousness expands into the *chinmaya* body, i.e. the transcendental state.

569

It is said in sloka 72 that the shakti enters the 'middle nadi'. This usually refers to sushumna, but as kundalini has already been flowing in sushumna from mooladhara, it is more likely to be referring to the inner layer chitrini.

PARICHAYA AVASTHA (stage of increase)

अथ परिचयावस्था ।

तृतीयायां तु विज्ञेयो विहायोमर्दलध्वनि: ।
महाशून्यं तदा याति सर्वसिद्धिसमाश्रयम् ॥ 74 ॥

*In the third stage is the experience of the sound of the drum. Then
there is the great void and one enters the place of total perfection or
siddhi.*

चित्तानन्दं तदा जित्वा सहजानन्दसंभव: ।
दोषदु:खजराव्याधिक्षुधानिद्राविवर्जित: ॥ 75 ॥

*Then the bliss of chitta being attained, natural or spontaneous
ecstasy arises. Imbalance of the three humours or doshas, pain, old
age, disease, hunger and sleep are overcome.*

Swatmarama is describing here the third stage in the
awakening of kundalini by nada yoga, when the kundalini
penetrates vishuddhi chakra. In *Theories of the Chakras*, Dr
Hiroshi Motoyama described this as the stage where one 'faces
the abyss of absolute void', and due to this experience comes
the falling away of worldly attachments. This is the absolute
prerequisite step before the place of total perfection and
accomplishment can be entered. There the indwelling bliss
of an undivided mind is experienced, and this is the source
of effortless and natural inner enjoyment and contentment.

In Buddhism, this corresponds to the fifth shoonya out
of the eighteen types of shoonya. The characteristic sound
heard at this stage of expansion and dissolution of mind is
described as the beat of drums.

The benefits when kundalini pierces vishuddhi are
also outlined. Balance of the three humours refers to the
ayurvedic concept of health as a state of equilibrium which
is experienced when wind, or *vata*, bile, or *pitta*, and phlegm,
or *kapha*, are in dynamic balance in the body.

What does it means to overcome pain, old age, disease, hunger and sleep? It does not mean that these naturally occurring experiences are eradicated but that their effects are overcome. The yogi who has awakened vishuddhi chakra has attained a level of consciousness from which the normal demands of pain, etc., do not disturb his equilibrium.

A small child who falls and grazes its knee will automatically cry and weep, but the consciousness of an adult who endures the same is barely perturbed. Similarly, the experiences of hunger, pain, old age, disease and desire for sleep, to which a normal individual succumbs, have less influence upon the mind and body of a yogi because of the expanded scope, depth and dimension of his awareness and prana. It is as though we are journeying deep in a valley and from this vantage point our aches and pains, hunger and tiredness, etc., often become our all-embracing needs and demand our entire attention.

However, a yogi is able to witness from a greater view point, as though he is simultaneously on top of a mountain pass, having a glimpse of the vista beyond. So the pains and demands of the body diminish in intensity, becoming only minor distractions. It is not that the body of a yogi does not become old. All bodies become old – eighty years old, one hundred years old, etc., but because of the greater vista of his experience, the yogi's endurance, vigour, vitality, dedication and energy far surpass the common man's.

How is it then that many great saints and enlightened ones have undergone tremendous suffering, such as acute or chronic diseases? For example, Ramakrishna Parama-hamsa and Shankaracharya suffered from cancer. In the first place we have to remember that all masters have not gained illumination by hatha yoga or nada yoga. Their chakras were surely awakened and they experienced the various stages of samadhi, but their awakening of kundalini was often achieved by less systematic discipline and austerities.

Suffering is a very powerful trigger in arousal of kundalini in those whose psyche is able to tolerate it. Intense and one-pointed bhavana and devotion, *bhakti*, has also been sufficient to trigger the greater awakening in devotionally minded aspirants. However, such awakening is not achieved systematically and scientifically and can be precipitated prematurely when the nadis remain blocked and unpurified. As a result the stages of higher awareness will be experienced in the midst of pain and suffering in the physical body. It is in order to avert this that hatha yoga has always emphasized purification of the body systems as the first step to awakening kundalini.

The next point which we must remember is that even though enlightenment and kundalini may supervene at a particular stage due to the intensity of practice and dedication, there remains the prarabdha karma of that individual body and mind. It has to be experienced, both positive and negative aspects alike, and this may include chronic disease or the tendency to it.

Thirdly, the suffering of the highly evolved ones is usually not their own. They are able to take upon themselves the painful karmic bonds of other less evolved souls and so manifest disease in their own bodies. Therefore, the sufferings of the great ones are explicable and do not detract from the inherent perfection of hatha yoga as a science to bring about awakening of kundalini. The quality of the karma of the aspirant and the quality of application of the practices are also to be considered.

The *Shiva Samhita* describes the state of *parichaya avastha* or 'the state of increase' as the condition in which: "The vayu does not move through the moon and sun (ida and pingala) but remains steady in sushumna. This takes place when one has control of kriya shakti or pingala and has pierced the six chakras." (3:60,61) This text has included the awakening of ajna chakra in the state of parichaya, but as we discuss nada anusandhana further we will find that ajna is included in the next state. In addition, the *Shiva Samhita* states that parichaya is achieved through pranayama, and the yogi should destroy his karma by the use of the *pranava* or *Om* mantra so that he need not be reborn.

NISHPATTI AVASTHA (stage of consummation)

रुद्रग्रंथि यदा भित्त्वा शर्वपीठगतोऽनिल: ।
निष्पत्तौ वैणव: शब्द: क्वणद्वीणाक्वणो भवेत् ॥ 76 ॥

If the Rudra granthi is pierced, the fire of prana moves to the place of Ishwara. Then in the stage of nishpatti or consummation is the tinkling sound of the flute resonating like a vina.

In the final stage of perception of the nada, kundalini pierces ajna chakra and the Rudra granthi. The sound heard is that of the flute. The flute is always associated with Lord Krishna, they are part and parcel of each other. However, this is not the only sound heard. In *Theories of the Chakras*, Dr Hiroshi Motoyama talks about hearing an echoing voice which called to him.

The *Shiva Samhita* also states that at this stage, "The yogi drinks amrita (the nectar of immortality), having destroyed the seeds of his karma." Nishpatti avastha is equated with nirvikalpa samadhi which renders one a jivanmukta.

When the Rudra granthi is pierced the kundalini moves to sahasrara chakra, the abode of paramshiva, the maha-bindu. This is above the state of manifested or differentiated Shakti. Here Shiva and Shakti abide together. It is *turiyatita*, even beyond the fourth dimension.

एकीभूतं तदा चित्तं राजयोगाभिधानकम् ।
सृष्टिसंहारकर्तासौ योगीश्वरसमो भवेत् ॥ 77 ॥

This is called raja yoga when there is one element in the mind or chitta. The yogi becomes Ishwara, being the creator and destroyer.

अस्तु वा मास्तु वा मुक्तिरत्रैवाखण्डितं सुखम् ।
लयोद्भवमिदं सौख्यं राजयोगादवाप्यते ॥ 78 ॥

Whether there is liberation or not, nevertheless there is pleasure. The pleasure arising from laya is derived from raja yoga.

Here, 'element' does not mean the tattwas of earth, water, fire, air or ether, nor the tattwas of manas, Shiva or Shakti. It is the experience of 'Thatness', the experience of atma, where the vrittis or mental modifications are nullified. Then 'the yogi becomes Ishwara'. Ishwara is another name for the totality of cosmic unmanifest Shakti, the total creative principle of the highest consciousness; the sattwic state of Shakti. It is the combination of Brahma, Vishnu and Maheshwara.

Experience of this state is supreme *anandam*, the highest bliss. However, we are told it is not the final liberation. Liberation can only occur when one's consciousness has been absorbed back into the mahabindu. Ishwara is a state of evolution after the mahabindu. Ishwara is the cosmic causal body. Hiranyagarbha is the cosmic subtle body. Few people attain the final state of jivanmukti whether through nada anusandhana or any form of yoga; but do not be discouraged because there is nevertheless abiding and indwelling pleasure inherent in this state. That pleasure is not derived from the senses but from the experience of ongoing absorption in the expanded unified cosmic mind which accompanies both creation and dissolution within itself. This is the pleasure derived from raja yoga. At the same time, one should not be satisfied only with this, but should continue striving for mahasamadhi, nirvana, kaivalya, moksha.

राजयोगमजानंत: केवलं हठकर्मिण: ।
एतानभ्यासिनो मन्ये प्रयासफलवर्जितान् ॥ 79 ॥

There are practitioners of hatha yoga who do not have the knowledge of raja yoga. I consider them as mere practitioners because they derive no fruits for their efforts.

Those people who practise hatha yoga merely as a form of bodily beautification and exercise are not using this science with the correct intention, and they therefore fail to progress to the path of raja yoga. They fail to gain the indwelling pleasure which unified consciousness bestows. The real purpose of hatha yoga is to open the gate to self-realization. A practitioner has to know its subtle influence on the nadis, prana and mind. He should at least know intellectually about shoonya, kundalini, samadhi etc.

The sloka states that no fruits are obtained if these things are not known. However, it is not completely correct. Even if the disciplines of hatha yoga are perfected without faith or belief in spiritual life, one's whole being is nevertheless affected by the practices. One becomes open to the greater experiences even if these are not sought after directly. Even if it is practised for good health, the higher brain centres are activated. The side effect of creating a harmonious psycho-physiological balance is definitely a worthwhile fruit.

Perhaps from the point of view of modern medical science, which is researching hatha yoga as a system of vitality and rejuvenation, this fruit is sufficient and enough. In fact, it is like diving for a pearl and bringing the whole oyster to the surface, opening the shell and then discarding the pearl of perfection for the sake of the lining which is only mother-of-pearl.

उन्मन्यवाप्तये शीघ्रं भ्रूध्यानं मम संमतम् ।
राजयोगपदं प्राप्तुं सुखोपायोऽल्पचेतसाम् ।
सद्य: प्रत्ययसंधायी जायते नादजो लय: ॥ 80 ॥

In my opinion, contemplation on the eyebrow centre leads to a mindless state immediately. It is a suitable method even for those with less intellect to attain the state of raja yoga. The laya attained through nada gives immediate experience.

Contemplation on the eyebrow centre refers to shambhavi mudra. It can be done with the eyes open or closed. Even simple concentration on ajna chakra itself is effective. It requires no intellectual capacity or brainpower to do this, only sincere application of the practice.

When the mind is absorbed in the point of concentration, the eyes spontaneously turn upwards. Samadhi develops thus. Shambhavi mudra stimulates ajna chakra in the brain directly behind the mid eyebrow point. Through this, mind is absorbed and the nada perceived.

Spiritual life and experiences are independent of academic ability and intellectual or mundane knowledge. Spiritual knowledge, power and experience exist on a different plane altogether. Even a debauchee can perceive the nada and dwell in the greater experience. Anyone who hears it should listen intently, excluding other experiences and thoughts so that the mundane state of consciousness is illumined.

We have to realize that when Swatmarama says that in his opinion, eyebrow centre gazing leads immediately to mindlessness, he is actually narrating from his own experience. Those who have become highly established in spiritual consciousness through hatha yoga and raja yoga, gain control of the mind and are able to transcend its modifications and enter into the samadhi states at will.

577

नादानुसंधानसमाधिभाजां योगीश्चराणां हृदि वर्धमानम् ।
आनन्दमेकं वचसामगम्यं जानाति तं श्रीगुरुनाथ एक: ॥ 81 ॥

There is plenitude of bliss in the hearts of the great yogis who remain in samadhi through nada anusandhana or exploration of nada, which is unequalled and beyond any description, known by the one and only Gurunath.

कर्णौ पिधाय हस्ताभ्यां यं शृणोति ध्वनिं मुनि: ।
तत्र चित्तं स्थिरीकुर्याद्यावत् स्थिरपदं व्रजेत् ॥ 82 ॥

Having closed the ears with the hands, the muni should listen to the inner sound with the mind steady on that, then the state of stillness is achieved.

अभ्यस्यमानो नादोऽयं बाह्यमावृणुते ध्वनिम् ।
पक्षाद्विक्षेपमखिलं जित्वा योगी सुखी भवेत् ॥ 83 ॥

Through sustained listening to the nada, awareness of the external sound diminishes. Thus, the yogi overcomes mental turbulence within fifteen days and feels the pleasure.

श्रूयते प्रथमाभ्यासे नादो नानाविधा महान् ।
ततोऽभ्यासे वर्धमाने श्रूयते सूक्ष्मसूक्ष्मक: ॥ 84 ॥

When he first begins to hear sounds during practice, there are various prominent nadas but with prolonged practice the subtlest of subtleties becomes audible.

When practising shanmukhi mudra and perceiving the inner sound, you must listen to it in such a way as if listening for another sound within or beyond that sound. Keep on searching for finer and subtler sounds. The four stages of vaikhari, etc., are not different from kundalini shakti. Vaikhari sound in the form of the mantra captivates the gross mind and moves the consciousness beyond the *swayambhulingam* or 'gross physical body'. In the form of madhyama shabda, in the heart, consciousness is awakened through *banalingam* or 'the subtle body'. Kundalini shakti in the form of pashyanti nada captivates the causal body or *itaralingam*. It then proceeds to parabindu and para nada.

In the initial stage of practice, there is awareness of the external sounds and movements but eventually this awareness drops away and only the nada remains. Just as in the dream state the external sounds and movements are not perceived, so is the mind withdrawn while consciously listening to nada. When the mind is absorbed in nada there are no vrittis. Mind is still like a crystal clear pool of water. The reflection seen inside is the nada.

Swatmarama asserts that once the nada is perceived, then sustained listening for fifteen days will pacify the mind and give the pleasure of perfect absorption. This is for the individual to verify.

Sound exists in the form of vibrations which are of varying frequencies. In fact, the brain is constantly emitting hundreds of vibrations every second. The more powerful your consciousness is, the greater the vibrations emanating from your brain will be. These vibrations are of varying intensity and frequency according to the individual. Just as there are spectra of electromagnetic and radio waves, etc., similarly there is a whole range of subtle sound waves which travel beyond the brain and which can be realized within the brain itself.

In the tradition of tantra, knowledge of the structure and combination of gross and subtle sounds is known as *mantra shastra*, and is considered to be very important. In fact, it has been said many times that without mantra there is no tantra. According to both the Vedas and the Bible, the seed out of which the gross manifestation of the material universe is emerging is a matrix of eternal sound.

Mantra exists as energy in the form of gross and subtle sounds. Different dimensions of nada have been perceived and passed on by the great yogis, rishis and munis in the

579

form of mantras. Mantras can bring about every kind of outcome and result. Inner knowledge of mantra is known as *mantra siddhi,* which confers the power to modify and influence the process of creation and destruction in the material world from the causal dimension.

However, it must be remembered that manifestation of, and attachment to, such psychic powers or siddhis is a major barrier to spiritual realization. Mantra is to be utilized for spiritual evolution and must be received from a guru. In the practice of nada yoga, these inner sounds are used as a pathway to pratyahara, dharana, dhyana and samadhi.

आदौ जलधिजीमूतभेरीझझ्रसंभवाः ।
मध्ये मर्दलशंखोत्था घंटकाहलजास्तथा ॥ ८५ ॥

The first fruits are the sounds of the ocean, then clouds, the kettledrum and jharjhara drum. In the middle stage the shankha (conch), gong and horn.

अन्ते तु किंकिणीवंशवीणाभ्रमरनिःस्वनाः ।
इति नानाविधा नादाः श्रूयन्ते देहमध्यगाः ॥ ८६ ॥

Now, reaching the inner point of conclusion, are the tinkling of bells, flute, vina and humming of bees. Thus, the various nadas are produced and heard from the middle of the body.

महति श्रूयमाणेऽपि मेघभेर्यादिके ध्वनौ ।
तत्र सूक्ष्मात् सूक्ष्मतरं नादमेव परामृशेत् ॥ ८७ ॥

Even when the sounds of clouds and the kettledrum are heard, attention should be kept on even subtler nada.

घनमुत्सृज्य वा सूक्ष्मे सूक्ष्ममुत्सृज्य वा घने ।
रममाणमपि क्षिप्तं मनो नान्यत्र चालयेत् ॥ ८८ ॥

Though the attention may go from the deep to the subtle or subtle to deep, the mind should not move to various things other than the sound.

यत्रकुत्रापि वा नादे लगति प्रथमं मनः ।
तत्रैव सुस्थिरीभूय तेन सार्धं विलीयते ॥ ८९ ॥

Whatever nada the mind initially adheres to, it becomes perfectly still in that and dissolves with it.

मकरन्दं पिबन्भृंगो गन्धं नापेक्षते यथा ।
नादासक्तं तथा चित्तं विषयान्नहि कांक्षते ॥ ९० ॥

Just as a bee drinking honey is unconcerned about the fragrance, so the mind engaged in nada is not craving for sensual objects.

In nada yoga various frequencies of sound are perceived. When you utter a word verbally, its frequency is within the limited range of your auditory capacity, and so your ears can hear it. However, when you hear a sound in the depth of meditation its frequencies are far higher and more rapid than those of external, audible sound. In fact, in scientific investigations of mental telepathy between two people it became evident that the higher the frequency of sound, the lower the audible volume; the greater the volume of sound, the lesser the frequency.

When you are talking to someone, the volume of sound increases and therefore it has a lower frequency. However, if you can increase the momentum of frequency, either by mechanical, mental or psychological devices, then sound travels through a different field altogether and can be heard at a greater distance.

Various energy fields are known to modern science: electromagnetic fields, radioactive fields, etc. If the chakras can be influenced so that the sound gains a certain momentum of frequency, it can also travel through what are called psychic fields.

In the symbolism of each chakra there is a bija mantra in the centre: *Lam, Vam, Ram, Yam, Ham, Om*. This means that every chakra has a confluent sound base. Just as the body is composed of bone, marrow, blood, flesh, muscles, mucus, etc., similarly a chakra is constituted of sound, symbol and light. Hence, when sound attains a certain momentum of frequency, it affects the chakras. It is therefore a fact that nada yoga is also an instrument in the awakening of kundalini.

When kundalini rises, the sounds are deep, monotone vibrations, like waves pounding on the shore, the clap of thunder and beating of various types of base drums. Or one might describe the sound and sensation as a jet plane or rocket taking off. This occurs in the arambha and ghata stages.

In the middle stage, parichaya, higher frequencies are experienced, but these are still loud and penetrating, those which grip the body like a gong or horn. The sounds heard might be described as a bassoon or organ, depending on one's cultural background and the type of sounds one has previously experienced.

In the last stage of consummation or nishpatti, melodious high pitched and reverberating sounds occur, something like a piano, harp or harpsichord. The *Hatharatnavali* explains: "In the beginning of the practice, loud and voluminous sounds of various types are heard. As the practice progresses, sharper and subtler sounds are heard."

In his book, *Chitshakti Vilas*, Swami Muktananda Parama-hamsa describes different kinds of nadas he experienced which not only resembled the ocean, but also thunder, drums, conch, bells, buzzing of insects: "the murmur of a brook, the rattle of a fast moving train, the drone of an aeroplane, the crackle of a funeral pyre, full-throated singing of the divine name by large groups of devotees, the cries of peacocks and songs of cuckoos". He states that while hearing the nada his mind would converge upon its source. He witnessed the centre which emits divine sparks when elevated by nada and all his senses were drawn towards it.

मनोमत्तगजेंद्रस्य विषयोद्यानचारिण: ।
समर्थोऽयं नियमने निनादनिशितांकुश: ॥ 91 ॥

By the sharp goad of nada, the mind, which is like a furious elephant roaming in the garden of the senses, is controlled.

बद्धं तु नादबंधेन मन: संत्यक्तचापलम् ।
प्रयाति सुतरां स्थैर्यं छिन्नपक्ष: खगो यथा ॥ 92 ॥

When the mind ceases to be fickle and is united by fixing it in nada, it becomes immobile like a wingless bird.

सर्वचिंतां परित्यज्य सावधानेन चेतसा ।
नाद एवानुसंधेयो योगसाम्राज्यमिच्छता ॥ 93 ॥

One who desires complete dominion of yoga should thus explore the nada with an attentive mind and abandon all thoughts.

Just as audible sound frequencies influence the brain, mind and body, the subtle frequencies affect their underlying layers. When you listen to music it arouses different emotions and states of mind, and affects different areas and centres of the body. In fact, music therapy for sick and disturbed people should not be overlooked. Sound is the most powerful tool in pacifying the restless mind. Sound exerts an influence upon the entire brain, body and mind of an individual who has come into manifestation because both are an aspect of Shakti. In fact, this Shakti is the matrix which underlies this entire phenomenal world.

The mind, under the sway of the senses, is likened to a raging elephant confined within a small garden. Nada, as the vehicle of Shakti, is then likened to a goad, because it draws and prods it towards internal absorption and union with its source. Just as music can calm and relax the mind, making one completely forget problems and worries, so absorption in the subtle nada brings forgetfulness of the external world.

नादोऽन्तरंगसारंगबंधने वागुरायते ।
अन्तरंगकुरंगस्य वधे व्याधायतेऽपि च ॥ 94 ॥

*Nada is like the net which snares the deer (mind) inside. It is also
like the hunter who slays the deer (mind) inside.*

अंतरंगस्य यमिनो वाजिन: परिघायते ।
नादोपास्तिरतो नित्यमवधार्या हि योगिना ॥ 95 ॥

*It is like the bolt locking a horse inside, for one who is self-controlled.
The yogi must therefore meditate regularly upon the nada.*

बद्धं विमुक्तचांचल्यं नादगंधकजारणात् ।
मन:पारदमाप्नोति निरालंबाख्यखेऽटनम् ॥ 96 ॥

*Just as liquid mercury is solidified by sulphur, so mind is bound by
nada and freed from restlessness. Then one moves unsupported in
void.*

नादश्रवणत: क्षिप्रमंतरंगभुजंगम: ।
विस्मृत्य सर्वमेकाग्र: कुत्रचिन्नहि धावति ॥ 97 ॥

*Hearing the nada, mind, which is like a serpent within, becomes
captivated and oblivious to all else, not moving anywhere else.*

काष्ठे प्रवर्तितो वह्नि: काष्ठेन सह शाम्यति ।
नादे प्रवर्तितं चित्तं नादेन सह लीयते ॥ 98 ॥

*As fire burns wood and both subside together, so the mind which
moves with nada is absorbed in it.*

घंटादिनादसक्तस्तब्धांत:करणहरिणस्य ।
प्रहरणमपि सुकरं शरसंधानप्रवीणश्चेत् ॥ 99 ॥

*Just as a deer attracted by the sound of bells is easily killed by an expert
archer, so is the mind silenced by an adept in nada yoga.*

Whatever process is adopted to attain a state of higher consciousness, it has to be one which can totally absorb and preoccupy the mind. Identification with the gross aspect of existence has to be forgotten or transcended for a period of time. Expansion of mundane consciousness has to be the motivation for the practice. Otherwise it is like expecting to fly to the moon with the whole contents of your house. Similarly, you cannot expect to attain higher states of consciousness with the gross mind. Some things have to be left behind on your journey, such as empirical awareness.

Conscious mind is experienced when the mind is attracted to external objects which appear separate from yourself or your ego. That mind is in a continuous state of hypnosis. It is hypnotized by the external objects. This hypnosis has to become an internal process so that the mind is now hypnotized by the internal object and oblivious to the mundane external reality. When there is total concentration upon the internal object then there is absorption of mind.

The nada heard in meditation easily captivates the mind. Once perceived, it exerts a magnetic force upon the functioning mind. At one time Swami Muktananda was unable to sleep for fourteen consecutive nights because the experience of nada and sleep are incompatible. His body would respond with a mildly painful quiver to whatever variety of nada he heard. "During this phase of heavenly music a yogi acquires the art of dancing." He would even hear the nada while working, moving, eating, and when he felt angry the nada became intensive.

Some methods of yoga advise renunciation of the material world to detach the mind from its externalizing tendency. However, hatha yoga approaches from a different point of view. Mind is energy. The energy appears as sound. If the consciousness can become aware of that sound it will realize its own nature because ultimately the two forces cannot be kept separate from each other.

586

अनाहतस्य शब्दस्य ध्वनिर्यं उपलभ्यते ।
ध्वनेरन्तर्गतं ज्ञेयं ज्ञेयस्यांतर्गतं मन: ।
मनस्तत्र लयं याति तद्विष्णो: परमं पदम् ॥ 100 ॥

*One hears the sound of the unstruck resonance (anahata shabda);
the quintessence of that sound is the (supreme) object (consciousness).
The mind becomes one with that object of knowledge and it dissolves
therein. That is the supreme state of Vishnu (sthiti).*

When you are concentrating there is awareness of the object,
awareness of the process of concentration and awareness of
yourself who is concentrating. When both the awareness that
there is nada and the sound of the nada dissolve into the
vibration of the nada, then nada alone exists.

"When, through constant practice, one's concentration
becomes objectless, then being divested of merits and
demerits, one attains the state of complete dissolution in the
Absolute through the dissolution of the object of concentration, but not before then." (*Avadhoota Gita*, 2:16)

Some say Vishnu is the highest state and everything
manifests from him. Even Brahma (the Creator) manifested
from his navel. Others maintain Shiva or Brahman as
the origin, with the three shaktis and the trinity having
originated from there.

Nada is a state of creative movement and is therefore not
the final state of absolute dissolution, or pralaya. According
to Kashmir Shaivism, nada is the continuum of the creative
descent. When it condenses into a dynamic point it is bindu.
From these two (nada and bindu) manifestation arises, which
are beyond the differentiation of time, space, subject and
object. When the two poles become one then nada is heard.

The *Avadhoota Gita* further states: "He attains to the
supreme, eternal Self, from whose essence the universe of
animate and inanimate objects is born, in whom it rests, and
in whom it dissolves; even as foam and bubbles are born of
the transformation of water." (2:34)

तावदाकाशसंकल्पो यावच्छब्द: प्रवर्तते ।
नि:शब्दं तत्परं ब्रह्म परमात्मेति गीयते ॥ 101 ॥

The conception of akasha (the substratum of sound) exists as long as the sound is heard. The soundless, which is the supreme reality, is called the supreme atma.

यत्किंचिन्नादरूपेण श्रूयते शक्तिरेव सा ।
यस्तत्त्वांतो निराकार: स एव परमेश्वर: ॥ 102 ॥

Whatever is heard of the nature of the mystical nada is indeed Shakti. That in which all the elements (panchatattwa) find dissolution, that is the formless being, the supreme lord (Parameshwara).

इति नादानुसंधानम्

Thus ends the enquiry into nada.

Each of the five elements (tattwas or mahabhutas) has a particular quality. Sound is the quality of akasha tattwa, the finest and subtlest of the five elements. As long as there is consciousness of the existence of sound or even that you are sound itself, dissolution into the highest state has not yet been attained.

In atma there is no 'is' or 'is not'. It cannot be said that there is or is not sound. We think now that we are not in atma. We are, but awareness of that state is not there. It is something like an old man saying that he was never a child just because he cannot remember it. Individual existence, like waves on the ocean, seems to be separate but nevertheless is part of the whole.

There are two schools of Advaita thought. One holds that there is only consciousness and that Shakti exists only as *maya*, illusion. *Chit*, the Supreme reality (Brahman or Atma), is without action or change, but is pure jnana or knowledge, *prakasha*. Therefore, the universe is *mithya* or 'unreal'.

However, the other school maintains that chit is both the consciousness and the creative potential. The display of the universe is the display of the creative principle. Therefore creation is real. Whichever may be true, in the final state of atma, there is completeness.

Atma is known according to its attributes, as *satchidananda*: existence-consciousness-bliss. The *Drigdrishya-viveka* explains: "The attributes of existence, consciousness and bliss are equally present in the ether, air, fire, water and earth elements, as well as in gods, animals and men, etc. Only names and forms make one differ from the other. I am Existence, Consciousness, Bliss, unattached, self-illumined, and free from duality. This is known as savikalpa samadhi, associated with sound (object)." (21–25)

Supraconsciousness or atma is the state where consciousness pervades even the potential force of Shakti. In that state, Shakti can be said to be the silent bystander. In creation Shakti is active, and consciousness can be said to be the silent bystander. Therefore, 'Existence-Consciousness-Bliss' is present even in the tattwas. In dissolution, the tattwas subside into consciousness.

"He attains the supreme, eternal Self who is devoid of manifoldness, oneness, many and oneness and otherness; who is devoid of minuteness, length and largeness and nothingness; who is devoid of knowledge and knowableness and sameness." (*Avadhoota Gita* 2:39)

सर्वे हठलयोपाया राजयोगस्य सिद्धये ।
राजयोगसमारूढ: पुरुष: कालवंचक: ॥ 103 ॥

All the processes of hatha and laya yoga are but the means to attain raja yoga (samadhi). One who attains raja yoga is victorious over time (death).

तत्त्वं बीजं हठ: क्षेत्रमौदासीन्यं जलं त्रिभि: ।
उन्मनी कल्पलतिका सद्य एव प्रवर्तते ॥ 104 ॥

Tattwa is the seed, hatha is the soil, total desirelessness (vairagya) is the water. By these three the kalpa vriksha (wish-fulfilling tree) which is the unmani avastha (mindless state) immediately sprouts forth.

Raja yoga means realization of, or being, Shiva, Brahman, Atma, the Self, cosmic consciousness. Hatha yoga is the same experience but from the reflection on the primordial Shakti, i.e. before nirvana samadhi. In the highest state of raja yoga there is no reflection in Shakti; Shiva and Shakti are in equanimity. Hatha yoga is the means to experience this; shakti or tattwa is the tool.

According to the sloka, through hatha yoga and absorption of mind and prana, i.e. laya, unmani avastha is attained. *Unmani* is the condition when finite mind ceases to function. *Avastha* is a state or condition achieved through effort but it is impermanent. It means that hatha yoga will arouse the condition of unmani but until it becomes an established condition or natural state, *sthiti*, you will remain at the level of hatha yoga and not attain raja yoga. Hatha yoga culminates in the union of ida, pingala and sushumna in ajna chakra, whereas raja yoga culminates beyond this, when the kundalini reaches sahasrara chakra.

The Supreme is neither state, experience nor condition. There are really no words to express it exactly as it goes beyond all thought categories, although the Upanishads and various other scriptures have attempted to put it into words. It is just 'beingness'.

In sloka 104 Swatmarama refers to the *kalpa vriksha* which is the 'wish fulfilling tree'. This is located in the subtle body just below the pericarp of anahata chakra, the heart centre. Kalpa vriksha is inside a red, upturned, eight petalled lotus, and is said to be one of the celestial trees in Indra's heaven.

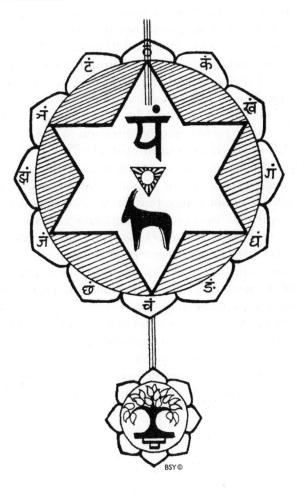

When anahata chakra is awakened, one's desires, however big or small, are fulfilled. This is also the case when the chakra in which kalpa vriksha grows is awakened. Some people call this psychic power. You may even have experienced this yourself to a small degree. Sometimes you wish something and within a short while or even five years later, it happens. In fact, there have been a few people who, developing this capacity, can manifest an object at will.

There is a story about a yogi who was practising his sadhana in the jungle and awakened his anahata chakra. One day he was sitting to meditate and thought: "What if a tiger should come and eat me?" At that instant a tiger appeared from behind the trees and did exactly as he had thought. It ate him. This is just to explain the necessity of mental purity in the path of spiritual life. The powers developed are intended for growth but the direction in which they are channelled depends on your individual will.

Kalpa vriksha has one excelling quality, that it not only grants whatever is asked of it, but it also bestows moksha. In actuality it is not a tree but the symbol of a particular state of spiritual evolution. In anahata chakra, directly above, is the symbol of the *akhand jyoti*, the 'eternal flame', which symbolizes the existence of jivatma, and the state of consciousness unperturbed by the external world. At this level of consciousness, vairagya becomes spontaneous, and the mind is in perfect equanimity.

Therefore, Swatmarama states that when one reaches this level of consciousness, i.e. if kundalini penetrates anahata, one attains the unmani avastha. However, it should be remembered that it is a state achieved by effort and one will have to endeavour further to attain a higher state.

सदा नादानुसंधानात्क्षीयंते पापसंचया: ।
निरंजने विलीयेते निश्चितं चित्तमारुतौ ॥ 105 ॥

'Bad karma' (sin) is destroyed by constant concentration on nada.
The finite mind and prana dissolve into the stainless (niranjana).

शंखदुंदुभिनादं च न शृणोति कदाचन ।
काष्ठवज्जायते देह उन्मन्यावस्थया ध्रुवम् ॥ 106 ॥

The body becomes like a log of wood in the unmani avastha and
not even the sound of the conch or dundhubhi (drum) is perceived
by the yogi.

सर्वावस्थाविनिर्मुक्त: सर्वचिंताविवर्जित: ।
मृतवत्तिष्ठते योगी स मुक्तो नात्र संशय: ॥ 107 ॥

The yogi who has gone beyond all the states (of consciousness), who
is freed of thought, who appears dead (impervious to stimulus) is
liberated without doubt.

खाद्यते न च कालेन बाध्यते न च कर्मणा ।
साध्यते न स केनापि योगी युक्त: समाधिना: ॥ 108 ॥

In samadhi a yogi is neither consumed by the processes of time
(death) nor is he affected by action (karma) nor affected by any
influence.

न गन्धं न रसं रूपं न च स्पर्शं न नि:स्वनम् ।
नात्मानं न परं वेत्ति योगी युक्त: समाधिना ॥ 109 ॥

In samadhi a yogi knows neither smell, taste, form, touch or sound
(tanmatras); he does not cognize his self (ego) nor that of others.

चित्तं न सुप्तं नोजाग्रत्स्मृतिविस्मृतिवर्जितम् ।
न चास्तमेति नोदेति यस्यासौ मुक्त एव स: ॥ 110 ॥

One whose mind is neither asleep nor awake, (whose mind) is devoid of memory and forgetfulness, neither oblivious nor active, is indeed liberated.

न विजानाति शीतोष्णं न दु:खं न सुखं तथा ।
न मानं नापमानं च योगी युक्त: समाधिना ॥ 111 ॥

In samadhi a yogi is unaware of (distinctions of) heat and cold, pain and pleasure, honour and dishonour.

स्वस्थो जाग्रदवस्थायां सुप्तवद्योऽवतिष्ठते ।
नि:श्वासोच्छ्वासहीनश्च निश्चितं मुक्त एव स: ॥ 112 ॥

He who seems asleep in the waking state, who is without breathing yet is perfectly healthy, is verily liberated.

In the state of samadhi there is total introversion of sense perception and cessation of mental processes until consciousness alone remains. The first sense which withdraws is smell, then taste, sight, feeling, sound and lastly ego. This corresponds to the ascent of shakti from mooladhara chakra through swadhisthana, manipura, anahata, vishuddhi and ajna to reside in sahasrara where consciousness of consciousness alone remains. That state of consciousness is no longer individual awareness but what is called universal or cosmic awareness.

All individual aspects are withdrawn at that time. Every aspect of the conscious, subconscious and unconscious realms become merged within the collective existence and non-existence. There is no fear, death, time, space, sleep, hunger, thirst, emotion, karma, anything. It is everything and nothing.

When you transcend the body in your sadhana and when matter is also transcended, the object within you is illuminated. Duality ceases to exist. The experience alone remains. That is nirvana or enlightenment.

There are two realities within us – time and space, which are the categories of the mind. As long as they are apart, there is external awareness. When you bring time and space together, there is a moment when they unite with each other. The moment there is union between time and space, individuality is lost, awareness of the limited 'I' diminishes and the greater experience dawns. It may be the experience of light. It may be divinity. It may be the experience of truth. It may be the experience of the experience of eternity. During the instant of this experience there is no duality of experience whatsoever. There is no notion that 'I am experiencing'.

Now there is duality. However, when you go inside yourself, duality becomes feeble. There is duality; 'I am experiencing imagination, I am experiencing feeling, I am experiencing a vision', but it becomes very feeble. It is no longer very significant.

As you go on purifying the ego, i.e. the notion of duality, the ego awareness becomes increasingly faint and dim until there is a very improbable moment in our life that can come. It does not come in the life of every individual. That is a rare moment when the ego is completely fused and lost. At that time there is only experience and not the experiencer of the experience. Such an experience is known as homogeneous experience or absolute experience. It has various names, some say transcendental experience, or nirvikalpa samadhi, some call it nirvana, emancipation or salvation, moksha; some call it advaita anubhuti, the non-dual experience. From time to time different people have given it different names and in tantra it is called darshan.

This experience is an experience which every great man has had. Every great yogi has had this experience. Without this you cannot be a yogi. One who does not hold time in one hand and space in the other and then has the experience of putting them together in one pocket cannot be a yogi.

Only when the duality of time and space is non-existent can you have darshan of the true Self. *Darshan* means to see, but not with the eyes. When the eyes are shut, and the senses have closed, the mind has retired and the ego has been permanently locked away, at that time there is a vision which is more real than this. At that time you are face to face with what you call 'God'. You are face to face with what you call your guru.

In India, for thousands of years the great ones have taught that by having darshan of that inner being there is nothing in this world that you need any more, because the darshan is the wealth of all wealth. It is not for a monkey, or a donkey or a dog to have darshan. It is only man who has got the evolution of inner vision; it is for him alone.

Darshan means jumping out of the mind, kicking off matter. There is no fire but the fire is there. There is no external light but still you see light. There is nobody making a sound, but still you hear the sound. There is no substance for life, but still one is alive. What does it mean? It means enlightenment. It means illumination. It means nirvana. It has nothing to do with the body, mind, senses or emotions.

The totality of existence is divided into two external realities. One is matter, the other is consciousness. Tantra calls them Shiva and Shakti. The Samkhya system of philosophy calls them purusha and prakriti. Scientists have begun to say matter and energy. Matter is the lower empirical substance and consciousness is the higher and transcendental substance. In our existence both are interacting. You have to withdraw yourself from prakriti and become aware of purusha, consciousness. That is called nirvana. That is the definition of tantra, hatha yoga and raja yoga.

In sloka 108 it is stated that there is no action or karma which affects one who has had samadhi, i.e. liberation or moksha. *Karma* has two meanings: 'cause and effect' is one meaning, the other is 'action'. After nirvikalpa or nirvana samadhi when the yogi returns to the mundane state he does it as a *jivanmukta* or 'liberated soul'. Whatever he does will bear no effect on his individual consciousness in relation to spiritual evolution and consciousness.

There are two broad classifications of karma or action; sakam karma and nishkama karma. These can be further classified into nityakarma, naimittika karma and kamya karma.

For example, you have active desires or ichchha and you also have latent desires or vasana. You have samskaras or impressions which are the cause of vasana. Whether you want to or not you carry them with you. What can you do? Even if you do not like it, you will be compelled to do action. That is what Lord Krishna told Arjuna in the battle of the Mahabharata at Kurukshetra – even if you do not like it, you will have to fight. Because the desire (ichchha), latent desires (vasana) and impressions (samskara) all compel you to do action, even if you want to renounce karma or action, you cannot renounce it. Your nature is like that.

Everybody has some sort of nityakarma. However, nityakarma does not really have any deep bearing on one's existence. It does not depend on your caste or social upbringing. Getting up in the morning, etc., is nityakarma. If these are properly organized they can give you good health, but they do not make any samskaras or karmas (cause and effect).

Karma or action which you do as an obligation, for example, taking part in marriage or funeral ceremonies etc., is naimittika karma. You have to participate whether you like it or not. These nityakarma and naimittika karmas do not go too deeply into the realm of karma (cause and effect).

Only the kamya karma has a great bearing on man's mind, his personality and life. Kamya karma is also said to be of different types according to one's nature. Sattwic people have their own motives, rajasic people also have motives, tamasic people also have motives. Therefore, kamya karma can be classified into these three types: tamasic, rajasic and sattwic kamya karma. A jivanmukta is beyond this type of karma.

If you desire to have a big institution, or orphanage or a hospital, it is kamya or desire; that is a motive, but it is sattwic. If you want a lot of money, cars, buildings, etc., it is also kamya but it is rajasic. If you want to kill, harm, torture or harass somebody, that is also kamya but it is tamasic kamya karma. So, according to tamas, rajas and sattwa the kamya karmas have a different impact on life, personality and mind.

To be nishkama or totally devoid of identification with desire is extremely difficult unless you are a jivanmukta, because without desire you are not going to be motivated to work or to do anything. However, if you go very, very deeply into it, you will find that this nishkama karma automatically comes when you change the quality of mind. Supposing that you are working in a government department, and you want things to be done there in a particular way. The desire is there, but its quality is different. It is nishkama because the ego is not involved there. Just because you desire to do something does not mean you are going to create karma (cause and effect). You have to avoid association of ahamkara, abhimana or ego with the desire, i.e. selfless desire. Nishkama does not mean desirelessness. Nishkama only means you detach your ego. The method of ego detachment comes through samadhi.

Letter from Swami Sivananda

8th November 1943

Beloved aspirants,

Samadhi is blissful union with the Supreme Self. It leads to the direct intuitive realization of the infinite.
It is an inner divine experience which is beyond the reach of speech and mind.
You will have to realize this yourself through self-meditation. The senses, the mind, and the intellect cease functioning. There is neither time nor causation here.

May you rest in samadhi.

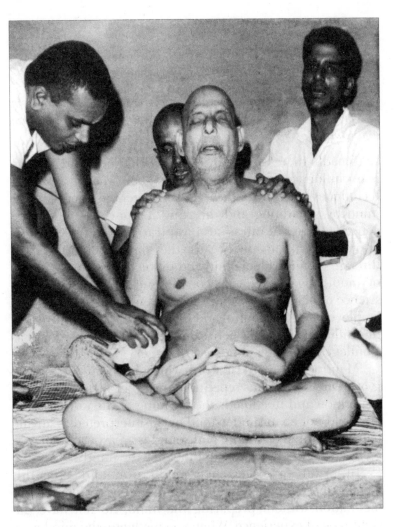

*Swami Sivananda Maharaj of Rishikesh
in mahasamadhi*

अवध्यः सर्वशस्त्राणामशक्यः सर्वदेहिनाम् ।
अग्राह्यो मंत्रयंत्राणां योगी युक्तः समाधिना ॥ 113 ॥

*In samadhi, a yogi is invulnerable to any weapon, unassailable by
any person, unsubjected to another's control by the use of mantras
and yantras.*

In samadhi there is no individual consciousness and so there
is no influence which can affect it. Mantra and yantra are
techniques of tantra, which awaken potential energy in the
mind by separating and directing it from the underlying
consciousness. Mantras and yantras become ineffectual
upon a yogi in samadhi because they direct and focus power
through the individual mind and prana, and are not capable
of modifying the eternal consciousness. Even where the
science of mantra and yantra has degenerated and has been
employed to exert control and influence upon an individual,
this influence is futile where samadhi has supervened, just as
a bullet cannot hit a non-existent target.

Mantra is a Sanskrit word which is composed of two
roots. One root means repetition, the other means freedom.
Repetition and freedom is the meaning of the word *mantra*.
It should not be misunderstood or misinterpreted as 'divine
name'. Mantra is a sound, and sound is an aspect of energy,
a powerful energy which can influence the mind.

In order to experience meditation and samadhi,
you need a certain quality of mind. Those who practise
meditation without preparing the mind, do not have the
right type of experience. When you meditate, the mind goes
into the subconscious and unconscious plane and there it
visualizes its own nature and its own contents. Therefore,
before the practices of concentration, you should clean the
mind. The sounds of specific mantras make the mind clean
of its impurities and impressions.

In the human mind there are millions and billions and
trillions of impressions embedded. You have a great past

hovering in your mind; not only of this incarnation, but also belonging to other incarnations. Concentration is necessary, but to first make the mind lighter there is the practice of mantra. Therefore, when you practise mantra, you should not try to concentrate.

Mantra does not mean concentration, and with mantra repetition concentration is unnecessary. If you can make your consciousness clean, concentration becomes spontaneous. When you practise your mantra, you should let your mind flow, because it is filled with lots of suppressions and agonies. Suppressing the tendencies of mind hinders spiritual experience. When you take the mantra and practise it you should just repeat it either verbally or mentally, and if you experience turbulence in the mind or dissipation in the mind, let them be. You should let them be and be bold enough to face yourself.

You must face your own frustrations, your own ambitions, your own passions and everything else that is in the mind. For that purpose you must completely detach yourself from the wanderings of the mind. Just as you look at the television, in the same way you should look at the 'television of your mind'.

Mantra should be practised in the way taught by your guru. There are thousands of sounds in the universe, but the universal sound is *Om*. *Om* represents time, space, object and transcendence. Apart from *Om*, there are many hundreds of thousands of other sounds existing at high frequencies which you cannot hear now. Some people who raise the frequency of their minds can hear these sounds which are known as mantras.

There are many types of mantras, but they are generally classified into three according to their effects: mantras which have gross or mundane effects, mantras which have subtle effects and mantras which have spiritual effects. This is the very general classification known.

There are also two other kinds of mantras. One is known as *bija*, meaning 'seed', and the other is a combination of many sounds. These are combinations of various sound frequencies. Every sound has a frequency and no two sounds have exactly the same frequency. *Ah* is one sound, *aah* is another and *ka* is another. Of course, they have a different pronunciation but they also have a different frequency. Each sound is different in colour from another sound. No two sounds have the same colour.

Three or four sounds of low frequency, if properly combined, can attain high frequency and therefore you will find many mantras with more than one syllable. There are certain sounds which, if combined, attain greater power. *Om* is monosyllabic, but other mantras are not. Besides *Om* only bija mantras are monosyllabic, like *Kleem, Aim, Hreem, Shreem*. However, these monosyllabic mantras are intended to purify the mind at a greater speed. So, when mantra is referred to it means the sound energy in the universe.

There are many kinds of energies: electrical, nuclear, etc. Similarly, sound is also energy which can be transmitted through space. A mantra is so powerful that it can create an effect within you and it can also create an effect in the objects of the universe.

When you receive the mantra from your guru, you are actually receiving a portion of energy from him in the seed potential form. When you practise the mantra, if it does not give you concentration it does not matter, because in the initial stage the mantra creates more explosions in the mind, but then concentration will come by itself.

Mantra is the very basis of yoga, tantra and spiritual life. Mantra can give contentment and mantra can influence your character and personality. Mantra can bring about communication between individuals on the astral plane; and mantra can influence the brain, body, subconscious and unconscious realms. *Yantra* is the form of mantra; mantra is the sound and yantra is the form of that sound. It is a precisely formulated geometrical figure through which the mantra shakti operates. Mantra and yantra, however, cannot influence the consciousness in the state of samadhi or turiya, that is the fourth dimension.

यावन्नैव प्रविशति चरन्मारुतो मध्यमार्गे
यावद्विंदुर्न भवति दृढ: प्राणवातप्रबंधात् ।
यावद्ध्याने सहजसदृशं जायते नैव तत्त्वं
तावज्ज्ञानं वदति तदिदं दम्भमिथ्याप्रलाप: ॥ 114 ॥

While the prana does not flow in the middle passage (of sushumna),
while the bindu is not steadied by restraining the prana, while mind
does not reflect spontaneous meditation, then those who speak of
spiritual knowledge are only indulging in boastful and false tales.

According to Swatmarama, to say anything about awakening
of shakti and consciousness as long as it has not taken place
within yourself, is hypocritical. However, anyone who talks
on such a subject must have had some sort of realization or
else he would not understand or perceive such a phenomenon. The principle of hatha yoga and tantra is 'practise
and realize' rather than talk and philosophize. Actions speak
louder than words, and practice makes perfect.

This is why the practitioner of kundalini yoga will not
be merely a preacher or a teacher. Others may occupy
themselves by teaching about spirituality but a yogi will live
it. His life is his teaching, and those who have an eye to see
and an ear to hear will be able to gain everything from him
effortlessly by a process of direct transmission. Those who
see only their preconceptions when they look at the world
will have to be content to listen to preachers until their own
blockages are loosened and their perception is illumined.

Which is the complete experience? To hear about
chocolate and imagine that its taste can be understood from
that, or to taste chocolate itself? To be told about spellbinding
music, or to hear it yourself? To see an enchanting scene in
a picture, or to be there yourself? To hear about physical,
psychic or spiritual experiences and imagine they can be
understood from that, or to experience them oneself – that is
the difference between a teacher and a yogi.

603

Appendicies

Appendices

Appendix A

Sanskrit Text

Chapter One

1. श्रीआदिनाथाय नमोऽस्तु तस्मै येनोपदिष्टा हठयोगविद्या।
विभ्राजते प्रोन्नतराजयोगमारोढुमिच्छोरधिरोहिणीव ॥

2. प्रणम्य श्रीगुरुं नाथं स्वात्मारामेण योगिना ।
केवलं राजयोगाय हठविद्योपदिश्यते ॥

3. भ्रान्त्या बहुमतध्वान्ते राजयोगमजानताम् ।
हठ प्रदीपिकां धत्ते स्वात्माराम: कृपाकर: ॥

4. हठविद्यां हि मत्स्येन्द्रगोरक्षाद्या विजानते ।
स्वात्मारामोऽथवा योगी जानीते तत्प्रसादत: ॥

5. श्रीआदिनाथमत्स्येंद्रशाबरानंदभैरवा: ।
चौरंगीमीनगोरक्षविरूपाक्षबिलेशया: ॥

6. मंथानो भैरवो योगी सिद्धिर्बुद्धश्च कंथडि: ।
कोरंटक: सुरानन्द: सिद्धपादश्च चर्पटि: ॥

7. कानेरी पूज्यपादश्च नित्यनाथो निरंजन: ।
कपाली बिन्दुनाथश्च काकचंडीश्वराह्वय: ॥

8. अल्लाम: प्रभुदेवश्च घोडा चोली च टिंटिणि: ।
भानुकी नारदेवश्च खंड: कापालिकस्तथा ॥

9. इत्यादयो महासिद्धा हठयोगप्रभावत: ।
खंडयित्वा कालदंडं ब्रह्माण्डे विचरंति ते ॥

607

10. अशेषतापतप्तानां समाश्रयमठो हठ: ।
अशेषयोगयुक्तानामाधारकमठो हठ: ॥

11. हठविद्या परं गोप्या योगिना सिद्धिमिच्छताम् ।
भवेद्वीर्यवती गुप्ता निर्वीर्या तु प्रकाशिता ॥

12. सुराज्ये धार्मिके देशे सुभिक्षे निरुपद्रवे ।
धनु: प्रमाणपर्यन्तं शिलाग्निजलवर्जिते ।
एकान्ते मठिकामध्ये स्थातव्यं हठयोगिना ॥

13. अल्पद्वारमरन्ध्रगर्तविवरं नात्युच्चनीचायतं
सम्यग्गोमयसांद्रलिप्तममलं नि:शेषजंतूज्झितम् ।
बाह्ये मंडपवेदिकूपरुचिरं प्राकारसंवेष्टितं
प्रोक्तं योगमठस्य लक्षणमिदं सिद्धैर्हठाभ्यासिभि: ॥

14. एवंविधे मठे स्थित्वा सर्वचिंताविवर्जित: ।
गुरूपदिष्टमार्गेण योगमेव समभ्यसेत् ॥

15. अत्याहार: प्रयासश्च प्रजल्पो नियमग्रह: ।
जनसंगश्च लौल्यं च षड्भिर्योगो विनश्यति ॥

16. उत्साहात्साहसाद्धैर्यात्तत्त्वज्ञानाश्च निश्चयात् ।
जनसंगपरित्यागात्षड्भिर्योग: प्रसिद्ध्यति ॥
अहिंसा सत्यमस्तेयं ब्रह्मचर्यं क्षमा धृति: ।
दयार्जवं मिताहार: शौचं चैव यमा दश ॥
तप: संतोष आस्तिक्यं दानमीश्वरपूजनम् ।
सिद्धान्तवाक्यश्रवणं ह्वीमती च तपो हुतम् ।
नियमा दश संप्रोक्ता योगशास्त्रविशारदै: ॥

17. हठस्य प्रथमांगत्वादासनं पूर्वमुच्यते ।
कुर्यात्तदासनं स्थैर्यमारोग्यं चांगलाघवम् ॥

18. वशिष्ठाद्यैश्च मुनिभिर्मत्स्येन्द्राद्यैश्च योगिभि: ।
अंगीकृतान्यासनानि कथ्यन्ते कानिचिन्मया ॥

19. जानूर्वोरन्तरे सम्यक्कृत्वा पादतले उभे ।
ऋजुकाय: समासीन: स्वस्तिकं तत्प्रचक्षते ॥

20. सव्ये दक्षिणगुल्कं तु पृष्ठपार्श्वे नियोजयेत् ।
दक्षिणेऽपि तथा सव्यं गोमुखं गोमुखाकृति: ॥

21. एकं पादं तथैकस्मिन्विन्यसेदुरुणि स्थिरतम् ।
    इतरस्मिंस्तथा चोरुं वीरासनमितीरितम् ॥

22. गुदं निरुध्य गुतफाभ्यां व्युत्क्रमेण समाहितः ।
    कूर्मासनं भवेदेतदिति योगविदो विदुः ॥

23. पद्मासनं तु संस्थाप्य जानूर्वोरन्तरे करौ ।
    निवेश्य भूमौ संस्थाप्य व्योमस्थं कुक्कुटासनम् ॥

24. कुक्कुटासनबंधस्थो दोभ्यां संबध्य कंधराम् ।
    भवेत्कूर्मवदुत्तान एतदुत्तानकूर्मकम् ॥

25. पादांगुष्ठौ तु पाणिभ्यां गृहीत्वा श्रवणावधि ।
    धनुराकर्षणं कुर्याद्धनुरासनमुच्यते ॥

26. वामोरुमूलार्पितदक्षपादं जानोर्बहिर्वेष्टितवामपादम् ।
    प्रगृह्य तिष्ठेत्परिवर्तितांगः श्रीमत्स्यनाथोदितमासनं स्यात् ॥

27. मत्स्येन्द्रपीठं जठरप्रदीप्तिं प्रचंडरुग्मंडलखंडनास्त्रम् ।
    अभ्यासतः कुंडलिनीप्रबोधं चन्द्रस्थिरत्वं च ददाति पुंसाम् ॥

28. प्रसार्य पादौ भुवि दंडरूपौ दोभ्यां पदाग्रद्वितयं गृहीत्वा ।
    जानूपरिन्यस्तललाटदेशो वसेदिदं पश्चिमतानमाहुः ॥

29. इति पश्चिमतानमासनग्र्यं पवनं पश्चिमवाहिनं करोति ।
    उदयं जठरानलस्य कुर्यादुदरे कार्श्यमरोगतां च पुंसाम् ॥

30. धरामवष्टभ्य करद्वयेन तत्कूर्परस्थापितनाभिपार्श्वः ।
    उच्चासनो दंडवदुत्थितः खे मायूरमेतत्प्रवदन्ति पीठम् ॥

31. हरति सकलरोगानाशु गुल्मोदरादी-
    नभिभवति च दोषानासनं श्रीमयूरम् ।
    बहु कदशनभूक्तं भस्म कुर्यादशेषं
    जनयति जठराग्निं जारयेत्कालकूटम् ॥

32. उत्तानं शववद्भूमौ शयनं तच्छवासनम् ।
    शवासनं श्रान्तिहरं चित्तविश्रान्तिकारकम् ॥

33. चतुरशीत्यासनानि शिवेन कथितानि च ।
    तेभ्यश्चतुष्कमादाय सारभूतं ब्रवीम्यहम् ॥

34. सिद्धं पद्यं तथा सिंहं भद्रं वेति चतुष्टयम् ।
श्रेष्ठं तत्रापि च सुखे तिष्ठेत्सिद्धासने सदा ॥

35. योनिस्थानकमङ्घ्रिमूलघटितं कृत्वा दृढं विन्यसे-
त्मेण्ढ्रे पादमथैकमेव हृदये कृत्वा हनुं सुस्थिरम् ।
स्थाणुः संयमितेन्द्रियोऽचलदृशा पश्येद्भ्रुवोरन्तरं
ह्येतन्मोक्षकपाटभेदजनकं सिद्धासनं प्रोच्यते ॥

36. मेण्ढ्रादुपरि विन्यस्य सव्यं गुल्फं तथोपरि ।
गुल्फान्तरं च निक्षिप्य सिद्धासनमिदं भवेत् ॥

37. एतत्सिद्धासनं प्राहुरन्ये वज्रासनं विदुः ।
मुक्तासनं वदन्त्येके प्राहुर्गुप्तासनं परे ॥

38. यमेष्विव मिताहारमहिंसां नियमेष्विव ।
मुख्यं सर्वासनेष्वेकं सिद्धाः सिद्धासनं विदुः ॥

39. चतुरशीतिपीठेषु सिद्धमेव सदाभ्यसेत् ।
द्वासप्ततिसहस्राणां नाडीनां मलशोधनम् ॥

40. आत्मध्यायी मिताहारी यावद्द्वादशवत्सरम् ।
सदा सिद्धासनाभ्यासाद्योगी निष्पत्तिमाप्नुयात् ॥

41. किमन्यैर्बहुभिः पीठैः सिद्धे सिद्धासने सति ।
प्राणानिले सावधाने बद्धे केवलकुंभके ।
उत्पद्यते निरायासात्स्वयमेवोन्मनी कला ॥

42. तथैकस्मिन्नेव दृढे सिद्धे सिद्धासने सति ।
बंधत्रयमनायासात्स्वयमेवोपजायते ॥

43. नासनं सिद्धसदृशं न कुंभः केवलोपमः ।
न खेचरीसमा मुद्रा न नादसदृशो लयः ॥

44. वामोरुपरि दक्षिणं च चरणं संस्थाप्य वामं तथा
दक्षोरुपरि पश्चिमेन विधिना धृत्वा कराभ्यां दृढम् ।
अंगुष्ठौ हृदये निधाय चिबुकं नासाग्रमालोकयेत्
एतद्व्याधिविनाशकारि यमिनां पद्मासनं प्रोच्यते ॥

45. उत्तानौ चरणौ कृत्वा ऊरुसंस्थौ प्रयत्नतः ।
ऊरुमध्ये तथोत्तानौ पाणी कृत्वा ततो दृशौ ॥

46. नासाग्रे विन्यसेद्राजदंतमूले तु जिह्वया ।
उत्तंभ्य चिबुकं वक्षस्युत्थाप्य पवनं शनै: ॥

47. इदं पद्मासनं प्रोक्तं सर्वव्याधिविनाशनम् ।
दुर्लभं येन केनापि धीमता लभ्यते भुवि ॥

48. कृत्वासंपुटितौ करौ दृढतरं बद्ध्वातु पद्मासनं
गाढं वक्षसि सन्निधाय चिबुकं ध्यायंश्च तच्चेतसि ।
वारंवारमपानमूर्ध्वमनिलं प्रोत्सारयन्पूरितं
न्यंचन्प्राणमुपैति बोधमतुलं शक्तिप्रभावान्नर: ॥

49. पद्मासने स्थितो योगी नाडीद्वारेण पूरितम् ।
मारुतं धारयेद्यस्तु स मुक्तोनात्र संशय: ॥

50. गुल्फौ च वृषणस्याध: सीवन्या: पार्श्वयो: क्षिपेत् ।
दक्षिणे सव्यगुल्फं तु दक्षगुल्फं तु सव्यके ॥

51. हस्तौ तु जान्वो: संस्थाप्य स्वांगुली: संप्रसार्य च ।
व्यात्तवक्रो निरीक्षेत नासाग्रं सुसमाहित: ॥

52. सिंहासनं भवेदेतत्पूजितं योगिपुंगवै: ।
बन्धत्रितयसंधानं कुरुते चासनोत्तमम् ॥

53. गुल्फौ च वृषणस्याध: सीवन्या: पार्श्वयो: क्षिपेत् ।
सव्यगुल्फं तथा सव्ये दक्षगुल्फं तु दक्षिणे ॥

54. पार्श्वपादौ च पाणिभ्यां दृढं बद्ध्वा सुनिश्चलम् ।
भद्रासनं भवेदेतत्सर्वव्याधिविनाशनम् ।
गोरक्षासनमित्याहुरिदं वै सिद्धयोगिन: ॥

55. एवमासनबंधेषु योगीन्द्रो विगतश्रम: ।
अभ्यसेन्नाडिकाशुद्धिं मुद्रादिपवनक्रियाम् ॥

56. आसनं कुंभकं चित्रं मुद्राख्यं करणं तथा ।
अथ नादानुसंधानमभ्यासानुक्रमो हठे ॥

57. ब्रह्मचारी मिताहारी त्यागी योगपरायण: ।
अब्दादूर्ध्वं भवेत्सिद्धो नात्र कार्या विचारणा ॥

58. सुस्निग्धमधुराहारश्चतुर्थांशविवर्जित: ।
भुज्यते शिवसंप्रीत्यै मिताहार: स उच्यते ॥

611

59. कट्वम्लतीक्ष्णलवणोष्णहरीतशाकसौवीरतैलतिलसर्षप मद्यमत्स्यान् ।
अजादिमांसदधितक्रकुलत्थकोलपिण्याकहिंगुलशुनाद्यमपथ्यमाहुः ॥

60. भोजनमहितं विद्यात्पुनरस्योष्णीकृतं रूक्षम् ।
अतिलवणमम्लयुक्तं कदशनशाकोत्कटं वर्ज्यम् ॥

61. वह्निस्त्रीपथिसेवानामादौ वर्जनमाचरेत् ।
तथाहि गोरक्षवचनम् ।
'वर्जयेद् दुर्जनप्रान्तं वह्निस्त्रीपथिसेवनम्।
प्रातःस्नानोपवासादि कायक्लेशविधिं तथा' ॥

62. गोधूमशालियवषष्टिकशोभनान्नंक्षीरराज्यखंडनवनीतसितामधूनि ।
शुंठीपटोलकफलादिकपंचशाकंमुद्गादिदिव्यमुदकंच यमींद्रपथ्यम् ॥

63. पुष्टं सुमधुरं स्निग्धं गव्यं धातुप्रपोषणम् ।
मनोभिलषितं योग्यं योगी भोजनमाचरेत् ॥

64. युवा वृद्धोऽतिवृद्धो वा व्याधितो दुर्बलोऽपि वा ।
अभ्यासात्सिद्धिमाप्नोति सर्वयोगेष्वतंद्रितः ॥

65. क्रियायुक्तस्य सिद्धिः स्यादक्रियस्य कथं भवेत् ।
न शास्त्रपाठमात्रेण योगसिद्धिः प्रजायते ॥

66. न वेषधारणं सिद्धेः कारणं न च तत्कथा ।
क्रियैव कारणं सिद्धेः सत्यमेतन्न संशयः ॥

67. पीठानि कुंभकाश्चित्रा दिव्यानि करणानि च ।
सर्वाण्यपि हठाभ्यासे राजयोगफलावधिः ॥

Chapter Two

1. अथासने दृढे योगी वशी हितमिताशनः ।
गुरूपदिष्टमार्गे प्राणायामान्समभ्यसेत् ॥

2. चले वाते चलं चित्तं निश्चले निश्चलं भवेत् ।
योगी स्थाणुत्वमाप्नोति ततो वायुं निरोधयेत् ॥

3. यावद्वायुः स्थितो देहे तावज्जीवनमुच्यते ।
मरणं तस्य निष्क्रांतिस्ततो वायुं निरोधयेत् ॥

4. मलाकुलासु नाडीषु मारुतो नैव मध्यगः ।
कथं स्यादुन्मनीभावः कार्यसिद्धिः कथं भवेत् ॥

5. शुद्धिमेति यदा सर्वं नाडीचक्रं मलाकुलम् ।
   तदैव जायते योगी प्राणसंग्रहणे क्षमः ॥

6. प्राणायामं ततः कुर्यान्नित्यं सात्त्विकया धिया ।
   यथा सुषुम्नानाडीस्था मलाः शुद्धिं प्रयांति च ॥

7. बद्धपद्मासना योगी प्राणं चंद्रेण पूरयेत् ।
   धारयित्वा यथाशक्ति भूयः सूर्येण रेचयेत् ॥

8. प्राणं सूर्येण चाकृष्य पूरयेदुदरं शनैः ।
   विधिवत्कुंभकं कृत्वा पुनश्चंद्रेण रेचयेत् ॥

9. येन त्यजेत्तेन पीत्वा धारयेदतिरोधतः ।
   रेचयेच्च ततोऽन्येन शनैरेव न वेगतः ॥

10. प्राणं पिबेदिडया पिबेन्नियमितं भूयोऽन्यया रेचयेत्
    पीत्वा पिंगलया समीरणमथो बद्ध्वा त्यजेद्वामया ।
    सूर्याचन्द्रमसोरनेन विधिनाभ्यासं सदा तन्वतां
    शुद्धा नाडिगणा भवंति यमिनां मासत्रयादूर्ध्वतः ॥

11. प्रातर्मध्यदिने सायमर्धरात्रे च कुंभकान् ।
    शनैरशीतिपर्यन्तं चतुर्वारं समभ्यसेत् ॥

12. कनीयसि भवेत्स्वेदः कंपो भवति मध्यमे ।
    उत्तमे स्थानमाप्नोति ततो वायुं निबंधयेत् ॥

13. जलेन श्रमजातेन गात्रमर्दनमाचरेत् ।
    दृढता लघुता चैव तेन गात्रस्य जायते ॥

14. अभ्यासकाले प्रथमे शस्तं क्षीराज्यभोजनम् ।
    ततोऽभ्यासे दृढीभूते न तादृङ्नियमग्रहः ॥

15. यथा सिंहो गजो व्याघ्रो भवेद्वश्यः शनैःशनैः ।
    तथैव सेवितो वायुरन्यथा हन्ति साधकम् ॥

16. प्राणायामेन युक्तेन सर्वरोगक्षयो भवेत् ।
    अयुक्ताभ्यासयोगेन सर्वरोगसमुद्भवः ॥

17. हिक्का श्वासश्च कासश्च शिरःकर्णाक्षिवेदनाः ।
    भवन्ति विविधा रोगाः पवनस्य प्रकोपतः ॥

18. युक्तं युक्तं त्यजेद्वायुं युक्तं युक्तं च पूरयेत् ।
    युक्तं युक्तं च बन्धीयादेवं सिद्धिमवाप्नुयात् ॥

19. यदा तु नाडीशुद्धिः स्यात्तथा चिह्नानि बाह्यतः ।
    कायस्य कृशता कान्तिस्तदा जायेत निश्चितम् ॥

20. यथेष्टंधारणं वायोरनलस्य प्रदीपनम् ।
    नादाभिव्यक्तिरारोग्यं जायते नाडिशोधनात् ॥

21. मेदश्लेष्माधिकः पूर्वं षट्कर्माणि समाचरेत् ।
    अन्यस्तु नाचरेत्तानि दोषाणां समभावतः ॥

22. धौतिर्बस्तिस्तथा नेतिस्त्राटकं नौलिकं तथा ।
    कपालभातिश्चैतानि षट् कर्माणि प्रचक्षते ॥

23. कर्मषट्कमिदं गोप्यं घटशोधनकारकम् ।
    विचित्रगुणसंधायि पूज्यते योगिपुंगवैः ॥

24. चतुरंगुलविस्तारं हस्तपंचदशायतम् ।
    गुरूपदिष्टमार्गेण सिक्तं वस्त्रं शनैर्ग्रसेत् ।
    पुनः प्रत्याहरेच्चैतदुदितं धौति कर्म तत् ॥

25. कासश्वासप्लीहकुष्टं कफरोगाश्च विंशतिः ।
    धौतिकर्मप्रभावेण प्रयांत्येव न संशयः ॥

26. नाभिदघ्नजले पायौ न्यस्तनालोत्कटासनः ।
    आधाराकुंचनं कुर्यात्क्षालनं बस्तिकर्म तत् ॥

27. गुल्मप्लीहोदरं चापि वातपित्तकफोद्भवाः ।
    बस्तिकर्मप्रभावेण क्षीयन्ते सकलामयाः ॥

28. धात्विंद्रियान्तःकरणप्रसादं दधाच्च कांतिं दहनप्रदीप्तिम् ।
    अशेषदोषोपचयं निहन्यादभ्यस्यमानं जलबस्तिकर्म ॥

29. सूत्रं वितस्तिसुस्निग्धं नासानाले प्रवेशयेत् ।
    मुखान्निर्गमयेच्चैषा नेतिः सिद्धैर्निगद्यते ॥

30. कपालशोधिनी चैव दिव्यदृष्टिप्रदायिनी ।
    जत्रूर्ध्वजातरोगौघं नेतिराशु निहंति च ॥

31. निरीक्षेन्निश्चलदृशा सूक्ष्मलक्ष्यं समाहितः ।
    अश्रुसंपातपर्यन्तमाचार्यैस्त्राटकं स्मृतम् ॥

614

32. मोचनं नेत्ररोगाणां तन्द्रादीनां कपाटकम् ।
यत्नतस्त्राटकं गोप्यं यथा हाटकपेटकम् ॥

33. अमन्दावर्तवेगेन तुन्दं सव्यापसव्यत: ।
नतांसो भ्रामयेदेषा नौलि: सिद्धै: प्रचक्ष्यटे ॥

34. मन्दाग्निसंदीपनपाचनादिसंधापिकानन्दकरी सदैव ।
अशेषदोषामयशोषणी च हठक्रिया मौलिरियं च नौलि: ॥

35. भस्त्रावल्लोहकारस्य रेचपूरौ ससंभ्रमौ ।
कपालभातिर्विख्या कफदोषविशोषणी ॥

36. षट्कर्मनिर्गतस्थौल्यकफदोषमलादिक: ।
प्राणायामं तत: कुर्यादनायासेन सिद्ध्यति ॥

37. प्राणायामैरेव सर्वे प्रशुष्यन्ति मला इति ।
आचार्याणां तु केषांचिदन्यत्कर्म न संमतम् ॥

38. उदरगतपदार्थमुद्वमन्ति पवनमपानमुदीर्य कंठनाले ।
क्रमपरिचयवश्यनाडिचक्रा गजकरणीति निगद्यते हठज्ञै: ॥

39. ब्रह्मादयोऽपि त्रिदशा: पवनाभ्यासतत्परा: ।
अभूवन्नंतकभयात्तस्मात्पवनमभ्यसेत् ॥

40. यावद्बद्धोमरुंहे यावच्चित्तं निराकुलम् ।
यावद्दृष्टिर्भ्रुवोर्मध्ये तावत्कालभयं कुत: ॥

41. विधिवत्प्राणसंयामैर्नाडीचक्रे विशोधिते ।
सुषुम्नावदनं भित्त्वा सुखाद्विशति मारुत: ॥

42. मारुते मध्यसंचारे मन:स्थैर्यं प्रजायते ।
यो मन:सुस्थिरीभाव: सैवावस्था मनोन्मनी ॥

43. तत्सिद्धये विधानज्ञाश्चित्रान्कुर्वन्ति कुंभकान् ।
विचित्र कुंभकाभ्यासाद्विचित्रां सिद्धिमाप्नुयात् ॥

44. सूर्यभेदनमुज्जायी सीत्कारी शीतली तथा ।
भस्त्रिका भ्रामरी मूर्च्छा प्लाविनीत्यष्टकुंभका: ॥

45. पूरकांते तु कर्तव्यो बन्धो जालंधराभिध: ।
कुंभकांते रेचकादौ कर्तव्यस्तूड्डियानक: ॥

46. अधस्तात्कुंचनेनाशु कंठसंकोचने कृते ।
मध्ये पश्चिमतानेन स्यात्प्राणो ब्रह्मनाडिग: ॥

47. आपानमूर्ध्वमुत्थाप्य प्राणं कंठादधो नयेत् ।
योगी जराविमुक्त: सन्षोडशाब्दवया भवेत् ॥

48. आसने सुखदे योगी बद्ध्वा चैवासनं तत: ।
दक्षनाड्या समाकृष्य बहि:स्थं पवनं शनै: ॥

49. आकेशादानखाग्राच्च निरोधावधि कुंभयेत् ।
तत: शनै: सव्यनाड्या रेचयेत्पवनं शनै: ॥

50. कपालशोधनं वातदोषघ्नं कृमिदोषहृत् ।
पुन:पुनरिदं कार्यं सूर्यभेदनमुत्तमम् ॥

51. मुखं संयम्य नाडीभ्यामाकृष्य पवनं शनै: ।
यथा लगति कंठात्तु हृदयावधि सस्वनम् ॥

52. पूर्ववत्कुंभयेत्प्राणं रेचयेदिडया तथा ।
श्लेष्मदोषहरं कंठे देहानलविवर्धनम् ॥

53. नाडीजलोदराधातुगतदोषविनाशनम् ।
गच्छता तिष्ठता कार्यमुज्जाय्याख्यं तु कुंभकम् ॥

54. सीत्कां कुर्यात्तथा वक्त्रेप्राणेनैव विजृंभिकाम् ।
एवमभ्यासयोगेन कामदेवो द्वितीयक: ॥

55. योगिनी चक्रसमान्य:सृष्टिसंहारकारक: ।
न क्षुधा न तृषा निद्रा नैवालस्यं प्रजायते ॥

56. भवेत्सत्त्वं च देहस्य सर्वोपद्रववर्जित: ।
अनेन विधिना सत्यं योगींद्रो भूमिमंडले ॥

57. जिह्वया वायुमाकृष्य पूर्ववत्कुंभसाधनम् ।
शनकैर्घ्राणरंध्राभ्यां रेचयेत् पवनं सुधी: ॥

58. गुल्मप्लीहादिकान् रोगान् ज्वरं पित्तं क्षुधां तृषाम् ।
विषाणि शीतली नाम कुंभिकेयं निहंति हि ॥

59. ऊर्वोरुपरि संस्थाप्य शुभे पादतले उभे ।
पद्मासनं भवेदेतत्सर्वपापप्रणाशनम् ॥

60. सम्यक्पद्मासनं बद्ध्वा समग्रीवोदरः सुधीः ।
मुखं संयम्य यत्नेन प्राणं घ्राणेन रेचयेत् ॥

61. यथा लगति हृत्कंठे कपालावधि सस्वनम् ।
वेगेन पूरयेच्चापिहृत्पद्मावधि मारुतम् ॥

62. पुनर्विरेचयेत्तद्वत्पूरयेच्च पुनः पुनः ।
यथैव लोहकारेण भस्त्रा वेगेन चाल्यते ॥

63. तथैव स्वशरीरस्थं चालयेत्पवनं धिया ।
यदा श्रमो भवेद्देहे तदा सूर्येण पूरयेत् ॥

64. यथोदरं भवेत्पूर्णमनिलेन तथा लघु ।
धारयेन्नासिकां मध्यातर्जनीभ्यां विना दृढम् ॥

65. विधिवत्कुंभकं कृत्वा रेचयेदिडयानिलम् ।
वातपित्तश्लेष्महरं शरीराग्निविवर्धनम् ॥

66. कुंडली बोधकं क्षिप्रं पवनं सुखदं हितम् ।
ब्रह्मनाडीमुखे संस्थकफाद्यर्गलनाशनम् ॥

67. सम्यग्गात्रसमुद्भूतग्रंथित्रयविभेदकम् ।
विशेषेणैव कर्तव्यं भस्त्राख्यं कुंभकंत्विदम् ॥

68. वेगाद्घोषं पूरकं भृंगनादं भृंगीनादं रेचकं मंदमंदम् ।
योगींद्राणामेवमभ्यासयोगाच्चित्ते जाता काचिदानंदलीला ॥

69. पूरकांते गाढतरं बद्ध्वा जालंधरं शनैः ।
रेचयेन्मूर्च्छनाख्येयं मनोमूर्च्छा सुखप्रदा ॥

70. अंतः प्रवर्तितोदारमारुतापूरितोदरः ।
पयस्यगाधेऽपि सुखात्प्लवते पद्मपत्रवत् ॥

71. प्राणायामस्त्रिधा प्रोक्तो रेचपूरककुंभकैः ।
सहितः केवलश्चेति कुंभको द्विविधो मतः ॥

72. यावत्केवलसिद्धिः स्यात्सहितं तावदभ्यसेत् ।
रेचकं पूरकं मुक्त्वा सुखं यद्वायुधारणम् ॥

73. प्राणायामोऽयमित्युक्तः स वै केवलकुंभकः ।
कुंभके केवले सिद्धे रेचपूरकवर्जिते ॥

617

74. न तस्य दुर्लभं किंचित्रिषु लोकेषु विद्यते ।
शक्त: केवलकुंभेन यथेष्टं वायुधारणात् ॥

75. राजयोगपदं चापि लभते नात्र संशय: ।
कुंभकात्कुंडलीबोध: कुंडलीबोधतो भवेत् ।
अनर्गला सुषुम्ना च हठसिद्धिश्च जायते ॥

76. हठं विना राजयोगो राजयोगं विना हठ: ।
न सिध्यति ततो युग्ममानिष्पत्ते: समभ्यसेत् ॥

77. कुंभकप्राणरोधांते कुर्याच्चित्तं निराश्रयम् ।
एवमभ्यासयोगेन राजयोगपदं व्रजेत् ॥

78. वपु: कृशत्वं वदने प्रसन्नता नादस्फुटत्वं नयने सुनिर्मले ।
अरोगता बिंदुजयोऽग्निदीपनं नाडीविशुद्धिर्हठसिद्धिलक्षणम् ॥

Chapter Three

1. सशैलवनधात्रीणां यथाधारोऽहिनायक: ।
सर्वेषां योगतंत्राणां तथाधारो हि कुंडली ॥

2. सुप्ता गुरुप्रसादेन यदा जागर्ति कुंडली ।
तदा सर्वाणि पद्मानि भिद्यंते ग्रंथयोऽपि च ॥

3. प्राणस्य शून्यपदवी तदा राजपथायते ।
तदा चित्तं निरालंबं तदा कालस्य वंचनम् ॥

4. सुषुम्ना शून्यपदवी ब्रह्मरंध्रं महापथ: ।
श्मशानं शांभवी मध्यमार्गश्चेत्येकवाचका: ॥

5. तस्मात्सर्वप्रयत्नेन प्रबोधयितुमीश्वरीम् ।
ब्रह्मद्वारमुखे सुप्तां मुद्राभ्यासं समाचरेत् ॥

6. महामुद्रा महाबंधो महावेधश्च खेचरी ।
उड्डीयानं मूलबंधश्च बंधो जालंधराभिध: ॥

7. करणी विपरीताख्या वज्रोली शक्तिचालनम् ।
इदं हि मुद्रादशकं जरामरणनाशनम् ॥

8. आदिनाथोदितं दिव्यमष्टैश्वर्यप्रदायकम् ।
वल्लभं सर्वसिद्धानां दुर्लभं मरुतामपि ॥

9. गोपनीयं प्रयत्नेन यथा रत्नकरंडकम् ।
कस्यचिन्नैव वक्तव्यं कुलस्त्रीसुरतं यथा ॥

10. पादमूलेन वामेन योनिं संपीड्य दक्षिणम् ।
प्रसारितं पदं कृत्वा कराभ्यां धारयेद्दृढम् ॥

11. कंठे बंधं समारोप्य धारयेद्वायुमूर्ध्वतः ।
यथा दंडहतः सर्पो दंडाकारः प्रजायते ॥

12. ऋज्वीभूता तथा शक्तिः कुंडली सहसा भवेत् ।
तदा सा मरणावस्था जायते द्विपुटाश्रया ॥

13. ततः शनैः शनैरेव रेचयेन्नैव वेगतः ।
महामुद्रां च तेनैव वदंति विबुधोत्तमाः ॥

14. इयं खलु महामुद्रा महासिद्धैः प्रदर्शिता ।
महाक्लेशादयो दोषाः क्षीयंते मरणादयः ।
महामुद्रां च तेनैव वदंति विबुधोत्तमाः ॥

15. चंद्रांगे तु समभ्यस्य सूर्यांगे पुनरभ्यसेत् ।
यावत्तुल्या भवेत्संख्या ततो मुद्रां विसर्जयेत् ॥

16. न हि पथ्यमपथ्यं वा रसाः सर्वेऽपि नीरसाः ।
अपि भुक्तं विषं घोरं पीयूषमपि जीर्यति ॥

17. क्षयकुष्ठगुदावर्तगुल्माजीर्णपुरोगमाः ।
तस्य दोषाः क्षयं यान्ति महामुद्रां तु योऽभ्यसेत् ॥

18. कथितेयं महामुद्रा महासिद्धिकरा नृणाम् ।
गोपनीया प्रयत्नेन न देया यस्य कस्यचित् ॥

19. पार्ष्णिं वामस्य पादस्य योनिस्थाने नियोजयेत् ।
वामोरूपरि संस्थाप्य दक्षिणं चरणं तथा ॥

20. पूरयित्वा ततो वायुं हृदये चुबुकं दृढम् ।
निष्पीड्यं वायुमाकुंच्य मनोमध्ये नियोजयेत् ॥

21. धारयित्वा यथाशक्ति रेचयेदनिलं शनैः ।
सव्यांगे तु समभ्यस्य दक्षांगे पुनरभ्यसेत् ॥

22. मतमत्र तु केषांचित्कंठबंधं विवर्जयेत् ।
राजदंतस्थजिह्वाया बंधः शस्तो भवेदिति ॥

23. अयं तु सर्वनाडीनामूर्ध्वं गतिनिरोधक: ।
    अयं खलु महाबंधो महासिद्धिप्रदायक: ॥

24. कालपाशमहाबंधविमोचनविचक्षण: ।
    त्रिवेणीसंगमं धत्ते केदारं प्रापयेन्मन: ॥

25. रूपलावण्यसंपन्ना यथा स्त्री पुरुषं विना ।
    महामुद्रामहाबंधौ निष्फलौ वेधवर्जितौ ॥

26. महाबंधस्थितो योगी कृत्वा पूरकमेकधी: ।
    वायूनां गतिमावृत्य निभृतं कंठमुद्रया ॥

27. समहस्तयुगो भूमौ स्फिचौ संताडयेच्छनै: ।
    पुटद्वयमतिक्रम्य वायु: स्फुरति मध्यग: ॥

28. सोमसूर्याग्निसंबंधो जायते चामृताय वै ।
    मृतावस्था समुत्पन्ना ततो वायुं विरेचयेत् ॥

29. महावेधोऽयमभ्यासान्महासिद्धिप्रदायक: ।
    वलीपलितवेपघ्न: सेव्यते साधकोत्तमै: ॥

30. एतत्त्रयं महागुह्यं जरामृत्युविनाशनम् ।
    वह्निवृद्धिकरं चैव ह्लणिमादिगुणप्रदम् ॥

31. अष्टधा क्रियते चैव यामे यामे दिने दिने ।
    पुण्यसंभारसंधायि पापौघभिदुरं सदा ।
    सम्यक्शिक्षावतामेवं स्वल्पं प्रथमसाधनम् ॥

32. कपालकुहरे जिह्वा प्रविष्टा विपरीतगा ।
    भ्रुवोरंतर्गता दृष्टिर्मुद्रा भवति खेचरी ॥

33. छेदनचालनदोहै: कलां क्रमेण वर्धयेत्तावत् ।
    सा यावद्भ्रूमध्यं स्पृशति तदा खेचरीसिद्धि: ॥

34. स्नुहीपत्रनिभं शस्त्रं सुतीक्ष्णं स्निग्धनिर्मलम् ।
    समादाय ततस्तेन रोममात्रं समुच्छिनेत् ॥

35. तत: सैन्धवपथ्याभ्यां चूर्णिताभ्यां प्रघर्षयेत् ।
    पुन: सप्तदिने प्राप्ते रोममात्रं समुच्छिनेत् ॥

36. एवं क्रमेण षण्मासं नित्यं युक्त: समाचरेत् ।
    षण्मासाद्रसनामूलशिराबंध: प्रणश्यति ॥

37. कलां पराङ्मुखीं कृत्वा त्रिपथे परियोजयेत् ।
सा भवेत्खेचरी मुद्रा व्योमचक्रं तदुच्यते ॥

38. रसनामूर्ध्वगां कृत्वा क्षणार्धमपि तिष्ठति ।
विषैर्विमुच्यते योगी व्याधिमृत्युजरादिभि: ॥

39. न रोगो मरणं तंद्रा न निद्रा न क्षुधा तृषा ।
न च मूर्च्छा भवेत्तस्य यो मुद्रां वेत्ति खेचरीम् ॥

40. पीड्यते न स रोगेण लिप्यते न च कर्मणा ।
बाध्यते न स कालेन यो मुद्रां वेत्ति खेचरीम् ॥

41. चित्तं चरति खे यस्माज्जिह्वा चरति खे गता ।
तेनैषा खेचरी नाम मुद्रा सिद्धैर्निरूपिता ॥

42. खेचर्या मुद्रितं येन विवरं लंबिकोर्ध्वत: ।
न तस्य क्षरते बिन्दु: कामिन्या: श्लेषितस्य च ॥

43. चलितोऽपि यदा बिंदु: संप्राप्तो योनिमंडलम् ।
व्रजत्यूर्ध्वं हृत: शक्तया निबद्धो योनिमुद्रया ॥

44. ऊर्ध्वजिह्व: स्थिरो भूत्वा सोमपानं करोति य: ।
मासार्धेन न संदेहो मृत्युं जयति योगवित् ॥

45. नित्यं सोमकलापूर्णं शरीरं यस्य योगिन: ।
तक्षकेणापि दष्टस्य विषं तस्य न सर्पति ॥

46. इंधनानि यथा वह्निस्तैलवर्तिं च दीपक: ।
तथा सोमकलापूर्णं देही देहं न मुंचति ॥

47. गोमांसं भक्षयेन्नित्यं पिबेदमरवारुणीम् ।
कुलीनं तमहं मन्ये चेतरे कुलघातका: ॥

48. गोशब्देनोदिता जिह्वा तत्प्रवेशो हि तालुनि ।
गोमांसभक्षणं तत्तु महापातकनाशनम् ॥

49. जिह्वाप्रवेशसंभूतवह्निनोत्पादित: खलु ।
चंद्रात्स्रवति य: सार: सा स्यादमरवारुणी ॥

50. चुम्बंती यदि लंबिकाग्रमनिशं जिह्वारसस्यंदिनी
सक्षारा कटुकाम्लदुग्धसदृशी मध्वाज्यतुल्या तथा ।

621

व्याधीनां हरणं जरांतकरणं शस्त्रागमोदीरणं
तस्य स्यादमरत्वमष्टगुणितं सिद्धांगनाकर्षणम् ॥

51. मूर्ध्नः षोडशपत्रपद्मगलितं प्राणादवाप्तं हठा-
दूर्ध्वास्यो रसनां नियम्य विवरे शक्तिं परां चिंतयन् ।
उत्कल्लोलकलाजलं च विमलं धारामयं यः पिबे-
त्रिव्याधिः स मृणालकोमलवपुर्योगी चिरं जीवति ॥

52. यत्प्रालेयं प्रहितसुषिरं मेरुमूर्धान्तरस्थं
तस्मिंस्तत्त्वं प्रवदति सुधीस्तन्मुखं निम्नगानाम् ।
चंद्रात् सारः स्रवति वपुषस्तेन मृत्युर्नराणां
तद्बध्नीयात्सुकरणमधो नान्यथा कार्यसिद्धिः ॥

53. सुषिरं ज्ञानजनकं पंचस्रोतःसमन्वितम् ।
तिष्ठते खेचरी मुद्रा तस्मिन्शून्ये निरंजने ॥

54. एकं सृष्टिमयं बीजमेका मुद्रा च खेचरी ।
एको देवो निरालम्ब एकावस्था मनोन्मनी ॥

55. बद्धो येन सुषुम्नायां प्राणस्तूड्डीयते यतः ।
तस्मादुड्डीयनाख्योऽयं योगिभिः समुदाहृतः ॥

56. उड्डीनं कुरुते यस्मादविश्रान्तं महाखगः ।
उड्डीयानं तदेव स्यात्तत्र बंधोऽभिधीयते ॥

57. उदरे पश्चिमं तानं नाभेरूर्ध्वं च कारयेत् ।
उड्डीयानो ह्यसौ बंधो मृत्युमातंगकेसरी ॥

58. उड्डीयानं तु सहजं गुरुणा कथितं यथा ।
अभ्यसेत्सततं यस्तु वृद्धोऽपि तरुणायते ॥

59. नाभेरूर्ध्वमधश्चापि तानं कुर्यात्प्रयत्नतः ।
षण्मासमभ्यसेन्मृत्युं जयत्येव न संशयः ॥

60. सर्वेषामेव बंधानामुत्तमो ह्युड्डियानकः ।
उड्डियाने दृढे बद्धे मुक्तिः स्वाभाविकी भवेत् ॥

61. पार्ष्णिभागेन संपीड्य योनिमाकुंचयेद्गुदम् ।
अपानमूर्ध्वमाकृष्य मूलबंधोऽभिधीयते ॥

62. अधोगतिमपानं वा ऊर्ध्वगं कुरुते बलात् ।
आकुंचनेन तं प्राहुर्मूलबंधं हि योगिनः ॥

63. गुदं पार्ष्ण्या तु संपीड्य वायुमाकुंचयेद् बलात् ।
वारंवारं यथा चोर्ध्वं समायाति समीरणः ॥

64. प्राणापानौ नादबिन्दू मूलबंधेन चैकताम् ।
गत्वा योगस्य संसिद्धिं यच्छतो नात्र संशयः ॥

65. अपानप्राणयोरैक्यं क्षयो मूत्रपुरीषयोः ।
युवा भवति वृद्धोऽपि सततं मूलबंधनात् ॥

66. अपान ऊर्ध्वगे जाते प्रयाते वह्निमंडलम् ।
तदाऽनलशिखा दीर्घा जायते वायुनाऽऽहता ॥

67. ततो यातो वह्न्यपानौ प्राणमुष्णस्वरूपकम् ।
तेनात्यंतप्रदीप्तस्तु ज्वलनो देहजस्तथा ॥

68. तेन कुंडलिनी सुप्ता संतप्ता संप्रबुध्यते ।
दंडाहता भुजंगीव निःश्वस्य ऋजुतां व्रजेत् ॥

69. बिलं प्रविष्टेव ततो ब्रह्मनाड्यंतरं व्रजेत् ।
तस्मान्नित्यं मूलबंधः कर्तव्यो योगिभिः सदा ॥

70. कंठमाकुंच्य हृदये स्थापयेच्चिबुकं दृढम् ।
बंधो जालंधराख्योऽयं जरामृत्युविनाशकः ॥

71. बध्नाति हि शिराजालमधोगामि नभोजलम् ।
ततो जालंधरो बंधः कंठदुःखौघनाशनः ॥

72. जालंधरे कृते बंधे कंठसंकोचलक्षणे ।
न पीयूषं पतत्यग्नौ न च वायुः प्रकुप्यति ॥

73. कंठसंकोचनेनैव द्वे नाड्यौ स्तंभयेद् दृढम् ।
मध्यचक्रमिदं ज्ञेयं षोडशाधारबंधनम् ॥

74. मूलस्थानं समाकुंच्य उड्डियानं तु कारयेत् ।
इडां च पिंगलां बद्ध्वा वाहयेत्पश्चिमे पथि ॥

75. अनेनैव विधानेन प्रयाति पवनो लयम् ।
ततो न जायते मृत्युर्जरारोगादिकं तथा ॥

76. बंधत्रयमिदं श्रेष्ठं महासिद्धैश्च सेवितम् ।
सर्वेषां हठतंत्राणां साधनं योगिनो विदु: ॥

77. यत्किंचित्स्त्रवते चंद्रादमृतं दिव्यरूपिण: ।
तत्सर्वं ग्रसते सूर्यस्तेन पिंडो जरायुत: ॥

78. तत्रास्ति करणं दिव्यं सूर्यस्य मुखवंचनम् ।
गुरूपदेशतो ज्ञेयं न तु शास्त्रार्थकोटिभि: ॥

79. उर्ध्वनाभेरधस्तालोरूर्ध्वं भानुरध: शशी ।
करणी विपरीताख्या गुरुवाक्येन लभ्यते ॥

80. नित्यमभ्यासयुक्तस्य जठराग्निविवर्धिनी ।
आहारो बहुलस्तस्य संपाद्य: साधकस्य च ।
अल्पाहारो यदि भवेदग्निर्दहति तत्क्षणात् ॥

81. अध:शिराश्चोर्ध्वपाद: क्षणं स्यात्प्रथमे दिन ।
क्षणाच्च किंचिदधिकमभ्यसेच्च दिने दिने ॥

82. वलितं पलितं चैव षण्मासोर्ध्वं न दृश्यते ।
याममात्रं तु यो नित्यमभ्यसेत् स तु कालजित् ॥

83. स्वेच्छया वर्तमानोऽपि योगोक्तैर्नियमैर्विना ।
वज्रोलीं यो विजानाति स योगी सिद्धिभाजनम् ॥

84. तत्र वस्तुद्वयं वक्ष्ये दुर्लभं यस्य कस्यचित् ।
क्षीरं चैकं द्वितीयं तु नाडी च वशवर्तिनी ॥

85. मेहनेन शनै: सम्यगूर्ध्वाकुंचनमभ्यसेत् ।
पुरुषोप्यथवा नारी वज्रोलीसिद्धिमाप्नुयात् ॥

86. यत्नत: शस्तनालेन फूत्कारं वज्रकंदरे ।
शनै: शनै: प्रकुर्वीत वायुसंचारकारणात् ॥

87. नारीभगे पतद्बिंदुमभ्यासेनोर्ध्वमाहरेत् ।
चलितं च निजं बिंदुमूर्ध्वमाकृष्य रक्षयेत् ॥

88. एवं संरक्षयेद् बिन्दुं मृत्युं जयति योगवित् ।
मरणं बिंदुपातेन जीवनं बिंदुधारणात् ॥

89. सुगंधो योगिनो देहे जायते बिंदुधारणात् ।
यावद् बिन्दु: स्थिरो देहे तावत् कालभयं कुत: ॥

90. चित्तायत्तं नृणां शुक्रं शुक्रायत्तं च जीवितम् ।
तस्माच्छुक्रं मन:श्चैव रक्षणीयं प्रयत्नत: ॥

91. ऋतुमत्या रजोऽप्येवं निजं बिंदुं च रक्षयेत् ।
मेंढ्रेणाकर्षयेदूर्ध्वं सम्यगभ्यासयोगवित् ॥

92. सहजोलिश्चामरोलिर्वज्रोल्या भेद एकत: ।
जले सुभस्म निक्षिप्य दग्धगोमयसंभवम् ॥

93. वज्रोलीमैथुनादूर्ध्वं स्त्रीपुंसो: स्वांगलेपनम् ।
आसीनयो: सुखेनैव मुक्तव्यापारयो: क्षणात् ॥

94. सहजोलिरियं प्रोक्ता श्रद्धेया योगिभि: सदा ।
अयं शुभकरो योगो भोगयुक्तोऽपि मुक्तिद: ॥

95. अयं योग: पुण्यवतां धीराणां तत्त्वदर्शिनाम् ।
निर्मत्सराणां वै सिध्येत्र तु मत्सरशालिनाम् ॥

96. पित्तोल्बणत्वात्प्रथमांबुधारां विहाय नि:सारतयांत्यधाराम् ।
निषेव्यते शीतलमध्यधारा कापालिके खण्डमतेऽमरोली ॥

97. अमरीं य: पिबेन्नित्यं नस्यं कुर्वन्दिनेदिने ।
वज्रोलीमभ्यसेत् सम्यक्सामरोलीति कथ्यते ॥

98. अभ्यासान्नि:सृतां चांद्रीं विभूत्या सह मिश्रयेत् ।
धारयेदुत्तमांगेषु दिव्यदृष्टि: प्रजायते ॥

99. पुंसो बिंदुं समाकुंच्य सम्यगभ्यासपाटवात् ।
यदि नारी रजो रक्षेद्वज्रोल्या सापि योगिनी ॥

100. तस्या: किंचिद्रजो नाशं न गच्छति न संशय: ।
तस्या: शरीरे नादश्च बिंदुतामेव गच्छति ॥

101. स बिंदुस्तद्रजश्चैव एकीभूय स्वदेहगौ ।
वज्रोल्यभ्यासयोगेन सर्वसिद्धिं प्रयच्छत: ॥

102. रक्षेदाकुंचनादूर्ध्वं या रज: सा हि योगिनी ।
अतीतानागतं वेत्ति खेचरी च भवेद् ध्रुवम् ॥

103. देहसिद्धिं च लभते वज्रोल्यभ्यासयोगत: ।
अयं पुण्यकरो योगो भोगे भुक्तेऽपि मुक्तिद: ॥

625

104. कुटिलांगी कुण्डलिनी भुजंगी शक्तिरीश्वरी ।
कुंडल्यरुंधती चैते शब्दा: पर्यायवाचका: ॥

105. उद्घाटयेत्कपाटं तु यथा कुंचिकया हठात् ।
कुंडलिन्या यथा योगी मोक्षद्वारं विभेदयेत् ॥

106. येन मार्गेण गंतव्यं ब्रह्मस्थानं निरामयम् ।
मुखेनाच्छाद्य तद्द्वारं प्रसुप्ता परमेश्वरी ॥

107. कंदोर्ध्वे कुंडली शक्ति: सुप्ता मोक्षाय योगिनाम् ।
वंधनाय च मूढानां यस्तां वेत्ति स योगवित् ॥

108. कुण्डली कुटिलाकारा सर्पवत्परिकीर्तिता ।
सा शक्तिश्चालिता येन स मुक्तो नात्र संशय: ॥

109. गंगायमुनयोर्मध्ये बालरण्डां तपस्विनीम् ।
बलात्कारेण गृह्णीयात्तद्विष्णो: परमं पदम् ॥

110. इडा भगवती गंगा पिंगला यमुना नदी ।
इडापिंगलयोर्मध्ये बालरण्डा च कुंडली ॥

111. पुच्छे प्रगृह्य भुजगीं सुप्तामुद्बोधयेच्च ताम् ।
निद्रां विहाय सा शक्तिरूर्ध्वमुत्तिष्ठते हठात् ॥

112. अवस्थिता चैव फणावती सा प्रातश्च सायं प्रहरार्धमात्रम् ।
प्रपूर्य सूर्यात् परिधानयुक्त्या प्रगृह्य नित्यं परिचालनीया ॥

113. उर्ध्वं वितस्तिमात्रं तु विस्तारं चतुरंगुलम् ।
मृदुलं धवलं प्रोक्तं वेष्टितांबरलक्षणम् ॥

114. सति वज्रासने पादौ कराभ्यां धारयेद् दृढम् ।
गुल्फदेशसमीपे च कन्दं तत्र प्रपीडयेत् ॥

115. वज्रासने स्थितो योगी चालयित्वा च कुंडलीम् ।
कुर्यादनन्तरं भस्त्रां कुंडलीमाशु बोधयेत् ॥

116. भानोराकुंचनं कुर्यात्कुण्डलीं चालयेत् तत: ।
मृत्युवक्त्रगतस्यापि तस्य मृत्युभयं कुत: ॥

117. मुहूर्तद्वयपर्यंतं निर्भयं चालनादसौ ।
ऊर्ध्वमाकृष्यते किंचित्सुषुम्नायां समुद्गता ॥

118. तेन कुंडलिनी तस्या: सुषुम्नाया मुखं ध्रुवम् ।
जहाति तस्मात्प्राणोऽयं सुषुम्नां व्रजति स्वत: ॥

119. तस्मात्संचालयेन्नित्यं सुखसुप्तामरुंधतीम् ।
तस्या: संचालनेनैव योगी रोगै: प्रमुच्यते ॥

120. येन संचालिता शक्ति: स योगी सिद्धिभाजनम् ।
किमत्र बहुनोक्तेन कालं जयति लीलया ॥

121. ब्रह्मचर्यरतस्यैव नित्यं हितमिताशिन: ।
मंडलाद् दृश्यते सिद्धि: कुंडल्यभ्यासयोगिन: ॥

122. कुंडलीं चालयित्वा तु भस्त्रां कुर्याद्द्विशेषत: ।
एवमभ्यसतो नित्यं यमिनो यमभी: कुत: ॥

123. द्वासप्ततिसहस्राणां नाडीनां मलशोधने ।
कुत: प्रक्षालनोपाय: कुंडल्यभ्यसनादृते ॥

124. इयं तु मध्यमा नाडी दृढाभ्यासेन योगिनाम् ।
आसनप्राणसंयाममुद्राभि: सरला भवेत् ॥

125. अभ्यासे तु विनिद्राणां मनो धृत्वा समाधिना ।
रुद्राणी वा परा मुद्रा भद्रां सिद्धिं प्रयच्छति ॥

126. राजयोगं विना पृथ्वी राजयोगं विना निशा ।
राजयोगं विना मुद्रा विचित्रापि न शोभते ॥

127. मारुतस्य विधिं सर्वं मनोयुक्तं समभ्यसेत् ।
इतरत्र न कर्तव्या मनोवृत्तिर्मनीषिणा ॥

128. इति मुद्रा दश प्रोक्ता आदिनाथेन शंभुना ।
एकैका तासु यमिनां महासिद्धिप्रदायिनी ॥

129. उपदेशं हि मुद्राणां यो दत्ते सांप्रदायिकम् ।
स एव श्रीगुरु: स्वामी साक्षादीश्वर एव स: ॥

130. तस्य वाक्यपरो भूत्वा मुद्राभ्यासे समाहित: ।
अणिमादिगुणै: सार्धं लभते कालवंचनम् ॥

Chapter Four

1. नम: शिवाय गुरवे नादबिन्दुकलात्मने ।
   निरंजनपदं याति नित्यं तत्र परायण: ॥

2. अथेदानीं प्रवक्ष्यामि समाधिक्रममुत्तमम् ।
   मृत्युघ्नं च सुखोपायं ब्रह्मानन्दकरं परम् ॥

3. राजयोग: समाधिश्च उन्मनी य मनोन्मनी ।
   अमरत्वं लयस्तत्त्वं शून्याशून्यं परं पदम् ॥

4. अमनस्कं तथाद्वैतं निरालम्बं निरंजनम् ।
   जीवन्मुक्तिश्च सहजा तुर्या चेत्येकवाचका: ॥

5. सलिले सैन्धवं यद्वत्साम्यं भजति योगत: ।
   तथात्ममनसोरैक्यं समाधिरभिधीयते ॥

6. यदा संक्षीयते प्राणो मानसं च प्रलीयते ।
   तदा समरसत्वं च समाधिरभिधीयते ॥

7. तत्समं च द्वयोरैक्यं जीवात्मपरमात्मनो: ।
   प्रनष्टसर्वसंकल्प: समाधि: सोऽभिधीयते ॥

8. राजयोगस्य माहात्म्यं को वा जानाति तत्त्वत: ।
   ज्ञानं मुक्ति: स्थिति: सिद्धिर्गुरुवाक्येन लभ्यते ॥

9. दुर्लभो विषयत्यागो दुर्लभं तत्त्वदर्शनम् ।
   दुर्लभा सहजावस्था सद्गुरो: करुणां विना ॥

10. विविधैरासनै: कुंभैर्विचित्रै: करणैरपि ।
    प्रबुद्धायां महाशक्तौ प्राण: शून्ये प्रलीयते ॥

11. उत्पन्नशक्तिबोधस्य त्यक्तनि:शेषकर्मण: ।
    योगिन: सहजावस्था स्वयमेव प्रजायत ॥

12. सुषुम्नावाहिनि प्राणे शून्ये विशति मानसे ।
    तदा सर्वाणि कर्माणि निर्मूलयति योगवित् ॥

13. अमराय नमस्तुभ्यं सोऽपि कालस्त्वया जित: ।
    पतितं वदने यस्य जगदेतच्चराचरम् ॥

14. चित्ते समत्वमापन्ने वायौ व्रजति मध्यमे ।
    तदामरोली वज्रोली सहजोली प्रजायते ॥

15. ज्ञानं कुतो मनसि संभवतीह तावत्
प्राणोऽपि जीवति मनो म्रियते न यावत् ।
प्राणो मनो द्वयमिदं विलयं नयेद् यो
मोक्षं स गच्छति नरो न कथंचिदन्य: ॥

16. ज्ञात्वा सुषुम्नासद्भेदं कृत्वा वायुं च मध्यगम् ।
स्थित्वा सदैव सुस्थाने ब्रह्मरंध्रे निरोधयेत् ॥

17. सूर्याचंद्रमसौ धत्त: कालं रात्रिंदिवात्मकम् ।
भोक्त्री सुषुम्ना कालस्य गुह्यमेतदुदाहृतम् ॥

18. द्वासप्ततिसहस्राणि नाडीद्वाराणि पंजरे ।
सुषुम्ना शांभवी शक्ति: शेषास्त्वेव निरर्थका: ॥

19. वायु: परिचितो यस्मादग्निना सह कुंडलीम् ।
बोधयित्वा सुषुम्नायां प्रविशेदनिरोधत: ॥

20. सुषुम्नावाहिनि प्राणे सिद्ध्यत्येव मनोन्मनी ।
अन्यथा त्वितराभ्यासा: प्रयासायैव योगिनाम् ॥

21. पवनो बध्यते येन मनस्तेनैव बध्यते ।
मनश्च बध्यते येन पवनस्तेन बध्यते ॥

22. हेतुद्वयं तु चित्तस्य वासना च समीरण: ।
तयोर्विनष्ट एकस्मिंस्तौ द्वावपि विनश्यत: ॥

23. मनो यत्र विलीयेत पवनस्तत्र लीयते ।
पवनो लीयते यत्र मनस्तत्र विलीयते ॥

24. दुग्धांबुवत्संमिलितावुभौ तौ तुल्यक्रियौ मानसमारुतौ हि ।
यतो मरुत्तत्र मन: प्रवृत्तिर्यतो मनस्तत्र मरुत्प्रवृत्ति: ॥

25. तत्रैकनाशादपरस्य नाश एकप्रवृत्तेरपरप्रवृत्ति: ।
अध्वस्तयोश्चेन्द्रियवर्गवृत्ति: प्रध्वस्तयोर्मोक्षपदस्य सिद्धि: ॥

26. रसस्य मनसश्चैव चंचलत्वं स्वभावत: ।
रसो बद्धो मनो बद्धं किं न सिद्ध्यति भूतले ॥

27. मूर्च्छितो हरते व्याधीन्मृतो जीवयति स्वयम् ।
बद्ध: खेचरतां धत्ते रसो वायुश्च पार्वति ॥

28. मन: स्थैर्ये स्थिरो वायुस्ततो बिन्दु: स्थिरो भवेत् ।
बिंदुस्थैर्यात्सदा सत्त्वं पिंडस्थैर्यं प्रजायते ॥

29. इंद्रियाणां मनो नाथो मनोनाथस्तु मारुत: ।
मारुतस्य लयो नाथ: स लयो नादमाश्रित: ॥

30. सोऽयमेवास्तु मोक्षाख्यो मास्तु वापि मतांतरे ।
मन: प्राणलये कश्चिदानन्द: संप्रवर्तते ॥

31. प्रनष्टश्वासनि:श्वास: प्रध्वस्तविषयग्रह: ।
निश्चेष्टो निर्विकारश्च लयो जयति योगिनाम् ॥

32. उच्छिन्नसर्वसंकल्पो नि:शेषाशेषचेष्टित: ।
स्वावगम्यो लय: कोऽपि जायते वागगोचर: ॥

33. यत्र दृष्टिर्लयस्तत्र भूतेन्द्रियसनातनी ।
सा शक्तिर्जीवभूतानां द्वे अलक्ष्ये लयं गते ॥

34. लयो लय इति प्राहू: कीदृशं लयलक्षणम् ।
अपुनर्वासनोत्थानाल्लयो विषयविस्मृति: ॥

35. वेदशास्त्रपुराणानि सामान्यगणिका इव ।
एकैव शांभवी मुद्रा गुप्ता कुलवधूरिव ॥

36. अंतर्लक्ष्यं बहिर्दृष्टिर्निमेषोन्मेषवर्जिता ।
एषा सा शांभवी मुद्रा वेदशास्त्रेषु गोपिता ॥

37. अंतर्लक्ष्यविलीनचित्तपवनो योगी यदा वर्तते
दृष्ट्या निश्चलतारया बहिरध: पश्यन्नपश्यन्नपि ।
मुद्रेयं खलु शांभवी भवति सा लब्धा प्रसादाद्गुरो:
शून्याशून्यविलक्षणं स्फुरति तत्तत्त्वं परं शांभवम् ॥

38. श्रीशांभव्याश्च खेचर्या अवस्थाधामभेदत: ।
भवेच्चित्तलयानंद: शून्ये चित्सुखरूपिणि ॥

39. तारे ज्योतिषि संयोज्य किंचिदुन्नमयेद् भ्रुवौ ।
पूर्वयोगं मनो युंजन्नुन्मनीकारक: क्षणात् ॥

40. केचिदागमजालेन केचिन्निगमसंकुलै: ।
केचित्तर्केण मुह्यन्ति नैव जानंति तारकम् ॥

41. अर्धोन्मीलितलोचन: स्थिरमना नासाग्रदत्तेक्षण-
चंद्रार्काविप लीनतामुपनयन्नि ष्यंदभावेन य: ।
ज्योतीरूपमशेषबीजमखिलं देदीप्यमानं परं
तत्त्वं तत्पदमेति वस्तु परमं वाच्यं किमत्राधिकम् ॥

42. दिवा न पूजयेल्लिंगं रात्रौ चैव न पूजयेत् ।
सर्वदा पूजयेल्लिंगं दिवारात्रिनिरोधत: ॥

43. सव्यदक्षिणनाडिस्थो मध्ये चरति मारुत: ।
तिष्ठति खेचरी मुद्रा तस्मिन्स्थाने न संशय: ॥

44. इडापिंगलयोर्मध्ये शून्यं चैवानिलं ग्रसेत् ।
तिष्ठते खेचरी मुद्रा तत्र सत्यं पुन: पुन: ॥

45. सूर्याचन्द्रमसोर्मध्ये निरालम्बान्तरे पुन: ।
संस्थिता व्योमचक्रे या सा मुद्रा नाम खेचरी ॥

46. सोमाद् यत्रोदिता धारा साक्षात् सा शिववल्लभा ।
पूरयेदतुलां दिव्यां सुषुम्नां पश्चिमे मुखे ॥

47. पुरस्ताच्चैव पूर्येत निश्चिता खेचरी भवेत् ।
अभ्यस्ता खेचरी मुद्राप्युन्मनी संप्रजायते ॥

48. भ्रुवोर्मध्ये शिवस्थानं मनस्तत्र विलीयते ।
ज्ञातव्यं तत्पदं तुर्यं तत्र कालो न विद्यते ॥

49. अभ्यसेत् खेचरीं तावद्यावत् स्याद्योगनिद्रित: ।
संप्राप्तयोगनिद्रस्य कालो नास्ति कदाचन ॥

50. निरालम्बं मन: कृत्वा न किंचिदापि चिंतयेत् ।
सबाह्याभ्यंतरे व्योम्नि घटवत्तिष्ठति ध्रुवम् ॥

51. बाह्यवायुर्यथा लीनस्तथा मध्यो न संशय: ।
स्वस्थाने स्थिरतामेति पवनो मनसा सह ॥

52. एवमभ्यसमानस्य वायुमार्गे दिवानिशम् ।
अभ्यासाज्जीर्यते वायुर्मनस्तत्रैव लीयते ॥

53. अमृतै: प्लावयेद् देहमापादतलमस्तकम् ।
सिद्ध्यत्येव महाकायो महाबलपराक्रम: ॥

631

54. शक्तिमध्ये मन: कृत्वा शक्ति मानसमध्यगाम् ।
मनसा मन आलोक्य धारयेत्परमं पदम् ॥

55. खमध्ये कुरु चात्मानमात्ममध्ये च खं कुरु ।
सर्वं च खमयं कृत्वा न किंचिदपि चिन्तयेत् ॥

56. अन्त: शून्यो बहि: शून्य: शून्य: कुंभ इवांबरे ।
अन्त: पूर्णो बहि: पूर्ण: पूर्ण: कुम्भ इवार्णवे ॥

57. बाह्याचिंता न कर्तव्या तथैवांतरचिंतनम् ।
सर्वचिंतां परित्यज्य न किंचिदपि चिंतयेत् ॥

58. संकल्पमात्रकलनै जगत समग्रं
संकल्पमात्रकलनैव मनोविलास: ।
संकल्पमात्रमतिमुत्सृज निर्विकल्प-
मश्रित्य निश्चयमवाप्नुहि राम शांतिम् ॥

59. कर्पूरमनले यद्वत्सैन्धवं सलिले यथा ।
तथा संधीयमानं च मनस्तत्त्वे विलीयते ॥

60. ज्ञेयं सर्वं प्रतीतं च ज्ञानं च मन उच्यते ।
ज्ञानं ज्ञेयं समं नष्टं नान्य: पंथा द्वितीयक: ॥

61. मनोदृश्यमिदं सर्वं यत्किंचित्सचराचरम् ।
मनसो ह्युन्मनीभावाद् द्वैतं नैवोपलभ्यते ॥

62. ज्ञेयवस्तुपरित्यागाद्विलयं याति मानसम् ।
मनसो विलये जाते कैवल्यमवशिष्यत ॥

63. एवं नानाविधोपाया: सम्यक् स्वानुभवान्विता: ।
समाधिमार्गा: कथिता: पूर्वाचार्यैर्महात्मभि: ॥

64. सुषुम्नायै कुंडलिन्यै सुधायै चन्द्रजन्मने ।
मनोन्मन्यै नमस्तुभ्यं महाशक्त्यै चिदात्मने ॥

65. अशक्यतत्त्वबोधानां मूढानामपि संमतम् ।
प्रोक्तं गोरक्षनाथेन नादोपासनमुच्यते ॥

66. श्रीआदिनाथेन सपादकोटिलयप्रकारा: कथिता जयंति ।
नादानुसंधानकमेकमेव मन्यामहे मुख्यतमं लयानाम् ॥

67. मुक्तासने स्थितो योगी मुद्रां संधाय शांभवीम् ।
श्रृणुयाद् दक्षिणे कर्णे नादमंतःस्थमेकधी: ॥

68. श्रवणपुटनयनयुगलघ्राणमुखानां निरोधनं कार्यम् ।
शुद्धसुषुम्नासरणौ स्फुटममल: श्रूयते नाद: ॥

69. आरंभश्च घटश्चैव तथा परिचयोऽपि च ।
निष्पत्ति: सर्वयोगेषु स्यादवस्थाचतुष्टयम् ॥

70. ब्रह्मग्रंथेर्भवेद्भेदो ह्यानंद: शून्यसंभव: ।
विचित्र: क्वणको देहेऽनाहत: श्रूयते ध्वनि: ॥

71. दिव्यदेहश्च तेजस्वी दिव्यगंधस्त्वरोगवान् ।
संपूर्णहृदय: शून्य आरम्भे योगवान्भवेत् ॥

72. द्वितीयायां घटीकृत्य वायूर्भवति मध्यग: ।
दृढासनो भवेद् योगी ज्ञानी देवसमस्तदा ॥

73. विष्णुग्रंथेस्ततो भेदात् परमानंदसूचक: ।
अतिशून्ये विमर्दश्च भेरीशब्दस्तदा भवेत् ॥

74. तृतीयायां तु विज्ञेयो विहायोमर्दलध्वनि: ।
महाशून्यं तदा याति सर्वसिद्धिसमाश्रयम् ॥

75. चित्तानंदं तदा जित्वा सहजानन्दसंभव: ।
दोषदु:खजराव्याधिक्षुधानिद्राविवर्जित: ॥

76. रुद्रग्रंथि यदा भित्त्वा शर्वपीठगतोऽनिल: ।
निष्पत्तौ वैणव: शब्द: क्वणद्वीणाक्वणो भवेत् ॥

77. एकीभूतं तदा चित्तं राजयोगाभिधानकम् ।
सृष्टिसंहारकर्तासौ योगीश्वरसमो भवेत् ॥

78. अस्तु वा मास्तु वा मुक्तिरत्रैवाखण्डितं सुखम् ।
लयोद्भवमिदं सौख्यं राजयोगादवाप्यते ॥

79. राजयोगमजानंत: केवलं हठकर्मिण: ।
एतानभ्यासिनो मन्ये प्रयासफलवर्जितान् ॥

80. उन्मन्यवाप्तये शीघ्रं भ्रूध्यानं मम संमतम् ।
राजयोगपदं प्राप्तुं सुखोपायोऽल्पचेतसाम् ।
सद्य: प्रत्ययसंधायी जायते नादजो लय: ॥

81. नादानुसंधानसमाधिभाजां योगीश्चराणां हृदि वर्धमानम् ।
आनन्दमेकं वचसामगम्यं जानाति तं श्रीगुरुनाथ एक: ॥

82. कर्णौ पिधाय हस्ताभ्यां यं शृणोति ध्वनिं मुनि: ।
तत्र चित्तं स्थिरीकुर्याद्यावत् स्थिरपदं व्रजेत् ॥

83. अभ्यस्यमानो नादोऽयं बाह्यमावृणुते ध्वनिम् ।
पक्षाद्विक्षेपमखिलं जित्वा योगी सुखी भवेत् ॥

84. श्रूयते प्रथमाभ्यासे नादो नानाविधा महान् ।
ततोऽभ्यासे वर्धमाने श्रूयते सूक्ष्मसूक्ष्मक: ॥

85. आदौ जलधिजीमूतभेरीझर्झरसंभवा: ।
मध्ये मर्दलशंखोत्था घंटकाहलजास्तथा ॥

86. अन्ते तु किंकिणीवंशवीणाभ्रमरनि:स्वना: ।
इति नानाविधा नादा: श्रूयन्ते देहमध्यगा: ॥

87. महति श्रूयमाणेऽपि मेघभेर्यादिके ध्वनौ ।
तत्र सूक्ष्मात् सूक्ष्मतरं नादमेव परामृशेत् ॥

88. घनमुत्सृज्य वा सूक्ष्मे सूक्ष्ममुत्सृज्य वा घने ।
रममाणमपि क्षिप्तं मनो नान्यत्र चालयेत् ॥

89. यत्रकुत्रापि वा नादे लगति प्रथमं मन: ।
तत्रैव सुस्थिरीभूय तेन सार्धं विलीयते ॥

90. मकरन्दं पिबन्भृंगो गन्धं नापेक्षते यथा ।
नादासक्तं तथा चित्तं विषयान्नहि कांक्षते ॥

91. मनोमत्तगजेंद्रस्य विषयोद्यानचारिण: ।
समर्थोऽयं नियमने निनादनिशितांकुश: ॥

92. बद्धं तु नादबंधेन मन: संत्यक्तचापलम् ।
प्रयाति सुतरां स्थैर्यं छिन्नपक्ष: खगो यथा ॥

93. सर्वचिंतां परित्यज्य सावधानेन चेतसा ।
नाद एवानुसंधेयो योगसाम्राज्यमिच्छता ॥

94. नादोऽन्तरंगसारंगबंधने वागुरायते ।
अन्तरंगकुरंगस्य वधे व्याधायतेऽपि च ॥

95. अंतरंगस्य यमिनो वाजिन: परिघायते ।
नादोपास्तिरतो नित्यमवधार्या हि योगिना ॥

96. बद्धं विमुक्तचांचल्यं नादगंधकजारणात् ।
मन:पारदमाप्नोति निरालंबाख्यखेऽटनम् ॥

97. नादश्रवणत: क्षिप्रमंतरंगभुजंगम: ।
विस्मृत्य सर्वमेकाग्र: कुत्रचिन्नहि धावति ॥

98. काष्ठे प्रवर्तितो वह्नि: काष्ठेन सह शाम्यति ।
नादे प्रवर्तितं चित्तं नादेन सह लीयते ॥

99. घंटादिनादसक्तस्तब्धांत:करणहरिणस्य ।
प्रहरणमपि सुकरं शरसंधानप्रवीणश्चेत् ॥

100. अनाहतस्य शब्दस्य ध्वनिर्य उपलभ्यते ।
ध्वनेरन्तर्गतं ज्ञेयं ज्ञेयस्यांतर्गतं मन: ।
मनस्तत्र लयं याति तद्विष्णो: परमं पदम् ॥

101. तावदाकाशसंकल्पो यावच्छब्द: प्रवर्तते ।
नि:शब्दं तत्परं ब्रह्म परमात्मेति गीयते ॥

102. यत्किंचिन्नादरूपेण श्रूयते शक्तिरेव सा ।
यस्तत्त्वांतो निराकार: स एव परमेश्वर: ॥

103. सर्वे हठलयोपाया राजयोगस्य सिद्धये ।
राजयोगसमारूढ: पुरुष: कालवंचक: ॥

104. तत्त्वं बीजं हठ: क्षेत्रमौदासीन्यं जलं त्रिभि: ।
उन्मनी कल्पलतिका सद्य एव प्रवर्तते ॥

105. सदा नादानुसंधानात्क्षीयंते पापसंचया: ।
निरंजने विलीयेते निश्चितं चित्तमारुतौ ॥

106. शंखदुंदुभिनादं च न शृणोति कदाचन ।
काष्ठवज्जायते देह उन्मन्यावस्थया ध्रुवम् ॥

107. सर्वावस्थाविनिर्मुक्त: सर्वचिंताविवर्जित: ।
मृतवत्तिष्ठते योगी स मुक्तो नात्र संशय: ॥

108. खाद्यते न च कालेन बाध्यते न च कर्मणा ।
साध्यते न स केनापि योगी युक्त: समाधिना: ॥

109. न गन्धं न रसं रूपं न च स्पर्शं न निःस्वनम् ।
नात्मानं न परं वेत्ति योगी युक्तः समाधिना ॥

110. चित्तं न सुप्तं नोजाग्रत्स्मृतिविस्मृतिवर्जितम् ।
न चास्तमेति नोदेति यस्यासौ मुक्त एव सः ॥

111. न विजानाति शीतोष्णं न दुःखं न सुखं तथा ।
न मानं नापमानं च योगी युक्तः समाधिना ॥

112. स्वस्थो जाग्रदवस्थायां सुप्तवद्यौऽवतिष्ठते ।
निःश्वासोच्छ्वासहीनश्च निश्चितं मुक्त एव सः ॥

113. अवध्यः सर्वशस्त्राणामशक्यः सर्वदेहिनाम् ।
अग्राह्यो मंत्रयंत्राणां योगी युक्तः समाधिना ॥

114. यावन्नैव प्रविशति चरन्मारुतो मध्यमार्गे
यावद्विंदुर्न भवति दृढः प्राणवातप्रबंधात् ।
यावद्ध्याने सहजसदृशं जायते नैव तत्त्वं
तावज्ज्ञानं वदति तदिदं दम्भमिथ्याप्रलापः ॥

Translation

Chapter One

1. Salutations to the glorious primal (original) guru, Sri Adinath, who instructed the knowledge of hatha yoga which shines forth as a stairway for those who wish to ascend to the highest stage of yoga, raja yoga.

2. Prostrating first to the guru, Yogi Swatmarama instructs the knowledge of hatha yoga only for (raja yoga) the highest state of yoga.

3. The highest state of raja yoga is unknown due to misconceptions (darkness) created by varying ideas and concepts. In good will and as a blessing, Swatmarama offers light on hatha yoga.

4. Yogi Matsyendranath knew the knowledge of hatha yoga. He gave it to Gorakhnath and others, and by their grace the author (Swatmarama) learned it.

5. Sri Adinath (Shiva), Matsyendra, Shabara, Anandabhairava, Chaurangi, Mina, Goraksha, Virupaksha, Bileshaya, Manthana, Bhairava, Siddhi, Buddha, Kanthadi, Korantaka, Surananda, Siddhipada, Charapati, Kaneri, Pujyapada, Nityanath, Niranjan, Kapali, Bindunath, Kakachandishwara, Allama, Prabhudeva,

Ghodacholi, Tintini, Bhanuki, Naradeva, Khanda, Kapalika. *(5–8)* These mahasiddhas (great masters), having conquered time (death) by the practice of hatha yoga, roam about the universe. *(9)*

10. For those continually tempered by the heat of tapa (the three types of pain – spiritual, environmental and physical) hatha is like the hermitage giving protection from the heat. For those always united in yoga, hatha is the basis acting like a tortoise.

11. Hatha yoga is the greatest secret of the yogis who wish to attain perfection (siddhi). Indeed, to be fruitful, it must be kept secret; revealed it becomes powerless.

12. The hatha yogi should live alone in a hermitage and practise in a place the length of a bow (one and a half metres), where there is no hazard from rocks, fire or water, and which is in a well-administered and virtuous kingdom (nation or town) where good alms can be easily attained.

13. This is the description of the yoga hermitage as prescribed by the siddhas for the hatha yoga practitioners. The room of sadhana should have a small door, without aperture (window), holes or cracks, being neither too high nor too low. It should be spotlessly clean, wiped with cow manure and free from animals or insects. Outside, there should be an open platform with a thatched roof, a well and a surrounding wall (fence). The appearance of the hermitage should be pleasant.

14. In this manner, dwelling in the hermitage, being devoid of all thought (excess mentation), yoga should be practised in the way instructed by the guru.

15. Overeating, exertion, talkativeness, adhering to rules, being in the company of common people and unsteadiness (wavering mind) are the six (causes) which destroy yoga.

16. Enthusiasm, perseverance, discrimination, un-shakeable faith, courage, avoiding the company of common people, are the (six causes) which bring success in yoga. *(i)*

Non-violence, truth, non-stealing, continence (being absorbed in a pure state of consciousness), forgiveness, endurance, compassion, humility, moderate diet and cleanliness are the ten rules of conduct (yama). *(ii)*

Penance (austerity), contentment, belief (faith) in the Supreme (God), charity, worship of God, listening to the recitations of sacred scriptures, modesty, a discerning intellect, japa (mantra repetition) and sacrifice are the ten observances (niyama). *(iii)*

17. Prior to everything, asana is spoken of as the first part of hatha yoga. Having done asana one gets steadiness (firmness) of body and mind; diseaselessness and lightness (flexibility) of the limbs.

18. I will proceed to describe some of the asana accepted by munis such as Vasishtha and yogis such as Matsyendranath.

19. Placing both soles (of the feet) on the inner side of the thighs, sitting equipoised with a straight body. This is called swastika (asana).

20. Place the right ankle next to the left buttock and the left (ankle) next to the right (buttock). This is gomukhasana and it resembles the face of the cow.

21. Placing one foot by the (opposite) thigh and the other (foot) under the (same) thigh is known as veerasana.

22. Press the anus firmly with the ankles positioned in opposite directions and sit well-poised. According to the yogis this is koormasana.

23. Assuming padmasana insert the hands between the thighs and calves, planting them (the hands) firmly on the ground, raise the body in the air. This is kukkutasana.

24. Sitting in kukkutasana, join both the hands at the shoulders and lie flat on the back like a tortoise. This is uttankoormasana.

25. Holding the toes with the hands, pull them up to the ears as if drawing a bow. This is called dhanurasana.

26. Place the right foot at the base of the left thigh, the left foot at the side of the right knee. Take hold of the left foot with the right hand, pass the left arm behind the waist and remain with the body turned. This asana is described by Sri Matsyendranath.

27. Practice of this asana (matsyendrasana) increases the digestive fire to such an incredible capacity that it is the means of removing diseases and thus awakening the serpent power and bringing equilibrium in the bindu.

28. Stretching the legs (in front) on the ground, like a stick; bending forward, holding the toes with both hands and placing the forehead on the knees, is called paschimottanasana.

29. Paschimottanasana is the best among asanas. By this asana the pranic currents rise through sushumna, the digestive fire increases, the abdomen becomes flat, and the practitioner becomes free from diseases.

30. Lie on the stomach, placing both hands on the ground (under the body) and the elbows at the sides of the navel. Raise the body high, keeping it like a stick. This is called the peacock pose by the exponents of yoga.

31. Mayurasana quickly alleviates all diseases like enlargement of the glands, dropsy and other stomach disorders. It rectifies imbalance of the humours (vata, pitta, kapha). It reduces to ashes all food taken indiscriminately, kindles the gastric fire and enables destruction of kalakuta (a deadly poison).

32. Lying flat on the ground with the face upwards, in the manner of a dead body, is shavasana. It removes tiredness and enables the mind (and whole body) to relax.

33. Eighty-four asanas were taught by Shiva. Out of those I shall now describe the four important ones.

34. Siddhasana, padmasana, simhasana and bhadrasana, these are the four main asanas. Always sit comfortably in siddhasana because it is the best.

35. Press the perineum with the heel of one foot, place the other foot on top of the genitals. Having done this, rest the chin on to the chest. Remaining still and steady, with the senses controlled, gaze steadily into the eyebrow centre; it breaks open the door to liberation. This is called siddhasana.

36. According to others, placing the heel above the penis and the other (heel) on top of that is siddhasana.

37. This is called siddhasana, others know it as vajrasana, some call it muktasana and lastly it is called guptasana.

38. Just as moderate diet is the most important of the yamas, and non-violence, of the niyamas, so the siddhas know that siddhasana is the most important of the asanas.

39. Of all the eighty-four asanas, siddhasana should always be practised. It purifies the 72,000 nadis.

40. The yogi who meditates on the self or atma, takes moderate and pure food and practises siddhasana for twelve years, attains perfection or siddhi.

41. When perfection is attainable through siddhasana, what is the use of practising many other asanas? When the flow of prana is stabilized, the breath stops spontaneously (kevala kumbhaka) and a mindless state (unmani) arises by itself.

42. Thus, through securing siddhasana, the three bandhas occur by themselves.

43. There is no asana like siddhasana, no kumbhaka like kevala, no mudra like khechari and no laya or dissolution of mind like nada, the inner sound.

44. Place the right foot on the left thigh and the left foot on the right thigh, cross the hands behind the back and firmly hold the toes. Press the chin against the chest and look at the tip of the nose. This is called padmasana, the destroyer of a yogi's diseases.

45. Place the feet on the thighs, soles upward, palms in the middle of the groin, facing upward.

46. Gaze at the nosetip, keeping the tongue pressed against the root of the upper teeth and the chin against the chest, and slowly raise the prana upward.

47. This is called padmasana, destroyer of all diseases. Ordinary people cannot achieve this posture, only the few wise ones on this earth can.

48. (Sitting in padmasana) keeping the palms one above the other, chin on the chest and concentrate the mind (chitta) on Him (the Self). Repeatedly draw the vital air up from the anal region and bring the inhaled prana downwards. (Thus joining the two) one gets the highest knowledge by awakening the Shakti.

49. The yogi who, seated in padmasana, inhales through the entrances of the nadis and fills them with maruta or vital air gains liberation; there is no doubt about it.

50. Place the ankles below the scrotum, right ankle on the left side, left ankle on the right side of the perineum.

51. Place the palms on the knees, fingers spread apart, keep the mouth open and gaze at the nosetip with a concentrated mind.

52. This is simhasana, held in great esteem by the highest yogis. This most excellent asana facilitates the three bandhas.

53. Place the ankles below the genitals on the sides by the perineum, left ankle on the left (side) right ankle on the right (side).

54. Then hold the feet, which are on their sides, firmly with the hands and remain motionless. This is bhadrasana which destroys all diseases. The yogis who are perfected (siddhas) call it gorakshasana.

55. Thus the best of yogis, being free from fatigue in practising asana and bandhas, should practise purification of the nadis, mudras and pranayama.

56. Asana, the varieties of kumbhaka, practices called mudras and concentration on the inner sound (nada) comprise the sequence of hatha yoga.

57. One who is brahmachari, takes moderate and pure food, is regular and intent on yoga and renounces (attachment to sensual experience) becomes perfected (siddha) after a year.

58. Mitahara is defined as agreeable and sweet food, leaving one fourth of the stomach free, and eaten (as an offering to please Shiva).

59. The foods which are prohibited (for the yogi) are: those which are bitter, sour, pungent, salty, heating, green vegetables (other than those ordained), sour gruel, oil, sesame and mustard, alcohol, fish, flesh foods, curds, buttermilk, horse gram, fruit of jujube, oil cakes, asafoetida and garlic.

60. Unhealthy diet should not be taken, that which is reheated after becoming cold, which is dry (devoid of natural oil), which is excessively salty or acidic, stale or has too many (mixed) vegetables.

61. Fire, women and long pilgrimages should be avoided. Therefore Gorakhnath said: bad company, mixing with women, bathing in the early morning, fasting and tasks which produce pain in the body should be avoided.

62. (The most conducive foods for the yogi are:) good grains, wheat, rice, barley, milk, ghee, brown sugar, sugar candy (crystallized sugar), honey, dry ginger, patola fruit (species of cucumber), five vegetables, mung and such pulses, and pure water.

63. The yogi should take nourishing and sweet food mixed with ghee and milk; it should nourish the dhatus (basic body constituents) and be pleasing and suitable.

64. Whether young or old, very old, sick or feeble, one can attain perfection in all the yogas by practising.

65. Perfection results from practical application. Without practising how can it happen? Just by reading the shastras perfection in yoga will never be attained.

66. Neither by wearing the garb of a siddha, nor by talking about it (is perfection attained). Only through practical application does one become a siddha. This is the truth without a doubt.

67.   Asanas, various types of kumbhaka, and the other various means of illumination should all be practised in the hatha yoga system until success in raja yoga is attained.

Chapter Two

1.   Thus being established in asana and having control (of the body), taking a balanced diet; pranayama should be practised according to the instructions of the guru.

2.   When prana moves, chitta (the mental force) moves. When prana is without movement, chitta is without movement. By this (steadiness of prana) the yogi attains steadiness and should thus restrain the vayu (air).

3.   As long as the vayu (air and prana) remains in the body, that is called life. Death is when it leaves the body. Therefore, retain vayu.

4.   The vital air does not pass in the middle channel because the nadis are full of impurities. So how can the state of unmani arise and how can perfection or siddhi come about?

5.   When all the nadis and chakras which are full of impurities are purified, then the yogi is able to retain prana.

6.   Therefore pranayama should be done daily with a sattwic state of mind so that the impurities are driven out of sushumna nadi and purification occurs.

7.   Sitting in baddha padmasana, the yogi should inhale through the left nostril and hold the breath to capacity, and then exhale through the right nostril.

8.   Then inhaling through the right nostril, gradually fill the abdomen, perform kumbhaka as before, then exhale completely through the left nostril.

9.   Inhale with the same nostril through which exhalation was done, hold the breath to utmost capacity and exhale through the other nostril slowly and not forcibly.

10.   When the prana is inhaled through the left nostril, then it must be exhaled through the other. When it is inhaled through the right, hold it inside and then exhale through the other nostril. The yamini who practises in this way, through the right and left nostrils, alternately purifies all his nadis within three months.

11.   Retention should be practised perfectly four times a day: early morning, midday, evening and midnight, so that retention is gradually held up to eighty (counts in one sitting).

12.   At first there is perspiration, in the middle stage trembling, in the highest stage complete steadiness, and therefore the breath should be withheld.

13.   Rub the body with the perspiration from the labour (of pranayama). The body derives firmness and steadiness from this.

14.   In the beginning stages of practice, food consisting of milk and ghee is recommended. Upon being established in the practice such restrictions are not necessary.

15.   Just as lions, elephants and tigers are gradually controlled, so the prana is controlled through practice. Otherwise the practitioner is destroyed.

16.   By proper practice of pranayama etc., all diseases are eradicated. Through improper practice all diseases can arise.

17.   Hiccups, asthma, coughs, headache, ear and eye pain, and various other diseases are due to disturbances of the vital air.

646

18. The vayu should skilfully be inhaled, exhaled and retained so that perfection or siddhi is attained.

19. When the nadis are purified there are external symptoms. Success is definite when the body becomes thin and glows.

20. When one is able to hold the vayu according to one's will, the digestive power increases. With the nadis purified, thus the inner sound or nada awakens and one is free from disease.

21. When fat or mucus is excessive, shatkarma: the six cleansing techniques, should be practised before (pranayama). Others, in whom the doshas, i.e. phlegm, wind and bile, are balanced should not do them.

22. Dhauti, basti, neti, trataka, nauli and kapalbhati; these are known as shatkarma or the six cleansing processes.

23. These shatkarma which effect purification of the body are secret. They have manifold, wondrous results and are held in high esteem by eminent yogis.

24. A strip of wet cloth, four angulas wide (i.e. seven to eight centimetres) and fifteen handspans (i.e. one and a half metres) in length is slowly swallowed and then taken out, as instructed by the guru. This is known as dhauti.

25. There is no doubt that coughs, asthma, diseases of the spleen, leprosy and twenty kinds of diseases caused by excess mucus are destroyed through the effects of dhauti karma.

26. Sitting in utkatasana, navel deep in water, insert a tube into the anus and contract the anus. This cleansing with water is called basti karma.

27. Enlargement of the glands and spleen, and all diseases arising from excess wind, bile and mucus are eliminated from the body through the practice of basti.

28. By practising jala basti the appetite increases, the body glows, excess doshas are destroyed and the dhatu, senses and mind are purified.

29. Insert a soft thread through the nose to the length of one handspan so that it comes out of the mouth. This is called neti by the siddhas.

30. Neti cleanses the cranium and bestows clairvoyance. It also destroys all diseases which manifest above the throat.

31. Looking intently with an unwavering gaze at a small point until tears are shed is known as trataka by the acharyas (teachers).

32. Trataka eradicates all eye diseases, fatigue and sloth and closes the doorway creating these problems. It should be carefully kept secret like a golden casket.

33. Lean forward, protrude the abdomen and rotate (the muscles) from right to left with speed. This is called nauli by the siddhas.

34. Nauli is foremost of the hatha yoga practices. It kindles the digestive fire, removing indigestion, sluggish digestion, and all disorders of the doshas, and brings about happiness.

35. Perform exhalation and inhalation rapidly like the bellows (of a blacksmith). This is called kapalbhati and it destroys all mucous disorders.

36. By the six karmas (shatkarma) one is freed from excesses of the doshas. Then pranayama is practised and success is achieved without strain.

37. According to some teachers, pranayama alone removes impurities and therefore they hold pranayama in esteem and not the other techniques.

38. Vomiting the things in the stomach by moving the apana into the throat is called gaja karani by those who have attained knowledge of hatha yoga. Thus, being accustomed to this technique, control of the nadis and chakras is brought about.

39. Even Brahma and other gods in heaven devote themselves to practising pranayama because it ends the fear of death. Thus it (pranayama) must be practised.

40. As long as the breath is restrained in the body, the mind is devoid of thought and the gaze is centred between the eyebrows, why should there be fear of death?

41. By systematically restraining the prana (breath) the nadis and chakras are purified. Thus the prana bursts open the doorway to sushumna and easily enters it.

42. The breath (prana) moving in the middle passage makes the mind still. This steadiness of mind is itself called the state of manonmani – devoid of thought.

43. By practising the various kumbhakas wondrous perfections are obtained. Those who are the knowers practise the various kumbhakas to accomplish them.

44. The eight kumbhakas are suryabheda, ujjayi, sheetkari, sheetali, bhastrika, bhramari, moorchha and plavini.

45. At the end of inhalation, jalandhara bandha is done. At the end of kumbhaka and beginning of exhalation, uddiyana bandha is done.

46. By contracting the perineum, contracting the throat and drawing the abdomen up, the prana flows into the brahma nadi.

47. Raising the apana upward and bringing the prana down from the throat, the yogi becomes free from old age and appears as if sixteen years of age.

48. Sitting comfortably, the yogi should become fixed in his posture and slowly breathe the air in through the right nostril.

49. Retention should then be held until the breath diffuses to the roots of the hair and tips of the nails. Then slowly exhale through the left nostril.

50. Suryabheda is excellent for purifying the cranium, destroying imbalances of the wind dosha and eliminating worms. It should be done again and again.

51. Closing the mouth, inhale with control and concentration through ida and pingala, so that the breath is felt from the throat to the heart and produces a sonorous sound.

52. Do kumbhaka as before and exhale through ida. This removes phlegm from the throat and stimulates the (digestive) fire.

53. This pranayama, called ujjayi, can be done while moving, standing, sitting or walking. It removes dropsy and disorders of the nadis and dhatu.

54. By drawing the breath in through the mouth, make a hissing sound, without gaping the mouth, and exhale through the nose. By practising this, one becomes a second Kaamadeva (god of love).

55. He is adored by the circle of yoginis and becomes the controller of creation and dissolution, being without hunger, thirst, sleep and laziness.

56. And the sattwa in the body becomes free from all disturbances. Truly, by the forementioned method one becomes lord of yogis on this earth.

57. The wise inhale air through the tongue and practise kumbhaka as (described) before, then exhale the air through the nostrils.

58. This kumbhaka called sheetali cures an enlarged stomach or spleen and other related diseases, fever, excess bile, hunger and thirst, and counteracts poisons.

59. Placing both soles of the feet on top of the thighs is padmasana which destroys all sins (bad karma).

60. Sitting properly in padmasana, keeping neck and abdomen in alignment, exhale prana through the nose.

61. And again the air should be quickly inhaled up to the heart lotus. Accordingly, the resounding is felt from the heart and throat up to the cranium.

62. In that way it (the breath) is inhaled and exhaled repeatedly, with the same motion as a pair of bellows being pumped.

63. Thus, in this way, one keeps the breath moving with mindfulness (awareness) and body steadiness. When the body is tired then inhale through the right nostril.

64. Accordingly, when the abdomen becomes full of air, then quickly hold the nostrils (and breath) firmly, without using the index and middle fingers (i.e. using the thumb and ring finger as in nasikagra mudra).

65. Having performed (pranayama and) retention systematically, exhale through the left nostril. Thereby imbalances of wind, bile and mucus are annihilated and the digestive fire increased.

66. This (bhastrika) quickly arouses kundalini. It is pleasant and beneficial, and removes obstruction due to excess mucus accumulated at the entrance to brahma nadi.

67. This kumbhaka called bhastrika enables the three granthis (psychic, pranic knots) to be broken. Thus it is the duty of the yogi to practise bhastrika.

68. Breathe in quickly, making a reverberating sound like the male black bee, and exhale slowly while softly making the sound of the female black bee. By this yogic practice one becomes lord of the yogis and the mind is absorbed in bliss.

69. At the end of inhalation gradually become fixed on jalandhara bandha, then exhale slowly. This is called the fainting or swooning pranayama as it makes the mind inactive and (thus) confers pleasure.

70. The inner part of the abdomen being completely filled with air, one can float like a lotus leaf on water.

71. Pranayama is said to be of three types: exhalation (rechaka), inhalation (pooraka) and retention (kumbhaka). Kumbhaka is again of two types: connected (sahita) and unconnected (kevala).

72. Until kevala kumbhaka is perfected, sahita kumbhaka has to be practised. When (you are) freed of inhalation and exhalation then the breath or prana is retained easily.

73. Perfection of isolated retention is freedom from inhalation and exhalation. This pranayama spoken of is verily kevala kumbhaka.

74. Nothing in the three planes of existence is unobtainable by him who has mastery of kevala kumbhaka and can retain the breath as desired.

75. There is no doubt, the state of raja yoga is also attained (through kevala kumbhaka). By retention kundalini is aroused, sushumna becomes unobstructed and perfection of hatha yoga takes place.

76. There can be no perfection if hatha yoga is without raja yoga or raja yoga without hatha yoga. Therefore, through practice of both, perfection is attained.

77. By stopping the prana through retention, the mind becomes free from all modifications. By thus practising (this yoga), one achieves the stage of raja yoga (supreme union).

78. Perfection of hatha yoga is achieved when there is leanness of the body, tranquil countenance, manifestation of the inner sound, clear eyes, diseaselessness, control of bindu (semen or ova), active digestive fire and purification of nadis.

Chapter Three

1. As the serpent (Sheshnaga) upholds the earth and its mountains and woods, so kundalini is the support of all the yoga practices.

2. Indeed, by guru's grace this sleeping kundalini is awakened, then all the lotuses (chakras) and knots (granthis) are opened.

3. Then indeed sushumna becomes the pathway of prana, mind is free of all connections and death is averted.

4. Sushumna, shoonya padavi, brahmarandhra, maha patha, shmashan, shambhavi, madhya marga, are all said to be one and the same.

5. Therefore, the goddess sleeping at the entrance of Brahma's door should be constantly aroused with all effort by performing mudra thoroughly.

6. Maha mudra, maha bandha, maha vedha, khechari, uddiyana, moola bandha and jalandhara bandha.

7. Vipareeta karani mudra, vajroli and shakti chalana, verily, these are the ten mudras which destroy old age and death.

8. Adinath said they are the bestowers of the eight divine powers. They are held in high esteem by all the siddhas and are difficult for even the gods to attain.

9. These must remain secret just like precious stones, and not be talked about to anyone, just as one does not tell others about his intimate relations with his wife.

10. Press the left heel into the perineum (or vagina), straighten the right leg, and with the hands, firmly take hold of the outstretched foot.

11. By locking the throat and retaining the breath, the prana rises straight, just like a snake beaten with a stick becomes straight.

12. So the kundalini shakti becomes straight at once. Then the two (ida and pingala) become lifeless as the shakti enters sushumna.

13. Then exhale slowly and gradually, not quickly. Indeed this is described as maha mudra by the great siddhas.

14. Maha mudra removes the worst afflictions (the five kleshas) and the cause of death. Therefore it is called 'the great attitude' by the ones of highest knowledge.

15. After practising on the left side, practise on the right side. When the number of rounds is even, discontinue and release the mudra.

16. For one who practises maha mudra, there is nothing wholesome or unwholesome. Anything can be consumed, even the deadliest of poisons is digested like nectar.

17. Abdominal disorders, constipation, indigestion and leprosy, etc., are alleviated by the practice of maha mudra.

18. Thus maha mudra has been described as the giver of great siddhis. It must be kept secret and not disclosed to anyone.

19. Thus maha mudra has been described as the giver of great siddhis. It must be kept secret and not disclosed to anyone.

20. Thus breathing in, bring the chin to the chest (jalandhara bandha), contract the perineal/cervical region (moola bandha) and concentrate on the eyebrow centre (shambhavi mudra).

21. Having retained the breath as long as comfortable, exhale slowly. Once completing the practice on the left side, practise again on the right side.

22. Some are of the opinion that the throat lock (jalandhara bandha) is unnecessary and it is sufficient to keep the tongue against the front teeth.

23. This stops the upward movement of energy in the nadis. Verily this maha bandha is the bestower of great siddhis.

24. Maha bandha frees one from the bonds of death, makes the three nadis unite in ajna chakra and enables the mind to reach the sacred seat of Shiva, Kedara.

25. Just as an extremely beautiful woman is nothing without a husband, so maha mudra and maha bandha are unfruitful without maha vedha mudra.

26. The yogi, in the position of maha bandha, should inhale, make the mind steady and stop the movement of prana by performing the throat lock.

27. Placing the palms of the hands on the ground, he should slowly beat the buttocks gently on the ground. The prana (then) leaves the two nadis (ida and pingala) and enters into the middle channel (sushumna).

28. Ida, pingala and sushumna become united and verily, immortality is attained. A death-like state occurs; then the breath should be exhaled.

29. This is maha vedha, and its practice bestows great perfections. Wrinkles, grey hair and the trembling of old age are evaded, thus the best of practitioners devote themselves to it.

30. These are the three great secrets which destroy old age and death, increase the digestive fire and bestow the siddhis of anima, etc.

31. They should be done daily at every yama (three hour period). They bring out the virtues and destroy vices. Those who have perfect instructions should practise them gradually.

32. Khechari mudra is turning the tongue backwards into the cavity of the cranium and turning the eyes inwards towards the eyebrow centre.

33. The tongue should be exercised and milked and the underneath part cut away in small degrees. Indeed khechari is perfected when the tongue touches the eyebrow centre.

34. With a clean thin blade, gently cut away the membrane under the tongue. Cut it by a fine hair's breadth each time.

35. Then rub in a mixture of powdered rock salt and turmeric. After seven days, again cut a hair's breadth.

36. One should continue doing this regularly for six months, then the membrane at the root of the tongue will be completely severed.

37. Having turned the tongue back, the three channels of ida, pingala and sushumna are controlled. This is khechari mudra and it is called the centre of ether.

38. The yogi who remains with the tongue going upwards for even half a second is freed from toxins, disease, death, old age, etc.

39. One who accomplishes this khechari mudra is neither troubled by diseases, nor death, lassitude, sleep, hunger, thirst or unconsciousness.

40. One who knows khechari mudra is unafflicted by disease, unaffected by the laws of cause and effect (karma) and free from the bonds of time (death).

41. Mind moves in Brahman (khe) because the tongue moves in space (khe). Therefore, the perfected ones have named this mudra khechari, moving in space or Brahman.

42. When the upper cavity of the palate is sealed by khechari mudra, the bindu or semen cannot be lost even if one embraces a beautiful woman.

43. Even when there is movement of the bindu and it enters the genitals, it is seized by closing the perineum and is taken upward.

44. With the tongue directed upwards, the knower of yoga drinks the fluid of the moon. Within fifteen days physical death is conquered.

45. The yogi's body is forever full of the moon's nectar. Even if he is bitten by the king of snakes (Takshaka), he is not poisoned.

46. Just as fuel kindles fire and oil a lamp, so the indweller of the body does not vacate while the body is full of the moon's nectar.

47. By constant swallowing of the tongue he can drink amaravaruni. I consider him of high lineage (heritage). Others destroy the heritage.

48. The word 'go' means tongue (and also means cow). When it enters into the upper palate, it is 'eating the flesh of the cow'. It (khechari) destroys the great sins.

49. When the tongue enters the cavity, indeed heat is produced and the nectar flows from the moon.

50. When the tongue constantly presses the cavity, the moon's nectar (flows and) has a saline, pungent and acidic flavour. It is like (the consistency of) milk, ghee, honey. Fatal diseases, old age and weapons are warded off. From that, immortality and the eight siddhis or perfections manifest.

51. Fluid drips into the sixteen petalled lotus (vishuddhi chakra) when the tongue is inserted into the upper throat cavity; the paramshakti (kundalini) is released and one becomes concentrated in that (experience which ensues). The yogi who drinks the pure stream of nectar is freed from disease, has longevity, and has a body as soft and as beautiful as a lotus stem.

52. The nectar is secreted from the topmost part of the Meru (Sushumna), the fountainhead of the nadis. He who has pure intellect can know the Truth therein. The nectar, which is the essence of the body, flows out from the moon and hence death ensues. Therefore khechari mudra should be practised, otherwise perfection of the body cannot be attained.

53. Five nadis convene in this cavity and it is the source of knowledge. Khechari should be established in that void, untainted (by ignorance).

54. There is only one seed of creation and one mudra – khechari; one deva independent of everything and one state – manonmani.

55. Uddiyana bandha is so-called by the yogis because through its practice the prana (is concentrated at one point and) rises through sushumna.

56. The bandha described is called the rising or flying bandha, because through its practice, the great bird (shakti) flies upward with ease.

57. Pulling the abdomen back in and making the navel rise is uddiyana bandha. It is the lion which conquers the elephant, death.

58. Uddiyana is easy when practised as told by the guru. Even an old person can become young when it is done regularly.

59. The region above and below the navel should be drawn backward with effort. There is no doubt that after six months of practice, death is conquered.

60. Of all the bandhas, uddiyana is the best. Once it is mastered, mukti or liberation occurs spontaneously.

61. Pressing the perineum/vagina with the heel and contracting the rectum so that the apana vayu moves upward is moola bandha.

62. By contracting the perineum the downward moving apana vayu is forced to go upward. Yogis call this moola bandha.

63. Press the heel firmly against the rectum and contract forcefully and repeatedly, so that the vital energy rises.

64. There is no doubt that by practising moola bandha, prana and apana, and nada and bindu are united, and total perfection attained.

65. With constant practice of moola bandha, prana and apana unite, urine and stool are decreased and even an old person becomes young.

66. Apana moves up into the region of fire (manipura chakra, the navel centre), then the flames of the fire grow, being fanned by apana vayu.

67. Then, when apana and the fire meet with prana, which is itself hot, the heat in the body is intensified.

68. Through this, the sleeping kundalini is aroused by the extreme heat and it straightens itself just as a serpent beaten with a stick straightens and hisses.

69. Just as a snake enters its hole, so kundalini goes into brahma nadi. Therefore the yogi must always perform moola bandha.

70. Contracting the throat by bringing the chin to the chest is the bandha called jalandhara. It destroys old age and death.

71. That is jalandhara bandha which catches the flow of nectar in the throat. It destroys all throat ailments.

72. Having done jalandhara bandha by contracting the throat, the nectar does not fall into the gastric fire and the prana is not agitated.

73. By firmly contracting the throat, the two nadis, ida and pingala are paralyzed and the sixteen adharas of the middle chakra are locked.

74. By contracting the perineum, performing uddiyana and locking ida and pingala with jalandhara, sushumna becomes active.

75. By this means the prana and breath become still. Thus death, old age and sickness are conquered.

76. The great siddhas practise these three best bandhas. Of all the sadhanas in hatha yoga and tantra, the yogis know this practice (maha bandha).

77. That nectar which flows from the moon has the quality of endowing enlightenment, but it is completely consumed by the sun, incurring old age.

78. There is a wonderful means by which the nectar is averted from falling into the opening of the sun. This is obtained by the guru's instructions and not from the hundreds of shastras (treatises).

79. With the navel region above and the palate below, the sun is above and the moon below. It is called vipareeta karani, the reversing process. When given by the guru's instructions it is fruitful.

80. Digestion is strengthened by continual, regular practice and therefore, the practitioner should always have sufficient food. If one takes only a little food, the heat produced by the digestion will destroy the system.

81. Therefore, on the first day, one should only stay a moment with the feet up and head down. The practice should be done daily, gradually increasing the duration.

82. After six months of practise, grey hairs and wrinkles become inconspicuous. One who practises it for yama (three hours) conquers death.

83. Even one living a free lifestyle without the formal rules of yoga, if he practises vajroli well, that yogi becomes a recipient of siddhis (perfections).

84. There are two things hard to obtain, one is milk and the second is a woman who can act according to your will.

85. By practising gradual upward contractions during the emission in intercourse, any man or woman achieves perfection of vajroli.

86. By slowly drawing in air through a prescribed tube inserted into the urethra of the penis, gradually air and prana traverse into the vajra kanda.

87. The bindu (semen) that is about to fall into the woman's vagina should be made to move upwards with practice. And if it falls, the semen and the woman's fluid should be conserved by drawing it up.

88. Therefore, the knower of yoga conquers death by preserving the bindu (semen). Release of the bindu means death; conservation of semen is life.

89. As long as the bindu or semen is steady in the body, then where is the fear of death? The yogi's body smells pleasant by conserving the bindu or semen.

90. A man's semen can be controlled by the mind and control of semen is life-giving. Therefore, his semen and mind should be controlled and conserved.

91. The knower of yoga, perfect in the practice, conserves his bindu and the woman's rajas by drawing it up through the generative organ.

92. Sahajoli and amaroli are separate techniques of vajroli. The ashes of burnt cow manure should be mixed with water.

93. After performing vajroli during intercourse, (being in a comfortable position), the man and woman should wipe the ashes on specific parts of their bodies during the leisure time.

94. It is called sahajoli and the yogis have complete faith in it. This is very beneficial and enables enlightenment through the combination of yoga and bhoga (sensual involvement).

95. Verily this yoga is perfected by virtuous and well-conducted men who have seen the truth and not those who are selfish.

96. According to the Kapalika sect, amaroli is practised by drinking the cool midstream of urine. The first part of the urine is left as it contains bile, and the last part is left as it does not contain goodness.

97. One who drinks amari, takes it through the nose and practises vajroli, is said to be practising amaroli.

98. The practitioner should mix the semen with the ashes of burnt cow manure and wipe it on the upper parts of the body, it bestows divya drishti (clairvoyance or divine sight).

99. If a woman practises vajroli and saves her rajas and the man's bindu by thorough contraction, she is a yogini.

100. Without doubt, not even a little rajas is wasted through vajroli, the nada and bindu in the body become one.

101. The bindu and that rajas in one's own body unite through the union by practice of vajroli, thus bestowing all perfections or siddhis.

102. She is verily a yogini who conserves her rajas by contracting and raising it. She knows past, present and future and becomes fixed in khechari (i.e. consciousness moves into the higher realm).

103. By the yoga of vajroli practice, perfection of the body fructifies. This auspicious yoga even brings liberation alongside with sensual involvement (bhoga).

104. Kutilangi, kundalini, bhujangi, shakti, ishwari, kundali, arundhati are all synonymous terms.

105. Just as a door is opened with a key, similarly the yogi opens the door to liberation with kundalini.

106. The sleeping Parameshwari rests with her mouth closing that door, through which is the path to the knot of brahmasthana, the place beyond suffering.

107. The kundalini shakti sleeps above the kanda. This shakti is the means of liberation to the yogi and bondage for the ignorant. One who knows this is the knower of yoga.

108. Kundalini is said to be coiled like a snake. Without a doubt, one who makes that shakti flow obtains liberation.

109. Between Ganga and Yamuna is the young widowed Balarandam practising austerity. She should be seized forcibly, then one can reach the supreme state of Vishnu.

110. Ida is the holy Ganga, pingala the river Yamuna. Between ida and pingala in the middle is this young widow, kundalini.

111. By seizing the tail of kundalini serpent, she becomes very excited. Abandoning sleep that shakti is released and rises up.

112. ,Breathing in through the right nostril (pingala) the serpent (shakti) should be seized through kumbhaka and rotated constantly for an hour and a half, morning and evening.

113. The kanda, situated above the anus, one hand span high and four fingers breath wide, is soft and white as if enveloped in cloth.

114. Firmly seated in vajrasana, holding the ankles, one should squeeze the kanda close to the anus.

115. In the position of vajrasana, the yogi should move the kundalini. Having done bhastrika pranayama the kundalini is soon aroused.

116. Contracting the sun in manipura, kundalini should be moved. Even if such a person should be on the verge of death, where is the need to fear death?

117. By moving the kundalini fearlessly for an hour and a half, it is drawn into sushumna and rises up a little.

118. In this way, it is easy for kundalini to issue from the opening of sushumna. Thus the prana proceeds through sushumna of its own accord.

119. In that way the sleeping kundalini should be regularly moved. By her regular movement, the yogi is freed from disease.

120. The yogi who moves the shakti regularly, enjoys perfection or siddhi. He easily conquers time and death. What more is there to say?

121. One who enjoys being brahmacharya and always takes moderate diet and practises arousal of kundalini, achieves perfection in forty days.

122. Bhastrika pranayama with kumbhaka should specifically be practised to activate kundalini. From where will the fear of death arise for a self-restrained practitioner who practises daily with regularity?

123. What other methods are there to cleanse the 72,000 nadis of dirt besides the practice of arousing kundalini?

124. This middle nadi, sushumna, easily becomes established, (straight) by the yogi's persistent practice of asana, pranayama, mudra and concentration.

125. For those who are alert and the mind one-pointed (disciplined) in samadhi, rudrani or shambhavi mudra is the greatest mudra for bestowing perfection.

126. The earth without raja yoga, night without raja yoga, even the various mudras without raja yoga are useless, i.e. not beautiful.

127. All the pranayama methods are to be done with a concentrated mind. The wise man should not let his mind be involved in the modifications (vrittis).

128. Thus the ten mudras have been told by Adinath Shambhu. Each one is the bestower of perfection to the self-restrained.

129. One who instructs mudra in the tradition of guru-disciple is the true guru and form of Ishwara.

130. By following explicitly his (guru's) words, and practising mudra, one obtains the qualities of anima, etc., and overcomes death/time.

Chapter Four

1. Salutations to the Guru Shiva, who is regarded as nada, bindu, kalaa (sound, nucleus and emanating ray). One wholly devoted to them, goes into the eternally stainless state.

2. Thus, I shall now expound the best process of samadhi which eliminates death and takes one to the greatest bliss of Brahma.

3. Raja yoga, samadhi, unmani, manonmani, amaratwa, laya, sahaja tattwa, shoonyashoonya, parampadam.

4. Amanaskam, advaitam, niralamba, niranjana, jivanmukti, sahaja and turiya are all synonymous terms.

666

5. As salt merges in the sea, likewise the mind and atma are considered united in samadhi.

6. When the movement of prana is completely annihilated, then mind is reabsorbed and then samadhi is considered attained.

7. When the twofold nature of the individual soul and cosmic soul becomes one, all desires and ideations are destroyed and that is considered samadhi.

8. Who really knows the magnitude of raja yoga? Through the guru's words, inner knowledge, liberation, perfection fructify.

9. Without the compassion of the true guru, renunciation is impossible, perception of the truth inaccessible and sahaja samadhi unobtainable.

10. When the maha shakti is aroused by the various asanas, pranayamas and mudras, the prana dissolves into shoonya.

11. The sahaja state is conquered on its own (occurs by itself) in him whose remaining karmas are abandoned and who experiences the rising of shakti.

12. When prana is flowing through sushumna, mind is in pure shoonya. Then all the karmas of the one knowing yoga are uprooted.

13. O immortal one, salutations to you who have mastery over time, by whose jaws the animate and inanimate alike are devoured.

14. When mind is in equanimity and (prana) vayu proceeds through sushumna, then amaroli, vajroli and sahajoli are attained.

15. How can there be inner knowledge in the mind, as long as prana is alive and mind is not dead? As long as the twofold nature of mind and prana

can be quiescent, liberation is attained. It is not possible for any other person.

16. Staying in the most suitable place, having found out how to penetrate sushumna and make the prana flow through the middle passage, it should be blocked in the brahmarandhra, the centre of higher consciousness.

17. The sun and moon divide time into day and night. Sushumna is the consumer of time. This is the conveyed secret.

18. There are 72,000 nadis throughout the cage of this body. Sushumna is the Shambhavi, the remaining nadis are unimportant.

19. When the vayu is increased then the gastric fire (samana) should be taken along with kundalini in the aroused sushumna and blocked.

20. When the prana flows in the sushumna this state of manonmani (consciousness devoid of mind) is established. Therefore, other forced practices are just laborious to the yogi.

21. Through restraining the prana, thought and counterthought are restrained and through restraint of thought and counterthought, prana (air) is restrained.

22. Chitta has two causes, vasana and prana. When one of the two is destroyed or inactivated the other also will become immobile.

23. Where mind is stilled, then the prana is suspended there, and where prana is suspended, there the mind is still.

24. Mind and prana are mixed like milk and water. Both of them are equal in their activities. Where there is pranic movement or activity there is mind (consciousness). Where there is consciousness there is prana.

25. Therefore, if one is annihilated, the other is eradicated; if one is active, the other becomes active, and while they exist, all the senses are active. If they are controlled, the state of moksha or liberation is attained.

26. Mercury and mind are unstable by nature. By stabilizing (seizing or fixing) mercury and mind what cannot be perfected?

27. O Parvati, when mercury and prana are made steady, disease is wiped out. When they are made torpid that is life-giving. When they are seized, one moves in space (Brahman).

28. When mind is still, prana is still, then bindu is still. By bindu being held still, there is always a sattwic state which produces steadiness in the body.

29. Mind is the ruler of the senses, prana is the ruler of the mind. Dissolution is the lord of the prana and that dissolution (laya) is the basis of nada.

30. This is verily called liberation or moksha, but others might not call it so. Nevertheless, when prana and mind are in laya, indescribable ecstasy is created.

31. When inhalation and exhalation are stopped (finished), enjoyment of the senses annihilated, when there is no effort, and a changeless state (of mind) occurs, the yogi attains laya or absorption.

32. All the prominent desires being entirely finished, and the body motionless, results in the absorption or laya, which is only known by the Self, and beyond the scope of words.

33. Where the sight is directed, absorption occurs. That in which the elements, senses and shakti exist externally, which is in all living things, both are dissolved in the characteristicless.

34. Some say 'laya, laya' but what is the characteristic of laya or absorption? Laya is the non-recollection of the objects of the senses when the previous deep-rooted desires (and impressions) are non-recurrent.

35. The Vedas, shastras and Puranas are like common women, but shambhavi is secret like a woman of good heritage.

36. With internalized (one-pointed) awareness and external gaze unblinking, that verily is shambhavi mudra, preserved in the Vedas.

37. If the yogi remains with the chitta and prana absorbed in the internal object and gaze motionless, though looking, he is not seeing, it is indeed shambhavi mudra. When it is given by the guru's blessing, the state of shoonyashoonya arises. That is the real state of Shiva (consciousness).

38. Shambhavi and khechari states, though there is a difference in the place of concentration or influence, both bring about ecstasy, absorption in void, in the experience of chit sukha or the pleasure of consciousness.

39. With perfect concentration, the pupils fixed on the light by raising the eyebrows up a little, as from the previously described (shambhavi), mind is joined and instantly unmani occurs.

40. Some people are confused by the agamas, some are confused by the nigamas and logic. They are bewildered, not knowing how to be liberated.

41. Mind steady, eyes semi-open, gaze fixed on the nose tip, the moon (ida) and sun (pingala) suspended, without any movement (physical or mental), that one attains the form of light (jyoti) which is endless and is complete, radiant, the Supreme. What more can be said?

42. Worship the lingam neither by day nor by night. By blocking the day and night the lingam should always be worshipped.

43. When the prana which is in the right and left nadis moves in the middle nadi (sushumna) that is the condition for khechari mudra.

44. The fire (of shakti) being swallowed (suppressed) midway between, ida and pingala, in that shoonya (of sushumna), is in truth the condition for khechari mudra.

45. The middle of the sun (pingala) and moon (ida) is the 'unsupported', in which is situated vyoma chakra or centre of ether (void). This mudra is called khechari.

46. In the flow from the moon (bindu) is the beloved of Shiva (consciousness). The opening of the unequalled divine sushumna should be filled from behind (by the tongue).

47. The sushumna being completely filled at the rear (upper palate) also is khechari. The practice of khechari mudra is followed by the state of unmani (consciousness devoid of mind).

48. In the middle of the eyebrows is the place of Shiva, there the mind is quiescent. That state is known as turiya or the fourth dimension. There, time is unknown.

49. Khechari should be practised until yogic sleep occurs. For one who has attained yogic sleep, time becomes non-existent.

50. Having made the mind unsupported without even a thought, indeed, one is like a pot filled inside and out with space.

51. When the external breath is suspended, likewise the middle one (i.e. shakti in sushumna is suspended).

Without a doubt, prana and mind become still in their own place (i.e. Brahmarandhra).

52. Verily, practising with the breath (prana) day and night through the course of prana (sushumna), prana and mind become absorbed there.

53. The whole body from the soles of the feet to the head should become filled with nectar. Thus, the one who perfects this has a superior body, superior strength and immense valour.

54. Having made shakti the centre of mind and mind the centre of shakti, observe the mind making the supreme state the object (of concentration).

55. Making the atma the centre of Brahman, and making Brahman the centre of atma, and making everything Brahman; remain without even a single thought (in samadhi).

56. Within is void, without is void; like an empty vessel in space, completely full internally, completely full externally, just like a pot in the ocean.

57. Without thought of the external or even internal thought, all thoughts abandoned, without even a single thought.

58. The entire world is only the fabrication of thought. Play of mind is only created by thought. By transcending the mind which is composed of constructed thought, definitely peace will be attained, O Rama!

59. As camphor (dissolves) in fire, and salt (dissolves) in the sea, in samadhi mind dissolves into 'Thatness' (tattwa).

60. All that can be known, all that is known and the knowledge, is called mind. When the knower and that which is known are lost together, there is no dual or second way.

61. All that is in this world, animate and inanimate, is the appearance of mind. When mind attains unmani, duality is lost.

62. All the known objects being abandoned, mind goes into absorption or is dissolved. When the mind is dissolved, then there will be kaivalya.

63. Thus, there are many various methods, depending on individual experience, of the path to samadhi, told by the great ones (mahatmas).

64. Salutations to sushumna, kundalini, the nectar flowing from the moon, to the mindless state of mind (manonmani), to the great Shakti, to the atma.

65. I will describe the concentration on nada as told by Gorakhnath which is attainable by even the unlearned who are unable to comprehend Thatness (tattwas).

66. There are one and a quarter crore ways told by Sri Adinath to attain laya, but we think the one and only thing is nada anusandhana or the exploration of nada.

67. The yogi, sitting in muktasana, concentrated in shambhavi, should listen closely to the nada heard within the right ear.

68. Closing the ears, nose and mouth, a clear, distinct sound is heard in the purified sushumna.

69. In all the yogic practices there are four stages; arambha, beginning; ghata, vessel; parichaya, increase; nishpatti, consummation.

70. The Brahma granthi being pierced, the feeling of bliss arises from the void; wondrous, tinkling sounds and the unstruck sound (anahata) are heard within the body.

71. When the yogi experiences arambha in the void of the heart, his body becomes lustrous and brilliant with a divine smell and diseaseless.

72. In the second stage, when ghata is achieved, the Shakti goes into the middle nadi. Being fixed in his asana the wise yogi is comparable to a divine being.

73. When the Vishnu granthi is pierced the greatest bliss is revealed. Then from the void the sound of the kettledrum manifests.

74. In the third stage is the experience of the sound of the drum. Then there is the great void and one enters the place of total perfection or siddhi.

75. Then the bliss of chitta being attained, natural or spontaneous ecstasy arises. Imbalance of the three humours or doshas, pain, old age, disease, hunger and sleep are overcome.

76. If the Rudra granthi is pierced, the fire of prana moves to the place of Ishwara. Then in the stage of nishpatti or consummation is the tinkling sound of the flute resonating like a vina.

77. This is called raja yoga when there is one element in the mind or chitta. The yogi becomes Ishwara, being the creator and destroyer.

78. Whether there is liberation or not, nevertheless there is pleasure. The pleasure arising from laya is derived from raja yoga.

79. There are practitioners of hatha yoga who do not have the knowledge of raja yoga. I consider them as mere practitioners because they derive no fruits for their efforts.

80. In my opinion, contemplation on the eyebrow centre leads to a mindless state immediately. It is a suitable method even for those with less intellect to attain the state of raja yoga. The laya attained through nada gives immediate experience.

81. There is plenitude of bliss in the hearts of the great yogis who remain in samadhi through nada anusandhana or exploration of nada, which is unequalled and beyond any description, known by the one and only Gurunath.

82. Having closed the ears with the hands, the muni should listen to the inner sound with the mind steady on that, then the state of stillness is achieved.

83. Through sustained listening to the nada, awareness of the external sound diminishes. Thus, the yogi overcomes mental turbulence within fifteen days and feels the pleasure.

84. When he first begins to hear sounds during practice, there are various prominent nadas but with prolonged practice the subtlest of subtleties becomes audible.

85. The first fruits are the sounds of the ocean, then clouds, the kettledrum and jharjhara drum. In the middle stage the shankha (conch), gong and horn.

86. Now, reaching the inner point of conclusion, are the tinkling of bells, flute, vina and humming of bees. Thus, the various nadas are produced and heard from the middle of the body.

87. Even when the sounds of clouds and the kettledrum are heard, attention should be kept on even subtler nada.

88. Though the attention may go from the deep to the subtle or subtle to deep, the mind should not move to various things other than the sound.

89. Whatever nada the mind initially adheres to, it becomes perfectly still in that and dissolves with it.

90. Just as a bee drinking honey is unconcerned about the fragrance, so the mind engaged in nada is not craving for sensual objects.

91. By the sharp goad of nada, the mind, which is like a furious elephant roaming in the garden of the senses, is controlled.

92. When the mind ceases to be fickle and is united by fixing it in nada, it becomes immobile like a wingless bird.

93. One who desires complete dominion of yoga should thus explore the nada with an attentive mind and abandon all thoughts.

94. Nada is like the net which snares the deer (mind) inside. It is also like the hunter who slays the deer (mind) inside.

95. It is like the bolt locking a horse inside, for one who is self-controlled. The yogi must therefore meditate regularly upon the nada.

96. Just as liquid mercury is solidified by sulphur, so mind is bound by nada and freed from restlessness. Then one moves unsupported in void.

97. Hearing the nada, mind, which is like a serpent within, becomes captivated and oblivious to all else, not moving anywhere else.

98. As fire burns wood and both subside together, so the mind which moves with nada is absorbed in it.

99. Just as a deer attracted by the sound of bells is easily killed by an expert archer, so is the mind silenced by an adept in nada yoga.

100. One hears the sound of the unstruck resonance (anahata shabda); the quintessence of that sound is the (supreme) object (consciousness). The mind becomes one with that object of knowledge and

it dissolves therein. That is the supreme state of Vishnu (sthiti).

101. The conception of akasha (the substratum of sound) exists as long as the sound is heard. The soundless, which is the supreme reality, is called the supreme atma.

102. Whatever is heard of the nature of the mystical nada is indeed Shakti. That in which all the elements (panchatattwa) find dissolution, that is the formless being, the supreme lord (Parameshwara).

103. All the processes of hatha and laya yoga are but the means to attain raja yoga (samadhi). One who attains raja yoga is victorious over time (death).

104. Tattwa is the seed, hatha is the soil, total desirelessness (vairagya) is the water. By these three the kalpa vriksha (wish-fulfilling tree) which is the unmani avastha (mindless state) immediately sprouts forth.

105. 'Bad karma' (sin) is destroyed by constant concentration on nada. The finite mind and prana dissolve into the stainless (niranjana).

106. The body becomes like a log of wood in the unmani avastha and not even the sound of the conch or dundhubhi (drum) is perceived by the yogi.

107. The yogi who has gone beyond all the states (of consciousness), who is freed of thought, who appears dead (impervious to stimulus) is liberated without doubt.

108. In samadhi a yogi is neither consumed by the processes of time (death) nor is he affected by action (karma) nor affected by any influence.

109. In samadhi a yogi knows neither smell, taste, form, touch or sound (tanmatras); he does not cognize his self (ego) nor that of others.

677

110. One whose mind is neither asleep nor awake, (whose mind) is devoid of memory and forgetfulness, neither oblivious nor active, is indeed liberated.

111. In samadhi a yogi is unaware of (distinctions of) heat and cold, pain and pleasure, honour and dishonour.

112. He who seems asleep in the waking state, who is without breathing yet is perfectly healthy, is verily liberated.

113. In samadhi, a yogi is invulnerable to any weapon, unassailable by any person, unsubjected to another's control by the use of mantras and yantras.

114. While the prana does not flow in the middle passage (of sushumna), while the bindu is not steadied by restraining the prana, while mind does not reflect spontaneous meditation, then those who speak of spiritual knowledge are only indulging in boastful and false tales.

Glossary

Abhinivesha – fear of death, clinging to life; last of the kleshas.

Abhyasa – constant, regular and uninterrupted practice.

Acharya – spiritual guide or teacher.

Adhara – receptacle, lower region.

Adhibautik tapa – physical hardship and pain.

Adhidevik tapa – environmental hardship and pain.

Adhyatmik tapa – spiritual hardship and pain.

Adinath – literally means the 'first lord'; primordial guru of all; cosmic consciousness; name of Lord Shiva given by the Nath sect of yogis; first guru of the Nath yogis.

Advaita – literally means 'without two'; monistic philosophy which says there is only one state of pure consciousness, all duality is illusory.

Agama – testimony, revelation; the philosophy and scriptures in which Shiva teaches Shakti; last books of the Vedas, appropriate to the Kali yuga; tantra shastra.

Agni –c fire.

Agni tattwa – one of the pancha tattwas; fire element.

Agnisar kriya – one of the shatkarmas, same as vahnisar dhauti.

Aham – ego, 'I'.

Ahamkara – faculty of ego, awareness of the existence of 'I'; centre of individual mental, emotional, psychic and physical functioning.

Ahimsa – first yama; non-violence, non-injury.

Ajapa japa – spontaneous repetition of *soham* mantra.

Ajna chakra – psychic centre situated at medulla oblongata; seat of intuition, higher knowledge; third eye; centre of command, monitoring centre.

Akasha – space, ether; sky.

Akasha tattwa – one of the pancha tattwas; ether element.

Akashi mudra – mudra which involves gazing upward.

Alamba – supported.

Amaroli – tantric practice according to the kapalika yogis in which the midstream of urine is drunk or applied on the body.

Amavasya – fifteenth day of the dark fortnight when there is absolutely no moon in the sky.

Amrita – nectar; without death.

Anahata chakra – psychic, pranic centre situated in the region of the heart and cardiac plexus; fourth chakra in human evolution.

Ananda – state of bliss, ecstasy.

Anandamaya kosha – fifth layer of human existence; sheath or body of bliss and supramental consciousness.

Ananda samadhi – fifth stage of sabija samadhi according to Sage Patanjali, after nirvichara and before asmita samadhi.

Ananta – endless; according to Hindu mythology, a serpent symbolizing eternity. See Shesha.

Anga – part, limb of the body, constituting part.

Angula – measurement of a finger's breadth.

Anima – one of the ashta siddhi; paranormal ability to become as small as desired.

Antah karana – literally means 'inner tool', inner organ of the consciousness. See Manas. See Chitta. See Buddhi. See Ahamkara.

Antar – inner, internal.

Antaranga – inner part, internal stage.

Antaranga trataka – internal gazing at a point of concentration.

Antar dhauti – internal cleansing techniques of shatkarma, divided into four classifications: vatsara, varisara, agnisara and bahiskrita.

Antar kumbhaka – internal breath retention. An essential step in the perfection of pranayama or yogic breathing.

Antar mouna – inner silence; practice of pratyahara constituted by five consecutive stages.

Anubhava – spiritual realization.

Anugraha – grace.

Anusandhana – exploration.

Apana – one of the pancha vayu; pranic air current operating in the lower abdominal region causing elimination through the excretory and reproductive organs.

Aparigraha – one of the yama; non-covetousness, non-acquisition.

Apas – water.

Apas tattwa – one of the pancha tattwas; water element.

Arambha – first stage of hearing the internal nada.

Ardha – half.

Ardha dhanurasana – half bow pose.

Ardha matsyendrasana – half spinal twist.

Ardha padmasana – half lotus pose.

Arohan – psychic, pranic passageway in the subtle body which passes up from mooladhara through each chakra kshetram in the front of the body and then to bindu and sahasrara. Another view is that it travels from mooladhara to vishuddhi and then to lalana chakra, the nosetip, ajna and sahasrara.

Artha – literally means 'object'. Also refers to wealth, one of the purusharthas.

Asamprajnata samadhi – negative phases of savikalpa samadhi which occur in between successive stages of samprajnata, the positive phases.

Asana – a steady and comfortable meditative pose according to Sage Patanjali; a specific position of the body which channels prana, opens the chakras and removes energy blocks.

Ashabda – without sound.

Ashrama – stage of life; place where a community of people live and practise spiritual life.

Ashta siddhi – the eight major paranormal accomplishments of anima, mahima, laghima, garima, prapti, prakamya, vaishitva, ishatva.

Ashtanga yoga – the eight-limbed yoga of Sage Patanjali: yama, niyama, asana, pranayama, pratyahara, dharana, dhyana, samadhi.

Ashwini mudra – practice of contracting the anal sphincter, resembling the movement of a horse's anus.

Asmita – one of the five kleshas; ego.

Asmita samadhi – sixth stage of sabija samadhi in which the last trace of ego survives; directly before nirbija samadhi.

Asteya – one of the yamas; honesty.

Astikya – one of the niyamas; faith in the teachings of the Vedas.

Atma, Atman – highest reality, supreme consciousness, individual soul, Brahman, Shiva. See Jivatma.

Atma darshan – the vision of the self.

Atma shakti – the power of the atma. See Kundalini shakti.

Atmabhava – awareness and experience of the self.

Aum – See Om.

Avarana shakti – hiranyagarbha; cosmic subtle body.

Avastha – state or condition of mind and consciousness achieved through effort.

Avatara – descent or incarnation of supreme consciousness, e.g. Rama, Krishna.

Avidya – ignorance, complete unawareness, nescience.

Avidya vidya – one of the kanchukas which restricts the capacity of an individual to know.

Avyakta – unmanifest.

Awarohan – psychic, pranic passageway in the subtle body which passes down from bindu to ajna, then within the spine through each chakra to mooladhara.

Ayama – extension, length, expansion.

Baddha – restrained, bound, locked.

Baddha padmasana – locked lotus pose.

Bahir – outside, external.

Bahiranga trataka – gazing with eyes open and concentrating upon an external object or point, e.g. candle flame.

Bahir kumbhaka – external breath retention.

Banalingam – lingam situated in anahata chakra; represents the jivatma or individual consciousness.

Bandha – binding, bondage; a posture in which organs and muscles are contracted and controlled, creating a psycho-

682

muscular energy lock which redirects the flow of energy or prana in the body and locks it into a specific area.

Basti – third shatkarma; yogic enema.

Bhadrasana – gracious pose; a sitting posture.

Bhagavad Gita – a part of the famous Hindu epic *Mahabharata*. Teachings of Lord Krishna to his disciple Arjuna at the commencement of the battle of Kurukshetra, with explanations on sannyasa yoga, karma yoga, bhakti yoga and jnana yoga.

Bhagavan – God; one who possesses the six aishavarya or superhuman powers of auspiciousness, power, wisdom, dispassion, glory and omniscience.

Bhairava – name of Lord Shiva, signifying the state beyond individual and mundane consciousness.

Bhakti – pure devotion.

Bhakti yoga – yogic path of devotion.

Bhalabhati – See Kapalbhati.

Bhalarandhra – See Brahmarandhra.

Bhasma – purified essence of ash.

Bhastrika pranayama – bellows breathing in which the breath is forcibly drawn in and out through the nose in equal proportions, like the pumping action of the bellows.

Bhava – intense inner attitude or feeling; state of mind and body.

Bhedan – to pierce, discriminate, differentiate.

Bhiksha – asking for alms, in particular food.

Bhoga – sensual gratification, enjoyment and experience.

Bhramari pranayama – breathing practice in which a soft humming sound is produced during exhalation like the murmuring of the black bee.

Bhujangasana – cobra pose.

Bhu loka – terrestrial plane of existence.

Bhumika – stages of evolution of the mind, five in number. See Mudha. See Kshipta. See Vikshipta. See Ekagra. See Nirudha.

Bhuvar loka – intermediate realm between earth and heaven; astral plane of existence.

683

Bija – seed, seed state.

Bija bindu – shakti bindu, the potentially creative bindu.

Bija mantra – seed mantra; particular vibration which has its origin in transcendental consciousness.

Bindu – point of potential energy and consciousness; nucleus; in tantra and hatha yoga it also represents a drop of semen.

Brahma – a deity of the holy trinity; cosmic creator; potentiality of mooladhara chakra.

Brahmachari – celibate; one who moves in consciousness of the true reality, Brahman.

Brahmacharya – one of the niyama; self-restraint, celibacy; state of living in constant awareness of Brahman.

Brahmacharya ashrama – first period of a person's life before marriage, when one lives with the guru as a celibate and student up to the age of twenty-five.

Brahma granthi – psychic 'knot' of creation situated in mooladhara chakra.

Brahman – etymologically it means 'ever expanding, limitless consciousness'; name of supreme consciousness according to Vedanta philosophy; monistic concept of absolute reality.

Brahma nadi – nadi within the innermost layer of sushumna nadi.

Brahmananda – the blissful realization of the ultimate reality.

Brahmarandhra – the aperture at the crown of the head through which the soul of a yogi passes in the final samadhi.

Brahma vidya – realized knowledge of Brahman.

Buddhi – intellect, discrimination; aspect of mind closest to pure consciousness.

Chakra – circle, wheel or vortex; pranic, psychic centre in the subtle body responsible for specific physiological and psychic functions; conjugating point of nadis.

Chakshu dhauti – cleansing of the eyes.

Chandra – moon.

Chandra nadi – ida nadi.

Chandra swara – flow of breath through the left nostril, indicating activation of ida nadi.

684

Chaturvarga – another word for purushartha. See Purushartha

Chela – disciple.

Chetana – consciousness.

Chid – consciousness.

Chidakasha – psychic space in front of the closed eyes, just behind the forehead.

Chidananda – bliss of pure consciousness.

Chin mudra – attitude of consciousness; gesture in which the first finger is kept at the root of the thumb, the last three fingers are separated.

Chit – supreme consciousness.

Chitra, chitrini – third layer inside sushumna nadi.

Chit shakti – the kinetic power akin to pure consciousness.

Chitta – individual consciousness, includes subconscious and unconscious layers of mind; one of the twenty-four elements constituting mind; part of the antah karana. Its functions are memory, thinking, concentration, attention and enquiry.

Chitta vritti – mental movement or modification.

Dakshina – right; also a gift offered to the guru during initiation.

Dakshina marga – commonly known as the 'right hand path' of tantra (as opposed to the 'left'), where one practices sadhana alone in order to attain self-realization. Suitable for aspirants of a sattwic nature. See Dakshina tantra.

Dakshina nauli – contraction of the abdomen and stomach in which the rectus abdomini muscles are isolated to the right; one of the shatkarma.

Dakshina swara – flow of the breath through the right nostril.

Dakshina tantra – path of tantra which excludes pancha makara and the sexual affairs between a man and woman. See Dakshina marga.

Danda – stick.

Danda dhauti – one of the shatkarmas; method of cleaning the oesophagus with a stick made of the soft core of a banana tree.

Danta dhauti – cleaning the teeth.

685

Deva – divine being; literally means 'illumined one'; higher force or power.

Devadatta – pranic air current creating yawning and sneezing.

Dhananjaya – one of the upapranas which remains in the body after death.

Dhanur – bow.

Dhana – wealth.

Dhanurasana – bow pose; one of the major backward bending postures of hatha yoga.

Dharana – practice of concentration; sixth stage of ashtanga yoga.

Dharma – quality; duty; righteous path; that which is established and firm; one of the purusharthas. See Purushartha

Dhatu – element of the physical body, altogether there are seven dhatus; also means semen in particular. See Sapta dhatu.

Dhauti – second of the shatkarmas; cleansing technique of the eyes, ears, tongue, forehead, oesophagus, stomach, rectum and anus; See Danta dhauti. See Jihva dhauti. See Karna dhauti. See Kapalrandhra dhauti. See Chakshu dhauti. See Varisara dhauti. See Vahnisara dhauti. See Vastra dhauti. See Moola shodhana.

Dhyana – meditation; one-pointedness of mind through concentration on either a form, thought or sound; absorption in the object of meditation; seventh stage of Sage Patanjali's ashtanga yoga.

Diksha – initiation given by the guru.

Dosha – three humours of the body. See Kapha. See Pitta. See Vata.

Drashta – seer.

Dugdha neti – milk neti.

Dukha – pain; unhappiness, sorrow; suffering.

Dvaita – philosophy of supreme consciousness in which one perceives his self separate from the supreme self and aspires for union with it.

Dwapara yuga – third age or cycle in the Day of Brahma, consisting of 864,000 years.

Dwesha – one of the kleshas; aversion or dislike.

Eka – one.

Ekadashi – eleventh day of the moon's phase; the rising phase of the moon having a strong influence upon the body and mind; in India fasting is recommended on this day.

Ekagra – one-pointed mind; fourth stage of evolution of mind.

Ekagrata – one-pointedness of mind.

Gaja karani – practice of hatha yoga similar to vyaghra dhauti..

Ganga, Ganges – great holy river of India flowing from Gangotri in the Himalayas to the Bay of Bengal. Has important spiritual, religious and esoteric significance in the Hindu culture; symbolizes ida nadi and chitta shakti in yoga.

Garima – one of the ashta siddhi; paranormal power to become as heavy as desired.

Ghata avastha – second stage of hearing the inner nada..

Ghrita neti – neti performed with ghee.

Gomansa – literally means cow's meat; refers to the tongue.

Gomukhasana – cow's face posture; one of the major yogic postures .

Gorakhnath – famous tantric guru and hatha yogi. Disciple of Matsyendranath, founder of the Nath school of hatha yoga, second in line of the eighty-four siddhas.

Gorakshasana – Yogi Gorakhnath's pose; an advanced yoga posture.

Granthi – knot, psychic, pranic knot in the subtle body.

Granthi sthan – kanda; junction of mooladhara and sushumna nadi.

Grihastha – householder.

Grihastha ashrama – the period of life from the age of twenty-five to fifty when one lives a married life.

Guna – quality of nature; threefold capacity of manifest shakti, prakriti, nature; viz. tamas, rajas, sattwa.

Gupta – secret.

Guptasana – secret pose, similar to siddhasana.

Guru – spiritually enlightened soul, who by the light of his own atma can dispel darkness, ignorance and illusion from the mind and enlighten the consciousness of a devotee or disciple.

Hamsah, Hamso – psychic sound and mantra of the breath. 'Hamsa' literally means swan. The swan is considered to be important symbolically as it has the unique ability to separate pure milk and water. Similarly the mantra *Hamsah* or *Hamso* when it is realized, arouses the perception of reality or essence of creation.

Hatha yoga – science of yoga which purifies the whole physical body by means of shatkarma, asana, pranayama, mudra, bandha and concentration, as a prelude to raja yoga and samadhi.

Hiranyagarbha – cosmic subtle body; the golden womb.

Hridaya akasha – psychic space of the heart centre.

Hrid dhauti – shatkarma consisting of the four practices of vastra dhauti, danda dhauti, vaman dhauti, vyaghra dhauti.

Ichchha – desire.

Ichchha shakti – willpower, the force of desire, flowing through ida nadi.

Ida nadi – major nadi running on the left side of the spine from mooladhara to ajna through which manas (chitta, ichchha) shakti flows, and which governs the mental processes.

Indra – chief of the gods or devas; god of thunder, lightning, rain; lord of the senses.

Indriya – sense or sense organ.

Ishatva – one of the ashta siddhi; the ability to create and destroy at will.

Ishta devata – personal deity, one's personal symbol of the supreme; form or vision of divinity.

Ishwara – cosmic causal body of sound, also known as parabindu, parashabda, supreme being, God.

Ishwara pranidhana – dedication to the supreme being in thought, word and action; one of the five niyamas according to Sage Patanjali.

Ishwara tattwa – See Ishwara.

Itaralingam – lingam situated in ajna chakra; represents supra-consciousness with a residual trace of ego; anandamaya kosha.

Jagrat – conscious reality.

Jagrat avastha – conscious state of perception.

Jagrit – awake; conscious.

Jagriti – conscious realm; material world of the senses.

Jala – water.

Jala basti – one of the shatkarmas; yogic enema using water.

Jala neti – one of the shatkarmas; nasal cleansing by passing saline water through each nostril alternately.

Jala tattwa – water element; See Apas tattwa.

Jalandhara bandha – throat lock in which the chin rests forward upon the upper sternum, arresting the flow of breath through the throat.

Jamuna – river in North India. See Yamuna.

Japa – continuous repetition of mantra.

Jihva – tongue.

Jihva dhauti – one of the shatkarmas; cleansing of the tongue.

Jiva – individual life.

Jivatma – individual soul.

Jivan mukta – one who has attained final samadhi or liberation and continues to live again in the body with the knowledge and realization of the supreme reality; liberated soul.

Jivan mukti – a state of consciousness achieved once the final samadhi has taken place and one continues to live in the world with the knowledge of that experience.

Jnana – knowledge; cognition; wisdom.

Jnana mudra – psychic gesture of knowledge in which the index finger is joined with the tip of the thumb, the other three fingers are spread apart.

Jnana yoga – yoga of knowledge and wisdom attained through spontaneous self-analysis and investigation of abstract and speculative ideas.

Jnanendriya – organ of sense perceptions and knowledge, five in number, viz. ears, eyes, nose, tongue and skin.

Kaala – one of the five kanchukas; limiting aspect of Shakti which creates the dimension of time and restricts individual consciousness and body within it.

Kaama – first of purushartha or chaturvarga; sensual gratification, passion, desire, lust.

Kaamadeva – name of the god or deva of sensual gratification, also known as Cupid.

Kaama roopa – in the form of kaama, named after Kaamadeva; also refers to the reproductive organs.

Kailash – a sacred mountain peak in the Himalayas, the abode of Lord Shiva.

Kaivalya samadhi – highest stage of samadhi. See Turiya. See Nirvana samadhi.

Kaki mudra – crow's beak mudra.

Kalaa – one of the kanchukas; limiting aspect of Shakti which restricts the creative power of individual consciousness and body.

Kali – primal manifestation of Shakti; deity, divine mother; destroyer of time, space and object, i.e. ignorance.

Kali yuga – the present age, last of the four ages or cycles in the Day of Brahma and maha yuga which began in 3,102 BC, with a duration of 432,000 years. During this cycle man is collectively at the height of technology, decadence, dishonesty and corruption of spiritual awareness.

Kalpa – period of 4,320,000,000 years; the Day of Brahma in which the four yugas or cycles recur 1,000 times.

Kanchuka – limiting or confining aspect of cosmic shakti as maya, five in number.

Kanda – a bulbous root; in the subtle body it is the source of the nadis, twelve inches high and four inches wide, situated from mooladhara to manipura.

Kandasthan – conjunction point of the nadis in both mooladhara and manipura.

Kanphatta yogi – a sect of yogis, tracing its lineage back to Gorakhnath. Means 'split-ear yogi' because their ears are pierced and carry a heavy ring made of various substances, preferably rhinoceros horn.

Kapal – skull or cerebrum.

Kapalbhati pranayama – 'frontal brain purification'; process of purifying the frontal region of the brain by breathing rapidly through the nostrils with emphasis on exhalation.

Kapal moksha – final liberation when the yogi's soul leaves the physical body by passing out through the crown of the head.

Kapalrandhra dhauti – one of the shatkarma; cleaning of the frontal sinuses.

Kapha – one of the three doshas; phlegm, mucus.

Karana – cause.

Karana sharira – causal or etheric body.

Karma – action; law of cause and effect; cleansing technique.

Karmashaya – storage of past impressions, actions, words and thoughts.

Karma yoga – yogic path of action; union with the supreme consciousness through action; discussed in *Bhagavad Gita*.

Karna dhauti – one of the shatkarmas which involves cleaning the ears.

Kati chakrasana – waist rotating pose.

Kaya – body.

Kaya sthairyam – practice of absolute steadiness and complete awareness of the physical body, making the body still like a statue; preparing for concentration and meditation.

Kevala kumbhaka – spontaneous breath retention, when fluctuation of the breath ceases spontaneously, without conscious effort.

Klesha – five-fold afflictions, tensions or fears accompanying human birth.

Koorma – tortoise.

Koormasana – tortoise pose; one of the advanced postures of hatha yoga.

Koorma vayu – pranic movement or current which causes the eyelids to blink.

Kosha – sheath or body; realm of experience and existence.

Krikara vayu – one of the subsidiary vital airs responsible for sneezing and coughing.

Krishna – literally means 'black' or 'dark'; eighth incarnation of Vishnu; avatara who descended in the Dwapara yuga and lived in Dwarka, in modern day Gujarat.

Krishna paksha – dark fortnight, when the moon is waning.

691

Krita yuga – See Satya yuga.

Kriya – activity; dynamic yogic practice.

Kriya yoga – part of kundalini yoga; kundalini yoga is the philosophy, kriya yoga is the practice.

Kshama – one of the yamas stated in the *Hatharatnavali*; forgiveness .

Kshana – a second.

Kshetram – field; trigger-point.

Kshipta – one of the five bhumikas; distracted or dissipated mind.

Kukkuta – cockerel.

Kukkutasana – cockerel pose.

Kumbhaka – breath retention.

Kundalini – man's spiritual energy, capacity and consciousness.

Kundalini shakti – also known as 'serpent power'; man's potential energy lying dormant in mooladhara chakra, which passes through sushumna nadi when awakened.

Kundalini yoga – philosophy expounding the awakening of potential energy and inherent consciousness within the human body and mind.

Kunjal kriya – one of the shatkarmas; method of cleansing the stomach by drinking warm, salty water and inducing vomiting.

Laghima – one of the ashta siddhi or paranormal powers to become as light and weightless as desired.

Laghoo shankhaprakshalana – one of the shatkarmas; 'quick intestinal washout'. Systematic and simple method of washing the alimentary canal by drinking six glasses of warm saline water and practising a series of five asanas.

Lakh – one hundred thousand.

Lakshmi – goddess of wealth, consort of Vishnu and creative power of manipura chakra.

Lalana chakra – nectar centre situated opposite the uvula, consisting of twelve petals; place where nectar collects if it is trapped as it falls from bindu visarga.

Laulika – name of nauli in *Gheranda Samhita*. See Nauli.

Laya – dissolution or absorption of mind.

Laya yoga – union with the supreme consciousness through pranayama or devotion; literally, union by absorption.

Lingam – naturally formed oval shaped stone; represents the subtle form of individual existence; Shivalingam is especially venerated as the symbol of atma and individual soul.

Lobha – greed, covetousness.

Loka – level or realm of existence; world.

Madhya – medium.

Madhyama – middle.

Madhyama nada – subtle sound vibration.

Madhyama nadi – sushumna.

Madhyama nauli – one of the shatkarmas; contraction and isolation of the rectus abdomini muscles in the middle of the abdomen.

Maha – great.

Maha bandha – great lock; the combination of moola bandha, jalandhara bandha and uddiyana bandha with kumbhaka.

Maha mudra – great attitude; one of the major practices of hatha yoga and kriya yoga, which includes practising moola bandha, shambhavi and khechari mudras simultaneously.

Maha nadi – literally means great nadi, sushumna.

Mahanirvana tantra – one of the sixty-four tantras on the practices of kaula marga tantra for householders.

Maha siddha – literally means great perfectionist; one who has achieved great paranormal and psychic power.

Mahat – cosmic consciousness, supraconsciousness.

Maha vedha mudra – great piercing attitude; major practice of hatha yoga done in siddhasana with shambhavi mudra and beating the buttocks.

Maha yuga – combination of the four yugas or ages.

Mahima – one of the ashta siddhi or paranormal powers; to become as large as desired.

Maithuna – sexual interaction between male and female in order to awaken kundalini shakti; fifth element of the pancha makara of kaulachara tantra.

Makara – crocodile; tantric practice of vama marga tantra; See Pancha makara.

Makarasana – crocodile pose.

Mala – garland or rosary of tulsi wood, sandal wood, rudraksha seed, coral, crystal, or other precious stones, or as specified by the guru, to count the number of mantras repeated during japa or mantra sadhana. Malas of flowers are also offered to the guru.

Man – mind.

Manas – finite mind, mentation; See Antah karana.

Manas chakra – six-petalled chakra situated above ajna chakra.

Manas shakti – mental energy channelled through ida nadi.

Manipura chakra – literally means 'city of jewels'; psychic and pranic centre behind the navel within the spinal column; corresponding to the solar plexus in the physical body.

Manomaya kosha – mental sheath or body.

Manonmani – literally means 'mind without mind'; state of samadhi; consciousness devoid of the functions of the individual mind.

Mantra – subtle sound vibration; process of tantra for liberating energy and expanding consciousness from the limitations of mundane awareness.

Mantra shakti – the power or force of mantra.

Mantra siddhi – the ability to make a mantra efficacious and to acquire its fruits.

Marga – distinct and well formulated path for liberation.

Maruta – wind, prana vayu.

Matsya – literally means 'fish'; one of the pancha makara. See Pancha makara.

Matsyendranath – first human guru of the hatha yoga tradition; guru of Yogi Gorakhnath. Though a Shaivite, he is also considered a Buddhist saint and guardian deity of Nepal.

Matsyendrasana – pose of Matsyendranath; major posture of hatha yoga in which the spine is twisted.

Maya – literally means illusion; veiling power of manifest shakti; the illusory nature of the phenomenal world.

Mayur – peacock.

Mayurasana – peacock pose; advanced posture of hatha yoga which awakens manipura chakra. Includes balancing the body on the hands.

Meru – mountain; famous mythological mountain comparable to Mount Olympus in Greece; also known as Sumeru, the abode of the gods.

Merudanda – the human spinal column.

Moha – confusion; infatuation.

Moksha – liberation from the cycles of birth and death and the illusion of maya.

Moola – root.

Moola bandha – contraction of the perineum in the male and the cervix in the female body.

Mooladhara chakra – lowest psychic and pranic centre in the human body and the evolutionary platform where kundalini shakti emerges; situated in the perineal floor in men and the cervix in women; connected to the coccygeal plexus.

Moola shodhana – practice of dhauti karma; anal cleansing.

Moorchha pranayama – fainting or swooning breath in which the breath is inhaled slowly and retained for an extended period.

Mouna – silence; remaining without speaking for a specific period of time.

Mudha – dull state of mind; first of the five bhumikas; preliminary stage of evolution of the mind.

Mudra – literally means 'gesture'; physical, mental and psychic attitude which expresses and channels cosmic energy within the mind and body; also means 'grain', one of the elements of the pancha makara sadhana in tantra.

Mukta – liberated.

Mukti – release; liberation, final absolution of the consciousness from the chain of birth and death and from the illusion of maya.

Muni – an ascetic; literally means 'silent one'.

Nada – subtle sound vibration; the vibration created by the union of shiva and shakti tattwas.

Nadi – flow; subtle channel in the pranic body, conducting the flow of shakti; comparable to the meridians of acupuncture.

Nadi shodhana pranayama – purifying breath which purifies the nadis by alternate nostril breathing; it balances the flow of shakti in ida and pingala nadis and the flow of breath through the right and left nostrils.

Naga vayu – pranic air current responsible for burping and hiccups.

Nama – name; gross form of sound.

Nasagra, nasikagra – nosetip.

Nasagra drishti, nasikagra drishti – gazing at the nosetip.

Nasagra mudra, nasikagra mudra – hand position adopted during pranayama to alternate the flow of breath through the nostrils.

Natha – lord.

Nauli – abdominal massage; fifth shatkarma in which the rectus abdomini muscles are contracted and isolated vertically.

Neti kriya – the third shatkarma; 'nasal cleansing' with either saline water or a waxed string.

Nidra – sleep.

Nigama – that part of the tantra shastras in which Shakti instructs Shiva; relevant scriptures in the Kali yuga, the present age.

Niralamba – unsupported.

Nirgarbha pranayama – pranayama without repetition of mantra.

Nirodha – blocking, stopping.

Niruddha – state of mind in which mind is blocked or prevented from functioning; beyond the three qualities or gunas.

Nirvana samadhi – highest state of samadhi in which only supraconsciousness or universal consciousness remains.

Nirvitarka – without confusion of the three processes of knowing, known and knower.

Nirvitarka samadhi – viz. vitarka asamprajnata samadhi; negative phase of vitarka samprajnata in which there is unconsciousness of the gross form of the object; without language.

Nishpatti avastha – fourth stage of hearing the inner nada.

Nivritti – renunciation of the external world and vrittis.

Niyama – fixed observance; rules of raja yoga, five in number according to Sage Patanjali.

Nyaya – logic, a branch of Indian philosophy.

Ojas – vitality; sublimated sexual energy; kundalini shakti.

Om – cosmic vibration of the universe; universal mantra; represents the four states of consciousness: conscious, subconscious, unconscious and supraconscious.

Pada – foot or leg; quarter section of a stanza or literary work.

Padma – lotus.

Padmasana – lotus pose; classical meditative posture.

Paksha – one fortnight.

Pancha makara – the five practices of kaulachara tantra: mamsa, madhya, matsya, mudra, maithuna, which uses meat, wine, fish, grain and sexual intercourse.

Pancha tattwa – the five elements, earth, water, fire, air, ether. See Prithvi tattwa. See Apas tattwa. See Agni tattwa. See Vayu tattwa. See Akasha tattwa.

Panth – path of manifestation.

Para – supreme.

Parabindu – cosmic causal body; Ishwara tattwa.

Paralingam – symbol of the self within sahasrara chakra; represents cosmic awareness.

Param – highest, supreme.

Paramatma – the supreme atma; universal or cosmic self.

Para nada – most subtle causal sound vibration; Ishwara tattwa.

Parichaya avastha – third stage of perception of nada.

Paschim – west or back part of the body.

Paschimottanasana – back stretching pose; one of the major hatha yoga postures.

Pashinee mudra – folded mudra.

Pashyanti nada – sound vibration in the cosmic subtle body.

Pawan – wind, prana vayu.

Pawan tattwa – air element. See Vayu tattwa.

Payaswini nadi – nadi terminating at the right big toe, between poosha and pingala.

Pinda – cage; physical body.

Pingala nadi – major nadi which conducts prana shakti. Emerges from the right side of mooladhara opposite ida and intersects each of the chakras before reaching the right side of ajna. Also associated with the mundane realm of experience and externalized awareness.

Pitta – one of the three doshas or humours; bile.

Plavini pranayama – gulping breath in which air is swallowed into the stomach and retained.

Pooja – worship.

Pooraka – inhalation.

Poornima – full moon day or night.

Poosha nadi – one of the ten major nadis; supporting pingala, it runs from the right ear to the abdomen.

Pragya, prajna – intuition; source of revelation in an individual.

Prakamya – certain fulfilment of desire.

Prakasha – light, illumination; internal or subtle illumination.

Prakriti – nature; manifested shakti; vehicle of purusha (consciousness) according to Samkhya philosophy.

Pramana – evidence or right notion.

Prana – vital energy force sustaining life and creation, permeating the whole of creation and existing in both the macrocosmos and microcosmos.

Prana shakti – the force of prana.

Pranava – Om mantra.

Prana vayu – pranic air current; also refers to a specific current centralized in the thoracic region, from the throat to the diaphragm, responsible for processes of inspiration and absorption.

Pranayama – technique of breathing and breath retention which increases the pranic capacity; fourth step of Sage Patanjali's ashtanga yoga.

Prapti – one of the ashta siddhi; ability to travel everywhere and anywhere as desired.

Prasad – an offering to and from the guru or higher power, usually in the form of food.

Pratyahara – sense withdrawal; first stage of concentrating the mind; fifth stage of ashtanga yoga.

Pratyaya – content of the mind; object.

Pravritti – involvement with the vrittis of the mind.

Prithvi – earth.

Prithvi tattwa – one of the pancha tattwas or bhutas; the earth element or principle.

Purana – eighteen books consisting of legends and mythological narrations dealing with creation, recreation and the genealogies of sages and rulers.

Purusha – pure consciousness according to Samkhya philosophy; can also refer to a man or human being.

Purushartha – purpose of the consciousness; the four basic needs or desires, viz. artha, kaama, dharma, moksha.

Raga – according to Sage Patanjali one of the kleshas; liking, attraction, attachment; according to tantra it is the kanchuka which restricts an individual's capacity to exert willpower and desire.

Raja – king.

Rajas – second quality of nature and mind; dynamism, movement or oscillation; also refers to a woman's menstrual and reproductive secretions.

Raja yoga – the supreme yoga; union through concentration of mind; the eightfold path as formulated by Sage Patanjali.

Rajo guna – the quality of mobility, activity and dynamism.

Rakta bindu – red bindu, same as bija bindu, shakti bindu; the potentially creative bindu from which creation springs; often refers to the ovum.

Rechaka – exhalation, emptying of the lungs.

Rishi – a seer of truth.

Ritam – ultimate, unchanging truth.

Ritambhara – full of cosmic experience, cosmic harmony.

Roopa – form.

Rudra – name of Lord Shiva in the Vedas; first aspect of nature, tamas; generally signifies transformation through destruction; Rudra is said to have sprung from Brahma's forehead and is one of the holy trinity.

Rudra granthi – 'psychic knot' located in ajna chakra.

Sabija – with seed or basis.

Sabija samadhi – supraconsciousness with continuation of ego in dormant or seed state. When the basis of meditation becomes the object, there is oneness of mind with the object but dissolution of the self is as yet incomplete.

Sada – always.

Sadha – to practise.

Sadhaka – spiritual practitioner; a person who is striving on the spiritual path for self-realization, true reality and cosmic consciousness.

Sadhya – the object of practice.

Sagarbha pranayama – pranayama practised with repetition of mantra.

Sage Patanjali – propounder of ashtanga yoga and author of the *Yoga Sutras*, contemporary of Lord Buddha.

Sahaja – spontaneous; natural.

Sahaja avastha – natural and spontaneous samadhi which is achieved through previous practice.

Sahaja samadhi – natural and spontaneous supraconsciousness.

Sahajoli mudra – practice of vajroli by a woman, involving contraction of the lower urinary muscles.

Sahasrara chakra – 'thousand petalled lotus' at the crown of the head associated with the pituitary gland.

Sahita kumbhaka – 'connected pranayama' in which there is a flow between inhalation, exhalation and retention.

Sahita pranayama – See Sahita kumbhaka.

Sahita samadhi – 'connected samadhi' in which there is a flow of consciousness from the witness, witnessing and witnessed.

Sakshi – aspect of individual consciousness which remains the 'silent witness'.

Sakshi bhava – attitude of witnessing.

Salambana samadhi – See Sabija samadhi.

Samadhi – culmination of meditation, state of oneness of mind with the object of concentration; supramental consciousness; the eighth stage of ashtanga yoga.

Samana vayu – pranic air current in the middle region of the body which facilitates assimilation of prana and food.

Samapattih – complete absorption of mind; when mind has completely accepted the object of meditation and become one with it.

Samkhya – atheistic philosophy underlying tantra, proposes the existence of two eternal realities: purusha (consciousness) and prakriti (energy, matter or manifestation).

Samprajnata samadhi – positive phase of samadhi where there is illumination and awareness.

Samsara – unending cycle of birth and death.

Samskara – mental impression stored in the subtle body and existing as an archetype in the brain.

Samyama – the threefold process of dharana, dhyana and samadhi occurring respectively.

Sankalpa – willpower, determination or conviction; concept formed in the mind; also spiritual resolve.

Sannyasa ashrama – fourth stage of a person's life which involves living free of social obligations in order to find the truth of existence.

Sannyasi – renunciate; one who has detached himself from worldly affairs and lives for the experience of self-realization.

Santosha – one of the yamas (observances); contentment.

Sapta dhatu – the seven bodily constituents, viz. bone, fat, flesh, blood, skin, marrow and semen or ova.

Saraswati – divine form of cosmic shakti, goddess; creative power of Brahma who bestows knowledge of fine arts and power of speech.

Saraswati river – subterranean holy river in India which connects with Ganga and Yamuna in Prayag, Uttar Pradesh; associated with sushumna nadi in the subtle body.

Sarvangasana – shoulder stand pose; an inverted posture.

Sat – true.

Satchidananda – truth, consciousness, ecstasy; the highest state of supraconsciousness.

Satguru – true preceptor; guru who has attained self-realization; the inner guru.

701

Sattwa – third quality of nature and mind, which is steady, pure and harmonious.

Sattwa guna – quality of steadfastness and unwavering purity.

Satya – one of the yamas; truthfulness, real, genuine.

Satya yuga – also known as Krita yuga, first of the cycles or ages in the Day of Brahma, consisting of 1,728,000 years in which the people born are honest, trustworthy and spiritually minded.

Savikalpa samadhi – See Sabija samadhi.

Sheetkari pranayama – hissing breath, which exerts a cooling effect upon the whole body.

Shabda – word; mantra; sound; nada.

Shabda Brahman – Ishwara tattwa; parabindu; cosmic causal state.

Shakti – vital energy force; creative, potential force; vehicle of consciousness.

Shakti chalana mudra – major hatha yoga mudra which is similar to 'churning' nauli.

Shambhavi – feminine counterpart of Shambhu.

Shambhavi mudra – an attitude or gesture indicating peace and concentration of mind in which one gazes at the mid-eyebrow centre.

Shambhu – Shiva; pure consciousness; literally means 'born of peace'.

Shanmukhi mudra – closing of the seven gates of perception in the head with the fingers of both hands.

Shashankasana – moon pose; from base position of vajrasana.

Shastra – an authoritative treatise on any subject, particularly science and religion.

Shatkarma – the six yogic techniques of purification, viz. neti, dhauti, nauli, basti, trataka, kapalbhati.

Shaucha – one of the niyamas; purity, cleanliness.

Sheetali pranayama – cooling breath which lowers the body temperature and diminishes thirst by drawing the breath in through the tongue.

Sheetkrama kapalbhati – passing of water from the mouth out through the nose.

Shesha – great serpent with a thousand heads upon which Vishnu reclines in the cosmic ocean; also the support on which the earthly world revolves. See Ananta.

Shishya – disciple. See Chela.

Shiva – state of pure consciousness, individual and cosmic; original source of yoga; Lord of yogis.

Shoonya – void.

Shoora nadi – energy flow running from manipura to ajna chakra.

Shuddhi – purification; purity.

Siddha – an adept or perfected person; one who has developed their psychic and pranic capacity to the point of mastery.

Siddhanta – established doctrines.

Siddhasana – pose of perfection; classical male meditative posture in which sustained pressure is exerted on the mooladhara chakra by the left heel pressing the perineum.

Siddha yoni asana – classical female meditative posture corresponding to siddhasana, in which the left heel presses the entrance to the vagina.

Siddhi – perfection; enhanced pranic and psychic capacity; paranormal or supernormal accomplishment; control of mind and prana.

Sirshasana – headstand pose in which the body is inverted and balanced on the crown of the head.

Sloka – verse.

Smriti – memory, that part of the Vedas recorded as the disciples' remembrance of what has been revealed by the great gurus regarding the truth of inner experience, expansion of awareness and evolution of mind. Smriti includes the six Vedangas; sutras, Manu's laws, puranas, itihasas and nitishastras. Principle smritis are *Manu, Yajnavalkya, Narada, Deval*.

Soham – literally, 'I am That'; psychic sound, mantra of the breath, mantra used in ajapa japa. 'So' represents cosmic consciousness, 'Ham' individual awareness and existence.

Soma chakra – sixteen petalled chakra situated above ajna and manas chakras.

Spandana – movement, vibration; to spring suddenly to life.

Srishti – creation.

Sruti – that part of the Vedas in which the disciple is listening and recording directly the instructions of the guru regarding truth and consciousness.

Sthala basti – dry basti, one of the shatkarmas in which air is sucked into the bowels and then expelled by ashwini mudra, contracting the anal muscles.

Sthiti – steadiness; steady state of created universe; upholding of creation.

Sthula – gross.

Sthula sharira – gross or physical body.

Sukha – happiness, delight, comfort.

Sukhasana – easy pose, sitting cross-legged.

Sukshma – subtle.

Sukshma sharira – subtle or astral body.

Surya – sun.

Surya bheda pranayama – vitality stimulating breath; pranayama in which inhalation is through the right nostril to activate pingala nadi.

Surya nadi – pingala nadi.

Surya swara – flow of breath in the right nostril.

Sutra – thread; aphorism.

Sutra neti – nasal cleansing with thread; one of the shatkarmas.

Sushumna nadi – main nadi in the centre of the spinal cord which conducts kundalini shakti.

Sushupti – unconscious realm and mind; deep sleep.

Swadhisthana chakra – literally means one's own abode; second chakra in the spinal column, above mooladhara, associated with the sacral plexus and governing the urogenital system.

Swadhyaya – one of the niyamas; self-study and study of the texts regarding realization of the self.

Swapna – subconscious realm and mind; dream state.

Swara – flow of the breath in one or both nostrils; also means sound or tone.

Swarodaya – beginning or rising of the swara in one nostril.

Swastika – Hindu and Jain mandala; symbol of creativity and auspiciousness; an equal cross with a smaller line in clockwise direction at the end each extremity.

Swastikasana – auspicious pose; meditative posture similar to siddhasana.

Swayambhu – self-existent; self-established; clear, obvious; self-proclaimed.

Swayambhulingam – symbol of the self in mooladhara chakra; the unconscious mind and body.

Tadasana – palm tree pose; a standing posture.

Tamas – the first quality of nature, shakti and mind; inertia; laziness, procrastination.

Tamo guna – the quality of ignorance or inertia; dull, inert state of mind and nature.

Tanmatra – subtle or primary principle of mind; gandha (smell), rasa (taste), roopa (form), sparsha (touch or feel), shabda (sound), from which the pancha tattwas arise.

Tantra – the oldest science and philosophy of man which expands the mind and liberates the potential energy and inner consciousness from matter; also, texts concerning the philosophy and techniques of expansion of mind and liberation of energy, sixty-four in number.

Tapa – a specific type of pain and hardship. See Adhibautik. See Adhidaivik. See Adhyatmik.

Tapah – one of the niyamas; austerity; elimination of mental impurities by suffering and endurance.

Tapas, tapasya – austerity.

Tattwa – element; true or real state.

Tejas – fire or lustre; brilliance.

Tiryaka bhujangasana – twisting cobra pose.

Tiryaka tadasana – swaying palm tree pose.

Tithi – date, day of the moon's phase.

Tivra – intense.

Trataka – one of the shatkarmas; technique of gazing steadfastly upon an object such as a candle flame, mandala or yantra.

Treta yuga – second of the cycles in the Day of Brahma, in which man becomes less spiritually inclined and motivated. Period of 1,296,000 years.

Triveni – the confluence in ajna chakra where ida, pingala and sushumna nadis merge.

Turiya – literally means 'fourth' state of consciousness; unmanifested state of purusha and prakriti, beyond conscious, subconscious and unconscious mind; supra-consciousness.

Twacha, twak – skin; one of the jnanendriyas; perception through touch or feeling.

Udana – pranic air current in the area of the throat and face.

Udarakarshan asana – abdominal massage pose.

Uddiyana bandha – abdominal retraction lock; drawing in of the abdomen towards the backbone after exhaling.

Ujjayi pranayama – psychic breath performed by contracting the epiglottis producing a light sonorous sound.

Unmani – literally means 'no mind' or 'without mind'; state of samadhi; consciousness devoid of finite mind.

Upanishad – books of the Vedas, traditionally one hundred and eight in number, containing knowledge revealed by guru to disciple; the realizations of the rishis and sages concerning reality and real identity and nature of individual consciousness.

Upaprana – subsidiary pranic function in the body.

Upasana – concentration; dharana; worship.

Utkatasana – squatting position with separated knees.

Uttankoormasana – stretching tortoise pose; one of the advanced hatha yoga postures.

Vahnisara dhauti – practice of antar dhauti in which the abdomen is drawn rapidly in and out.

Vaikhari nada – gross sound and letters.

Vairagya – absence of sensual craving and desires; detachment; supreme dispassion.

Vajra – thunderbolt; the weapon of Lord Indra shaped like a circular disc, and said to be made of the bones of Rishi Dadhicha.

Vajra nadi – second layer of sushumna; also the nadi governing the male sexual organ and processes.

Vajrasana – thunderbolt pose; kneeling posture.

Vajroli mudra – thunderbolt attitude in which the muscles of the male sexual organ and lower urinary tract are contracted, redirecting sexual energy upwards; a practice of hatha yoga and tantra.

Vak – nada; shabda; word; manifest sound.

Vama – left; contrary; opposite.

Vamachara – one who follows the practices and doctrines of vama marga tantra, including sexual interaction where the wife is considered the guru.

Vama marga – commonly known as the left hand path of tantra, as opposed to dakshina marga; path of spiritual unfoldment which includes the pancha makara sadhana.

Vama nauli – left side abdominal massage in which the rectus abdomini muscles are contracted and isolated on the left side of the abdomen.

Vaman dhauti – one of the shatkarmas; method of cleansing the stomach by voluntary vomiting. There are two types: kunjal kriya (regurgitating of water) and vyaghra (regurgitating of food).

Varisara dhauti – shatkarma in which a large quantity of water is drunk in conjunction with asanas to cleanse the entire digestive tract; also known as shankhaprakshalana.

Vama swara – flow of breath in the left nostril.

Vasana – a deep-rooted desire in the unconscious mind.

Vasishtha – celebrated rishi and seer of the Vedas; author of many vedic hymns and owner of the 'cow of plenty'; family guru of King Sudhas, Ikshvaku and Sri Ramachandra; one of the ten patriarchs produced by Manu Swayambhuva, and one of the rishis forming the Great Bear constellation in the heavens. His teachings are recorded in *Yoga Vasishtha*, one of the greatest expositions of jnana yoga.

Vashitva – one of the ashta siddhi; the ability to control all objects, living and non-living.

Vastra dhauti – cloth cleansing technique in which a specially prepared cloth is swallowed and removed after ten minutes, in order to remove mucus from the stomach.

Vata – one of the three doshas; wind and gas.

Vatakrama kapalbhati – See Kapalbhati.

Vatsara dhauti – similar to plavini pranayama but the air swallowed into the stomach is belched out instead of being retained.

Vayu – wind; pranic air current.

Vayu tattwa – one of the pancha tattwas or mahabhutas; the air element.

Vedas – most ancient texts revealed to the sages and saints of India which explain and regulate every aspect of life from supreme reality to worldly affairs. Four in number: *Rig, Yajur, Sama, Atharava*, which are further divided into *Samhita, Brahmana, Aranyaka* and Upanishads. The oldest books in the library of mankind.

Vedanta – culmination of the essential knowledge of the Vedas; concerning the truth of existence, creation and soul and the illusion of all duality; monistic philosophy of the Hindus.

Veera – hero, courageous person.

Veerasana – hero's pose; specifically for concentration and discriminative thinking.

Veerya – energy; strength of will; courage; virility; semen.

Vichara – reflection.

Vichara asamprajnata samadhi – vichara samadhi in which there is unconscious supraconsciousness; the negative phase of vichara samprajnata samadhi .

Vichara samprajnata samadhi – second stage of samadhi or supraconsciousness in which there is no confusion of the witness, witnessed and process of witnessing, and there is thought existing but not in the form of language.

Vidya – knowledge or science, particularly knowledge of spiritual truth and non-mundane reality.

708

Vijnana – science or intuition.

Vijnanamaya kosha – sheath or body of intuition or higher knowledge.

Vikalpa – fancy, imagination, thought or conclusion without factual evidence; counter-thought.

Vikas – active effort; there are two paths of yoga, one is laya, the other is vikas or active effort.

Vikshepa – oscillation of mind especially during the practice of dharana.

Vikshipta – one of the bhumikas; dissipated state of mind fluctuating between concentration and distraction, when mind strays from the point of dharana to some other abstract or irrelevant thing.

Viparyaya – misconception.

Vishnu – a deity of the holy trinity, the cosmic preserver; also refers to the vital capacity of manipura chakra, which stores and distributes prana so that health and stamina are maintained in the body.

Vishnu granthi – psychic 'knot' in anahata chakra; the blockage to spiritual progress posed by personal attachments.

Vishuddhi chakra – psychic and pranic centre in the spine behind the throat and connected with the cervical plexus, tonsils and thyroid gland.

Vishwa – universe, entire cosmos.

Vitarka – reasoning; conjecture.

Vitarka asamprajnata samadhi – negative phase of vitarka samadhi; unconscious supraconsciousness in which there is no language.

Vitarka samprajnata samadhi – first stage of samadhi according to Sage Patanjali, in which the three states of witness, witnessed and witnessing remain confused and thought remains in the form of language.

Viveka – discrimination.

Vrata – spiritual vow or practice, e.g. fasting.

Vritti – pattern of individual consciousness; mental modification.

Vyaghra kriya – tiger action. See Vaman dhauti.

709

Vyana – pranic air current pervading the whole body.

Vyutkrama kapalbhati – technique in which water is passed through the nose and out the mouth.

Yajna – fire ceremony in which oblations and mantra are offered into a sacred fire.

Yama – self-restraints; first stage of ashtanga yoga; also is a period of three hours.

Yamuna river – emanating from Yamnotri in the Himalayas and joining Ganga near Allahabad, North India; celebrated river beside which Lord Krishna lived and played in Vrindavan; refers to pingala nadi in the pranic body.

Yantra – precisely calculated geometrical symbol representing specific conformations of forces of shakti and consciousness; a process of concentration upon specific forms employed in tantra to liberate potential energy and consciousness within an individual.

Yoga – state of union between two opposite poles, viz. Shiva and Shakti, body and mind, individual and universal awareness; process of uniting opposing forces in the body and mind in order to realize the spiritual essence of being.

Yoga abhyasa – practice of the philosophy of yoga.

Yoga danda – specifically designed rod which yogis rest in the armpit to change the flow of the breath in the nostrils.

Yoga nidra – yogic sleep in which the conscious mind is asleep but awareness remains active.

Yogi – accomplished practitioner of yoga, who has achieved internal union.

Yoni – womb, source; specially carved stone in which the shivalingam rests, representing the source which supports and sustains spiritual consciousness (atma).

Yoni mudra – specific hand gesture symbolizing the source and sustenance of consciousness during meditation.

Yuga – an age or cycle of earth and mankind. See Satya yuga. See Treta yuga. See Dwapara yuga. See Kali yuga.

Index of Practices

712

Index of Illustrations

----- Notes -----

Notes